A *tour de force* uncovering Scotland's post-devolution journey, as much as the Centre's. An inspiration to the next generation of public intellectuals. **Wendy Alexander, ex Scottish Labour Leader**

Carol Craig understands Scotland's psyche better than most – what holds us back from realising our full potential and what drives the inequity which still damages so many lives and communities. Her life's work, chronicled in this important book, provides all of us with a blueprint on how we can flourish, both as individuals and as a nation. Every politician should read it.

Susan Dalgety, co-editor *The Women Who Wouldn't Wheesht*; *Scotsman* columnist

In *A Time of Hope,* Carol Craig – a seasoned observer of Scottish society – provides a critical analysis of the deep historical roots of the challenges facing Scottish children today. No one does it better.

John Frank, Professorial Fellow (public health), Edinburgh

This book is much more than the record of twenty years work. It offers a lens on an important period of recent history from the perspective of an astute and challenging participant. It goes deep into the subterranean world of Scottish society and culture not captured by other, including academic accounts drawing on work by or facilitated by the author. **Professor James Mitchell, Politics and International Relations, Edinburgh**

In 2004 I felt Scotland was really at a tipping point: more diverse, creative, ambitious, entrepreneurial and confident. Carol Craig embodied that spirit and the Centre was a bold initiative reflecting those times. This book remembers optimistic days and helps us see the new challenges.

Rt Hon Lord Jack McConnell of Glenscorrodale

. . . such a beautifully written and compelling account of a remarkable story of collaborative inquiry into confidence, well-being and the Scottish psyche. Every illuminating chapter is rich with creative initiatives, humane insights, remarkable thinkers and practitioners and honest reflection. . . (a) superb book.

Will Storrar,
Director, Center of Theological Inquiry, Princeton, New Jersey

Previous books by the author

The Scots Crisis of Confidence (2003, Big Thinking) (2011, Argyll)

Creating Confidence (2007, CCWB)

The Tears that Made the Clyde (2010, Argyll)

The Great Takeover (2012, Argyll)

Hiding in Plain Sight (2017, CCWB Press)

A Time of Hope

The Story of Scotland's Centre for Confidence and Well-being

CAROL CRAIG

ARGYLL PUBLISHING

First published by Argyll Publishing in 2024
Argyll Publishing is an imprint of thirsty books
www.thirstybooks.com
www.postcardsfromscotland.co.uk

**British Library Cataloguing-in-Publication Data.
A catalogue record for this book is available
from the British Library.**

ISBN 9781739318147 hardback

Typeset and design:
derek.rodger21@outlook.com

Printing:
Bell & Bain Ltd, Glasgow

To all the people who attended Centre events
or listened to me speak on confidence and well-being.
Your interest and encouragement
have been a vital part of this story.

Contents

Contents of boxed panels/figures/tables

Foreword
Professor William Storrar

'What a time it was... a time of confidences... preserve your memories.'

THESE THREE PHRASES from the Simon & Garfunkel song 'Bookends' came back to me as I read Carol Craig's story of the Centre for Confidence and Well-being. They reveal not only my age but also the genius of this book.

What a time it was in Scotland in the opening decade of the twenty first century, the start of this story. It was a time of confidences. Scotland's ancient and adjourned parliament had just been recalled by popular vote as a modern democratic legislature for Scottish affairs. The new body carried with it my generation's confidence in the power of constitutional change to create a better country. But while the Scottish Parliament was attracting fierce criticism at the rising cost of its new home at Holyrood, another Scottish institution emerged in those years, one which put its trust in the power of cultural change to bring about a better country.

When the Centre for Confidence and Well-being was founded in 2004 by its visionary Chief Executive and Board, it launched a remarkable series of events and publications to address what Carol Craig perceived as the Scots' crisis of confidence. In *A Time of Hope*, Dr Craig has not only preserved the memory of these gatherings and writings. She has distilled their wisdom for our time of widespread despair, when we need her insights more than ever.

The 'Bookends' lyrics also speak of a time of innocence. The mixed record of the first twenty-five years of the Scottish Parliament has certainly shaken my innocence as a home rule campaigner in the 1990s, believing in constitutional change as the key to societal transformation. Deeper cultural and psychological forces have clearly been at work in Scottish society like an undertow, pulling against every surface political current. The genius of the Centre for Confidence and Well-being was to see that and to act on it.

Three strands of that genius stand out for me in this book. I am confident they will for every reader of *A Time of Hope* who is open to Carol Craig's honest account of the work well done, paths not taken, and lessons learned by the Centre in its twenty year history.

To See Ourselves: The Genius of the Centre's Humanism

In reading this book, we see ourselves as Scots. I recognise so much of my life growing up in the Scotland of the 1950s and '60s, and stepping into adulthood in the '70s. *A Time of Hope* holds up a light to many features of Scottish experience that hid in the shadows, or strutted around in public like the emperor wi' nae claes – the vaunted schools whose most lasting impression was too often the terror of the tawse; the full churches that were too often pillars of establishment respectability rather than beacons of emancipatory religion; the heavy industries with their proud litany of Scottish firsts, but where too often the workers were the last to share in the wealth; the dominant male culture across all social classes and institutions that excluded, marginalised, or demeaned women and girls.

The work of the Centre has documented the human cost of so many lives scarred by this culture of fear and violence, poverty and ill health, addiction and abuse, and the censorious moralising marbled through it all, leading to a devasting loss of confidence and lack of well-being. In response, the Centre sought to find and map compassionate and credible pathways out of the emotional, mental, physical, and social morass of such harmful ways of being human, especially due to adverse childhood experiences. This is the story of a hopeful humanism that believes a healthier and happier Scotland is possible, but a humanism based on hard evidence, not hollow pieties.

As Others See Us: The Genius of the Centre's Internationalism

In reading this book, we see Scotland as others see it. One of the most effective ways in which the Centre addressed the distinctive Scottish problems on its agenda was by inviting leading thinkers, writers, researchers and practitioners to Scotland to share their ideas and international comparisons with interested local audiences. Star speakers like Martin Seligman on positive psychology or Malcolm Gladwell on change makers cast light on the complexities of the human condition as they played out in Scottish history and society. The author documents the ways in which so many of these Centre events were life-changing for the participants, giving them illuminating new perspectives on their personal, professional and civic responsibilities for fostering confidence and well-being in different sectors of Scottish society.

The Centre's commendable internationalism did not mean that it accepted visiting approaches to fostering confidence and well-being uncritically or did not look to its own resources in fostering a transnational dialogue on those concerns. Craig notes with a certain pride that none of the distinguished guest speakers could capture the attention and command the respect of the Centre's audiences as well as its own eminent expert on public health and well-being, Professor Phil Hanlon of Glasgow University. One of the most impressive stories told in this book is the way in which Craig and her colleagues come to see the limitations of the positive psychology movement they initially promoted, not least in its impact on educational policy and practice, where children who only knew praise were at risk of not developing the resilience that comes from overcoming disappointments, failures, and challenges. Is it mischievous of me to wonder if the Centre's idea of confidence owes something to the Calvinist school of hard knocks? Whatever its sources, the Centre's evolving understanding of confidence shows a reflective learning community at its very best.

Intellectual Democracy: The Genius of the Centre's Generalism

In reading this book, we become fellow citizens with the author in that intellectual democracy known as the Scottish generalist tradition. The generalist thinks across academic disciplines to find wisdom from many sources on how to make sense of things and live well. Carol Craig is a generalist thinker *par excellence*. Under her leadership as director, author, mentor, and speaker, the Centre has been a powerhouse for that generalist approach in Scotland. She has paid a high price for it in being subject to unwarranted dismissal by some reviewers. Yet specialist interests do not always equate with the public interest. In the work of the Centre for Confidence and Well-being under Craig's direction, we see a welcome confluence of many specialisms for the common good.

More than that, we see a thinker and writer who is willing to make bold generalist claims that invite a response. I should know! As an émigré Kirk minister in Presbyterian Princeton, why am I commending a book which concludes that Calvinism is the root cause of Scotland's lack of confidence and well-being? I am doing so because the author is making important arguments that Christians like me need to hear, even as we struggle with our own lack of institutional confidence in an increasingly secular society that no longer looks to organised religion for its well-being. This book should make us all think about our complicity in the Scots' crisis of confidence and well-being, whatever our beliefs, values or part in history.

An Album of Hope

As the 'Bookends' song reminds us, one of the most powerful ways of holding on to the past is with a photograph. It may be all that is left to us. In commending Carol Craig's book to readers in and beyond Scotland, I treasure the photograph she has developed in its pages to preserve our memory of what it means to cultivate a culture of hope. More than a photograph, she has given us a whole album of hope. It is filled with vivid pen portraits of the contributors, colleagues, and citizens she convened under the auspices of the Centre for Confidence and Well-being. But that's not all we have from those twenty extraordinary years.

The story of the Centre reminds us Scotland desperately needs such research institutions, whether on cultural or political questions. It turns out the new Scottish Parliament was necessary but not sufficient to ensure a better country. Nothing long term happens to advance human well-being without the sustained effort of innovative public policy centres in an autonomous civil society. *A Time of Hope is* a compelling case study of one such institution. In saluting its accomplishments, we should be inspired by its ambition to go and do likewise. We need a Scotland seeded with centres for fresh thinking across the civic and democratic spectrum. Without them we are in a policymaking desert. We shall be blessed if any are as life-enhancing as the Centre run and recorded here by Carol Craig.

William Storrar
August 2024

William Storrar is Director of the Center of Theological Inquiry in Princeton, New Jersey, an independent institute for interdisciplinary research. He was formerly Director of the Centre for Theology and Public Issues at the University of Edinburgh.

Introduction

I HAVE CALLED this book *A Time of Hope* as the Centre for Confidence and Well-being was born in 2004 into a culture of hope and optimism. Those of us involved in the Centre, and those who attended our events, believed passionately that positive change could happen. We were all too aware of problems and believed that some old attitudes, structures and ways of doing things needed to change but we thought this could happen. Indeed, this is what we were working towards. The belief that we could enhance well-being and tackle many of the problems in our midst remained for years thereafter, despite the 2008 financial crash and the age of austerity.

I started to become interested in confidence in Scotland in 1991 when I became an assertiveness trainer. In the following twelve years I ran lots of workshops with literally thousands of Scots and learned a lot about how they felt about themselves and their lives. I also listened to people who were not born in Scotland expressing surprise at Scots' reticence and paralysing self-doubt. And, of course, I had my own personal experience to learn from. I remember having an epiphany in my 30s when writing an article on the novels of the Scottish writer, William McIlvanney. I suddenly realised that the desire to develop myself and do something with my life was against the grain of Scottish working-class culture, particularly for women.

My book, *The Scots' Crisis of Confidence* (2003), emerged from my desire to weave together insights from three separate strands of my life: my own struggle to raise my head above the parapet; the personal and team development work I had undertaken with fellow Scots; and my enduring interest in what it meant to be Scottish. Indeed, over the years I had acquired a considerable library of books on Scottish culture and identity. Many of these works, though written by Scots themselves, were disparaging about Scotland and the Scottish people.

The Scots' Crisis of Confidence sold well as it resonated strongly with so many people in Scotland and elsewhere – even men who came from privileged backgrounds endorsed the idea that confidence was an issue for them. The book also received considerable press coverage, thus attracting interest from people at the top of many organisations, including the then Scottish Executive.

In November 2003 I was the joint organiser of an event called 'Towards a Confident Scotland' and this ultimately led to the creation of the Centre for Confidence and Well-being in late 2004, with financial support from the Scottish Executive.

These early years of the twenty-first century felt like an auspicious time for the foundation of such an organisation. The Scottish Parliament had been 'reconvened' in 1999 after nearly 300 years and though initial opposition was loud and long from certain predictable quarters this new institution ultimately found wide support among the Scottish people.

This was also the time when confidence and personal development issues were now part of the *zeitgeist*, even in Scotland which had not traditionally been influenced by such ideas. Books on personal development lined our bookshops and organisations were now offering employees courses on these themes: this is why I was so busy running workshops.

The Centre was ideally placed to become a focus for anyone who wanted to see substantial cultural, personal and organisational change in Scotland. This is palpable in the glowing endorsements the Centre received on its foundation. Our launch event was the memorable 'Scotland's Tipping Point' conference, held in December 2004 in Glasgow's Òran Mór, depicted on this book's cover. The internationally famous Canadian writer, Malcolm Gladwell, was the keynote speaker. The popularity and influence of the Centre can also be seen throughout this book in the involvement we had with so many Scots in various facets of their lives.

In the early days of the Centre most of the communication of our ideas was via events, our website and the large number of talks I gave to a variety of organisations in Scotland. In 2012 we launched our book series, *Postcards from Scotland,* and again many of these books struck a hopeful note, as is clear from some of the early titles – *The New Road: Charting Scotland's inspirational communities; Scotland's Local Food Revolution;* and *Raising Spirits*. In 2019 we published *The Dear Wild Place: Green spaces, community and campaigning* about a successful local campaign in Glasgow's west end where developers of proposed 'luxury' apartments were defeated and land was turned over for much-needed community use.

But when we held an event there in June 2022 on what had become a community garden the mood was sombre. The Covid-19 pandemic was over but we were now grappling with its legacy. As a society we were also gripped by several troubling events which diminished a sense of well-being: a cost-of-living crisis, the war in Ukraine, and the knowledge that vital services such as health and care of the elderly were not just bursting at the seams but potentially broken. Most of us also sensed that the climate crisis we had talked about for years was now upon us.

So, as I write this book in 2023 and 2024, I'm aware *survival* is now uppermost in many people's minds rather than an expansive sense of hope and optimism which was commonplace when the Centre appeared on the scene in 2004. But as optimism and a belief in positive change was a vital part of the Centre's work for most of our existence, *A Time of Hope* still seems an appropriate title.

I founded the Centre at the end of 2004 and have been at the forefront of its work for these 20 years. My centrality to the organisation has much less to do with egocentrism than practicality. We have always been a tiny organisation with a tight budget and a small, and sometimes non-existent, staff. This inevitably means that the Centre's evolution is inextricably linked with my own story. So, I could never have written an objective account, or history, of the Centre's activities and decisions. I have tried to make a virtue of this by creating a personal narrative in most chapters, and explaining what we did and why from my point of view. In fact, as I dislike the way some researchers or writers feign objectivity, I've deliberately outlined my personal reasons for being motivated by certain courses of action.

This doesn't mean that I am the only actor in this story about the Centre: far from it. The book teems with people – employees (when we had the cash to pay wages), board members, associates, funders, authors, speakers, collaborators, volunteers. As there has been so much to write about – our publication of almost 20 books, and our large number of events and numerous projects – I was continually aware that I haven't always been able to give due prominence to some of the people involved. So, I have included a section with mini pen portraits and photographs of the people who did much of the Centre's work, often behind the scenes.

I have devoted many pages to the ideas which influenced the Centre and our own beliefs and values. If I hadn't given salience to these ideas and their continuing relevance the book would read like a turgid 20-year activities report. Besides, we always saw our role as a catalyst for change. Ideas were our currency. But this doesn't mean that we stuck with what initially seemed helpful if it later seemed questionable. We paid attention to how ideas evolved and were translated into action. We observed the impact ideas had on people and organisations; sometimes we didn't like what we saw. Rather than keep going with the idea or approach we would talk openly about our reservations and criticisms. We suggested alternatives. At one point we even completely changed the main focus of our attention. And we did this even though we could have profited from the original ideas.

Positive psychology, particularly Professor Martin Seligman's work, is the best example of a set of ideas that we were originally attracted to but then qualified our support for. We were one of the first organisations internationally to disseminate positive psychology research and ideas to a lay audience and in the early days of the Centre we attracted 300-400,000 hits a year on our website from around the world. Given how undeveloped the internet was in those days that was a lot of website traffic. I even became secretary of the International Positive Psychology Association and was regularly asked to speak at conferences. But the more we became involved in thinking about well-being the more we realised that positive psychology wasn't the only, or even the best, way to improve it.

Indeed, one of the key learning points for me and others at the Centre is how people can benefit from some exposure to ideas or interventions, but more is not necessarily better. Just as with medication, dose matters. However, in our highly networked, interconnected world if an idea gets traction, it then becomes reinforced and reiterated at every turn. A whole cadre of professionals soon appears to take on this work and argue that it's the best thing since sliced bread. These professionals then have a vested interest in maintaining the efficacy and importance of their approach.

As I shall argue in later chapters, this happened with the self-esteem movement, emotional intelligence, positive psychology, and is happening now with the emphasis on trauma. Yes, there can be substantial insights in such approaches, but they are often not enough on their own to effect changes in individuals and organisations. Despite this their advocates often present the approach as a stand-alone panacea or quick fix. Sometimes, as is the case with the self-esteem movement, the approach can backfire and paradoxically produce negative effects. In this case, the loss of resilience, the growth of narcissism and the desire to blame others for misfortunes and mistakes. The Centre always tried to be aware of, and honest about, how ideas could rebound and have a deleterious effect.

One of the main challenges in writing this book is how to manage the sheer volume of material. In other words, given how much we did in that 20-year period, how could I convey the extensive factual information alongside an explanation of the ideas that motivated us and how these ideas changed in the course of our work? To help organise this potentially disparate material and create coherence for the reader I present our work in two distinct phases. Phase 1 begins at the end of 2004 with the official set-up of the Centre and continues until the autumn of 2008. During this phase we concentrated on positive psychology, confidence and psychological approaches to well-being. This means that it's easy for me to explain what we did and why in this phase *chronologically.*

This phase ended in the closing months of 2008 primarily because we moved away from positive psychology, no longer seeing it as the best way to pursue well-being. As we thought positive psychology still had some merit, we didn't turn our back on it completely and knew that we might still do some work related to it. In a nutshell, as we moved into Phase 2, we deliberately broadened our approach to well-being much beyond psychology, positive or traditional. Now we started to consider a range of factors that influenced people's well-being such as community projects, contact with the natural world, music, physical exercise, workplace activities and ethos, materialist values, inequality – in other words external, societal factors. The list of topics in the extensive index at the end of this book is an indicator of the depth and breadth of the Centre's interest over the years.

The work we did in Phase 2 was not just varied in terms of subject matter. We also participated in a variety of projects and launched a book series. This means that, unlike Phase 1, it's difficult to recount the Centre's activities and thought in this period chronologically. So, in the second part of the book on Phase 2, I describe what we did and why *thematically*, grouping our work in broad themes such as Glasgow, materialism, organisations, or play. This means that some of these chapters span ten years or more.

Chapter 22 is the final chapter in the part of the book dedicated to our work in Phase 2. It's on the trajectory of the Centre's work from focusing on confidence and positive psychology in our early years, to looking at trauma, abuse and adverse childhood experiences (ACEs). In 2017, for example, I wrote *Hiding in Plain Sight: Exploring Scotland's ill health* in which I argue the country's punitive, insensitive, approach to child-rearing is the cause of much of our health and social problems. As I explain, this shift was partly caused by changes in my own life but, more importantly it was completely in tune with the *zeitgeist* as these are issues which now dominate. The first of the chapters here documents how there has been a substantial change in the way certain issues are understood in the past 20 years. The word 'trauma' now characterises how we think about negative experiences, even when they are just mildly stressful and, following the USA, we're now moving towards a 'victimhood culture'.

I've also included a third section called Reflections on Scotland and the three chapters here are different from those which outline the work we did in Phases 1 and 2. These chapters are more intellectual – driven by ideas rather than Centre events and activities.

When I gave talks on my book on ACEs in Scotland, I was aware that people were happy to accept that poor and abusive child-rearing was the cause of many of the country's problems but they were also eager to attribute them to some kind of 'national trauma'. As the word trauma is likely to increase in use, I devote the first chapter in this section to looking at whether Scottish history shows that there were national events which can be interpreted as traumatic. I look specifically at the Act of Union in 1707 and the Highland Clearances as these are the events Scots are most likely to mention when claiming Scotland has suffered a national trauma. I argue that we can't draw that conclusion from these two events but that rapid industrialisation and urbanisation, particularly in the West of Scotland in the eighteenth and nineteenth centuries was very stressful for families and established a culture which has not been conducive to bringing children up in the type of environment which lays the foundation for good health.

But I still do not think any aspect of Scotland's constitution or economic and social history completely explains enduring problems with health, addictions or violence. So, in Chapter 24 I move on to look at the legacy of the Reformation on Scotland, specifically how the Calvinist belief in human worthlessness and the division into the saved and the damned has undermined individual well-being, and particularly affected children. I believe that this aspect of our history also explains the punitive nature of Scottish culture. As I explain in Chapter 19, it was only a decade after writing *The Scots' Crisis of Confidence* that I realised just how much an outlier Scotland was in the use of corporal punishment in state schools.

Chapter 25, the last chapter in this section, is on the Scottish independence referendum held in September 2014. I explain why I didn't agree that the vote was largely about confidence and optimism as well as my own reasons to vote as I did. I then argue that the Presbyterian dream to build the New Jerusalem, which animated Scotland for over three hundred years, can still be seen in many Scots' longing for utopia and collective redemption. Indeed, these longings energised the popular Yes campaign.

After writing the three chapters in Reflections on Scotland, I was aware that this section is so different that it could be a separate book. However, we decided to include it here as it gives a symmetry to the Centre's work. We were born out of my reflections on Scotland in *The Scots' Crisis of Confidence,* so it seems apposite to end on how my thinking has changed on these issues in the light of the work the Centre has done in the past twenty years. Of most relevance is the fact that I've become much more interested in well-being, not just confidence, and in what children need to flourish in childhood and later life. The importance of early years experiences and family influences can be seen throughout the book. The hidden, but potent, influence of Scotland's religious past provided the backbone for my argument in *The Scot's Crisis of Confidence* and it does again here. Eerily, and quite by chance, it's also hinted at in the book's lovely cover picture of Òran Mór, now an arts and entertainment venue but once Kelvinside Parish Church in Glasgow's west end.

Until twenty years ago so much of what was written about Scotland and the Scots was negative and full of self-hate. I'm glad these instincts have gone. But we've now gone to the other extreme. There's now a strong impulse to put a positive spin on everything: to show the country in the most flattering light. I'm not doing that here. In *The Scots' Crisis of Confidence* I very deliberately set out to give a balanced, generous perspective on Scotland. I agreed we had weaknesses but I argued these were the downsides of our strengths. Here I'm very deliberately focusing on problems and asking questions: why have so many of the children I grew up with in Milngavie's council estate died prematurely or suffered from ill health; why does Scotland have such a problem with addiction; why do we have so many looked-after children; why have we been so keen to punish children? Some people in Scotland will not just disagree with me but thoroughly dislike the answers I give.

Indeed, some may be annoyed that I'm not only putting a spotlight on Scotland's problems, I'm also digging up their roots to expose them to light. But it's worth remembering that what I set out here by way of explanation are only my ideas. They are tentative and speculative. They also come from a blend of ideas and theories spanning psychology, sociology, public health, politics, religion and literature. And I freely admit that I have no professional academic expertise in any of these topics. However, if I were an expert based in a university, I wouldn't be attempting a broad, speculative analysis. The academic world encourages depth not breadth. Of course, I will make mistakes by having insufficient expertise. But the experts also make mistakes by focusing myopically on one narrow topic when life is inevitably complex and multi-faceted.

It has taken me a lifetime to fathom what it means for me to have, in the words of Robert Louis Stevenson, 'a strong Scots accent of the mind'. So I offer my analysis of Scotland simply as something which may help readers understand themselves or the nation better. If, as a reader, you don't find it useful or insightful, then that's fine. I hope it has helped sharpen your own ideas.

Finally, I want to point out that those of us who were involved with the Centre often shared similar views. This is why we were able to operate so well as a board. But we didn't agree on everything and the board has always held a range of views. For example, we have been of one mind when it comes to the toxic nature of materialist values but we had different views on Scottish independence and Scottish politics. Generally, my board gave me free rein to pursue certain themes and ideas even when they didn't necessarily share my enthusiasm, commitment or perspective. 'We're here to support you, Carol,' has been one of their frequent refrains and one I always appreciated. Indeed, I owe the people who have sat on the Centre's board, and those who worked alongside me, an enormous debt of gratitude for their generous support.

Carol Craig
September 2024

Part 1

Phase 1: 2004-2008

Chapter 1

The difficult birth of the Centre for Confidence and Well-being

Towards a Confident Scotland conference;
Professor Martin Seligman as keynote speaker;
Gregor Henderson's suggestion;
Scottish Executive interest in supporting a centre;
propelling the Scottish Executive to act;
Scotland's Tipping Point conference with Malcolm Gladwell;
a challenging alteration to the funding offer.

IN NOVEMBER 2003 the writer and activist, Gerry Hassan, and I held a conference at Glasgow's Science Centre called 'Towards a Confident Scotland'. Gerry was at that time involved with a small think tank called Big Thinking which had published my first book *The Scots' Crisis of Confidence* in February 2003. I was new to the world of publishing but Gerry was not. And he knew that one of the ways to get a book noticed and talked about was to organise an event linked to its publication.

As Gerry and I had little capability to organise the large-scale event we envisaged the only way forward was to engage conference organisers. This proved to be calamitous as weeks before the event the company went into receivership. Stressful times followed but all was not lost. We ultimately managed to go ahead with new organisers and 150 participants.

There's little doubt that if our organising fiasco had not slowed our momentum and stunted publicity in the weeks running up to the conference, we would have attracted a lot more people. *The*

Scots' Crisis of Confidence had received considerable attention in the Scottish media – not all of it favourable, of course – and I had been asked to speak at numerous events. The book was also attracting interest in high places.

The then First Minister, Jack McConnell, was intrigued by the book and asked the Scottish Executive's Strategy Unit to consider whether there was any merit in my argument that Scottish culture conspires to drain Scots individually of confidence. In 2004 they issued a preliminary paper on what was known about confidence in Scotland. This was then published more formally in February 2005 as a discussion paper called 'Confidence in Scotland'. It showed that there was some, albeit patchy, direct evidence to support the view that Scots often lack confidence. It quotes the Scottish Council Foundation's research published in 2002 which shows that only about a quarter of Scots would describe Scotland as 'a confident place'. The Strategy Unit paper also accepted that many of Scotland's poor economic, social and health statistics (rising rates of suicide, depression, violence, and lower life expectancy) may be linked to low self-esteem and pessimistic thinking.

There's little doubt that the topic of confidence resonated personally with many Scots. Indeed on numerous occasions people who had read the book or heard me speak would say, 'You must know my granny' or 'You've written this book about me'. As the author this surprised me as I felt the book was overly historical and analytical and didn't focus enough on people's everyday lives. Nonetheless individuals' desire to have this aspect of their experience explored and validated meant that they were still able to identify with my arguments.

Aside from the individual resonance, many readers and conference goers could also apply my arguments on the Scots' lack of individual confidence to people they worked with. For managers this meant their employees and for lots of different professionals it meant the people they were supposed to educate, develop, treat, or support. So the book, and particularly the conference, appealed to educators, social workers, public health professionals, sports and arts organisers, business development people, managers and leaders. Indeed attendees found the event particularly refreshing because it was 'cross sectoral' and attracted people from other sectors and organisations with whom they did not usually meet up at more targeted events.

Another source of satisfaction with the event was the keynote speaker, Professor Martin Seligman. We were only able to afford his hefty fee as Scottish Enterprise agreed to be a sponsor on condition that we used the money to secure a heavyweight international speaker. Seligman certainly complied. Not only was he an American author and academic but he was also one of the world's leading psychologists.

Future chapters set out the thinking and research behind Seligman's work and how we employed positive psychology as an organisation. What's relevant here is why participants at 'Towards a Confident Scotland' were so taken with him as a speaker.

There's nothing flashy about Professor Martin Seligman. In fact, he's not even a very articulate or polished performer. He comes over as stolid and academic and likes to describe himself as a 'scientist'. But this is precisely what so many policymakers, civil servants and leaders at the event appreciated. In later conversations with a number of them I repeatedly heard that they knew individual psychology mattered but that they didn't know how to take the matter forward. They were aware that those who were currently involved in various types of personal development programmes were, inevitably, good at selling themselves and their work and this made the professionals nervous. How could these Scottish policymakers or practitioners know there was anything in these claims? And so they repeatedly feared being taken in and made to look foolish.

So Seligman's 'scientific' approach, which purported to show the statistical effect of various interventions, was alluring. What's more, Seligman is a substantial intellectual and appeared at home talking about Greek philosophy or some of the figures of the Scottish Enlightenment. All of this played well with the Science Centre audience in November 2003.

One of those impressed, not only by Seligman's keynote speech but the whole event, was Gregor Henderson. The year before he had been appointed as the Scottish Executive's Director of the

National Programme for Improving Mental Health and Well-being, a role he held until 2008. The programme aimed to eliminate stigma, increase public awareness, reduce suicide and promote recovery. One of its priorities was community mental health and well-being. There's little doubt Gregor was a visionary and the National Programme he created attracted interest and plaudits internationally.

Gregor sought me out at the event to suggest that I should keep working on the conference themes of confidence, optimism and well-being and that he might be able to support me to get some kind of project launched. If he hadn't taken this step the Centre would never have been created and I wouldn't be writing this book.

Talks and planning

Over the next six months Gregor and I had numerous stimulating meetings to talk about how confidence and positive psychology interventions could be advanced in Scotland and how these ideas could be funded by the Scottish Executive. Two things were immediately important to me: any organisation set up had to be a charity or not for profit and I needed to be an employee.

I knew the importance of this from my experience of a loose organisation set up in 2003 called 'Confident Scotland'. The TV journalist Bill MacFarlane and the psychiatrist Dr Alex Yellowlees were the driving forces. I went to a large-scale discussion on confidence which they held at the Gleneagles Hotel. About 60 people attended this lively event including Phil Hanlon, then a professor of Public Health at Glasgow University. Phil and I found we shared an interest in culture and our meeting was the beginning of a fruitful collaboration which still continues.

But my relationship with Bill and Alex was more complicated. It wasn't clear to me what Confident Scotland was – an umbrella organisation to bring people together in their interest in confidence or their own training consultancy? So clarity on the status of any organisation I set up was one of my immediate concerns.

Gregor set about finding allies and support within the Scottish Executive. He knew that the First Minister and Strategy Unit were interested. So too was Angus Skinner who was then Chief Social Work Inspector and very keen on Seligman's work. Peter Peacock, Education Secretary, was also supportive. In time it transpired that three departments were willing to fund a centre. They were: Mental Health Division, Teachers' Division in the Education Department and Social Services.

State aid regulations limited the amount of money the Scottish Executive could put into the creation of this type of organisation to £150,000 per annum and so the proposal was for these three departments to contribute £50,000 each for three years.

So far so good but trouble lay ahead. A senior person working at the Scottish Executive, someone I knew well, was completely opposed to the proposal for a confidence centre ostensibly because it would not be greeted favourably by the press. My nemesis then started to phone some of those involved in the negotiations at home, shouting at them 'The First Minister does not want this centre.' They knew this not to be true as Jack McConnell consistently gave his support but it certainly made people feel fearful and the negotiations more difficult. As we shall see this person's negativity had a lasting impact on how the Centre functioned for its first three years.

And when I think about her malign influence I am reminded of Madeleine Albright, the former American diplomat, who once said: 'There is a special place in hell for women who don't help other women.'

Even after I had received a draft agreement all was not certain. In the summer of 2004 Professor Ed Diener was in the UK and offered to come to Glasgow to speak. He was another senior American psychologist and he had just co-authored an important journal article with Martin Seligman called 'Beyond Money' (2002). In it they argued that Gross Domestic Product (GDP) should no longer be used as the sole measurement for societal progress and we should be looking for a range of well-being measures instead. This argument now seems obvious but it was quite radical twenty years ago. Scottish Enterprise agreed to host a dinner to allow a discussion between Professor Diener and various Scottish thinkers, journalists and leaders. One of those present was a senior civil servant who took exception to me talking openly that night about the plans for a centre which, amongst other things, would promote positive psychology. The following day I was contacted by a junior civil servant and told that I was not to say to anyone that the Scottish Executive was going to fund a centre.

By this stage I had drafted a 35-page business plan for what I was now calling the Centre for Confidence and Well-being. Confidence clearly had to be in the name but I was aware that positive psychology, which the Scottish Executive was keen to promote, was more about well-being than confidence. What's more, I could see that interest in well-being was developing internationally. I would have preferred to put Scottish at the top of the name but was told that I was not allowed to do this without permission. So this is how the Centre's somewhat grandiose name came about.

Gregor and I then entered a period of limbo. Was the Centre going to happen or not? Would the Scottish Executive move on from draft proposals and make a legally binding offer? I suspect that years later we would still have been waiting for approval and it was only by taking action that I inadvertently made it happen.

Propelling the Scottish Executive to act

I was very keen to hold a celebratory launch event. Malcolm Gladwell's book *The Tipping Point: How little things can make a big difference* (2000) had become very popular in the UK and its analysis was relevant to anyone interested in large scale social change. I phoned his agent and found that he was going to be in the UK in late November and early December and had one free day. Within a week I was able to raise a substantial sum in sponsorship from a range of organisations such as Scottish Enterprise Glasgow and the City Council. I made a temporary booking with Òran Mór for December 2nd. And then I waited for confirmation from the Scottish Executive that this would indeed be the launch event for the Centre. It didn't come. I had a few agonising days when I considered forgetting all about the event. But it seemed such a pity and some of the people I had asked for support were disappointed to think it wouldn't go ahead. So I took a gamble. I decided I would just run it myself and if it made a loss I would bear that cost.

I had also been discussing the idea of the Centre with William Roe as I was keen for him to be its first Chair. At that time Willy had just been appointed Chairman of Highlands and Islands Enterprise and involved with various organisations in Scotland so he was very well connected.[1] This was something that we were going to need. Willy and I both agreed not just to hold the event but also to launch the Centre at it even if we didn't have the Scottish Executive's financial support.

Taking this decisive action forced the Executive's hand. I suspect they feared the press writing that they weren't confident enough to support a confidence centre that they had been discussing for months. It was good news for all of us wanting to establish the Centre for they confirmed that the First Minister would open 'Scotland's Tipping Point' and publicly announce financial support for the Centre for Confidence and Well-being.

The event was a huge success. The 300 places sold out within a week and there was a large waiting list. Malcolm Gladwell was an engaging and captivating speaker. Indeed the speaking contributions from Jack McConnell, myself, Professor Phil Hanlon and Professor Tom Devine went down exceedingly well with the audience. Two sets of workshops followed – one according to sector (education, enterprise etc) and then geographically. For some participants this was an important experience and some were still meeting in their own city over a decade later under the banner of 'Go Dundee' (See Appendix).

At that time Julie Morrison was working in public relations at Royal Mail Scotland and, thanks to support from its Director of Scottish Affairs, Ian McKay, Julie helped us with PR in the first few years of our existence.[2]

Julie's professional PR advice and support undoubtedly resulted in us attracting widespread press coverage. Julie put together a

---

1. Willy Roe chaired the Centre for Confidence and Well-being board from December 2004 to December 2007.
2. Ian McKay joined the Centre's board in 2007 and remained a member until 2010.

Endorsements for the Centre of Confidence and Well-Being on its launch day, 2nd December 2004

Rt. Hon. Alistair Darling - Secretary of State for Scotland and Secretary of State for Transport

'We need a new generation of determined, confident innovators and entrepreneurs to keep Scotland's economy growing in the face of globalisation. It is sometimes said that Scotland 'does not do optimism' – it must do now. The Centre has the potential to help this happen and I strongly support it.'

Peter Peacock MSP, Education Minister, Scottish Executive

'Developing confidence in young people is vital to ensure they reach their full potential. Confidence will help them adopt a "can-do" approach, encourage them to take all the opportunities that come their way and will ensure there is no limit to their ambition.'

Jack Perry, Chief Executive of Scottish Enterprise

'The development of greater confidence and greater levels of collective self-belief are essential elements of an enterprising society. I believe the Centre can provide real leadership in this area and help inspire more people through its message of positivity and optimism. The Centre and Scottish Enterprise share the same goals and we look forward to working with them.'

Adam Crozier, Chief Executive of Royal Mail

'This new Centre is all about changing attitudes in Scottish culture and celebrating the success of the nation going forward. This is a fantastic idea and will help to remind Scots that Scotland is full to the brim with success.'

David Clayton, Partner, PricewaterhouseCoopers

'This initiative is an example of what is right in Scotland today. By marshalling the energy and commitment of talented Scots who care about their country and wish to make a positive difference, the new Centre potentially could be a significant beacon for Scotland's future. Scotland can compete in the global economy for the benefit of all our citizens, and this new Centre may help us believe it.'

Dr Harry Burns, Director of Public Health, Greater Glasgow NHS

'There is increasing evidence that psychological factors such as confidence, resilience and self-esteem play an important role in determining how healthy we are. I am strongly supportive of the Centre for Confidence and Well-Being and look forward to working with it to help enhance quality of life for all Scots, and Glaswegians in particular.'

Jeremy Purvis MSP, Tweeddale, Ettrick and Lauderdale
'Supporting someone to gain greater self-confidence and build esteem is an important element in allowing everyone to achieve their own personal ambitions in life. I therefore warmly welcome the initiative that will allow this support to be given.'

Archie Hunter, Chairman of the Court, University of Strathclyde
'It is very progressive for Scotland for this new Centre to be exploring these areas and in the long run it could produce a lot of material and approaches which will be useful for the educational sector.'

Professor Phil Hanlon, Professor of Public Health, University of Glasgow
'Scotland's health is very poor and in some key areas (Obesity, Mental Health, Alcohol Related Harm, Sexual Health) is getting worse. 'Confidence' will be one of the keys needed to open the door to a healthier future. For this reason alone, I welcome the creation of this new Centre, it is, however, about much more than just confidence. The work Carol Craig is leading opens up a much more positive way of looking at health and health improvement.'

Wendy Alexander MSP, Paisley North
'The Centre's founding is an exciting step in Scotland's journey from debilitating self-doubt to stimulating self respect.'

Sandy Cumming, Chief Executive, Highland and Islands Enterprise
'The HIE network supports the formation of the Centre. Its aspirations and activities have the potential to make significant impact on many aspects of life in the Highlands where growing confidence has underpinned recent success and will be equally important in the future.'

Tom Devine, Glucksman Professor of Irish & Scottish Studies, University of Aberdeen
'The issue of confidence and well-being has been an important source of debate and controversy in Scotland over the past few years. It is therefore welcome that this fundamental aspect of our national life is to be discussed in a professional and rigorous manner.'

Tom Hunter, Chairman of The Hunter Foundation
'If you accept that you should give a hungry man a fishing rod, not a fish, then confidence underpins his ability to use that fishing rod – we need to continue to move away from dependency and on to self-belief if Scotland is to flourish. This Centre will support this movement and I hope aid in tipping us over the edge in becoming a leading small nation of the world. . .'

lengthy press release for our launch at Scotland's Tipping Point and included within it a large list of endorsements for the Centre. This is something I wouldn't have thought of doing but it was helpful in demonstrating the widespread, and enthusiastic, support the Centre was attracting across Scottish life.

The fly in the ointment

At the event the First Minister announced that the Scottish Executive was giving £450,000 to set up the Centre for Confidence and Well-being. This was over three years so it was not as generous as it sounded. More importantly, at the last moment the Scottish Executive changed its offer from 'core' funding, which covers salaries, accommodation and other running costs, to 'project' funding where only agreed activities are financed. I have good reason to believe that my nemesis had a hand in that. This apparently small change had important repercussions for how the Centre was able to operate.

This became painfully clear at the first official meeting I had with the three funding departments a week or so after the event in Edinburgh. In the chair was Geoff Huggins who was at that time head of Mental Health Division. This was one of the three funding departments but Geoff had also agreed to be the partners' main link with the Centre. We had never met before and had no relationship of goodwill or trust to draw on. My recollection of the meeting is that everything I proposed was knocked back on the basis that it was 'core' funding. Nor did my idea of a large-scale event on positive psychology with Professor Martin Seligman find favour. They wanted to 'pilot' a one day training course with 30 people. My vision was for an ambitious programme involving at least a few hundred. 'You'll have to organise and fund that yourself,' they told me.

What was now being proposed was substantially different from what Gregor and I had been discussing for months and from the bold vision set out in our Business Plan. Yes we now had a Centre but every pound it spent would be controlled by the Scottish Executive through project funding. They would have to sign off everything we did with a penny of their money. From experience

Extract from the Summary of the Centre's Business Plan

In autumn 2004 The Centre for Confidence and Well-Being Ltd. will be set up in Glasgow.

The new Centre's mission is to bring about a change in attitudes in Scottish culture so that it –

- encourages confidence and creativity
- celebrates success
- fosters positive attitudes
- highlights and promotes the importance and understanding of well-being.

The Centre will be outward looking and aims to establish itself as an internationally recognised centre for research, thinking and interventions on confidence and positive psychology.

The Centre will be set up as a company limited by guarantee with charitable status. Its Chief Executive will be Dr Carol Craig. It will employ a small core team of people and it will be governed by a board of directors.

The Centre's broad role will be to –

- Provide strategic thinking for national culture change.
- Create a movement for such change.
- Provide leadership.
- Span different sectors in Scottish life and add value to all of them.
- Network interested parties.
- Take an international perspective.
- Develop rigorous tools and methodologies for research, evaluation and dissemination.
- Run large-scale interventions such as campaigns, training courses and conferences.

The Centre's core activities will include providing information, networking interested parties and improving the quality of confidence building approaches and activities through the provision of workshops and conferences and the dissemination or development of tools for evaluation. It will also pursue a number of large-scale projects, campaigns and interventions. It is envisaged that in the first few years of existence the Centre will work mainly on the confidence agenda and that the emphasis on well-being will become more significant with time.

I could see that caution, not creativity or confidence, would be their guiding principles. Or at least that is how it looked to me as I slunk to the station on a grim December day to get the train back to Glasgow. Indeed the euphoria and optimism of the two events that had led up to the creation of the Centre for Confidence and Well-being seemed to belong to another world.

Chapter 2

In the Vanguard: the early years and the development of positive psychology

Why I was keen to promote Martin Seligman's work and positive psychology;
the main ideas of 'Authentic Happiness';
support from Scottish MSPs at the official Centre launch in March 2005;
designing and running the Centre's first big event on positive psychology –
the Vanguard Programme;
reflections on its success;
subsequent Vanguard events in 2006;
the creation of positive psychology Resources on the Centre's website.

THE CENTRE for Confidence and Well-being started in earnest on 4th January 2005 and we launched our programme in the Scottish Parliament on 9th March. (See page 43) Another stroke of good fortune is that I had a good relationship with Dr Carol Tannahill as I had worked with her team when she was at Public Health Glasgow. She had just been appointed to run the Glasgow Centre for Population Health. The organisaton was founded in early 2004 by the Scottish Executive but run by various partners, namely the local NHS health board, Glasgow City Council and the University of Glasgow. Its remit was to study why people in the city had such poor health and to suggest ways this could be tackled. They were being given substantial funds from the Scottish Executive and had taken offices in Glasgow's St Vincent Street. Carol generously offered me a few spare desks in their office until we could get our own accommodation. We moved into our own office in 45 Union Street in November.

Funding was difficult from day one as the Scottish Executive decided that it wouldn't start our grant until April 2005. This meant that we had no money. Fortunately we received some money from a benefactor: in November 2004 Ewan Hunter, who worked for Tom Hunter at the Hunter Foundation, asked for a meeting with me and said they were interested to know more about the organisation I was planning to set up. After several meetings and lots of discussion the Foundation gave the new Centre a one-off payment of £50,000. This was contingent on us getting charitable status which we were awarded in due course. That £50,000 was a lifesaver for us.

Discovering Martin Seligman

We immediately started on a number of projects which I had set out in our business plan. My heart, however, was on delivering a large positive psychology training programme. Why?

When I wrote *The Scots' Crisis of Confidence* I hadn't read much academic psychology, though it's fair to say there isn't much of a scholarly literature on confidence as it's too general a concept. So my interest in the topic was a fusion of my personal development work with literally thousands of Scots – mainly in small discursive workshops – with my interest and knowledge of Scottish culture.

But all of this was about to change. At the end of one of my talks on confidence two people – Johnny Walker and Elaine Reilly – quite independently of one another, recommended I read *Learned Optimism* (1990) by Professor Martin Seligman. I was intrigued and went immediately to a book shop. As the book was more than ten years old it wasn't in stock. But what was prominently displayed was Martin Seligman's latest book *Authentic Happiness*(2002). Its title wouldn't have normally appealed to me – sounding too gushy and American – but I bought it anyway. (Interestingly Seligman used to say that he also disliked the title and his publisher chose it for its commercial appeal.)

I loved the book. I learned things which I knew would benefit my own life but, more importantly, it resonated strongly with what I thought would benefit many Scots – an injection of positive emotion and optimism. Also much of it was completely in tune

Programme launch of the Centre for Confidence and Well-being 9th March 2005, in the Scottish Parliament's Garden Lobby

In welcoming the 160 guests from across Scotland, George Reid msp, the Parliament's Presiding Officer, made it clear that confidence is now a major priority for Scotland's policy-makers: 'I welcome the work that is being done by Dr Carol Craig as it fits well with the role of the Parliament and what we are trying to achieve here,' he said.

He recalled that at the official launch of the Parliament the previous year, many of the speakers asked: 'what is wrong with you Scots, why do you go around whinging? You have a lot to be confident about – an environment to die for, world-class universities, major financial institutions and high tech industries.'

Politicians from across the political spectrum also spoke in support of the Centre.

Kenny MacAskill MSP (Scottish National Party)
'The confidence issue transcends parties and cultures. The Centre will help to encourage people to become much more confident in the country, together.'

Susan Deacon MSP (Scottish Labour)
'I think that this is the most exciting work being undertaken in Scotland at the moment. It will allow us to see the true potential in our nation. It will reveal what makes us tick – and will give us the confidence to go forward and make the country a better place.'

Margaret Mitchell MSP (Scottish Conservative & Unionist Party)
'I could never understand why, in history lessons at school, we focused on the Tudors and not on our own illustrious heritage. That's all about confidence. We need to look at what happens to the confidence of our children in primary school, on through secondary school and into adulthood – and why their confidence changes. I am pleased that we are starting to look along this road – it can only help Scotland in the future.'

George Lyon MSP (Scottish Liberal Democrats)
'I think that we need to learn from the experiences in Ireland. What was the catalyst that made Ireland one of the most confident nations in the world today? I am fed up with us Scots as a nation, where we see our glass as half empty rather than half full. I hope through this new centre we can end this self-doubt and signal to everyone that we are a confident nation.'

Mark Ballard MSP (Scottish Green Party)
'I welcome the Centre. It will give us a real opportunity to think about what it takes to turn us into a confident nation.'

At the event it was clear that there was a cross-party consensus that a more confident Scotland could transform our health, well-being, economic, educational and employment prospects. It would also help to create more dynamic organisations. Most of the people who attended the event commented on how refreshing it was to hear politicians agreeing with each other, rather than quibbling over tiny points of difference.

with the type of strong Scottish values I outlined in *The Scots' Crisis of Confidence*, such as a robust work ethic and the importance of meaning and purpose promoted by a once dominant Presbyterian church.

Seligman focuses attention on the real meaning of happiness. Ultimately he concludes that there are three different types of happiness. He calls the first 'the pleasant life' as it's the type of happiness which emanates from pleasure and positive emotion. Such pleasure can come from a variety of different sources such as sensory experience, or emotions induced by relationships or achievements. Much of what we are encouraged to desire in modern consumer society belongs to this type of happiness – big houses, cars, expensive clothes. However, while these experiences can be intensely pleasurable the problem is that they're transitory and so add little to a lasting feeling of satisfaction in life. This is exactly the problem that Robert Burns described in verse more than 200 years ago.

> But pleasures are like poppies spread
> You seize the flow'r, its bloom is shed
> Or like the snow falls in the river
> A moment white – then melts forever
>
> 'Tam O'Shanter'

One of the main reasons why pleasures do not last is that, as human beings, we have incredible powers of adaptation. Novel experiences, such as driving a new car, may make us feel great but soon the novelty wears off and we hardly notice the experience any more.

Seligman's second type of happiness he calls 'the engaged life' and this involves participation in activities which are intrinsically interesting and rewarding for the individual and induce what Professor Mihaly Csikszentmihalyi describes as 'flow'. People who lose themselves in work or activities will know the satisfaction and indirect feeling of happiness which can arise. While Seligman thinks this type of happiness deeper than pleasure he considers it a less important type of happiness than that gained from meaningful activities.

So, for Seligman, the third and most important type of happiness is 'the meaningful life'. However, this is becoming more difficult for people to achieve. Indeed Seligman attributes many of the problems of modern society to the rise of individualism and what he calls 'the big I and the small we'. At the turn of the twentieth century, even in an individualistic culture like America, people were focused on serving institutions such as the church, the family and the nation. But in today's world these have been eclipsed by what he often describes as the 'bloated self': a self overly obsessed with its own interests and vulnerable to depression since it exaggerates the significance of life's inevitable adversities.

For Seligman the antidote to depression is for people to live more meaningful lives and meaning, he argues, is by definition serving a goal bigger than yourself. This can be about having a clear idea of the mission and purpose of your life, contributing to charity, putting others' needs before your own and so forth. But, according to Seligman, the best way we can do this is to know what our 'signature strengths' are and then to be in a role – either at work or through volunteering – where every day we can use these strengths 'in the service of other people'. For me, one of the most useful aspects of Seligman's formulation of the meaningful life is that it unites the individual and the collective. It recognises the importance of individuality and the fact that individuals will be most motivated to undertake activities where they have a particular contribution to make. But it suggests the best way to direct these strengths and interests is in the service of other people – not the aggrandisement of the self.

According to Seligman's research at the time, the pursuit of pleasure is the least important for happiness. This rather turns normal thinking on its head, given that we so often equate happiness with money, leisure, good looks etc. It's in the pursuit of engagement and meaning that we find contentment, long term satisfaction and happiness. Speaking at the event I was planning for later in the year (September 2005) Seligman summed up the results of his latest research on how to live a happy life:

> What should we pursue if we want the most life satisfaction? The results are quite surprising. Basically, you can ask people

> the extent to which they pursue positive emotion in life, the extent to which they pursue engagement in life and the extent to which they pursue meaning in life. And we found that pleasure doesn't matter very much. If you'd asked me in advance, I would have said that pleasure was the big one – but it is the small one. So it's the pursuit of engagement and the pursuit of meaning that have the substantial effects on life satisfaction. It turns out pleasure matters but it seems to matter only if you have the other two. So if you have engagement and meaning in your life then pleasure adds significantly. The whole is greater than the sum of the parts if you have all three.

Positive psychology

After studying *Authentic Happiness* I read more online about Seligman's desire to promote positive psychology. Seligman's groundbreaking research on 'learned helplessness' in the 1960s led him to study depression and then from there to research into optimism and pessimism. In 1998 he became President of the American Psychological Association. As presidents usually have a theme they pursue during their year of office, Seligman's came in the form of an epiphany while gardening with his five-year-old daughter. This consisted mainly of an understanding that raising children should not be about fixing what is wrong with them but about recognising and building on their strengths.

Seligman believed that this insight did not fit with the usual preoccupation of psychology: his discipline had become increasingly focused on what was wrong with people and paid scant attention to what was right. This had not always been the case. In the 1920s and 30s psychology had three main areas of interest: understanding ordinary human life to help people become more productive and fulfilled, understanding and nurturing genius and the study and treatment of mental illness. But after World War II, in the US and the UK, new government spending priorities allowed psychologists to make a living treating or researching mental illness. This meant that a disease focus came to dominate psychology. Thus Seligman and his main collaborator at this time, Mihaly Csikszentmihaly, write of this era of psychology – 'practitioners went about treating the illnesses of patients with a disease framework by repairing damage: damaged habits, damaged drives, damaged childhoods, and damaged brains.' This deficit model, they argue, has also influenced the thinking of other professional groups.

Seligman and Csikszentmihaly then set about finding allies for a new discipline of 'positive psychology' and they were spectacularly successful. Many psychologists in the US were keen to support it. So too were students and members of the public. When Harvard University launched a new course on positive psychology it attracted so many students that it was the most popular course in Harvard's history.

Much has now been written on positive psychology but it has four main pillars:

- An interest in what it calls 'the science of optimal human functioning'.
- Its desire to learn what works from studying human *success* rather than human failure or weaknesses.
- Its attention on positive subjective experiences such as happiness and well-being as well as positive human characteristics such as strengths and virtues.
- Its desire to study not just individuals but group structures such as organisations, families or cultures to learn how they can induce positive emotion and encourage the use of strengths.

It's important not to confuse positive psychology with 'positive thinking'. The former is a development in social science supported by extensive academic research while the latter is a branch of personal development literature where gurus promote the idea that our success in life can come from thinking positively all the time. Positive psychology, by contrast, stresses the power and the pull of the negative. Indeed intrinsic to both Seligman's and Csikszentmihaly's work is the idea that the brain tends to prioritise negative information.

So there is a paradox at the heart of positive psychology. And it is this: the brain finds it very easy to be negative but it is very important for human beings to experience positive emotions as it is in this emotional state that we build our health, our relationships and our intellectual and psychological reserves. These insights have been drawn from the pioneering experiments carried out by Professor Barbara Fredrickson. Seligman described her as 'the genius' behind positive psychology as her 'broaden and build theory of human emotion', based on extensive empirical research, showed the importance of 'positive affect', (positive emotions in everyday language), to human flourishing.

The positive psychology paradox leads ultimately to the conclusion that it's crucially important for human beings to learn how to side-step the natural negativity of the brain and to experience more positive emotion. Positive psychologists believe that the research into happiness and other emotional states now gives people access to information on how to minimise negativity and live more positive and fulfilling lives.

A great opportunity

In the spring of 2003, as I was researching positive psychology I discovered that a large scale telephone-based coaching programme on *Authentic Happiness* was about the begin. I found out about the course just as they were closing the list so I was very lucky to get a place. I was one of about three hundred participants and the only one from Scotland. It was the first course of its type but more were planned given the developing interest in positive psychology.

The course was an intensive learning experience. There were twenty, weekly one hour telephone lectures mainly given by Martin Seligman but also by some guest lecturers such as Mihaly Csikszentmihalyi and Barbara Fredrickson. There was some opportunity in these hourly sessions for a few course participants to ask questions and become involved in discussions. But the main arena for course members to participate was in a weekly telephone 'pod' – or tutorial group – which was led by a coach and involved about 16 people. On the pod calls, course members were allocated homework exercises and had the opportunity to discuss this and other aspects of the course.

I learned that there was going to be a 2nd European Conference on Positive Psychology in Italy in July 2004. I attended the conference and learned that other countries, such as Portugal and Australia, also perceived barriers in their culture to the development of confidence, optimism and resilience and were now developing programmes for improvement.

The Vanguard Programme

All this learning was not only life changing for me but also pertinent to plans for the Centre's work. The pressing question was how we could replicate my experience on the Authentic Happiness Coaching Programme to allow others in Scotland to share what I had learned? One thing I knew – it needed another name and it didn't take long to come up with it. Seligman often referred to the first cohort of his training programme as 'the vanguard' and that seemed a perfect name for what we were planning for Scotland. We decided to call it the **Vanguard Programme** with the subtitle 'the new instrument for change'. Since we envisaged most of the participants being in Scotland we didn't need to devise a programme that was exclusively phone-based.

The shape of the programme soon emerged: two days of lectures and some discussion at a conference style event at the Radisson Hotel in Glasgow on September 5th and 6th 2005 followed by seven hour-long telephone lectures. There were also telephone-based small group discussions with facilitators. Thanks to support from the Scottish Parliament's Future Forum, the final day of the training course was to be in the Scottish Parliament's debating chamber in December.

As you can imagine this 35-hour long training programme was expensive to run and this had to be reflected in its price. We charged £800 per head. Despite the cost 300 people ultimately signed up, not all of them paying the full price, however. Many of them were senior managers and policy makers. For example, the then head of the civil service in Scotland, John Elvidge, booked a place. So too did two MSPs – Kenny MacAskill and Susan Deacon. I offered a few free places to people who were opinion formers and commentators, such as Iain Macwhirter.

And what of the speakers and contributors? The main speaker was, inevitably, Martin Seligman. He gave five one-hour lectures over the two days at the Radisson on positive psychology, learned helplessness, depression, pessimism, optimism, happiness and the importance of meaning. Professor Felicia Huppert, from Cambridge University, an expert on well-being, talked about how to bring about change at a population level. The economist Professor Richard Layard who had just published a best-selling book called *Happiness: lessons from a new science* (2005) talked about why he thought happiness should become a major focus of public policy.

Another speaker at the event was Richard Eckersley from Australia. When one of the temporary staff phoned to ask him if he would give a telephone lecture she mistakenly asked him to give a talk at the Glasgow event. He was very keen to do so. When I later explained the mistake and that we couldn't afford to pay him expenses from Australia he offered to come anyway as he was so keen to participate. He gave a tremendous talk based on his book *Well and Good* (2004) in which he argues that despite material progress people's lives were not getting better.

I also spoke at the Radisson on 'improving change programmes by understanding and respecting cultural and individual differences'. In my talk I argued, for example, that I didn't think the Scots warmed to the concept of happiness and that well-being and optimism are more motivational for us.

Phil Hanlon also spoke. His theme was 'the Scottish effect and the need for transforming change to improve health and well-being'. A few years later I spoke to Nic Marks who was working at the New Economics Foundation. He hadn't been to the event but had spoken to a few who had. 'I hear the local guy [Phil Hanlon] stole the show', is how he put it. And it was true: Phil's talk was, as usual thought provoking, relevant and inspiring and extremely articulate. There's no doubt it wowed the audience.

Another conference theme was the Scottish Enlightenment. The reason for this was simple. Positive psychology was being hailed as a new development in social science and it is the Scots of the Scottish Enlightenment who created social science. So the introductory lecture was given by Professor Tom Devine and called 'the roots and impact of the Scottish Enlightenment on Scotland and America'. The final (optional) lecture at the end of day two was from Scotland's foremost Scottish Enlightenment expert, Professor Alexander Broadie. He gave a lecture on 'the confidence, optimism and well-being agenda through the eyes of gifted Scottish thinkers such as Adam Smith, David Hume and Francis Hutcheson'. And the last telephone lecture was given by Professor Arthur Herman whose book on the Scottish Enlightenment, *How the Scots Invented the Modern World* (2001), had been a huge international success. Martin Seligman was very taken by this book.

Martin Seligman's claim that 'the Scots invented positive psychology'

In August 2005 Martin Seligman wrote a review of Arthur Herman's book *How the Scots Invented the Modern World* on the 'Reflective Happiness' website. In it he admits that he finds the French Enlightenment 'lightweight' and thanks to Herman is now 'astonished by the depth and modernity' of the Scottish Enlightenment. He does not consider it far-fetched to argue that the Scots 'may indeed have invented the modern world'. Seligman is particularly taken by Francis Hutcheson and his thoughts on morality and altruism – thoughts which influenced both David Hume and Adam Smith. Seligman ends the short review proclaiming: 'But one aspect is compelling to me: The Scots invented positive psychology.'

Willy Roe skilfully chaired the Radisson event and is fond of saying that what he learned over these two days 'changed his life'. Many participants were ecstatic about the two-day event and like Willy said it had made a significant impact on them personally and professionally.

These two days were then followed by an additional fifteen hours of distance learning. This involved six telephone-based discussions as well as seven one-hour long telephone lectures. Some of these were given by people prominent in the field of positive psychology: Professor Barbara Fredrickson, Dr Karen

Reivich, and Professor Barry Schwartz. Professor Howard Gardner, famous internationally for his work on multiple intelligences, gave a lecture on 'creating a positive climate for learning'. Dr Nick Bayliss from Cambridge University, the UK's first positive psychology lecturer and columnist on 'the Science of Happiness' for *The Times Magazine*, talked about the necessity of a holistic approach to well-being. Scotland's Chief Medical Officer, Dr Harry Burns, gave a lecture linking poor health outcomes in Glasgow to feelings of hopelessness.

We held the programme finale on 12th December in the Scottish Parliament and it was chaired by the Parliament's Presiding Officer, George Reid. It was an 'open space' event with the day's programme being partly decided on the day by participants. It was largely designed for people to reflect back on what they had learned from the programme. Eight 'Community of Practice' groups on a range of topics such as education, sport, mental health and well-being had met during the Radisson event and many of these reconvened. There were also small group sessions to allow participants to review a special folder of material put together on tools, tips and techniques to advance positive psychology.

I was slightly disappointed in the final day. Many of those who attended the Radisson event were in senior positions. It was great that they committed two days of their precious time but many found it difficult to sustain their involvement. So there was an inevitable fall-off with the distance learning and attendance on 12th December. Attendance was also reduced because of bad weather.

I had been so looking forward to us being in the Scottish Parliament's debating chamber but this is what I found most disappointing. It is a beautiful space and works well as a chamber for political debate but it was not good for creating the atmosphere we had experienced in the Radisson. People were sitting too far apart for there to be a sense of togetherness. Even Phil Hanlon's talk fell somewhat flat. Nonetheless there had been so many highs in the whole programme that ending on a lower note was fine. I'm also sure that I was more disappointed in the final day than most of those attending. The overall evaluations of the programme were outstanding with many saying it was 'intellectually challenging' as well as 'emotionally satisfying'. Many said they found it inspirational and/or 'life-changing.'

Reflections on the Vanguard Programme

Considering the programme as a whole there's little doubt that the Centre pulled off something remarkable. This was largely down to Zoe Conlin and Hazel Black. Zoe, formally the Programme Manager, was on a six-month secondment from Standard Life; Hazel Black was the Centre's Business Development Manager and she was on a two-year secondment from Scottish Enterprise. I helped out when I could and we also had occasional support from volunteers and temporary staff.

In late August, a week or so before the Vanguard started, I became ill, no doubt with stress, and had to go to bed for a few days. Zoe and Hazel assured me that I should rest as they had everything in hand. And they did.

The Vanguard Programme cost about £120,000 to run and some of this had to be paid in advance. There was no Scottish Executive financial support for the programme, though many officials paid to attend, and minimal direct sponsorship from other organisations. I knew David Thorburn, who was then CEO for the Clydesdale Bank, and he was very keen on what the Centre was doing. The bank was the main sponsor for the programme and we put their logo on the folders handed out at the event. BT gave some help with the telephone element of the programme and, of course, the Scottish Parliament's Future Programme provided the accommodation for the final day. *The Herald* gave us three free adverts to publicise the event. And that's it.

Looking back I see how extremely risky the whole venture was. If we had made a substantial loss or the event had been deemed a failure the Centre might have been a one-year wonder. I came across an email the other day where I mention in passing that I had agreed to 'financially underwrite' the Vanguard. In other words, I would have had to personally make good any financial loss. This stunned me. I am not that well off and I had spent a year setting up the Centre and doing virtually no paid work. I am also very conservative with money and don't take financial gambles. So I must have thought that the Vanguard Programme was bound to succeed. I must have been extraordinarily confident that people would want to attend.

And I was right. With all fees and expenses paid, but not accounting for staff time and overheads, we made a profit of £70,000.

The Vanguard rolls on

Given the success of the Vanguard Programme, the Centre's board was very keen to maintain momentum. We agreed that we would run smaller scale events round the country. In 2006 we held three separate regional events under the banner of the **Vanguard Series** in Glasgow, Inverness and Dundee and attracted about 200 people in total. At all the events I gave an overview of positive psychology and Phil Hanlon facilitated a discussion on themes related to health and well-being. A variety of other people and organisations participated in putting on these sessions.

The Glasgow event was chaired by the well-known journalist Ruth Wishart and the leader of Glasgow City Council, Stephen Purcell, outlined how 'social renewal' was now a major priority for the city. We held the second event in Inverness and it was sponsored by Highlands and Islands Enterprise (HIE). Professor Jim Hunter, a historian and former Chair of HIE, chaired the event and gave an introductory talk. We held the third of these Vanguards in Dundee and it was sponsored by the University of Abertay. Professor John Palfreyman from Abertay gave an interesting and informative introduction which included his involvement in 'Go Dundee' – an action group which formed as a result of the Scotland's Tipping Point conference. (See Appendix 1). Susan Deacon msp, and former Health Minister, talked about the negativity of the press in Scotland and how individuals could challenge this and turn it around.

In October 2006 Martin Seligman returned to Scotland to participate in another two half-day events run by the Centre. We called these **Vanguard Extra Events** and held them at the Hub,

Edinburgh. The afternoon session was an opportunity for Professor Seligman to talk about recent developments in positive psychology and some of his own thinking and research. These two events attracted almost 300 people and demonstrated that there was still a lot of interest and energy behind positive psychology in Scotland.

Positive psychology resources

To access our dedicated funding from the Scottish Executive we had to come up with 'projects' which they would then agree to fund. One of the these was the creation of 'positive psychology resources' on our website. This was a huge undertaking as it involved the creation of eleven sections on topics such as positive psychology, optimism, happiness, resilience etc. Each section had a variety of resources available – overview essays introducing the topic, audio lectures, evidence summaries, tools, tips and techniques, summaries of projects, web links and booklists.

As far as we could tell our positive psychology resources section on our website was at that time the most comprehensive, free resource library on the subject on the web. It attracted considerable international attention and undoubtedly put Scotland in the vanguard when it came to positive psychology. In 2006, when internet use was not nearly as developed as it is now, we still had over 127,000 individual visitors to our website. It also meant that while we were not a drop-in centre, we were a valuable resource centre which could be accessed anywhere in the world.

Despite the interest these internet resources attracted, creating a huge presence online would not have been how I would have chosen to spend the Scottish Executive's funding. Apart from anything else it made our website unwieldy and very difficult to maintain. I'm also sure there were better ways to spend the money allocated to us. But nonetheless, in the early years of the Centre we were going from strength to strength.

A few numbers from our extensive Activities Report[1] for 2006 astound me now. Around 800 people attended Centre events in

1. All of the Centre's Activities Reports are accessible documents

2006 and I spoke at 35 external, mainly Scottish, events to almost 3,500 people on themes of confidence, positive psychology and optimism. So there's little doubt: the Centre had a significant, and appropriately positive, impact on Scottish life in these early years of operation. But much, much more was to come.

CHAPTER 3

'The costly pursuit of self-esteem': what every Scottish teacher needs to know

Seligman's warning on self-esteem;
the Curriculum for Excellence;
the self-esteem bandwagon;
Seligman's critique;
Generation Me;
implications for Scotland;
the Centre's *Creating Confidence Handbook*;
other activities promoted by the Centre to foster young people's confidence and well-being;
the Centre's model of confidence & well-being.

WHEN MARTIN Seligman spoke in Glasgow in November 2003 at the 'Towards a Confident Scotland' conference he said something in conversation which had an enduring impact on my thinking and ultimately led to insights for which I'm eternally grateful. 'Great what you are doing on confidence,' he told me 'but don't go down the self-esteem route as it's toxic to young people.' Adding, 'It undermines their resilience and well-being' as well as academic standards. He then explained briefly why there's a problem with the pursuit of self-esteem.

As I wasn't a psychologist and hadn't read a lot of psychology at that stage I didn't really know what to make of his observations. I hadn't written much about self-esteem in *The Scots' Crisis of Confidence* and I wondered if what he said had much more significance for America than Scotland. After all, to Scots' eyes Americans often seem overly full of themselves. But I listened politely, filed away this important warning and vowed to explore the topic fully at a later date.

The impulse to explore Seligman's comments further was heightened in 2005 when I realised that Scotland's proposed Curriculum for Excellence envisaged a schools curriculum that would develop pupils' 'four capacities'. This meant that Scotland's school system would, amongst other things, be redesigned to create: 'successful learners, confident individuals, responsible citizens and effective contributors'. With confidence soon to be at the heart of Scottish education I had to understand Seligman's warning.

So in my spare time I started to find out why important psychologists like Martin Seligman thought the pursuit of self-esteem toxic to young people. In the following pages I outline what I discovered and why it disturbed me.

The self-esteem bandwagon

> Though an overweening conceit of our own merit be vicious and disagreeable, nothing can be more laudable than to have a value for ourselves, where we really have qualities that are valuable. . . it is certain that nothing is more useful to us, in the conduct of life, than a due degree of pride, which makes us sensible of our own merit, and gives us a confidence and assurance in all our projects and enterprises.
>
> David Hume

As the quote from the great eighteenth century Scottish Enlightenment thinker, David Hume, shows the idea that it's important to value and think well of yourself has been around for a long time. The first pure psychological use of the term self-esteem can be traced back to 1890 and the work of William James who is generally seen as the father of modern psychology.

Martin Seligman argues that James's work was then largely ignored for 75 years as a result of academic and socio-economic factors. World wars and economic depression did not create fertile territory for a focus on how people feel about themselves and psychology itself was dominated during this period by two schools of thought – Freudianism and behaviourism – and both held the belief that individuals' lives were determined largely by forces outwith their control.

Seligman argues that the 1960s changed all this. First the rise of wealth and consumerism made it easier to conceptualise the individual at the centre of his/her destiny. And psychology, partly as a result of Seligman's own learned helplessness experiments, created theories which put the 'self-directed' individual at the centre of his or her own life.

From the late 1960s on, self-esteem became a fashionable and influential idea. Self-esteem may simply have remained a largely philosophical concept, debated by academics, if it hadn't been taken up by politicians in California in the late 1980s who saw it as a 'social vaccine' which would protect young people from all ills. The enduring problem was a lack of evidence.

Roy Baumeister was a psychology professor in the US. Although he was a supporter of the self-esteem movement he was concerned about the paucity of hard evidence to support the claims being made for self-esteem. He was also concerned about some of the approaches and underlying assumptions of the research which had been undertaken. From research he carried out in the 1990s, Baumeister concluded that the premise that low self-esteem was a problem, and that curing it could cure many social ills, was 'completely false'. On the plus side he did find that people with high self-esteem tend to be happier and show more initiative. But crucially he no longer believed that it was desirable to artificially boost self-esteem. Later Baumeister said that coming to these conclusions was 'one of the biggest disappointments of his career'.

The demise of the notion that raising self-esteem is some kind of panacea was further hastened in 2001 with the publication of Professor Nicholas Emler's work. Emler was at that time a professor of psychology at the London School of Economics. His research, including longitudinal studies of children, supported Baumeister's findings that low self-esteem was not a risk factor for educational problems, violence, bullying behaviour, delinquency, racism, drug-taking or alcohol abuse. Other trenchant critiques followed.

But none of this stopped the self-esteem bandwagon from rolling on. Almost every school in the US made it its expressed mission to bolster students' self-esteem and parents did likewise. The UK, with its inclination to a 'put down' rather than a self-worth culture seems less fertile territory for the importance of self-esteem but this was not the case.

In 2004 two prestigious, and influential think tanks published reports on self-esteem. One was for Demos and called *The Self-Esteem Society*. In it the author acknowledges the research by Baumeister and Emler but still proposes widespread action to create a self-esteem society. The Work Foundation produced a similar paper in 2004. It's called *Me, Myself and Work*. It makes passing reference to Emler's work but largely ignores his conclusions and those of Baumeister. The author then exhorts the Labour Government to do more to ensure that self-esteem is increased in 'early years, general education. . . welfare to work' and so forth, without one question of the merit and empirical justification for such an approach.

Perhaps one of the reasons why self-esteem has become such an important concept in modern society is that we all understand what it is and its relevance to our own lives. David Hume was right: it feels great when we are proud of ourselves. Even Martin Seligman, an arch critic of the self-esteem movement, acknowledges that self-esteem is a 'delicious feeling'. The issue then is not whether self-esteem exists or even if it's important in people's lives – it is, according to the research, a salient characteristic of happy people. The issues are whether it is something which can be artificially boosted by professionals, the techniques we might employ to do this and whether this is beneficial for individuals and society.

Seligman's critique

Seligman points out that most definitions of self-esteem from the time of William James include the notion of 'doing well' and 'feeling good'. He also argues that he knows 'no effective technology' for teaching children to feel good about themselves which does not first teach them how to do well. But if you look at the standard self-esteem boosting practices of American schools outlined in Box 1, you will see that these deliberately try to disconnect how the child feels about him or herself from any talent, success or achievement. Indeed for these practitioners self-esteem

Box 1: Under the banner of boosting self-esteem the following became standard practice in schools across America

- Children are repeatedly told that they are 'special'; they may have to repeat this on numerous occasions or colour in 'I'm special' worksheets.
- Children are told that they must 'love' themselves and are given various exercises to help this sink in.
- Children are given lots of talking exercises where they have to talk about themselves and their special qualities. Usually they are only allowed to use positive adjectives.
- Children are constantly praised, or even rewarded, when they achieve very little.
- Children are protected from criticism and failure as it might make them feel bad.
- Competition or other activities which might allow some children to shine and others to feel bad are avoided.

It became commonplace in American schools to:

- Encourage self-esteem based on nothing tangible.
- Encourage 'pseudo' self-esteem simply based on praise and how you are subjectively viewed by others.
- Ignore the child's own value system or preferred approach. These self-esteem exercises do not recognise or validate differences. All children have to fit into this approach even if they are naturally modest or feel patronised by routine praise.

should not be contingent on performance, how the child behaves to others or on their ethics.

Seligman's critique of self-esteem boosting practices, outlined in his book *The Optimistic Child* (1995), concludes that they undermine both children's learning and their mental health. It's certainly easy to see how they can undermine learning. If you focus on how a child feels about him or herself it's easy to become overly concerned if the child has negative feelings and want to allay them. However, as a psychologist Seligman is very aware that 'strong emotions such as anxiety, depression, and anger, exist for a purpose: they galvanize you into action to change yourself or your world, and by doing so to terminate the negative emotion.' He also argues that trying to protect children from bad feelings, such as frustration, will undermine their quality of life and development, not enhance it.

Seligman also explains that bad feelings can be put to good use by encouraging 'persistence'. He points out that any complex task involves a series of steps which can lead to failure. If the child gives up too early then they will learn to become 'helpless'. 'In order for your child to experience mastery,' he writes, 'it is necessary for him to fail, to feel bad, and try again repeatedly until success occurs. None of these steps can be circumvented. Failure and feeling bad are necessary building blocks for ultimate success and feeling good.'

America's report card and the warning for Scotland

During the time that self-esteem practices were influential in American schools and colleges their educational standards plummeted and American students continually performed badly in international league tables for maths and science. One statistic which shocked me while I was doing this research is that around half of American college students need to attend remedial classes in maths or English. Interestingly, during a period which witnessed an acute drop in academic standards, America suffered from grade inflation. In 2004, 48 per cent of first year college students reported getting an A average in high school. The equivalent figure in 1968 was 18 per cent.

Another great irony about standards in America is that while their young people don't score well academically, they are very positive about their own achievements. For example, one survey showed that American pupils were likely to rate themselves as good at maths even though their competency was low on tests. The opposite was true for Korean students.

It's hardly surprising that a variety of books appeared on the topic such as *Dumbing Down Our Kids: Why American Children Feel Good About Themselves but Can't Read, Write, and Add* by

Charles Sykes (1995). It certainly doesn't take much imagination or analysis to see how grade inflation, demotivation and lowered standards could be linked to: unwarranted praise; protecting children from criticism, failure and mistakes; not encouraging children to persevere in case it makes them feel bad; outlawing competition or opportunities for some children to be seen to achieve; and taking time in the school day for children to focus excessively on themselves and their feelings.

Nor is it difficult to imagine why my reading on the influence of self-esteem building on American schools concerned me. Historically, educational standards had been one of Scotland's assets. I didn't want to see them fall as a result of teachers adopting such practices. But there was even more bad news. Young people's well-being, not just their learning, is also undermined by such practices.

Seligman feared that artificial self-esteem building would not only fail to counteract, but actually boost, the epidemic of depression. Remember that Seligman believed that this was due in part to the rise of individualism, the loss of meaning and 'the bloated self' obsessed by its own doings. The practices designed to boost children's self-esteem undermined meaning and a sense of purpose by telling them that they were the centre of the world. They were also encouraged to blow out of proportion any small adversity in life rather than keep it in perspective.

Writing in 1995 Seligman also predicted that what was happening in schools, and the 'feel good ethic' in general would lead to the production of low self-esteem 'on a massive scale'. He was right about a lot but not this.

'Generation Me'

Dr Jean Twenge's book, *Generation Me*(2006), was the result of thirteen years of unique research into generational differences. When she was a young psychology researcher, Twenge realised that from the 1950s onwards psychology students and more serious researchers had undertaken a myriad of research projects into the attitudes and personality traits of school children and college students. Many of them had used exactly the same questionnaires as measurement tools. What Twenge did was locate all these thousands of studies and put them together into a meta-analysis, with data from 1.3 million young Americans. Her goal was to assess shifts over time. The book is the outcome of twelve different research projects she has been involved in along the way.

Twenge is not the first researcher to talk about generational shifts in attitudes. Ideas of this type are the mainstay of market research. But her work is unique because it's based on detailed psychological data from the 1950s onwards. From her research Twenge describes two generations. The first comprises the baby boomers who were born between 1946, at the close of World War II, and the late 1960s. The second generation includes the people born in the 1970s, 80s and 90s. Twenge calls this group 'Generation Me' (GenMe).

Twenge discovered that by the mid 1990s, the average GenMe college man and woman had higher self-esteem than those in 1968. Some psychologists had warned that what was happening in schools could encourage 'an excessive preoccupation with one's self' and boost narcissism not just self-esteem. Psychologists agree that narcissism is not a positive personality trait. Narcissists are overly focused on themselves, find it difficult to empathise with others, often manipulate others to achieve their goals and can be very hostile, if not downright aggressive, if they do not get the respect they think they are due. As a result of these traits, narcissists often find it difficult to sustain relationships with others.

These siren voices were right. Twenge's research did indeed find that narcissism is much more common now than in past generations. Only 12 per cent of teenagers in the early 1950s agreed with the statement 'I am an important person' but by the late 1980s this had risen to 80 per cent. Twenge links the rise of narcissism with the growing sense of 'entitlement' among Generation Me. She says this can take the form of students 'demanding' better grades, irrespective of the effort they have put in.

Twenge, like Seligman, presents evidence of the rise of depression in the USA, particularly in young people. But she goes further and looks at the incidence of anxiety. Her data show that the average college student in the 1990s was more anxious than 85 per cent of students in the 1950s and 71 per cent of students in the 1970s. The trend for children was even more striking: children as young as nine years old were markedly more anxious than kids had been in the 1950s. The change was so large that 'normal' schoolchildren in the 1980s reported higher levels of anxiety than child psychiatric patients in the 1950s.

Like Seligman, Twenge argues that one of the reasons why depression and mental health problems have increased is that the pre-occupation with 'the self' means that when life is challenging or disappointing young people cannot put it in perspective. But she believes that it's also because young people are much more lonely and isolated than before. Echoing the famous line from *Me and Bobby McGee*, 'freedom's just another word for nothing left to lose', Twenge argues that young people pay dearly for their values of independence, freedom and putting themselves first. She writes: 'I often feel that many of us are one breakup, or one move away from depression – our roots are not deep enough, our support system too shallow.'

An important concept in psychology is 'locus of control'. A significant difference between people is whether they believe they are in control of their own lives and have an 'internal' locus of control or whether they think their lives are determined by others or by fate – an 'external' locus of control. Twenge's research shows that in the USA 'external control beliefs increased about 50 per cent between the 1960s and the 2000s.' She also argues that the emphasis on the self, and self-esteem in particular, is mainly responsible for this increase. This is how she explains this apparent paradox:

> Suppose that you're a student and you fail a test. If you acknowledge that you were lazy about studying – or just plain stupid – your self-esteem will suffer. If you can blame the teacher's unfair test, however, you can slide through the experience still feeling good about yourself. We say that bad things aren't our fault...

In other words, if you continually tell young people that they can achieve anything in life if they just believe in themselves and want it badly enough then failure can be so difficult to bear, and so much a poor reflection on the self, that it is often better for them to believe life has treated them unfairly than to accept the truth of their own shortcomings.

What I find fascinating about Twenge's research on very significant increases in narcissism, loneliness and anxiety in young people is that it was done before the era of social media. Facebook didn't start until 2004, years after the period under review.

Of course, Twenge's findings cannot all be attributed to self-esteem building. Changes in society, economy and culture, such as the rise of materialism and the decline of outdoor play, undoubtedly contributed. Twenge regularly pays attention to changes in work patterns and politics, for example. But, nonetheless, a parenting and school style, aimed to make children feel special and always good about themselves, by protecting them from the inevitable vicissitudes of everyday life, must be a significant part of the generational psychological shifts she documents.

The implications for Scotland

Twenge's research, like Seligman's and other critics of artificial self-esteem building, warns us to take heed and not blunder into the mistakes made by our American cousins. And, for me, that was particularly important given that Scotland was now on the brink of orienting its education system towards confidence building.

I passionately believed that practitioners needed to be armed with the knowledge and insights of this predominantly American literature. I remember thinking at the time that in years to come I didn't want to look back on the work of the Centre and feel responsible for encouraging Scottish schools down a dangerous road.

But I also want to make clear that I don't think my book *The Scots' Crisis of Confidence*, published in 2003, had any bearing on the development of the Curriculum for Excellence (CfE). In 2002 when the Scottish Executive minister, Cathy Jamieson, announced the National Debate on Scottish education, the beginning of the process which culminated in Curriculum for Excellence, she specifically said she wanted 'young people to be creative, confident and capable citizens'. That particular Labour/Liberal administration was particularly keen to pursue confidence themes and that's why they established the enterprise in schools initiative, 'Determined to Succeed', in 2002 and 'Schools of Ambition' in 2005. Of course, I also benefited from this interest by being given funding for the Centre in 2005.

In those years confidence was part of the *zeitgeist*: I had been as influenced by it as other people. But all that reading on self-esteem in the US led me to believe that part of the Centre's purpose was to make sure that any work done under the confidence banner in Scotland would enhance, not undermine, learning and well-being. Thus the Centre embarked on a significant programme of activity. (See Box 2 for a summary of things we did in this period.)

Educating Scotland on the dangers of artificial self-esteem boosting

The first thing we did was ensure that our latest Vanguard events included some of the material outlined in this chapter. The event in Edinburgh on the morning of October 25th 2006 was called 'Creating Confidence' and had both Martin Seligman and the British psychologist Professor Nicholas Emler as speakers. The event was sponsored by Learning and Teaching Scotland and Gill Robinson, who was the main person working on Curriculum for Excellence at that point, also spoke. In 2006 we recorded an hour-long lecture with Jean Twenge to put on our website.

I was increasingly asked by schools and education organisations to run workshops or give talks on confidence. Apart from setting out the critique of self-esteem outlined in this chapter I would often ask those present, usually teachers or headteachers, to define confidence. What I commonly heard concerned me as it was usual for them to define confidence as speaking and performing. Indeed sometimes they would say 'being confident all the time'. In other words, the dominant way of defining it was social confidence and that's essentially about having an extrovert personality. I pitied the introverted pupils who might feel confident about a whole range of skills, such as maths or writing, but who now didn't measure up to how their teachers thought they needed to behave. This I thought was more likely to drain confidence from some young people rather than boost it.

The Centre's response to all this was to put skills at the heart of our definition of confidence. So we defined it as self-efficacy + optimism. Self-efficacy, like self-belief, is the feeling that you can reach your goals as you have the skills and experience required. Optimism is a view of the world and ourselves which helps us to be resilient in the face of adversity. So our definition of confidence relates to doing and making things happen, not how we feel about ourselves.

When I set out in talks the type of things schools and parents in America have done to boost self-esteem I would ask those present how far down this road they thought the average Scottish classroom and teacher were. Some said we were already half way there. Others said we were already as far down the road as America. Many gave lots of examples of parents who were overly protecting their child from any adversity. Those who were parents themselves could understand why parents were doing this but as teachers they could see how it was undermining learning and children's resilience.

From these discussions I could see that Scottish parents and teachers needed to be aware of the dangers of this approach. So I started to write a book covering what I had learned in the previous months plus my own increasing focus on the meaning of confidence and well-being. The Centre published 3000 copies of *Creating Confidence: A handbook for professionals working with young people* in August 2007. It was launched at the Edinburgh Book Festival where I was giving a talk. The 200 strong event was very popular, selling out a week in advance. Within a few months the book had sold 1200 copies. It sold out within a few years and then was available to download for free.

We were very fortunate in attracting substantial sponsorship to publish the book from George Morris, who was head of his family business Morris & Spottiswood. George was very taken with what we were doing at the Centre and wrote a very supportive and insightful introduction.

Box 2: Centre projects/events to foster young people's resilience, confidence, self-efficacy well-being and divert from artificial self-esteem building

Bounce Back!

We promoted the award winning Australian resiliency programme for schools created by Dr Toni Noble and Helen McGrath. Much of its approach on how to encourage young people to endure adversity is a good counterpoint to the negative effects of artificial self-esteem building. Dr Noble gave talks/ran workshops for the Centre on her programme in February 2007 and again in 2008. A number of Scottish schools and local authorities pursued this approach. (For more on the Centre and *Bounce Back*, see p. 288.)

Mindset

We were also very keen on Stanford Professor Carol Dweck's work on 'mindset'. Her important research was mainly known by psychologists but in early 2007 she popularised her ideas in a book called *Mindset: the new psychology of success*. We informed the largely sports oriented organisation Winning Scotland about Dweck's work and we jointly brought her over to Scotland. In June 2007 the Centre held **a half-day masterclass with Professor Dweck** in Òran Mór Glasgow particularly aimed at business, education and sport. One of the panelists was Gregor Townsend, then a Scottish rugby player and now team coach. We also had Professor Dweck back for **two half-day events in September 2008**. Mindset has become an enormously popular approach internationally. It has also been very influential in Scotland and we believe that much of this can be traced back to the Centre's events and prominence we gave to Dweck's thinking. Like all approaches some proponents have over-hyped mindset and present it as a panacea which it certainly is not. We also collaborated with Professor Dweck's colleagues at Stanford University in a research project on Brainology. This was led for the Centre by Derek Goldman. We were also involved in a University of Glasgow mindset research project. (See page 112/113 on the Centre's research projects.)

Assertiveness

In 2006 and 2007 the Centre used some of its funding from the Scottish Executive to devise and pilot assertiveness training for secondary school pupils. Assertiveness (being able to say 'no' for example, or set limits) is linked to positive mental health. In 2007 Centre associate Isobel MacNaughtan trained some teachers to use our courses and materials with young people. These were then put online in 2008. Included in our resources to support assertiveness development was a DVD with scenarios which we made in conjunction with CollusionTheatre. These were designed to stimulate discussion with young people on assertive and non-assertive behaviour.

Creating Confidence

The book covers a large amount of material. It begins with the critique of self-esteem and the dangers of this type of psychological approach but then outlines 'good ways to create confidence' including Professor Carol Dweck's growth mindset, self-efficacy, optimism and hope, resilience, fostering positive teacher-pupil relationships and new educational approaches such as Assessment for Learning, the Motivated School and cooperative learning. I also included a chapter called 'Activities to Foster Confidence' which included a section on Young People's Orchestras in Venezuela. This was a few years before Richard Holloway and others set up *Il Systema* in the Raploch in Stirling. In this section I particularly advanced the importance of activities such as sport and outdoor education for fostering confidence.

Confidence model and well-being compass

In *Creating Confidence* I present for the first time the Centre's model of confidence (See Figure 1). This is made up of four core elements: *optimism* and *self-efficacy* (the Centre's definition of confidence) plus another two elements which sustain and foster confidence – *support from others* and *learning from others*. This means that in the Centre's whole notion of confidence other people play a vital role. This seemed particularly relevant in a book aimed at teachers and others working with young people and was also why I gave lots of examples of how this can be done effectively throughout the handbook.

In the penultimate chapter I ask an important question: confidence for what? Confidence may or may not be a good thing, depending on what it is related to. A thief could be confident that he could rob a bank; Hitler was confident that Germany could conquer Europe. In short, confidence may be good in as much as it helps individuals to accomplish goals in life but these goals can be judged as good or bad, worthless or worthwhile, depending on what they seek to achieve.

And this takes us to the heart of what was becoming an increasingly important dilemma for us at the Centre for Confidence

Figure 1: The Centre's model of confidence and compass of well-being

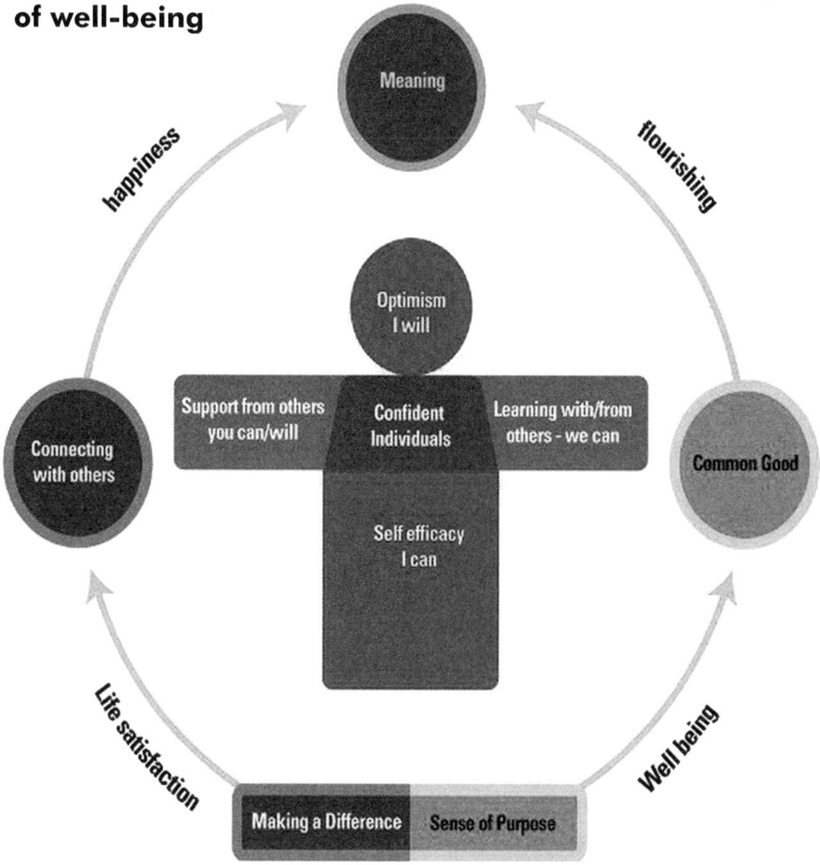

and Well-being. We were beginning to fear that the two parts of our agenda (confidence and well-being) may not only be misaligned but actually at odds with one another.

In Western societies – particularly the USA and the UK – there is a strong, pervasive achievement and materialistic ethic which helps to shape people's individual ambitions and motivations. This is an ethic which encourages us to believe that the main aim in life is to become a successful individual. What's more, as a result of the rise of the mass media and its ideas and values, success is increasingly couched in terms of power, fame, money and looks. This media agenda also encourages us to believe that becoming successful in this way will give us access to all the material trimmings which we believe will bring us happiness.

So the Centre's (and Scottish schools') confidence agenda could easily become part of this endless, individualistic quest for achievement and success. If so we may simply be encouraging, and equipping, young people to go down a very materialistic, and often lonely, path – a journey which may well undermine their well-being.

Research undertaken by Professor Jennifer Crocker, who coined the term 'the costly pursuit of self-esteem', shows that people's well-being is undermined by pursuing egotistical goals and enhanced by what she calls 'eco goals' which are based more on other people or the environment. So one of the problems with the confidence agenda is this: it could encourage people to put their personal development before their relationships and if they do this may undermine their well-being rather than foster it. (And if you think this is an airy fairy idea just look at all those celebrities who have a very successful life but who then engage in good works to allay the emptiness and find meaning.)

To get round this problem we situated our model of confidence within what we termed our 'well-being compass' to guide individuals' confidence towards a meaningful, flourishing and fulfilling life (See Figure 1, Page 71). This compass highlights the importance of sense of purpose, common good, making a difference and connecting with others. The ultimate destination is a sense of meaning, one of the main antidotes to depression and an important ingredient in life satisfaction, well-being and happiness.

This exhortation to social improvement and connection is very much in tune with Scottish values. The Scots have always had a very strong notion of society and social progress – this is why the origins of social science as we know it can be traced back to the Scottish Enlightenment. The belief that we are all Jock Tamson's bairns still appears to be strong in modern Scotland as is the desire to strengthen these ties.

The great Scottish Enlightenment thinker, Adam Smith, is the founder of economics, and is often portrayed as a stalwart defender of the free market. But Smith considered himself a moral philosopher. There's little doubt he was a thinker who believed in strong social ties, facilitated by human beings' capacity for sympathy. Smith writes:

> How selfish soever man may be supposed, there are evidently some principles in his nature, which interest him in the fortune of others, and render their happiness necessary to him, though he derives nothing from it except the pleasure of seeing it.

So, given our Enlightenment past, it seemed very appropriate to us at the Centre that in Scotland we should stress human strengths, action and agency and encourage such confident action towards social improvement, compassion and meaning in life.

The Centre, and I, had come a long way from Seligman's useful warning on self-esteem in November 2005.

confidentfutures

Personal Skills for Prefessional Development

In the spring of 2005 Napier University in Edinburgh approached the Centre and asked us to tender for a project designed to build the confidence of graduates. During the summer of 2005 the Centre collaborated with Isobel MacNaughtan, an educational consultant, to devise a programme of activities for undergraduates which would increase their confidence. The Centre's proposal envisaged students benefiting from coaching, mentoring, personal development workshops and inspirational lectures from people who have overcome major challenges in their lives.

The rationale behind the initiative was that in a fast-changing world graduates need more than academic qualifications. To ensure their adaptability in the face of constant change they also need self-confidence, self-knowledge and interpersonal skills. Those graduates who can combine academic qualifications and experience with self-confidence and a readiness to cope with change will become 'first choice' for employers.

The programme aimed to ensure that the confident graduate would:

- Be strongly internalised – much more likely to show practical intelligence.
- Have a strong self-belief and the ability to make a difference.
- Be resilient in the face of difficulty, with curiosity and problem-solving as their preferred response.
- Take risks, make mistakes and ask for help.
- Be adaptable and seize new opportunities for learning.
- Be creatively reflective.

Napier University staff were aware that their students needed this development as 50 per cent of their students were the first in their families to attend higher education. Students had some say in the programme as Isobel engaged a group of 30 to help design cooperative learning sessions and, as she said at the time, these students 'weren't in any way cynical about the whole approach to positivity – in fact they were blown away by it all.' Staff also freely bought into the project.

Napier University launched its Confident Futures Initiative in the autumn of 2006 and attracted considerable press coverage. Isobel MacNaughtan delivered one of the training strands on behalf of the Centre and other companies then provided the training for other modules.

Chapter 4

Positive organisations, optimism, pessimism and the power of small change

Michigan University's Positive Organizational Scholarship course;
ways to think about optimism and pessimism;
relevance to Scotland;
working with business;
measuring optimism;
the role of pessimism;
how to boost optimism;
the Centre's ideas for a 'small change' programme;
how large scale change happens;
creating a project plan;
applying to the Big Lottery; rejection.

BEFORE THE CENTRE was set up in 2005, I had been working for myself as a trainer specialising in personal, team and management development. It was my repeated exposure to staffs' lack of confidence that led me to write *The Scots' Crisis of Confidence*. I was acutely aware that many people were working in jobs well below their potential and that many managers and leaders did little to develop or encourage their employees. This worried me; in a globally competitive world Scottish organisations and businesses would lose out. And that means fewer jobs.

In 2006 a senior faculty member in the School of Positive Organizational Scholarship at the University of Michigan, Jane Dutton, came into our Union Street office to introduce herself and hear what we were doing. Jane was a very personable woman and it wasn't surprising to learn that compassion in organisations was her thing. Jane arranged a free place for me on a five-day executive education course in May 2006. Hotel and flight costs were all the Centre had to fund.

I was very grateful to Jane and others in Michigan for their generosity but it turned out to be a miserable experience. While in Michigan I continually wished that I had stayed at home and simply read the speakers' books and research papers.

Positive organisation courses at the University of Michigan were usually held in a university building in the lovely, historic town of Ann Arbor, one of America's most popular places to live. But for whatever reason this course was held in a hotel on the edge of town. From 8 o'clock in the morning till 6 o'clock at night we sat in a dark, windowless conference suite in the hotel basement being blasted by cold air from a merciless air conditioner. And we did this for the best part of five days. Breaks were infrequent and unsatisfying – huge, stale muffins and unpalatable tea and coffee served in plastic cups.

I excused myself and left early on a couple of afternoons only to discover how difficult it is to walk anywhere in that type of urban environment: there are virtually no pavements and the car is king. I managed to get to the local, ultra-sterile shopping mall on one occasion and see something of Ann Arbor on my other escape.

I find it fairly easy to connect with most people but had little in common with the other participants – all male middle managers from the Midwest. Though I did share one thing with them – the view that the programme was too drawn out and that what was happening over five days could easily be telescoped into two. Many of them were sceptical of much of the input which they saw as impractical and overly soft. Like me, however, they particularly enjoyed the presentation from one guest lecturer – Professor Barbara Fredrickson – and appropriately brightened up hearing her 'broaden and build' theory of positive emotions.

I couldn't wait to fly home at the end of the week. I had enjoyed previous trips to both the east and west coasts of America but this exposure to middle America meant that I returned to Scotland not just feeling distinctly European but also deeply appreciative of European culture.

I tell this story because it's mildly therapeutic to have a moan about negative experiences even fifteen years after the event, particularly when I suspect that no one at Michigan University will read this book and feel offended. But I also want to point out a paradox in myself: while at the Centre I invited lots of US speakers to Scotland and frequently cited American research but I'm no fan of American culture. This was evident when I wrote *The Scots' Crisis of Confidence* at the turn of the century. Nonetheless as the UK as a whole was progressing down a road the US had been on for some time, I also thought they had some things to teach us.

The idea of 'positive organisations' had a particular resonance not just for me but for many managers in Scotland as they had to deal with staff negativity. However, I soon came to realise that the most pertinent material for us in Scotland was not what I had learned in Michigan. What was most relevant was a concept at the heart of Seligman's positive psychology; optimism was in short supply and pessimism was casting a dark shadow on some key Scottish businesses. Before explaining why I had this epiphany I'll outline different ways to see optimism and pessimism.

Optimism

The poet Alexander Scott satirised a tendency in Scotland to always think the worst in two of his definitional poems:

> *Scotch Optimism*
> Through a gless, Darkly.
>
> *Scotch Pessimism*
> Nae Gless.

Some define pessimism as focusing on the downside of life – seeing the glass as half empty, not half full. Optimists, in this definition, are people who look on 'the bright side', a viewpoint which some psychologists call 'dispositional optimism'. But Martin Seligman and his colleagues have a different way of defining optimism and pessimism and in the mid 2000s it provided the Centre with a useful insight into a thinking style very evident in Scotland.

For Seligman, 'The basis of optimism does not lie in positive phrases or images of victory, but in the way you think about causes.' Indeed he argues that each of us has an 'explanatory style', a way of thinking about the causes of things that happen in life. We develop our explanatory style during childhood and, unless we take deliberate steps to change, it will last for the whole of our lives, acting as a prism through which we explain to ourselves why things, both good or bad, happen.

Seligman argues that there are three central dimensions which we use to interpret events in our lives. He refers to these dimensions as *permanence, pervasiveness* and *personalisation*. Permanence simply means believing that when something goes wrong, then it will *always* go wrong. In short, pessimists believe that bad fortune lasts. Pervasiveness refers to the belief that misfortune is not simply confined to one domain but pervades *everything*. For example, a pessimist who fails an examination will tend to believe that everything is going wrong with his/her life. This is why pessimists tend to 'catastrophise' after one negative incident. Personalisation involves the attribution of responsibility when things go wrong. Pessimists usually blame themselves; so for the pessimist the problem is *me*.

An optimistic thinker by contrast is someone who, when a problem arises, believes that it's temporary, restricted to this one thing and emanates from specific circumstances that aren't necessarily about what he or she has done. (Seligman changed his mind about the value of the last dimension as he thought it could encourage individuals to shift blame on to others.)

Explanatory style is not just relevant to how people look at bad events but also to how a person interprets good things as well. And this is where Seligman's work becomes really interesting when applied to Scottish culture. To understand optimism and pessimism in the face of good events, we need to reverse the pattern outlined above. Optimists see good fortune, such as passing a maths exam with flying colours as permanent (I'm going to keep doing well in maths), pervasive (I'm going to keep doing well at school) and something about themselves (I really worked hard/I'm good at maths). Whereas pessimists are more likely to see something good as temporary (the work will get harder next year), specific (it was just this one subject) and something they aren't responsible for (it was an easy exam, I was lucky).

From my experience I could see that the Scots are often pessimistic in the face of bad events but, unexpectedly, are just as likely to be pessimistic in the face of good events. A telling example is Scottish football, particularly our bids to qualify for the World Cup finals. In October 2007 I was at Hampden for the Scotland v Ukraine match. Scotland had 21 points from the games they had played so far and across the seven groups only two countries – Germany and Croatia had better scores. Scotland had also beaten World Cup finalists France twice in the last year – and one of these victories was still ringing in our ears yet pessimism abounded: we were fated to lose. Despite a great deal of pessimism, Scotland did win against Ukraine. The following game was against then World Champions, Italy. The day before the match I was asked to write a short piece for a national paper on how the Scots should prepare themselves for defeat. It was easy to see the psychology at work here: let's assume we'll lose and then we'll avoid being on an emotional roller-coaster – high and positive one minute and down in the dumps the next. If we're negative and we win then it'll be a great bonus.

Now I can well understand why in those days there was a fear in Scotland about becoming super-confident. In 2007 the spectre of the 1978 World Cup in Argentina still hung over the nation. All that stuff about Ally's army and Scotland winning the World Cup was so embarrassing given our subsequent performance. That's why many still believed that, for our dignity, it's much better to keep aspirations in check and when we lose we'll have the comfort of saying: 'We were right. We knew we would get beat.'

But I think there's more to it than this. Pessimists believe that good fortune does not happen as a result of your own actions. For them success is more of a fluke, a miracle or magic. And the whole point about miracles and magic is that they don't happen every day and they certainly aren't under your control. If the Scotland team wins against strong opponents then it's simply a fluke and not because Scotland has played well. What's more, there's an added twist here which we could call 'the pay-back factor'. Life is not meant to be easy; we are all miserable sinners therefore if life's going well some compensatory mechanism will soon be at work to ensure that we'll have to pay for this good fortune. Like many Scots I regularly catch myself having such thoughts.

Working with businesses

In March 2004, a year after the publication of *The Scots' Crisis of Confidence*, I was asked to give a keynote speech on confidence at the Scottish Council Development and Industry's prestigious annual meeting in St Andrews. This gave me, and the Centre once it was established, a high profile within Scotland's business community. This exposure meant that I was then invited to speak at a number of events or dinners held by Scottish Enterprise or the Institute of Directors. I also spoke at a couple of large -scale gatherings on Scottish manufacturing. In these talks I often focused on optimism/pessimism and it really resonated with the audiences.

The Centre was approached by an American company which had recently invested a large sum of money in their Scottish plant. When they announced the decision to invest to their staff they were not pleased as they were looking for the catch. 'Where are you going to cut back?' the employees asked.

In 2007 I agreed to run some workshops with management and staff at that plant and I could see that the American management were unnerved by the staff's pessimism, and lack of enthusiasm and confidence. I ran four workshops with large numbers of staff and had a useful and frank discussion about their jobs and attitudes. The staff were pessimistic and insecure but as we talked they began to see that their negativity could easily become a self-fulfilling prophecy. Why would the parent company keep investing there if the employees themselves were negative about it? The following year staff members gave a more positive response in the international survey of employee attitudes, something this company really cared about. I'm pleased to say that in 2024 this Scottish plant is still in business and provides some of the best jobs in the area.

Nonetheless I want to make clear that I've never been an unqualified fan of inward investment and have always felt more positive about the idea of trying to stimulate indigenous enterprise. After all, with global companies there's always a danger they will restructure and close plants to reduce costs. Since profit is all that really matters to them, they have no long-term commitment to their Scottish workforce regardless of how enthusiastic, positive and confident they are.

Does pessimism matter?

In the mid 2000s more than a hundred studies showed that whether people think optimistically or pessimistically affects various life outcomes such as sport and sales. What should be of even more interest to us in Scotland is the relationship between optimism / pessimism and health. At the time, research seemed to indicate that as much as seven years of life expectancy may be at stake in whether a person is an optimist or a pessimist. This is more significant for life expectancy than whether someone smokes a pack of cigarettes every day. The mechanism is not entirely known but there are two main explanations. The first is that negative emotions release stress hormones which undermine well-being. The second is that pessimism can encourage people to lose heart and give up. This is understandable: if you think the outcome is bound to be bad then why bother doing anything such as taking exercise or giving up smoking?

When I was organising the Vanguard Programme in 2006 a Scottish journalist was instructed to write a feature about it and phoned me up for a few quotes. Unable to keep the cynicism out of his voice he asked: 'And what has this got to do with the man coughing his guts out in Shettleston?' I think I said 'everything' in reply and if I did I was wrong. 'It's a contributory factor' was a more accurate answer. Other areas in Europe, particularly Eastern Europe, also have challenging conditions yet better life expectancy for this group. Excess smoking and drinking play a part but aren't themselves the cause as men in other cultures smoke more with less damaging consequences. As there was at that time an accepted link between pessimism and ill health, I was convinced that the prevailing culture and personal psychology must play *some* part. I was not alone. When Sir Harry Burns was Scotland's Chief Medical Officer, he constantly argued that many of Scotland's health inequalities are driven by feelings of hopelessness, pessimism's close cousin.

Elaine Duncan and measuring optimism

When I met Dr Elaine Duncan at a European Positive Psychology conference in 2004 she was a lecturer in psychology at Glasgow Caledonian University. One of Elaine's interests was positive emotion so she was an early adopter of positive psychology. For the first ten years of the Centre's existence Elaine acted as one of our advisers and was also a co-trainer, with Keith Hunter, on the Centre's action research courses. Elaine also selected the psychological questionnaires for us to include in our Confidence Research System. This allowed anyone running an intervention to measure its impact by arranging for participants to complete pre and post assessments online. Martin Seligman had devised a questionnaire for his 'explanatory style' type optimism and pessimism but it had a commercial price tag and so was well outwith our limited budget. This meant that we weren't able to measure the type of pessimism in the face of good events which I outline above and which I think was prevalent in Scotland. Therefore we had to make do with LOT-R (the Life Orientation Test – Revised) which measures dispositional optimism.

I'll outline some of our findings from the Confidence Research System in Chapter 7 but it's worth pointing out here that we found low levels of optimism in Scottish university and school students. Elaine regularly worked with psychology researchers in Italy. In one study of Scottish and Italian students they found that the Scottish students had significantly lower optimism than their Italian counterparts. Elaine was also involved in a 2009 study in Wellhouse, a housing scheme in Easterhouse, Glasgow. This showed exceptionally low levels of optimism in the participants who took part. Indeed they were the most pessimistic group we ever encountered in terms of LOT-R results.

How optimism and pessimism develop

Optimism and pessimism, according to Seligman, are partly genetic but also the consequence of the attitudes we observe in parents, particularly our mothers. In short, we learn to explain good and bad events optimistically or pessimistically. However, Seligman argues that if a bad thing happens early in a child's life, and that bad thing is permanent (such as the death of a parent), then this event predisposes the child to pessimistic thinking. In such cases, '. . . all setbacks are soon catastrophised into permanent and pervasive losses,' he writes.

Seligman tends to take an individualistic focus when studying optimism but recognises that culture plays some part. He argues that the USA has traditionally had an optimistic culture because historically it was founded and developed by people who left Europe and Asia and emigrated to this new land:

> What kind of mentality does it take to feel oppressed by caste and class, to leave family and possessions behind, and to journey in the hope of a better life? Optimism. These men and women had it in abundance and so it's not difficult to see how the USA became a nation of optimists.

If America is the land of migrants and optimism then is Scotland the land of emigrees and pessimism? In *To the Ends of the Earth: Scotland's Global Diaspora* (2012), Professor Tom Devine sets out the massive scale of migration from Scotland and makes clear that those who migrated were often the most skilled, leaving 'their native land in search of more opportunity, "independence" and through an ambition to "get on". . .' So it's very likely that emigration siphoned off many Scots who were the most optimistic thus intensifying pessimism within Scottish culture.

But there are other pessimism-inducing factors at work in Scottish culture. It's all too easy to look at Scottish history and see how rapid, and potentially traumatic, events would have set many

Scottish children up for pessimism in a similar way to the bereaved child who learns to 'catastrophise'. I'm specifically thinking of the speed of industrialisation and urbanisation in Scotland, losses from emigration, the extent of Scotland's war dead and the stress of deindustrialisation. These are topics I'll return to in a later chapter so all I want to say here is that we can see from this list that the stress and insecurity many Scots historically endured would have affected the culture, predisposing the country to pessimistic attitudes.

How to become more optimistic

Seligman and others who use explanatory style as a way to describe optimism and pessimism maintain that it isn't stable and can change over time. In short, we can learn to become more optimistic. The first thing we need to do is to become more conscious of our internal, critical voice and detach ourselves from it. Indeed, according to Seligman, it's helpful if people with a proclivity for pessimism can teach themselves to see this inner critic as an enemy who is out to make life as difficult for them as possible.

The next stage in the process is to engage in a 'disputation' with this critical voice. Bearing in mind the tendency in pessimists to see problems as long-lasting, pervasive and somehow their fault, what's involved here is trying to come up with *factual* information which disputes the pessimistic charge of the inner critic. Note that this does not mean the type of wishful, affirmative approach often advanced by positive thinking courses. Disputation encourages the individual to stick to facts, or at least to alternative, realistic ways of viewing the problem. Much of pessimistic thinking is driven by fear, not fact, and so what we need to do is build a more optimistic perspective by generating alternative interpretations. Even if you have to admit that you've done something wrong you can still 'decatastrophise' the difficulty either by looking at how you could get help with this problem or finding other ways to improve.

As Karen Reivich, a resilience expert, explains, to become more optimistic people have to become much more attuned to how they are using the formulation of 'always', 'everything' and 'me' when they meet difficulties in life.

A note of caution is required, however. Like all things in life optimism can be overdone. People who are overly optimistic can take unacceptable risks or be called foolhardy, cavalier or just plain foolish. Thinking that the worst may happen has a protective function. It keeps us alert to possible danger and is part of our survival instinct. If we are in risky situations where the cost of failure is high then it pays to be pessimistic rather than optimistic. Seligman talks about 'realistic optimism' and gives specific advice for when to use, and not use, optimism techniques.

Small Change: Big Change programme

I used optimism and a variety of other positive psychology and personal development techniques in workshops with a whole range of people: office staff at McAlpine's Business Services, staff at Careers Scotland, workers in a couple of Scottish factories, council staff in West Renfrewshire. The feedback from these programmes was excellent with most participants saying that it gave them vital insights into how they could make their lives, or their jobs, better. When we had set up the Centre in 2005 we set ourselves a bold mission – to help transform Scottish culture to make it more supportive of positive attitudes and well-being.

To have any hope of influencing Scots, never mind fulfilling our ambitious mission, we needed to have a direct impact on, and involvement with, the Scottish population rather than professional groups. Rather than stressing the potentially life-changing nature of involvement with these types of activities, we wanted to play this down and suggest that for individuals not too much was at stake.

We called the programme that we started to work on '*Small Change: Big Change*' but it soon simply became '*Small Change*'. We thought the benefit of this name is that it suggests that what's at stake for individuals is fairly trivial – like the loose change in our pockets. However, it also conveyed the idea that if we paid more attention to these small details in our daily lives it could have a cumulative effect, not just for ourselves as individuals, but for the nation as a whole. So *Small Change* was very much in tune with the thinking behind that well-worn proverb – 'Take care of the pennies and the pounds will look after themselves.'

The underlying message of *Small Change* is that as individuals, and as a country, we could become richer if we paid more attention to the small interactions and thought processes in our daily lives. The riches here refer, of course, to social, emotional, and health benefits as well as the indirect benefits associated with achieving educational, sporting and work goals.

Another advantage we perceived in the *Small Change* idea is that it demystifies personal development. For example, at the Vanguard Programme participants constantly insisted that they needed tools and techniques to take positive psychology forward. This illustrated how difficult people find it to grasp that what's often required are small and subtle changes in perception or behaviour in everyday life. Box 3 gives a few examples.

So the thinking behind our proposed initiative *Small Change: Big Change* was two-fold: i. If individuals make some small changes

Box 3: The type of changes envisaged by the *Small Change* programme

■ In the classroom or workplace it's about that hard-driving, critical teacher/leader saying more often 'well done, I can see you've really put in a great deal of effort today'.

■ In relationships at home and with peers it's about being more positive and supportive about others' success and good fortunes.

■ In our own thought processes it's about challenging ourselves to see that the problems we confront may be temporary and not permanent.

■ In dealing with people it's about trying to see the best in their intentions rather than the worst.

■ It's about focusing more on what we like, rather than don't like.

■ It's about being kinder and less critical of ourselves.

in their day to day attitudes and behaviour the cumulative effect on their lives could be big. ii. If enough individuals make a small change in their everyday attitudes and behaviours this could have a big, transformatory effect on Scottish culture and various outcomes in health, education, the economy and so forth.

How large scale change happens

In reading the proposals for our *Small Change* programme I'm struck by how much time we devoted to thinking through how change happens. At the top of our list was Malcolm Gladwell's book *The Tipping Point*. You will remember that he spoke at the Centre's launch event in Glasgow in 2004 and had influenced our thinking. Box 4 overleaf sets out some of the ideas which are most relevant to *Small Change*. In the first few years of working, Gladwell's ideas were very relevant to us. For example, we weren't only concerned about confidence but we knew confidence was the 'sticky' word which was more likely to attract people's attention than positive psychology, happiness, or cognitive psychology. That's why we had the word 'confidence' in our title. In creating and selling the Vanguard Programme too we deliberately tried to make it seem fashionable and attractive and created a sense of momentum through cross-sectoral meetings about the forthcoming event.

We also very deliberately wanted to stand the conventional approach to personal development on its head, as it tended to hype up and oversell the benefits. This was obvious in the approach taken by figures like Jack Black, Paul McKenna, Tony Robbins and countless others. We could see that this approach only appeals to a small, and rather untypical, set of people – those who are ambitious and individualistic risk takers. Given the collectivist, play-it-safe, conformist nature of Scottish society we have proportionately fewer individuals like this than the US (the home of personal development) where high-achieving individuals are highly prized.

Another type of personal development is sold primarily as leadership development. For example, Stephen Covey's *Principle-Centred Leadership* (1989), the work of countless management gurus, and Norman Drummond's work with Scottish school pupils

Box 4: Relevant aspects of Malcolm Gladwell's analysis in The Tipping Point

- Change happens often and more quickly than people often think.
- A small thing, like adding a few grains of sand to a pile, can have a huge effect – e.g. a landslide.
- Small things, and details, are often more important in change than we usually imagine.
- Some messages are more 'sticky' and hence more powerful in activating change than others.
- People are more likely to be influenced by friends, family, neighbours and work colleagues than they are in a top-down fashion by bosses or politicians.
- For ideas to become social epidemics and cause population-wide changes they need to jump sectoral and geographical boundaries (eg cross from health to social work or from one business sector to another).
- If something becomes 'fashionable' it is more likely to create changes in behaviour as we care very much about how we are seen by others.
- Word of mouth is the cheapest and best sales technique.
- Big changes can come about often by the simple repackaging of an old idea.

in Columba 1400. The thinking here is that transformational change will happen in organisations (and ultimately in society) if leaders pave the way by personally undergoing major personal development and then modelling the behaviour and encouraging others to follow suit. Again what is at stake here is a big step-change by an individual which will, in the short term at least, make this individual different from those around them. However, we didn't see this as a very attractive proposition for leaders in Scotland as it potentially makes them too different from others. What's more, Scotland does not only have a strong tendency to collectivism but also we operate in a culture which does not see leadership as positive. In the words of the poet Hamish Henderson, in Scotland there are 'No Gods and Precious Few Heroes'.

We also drew on the work of complexity theory, particularly Richard Steel's ideas. At that time he was an organisational development specialist in the UK who was interested in how complexity theory could help us understand organisational culture change. He points out that culture is often seen as something static when in fact it's something which as individuals we're 'constantly creating, affirming and expressing'. In other words, culture is 'emergent'. It emerges through our conversations and interactions with one another. One of the reasons why organisations often fail to make inroads with change programmes is that they focus too much on structures and rewards rather than on conversations and interactions. (This is exactly what we would focus on with *Small Change*.)

A second point is that in this complex system, where culture is formed through the interactions, conversations and paradigms of the individual agents, change can happen quickly and dramatically as a result of small outside influences. When a complex system is in a critical state even the smallest stimulus may cause major changes. The beating of a butterfly's wings causing a storm is how this idea is often expressed.

A third point about how to bring about change concerns increasing connectivity and diversity. Connectivity means that the agents in the system have heightened interaction with one another. Richard Steel talks about the challenge for change makers to be 'similar enough to be listened to, and different enough to be heard'. Elsewhere he describes this role as 'support and subvert'.

The proposal for a *Small Change* project

Armed with these ideas, a set of techniques which would help individuals to change their thoughts and behaviour, and some suggestions for how we could engage large sections of the Scottish population we applied to the Big Lottery for one of their 'Awards for All' grants. We were successful. This gave us £10,000 to engage a consultant to work with us to create an indepth project plan which we could then submit to the Big Lottery for a substantial sum of money to run the project. We chose Anne Brooks to work with us and over the next few months a large, fully costed and detailed project plan took shape. We envisaged working with lots of partnering organisations, having well-crafted materials online, an interactive forum, training of trainers' events, workshops. We also intended to involve the media, particularly radio. We envisaged working intensely with three geographical areas – Ruchazie in Glasgow, Dunfermline and Oban. Indeed we suggested these places as we knew that local leaders in these areas were eager to work with us.

Our proposal was rejected by the Big Lottery as they thought the project too broad in scope and didn't fit well enough with their priorities. We were disappointed at the time but, looking back, I've no regrets that lack of funding meant we couldn't go ahead. I see now that our focus was too psychological. Indeed we came to understand the limitations of psychological approaches and broadened our agenda substantially in future years. This is something I'll explain in subsequent chapters.

When rereading the project plan I was struck by the section setting out some of the rationale for why such a programme was needed in Scotland. I've included the most pertinent of these points in Box 5.

In 2007 it was clear that in Scotland people were neither at ease with themselves nor ready for the challenges that inevitably lay ahead. *Small Change* may not have been the answer, but that begs the question what, if anything could be done? There were many Scotland-wide initiatives to tackle specific problems – for example, the schools' enterprise initiative 'Determined to Succeed', the suicide prevention organisation 'Choose Life', a variety of public health initiatives and, of course, the Centre. We were making good headway in our work advising teachers on the confidence of teenagers but, now the *Small Change* project was shelved, our opportunity to tackle the Scots' crisis of confidence, particularly low levels of optimism in the adult population, had receded. But there was one silver lining – it freed up my time to wrestle with other challenges.

Box 5: Data collected between mid 1990s and 2007 suggesting confidence, optimism and mental health problems in Scotland

■ OECD 24 (2007) shows that over a range of indicators (including health, life expectancy, education, GDP etc), Scotland is the worst performing small country of the 10 recorded.

■ A World Health Organisation study from the mid 1990s on the self-confidence of fifteen year olds in twenty-five countries found that Scottish teenagers were third bottom of the list 'only higher than Estonia and Slovakia' for feelings of self-confidence.

■ In 2005 the Scottish Executive published research related to the development of 'Determined to Succeed' (DtS) the school enterprise initiative. The research aimed, 'to benchmark young people and children's attitudinal values, perceptions and opinions about 'enterprise', including confidence, self-expression, notions of success and career success'. The research indicates that 42 per cent of S4 students appear deficient in these positive attitudes to themselves and that 29 per cent of the others would also benefit from more nurturing of self-belief, presumably to help them become more dynamic and ambitious. Of the P7 students, 71 per cent of the group are seen to be lacking in self-belief or confidence.

■ The Centre for Confidence and Well-Being's research shows that young people in Scotland have a significantly lower level (on average) of self-esteem and confidence than young people of a similar age in the US and many other countries. The self-esteem and optimism figures for some students in deprived areas are particularly low.

■ 40 per cent more per head is spent on prescriptions for antidepressants in Scotland than in England. Depression is among the top 5 reasons a person in Scotland will visit their GP.

■ People aged 15-74 in Scotland have a higher rate of suicide than people of the same age in Greece, Italy, Portugal, Spain, England and Northern Ireland. (WHOSIS 2004)

CHAPTER 5

The Centre mounts a challenge to an Orwellian development in English education

The Westminster Government's Social and Emotional Aspects of Learning {SEAL) programme;
the Centre's critique of the theory and evidence underlying SEAL;
why this psychological intervention could backfire;
SEAL's inherent social control and conformity;
rebelliousness and an overly feminine agenda;
what happened next.

IN THE SPRING of 2007 I had a meeting with Geoff Huggins, then Head of Mental Health Division in the Scottish Executive and the main purse-holder for the Centre's funding. As I was leaving he handed me a large report saying he was eager to hear my views as he was continually being asked to fund these types of projects.

The report was a Guidance document for English and Welsh primary schools on 'Social and Emotional Aspects of Learning (SEAL)' issued in 2005 by the Department for Education and Skills (DfES) in London. (In 2007 it became known as the Department for Children, Schools and Families and here I mainly call it the Education Department.) At first glance the Guidance notes appeared to be uncontroversial and simply suggested ways to enhance children's broad social and emotional skills. But as I got into the substance of the report and grasped its ambition for how such skills should be taught in schools I was not just taken aback but ultimately opposed to what I thought was an essentially Orwellian vision.

It's important to make clear that the Centre was not opposed to some teaching of social and emotional skills or to everything in the SEAL Guidance. (See Box 6) What we objected to was that SEAL suggested that **every** child from the age of 3-18 should be formally and explicitly taught social and emotional skills in the classroom according to a 'spiral curriculum' and, in time, evaluated against a checklist of 'learning outcomes'. For 3-11 year olds there were 42 learning outcomes and for secondary students there were 50. This was a huge shift in educational policy.

On the surface SEAL seemed 'holistic' and child-centred and it was easy to believe that talking about the importance of emotions and feelings for children was a good antidote to the cold logic of business as usual education. But if you dug deeper into the SEAL Guidance you could see that the Education Department had ultimately grafted this new focus on emotions onto its standard practices: if this initiative had succeeded as planned, and schools fully implemented the recommendations, all young people's emotional lives (not just the few who have obvious difficulties) would become the focus of checklists of learning outcomes and assessments. This would have meant that the way children and young people dealt with their emotions, perceived themselves and related to others was predetermined by the Education Department and their learning outcomes.

Thankfully this didn't happen. SEAL Guidance never became mandatory and within a few years this unified approach lost momentum. And we believe that the Centre's arguments were influential.

When I first found out about SEAL I was in the middle of writing *Creating Confidence* so I included emotional intelligence in my research. When we published the book in September 2007 I included a chapter on SEAL. The Centre also made available on its website a 112-page free downloadable paper I compiled called 'The potential dangers of a systematic, explicit approach to teaching social and emotional skills (SEAL)' as well as a 17-page summary paper.

Before a quick resumé of some of the key points I advanced in that paper, it's worth introducing you to Professor Katherine Weare,

Box 6: Preamble to the Centre's large SEAL report

Please note this document is not critical of classroom teachers, head teachers or other professionals who, in the course of their working lives have to help young people improve their social and emotional skills. The critique advanced here solely focuses on a centralised, systematic, programmatic approach which recommends that all children, in all schools should be formally taught these skills on a year on year basis from 3 to 18.

The Centre for Confidence and Well-being is committed to improving the well-being of young people. We think it is being eroded by a complex interaction of various cultural changes and we do not believe there are any short-cuts or panaceas. We think SEAL is being presented as a panacea and may not simply be diversionary but ultimately part of the problem.

SEAL covers a huge range of disparate approaches and strands. Of course, there are elements to this work which we would not only accept but also recommend. For example, we are in favour of improving the climate in schools to make the atmosphere more positive and supportive of young people. We promote the idea of fostering good relationships between teachers and pupils. We are all for pupils being given more of a voice. We also think that some amount of skill based training for older secondary school pupils may be beneficial. What we question is the explicit teaching year on year of social and emotional skills to all children and the accompanying framework of learning outcomes and evaluations.

We think that what is required above all else at the moment is a debate on the merits of the SEAL approach.

the main adviser on SEAL. At that time she was an education professor at the University of Southampton. A former secondary school teacher turned educationalist, she had written extensively on young people's social learning and emotional well-being, and had been a major advisor in the development of SEAL. In 2004, at the beginning of the SEAL roll out she published a book called *Developing the Emotionally Literate School*. She certainly had considerable experience in the area and I never doubted her commitment to improve young people's well-being.

Critiquing the evidence and rationale for SEAL

From what we could ascertain there was a lot of resistance in schools south of the border to SEAL. Many teachers, particularly in secondary schools, were very sceptical of SEAL's value and did not want to deliver this type of programme. The Education Department's response to this resistance was to stress that there was strong evidence showing that its proposals would be good for children's well-being. But we took issue with this and found it woefully easy to poke holes not just in their proposals but in the so-called underlying evidence for its efficacy and benefits.

It was particularly easy to show the weakness of SEAL's intellectual base. The SEAL documents and Weare's work in particular make frequent reference to emotional intelligence (EI). It is Daniel Goleman's 1996 book of that name which is the intellectual rationale for SEAL and the five SEAL areas (self-awareness, managing feelings, motivation, empathy and social skills) are derived from Goleman. So too is the rationale for the importance of SEAL. The Guidance quotes Goleman and asserts:

> Emotional and social competences have been shown to be more influential than cognitive abilities for personal, career and scholastic success, so they need to be central to schools and learning to increase school effectiveness. Working in this area can improve educational and life chances.

But this hasn't been shown. Daniel Goleman was a journalist and his book has been seriously, and extensively, critiqued by a large number of psychologists. His claims for the importance of emotional intelligence have been discredited as there is no credible evidence to support them. Even Goleman tacitly accepts this. What's more, many psychologists claim that his notion of emotional intelligence is a ragbag which includes any positive human characteristic other than IQ. They also point out that many of the characteristics he cites are at odds with one another or largely emanate from personality.

Two psychologists – Mayer and Salovey – were the originators of the term 'emotional intelligence'. They are very critical of Goleman's work, including his outlandish claims. Also, a large academic tome on emotional intelligence, wrtten by Matthews *et al*, warned '. . . in spite of current theorising about EI programs, we really do not know that much about how they work, for whom they work, under what conditions they work, or indeed, whether or not they work at all.' They also refer to many EI programmes as 'snakeoil' and conclude that emotional intelligence is more 'myth than science'. In short, Goleman's work and the idea of emotional intelligence cannot be used to justify the type of programmes envisaged by SEAL.

It was also easy to undermine the credibility of another key aspect of Weare's rationale for the SEAL approach, namely that teaching all children social and emotional skills would end the current deficit whereby some children were seen to be lacking and require remedial help. This was a completely false argument.

The SEAL Guidance envisaged three tiers of intervention: classes for all children; small group work for children who were particularly lacking such skills; and then one-to-one work for some individual pupils. Indeed apart from there being a clear hierarchy of needs, the SEAL approach now extended a deficit approach to all children: effectively they were all now perceived to be lacking social and emotional competencies and needed formal teaching by adults. In this respect we agreed with academic critics, such as Professor Frank Furedi or education Professors Ecclestone and Hayes that such therapeutic approaches ushered in an era of a 'fragile' or 'diminished self': a self that now constantly needed help from professionals.

Like many others, we thought the empirical studies, cited in the SEAL Guidance as evidence of efficacy of these types of programmes, were too varied (and American) to be convincing evidence for what was proposed in England. (See Box 7) I was also shocked that the Education Department would claim that its pilot on SEAL generated positive data. It did not. Indeed for my big paper I pored over the empirical data from the SEAL pilot and presented it clearly in ways which showed how the intervention mainly had a nil or negative effect on the children. In this endeavour I was greatly indebted to my friend Dr Fran Wasoff who checked all my calculations. (As she has a Ph.D in maths and at that point taught statistics to social policy students, her support was a great comfort.)

Box 7: The weakness of SEAL's empirical evidence base

Empirical studies

The SEAL documents cite as additional supporting evidence for their approach 17 international studies (15 of which are American) which apparently demonstrate the necessity of whole-school, taught approaches to this type of work with young people. However, even proponents of SEAL acknowledge that these studies report interventions which are hugely different in design, goals and methodology and that it is very difficult to ascertain their effectiveness. What's more, while these studies may have been effective on their own terms, none of these pilot studies is anything like what is proposed by the SEAL Guidance – i.e. that children will be taught social and emotional skills on an annual basis from 3 to 18. As this has never been done before, only a longitudinal study, with a control group could allow us to assess what the impact might be of this type of intervention. Even if a large study of this kind had been done and proved effective, this would not provide evidence that rolling it out across a whole education system (where there would be fewer resources and well-trained staff) would be beneficial.

The DfES pilots on SEAL

Between 2003 and 2005, the DfES ran a multi-strand pilot. The results were then published as 'Evaluation of the Primary Behaviour and Attendance Strategy Pilot'. One of the strands piloted was SEAL. This was a very poorly designed study which had no control group. The report gives a positive impression as it mainly draws on the subjective feedback of teachers who were hand-picked on the basis of largely unspecified criteria. What's more the empirical data presented show that SEAL had no impact on attendance and virtually no effect on academic performance. More worryingly, the empirical data presented on the impact on pupils shows that for most of the attitudes measured the results went down, not up, after the pilot, particularly for boys. The report authors write: 'there were statistically significant gender differences in relation to almost all of the scales prior to and following the programme with the girls exhibiting more positive responses in all cases.' What they should have said is that the girls displayed fewer negative responses overall when compared with the boys.

This pilot did not show that SEAL was a success. Indeed it showed that explicitly teaching children social and emotional skills was much less effective than using classroom coaches to help improve teachers' skills. Nonetheless the DfES argued that the pilot was successful and cited it as part of the rationale for rolling SEAL out nationally to primary schools.

Another telling result from the SEAL pilot (see Box 7) was that the pre-intervention results for self-esteem, social skills and relationships and emotional awareness did not suggest there was a problem to be addressed in these children's social and emotional skills. For example, pre-intervention, the mean for self-esteem across the various stages was over 90 per cent; and for social skills and relationships over 80 per cent. The lowest figure (61 per cent) was ironically 'anxiety about school work'.

These types of conclusions could have led us to argue that SEAL looked like a major waste of public money and school time. But this was the least of our concerns. We were only too aware that the main project to change children's views of themselves and their relationships, and conducted routinely on a year on year basis by classroom teachers, was the American attempt to raise young people's self-esteem. From the arguments and evidence presented in Chapter 3, we knew that this yielded negative, not positive, results both for learning and for young people's mental health. We could see that those devising SEAL did not heed any of these warnings and appeared unaware of the evidence and arguments. Daniel Goleman was not an advocate of self-esteem and never mentions it in his book yet self-esteem appears frequently in SEAL and there is even a 'Good to be me' unit where the emphasis is on the child feeling 'special'. This is similar to what happened in American schools, a development which some psychologists warned would boost narcissism – something which did increase greatly in young people there.

Psychological interventions can backfire

A major aspect of my paper was to point out some of the inherent dangers in SEAL's proposed psychological interventions. Professor Robert Sternberg is a leading American psychologist and he is acutely aware of the dangers of psychology. He writes: 'We would not want drugs to go to market that are essentially untested and that have only their promoters' claims to back them up. Yet we routinely rely on such claims to buy educational and organisational products and services.' He then adds, 'People's lives may be affected in much the same way as their lives can be affected by drugs.'

We have already seen how this happened with artificial self-esteem building. But it's worth giving a few examples, from the many we advance, of why we considered SEAL to pose a threat to young people's well-being.

Calming techniques

In the SEAL document there is a heavy emphasis on the importance of young people learning how to 'calm themselves'. In the primary schools resources unit there is a wall poster for the classroom which reads: 'Have you used any of these calming techniques today?' and there are also cards for pupils urging them, 'Say to yourself – be calm – be calm – be calm'; 'Tell someone how you feel'; 'Feel your pulse. . .'

Of course, professionals working with very young children have always had to devote considerable time to helping children calm themselves and recover from upset feelings so that they can concentrate on other activities. Few professionals would survive working with young children if they weren't able to do this. However, introducing the idea of 'calming yourself' into the formal and 'taught' curriculum for three to eleven year olds is something different. Gone is the expectation of calmness – this is now something children have to learn. As soon as we put it in these terms we see that it introduces the idea of failure – of not being able to induce a calm state. It's very easy to see how by emphasising how important it is to be calm, rather than providing a context where calm is expected, teachers could unwittingly increase children's feelings of nervousness around not being calm.

There is another psychological mechanism at work which suggests that an emphasis on calming down in the classroom is likely to backfire. Dan Wegner, a social psychologist, has published many articles on what he calls 'ironic processes of mental control'. What this means is that often by trying to control our minds in some way – e.g. trying not to think about cigarettes or trying to fall asleep – we often, ironically, induce the opposite.

Ironic effects are particularly common around relaxation – the more we try to relax the more aware we become of being tense.

Wegner *et al* write: '. . . too often our efforts to cool down, withdraw, or calm ourselves seem to backfire – producing greater agitation than we had suffered before we even tried to relax.' In short, all that emphasis on being calm in the classroom could well make young people's excitability and lack of control worse – not better. And the idea that SEAL could unwittingly make more children anxious led us to feel anxious.

The problem with self-expression

Another key aspect of SEAL is the emphasis it places on young people not just recognising and managing their feelings but 'expressing' them as well. Students will be encouraged to talk about their feelings. Professor Weare believes, 'We all need to learn to express our emotions, because expressing an emotion is an integral part of experiencing it.'

In his great little book *Emotion* (2001) Dylan Evans writes:

> We look back at the stiff-necked Victorians with a smug sense of superiority. 'Emotional literacy' is held in high esteem. People who cannot talk openly about their feelings are regarded as psychologically immature, relics of a bygone age when repression reigned supreme. However, psychologists are increasingly realising that the hydraulic theory of emotion is too simplistic. It may well be good on some occasions to indulge in the spontaneous expression of emotion. On other occasions, however it can be positively harmful.

This has become evident partly as a result of research into post-traumatic stress/critical incident debriefing – something which has become the norm in contemporary society. Following any disaster– – rail crash, pile up on the motorway or shooting incident – counsellors are taken in along with emergency staff. The idea here being that the 'victims' need help with their psychological injuries as well as any physical ones. However, research shows that this type of debriefing/counselling after such events can make people worse not better, perhaps because psychological interventions can get in the way of spontaneous healing.

So talking about how you feel is not necessarily 'the good thing' which the SEAL document suggests. Authors of *One Nation under Therapy* (2005), Christina Hoff Sommers and Sally Satel (a practising psychiatrist), also fundamentally challenge the predominant notion that 'uninhibited emotional openness is essential for mental health'. And what they go on to say has direct applicability to the classroom – '. . . recent findings suggest that reticence and suppression of feelings, far from compromising one's psychological well-being, can be healthy and adaptive. For many temperaments, an excessive focus on introspection and self-disclosure is depressing.'

Salovey, one of the psychologists who coined the term emotional intelligence, admits that sometimes the best course of action is not to pay attention to one's feelings. 'A person might run the risk of becoming overwhelmed or even paralysed by negative emotion or unnecessarily bogged down with emotional information from the external world,' he writes and adds: 'There might be times when being oblivious to emotional states is adaptive'. This may be particularly the case for young people from abusive backgrounds. Dissociating from their feelings may not be healthy but it may be better (more adaptive) than experiencing the bad feelings such neglect and abuse engenders. It doesn't take a professional to see that getting abused or neglected children to focus more on how they are feeling might make them feel worse – not better.

What's more, psychologists are aware that ruminating on feelings can lead to depression. For example, research published in the *Journal of Developmental Psychology* in 2007 found that girls who excessively discuss problems and who constantly vent over personal problems, show increased levels of anxiety and depression.

An overly sophisticated approach

The architects of SEAL would no doubt rebut these arguments by saying that what they propose is much more sophisticated than I suggest. They may argue, for example, that young people won't get depressed as a result of encouragement to express their feelings as they will be taught how to regulate their feelings and manage their moods. But this is the problem with SEAL – it is too sophisticated. If you read the Primary and Secondary Guidance on the 'learning outcomes' for this work, you could swear you were reading the prospectus for a management training programme or a post-graduate diploma in counselling skills as they are such complex and sophisticated lists of desired outcomes. Here are two examples:

> I know that it is OK to have any feeling, but not OK to behave in any way I feel like. (Primary/pre-school);
>
> I understand that changing the way I think about people and events changes the way I feel about them. (Primary/pre-school)

Professor Mark Greenberg, an expert on emotional development, acknowledges that most young people 'often cannot separate their feelings from their behaviour' adding 'many adults have a hard time doing this. It is complicated and occupies much time in most forms of adult psychotherapy.'

The Orwellian aspect of SEAL – political control and social conformity

Until the emphasis on emotional literacy/intelligence, schools were mainly concerned about behaviour – it was how you behaved or what you said which mattered. What you felt was your own business. But for children in England this would go with SEAL's implementation – feelings, the most intimate part of our lives would be managed by the people drawing up the lists of emotional and social competences. As Professor Weare herself says, deciding what goes into such a list 'cannot be value-free, culture-free or an apolitical exercise.'

Secondary SEAL makes clear that young people are expected to develop in line with the 50 learning outcomes. The Guidance booklet states that Assessment for Learning can be used alongside SEAL to: 'Encourage pupils to set success criteria for meeting the SEAL learning outcomes'. In other words, they will be encouraged not to realise their own specific potential and develop their own personalities. No, they will be actively encouraged, and trained, to become more like the personality outlined in the learning outcomes. This means that young people who do not want to express their feelings will be expected to learn how to do this, even though this might not be their preference.

The problem of control goes much further than who draws up the lists of competences on which children are to be judged and trained. The SEAL document has learning outcomes linked to 'managing feelings' such as 'I can adapt the way I express my feelings to suit particular situations or people'. But this immediately raises the question of control. Who decides what level of self-expression is appropriate for a child or which feelings 'suit' particular situations or people?

By defining appropriateness and suitability of feelings, teachers will understandably mould young people in their own image. Even if this is done with subtlety and good intent, it's more oppressive and restricting of children's individuality than clear boundaries and rules on behaviour. To be fair to teachers, many of them don't want this power over children. In her book on emotional literacy in schools Professor Weare reports teachers' concerns that this type of work is 'manipulative and coercive.'

The micro management of children's lives will extend to their friendships. For example, the learning outcomes expressly mention the importance of not hurting others' feelings: 'I can express a range of feelings which do not hurt myself or other people'; 'I can make, sustain and break friendships without hurting others'; 'I can resolve conflicts to ensure that everyone feels positive about the outcome'.

Of course, there are better ways to break off friendships but there is no guarantee with even the most diplomatic method that the other person will not be hurt – and we are thinking about adults here, never mind children. Is it not disingenuous to make out, as this SEAL document does, that it's possible to break off friendships without the other person being hurt? Likewise is it always possible to resolve conflict to ensure that everyone feels positive about the outcome? Unfortunately we don't live in that perfect world. And it certainly appears to us that SEAL won't equip children with the experiences to deal with that reality.

Rebelliousness and an overly feminine agenda

As soon as we start to talk about the dangers of social control and conformity the prospect of rebellion rears its head. This is exactly what emerges from the SEAL pilot. Some headteachers actually reported a rise in 'fixed term exclusions' since the SEAL programme had been introduced. One headteacher reported: 'The children who normally behave well continued to behave well and for the ones who are lacking in emotional literacy it probably has not made much of a difference and. . . I think in some cases has made children worse'. Another head teacher reported that some children 'have rebelled against the SEAL programme'.

The authors' response is not to wonder whether this is the wrong approach but to say that the SEAL programme 'for a small minority was insufficient and more work was needed'. Is this simply a euphemistic way of saying that that these children needed to be subjected to more influence, if not more coercion?

One of the most worrying aspects of the SEAL document is its treatment of boys. As we have seen, SEAL encourages and values the development of a particular 'nice' type of person who expresses their feelings and is empathetic. In other words, they are keen to promote a way of being which is perceived as more feminine than masculine. Even the SEAL document accepts this. Here, in its entirety, is how the authors acknowledge the problem:

> Boys and girls are likely to respond differently to some of the activities, and may find different areas more or less difficult. Teachers/practitioners will need to be sensitive to these potential differences, and to the fact that the expression of emotion, talking about feelings and being seen to be empathetic and caring tend to be seen as feminine traits, with the consequence that boys may actively reject them rather than risk potential ridicule from peers and criticism at home. Teachers and practitioners will need to be aware of these issues during the planning and delivery stages and it would be useful for schools and settings to have developed a consistent response to them. Positive male role-models are a useful source of countering such responses, and examples of

> situations, stories and role-play should, wherever possible, engage the interest and motivation of boys.

That's it. That's all the SEAL document has to say, on the authors' own admission that this whole-school, taught, year-on-year activity may not suit 50 per cent of those sitting in the classroom – boys. Any difficulty that this is likely to cause is being passed, like a hot potato, onto teachers and schools to sort out and the main tool in their box is, as usual, likely to be nothing more than *sensitivity*. In short, schools and settings are going to have to work out for themselves how to respond to the problem of gender differences and emotional expression which, if not actually hard-wired into the brain, have been around for millennia.

The whole SEAL approach is effectively ensuring a further feminisation of primary education: not only are teachers and head teachers increasingly female but now the whole ethos of English schools is going to be dominated by the idea that a major priority is to pay attention to our own and others' feelings. Girls who do not share these values are unlikely to feel at home in the overly feeling classroom but they are unlikely to feel as uncomfortable as the legions of boys who will feel that this is not their preferred way of being.

What happened next

The Centre published the SEAL paper and handbook in 2007 before the advent of social media. Our growing list of supporters found out about them from emails, newsletters and from visiting our website. My talks were also an important way to inform teachers and educationalists on our views. That year I spoke at a large Scottish secondary headteachers' conference. I was then invited to speak to equivalent organisations in England, Northern Ireland and the Republic. These talks also proved popular and received some press coverage. Indeed media reports led to my SEAL paper making it into a favourable blog written by the famous American philosopher Ken Wilber.

As a result of all this publicity the SEAL report was downloaded thousands of times from our website. Much to my surprise I was contacted either by email or phone by about ten people in England, many of them in senior positions such as education officers, advisers, researchers and educational psychologists. They wanted to tell me how much they agreed with my paper and how much they appreciated the research I had undertaken. They all said that they found SEAL deeply worrying. Most also said that it was being promoted so strongly by the Education Department that it was not good for their careers to be openly critical of it. In fact a couple of them would not give their names for fear of reprisals.

There's little doubt that my large paper undermined the SEAL document's claim that everything proposed had a strong evidence base and was good for child well-being. In short, the paper weakened SEAL's credibility. This then gave teachers and head teachers, who were not keen on SEAL, justification for not implementing its recommendations for formal teaching of its curriculum.

In 2010 the Department for Education, as it had now become, published a report on the large scale secondary school pilot of SEAL. It was not happy reading for proponents. The researchers conclude:

> in terms of impact, our analysis of pupil-level outcome data indicated that SEAL (as implemented by schools in our sample) failed to impact significantly upon pupils' social and emotional skills, general mental health difficulties, pro-social behaviour or behaviour problems.

The Labour governments of Tony Blair and Gordon Brown had been very keen on an approach that emphasised self-esteem and individual psychology. Since SEAL could not be shown to be making a difference to the young people participating in programmes, it's hardly surprising that when the Conservative-Liberal Coalition Government took power in 2010 it discontinued SEAL as a national programme. Schools were free to use SEAL resources if they wished but the programme was no longer promoted by government.

By then schools and local authorities were experimenting with a variety of different approaches to social and emotional learning:

positive psychology, a strengths-based approach, happiness lessons, mindfulness. . . All these became quite popular with schools and for the Centre they were all preferable to the emotional intelligence competency framework at the core of SEAL.

It's worth noting that the authors of the Secondary schools review of SEAL which reported nil effects expressly say that in reporting this:

> We do not share the rather radical views of authors such as Craig (2007), Ecclestone and Hayes (2008) and Furedi (2004), who have argued that approaches such as SEAL are at best ill-conceived and at worst potentially damaging to children and young people.

Furedi, Eccleston and Hayes are uncompromising in their critique of any development in education which they see as 'therapeutic' and only see value in an intellectual education. But this wasn't true of our approach. We always made clear that there were aspects of the SEAL Guidance that we did not take issue with such as improving the school climate and fostering good relationships. (See Box 7) In addition we actively encouraged some types of social and emotional learning (SEL). Indeed the Centre devised an assertiveness programme for teenagers that would fall under the SEL banner and we also promoted the resiliency programme *Bounce Back!*. We specifically objected to one aspect of SEAL – a year-on-year emotional intelligence taught programme with learning outcomes and evaluations for 3-18 year olds.

We had hoped to initiate a debate on some of the issues raised in our report but this didn't happen. By 2007 too many people in education were genuinely fearful of contradicting what was fast becoming orthodoxy – schools should be formally teaching children skills to improve emotional well-being. There were also lots of people who had a vested interest in the development of emotional education – psychologists, counsellors, educators and researchers who had invested time in this area and had a professional interest in it continuing. And one of the questions they rarely asked is why was young people's well-being deteriorating? What was the origin of the problem SEAL was trying to address?

We saw the issue as deeply cultural, and related to big and important socio-economic developments in children's lives – family breakdown, materialism, and the rise of inequality to name a few – developments we shall return to in later chapters.

In many ways we were the exceptions. It was not in our interest to take issue with SEAL and be so vocal about it. As an organisation set up to advance confidence and well-being it would have been so easy for us to come up with an alternative programme or to say that we would promote SEAL in Scotland. We could have created a good income stream for ourselves if we had chosen to do this. Or we could just have kept quiet. But we didn't as we were genuinely concerned that an English and Welsh roll-out of SEAL would in the long term damage child well-being in the same way that artificial self-esteem building had undermined the mental health of American children.

There's little doubt our approach ruffled feathers. Some organisations in Scotland were involved in emotional literacy interventions and they didn't like what we were saying. One of our valued board members, a civil servant, resigned because we were too sharply critical of Westminster Government education policy. But fortunately Geoff Huggins, head of Mental Health Division in Scotland, and the person who had initiated the Centre's SEAL journey by handing me the Guidance and soliciting my opinion, took a different view. I'm not saying he welcomed the controversy but he accepted it and valued the fact that he received a clear answer to his question.

Over the years I have changed my mind about a lot of things but SEAL is not one of them. If I had my time over I would still write that challenging report.

The Centre and sport in Scotland

In Phase 1 of Centre activities most of what we were doing on confidence, optimism and mindset was relevant to those involved in sport. As well as talking about sport and optimism in talks and articles, here's a list of specific activities:

Npower Raise Your Game Manual

In June 2005, the Centre was approached by a PR agency and asked to collaborate with npower and the SFA in the preparation of a slim manual which would, amongst other things, help to address confidence issues for young footballers. The chartered psychologist Alan McLean, an expert on motivation, and I then co-authored 'Raise Your Game'. The manual was aimed at parents and others involved in school football and was designed to show readers how to improve young people's skills as well as training techniques to boost motivation and confidence. We also compiled a separate list of 'Top Touchline Tips for Parents' on how to keep youngsters' confidence and motivation high. The Tips were released to the press in July when npower launched the summer football classes it was sponsoring. These Tips attracted much interest from the media and I was interviewed on both radio and television. The Herald and Evening Times also covered the story favourably.

Alex McLeish's guest blog

In 2008, as part of a revamp of our website, we launched a 'guest blog' feature which allowed various people to reflect on how they thought that Scots could realise their potential. The first in the series was written by a former manager of the Scotland football team, Alex McLeish. This received some positive coverage in the press.

Sport, mindset and famous Scottish panellists

In 2007 we ran a masterclass with Professor Carol Dweck called 'the Psychology of Success'. It was aimed at people in business, education and sport and was sponsored by the Scottish Institute of Sport Foundation (later called Winning Scotland) as we had introduced them to Dweck's ideas. At this event we had three panels following Dweck's talk. The sports panel included Gregor Townsend who is now coach of Scotland's rugby team and a fan of Dweck's ideas on the fixed and growth mindsets; Scotland's famous athletics coach Tommy Boyle; and Susan Jackson, a rifle shooter and one of Scotland's most successful international competitors.

Chapter 6

Funding, findings, flexibility and facing the future

Funding crisis; the new funding settlement; findings from the Centre's research – positive writing, Confidence Research System, outdoor learning and Carol Dweck's Brainology; opportunities; the Centre's 'brand' identity; SWOT analysis; facing the future.

WE ALWAYS KNEW that the funding arrangements announced by the Scottish Executive in December 2004 would be difficult as they were giving us project, not core, funding. But we were unprepared for how impractical and stressful the arrangements would become. I spent an inordinate amount of time either drafting project proposals for funding or writing end of project reports. But this wasn't the only problem with the arrangement.

The £150,000 earmarked for the Centre per annum was coming from three departments – Mental Health, Teachers' Division in the Education Department and Social Services. So our project proposals had to be agreed and signed off by these departments. They didn't have many common interests so designing projects to appeal to them all was difficult. Something on young people was always the best option. But no matter what our proposals, the staff involved would take ages to meet up to decide what they wanted to fund. As a result the Centre could submit project proposals for our funding in April and they wouldn't be formally agreed till the end of September or even later. This then meant we had a mad dash to complete the projects by the end of the financial year in

March. It also meant that we wouldn't get any of our annual allocation of money till the autumn.

In 2007 the difficulties inherent in this arrangement came to a head. The delay in agreeing our proposed projects meant that by the summer we were running out of money and didn't have enough to pay staff. Fortunately, an organisation we were working with lent us some money to bridge the gap and we duly paid it back when we finally got our Scottish Executive funding. This was not a good way to run an organisation.

SNP Government support?

That year was also particularly stressful as we were unsure whether our funding would continue beyond the agreed three-year period: 2005-2008. First Minister's Jack McConnell's Labour administration had agreed our initial funding but they were voted out of office in May 2007. Scotland now had a minority SNP administration. Would this new Scottish Government, as they now called it, want to continue support for the Centre? I devote a whole chapter to the Centre's, and my own, relationship with Scottish politics in Chapter 22 but it's relevant here to make some brief comments.

As Scotland is a small, networked country, I was on good terms with three senior SNP politicians and they were very keen to support the Centre: Michael Russell, Jim Mather and Kenny MacAskill. They all held government posts so this clearly was an advantage for continued funding. But I also knew from *sotto voce* comments that some of the senior women were not particularly predisposed towards me, *The Scots' Crisis of Confidence* or the Centre – Shona Robison, Nicola Sturgeon and Fiona Hyslop. I hadn't met any of these women personally. Shona Robison's lack of enthusiastic support could have made a difference to whether our funding was continued as she was appointed minister for public health in 2007 – a department relevant to the Centre's work.

But this didn't happen and the settlement, while smaller, was much better than it had been for the first three years. We were now offered three years of core funding of £125,000 per year and it was coming from one department only – Mental Health run by

Geoff Huggins. Geoff had been the purse holder for the three departments under the previous arrangement and knew first-hand how difficult it was for the Centre to operate with these financial arrangements. Geoff also respected the Centre as we could be challenging and didn't support ideas simply because they were advantageous to us.

The Centre is eternally grateful for the core funding we got from Geoff Huggins' departmental budget. It guaranteed that we would be in business for the next three years – until 2011 – and that we would have much more financial stability.

Findings from Centre research

Between 2005 and 2009 the Centre was involved in four research projects related to young people's confidence and well-being. Some of these were completed when the Centre was in the second phase of its activity but I'm reporting them here because most of the groundwork was done before 2009.

Positive writing

In 2006 we used some of our funding to conduct a research project on 'positive writing'. We were keen to try to replicate Martin Seligman's research findings that a very simple task – keeping a diary for a couple of weeks listing three good things which have happened that day – could increase happiness and lead to a decrease in depressive symptoms. Seligman's participants completed the diary nightly but additional research showed that this exercise need not be undertaken every night and that two to three times a week was sufficient to produce results.

Seligman believes that the reason why this exercise is so helpful in raising positive emotion and decreasing depression scores is because it trains the brain to pay attention to the positive. It's all too easy for us to focus on rejection, failure and a low mood, rather than what's good in our lives. This could be an enjoyable conversation, a success, or something simple like enjoying a sunset.

We decided to try the exercise on S2 pupils in a two-week intervention in four schools across Scotland. In consultation with teachers, we agreed that the control group intervention would be completing a food diary of what the young person had eaten the day before. A psychology researcher, Lisa McGilvray, helped carry out the research and the data generated was then analysed by Dr Fabio Sani, a psychology lecturer at the University of St Andrews, who was very interested in our project. He then wrote a detailed report.

In his report Dr Sani summarises the results which showed that the positive writing exercise had a positive effect on the young people's self-esteem, happiness, satisfaction with life, and optimism and that depression scores decreased. However, this was also true of the pupils in the control group who had kept a food diary. Further analysis showed that the positive writing group's results varied by gender: the intervention had more positive results for the girls than the boys. In fact, keeping a diary of positive things had a negative effect on a majority of boys as their happiness decreased. From follow-up interviews we learned that some of the boys became frustrated as they couldn't always think of three good things.

Those who are interested in young people's well-being may find it useful to read Dr Sani's content analysis of the notebooks as there are some insights into what young people appreciate in their lives and how this differs by gender.[1]

Confidence Research System (CRS)

As I explained in a previous chapter, in 2005 the Centre set up an online system to allow people running confidence or well-being projects to measure the results of their interventions by asking participants to complete pre and post questionnaires. As confidence is a multifaceted concept, the term is not often used by psychologists. This also means that there is no simple validated questionnaire to measure confidence. To get round this problem Dr Elaine Duncan identified a number of questionnaires which together measured something approximating to what we think of as

[1] Most studies internationally show that males generally have higher self-esteem but many studies have shown that self-efficacy does not usually vary by gender.

Box 8: Findings from the Centre's Confidence Research System

- **Males** have **higher self-efficacy and higher self-esteem** than females.
- With regard to ethnic origin, the **white-Scottish group scores lowest on the scales optimism and self-efficacy but higher on self-esteem**.
- The group identifying as **'non-white' scored lowest on self-esteem**.
- Comparing different schools we find significant differences on the **optimism, mindset and self-esteem scales**. Interestingly, on all scales (except the mindset scale) it was one and the same school that consistently ranked first while the rest of the rank order differed widely across the different criteria.
- There are significant group differences between the **five socio-economic status groups** on the scales **self-efficacy, mindset and self-esteem. The most deprived quintile consistently scores worse than the others.** By and large for all of the scales (except mindset) the order formed by the socio-economic groups was replicated in the scoring order of those groups.
- The average scores for **the region West of Scotland** have been compared to the rest of the country. It was found that those belonging to the region score **lower on self-efficacy and mindset but slightly higher on happiness**. However, the total differences based on this grouping were rather small.
- What is interesting is that **none of the factors analysed led to a significant difference on the life satisfaction** scale.

confidence – optimism, self-efficacy, self-esteem, life satisfaction and happiness. In the following years we added two more questionnaires to the CRS – one on resilience and one on Professor Carol Dweck's concept of the fixed and growth mindsets.

The Centre made the CRS available to anyone wanting to use it and maintained the system until 2011. By then it contained responses from almost 6,000 participants. In 2009 David Walsh from the Glasgow Centre for Population Health analysed the data and confirmed that the largest data set we had collected – 13-15 year olds – was representative both of the Scottish and Glasgow populations.

The CRS was used extensively by Schools of Ambition and Determined to Succeed, and some other youth and school projects such as the Duke of Edinburgh's Award scheme, Outward Bound and Fife Young Carers. As a result the respondents were overwhelmingly young people though it also contained some responses from university students.

In 2009, Diana Wernisch, a young post-graduate from Austria came to work at the Centre for the summer as an intern. Her chosen piece of work was to analyse the data in the CRS. The average age of respondents at that time was 16.5. Diana wrote a number of reports on the data and some of her main findings are included in Box 8.

Outdoor learning

In 2009 the Centre produced a report on research it had conducted on the impact of different types of outdoor education interventions. We carried out the research in partnership with Scottish Outdoor Education Centres. The research involved 114 pupils who had participated in an outdoor education experience. The pupils were divided into four groups. One group only participated in outdoor education and the other three had this experience plus involvement in positive writing, or input/training from instructors on either mindset or optimism.

Overall the outdoor education programme alone produced consistently positive results across six confidence and well-being measures, for both males and females. The results show that the group which participated in the mindset and outdoor education experience showed the largest increase for self-efficacy, mindset and optimism, compared to all other groups. The gender results show that though there was an increase for both males and females, females especially benefited from the mindset intervention.

The optimism intervention seemed to have a small positive effect on self-efficacy, mindset and optimism. However, when looking at the gender difference, the evidence suggests that for girls the combination of outdoor education and optimism may have created more of a fixed mindset and ironically lowered levels of optimism. The males responded very well to this intervention.

The least successful intervention was positive writing. The group showed a decrease for both happiness and mindset; self-efficacy stayed the same. Looking at the gender differences, happiness decreased for males. The girls' life satisfaction decreased and their mindset became more fixed.

However, the numbers of those participating in the positive writing, mindset and optimism interventions were small and the results may have arisen not simply from chance but from poor instruction by the outdoor educators who had only participated in short training sessions provided by the Centre.

Brainology

As I outline on page 69 the Centre had held a few events with Professor Carol Dweck in 2007. In September 2009 she spoke to 2000 educationalists at Glasgow's Learning Festival and this engendered even more interest in her work. The Centre was delighted when she approached us to see if we would help her run a major controlled trial of a mindset intervention in Scotland. The trial involved the use of 'Brainology' – a computer animation programme to assist children and young people to develop growth mindsets. We appointed Derek Goldman to liaise with Stanford University on this and to approach local authorities and schools in Scotland to recruit the large number of classrooms required. Brainology is a fairly expensive programme for schools to access but we managed to secure a three-year free licensing agreement for the participating schools.

Dweck's researchers were mainly interested in whether exposure to Brainology improved academic performance when compared to pupils in a control group. Given that the Centre is more interested in resilience and well-being, they added a satisfaction with life scale to the pre and post measures.

At the end of the research two short papers were published authored by Dave Paunesku, Derek Goldman and Carol Dweck. One outlines the results of the study involving 14 primary schools in Renfrewshire; the other outlines the results from 26 Scottish secondary schools across the country.

The primary school results show that children involved in Brainology, in comparison with those in the control group, reported more growth mindset beliefs after the study. The experience improved their 'standing on a standardised reading assessment' (relative to the control groups) and they reported greater life satisfaction. Indeed the life satisfaction rating of the average pupil in the growth mindset classes was about 10 percentile points higher than that of the average pupil in the control classes. Pupils with lower pre-study life satisfaction ratings benefited to an even greater extent. Life satisfaction is an important dimension of well-being. Those participating in the growth mindset intervention also saw failure differently – attributing it to lack of effort and preparation rather than something stable about the self. This implies a growth in resilience.

In the secondary school study those involved in Brainology also reported a very small increase in life satisfaction whereas life satisfaction dropped slightly in the control group. The study also showed a small increase in the study group's self-efficacy whereas there was a drop in the control group's self-efficacy. When it comes to academic results the study showed a small improvement of 1 per cent in the maths scores of the boys doing Brainology from pre to post test, whereas the control group's results showed that boys lost almost 11 per cent from pre to post test. The girls' results were not changed by Brainology.

Given that there was some benefit to life satisfaction and/or the ways that youngsters viewed failure as a result of this mindset intervention, we think that the results more than justified the Centre's involvement in this research.

Opportunities

In the first few years of its existence a large number of organisations wanted to work with the Centre. There was a constant stream of people coming into the office to tell us about their projects and to ask us to be involved in some way. Often this just meant that I would speak to staff on confidence and well-being themes at one of their events. Sometimes we would deliver training for the organisation. For example, in 2008 a Centre associate, Derek Goldman, was involved in extensive training sessions with social work staff in West Dunbartonshire Council and the following year we held a large conference for all staff and some service users. In 2008 Careers Scotland agreed to allow a member of staff, Brian Waddell, to base himself in our office and to work on how they could utilise some of our ideas.

Around the same time Alan Sinclair, who had become an associate with the Work Foundation, took a desk in our office. Alan had set up the Wise Group and had recently stood down as Senior Director for Skills and Learning at Scottish Enterprise. Alan had become very interested in how early years experiences affect the later development of skills necessary in the modern workplace and his work on this ultimately became integral to the Centre's agenda, as I'll explain in Chapter 18.

Zoe Van Zwanenberg had been head of the Scottish Leadership Foundation. She had also been a Centre board member for three years from 2005. In August 2008 she left the board and became the Centre's Project Coordinator. This was vital when we got into our second phase of activity.

The Centre's brand

I dislike charities aping business organisations though sadly this has become commonplace across the voluntary sector. Nonetheless it can be helpful to think about an organisation's 'brand' identity or values and this was something I included in my 2008 business plan. I asserted then, and still believe, that one of the Centre's main assets was its strong brand identity. The Centre managed to establish this quickly thanks to Pete Fletcher the designer who created our logo early in 2005 and worked with the Centre until 2020. The Centre's board was conscious of these values and worked to reinforce, rather than undermine, them.

The Centre's brand values are communicated not only in the logo but also in the style and feel of our events, our website and our marketing materials. In 2008 we defined these as –

- Creative and entrepreneurial (as opposed to safe, traditional or corporate)
- Positive and optimistic
- Intellectual (as opposed to touchy-feely)
- Values led/committed (as opposed to commercially driven or objective).

As well as these brand values which were, and still are, communicated outwards, the Centre has values which guide the running of the organisation. In those early days these were –

- Flexibility
- Transparency
- Care and compassion
- Equality
- Sustainability.

As befits an organisation which wants to make sustainability a major value we made, and still make, business decisions on the basis of conserving resources. For example, we used email for most of our communication and as early as 2006 we did not give out folders or freebies at our events. Instead we gave participants centre for confidence and well-being

access to information on our website which they could download if they wanted supporting notes. It's because we seriously tried to live up to our values that underlined our claim to be 'values led'.

When we ran conferences we always emphasised content rather than appearance. This meant that those who came to our events knew that they would hear first rate speakers and participate in meaningful discussion. They also knew that the style of the event would be 'honest', in the architectural use of the term, rather than glitzy or glamorous.

SWOT analysis

In 2008 I compiled a SWOT analysis of the Centre – Strengths, Weaknesses, Opportunities and Threats and looking at it today it seems pretty accurate.

Our *strengths* undoubtedly came from our flexibility and our proven ability to seize opportunities. In other words, we were nimble and entrepreneurial. We had a very high profile and lots of organisations (too many in fact) wanted to work with us. There was a lot of interest in what we were doing both in Scotland and internationally. We also had lovely, and cost effective, offices in the middle of Glasgow.

We had undoubted *weaknesses*. Our funding was limited and insecure. We didn't have enough staff and, as we couldn't pay attractive salaries, those we hired tended to be young and inexperienced. The downside of flexibility is that we didn't have many formal processes in place. We also didn't have enough products, such as training courses, or services to cater for the huge interest in what we were doing. The organisation as a whole was too dependent on me and we needed more senior staff or associates.

There were undoubted *opportunities* for us as what we were doing was in tune with the *zeitgeist*. We were particularly aware that there was now a growing interest in sustainability and believed at that time that positive psychology, with its inherent critique of materialism, could have a role to play in developing a green consciousness.

There were also clear *threats*. The biggest was staff burnout – particularly for me given how much I was doing. Could I keep up travelling about the country giving talks as well as writing endless papers and worrying about money? Would we lose momentum and direction? Would our agenda become so mainstream that we would lose our edge?

Facing the future

In papers I wrote in early 2007 it was clear that we still envisaged continuing to work extensively on positive psychology. By the spring of 2008 we were beginning to talk amongst ourselves about broadening our agenda. By 2009 we were holding a variety of different events – events I'll describe in the section of the book outlining what we did in Phase 2 of our work.

The reasons for this different agenda will become clear from the next two chapters as they explain why we began to turn away from psychology, and positive psychology in particular.

Chapter 7

The shine goes off positive psychology

The supposed 'science' of positive psychology;
the Penn Resiliency Programme;
psychology's 'replicability crisis';
Fredrickson's 'positivity ratio' and 'voodoo science';
why 'science' matters to positive psychology;
the importance of negativity;
some inherent problems in the strengths-based approach (the VIA);
weighing up the positives and negatives of positive psychology;
what positive psychology offered Scotland;
events in Dundee and Glasgow with Tal Ben-Shahar.

I HAVE LIVED with Alf Young, one of Scotland's leading journalists, for over forty years. He has been a good friend to the Centre. He lent us money early in 2005 to tide us over till we received our government grant; he helped out at events when needed; and even now does the heavy lifting for the Centre's book business.

In 2005 he attended the Vanguard Programme in Glasgow in case we needed another pair of hands. He particularly valued the contributions from Phil Hanlon and Richard Eckersley but when it came to Martin Seligman, he was sceptical. As anyone who has read his columns can testify, Alf is a professional sceptic and critic. He asks trenchant questions and, unlike a lot of journalists, is skilled at analysing numbers. There's little doubt that he's confident in this realm as he studied physics and maths at Glasgow University and later became a physics teacher. However, he also has a good grounding in social science as he completed an M.Ed which included a major strand on educational psychology and then taught trainee teachers at Jordanhill College.

Alf particularly bristled at Seligman's claims that what he was presenting to us was 'science'. 'This isn't science as I know it,' he would later say to me. 'In real science all knowledge is provisional but Seligman, by contrast, is completely certain about what he's saying. He's got the answer and he's sticking to it.'

The fact that Seligman had a financial interest in the Penn Resiliency Programme (PRP) for school children, which he presented as scientifically proven, made this worse in Alf's eyes. I should point out that Seligman was always careful to declare his financial interest in the programme.

Finally, having studied both science and social science Alf was dubious about the scientific claims of the latter. 'There are too many variables; people and their life circumstances are too complex to really know what you're studying and what the results actually mean. Yes an intervention might work with one group but that doesn't mean it will elsewhere.'

It didn't take much to convince me that some scepticism was in order as I'd already had some of those thoughts myself. But I was also aware that it was the 'scientific' claim that so many policy makers liked. One policy maker at the Vanguard programme who was really taken by Seligman's claims on the PRP, and how it could 'inoculate young people against depression', was another speaker at the event – Professor Richard Layard. Layard was then instrumental in bringing the PRP to England.

In this chapter I outline my growing disenchantment with the so-called 'science' of positive psychology and psychology in general along with other reservations about the field. Up till now I have tried not to skip forward in time but I'm going to do this here as there's no appropriate place in a later chapter to convey some of this vitally important research.

The replicability of the Penn Resiliency Programme

The PRP is an in-depth school programme to promote resilience by blending material on optimism, cognitive behavioural therapy, assertiveness training and decision-making skills. It requires intensive training of facilitators and so is very expensive to run. At the Vanguard Programme Seligman quoted research which showed that after two years, the students in the PRP condition were half as likely as students in the usual-care condition to report moderate to severe levels of depressive symptoms.

Thanks to Richard Layard, in 2007-08, three English local authorities delivered the PRP in a large number of primary and secondary schools but they called it 'the UK resiliency programme'. The report on results is not encouraging:

> In summary, we find some impact of participation in UK Resilience Programme workshops on depression scores, absence rates, and academic attainment. The impact is small, and relatively short-lived: for no outcome measure does it persist until two years after the end of workshops. We also find no impact on behaviour scores, whether measured by pupil self- reports or by teacher reports, or on life satisfaction scores.

Other researchers have also found that the Penn Resiliency Programme has 'mild to moderate' results which don't last. The findings certainly don't suggest that the programme 'inoculates young people against depression' as Seligman claimed in Glasgow. In 2016 one meta-analysis of nine studies from Australia, the Netherlands and the USA found 'No evidence of PRP in reducing depression or anxiety and improving explanatory style... The large-scale roll-out of PRP cannot be recommended.' I'm so pleased that as a Centre we chose not to import this into Scotland.

The issue here is not whether the PRP has sometimes generated positive, though perhaps temporary results, but whether the results are consistently replicable. We ran into our own replicability problem with positive writing (see page 113). Writing three good things, sometimes called 'the three blessings exercise', was consistently portrayed by positive psychologists as having an anti-depressant effect and generating positive emotions. But we didn't find that it had this effect on the boys in our sample; their happiness decreased. When I was in Washington in 2007 at a positive psychology summit I spoke to one delegate who had also tried out this exercise with school students and his results were similar to ours. We both agreed that this result was like getting the wrong answer in a test as the exercise was continually portrayed in the positive psychology community as something that worked.

Other psychologists have replicated the three blessings exercise with adults but found the results much weaker than the original study. However, since 2015 psychology as a whole has been plunged into a 'replicability crisis'. Teams of psychologists cooperated to see if they could replicate 100 classic psychology studies: around 40 per cent failed to replicate and some others were inconclusive. The ones that did had weaker results. Other studies have found replication problems across social sciences and, worryingly, medicine. All of the original studies had been published in peer-reviewed journals. Other researchers reviewed the research findings from studies and came to very different conclusions from the original researchers. Some argue that this crisis will ultimately make psychological research stronger; my conclusion as a layperson is that we should be somewhat sceptical about the findings from empirical research conducted by social scientists. The results may or may not be relevant to life in the world we inhabit.

The replicability crisis has come to affect not just psychology but social science as a whole and some natural sciences. Positive psychology studies have not done well on replicability according to some researchers but ultimately this has not been as challenging as the huge scandal it has had to face on the 'voodoo science' at its heart.

Barbara Fredrickson's 'positivity ratio'

Barbara Fredrickson is undoubtedly the poster girl of positive psychology. Both Martin Seligman and Mihaly Csikszentmihalyi described her as the discipline's 'genius'. She gave a telephone lecture at the Centre's Vanguard Programme and she also spoke at the Michigan course I attended. I was instinctively drawn to her 'broaden and build theory of positive emotions'. Basically business-as-usual empirical psychology isn't too interested in positive mental states; it's negative emotions which they tend to study. Fredrickson's laboratory based research shows that it's when people are in a positive emotional state (previously primed by a feel-good film, for example) that they are best able to accomplish certain tasks. Her research shows that while negative emotions narrow our attention, positive emotions broaden our attention and it's in this frame of mind that we build our relationships and psychological resources.

Fredrickson teamed up with Marcial Losada, a social and organisational psychologist, and they published a paper called 'Positive affect and the complex dynamics of human flourishing'. In it they claim that there is a 'critical positivity ratio'. The finding was supposedly derived from their application of the famous Lorenz equation in physics which uses the mathematics of nonlinear dynamic systems. Fredrickson and Losada's mathematical calculations defined the positivity ratio precisely as 2.9013. If your ratio of positive emotions was 2.9013 to 1 negative emotion then you would be flourishing and if less than this you were languishing. This ratio applied to individuals, couples and any human group.

The paper was published in the peer-reviewed, prestigious journal, *American Psychologist* and attracted virtually no questioning or critical comment. In fact, it was repeatedly cited. In 2009 the paperback version of Fredrickson's book *Positivity* was subtitled *Top-Notch Research Reveals the 3-to-1 Ratio That Will Change Your Life*. In it Fredrickson even writes: 'Just as zero degrees celsius is a special number in thermodynamics, the 3-to-1 positivity ratio may well be a magic number in human psychology.'

When I did talks to organisations I would occasionally refer to Losada's empirical research with high performance teams but I didn't fully understand what the Lorenz equation was supposed to convey and I was inherently suspicious of the idea that there was some kind of universal positivity law. If this were true, Scots would never have learned or achieved anything given the inherent negativity of our culture.

When I attended positive psychology events in the UK and internationally I became increasingly aware that people were fearful of saying anything critical as this would affect their positivity ratio. I thought this dangerous as it would lead to complacency, hero worship and stultification. In fact, Fredrickson acknowledged that above a certain ratio of positive to negative emotions there would be no criticism and so no new thinking would emerge. In a review of Martin Seligman's new book *Flourish* (2011), I complained that the growing positive psychology obsession with the ratio of 'positive to negative emotions. . . implicitly encourages people to shy away from the critical analysis we require to square up to some of the big issues of our time.' But this criticism was small beer in comparison to what would undermine Fredrickson's positivity ratio a year or so later.

In 2013 Nick Brown was a very mature student on the Masters of Applied Positive Psychology course in London as he was about to retire as head of IT network operations at a European company. He had an engineering and computer science degree from Cambridge. When Brown was introduced to Fredrickson and Losada's positivity ratio of 2.9013 he thought it 'incredible' – as if it had been made up.

The story of how a psychological nobody took on America's psychology elite was the focus of an interesting feature in *The Observer* in 2014. In it Brown says that he was able to critique this work precisely because he was a 'nobody' and had 'independence': he wasn't a psychologist so his job and mortgage weren't on the line.

Brown's grasp of maths was good enough for him to see that the equation was bunkum but to really demolish it he sought the help of an academic mathematician, Professor Alan Sokal. He looked at the Fredrickson and Losada paper and 'in 10 seconds' could see it was 'total bullshit'. In 2013 Brown, Sokal and a professor of research psychology, Harris Friedman, published a paper in *American Psychologist* called 'The Dynamics of Wishful Thinking: The critical positivity ratio'.

Losada has never defended his work publicly but Fredrickson has. She accepts that Losada's maths was wrong and admits she never really understood it anyway. But she still clings to the idea that there is a positivity ratio around three – a tipping point to flourishing. In a later paper Friedman and Brown are rightly dismissive of the claim of a positivity ratio even when it's extracted from the 'bogus' maths:

> It can easily be seen that even this softened claim is based on flawed reasoning, because it implicitly requires all experiences of emotion to have the same magnitude and duration to be comparable, which is absurd. A moment's thought will show how impossible it is to actually measure a person's experience of positive emotions on this basis. If someone laughs at a joke on TV, eats an ice-cream, sees their dog get run over, and watches a nice sunset, are they at a 3 to 1 ratio of positive to negative emotions and flourishing? And so it is with any comparison of emotions, as who can provide a value-free metric on which to draw any comparison in a universal–invariant way?

Does it matter if positive psychology isn't 'scientific'?

The founders of positive psychology assert that 'business-as-usual psychology' is primarily interested in negative emotions and what's wrong with people. But to say this they have to sideline the humanistic psychology of important figures like Abraham Maslow and Carl Rogers. And this is what Seligman and Csikszentmihalyi do in their seminal *American Psychologist* article in 2000 where they set out why positive psychology is a new discipline:

> Unfortunately, humanistic psychology did not attract much of a cumulative empirical base, and it spawned myriad therapeutic self-help movements. In some of its incarnations, it emphasised the self and encouraged a self-centeredness that played down concerns for collective well-being. Further debate will determine whether this came about because Maslow and Rogers were ahead of their time, because these flaws were inherent in their original vision, or because of overly enthusiastic followers. However, one legacy of the humanism

> of the 1960s is prominently displayed in any large bookstore: The 'psychology' section contains at least 10 shelves on crystal healing, aromatherapy, and reaching the inner child for every shelf of books that tries to uphold some scholarly standard.

For them 'some scholarly standard' inevitably means first rate empirical research which produces tangible, replicable results which are scientifically credible. So Seligman and followers' claim that positive psychology is 'scientific' is fundamental to its *raison d'être* and its difference from humanistic psychology.

Psychology's replicability crisis and Brown *et al*'s claim that the positivity ratio, which at that point lay at the heart of positive psychology, is 'wishful thinking' or 'voodoo science' has weakened this credibility. Critics like Brown are still broadly supportive of positive psychology but they think it needs to reflect more on its chosen research methods and embrace qualitative, not just quantitative, methods.

Questioning positive psychology

From the beginning of the Centre in 2005 I've always had reservations about aspects of positive psychology. *Authentic Happiness* was the key text, and I liked much of its content, but I didn't like the emphasis on happiness which I thought overly American. I also thought that happiness was too transitory an emotion. Richard Layard set up 'Action for Happiness' and tried to get the Centre involved but we declined. In September 2007 Seligman himself publicly declared that he had 'got it wrong' on happiness and had revised his thinking. He now accepted that happiness is 'a mood' and that it was much better to focus on well-being (something we were doing). *Flourish* was the title of his next book.

In March 2006 I wrote a blog called 'In praise of negativity' in which I express my concern that the message people would take from positive psychology, and hence from what we were doing, is that they should be positive all the time and that they should encourage others to do likewise. I go on to say that from experience I know that life is complicated and it's not as simple as saying 'positive good, negative bad' as this can end up being repressive and hence counter-productive. And I then give the following example:

> At an event I attended recently, aimed at getting more businesses involved with schools, one local businesswoman, who was already very involved in her local primary school, demonstrated that she was a devotee to the positive thinking cause. Indeed she told us that if we went into the school she was involved with and asked any pupil how they were, they would say 'fantastic' as 'nothing else is acceptable'. I've little doubt that we live in a culture where people routinely never report being anything other than 'not bad'. It is a pity that when things are going well for us we fear registering our pleasure or success in case others think we're crowing or that somehow we'll get our comeuppance. . . But surely we don't want to encourage a culture where people are expected to say they are 'fantastic' if they don't genuinely feel like that? Surely we don't want to create a culture which undermines authenticity in relationships or ushers in another era where it's not possible to express yourself for fear of being told off?

So even way back in 2006 I could see that solely expressing positive emotions is beneficial only when it's appropriate to the situation and not overdone.

As I explain in that article, I had a powerful experience a decade or so earlier which taught me that we ignore negative feelings at our peril. In 1991 my BBC post (Continuing Education Officer, Scotland) was made redundant. I saw it coming and had made some plans. When the axe fell I immediately went into positive thinking mode. I convinced myself it was for the best and busily set about training for the new business I was going to set up. I didn't spend one second complaining or talking about how I felt. But a few months down the line when the BBC sent me my P45 and removed my free television I developed terrible sinusitis. I felt dreadful and finally had to admit to myself and others that emotionally I found the redundancy difficult to accept. I had worked there for thirteen years. I felt undervalued and rejected and not admitting that earlier hadn't been very good for my health. Despite the opportunities, I had negative feelings about the loss of my job and I would have benefitted from acknowledging this, ideally in writing, and letting others express their sympathy before I tried to embrace my new life. Of course, some people, when they're made redundant, spend too long in a negative, pessimistic state and need some encouragement to see the best in their circumstances. But each situation is different and there's a balance to be struck.

Within a few years of the launch of positive psychology, significant critiques emerged across psychological thinking. Critics raised various objections: emotions can't be neatly divided into positive and negative; the continual emphasis on positivity will make people feel worse when they, understandably, feel negative; people are different and not everyone will benefit from these interventions. Indeed Julie K. Norem's research on pessimism showed that some people, whom she described as 'defensive pessimists', do best when they think the worst will happen and plan accordingly. Being optimistic is not a good strategy for them. Where relevant I would acknowledge these findings or criticisms when I talked about positive psychology.

The limitations of positive psychology's strengths-based approach

Traditional, disease focused psychology revolves around the Diagnostic and Statistical Manual (DSM) of the American Psychiatric Association. It's here that we can find a description of everything that can go wrong with the human brain and personality. Positive psychology's answer to the DSM is the *VIA* (Values in Action) *Classification of Strengths* (2004) compiled by Chris Peterson and Martin Seligman which the latter often calls the 'classification of the sanities'. Peterson argued that the point of the VIA is to focus on 'what is right about people and, specifically, about the strengths of character that make the good life possible.' But the VIA is not just about character strengths it's also about virtues.

To compile their list Seligman and Peterson surveyed history and all the great philosophers. They end up with their 'high six' virtues which then break down into 24 individual character strengths. (See Box 9 for the full list.)

Box 9: Character Strengths and Virtues

The following are the 24 strengths and virtues outlined by VIA (Values in Action). These character strengths have been identified by Christopher Peterson and Martin Seligman:

Strengths of Wisdom and Knowledge

Creativity (originality, ingenuity)

Curiosity (interest, novelty-seeking, openness to experience)

Open-mindedness (judgement, critical thinking)

Love of learning

Perspective (wisdom)

Strengths of Courage

Bravery (valour)

Persistence (perseverance, industriousness)

Integrity (authenticity, honesty)

Vitality (zest, enthusiasm, vigour, energy)

Strengths of Humanity

Love

Kindness (generosity, nurturance, care, compassion, altruistic love, 'niceness')

Social intelligence (emotional intelligence, personal intelligence)

Strengths of Justice

Citizenship (social responsibility, loyalty, teamwork)

Fairness

Leadership

Strengths of Temperance

Forgiveness and mercy

Humility and modesty

Prudence

Self-regulation (self-control)

Strengths of Transcendence

Appreciation of beauty and excellence (awe, wonder, elevation)

Gratitude

Hope (optimism, future-mindedness, future-orientation)

Humour (playfulness)

Spirituality (religiousness, faith, purpose)

I encountered the VIA in 2004 when I completed my Authentic Happiness Coaching course and I wasn't overly taken with it. A free online questionnaire gives you immediate results on your top five strengths (usually referred to as 'signature strengths'). Perhaps I simply wasn't too pleased at my top strength –'curiosity about the world'. (In fact, I don't see this as a particular strength as it means my life is full of endless, often unsatisfying, distractions.) I used the VIA with a few groups but they were underwhelmed, though my inexperience with the instrument may have been partly to blame.

In the VIA classification there is no hierarchy in the virtues or character strengths. So playfulness, vitality, curiosity and hope are on the same level of character strengths as fairness, integrity and courage. But this is emphatically not the case in the philosophies or religions they surveyed as they have one or two overarching virtues. Also, in the VIA there's little acknowledgement that when strengths are overdone they can become weaknesses, yet this understanding is fundamental in Aristotle's concept of 'the golden mean'.

Barry Schwartz and Kenneth Sharpe published an important paper in 2005 called 'Practical Wisdom' in which they contrast the VIA with 'the Aristotelian view that virtues are interdependent, that happiness (eudaimonia) requires all the virtues, and that more of a virtue is not always better than less.' They go on to argue, convincingly in my view, that 'virtues and strengths should not be treated in isolation from each other'; that 'nurturing a single signature strength can produce *deformations* of character'; and, most importantly, they follow Aristotle in arguing that people need 'practical wisdom' to properly deploy strengths and resolve potential conflicts between them.

Despite these potential flaws Seligman advocated that schools use a strengths-based approach in the classroom. In *Creating Confidence* I inform readers that a young person's version of the VIA is available and give a few examples of engaging young people on their signature strengths but I'm generally not positive about the idea of strengths-based education. I acknowledge that there's a place for kindness, self-control, justice and so forth in the classroom but state that making signature strengths the *basis* of children's educational development is impractical and beyond the experience of most teachers. I also argue that it would also be antithetical to the basic tenets of Scottish education as Scotland has always valued breadth in the curriculum, rather than depth.

Weighing up the positive and the negatives

In 2007 Dr Fabio Sani who had worked with the Centre on our positive writing exercise attended the European Positive Psychology Conference in Croatia. He was not impressed. Unlike conventional psychological conferences where the emphasis is on critical evaluation of papers and results, he thought this conference was more about the promotion of books and programmes. In short, he felt the conference ethos was commercial. I was there too and agreed with Fabio on this. I was particularly taken with a talk from an up-and-coming young positive psychologist, Todd Kashdan, who warned that there was too little criticism and too much hero worship. Another young positive psychologist at the conference was Robert Biswas Diener, son of Ed Diener whom I mentioned in a previous chapter. He liked to be referred to as 'the Indiana Jones of positive psychology' as he had conducted a number of studies on happiness in India and other developing nations.

I mention these two as they were early positive psychologists whose commitment to the field changed substantially in the next few years. In 2014 they published a book called *The Upside of your Dark Side: Why being your whole self – not just your 'good' self – drives success and fulfilment*. A couple of years later they published *The Power of Negative Emotion* (2015). In the latter they write:

> . . . as we tilled the fields of positive psychology both of us were also increasingly put off by the gung-ho happiology we often witnessed. Over the past fifteen years positive psychology has been transformed from a reminder that 'positive experiences are important' to a kind of smiling fascism.

These comments particularly refer to how positive psychology is being used in organisations.

Later they set out in eloquent terms why they are now promoting a psychology which embraces the whole person:

> We are no different from you, dear reader. We prematurely discard our painful feelings, thoughts, and urges without giving them a fair chance. Seduced by the obvious benefits of kindness, compassion, mindfulness, optimism and positivity on our health, social relationships, and work, we often forget the value of uncomfortable states. Our minds were changed on this issue, however, when we considered results from a number of studies showing the counterintuitive truth: happiness sometimes backfires and bad states are sometimes good.

I could not have expressed myself so eloquently, or written with such certainty, but I was consciously struggling with this paradox from 2006 – the second year of the Centre's life. The awareness that bad feelings have a purpose and galvanise us to do things differently was inherent in the critique of self-esteem in the *Creating Confidence* handbook. I worried about the erosion of children's resilience from adults' overprotection and desire that they only experience positive emotions. Even in that 2006 blog, 'In praise of negativity' I write: 'There are no hard and fast rules. Not only do we need self-awareness but also wisdom to navigate the complexities and paradoxes inherent in human experience.' I then go on to write: '. . . brain imaging techniques show that Buddhism produces some of the happiest people on earth. The irony is that Buddhism does not teach its followers that life is fantastic. Far from it – it is a philosophy of suffering.'

I also knew from my reading of the 'ironic effects' literature that the more people try to be happy the less likely they are to achieve it as they will magnify the significance of any fleeting dip in their mood.

Given these reservations should the Centre have promoted positive psychology? Were we wrong to stage the Vanguard Programme of events and create related resources on our website?

What positive psychology offered Scotland

In 2005 when we were sharing offices with the Glasgow Centre for Population Health, I met Ken Thomson, a community psychiatrist from Pittsburgh with an abiding interest in the effects of deindustrialisation on public health. He was in the UK visiting Glasgow, Newcastle and other deindustrialised cities. We spent over an hour together having an informal discussion and we both enjoyed it so much that we are still in contact over eighteen years later. There was one part of that original conversation which is relevant here: America didn't need positive psychology as the injunction to be positive was already too strong but Scotland could benefit as it was an inherently negative culture. Ken could see this even in his brief visit to Scotland just as I could detect the over-positivity of American culture in the Authentic Happiness group telephone-coaching sessions I had been involved with a year earlier.

Ken was not alone in this observation about Scotland and I'll return to the topic in detail in a later chapter. But it's worth adding one thing here. After his visit to Scotland to discuss happiness and well-being measures Professor Ed Diener was fond of saying in his presentations that the 'Scots didn't want to be happy and were content being miserable'. He said this for a laugh and it wasn't an entirely accurate description of the discussion but there's little doubt that many Scots were, and still are, uncomfortable with positive emotions.

In my 2006 blog, cited earlier, I end writing that there's so much negativity in Scotland in the form of excessive criticism, blame and pessimism that as a culture we could benefit from what the new discipline of positive psychology has to offer. But I also say that we must be careful lest well-meaning zealots try to demonise negativity and end up making things worse for individuals, not better.

Even if the Centre hadn't introduced positive psychology to Scotland it would have been influential. In 2006 information about it was commonplace in magazines and the popular press. In January 2006 Mark Easton presented a six-part BBC tv series, 'The Happiness Formula'. In the 2008 Scottish parliamentary elections the SNP's campaign drew on the importance of optimism in elections: research based on Martin Seligman's study of American Presidential campaign winners. And, as I shall outline fully in Chapter 22, the ideas for this did not come from the Centre but from the Really Effective Development Company, based in Nottingham.

I also believed that for all its limitations and my growing concerns, positive psychology was preferable to what was mainly available in the psychology section of bookshops or some of the large commercial personal development programmes. At that time 'the law of attraction' was very fashionable as a result of Rhonda Byrne's book *The Secret* (2006). This was based on the idea that our lives are shaped simply by our thoughts. Thus we can 'attract' the things we want in life just by thinking about them enough. We send our thoughts out to 'the universe' and if we get the vibrations right some godlike creature sends us back what we desire. This belief leads to truly awful politics as it communicates the idea that people who lack essential things in their lives don't have the right thoughts.

I once asked a speaker espousing these ideas what it meant about people in third world countries who didn't have enough to eat. 'Are they not wanting food enough?' He considered and answered: 'They aren't at a high enough level of development.' For all positive psychology's limitations, it was certainly better than this. No wonder policy makers liked positive psychology as it came from university research and claimed to be 'scientific'.

The Centre's positive psychology experience in 2008 – the highs and lows

In January 2008 we held two impressive positive psychology events attracting almost 700 people. The speaker was the famous Harvard psychology lecturer, Dr Tal Ben-Shahar, whose positive psychology lectures were the most popular in the university's history. Around 300 people attended an event in Dundee called 'Leadership and the positive city' which we organised jointly with Go Dundee and the Dundee Chambers of Commerce. The event also featured some local speakers including Joe Lafferty from Go Dundee and Jackie Roberts of the Care Commission. The journalist Iain

Macwhirter was in the chair and the whole event was extremely popular, inspiring and energising.

The following evening Dr Ben-Shahar spoke to around 400 people in Glasgow. This event, chaired by the journalist Kirsty Wark, was called 'Is happiness the answer to Scotland's problems?' and also included a talk from Professor Phil Hanlon who didn't support the idea that happiness was the answer. To be fair to Dr Ben-Shahar, he gave a sophisticated answer to the question and was more interested in well-being than happiness. One of the most memorable things he said at both events regarded the link between exercise and positive emotions, something rarely mentioned by positive psychologists who were usually oblivious to anything happening from the neck down. Tal reinforced the idea that exercise was vital for good mental health by saying 'it's not just that exercise acts like an anti-depressant; not taking exercise is depressing.'

But within a few months of this undoubted high with positive psychology we were no longer seeing it as the main focus of the Centre's work. It wasn't the hype and the supposed 'science' which ultimately tripped us up and forced a hasty re-evaluation: I became the target of Seligman's self-confessed 'grouchiness' and the majority of us on the Centre's board found it impossible to ignore what we considered his lack of judgement and moral courage. We didn't part company with Seligman over a trivial issue as the conflict arose from the worst episode in America's contemporary history: state sanctioned torture.

CHAPTER 8

An untold story: the rift with Martin Seligman

A brusque email from Seligman;
allegations that Seligman advised the CIA on torture;
the Centre's contact with IPPA;
the Centre's statements;
why the Centre didn't publish my paper on the topic;
Seligman's desire for revenge;
how Seligman's reticence
caused many of his difficulties.

MY COPY of *Authentic Happiness* has a dedication from the author, Martin Seligman. It reads: 'To Carol Craig from your friend and admirer'. It's dated 23rd November 2003, the day of the Towards a Confident Scotland conference at which he was the keynote speaker. Almost five years later – the summer of 2008 – he was referring to me as 'that woman' and saying that I should be 'sacked'. So what happened?

On 19th May 2008 Martin Seligman sent me a brusque email with 'Anna Patty', an Australian journalist, as the subject line. It simply read: 'Do you know that you are being cited as evidence against our programs? Is this accurate?' and he attached his rebuttal to Patty's article. There were no social niceties, not even a signature. I felt taken aback not just at the rudeness but at the subtle rebuke. I also felt annoyed at the use of 'our programs' – what he meant was the Penn Resiliency Programme – a programme in which he had a financial interest.

Given the relevance of this to what followed I want to make

clear that I may have overreacted to this email. I didn't have a good relationship with my own father who was routinely disrespectful and authoritarian to me and my sisters. So this email from a male authority figure – the patriarch – provoked anger. I let this pass before I replied. I explained that Anna Patty had talked to me on the phone about my SEAL article but my criticisms were about emotional intelligence not positive psychology.

However, in the email I said that I was very concerned about one thing and I really wanted to know what he thought. The growing emphasis on young people's happiness in schools in the UK was leading adults to worry about children feeling good in the moment in a way which could then undermine their resilience, well-being and performance. This is what had happened in the USA with self-esteem and which Seligman had written about with such insight.

I didn't receive a reply. Nothing. This rankled not just because of the tone of his previous email but also because, for the past year, I had not just been a member of the board of the International Positive Psychology Association (IPPA) but also its titular secretary. And this was an organisation which Seligman and some colleagues had set up. What's more, I felt that, given our previous work together, he owed me a reply.

Seligman has a reputation for being rude and he acknowledges this characteristic frequently in his autobiography, *The Hope Circuit* (2018). I had managed to not let this bother me previously but now that my defences against the insensitive, arrogant patriarch were activated I was finding it much more difficult to ignore or forgive this failing. This was relevant to my next personal contact with IPPA.

Torture

One fateful morning in the middle of May 2008, a friend sent me an email telling me there were allegations all over the internet that Martin Seligman had advised the CIA on the torture techniques they were employing in places like the Guantanamo Bay Detention Centre. These allegations were indeed very easy to find. Jane

Mayer, a *New Yorker* journalist was about to publish a book called *The Dark Side: The inside story of how the war on terror turned into a war on American ideals* (2008). In advance of publication a variety of bloggers were claiming that Seligman had actively advised the CIA on how they could 'reverse engineer' the findings from his learned helplessness experiments and then use this for torture. This wasn't just an internet sensation, Jane Mayer was now appearing on cable television in the USA. One of the issues for Mayer is that since 2005 she had been linking Seligman with the CIA but all he would say was 'no comment'.

Of course, I didn't know whether there was any truth in what Mayer was saying but I did know from my American friend, Fran Wasoff, that Mayer was a first-class journalist whose work should be taken seriously. I was acutely aware that leaving aside the importance of the issue, this was potentially a public relations disaster for the Centre. As has been clear from the previous chapters, the Centre was very closely identified, not just with positive psychology, but with Martin Seligman. I rang Fred Shedden, the Chair of the board of trustees, to explain what was happening and he agreed to meet me that afternoon after he had read some of the online material.[1]

Until his retirement from legal practice a few years before, Fred was one of Scotland's leading corporate lawyers. But he wasn't, as this might suggest, an establishment figure. He was a working-class boy from Arbroath with left-leaning views. He had supported the Labour Party for years but, like many, had taken a scunner at the party as a result of the Iraq War. In 2007 he joined the SNP. Like me he felt appalled at how President Bush's administration was abusing human rights and using torture techniques such as water-boarding.

We both thought that the positive psychology community should say something publicly to clarify that we weren't supportive of the use of torture. We discussed whether we should write to Martin Seligman himself but decided not to as we didn't think he would reply. So jointly we drafted a short, measured email to the

1. Fred Shedden was Chair of the Centre's board from 2008 to 2015. He retired from the board on 30 June 2024.

IPPA board, of which I was a member. All it said was that given the allegations online, we were concerned about the reputational risk to positive psychology and did any of them think that anything should be done? We also asked if they knew what Martin Seligman's response was to what was being said online. There was no immediate reply.

The next day I rang various supporters of the Centre, including Joe Lafferty from Go Dundee, to ask them what they thought we should do. They were unanimous: please don't ignore or try to cover this up. Put something about it on your website. With Fred's approval, I drafted a simple statement on behalf of the Centre and posted it online. It gave the basic story of the allegations from Jane Mayer, but added that we now knew that she wasn't saying that Seligman had actively assisted the CIA in devising torture techniques.

By that stage Martin Seligman had issued a statement and we put the whole text in our article. In it he explains that he gave a three-hour lecture at a naval base in 2002 on 'how American troops and American personnel could use what is known about learned helplessness and related findings to resist torture. . . ' He accepted that two CIA agents were present in the audience but 'to the best of my knowledge' that was the sum total of 'my assisting them in the process.' He ends by writing: 'Most importantly, I strongly disapprove of torture and have never and would never provide assistance in its process.'

We then write:

> Seligman's statement that his contact with the military was to help protect American troops may well appease many fellow Americans. However, at the Centre we are picking up that his statement is not going down well in the UK. George Bernard Shaw reputedly said that Britain and America are two nations 'divided by a common language'. Americans are much more patriotic than the British in their support for the military. . . Given how hated the Iraq war and the Bush administration is currently in the UK, the idea that Seligman gave the regime support and advice on war matters is still likely to alienate potential supporters.

The same day I finally got a response from one member of the IPPA board, one of the many Americans I didn't know. I can't track it down but it was a short email and its contents are seared into my mind: I should feel ashamed of myself for writing that email and who did I think I was to criticise, or even question, such a great man as Martin Seligman? It was copied to the whole Executive Board. Naively I thought that Seligman himself would reply to say that I was quite within my rights to send the email. But I was wrong.

I waited a couple of days and then, with my board's support, I wrote a resignation email to IPPA. We all felt that given what had happened I could not continue to be a member of the IPPA board. Professor Ed Diener was the Chair and he had been away when the torture allegations erupted. He had now returned to my resignation email and was keen for me to reconsider. When we spoke on the phone he told me that positive psychology was much bigger than Martin Seligman and that IPPA was being undermined by the fact that many traditional psychologists simply dismissed it as 'the Martin Seligman appreciation society'. He told me that if I continued to be a member of the IPPA board, and critical of Seligman, this would be good for positive psychology and absolutely fine by him. But reconsidering wasn't an option as it had been a board decision not just a personal choice.

On 20th July we posted another statement as we had now read *The Dark Side* and were able to comment knowing what Jane Mayer had actually written in the book. Our statement includes the following:

> There are many 'baddies' in Jane Mayer's book but Martin Seligman is not one of them. Jane Mayer spends less than one page on Seligman. In it she recounts how he gave a lecture at the SERE school and how he thought it was to help US troops cope with torture.
>
> . . . the nub of Mayer's criticism is simply that Martin Seligman has not been forthcoming on his views and often says 'no comment' when faced with questions. When the topic is torture and the use of his ideas this does not look good and appears to be misjudged. But we have to bear in mind that this reticence is part of Seligman's personal style and, unless there

> is evidence to the contrary, we cannot read bad intent into it. If you asked anyone who attended our events in Scotland with Seligman about what they remember about him, the chances are they'll mention how he would say 'no comment' or 'I don't have a view' when asked questions.

Given the shirracking I had received at the hands of IPPA I think this was a fairly generous statement. But we do go on to criticise positive psychology leaders and gatekeepers who were trying to stop people discussing the matter. Our researcher Emily Cutts was a student on the Applied Positive Psychology Masters Programme in London and was well connected with similar students worldwide. She was hearing that various people had posted questions or innocuous comments on positive psychology sites on the issue only to have them deleted immediately. We also thought that since Seligman had very deliberately tried to stimulate a movement of supporters for positive psychology he owed these followers more detailed answers than he had given.

We announced that I was no longer on the IPPA board and concluded by saying:

> 'No matter what happens, the Centre hopes that all those involved in positive psychology, including Martin Seligman, can move on from this stressful episode and start focusing on what they have to offer to the understanding of flourishing lives. It goes without saying that a flourishing life is one which manages to handle problems rather than buries them.'

The fall out

In the autumn of 2008 Martin Seligman was in London speaking at events. At the end of one of them Gregor Henderson approached him to ask 'what should we be doing in Scotland now on positive psychology'? Seligman brusquely replied, 'Sacking your leader'. More was to come. Another friend who was senior in positive psychology in London also spoke to Seligman on this visit. She told me that she was taken aback at how vengeful he felt towards me. 'I'll get her back', he told her, adding, 'when her board comes running asking me to speak in Scotland I'll tell them I'll do it only if she's sacked.' My friend tried to explain that I had the backing of my board for everything I had done but he wouldn't listen.

The following year Ilona Boniwell, a positive psychologist working in the UK and member of the IPPA board, was charged with finding an English venue for the 2011 IPPA World Congress. She couldn't find anything down south. She then came to Edinburgh and thought it would make an ideal conference destination. The only fly in the ointment was me, or Seligman, depending on your point of view.

James Pawelski from IPPA arranged to speak to me on the phone. After the civilities he moved on to the task in hand. Seligman would agree to the IPPA Congress being held in Edinburgh on one condition: I had to give him a public apology at the event. But I wasn't prepared to do that as I hadn't committed any crime. What's more, given the nasty email I received from a person involved in IPPA I felt I was due an apology. So we said our goodbyes and the Congress was held yet again in Philadelphia.

What's curious about this whole affair is how vengeful and sensitive to even indirect criticism Martin Seligman is. I've little doubt that if I had been an academic psychologist he would've tried to use his undoubted influence to get me sacked. Luckily, he wasn't able 'to get me back'.

The answer to why he had such an extreme response to my email lies, at least in part, in his autobiography. On two occasions he tells us that early in life his ambition was 'to be like Ludwig Wittgenstein, surrounded by devoted students and followers.' Seligman loved and was motivated by adulation. This meant that he didn't welcome any criticism, or even questioning, particularly from those he thought were followers. I've little doubt that even if I hadn't sent that email to the IPPA board I would've been ostracised for having the temerity to post even mildly critical comments about the sorry affair online. As for any criticism of his Penn Resiliency Programme, that too would have been a punishable offence.

Shortcomings

At the end of our second online statement I wrote that we were drawing a line and wouldn't comment any further. However, I was unnerved by reading *The Dark Side* and just couldn't let the matter drop. I kept reading and researching in my spare time. And I went from thinking Seligman had no real case to answer to feeling that he was partly responsible for the position in which he now found himself. For example, Jeff Kaye, a psychologist who was campaigning against psychologists' role in torture techniques, specifically asked Seligman in an email: 'what is your position on the use of your research by others, and on psychologists involved in military/CIA interrogations under the current administration?' Martin Seligman replied: 'The only "position" I am comfortable staking out is good science always runs the risk of immoral application. It goes with the territory of discovery.'

Kaye thought this reply 'startling' as Seligman seems to believe it's okay 'to settle for a "see no evil" approach' . . . If his work might be abused, that is not a concern of his.'

My reading of Seligman's reply is that it is a helpless response which isn't warranted. Seligman was a past president of the American Psychological Association (APA). He was one of the country's most distinguished psychologists. Surely if he had spoken out against the use of torture in detention centres, he would have generated publicity and would have been listened to by other psychologists? If Seligman had made frequent and robust statements against torture and acknowledged that what was happening in the USA was wrong he would have squelched the unfounded accusations against him. But he *chose* not to do so.

In his autobiography he includes a chapter on the CIA and ends by saying: 'when in doubt we should err on the side of helping our nation'. Elsewhere he talks about being 'a patriotic American'. A chapter on the military follows. In it he writes about the work he has done in the creation of the 'Comprehensive Soldier Fitness programme' – a $31million contract that his university was awarded, without any competitive tender, to train US army personnel on resilience and positive psychology.

Seligman ends his chapter on the army by declaring:

> . . . critics accuse me of 'blind patriotism'. My patriotism is not at all blind. I view the United States as the country that gave my relatives persecuted unto death in Europe, a sanctuary where their children and grandchildren would flourish. I view the US Army as the force that stood between me and the Nazi gas chambers, and thus I count my days with the sergeants and the generals as the most fulfilling of my life.

I have no objection to psychologists working with soldiers to help them cope with what they have endured, or may in the future. The rate of suicide and PTSD in soldiers is shockingly high. Whether Seligman's techniques in the Comprehensive Soldier Fitness programmes are the right ones to prevent such problems is outwith my interest or expertise. (Though it's worth saying that it's based on the Penn Resiliency Programme originally devised for school children and, as we saw in the last chapter, this has not had consistently positive results.)

What I find difficult to embrace is the way Seligman lives in his own private world, blind to reality. Did he ever read Jane Mayer's *The Dark Side* on how America's torture programme was antithetical to its ideals? Has he ever heard James Reisen, one of the main activists for ethical psychology, declare that he comes 'from a family where people were tortured in the Holocaust. I have seen what happens when standards of decency, human rights and ethics are thrown out in a wave of totalitarian or government zeal.'

For me Seligman's declaration of patriotism as an explanation for his benign view of the CIA and the American military is wilfully blind to what had happened in America and the war on terror. What interests me is not whether Seligman's failure in this instance is personal but whether it indicates an inherent problem in positive psychology.

Positive psychology's inadequate moral compass

Seligman frequently talks not just about strengths but virtues. Remember Chris Petersen and Seligman published a large manual on character strengths called Values in Action (VIA) and an emphasis on strengths is an important pillar in positive psychology.

Justice is one of the six virtues in the VIA inventory and comprises the following character strengths – Citizenship/Duty/Teamwork/Loyalty; Fairness and Equity; Leadership. In other words, justice is no more than a combination of disparate, positive character traits. However, justice inevitably refers to the real world, and the distribution of power.

Seligman is an admirer of the French philosopher Andre Comte-Sponville's book *A Short Treatise on the Great Virtues* (1995). According to Comte-Sponville it's common to define justice with reference to two things: conformity to the law and equality among individuals or a sense of proportionality. Comte-Sponville also argues convincingly that it's justice alone which underpins every virtue. He writes: 'We need justice no matter what virtue we mean to discuss. . .' In other words, virtues such as courage, prudence or temperance cannot exist without reference to justice. A prudent murderer or a sober tyrant cannot be seen as truly virtuous despite what might appear at first glance, virtues or character strengths. This is why it's impossible to see strength and virtue in someone who has chosen to turn a blind eye to injustice. By the reckoning of most systems of morality, ignoring America's dark side shows a lack of moral judgement or courage.

Seligman's wilful blindness is not only evident in relation to American military policy and interrogation techniques. It has been evident, though to a lesser degree, in his writings since 2011 when he published *Flourish* – something I argued in my review of his book.

An inaccurate portrayal of the world

In *Flourish* Seligman makes clear that he is a believer in 'human progress' and that you have to be 'blinded by ideology' not to see it. He lists many of the achievements of the twentieth century and ends with the following: 'We extended the life span. We began to curb pollution and care for the planet, and we made large inroads into racial, sexual and ethnic injustice. The age of the tyrant is coming to an end, and the age of democracy has taken firm root.'

Yes. . . but. Perhaps the writing on the wall was not as clear in

2011 as it is now but the signs that trouble lay ahead were evident to anyone not trying to live in a bubble of positivity. I'm specifically thinking about climate change and the increase in adverse events such as fires, floods and storms (I've never seen Seligman acknowledge or write about these things); racial strife; the rise of strong men throughout the world; and the erosion, not strengthening of American democracy. In fact, at the time of writing this in 2023, Guantanamo Bay still held around 30 prisoners, some in custody without trial for twenty years.

In *Flourish* Seligman then goes on to outline 'the long mission for positive psychology': by the year 2051, 51 per cent of the people of the world will be flourishing.' He admits this is a challenge as more than half the population live in China and India but he is confident that well-being 'must also take root there'. Besides we needn't worry as a positive psychology conference took place in China and India in 2010 and since happiness is contagious 'upward spirals around positive goals will occur'.

This is what I mean about Seligman being blind to reality. He is so desperate to believe that the world is getting better and that positive psychology's limited toolkit is bringing well-being to the world that he can't look reality in the face. His grandiose vision prevents him from being a reliable witness to current reality. This concerned all of us at the Centre and why we would have parted company with Seligman even if we hadn't fallen out.

There are other reasons why positive psychology cannot *on its own* make a substantial difference to people's lives: it downplays external realities. All that really matters to Seligman is the subjective realm. Yes, that's important but so too are objective life circumstances. What's more, as I argued in the last chapter, positive psychology, particularly the so-called 'positivity ratio' leads its adherents to eschew criticism as this takes them away from positive emotions. This leads to unhealthy hero worship and is also the exact opposite of what's needed to tackle injustice or campaign on social justice and humanitarian issues. Not only is complaint often the driving force of campaigns but also the emotions fuelling action against gross injustice are disgust, anger and revulsion.

These are precisely the emotions that many people report when reading *The Dark Side*. In the words of one reviewer: 'Reading this book will make the hair on your nape stand up, as if electrified, and shock you to the very core, and leave you speechless.' Revulsion and outrage are needed to galvanise people to take steps to ensure that these types of activities do not happen in the future and it's imperative that we don't urge others to shy away from these strong, negative emotions. Of course, positive emotions such as optimism and hope have a role to play in political and social activism but the best movements are those which still manage to provide hope, instil trust and celebrate achievements alongside righteous anger.

'The ultimate tragedy' wrote the black American campaigner Martin Luther King Jr, 'is not the oppression and cruelty by the bad people but the silence over that by the good people.'

Part 2

Phase 2: Themes 2009–2024

CHAPTER 9

Surviving austerity

The Centre's new financial settlement;
broadening our focus beyond positive psychology;
overview of financial, staffing and structural changes at the Centre;
the book series *Postcards from Scotland*
and how it helped contribute to the Centre's independence.

THE YEAR 2008 was challenging for people around the world. Some financial institutions collapsed and the problem was so acute that in October the head of the International Monetary Fund warned that the global financial system was 'on the brink of systemic meltdown.' By the end of the year the UK was plunged into economic crisis. In response to the chaos, the Centre held an event in early December called **Thriving in Turbulent Times**.

With all this change in the air it seemed appropriate that the Centre was moving into a new phase of activity. Phase 1 had been dominated by two strands of work: first promoting confidence-building approaches, particularly for young people, and second promoting the type of well-being envisaged by the leaders of positive psychology. Now we wanted to broaden our agenda and definition of well-being. The plan was not to ignore positive psychology. We still believed it held some important insights, but we were not going to be limited by the way it defined well-being. In the words of the integral philosopher Ken Wilber, we wanted the Centre's future work to simultaneously 'transcend and include' positive psychology.

Fortunately, the Scottish Government's new grant settlement for the Centre was in tune with what we hoped to do in Phase 2. It was giving us £125,000 per annum for 2008-11. This was down £25,000 p.a. from the previous three years but it was a better settlement as it was now core funding from one department – Mental Health Division (MHD). Helpfully, our funders also gave us three core priorities to guide our work. These not only validated what we had already been doing but also encouraged us to broaden our focus. These were: continuing to deliver on our on-going work on promoting a greater understanding of positive mental health and well-being in Scotland; maintaining the Centre's position as the focus for policy and practice development in this area and working in collaboration with partners; and contributing a key independent perspective to wider work on cultural change which underpins objectives in respect of the Government's over-arching economic strategy. We particularly welcomed the reference to 'wider work on cultural change' as this fitted with how we envisaged our future activities.

This broadening focus makes the story of the Centre more challenging to tell. In the first part of the book on Phase 1 it was easy to recount our activities and events chronologically. But our interests and activities widened from 2008 on, so I now need to lay out the Centre's activities and thinking thematically. In the chapters which follow in this section on Phase 2, I aggregate these into eleven broad themes:

Flourishing

Glasgow

Materialist values

Organisations

Community, nature and the environment

Inequality and poverty, alcohol and drugs

Diversity and inclusion

Education

Early years and play

Personal development for children, youth and adults

Scotland, health and adverse childhood experiences

To ensure that some vital information about the Centre is not missed in this focus on themes, I set out some structural and financial changes which took place after 2008 in the rest of this chapter.

Financial and structural changes at the Centre

Given the drastic cuts to public sector finances during this time of austerity, we were not surprised that in 2011, at the end of the three-year settlement period, Mental Health Division radically cut its funding to us. It reduced the £125,000 to £50,000 p.a. but fortunately it maintained its funding commitment till 2014. Of course, we would still have additional income from events, projects and my talks but this 60 per cent reduction in core funding inevitably meant we had to restructure the organisation.

Over the years budget constraints meant that we had to whittle down our staffing and in the early part of 2011 this consisted of myself, Archie Dalrymple as Centre manager and Anna Wilson, my personal assistant. Now we had to lose Anna and Archie agreed to give up his full-time post and work a few days a week as an admin and financial assistant. I took a further cut in salary. We also had to give up our lovely office in Glasgow's Union Street, where we had been happily based since 2005. Archie and I would now work from home.

Table 1: Summary of funding from the Scottish Government for the Centre for Confidence and Well-being 2005-2015

Years	Funding	Funding department
2005-2008	£150,000 p.a. Project	Mental Health Division, Teachers' Division (Education), Social Services
2008-2011	£125,000, p.a. Core	Mental Health Division
2011-2014	£50,000 p.a. Core	Mental Health Division
2015	£10,000 Core	Mental Health Division

Nonetheless as you will see from the ensuing chapters the slimmed down Centre still had an impressive work programme and continued to run events, cooperate on various projects and maintain the burgeoning website. In 2012 we even launched our book series *Postcards from Scotland*. Until 2016 these were jointly published by the Centre and Argyll Publishing. During the early days of our cooperation, Argyll was owned by Derek Rodger and he had published my book *The Tears that Made the Clyde* in 2010 and issued a new edition of *The Scots' Crisis of Confidence* in 2011. In 2014 Derek sold the company to someone who was much more difficult for us to work with. In 2016 we bought all the stock and titles from the new owner and since then have published the books ourselves. (Latterly with support from Derek.) At the end of 2019 we brought out *Play is the Way*, edited by Sue Palmer. It's number 17 in the series and our most popular book to date. By 2023 it had sold in excess of 4000 copies and played a major part in discussions about the role of play in early primary school.

Our core funding was further cut in 2014. Mental Health Division reduced the £50,000 grant to £10,000 and awarded it for one year only. So by March 2015 we were no longer receiving any Scottish Government funds.

During this period of tapering finances the board regularly discussed applying to other organisations for funds. In the early years of the Centre we had received some sponsorship and other funding from the Clydesdale Bank, Logica and Alfred McAlpine Business Services. In those early days our work on confidence and positive psychology had an immediate appeal for some Scottish businesses as they perceived their staff to lack these attributes and, at the time, we didn't have any objection to this. But within a few years we were not keen to receive funding from businesses: from 2008 on our perception of business became more jaundiced. This wasn't simply about the financial crash and the financial practices that had brought it about. We were also concerned about rising inequality and the well-publicised scandal of huge bonuses for senior executives. So going to business organisations for support or sponsorship was no longer something we would countenance though I doubt we would have been an appealing prospect for them.

The Centre could still have applied to lots of different funding organisations – charitable trusts, government departments or public sector agencies – and again this is something that the board regularly discussed. There were practical reasons for not doing so – applying for funding is a time-consuming task and we simply didn't have the capacity to do this. In this respect we were like most small businesses who find it difficult to expand. As the main member of staff I was too busy working **in** the business (talks, website, writing) to work **on** the business and its development.

But there was a barrier which was even more important than that. Funding organisations have their own agendas and usually give grants so that the funded organisation delivers the funder's objectives. If you look at the charitable sector you will find lots of organisations, often with multi-million pound annual turnovers, transformed into delivery agents for their funders' objectives. Usually, the price of such funding for the delivery organisations is compliance. When this is government funding this can have a chilling effect on organisations who once had a radical agenda but have now adopted the language of government and ways of operating.

The Centre had been relatively free of constraints as a result of our government funding. Yes we had to agree on activities during our period of project funding but this never meant that we weren't free to do what we liked outwith this funding. Rarely did we feel that we had to fit in with government thinking. The subsequent core funding from MHD did not come with obvious constraints and, as I explained in Chapter 6, we were lucky to have Geoff Huggins, who ran MHD, as our main funder as he did not shy away from controversy and respected the Centre's views even if he did not always share them.

So the nub of the issue here is that the Centre valued its independence too much to seek outside funding. Indeed we thought that one of the Centre's main assets was its independence.

In Spring 2014 I wrote a paper for the board called 'A 20/20 vision for the Centre'. In it I acknowledge our dwindling finances, some of the reasons why we should not submit funding applications and the difficulty we now faced in making money from events as there was less money around in organisations for these types of fees. I envisaged us becoming more of a voluntary organisation and perhaps attracting individual donations to support our work. And I certainly thought that we could still be going in 2020 – six years hence.

We certainly did become more of a voluntary organisation. I ceased to be an employee in 2016 and no longer received payment for any of the work I did for the Centre. Archie left and was replaced latterly by Helen Carmichael who provided some admin support for me until 2022. We never solicited donations from people interested in our work so this did not provide a source of income. Instead we managed to exist on what we had in the bank, on the money we got from associates' speaking fees and the small amount we generated from events. We managed to maintain our internet resources and considerable presence online until 2020. After that we simply used our much more streamlined *Postcards from Scotland* website.

Our financial saviour in the last five years has been the book series. Most of the books have at least covered their costs and some have generated income for the Centre. It hasn't been a lot but it has been enough to keep the organisation going and to preserve our cherished independence. More importantly we might not be going strong, but we're still here and doing some interesting work. Despite our lack of finances we at least managed to survive these turbulent times.

CHAPTER 10

Defining and promoting flourishing lives

The limitations of psychology;
Foundations for Flourishing events;
creation of Flourishing Lives web resources;
Four Centre events – Nations, culture and well-being, Confidence and Well-being in motion, the Brain that Changes itself, and If Music Be. . .;
Ken Wilber's integral theory and what attracted the Centre; the quadrants;
Well-being and 'psychosocial integration'.

I COME FROM a working-class background. I grew up in a council house, my father was a railwayman and my mother worked in a bar. My parents weren't politically active but described themselves as 'socialists' and I inherited this political orientation. I graduated from university with a politics degree and then did a Ph.D. in politics on Simone de Beauvoir's *The Second Sex* (1949). I chaired BBC Scotland's Equal Opportunities Committee for seven years. In my book *The Scots' Crisis of Confidence* I consider a large number of structural and cultural influences on the Scots, collectively and individually.

I recount all this to make clear that understanding the world through the lens of power, class, inequality and culture was as natural to me as breathing. So, when I became interested in psychology I didn't see it as replacing the importance of structural and cultural factors: for me, it was simply a helpful addition. In a world of mounting depression, inequality and the failure of politicians to address societal issues, it was useful to know that there may be things individuals and communities could do to improve their lives. It was another tool to use in the quest for societal and individual change.

But I soon realised that psychologists, particularly American psychologists, were blind to wider societal factors and only interested in psychological interventions with individuals and sometimes small groups. Some of them, most notably Martin Seligman, made great claims for the interventions they favoured, arguing that they could lead to significant social change.

In his book *The Quick Fix: Why fad psychology can't cure our social ills,* published in 2021, Jesse Singal argues convincingly that the techniques psychologists favour are little more than 'hype'. Singal describes how psychologists and some other social scientists present complicated issues as simple and easily eradicated by their often 'half-baked solutions' to problems; problems that deserve more serious treatment. Singal argues that a major characteristic of their work is the assumption that 'big imposing structures and systems are invisible, unimportant or improved fairly easily.' They aren't.

As Singal also points out it's easy to see why politicians, policy-makers and practitioners, grappling with problems like the educational attainment gap, poverty or rising mental health problems in children, will seize on these hyped solutions.

Undoubtedly the Centre benefited from the desire for a 'quick fix'. I'm sure that many of the Centre's funders and adherents wanted what we offered to be the answer to the problems they faced. I was taken by positive psychology and thought that a country like Scotland, with a particular predilection for negativity, could benefit from its insights. Nonetheless I never presented confidence or positive psychology as a panacea. In fact, in my blogs, and in a conference paper to the European Positive Psychology Association in July 2008, I argued strongly that the tools in positive psychology's toolbox were woefully inadequate for its expressed mission to change people's lives. I urged more humility and a need for partnership with those working in other disciplines.

Broadening the Centre's focus

When I wrote *Creating Confidence*, barely two years after we set up the Centre, I covered a number of psychological interventions, such as Carol Dweck's mindset work or promoting resilience and self-efficacy, but end by listing ten non-psychological approaches to building confidence such as the Duke of Edinburgh Award Scheme, outdoor learning, sport, art and music, cooperative learning. . .

In the years that followed I also wrote a number of blogs railing against reductionism and how commonplace it had become for people to claim that their approach was 'the answer'. But there simply isn't a single answer. I found it particularly disturbing that those interested in children's and young people's well-being were blind to myriad forces influencing these young lives and focused myopically on one thing, such as boosting optimism or happiness.

It was because the Centre wanted to draw attention to these wider cultural influences on young people's lives that, in the spring of 2008, we organised two back-to-back events called **Foundations for Flourishing: creating the conditions for flourishing children and responsible youth**.

We designed the first day to attract people working in early years or primary school. The keynote speaker was Sue Palmer whose 2006 book *Toxic Childhood* had attracted a great deal of publicity and acclaim. Sue set out the evidence for children's loss of resilience and well-being and how this is happening as a result of wider societal changes such as media consumption, advertising, lack of physical activity and sleep and poor diet. Tim Gill, author of *No Fear: Growing up in a risk averse society* (2007), captivated the audience with his argument on the need for risky play and what he called 'benign neglect'. Alan Sinclair talked about the importance of the early years not just for a good childhood but for adult skills and relationships.

The following day focused on adolescence. Dr Robert Epstein, a distinguished American psychologist whose book *The Case Against Adolescence: Rediscovering the Adult* (2007) had created a huge impact in America, challenged the notion of the deficient teen brain, arguing that the problem is our low expectations of young people and their lack of responsibility. If we don't treat teenagers as responsible adults (something that had happened in previous times) then why should they act like adults? These types of arguments were built on by Sandy Campbell who at that time was running an acclaimed mentoring project for young men in Leith called Working Rite and by Glasgow-based psychologist and Centre collaborator Alan McLean who argued cogently for the need to give young people more responsibility by 'letting go of the reins'. Dr Alex Richardson, author of *They are What You Feed Them* (2006), added another dimension to our understanding of young people's mental and physical health. We also had some young people talking about how their experience of volunteering in Latin America had completely transformed their lives.

From this you can see how keen the Centre was to broaden its agenda, break out of a narrow psychological perspective on the world and start to focus more on the cultural and structural influences on well-being.

Flourishing lives web resources

To play up the importance of the broad factors which influence well-being, we had to downplay positive psychology on the website. At that point the main section on our website was called 'positive psychology resources' and it contained a large amount of background material as well as research summaries, tools, tips and links. This was the part of the website which attracted most visitors, many of them from abroad.

We wanted to maintain much of this material while conveying the idea that a focus on subjective well-being (how people feel) wasn't the whole picture. Other factors contributed and might even be more important. So, we created a new section called 'Flourishing Lives' and used an unfinished jigsaw as an entry point into the material. We launched this new feature on the website in the spring of 2009. We placed much of positive psychology in the 'emotional well-being' piece and began by including income equality, spirituality, nature, learning and playing outdoors, physical activity, relationships, values and freedom from stereotyping. We kept on adding more material and jigsaw pieces. As each section had various subsections it soon became unwieldy and we divided Flourishing Lives into two sections – one on adult well-being and the other on children and youth.

Over the years we changed the names of pieces and aggregated sections. It was always a work in progress and never anything like complete. It devoured time and resources. We were very fortunate that a young undergraduate, Mable Nakubulwa, received funding from the Chancellor's Fund at Glasgow University in 2009 to work with us for six weeks. During that time she researched and wrote the relationships section.

Figure 2: Graphical interface for the Flourishing Lives (adult) section of the Centre's website

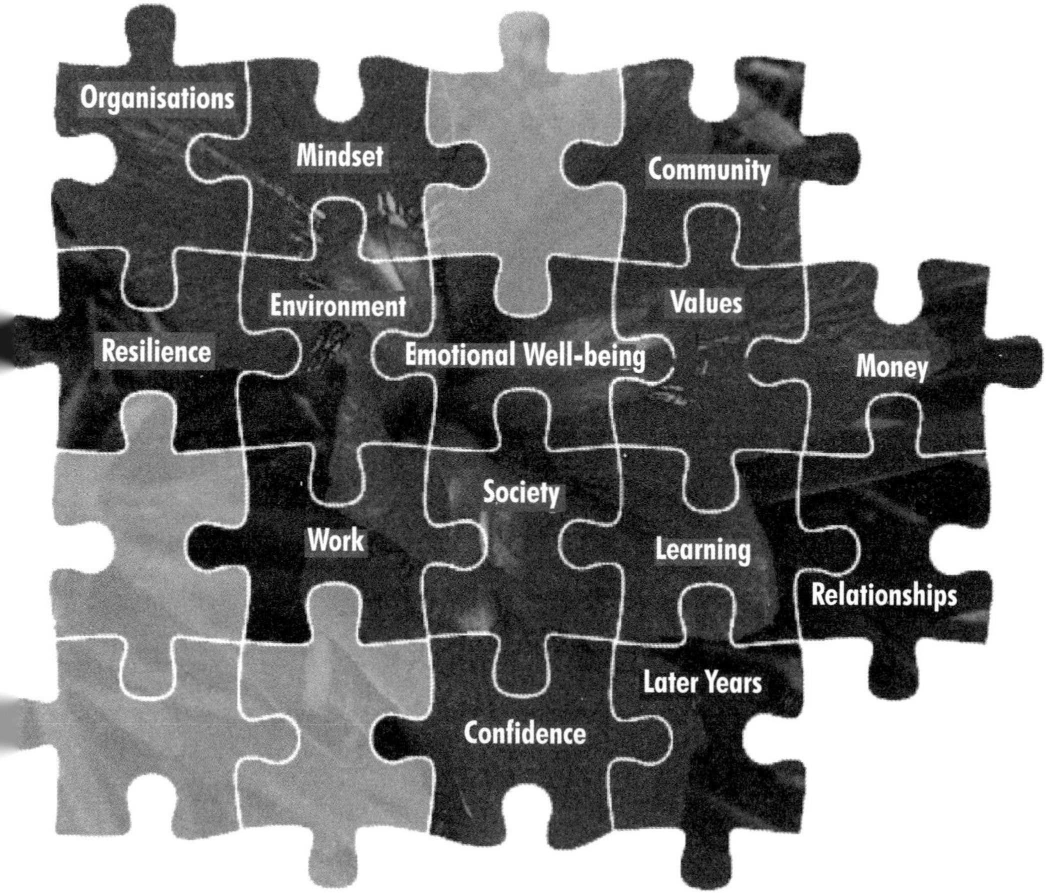

Relevant Centre events

This broadening of the Centre's agenda also led to six large-scale events in 2009. I'll only outline the four here which fit this widening perspective and which won't be mentioned in later chapters.

We held the first of these events, **'Nations, culture and well-being'** in March 2009. The focus of this half-day event was national culture and well-being. Speakers included Nic Marks of the New Economics Foundation who talked about the 'real wealth' that comes from relationships, connection and engagement. He reported that, in comparison with Scandinavian countries and others with high levels of well-being, the UK scores poorly for 'trust and belonging'. Dr Jim White based his talk on improving mental well-being on his extensive work with people suffering from depression in Glasgow's East End. And Phil Hanlon reflected on the previous two speakers' contributions as well as outlining his own work on 'the Scottish effect' – why Scotland's health is worse than its neighbours.

The Centre collaborated with a number of organisations – NHS Health Scotland, Culture and Sport Glasgow, The Scottish Urban Regeneration Forum (SURF), the Forestry Commission and Scottish Natural Heritage – to put on another half-day event in September called **Physical Activity: Confidence and Well-being in Motion.** Two professors – Nanette Mutrie and Ken Fox – who had undertaken considerable research on the importance of exercise for physical and mental health were the main speakers.

In September we then held an extremely successful evening event at Caledonian University which attracted 470 people and was chaired by the journalist Iain Macwhirter. Many attendees travelled from Aberdeenshire, the Highlands and Dumfries and Galloway. It was called *The Brain that Changes Itself* and the keynote speaker was Dr Norman Doidge. His 2008 book of the same name was an international bestseller and won many plaudits, most notably from Professor Carol Dweck.

Some of those who attended had been at previous Centre events and were interested in Carol Dweck's work on the fixed and growth mindsets but the majority had never attended anything we had run before. Many attended because they, or a family member, had suffered a stroke or brain injury.

Doidge's message is remarkably simple. Our mechanistic view of the universe has encouraged us to see the brain as a machine, or nowadays as a computer. Commonly people talk about the brain being 'hard-wired'. The brain as a machine metaphor has led us to believe that once it is fully working at the end of childhood then not much happens to it apart from the decay which sets in with old age. But Doidge helps us to see that the brain is plastic. This neuroplasticity means that the brain grows and develops in response to learning. While the brain tends to use certain areas for specific tasks this is not fixed and the brain is capable of reorganising itself.

Norman Doidge showed a few films featuring some of the people he talked about in the book. Some of these were sensational – blind people shooting basketball, stroke victims walking again and a woman cursed with extreme balance problems making a full recovery.

Many of those who attended did so because they were interested in dyslexia or special needs and so were particularly interested in the film Norman Doidge showed about Barbara Arrowsmith Young who runs a school in Toronto. She has now catalogued 19 specific brain weaknesses and has exercises to strengthen them. This is not the usual approach to learning difficulties. It is much more common to try and work round problems rather than tackle the weak areas directly. So, for example, dyslexic students will be allowed scribes, given extra time or told to listen to audio books rather than read.

Norman Doidge was inspiring but he didn't oversell his argument. Of course, he argued, not all brain conditions can be cured and there was little hope of change if people were not able to perform exercises. He also pointed out that brain plasticity has a downside, making people more vulnerable to negative influences such as pornography or indoctrination.

Despite Norman Doidge's note of realism the vast majority of people who left the lecture hall did so with more hope. They now knew that things are not as fixed as we think. Our brains are living organic things which can grow, develop and even heal.

We held the fourth relevant event in October. It was called **'If**

Music Be. . .' and was largely organised by Zoe Van Zwanenberg. Zoe worked as an associate and part-time project manager with the Centre but she was also Chair of Scottish Ballet. She used her contacts in the arts to put together an inspiring evening event run jointly with the Royal Scottish Academy of Music and Drama (RSAMD) on the importance of music for well-being. Raymond MacDonald, Professor of Music Psychology and Improvisation spoke at the event. So too did Richard Holloway on why he was so keen to import the ideas of El Sistema, a classical music project involving children in poor communities in Venezuela, to the Raploch in Stirling. Several RSAMD students also treated the 80 strong audience to a short recital. The event was so successful that the Centre and the RSAMD were keen to run a further four events the following year but sadly we were too busy with other projects to take this forward.

Theoretical underpinning for the Centre's work – Integral

As we moved away from positive psychology, we were influenced by Cambridge Professor Felicia Huppert's book *The Science of Well-being*. In 2005 she had published this large multi-authored book which gives positive psychology its place but also includes a range of other factors such as brain development, work, contact with nature and physical activity. That said, our conscious adoption of 'the science of well-being' was fairly short-lived as we became increasingly interested in the American philosopher, Ken Wilber, and his writings on 'Integral'. We knew that life was too complex and interactive for there ever to be 'one answer'. We also despaired at the myopia caused by narrow subject specialism within academia. We saw Integral as a way out of this bind.

I first encountered Ken Wilber's work in the autumn of 2006 through John Orr who, at that time, ran the Centre for Integral Education. John introduced me to Wilber's 'quadrants'. I liked John but I can't say I was overly impressed by these ideas at that stage. Nonetheless, I committed to reading Wilber's book – *A Theory of Everything* (2001).

I then discovered that Phil Hanlon had recently been reading Wilber's work and found much of it insightful. So too did Charlie

Miller, the famous Edinburgh hair stylist and entrepreneur, who had gone out of his way to meet me by attending the Carol Dweck event in Glasgow in June 2007. When I did finally meet up with Charlie a few weeks later I realised two things – first that he was an extremely intelligent and thoughtful man and second that his main intention in meeting up was to introduce me to Wilber's work. I invited Charlie to attend a board away day at the end of October in the fabulous Boathouse in Aberdour, home of the International Future's Forum. Go Dundee's Joe Lafferty, an experienced facilitator, led the session. Unsurprisingly we spent some time discussing Integral. Charlie joined the board a few months later primarily to discuss Wilber's work and its relevance to the Centre. From May to November 2010 Dr Ian Wight from the University of Manitoba in Winnipeg chose to spend his sabbatical at the Centre. As he was also interested in Integral, he was another source of help with developing this perspective.

In 2011 we created a section on the Centre's website called 'Scottish Integral'. In it we set out some background information on Ken Wilber and then gave some information on the quadrants and why we found it so helpful. Over the years we ran a few small workshops on the topic, mainly for board members.

So why did we find Integral so helpful?

Ken Wilber numerous books employ's his Integral perspective to all human knowledge. Key to this highly complex body of work is the concept of four quadrants and it was this part of his work that we found most useful.

Wilber's quadrants

Each quadrant represents a broad category of knowledge and a basic dimension of the world as we perceive it. Wilber had studied a huge array of thinkers: scientific theorists, Eastern and Western philosophers, religious scholars, feminists – anyone whose work contributed to human knowledge. He then tried to categorise these perspectives. After much sorting this yielded four quadrants which 'were divided along two axes: inner and outer, singular and plural.'

	INTERIOR	EXTERIOR
INDIVIDUAL	**I** **Psychological** **Spiritual**	**It** **Physiological** **Behavioural**
COLLECTIVE	**We** **Relational** **Cultural**	**Its** **Structural** **Social**

A helpful way to think about the division into four quadrants is that the individual and collective axis is about what is personal to an individual and what is shared with others. The inner/outer axis is about what can be easily seen (exterior) and what's hidden from view (interior). For example, we can see an individual's behaviour and body (in minute details given the right procedures and implements) but there is no technology to see a person's innermost thoughts and feelings. Likewise rules and procedures are clearly visible (lower right) but what is going on between people emotionally or the impact of culture (lower left) is not immediately apparent and requires elucidation and interpretation. This division into these categories reflects everyday experience: all languages have a distinction between the subjective (I) the intersubjective (we) and the objective (it). The only complicating factor here is that Wilber has divided the objective into the singular and the collective (i.e. groups of objects such as systems) into it and its.

The upper left quadrant pertains to the interior of the individual. This is about subjective experience as well as how we think and feel about these experiences. In terms of academic subjects or schools of thought, this quadrant has been the focus of psychologists and psychoanalysts concerned with human beings' inner life or their development. As this quadrant is also about consciousness (what it is and how it arises) philosophers have contributed enormously to our understanding of individuals' interior lives. Spiritual experience also belongs in this quadrant.

The Interior Collective quadrant comes into play when two 'I's meet and there is shared perception, connection or any emotional state generated by social interaction. 'We' then relates to anything where we are in relationship with others – communities, families, romantic relationships, workplaces, neighbourhoods, national sentiment and so on. This quadrant also relates to culture and shared beliefs as these have the power to shape perceptions not just of me as an individual but for me as a member of a 'we' group.

The two quadrants on the right concern the physical, material world. In a sense they are the natural domain of science. From an individual's perspective, the upper right quadrant relates to how he/she actually experiences the world through his/her five senses. So, anything to do with our individual bodies (e.g. health) and our concrete experience of the world and our behaviour relate to this quadrant. Indeed, anything about a person or thing that we can actually see belongs to the upper right quadrant.

The Exterior Collective quadrant (its) refers to collections of events/things. This means that anything which is a 'system' belongs here such as the political, governmental, legal, health, educational systems as well as the ecosystem or planetary system. Communication networks including the mass media and the internet belong here as does transportation and manufacturing as these too are about systems.

We were attracted to Wilber's mantra that 'it all matters' as this encourages respect for different thinkers and different approaches as they all have a specific contribution to make to our knowledge and understanding. This is a theory that respects the theoretical and practical insights of individual thinkers such as Marx, Freud, Jung, Levi-Strauss, Chomsky. . . as well as valuing the whole spectrum of Eastern and Western religious philosophies, feminism, and even structuralism and post-modernism.

Widening horizons

This widening of the Centre's perspective meant that we ultimately changed our Memorandum of Association to reflect how we now saw our role. In 2005 we had gained charitable status on the basis that we would 'promote interest in, educate and facilitate research into all aspects of confidence, well-being and related attitudes in Scotland and more generally in the United Kingdom and internationally for the public benefit.' In 2011 we amended this to read:

> The Centre for Confidence and Well-being Limited aims to be a catalyst for change – individual, organisational and cultural. Through its web resources, publications and events it aims to stimulate new thinking and disseminate research findings on confidence and well-being. It believes that there is a place for psychological interventions but particularly favours a broad, integral approach which stresses the importance of various factors. . .

We also believed that this 'Integral' approach, which deliberately tries to bridge subject specialisms and eschews a narrow perspective, was in tune with Scotland's Enlightenment tradition with its emphasis on generalism and commitment to social change. We proclaimed little of this attachment to Integral to our wider audience but it guided the Centre's board and allowed us to feel confident in our strategy.

Defining well-being

Finally, a word on well-being. In the course of the Centre's work, I encountered many different definitions of well-being. The one which I found most helpful is set out by Professor Bruce Alexander, a Canadian psychologist, who published a paradigm-shifting book called *The Globalisation of Addiction: a study in the poverty of the spirit* (2008) which I shall return to in Chapter 15. Alexander argues that human beings have a need for what the psychologist Erik Erikson calls 'psychosocial integration'. What this means is that human beings simultaneously need to 'express their individuality' and feel free but at the same time feel they belong to a wider social group in which they can make a positive contribution. This means that well-being is a complex term encompassing both a sense of individuality as well as the feeling of being part of a collective.

'Dislocation' is the term Alexander uses to describe the negative feelings human beings experience when their need for psychosocial integration is not met. Alexander does not romanticise ancient tribal or peasant societies, accepting that they were often barbarous to outsiders or individuals within their tribe. Nonetheless, he argues that such societies were able to fulfil their members' needs for psychosocial integration. 'The genius of a successful culture,' writes Alexander, 'is that it provides adequately for individual autonomy and social belonging at the same time – a balancing act of great virtuosity, since the needs often conflict with one another.' Viewed in this light we can see why socialist societies have often failed this test as they are too centralised to allow for individual expression. Free market capitalist society, with its emphasis on individual activity and weak social ties, is also poor at providing this balance and, in its extreme forms, often leads to 'mass dislocation' whereby the culture results in many people lacking psychosocial integration.

According to Alexander's theory, dislocation is not only 'socially destructive' but is also painful for individuals. The dislocated individual feels empty and overwhelmed by 'the poverty of spirit' or the sense of his or her lost soul. To help fill this void, dislocated individuals don't simply turn, but become addicted, to other things in life – alcohol, drugs, gambling, romantic love, work, shopping, sex. In their different ways, all can provide a diversion and/or numb the pain. What a dislocated individual chooses is dependent on his or her psychology and what is available in that society. These types of addictions can ruin people's lives to varying degrees, yet Alexander asserts that they should be seen as 'adaptive' in the sense that they provide a way for the individual to cope with dislocation. 'Without addictions,' writes Alexander, 'those who lack psychosocial integration would have 'terrifyingly little reason to live.'

These ideas on what constitutes well-being and what triggers addiction are useful to bear in mind in the next two chapters: the first is on *The Tears that Made the Clyde* and it sets out a historical perspective on Glasgow's social problems and drink culture and the second is on materialism and how we now live in a society obsessed with the acquisition of stuff.

Chapter 11

The Tears that Made the Clyde

Background to writing the book;
the inspiration from Professor Richard Wilkinson's books on inequality;
Wilkinson's thesis; applicability to Glasgow;
the origins of industrial Glasgow; the city's housing crisis;
the role of inequality in the making of Glasgow;
the social effects of inequality in the city;
how the city's history and economy weakened women's position and detached men from family life;
publishing the book; a scurrilous and misogynist review.

WEEKS BEFORE the first Coronavirus lockdown in 2020 I gave a talk on my book *The Tears that Made the Clyde* in Glasgow's City Chambers. The event was organised by a group from various city-wide organisations active in trying to understand and tackle Glasgow's considerable health and social problems. I was the main speaker and was pleased to see the leader of the Council, Susan Aitken, and various departmental heads, including Maureen McKenna the education chief, in attendance. I was also extremely heartened to hear a number of those present say that no one should be in the type of jobs they held in Glasgow unless they had read my book. From our discussions it was clear that they found the book's historical perspective particularly enlightening.

I wrote *The Tears that Made the Clyde* more by accident than design. In 2007 Fred Shedden became Chair of the Centre's board of trustees. He had recently retired as a lawyer and was now on the board of the Glasgow Housing Association. At meetings he often said that he wanted the Centre to contribute to an understanding of the city's problems and what might be done to remedy them.

The Centre was based in Glasgow and I regularly gave talks to organisations in the city. We also held most of our events there and we had been involved in a project called Drumchapel Life. I had put forward various proposals to the Scottish Government for projects with some of the city's poorer communities, but they hadn't been funded. So I just couldn't see how we could do anything to comply with Fred's request. What's more, the Glasgow Centre for Population Health (GCPH) had been expressly set up in 2004 to undertake research into why Glasgow had the worst health in Western Europe and what the solutions might be. That organisation had considerable resources and lots of staff and they had published a number of incisive papers on the extent of the city's health challenges. I thought they were doing a good job. But then, quite by chance, I read Richard Wilkinson's book *The Impact of Inequality: How to make sick societies better* (2005) and suddenly I felt I had something to say on Glasgow and its problems.

Wilkinson's thesis

When *The Impact of Inequality* was first published Richard Wilkinson was a Professor of Social Epidemiology. His work, including this book, was aimed at an academic audience. But a few years later he co-authored another book, essentially on the same lines as *The Impact of Inequality*, with a colleague, Kate Pickett. It was more aimed at the general reader and published with a much catchier title – *The Spirit Level: Why more equal societies almost always do better* (2009). By 2012 it had sold 150,000 copies and been translated into 23 different languages. As it was Wilkinson's previous book that inspired me to start reading and writing about Glasgow, I'll mainly concentrate on this book here.

The essence of Wilkinson's argument is that it is inequality rather than 'absolute material want' that leads to pronounced health inequalities and social problems. In short, it is socio-economic status rather than poverty which really matters. He cites data which show that more equal societies have higher levels of trust, enhanced social capital and social cohesion as well as lower levels of homicide and violence. More equal societies also have better health. But why should inequality have such an effect on societies? To help understand Wilkinson's answer we need to appreciate his basic thesis about human society and individual psychology.

Wilkinson argues that human evolution shows that as a species we have lived through periods with pronounced dominance hierarchies based on fear and submission and also the more egalitarian, cooperative structure of hunter-gatherer periods. This means that we have the capacity to operate in either type of social system.

Citing researchers such as Robin Dunbar, Wilkinson also argues that human beings' large brains, and speech, have evolved to allow us to interact socially with others and that we have great powers to empathise and identify with others' predicament and feelings. While we are capable of excluding and discriminating against others, thereby reinforcing our own status, our psychological make-up leads us to experience real shame and embarrassment if others treat us as inferiors or if we even think we are being judged as unequal in their eyes.

Wilkinson cites studies of non-human primates where hierarchies are central to the social structure which show that animals forced into submission by a higher-ranking animal then turn and attack others lower in the pecking order. Primatologists call this the 'bicycling reaction' because 'animals show their back to the top while kicking towards the bottom'.

The term (*Radfahrer-Reaktion*) originally came from Theodor Adorno's work *The Authoritarian Personality* (1950), which was written in an attempt to understand why the Jews had been scapegoated in Nazi Germany. Wilkinson asserts that the 'bicycling reaction' can be seen in the increased number of racist attacks during periods of unemployment and economic hardship. He also cites data which show that the worst problems of racism in the USA are in states with the most pronounced income inequality.

This bicycling reaction can also be seen in men's relationships with women. The domestic violence researchers, Russell and Becky Dobash, argue that women are much less likely to be assaulted in societies where there is relative equality of the sexes. Conversely, research in the USA shows that women married to men employed in hierarchical settings, such as the armed forces, are twice as likely to be beaten by their husbands as other women in their society. Wilkinson claims that women's position in general is prejudiced in societies with pronounced income inequality as it fosters a strong dominance hierarchy among men.

It is important to realise that in societies with a pronounced dominance hierarchy, it's not just women who suffer – men do as well. He writes: 'The costs are shown in their increased levels of violence, more risk-taking behaviour (from car crashes to sexually transmitted diseases), excessive drinking, and cardiovascular diseases. . . there is a "culture of inequality" that is not only more violent and aggressive, but more macho.'

Wilkinson claims that 'there have now been over fifty studies showing a clear tendency for violence to be more common in societies where income differences are larger.' This violence manifests itself in homicide figures or in violent attacks. The argument here is that men at the bottom of the dominance hierarchy feel bad about themselves but are not likely to tackle the dominant males. Instead they are more likely to attack one another in an attempt to achieve some respect. Indeed Wilkinson argues that 'the most frequent trigger of violence is people feeling they're disrespected and dishonoured.'

Everything Wilkinson writes in *The Impact of Inequality* and later in *The Spirit Level* about what happens in societies with pronounced dominance hierarchies screams Glasgow – violence, macho culture, heavy drinking, domestic abuse, sectarianism, suicide, and teenage pregnancies. This isn't just a media stereotype of the hard man fostered by books like *No Mean City* (1935) or *Laidlaw* (1977) or the numerous violent and bleak films set in Glasgow: a male dominance hierarchy, of the kind Wilkinson identifies, is easy to observe in the city.

In the early 2000s, before the activities of the Violence

Reduction Unit, Glasgow was the murder capital of Europe. In fact, the rate of murder committed with a knife in Glasgow was three and a half times the figure recorded for England and Wales. As much of this was gang violence there's no doubt that Glasgow had a macho, territorial culture which fitted with the notion of the bicycling reaction. As we've also heard, Glasgow had the worst health in Europe, including similar deindustrialised cities. One GCPH study carried out in late 2011 by Walsh *et al* showed that Glasgow has 30 per cent higher premature mortality (under 65 years) than Liverpool and Manchester.

But here's the conundrum: in various research studies, including the one cited above, Walsh *et al* could not substantiate the thesis that Glasgow, or the west of Scotland more generally, had particularly bad health simply because the region had extreme inequality. Indeed deprivation and inequality were similar in Glasgow, Manchester and Liverpool in Walsh *et al's* study. Even more curious is the fact that in that study Glasgow's significantly higher mortality did not just affect those in lower socio-economic groups – even middle-class Glaswegians have poorer health and die earlier than those in Liverpool and Manchester.

The similarities between Wilkinson's description of the effects of inequality and the data on Glasgow's health and social problems are uncannily suggestive and, to my mind, needed further investigation. Given the lack of supporting evidence that Glasgow's health and violence problems are due to excessive inequality I thought it important to consider if a modified version of Wilkinson's thesis may be applicable: one that involved considering whether Glasgow (or the West of Scotland in general) *historically* suffered from such extreme inequality that the type of mentality Wilkinson describes has become deeply embedded in the local culture.

It was my desire to answer this question that led me to embark on a great deal of reading on Glasgow's history and ultimately to write *The Tears that Made the Clyde: Well-being in Glasgow*. I hoped that my knowledge of well-being and various contemporary theories and perspectives on health meant I had something to offer our understanding of the city and its problems and offset the fact that I am not a trained historian. But I was also aware that I had to ensure that whatever I wrote was historically robust. To give me this assurance I asked Professor Tom Devine, Scotland's leading historian, if he would be my historical adviser. Not only did Tom meet up with me from time to time to give advice and read what I had written, he also he wrote the foreword to the book.

The origins of industrial Glasgow

In the seventeenth century and the first half of the eighteenth Glasgow was considered to be one of the most beautiful cities in Britain. It had an important university and a cathedral round which the city's attractive buildings clustered. The adjacent streets were originally laid out in the shape of a cross. The city was noted for its mild climate and abundant gardens and orchards. But, by the middle of the nineteenth century, for most of its inhabitants, Glasgow was a living hell.

It's impossible to understand Glasgow without grasping the bare bones of its industrial history. Glasgow had always depended on its river which originally afforded good links with Ireland. But with the advent of American colonies the city became ideally placed for trade with these new markets and soon became much more important than Scotland's eastern ports which had become wealthy from European trade. However, Glasgow could only exploit the Atlantic economy after the Act of Union in 1707 and the repeal of England's Navigation Acts which had debarred Scots from trading with England's colonies.

Glasgow merchants invested in ships and began trading in plantation commodities – tobacco, sugar and cotton. Tobacco was particularly lucrative and some merchants known as 'the tobacco lords' amassed huge fortunes. Following American independence in 1776 this business went up in a puff of smoke. But soon whole industries developed round the city to provide goods to export to the growing American population – linen, woollen cloth, furniture, pottery and other items. Glasgow, with its damp climate, became ideally placed for the manufacture of cotton which was increasingly produced in large mills.

The city's ready access to fuels and raw materials also meant it was particularly suitable for heavy engineering and manufacturing. From 1830 shipbuilding became Glasgow's forte and the term 'Clydebuilt' was used internationally to mean an engineered product of quality. In the nineteenth century most workers in Glasgow, as elsewhere in urban Britain, endured horrific working conditions: the hours were long, the work hard and the conditions appalling.

But there's another reason why Scotland was able to industrialise so quickly: it had ready access to large numbers of workers. Until the early part of the eighteenth century the vast majority of Scots lived in rural areas and Scotland was 'one of the least urbanised in Western Europe in the seventeenth century.' However, in the hundred years between 1750 and 1850 Scotland rose to third top of the urban league table, only below that of England and Wales. People from all over Scotland, highlands and lowlands, went to Glasgow to secure employment in the new textile industries or the range of jobs required in a burgeoning city. The development of industry in the west of Scotland also acted like a magnet for poor Irish people.

So, as a result of 'push pull factors' – expanding economic opportunities in Glasgow and changes in the rural economy – the city's population exploded. In 1830 there were more than a quarter of a million Glaswegians. This doubled by 1871 and doubled again by 1914. By the turn of the twentieth century 70 per cent of those employed in Glasgow were working in manufacturing of some kind. Glasgow was truly 'the workshop of the world', with a high proportion of her workforce in skilled or semi-skilled jobs.

The housing crisis

Tenements became a common type of urban housing in Scotland, including Glasgow, in the second half of the sixteenth century. The early tenements built in the heart of Glasgow were usually four storeys or more in height, with thick walls. They were mainly large rectangular buildings with back greens for drying or bleaching clothes and growing flowers and herbs.

As wealth increased the rich, and the middle classes, moved

out of the city centre to town houses, terraces or new elegant tenements in the west and south of the city. The tenements vacated by the well-to-do were soon occupied by the hordes flooding into the city to take up jobs available as a result of Glasgow's economic expansion. The demand for housing, and the limited amount of space in the area, meant that the back-greens were now used for new tenement blocks. The 'back lands' development, as it was called, immediately created wretched living conditions for everyone. The in-fill tenements were erected so close to the original buildings that people from different tenements could shake hands. This cramming meant that many of the tenements lacked ventilation and light. It also created a warren of dank, stinking wynds. Even without the back lands the old tenements became overcrowded by the creation of 'single-ends' or 'room and kitchens'. In other words, the old tenements were divided to create one- or two-roomed dwellings. Most lacked their own cooking or toilet facilities (privies or dry toilets) and these were shared with dozens of other families in the tenement.

As early as 1840 it was clear that Glasgow had a severe housing problem and that for many of its citizens living conditions were squalid, if not inhuman. The UK sanitary reformer, Edwin Chadwick declared that the Glasgow wynds were the worst he ever saw. Even in 1940, 700,000 people lived in 1800 acres in the city centre. These figures mean that Glasgow was the heaviest populated area in Europe.

Unsanitary, overcrowded living conditions are closely related to ill health. Abysmal living conditions undermined the health of generations of Glaswegians; rickets was common, as was tuberculosis which was higher in the city than elsewhere. Infanticide and infant mortality were high, stature was not. Living conditions were so bad that numerous cholera and typhus epidemics broke out in the first half of the nineteenth century, prompting a campaign for sanitary reform and energetic municipal activity to cleanse and improve the city. By the 1890s Glasgow – with its public water supply, baths, public lighting, gas supply, libraries, trams and so forth – had more municipal services than any other city of its size.

There were various official attempts to tackle the housing problem. The Town Council acquired powers to clear out unsanitary areas, widen streets, and make new streets. Often these powers led to the demolition of properties which were seen as a public health or public order hazard but not to the rehousing of the poor tenants who were displaced in the process. Indeed the poor were often seen as the *cause* of the slums – not the victims.

Given the atrocious housing conditions it is understandable why T.C. Smout should write on the topic of deprivation in Scotland in the nineteenth century:

> It was Glasgow. . . growing in population and in wealth as no city in Scotland had ever done before, that remained the most dramatic and squalid example of urban deprivation. Everyone wanted to reform it – evangelist, temperance crusader, socialist, municipal activist.

The role of inequality in the making of Glasgow

The Tears that Made the Clyde is almost 400 pages long so it's impossible to summarise the material and argument I include there in this single chapter. So, I'll concentrate on the subject of inequality, which I outline mainly in the chapter aptly called 'The Tiers that Made the Clyde'.

Scotland is a country which loves to proclaim its commitment to equality – it is the land of Robert Burns' 'a man's a man', and the democratic Presbyterian Church. A country that fulfilled John Knox's vision for a 'school in every parish', educating the poor alongside the middling classes. Undoubtedly there were, and still are, deep democratic instincts within Scotland but this is by no means the full story. When reading about Glasgow's industrial past it quickly became evident to me that the city's story is indeed one of profound inequality.

As the second city of the Empire, Glasgow was an extremely wealthy city – wealthier than Manchester, Edinburgh or Liverpool, for example. The well-to-do lived in handsome buildings and streets – indeed the city they inhabited was one of the finest in the UK and on a par with the best of the continent. On the other hand, there is general agreement that the conditions in Glasgow for the poor were the worst in Europe. Historical records show that Glasgow topped the bill when it came to the sordidness of the conditions, the extent of overcrowding, the sheer numbers living in slum conditions, infant mortality and other health problems.

The problems for Glasgow's workers were caused not just by poor housing but low wages. One of the strategic cost advantages throughout the nineteenth century for Glasgow bosses was that wages were low in comparison to the average for the United Kingdom. Indeed in 1872 the United States Congress heard that the 'worldwide success of Clyde-built ships was to be explained in the final analysis by "the abundance of skilled workmen and the low wages paid to them".'

Inequality also lies at the heart of the way the industrial city developed. Here's a summary of five key contributory factors:

Urbanisation and landownership

According to Tom Devine what is most remarkable about Scotland's urbanisation is its speed. England became the most urbanised country in Europe as a result of 'a continuous and protracted process of steadily intensifying urban expansion'. Scotland's urbanisation, by contrast was 'abrupt and fast'.

Agricultural improvement lay behind this rapid urbanisation but this derived its energy in part from the power of Scottish landlords. Ironically, for a country which likes to pride itself on its egalitarianism and fairness, Scotland had, according to Devine, 'probably the most concentrated pattern of land ownership in Europe.' What's more, in Scotland there was virtually no peasant class with legal rights and this helped to cement the hegemony of the landed class. This class was able to bring about rapid agricultural improvements, involving changes in land usage partly because they had the power to evict tenants at the end of a lease. These rights were not common in other countries. So Scottish landowners, in both lowland and highland Scotland, cleared people from the land and many of these virtual refugees streamed into Glasgow to become industrial workers and live in squalid slums.

Rampant capitalism, slavery and conspicuous consumption

Glasgow became 'the Second City of the Empire' because it was an industrial and commercial hub – an entrepôt. It was money, in the form of capital and investments, which fuelled the rapid expansion of Glasgow's commercial and industrial activities and money, in terms of profits, which provided the motivation for the expansion. Some successful west of Scotland families such as the Tennants, Bairds, Weirs and Coats were among the wealthiest in Britain.

Unlike Liverpool, Glasgow did not play an active part in the transportation of slaves but the Scots were heavily involved in plantation crops – cotton, tobacco and sugar – and many owned and ran numerous plantations, particularly in the Caribbean. By all accounts these plantations were the most inhumane. The horrible truth is that much of the money made through the work of slaves financed the making of Glasgow as a major industrial centre. If we are interested in 'the tears that made the Clyde' we must not forget those shed by African slaves and their families.

In commentaries on Glasgow's history what typically emerges is the view that 'the dear green place', once a spiritual centre full of herbs, orchards and pleasant smells, was transformed into a stinking cesspit of unbelievable human degradation. It is also common for commentators to argue that the people responsible for this calamity were ruthless, indigenous entrepreneurs. For example, the late Sydney Checkland, a great admirer of the sheer energy and productivity of Glasgow's economic past, was nonetheless appalled at what was done in the name of progress. He asserts that 'the fate of the mass of Glaswegians derives from the exploitation and short sightedness of the men of business who built the place'; that they were content to allow huge numbers of people to gather and set them to work 'without regard to dignity or suffering.'

It has also been commonplace for commentators on Glasgow to talk about its rampant, 'me first', individualism. The idea that Scotland's economic engine – Glasgow – was dominated by ruthless, money-oriented capitalists is at odds with the story we often tell ourselves in contemporary Scotland about the country's proclivity for equality and fair treatment of the poor. The truth is that, as money was amassed in nineteenth century Scotland, little was done to improve the terrible living conditions of the masses.

Of course, the logic of capitalism helps to explains this. For Scots with money to invest, a much greater return was likely from various projects in the New World, such as the construction of railways or factories, than from investing in local housing. Indeed Scotland invested more money per capita abroad than England or most other developed nations. This was of great benefit to the Scottish banks and those with money to invest in risky, but potentially profitable, overseas ventures but it did little for the poor Glaswegian or for the Scottish people as a whole.

The tobacco lords paved the way for Glasgow to become a money-making centre and they were particularly noted for their conspicuous consumption so it is hardly surprising that Glasgow spawned a particular type of money-oriented industrial elite. This opulence can still be seen in the houses in Glasgow's west end.

Class segregation

As a result of accumulating wealth and fear of contamination by disease from the slums, from the 1820s on, the wealthy and the middle classes moved out of the Old Town into new houses mainly to the west and south. This geographical segregation was not simply about housing but also about recreational use of the city. Only in some streets in the city centre did the classes ever mingle and cross paths.

Of course, Glasgow was not alone in having a city split geographically on class grounds. The west-end, east-end dichotomy can be found in many Western European cities. However, one of the reasons why this division into rich and poor appeared so stark in Glasgow is that the city had a very small middle and professional class, in comparison with most other cities, including Edinburgh. Glasgow was a working-class city with a huge number of very poorly paid and poorly housed workers.

Blaming the poor for their misfortunes and fearing their anger

Prior to the industrial revolution, in Scotland at least, various classes in society lived side by side. In Glasgow they often lived in the same tenements. However, as the rich in Glasgow felt compelled to move away from streets inhabited by the poor to escape contamination, they began to think of the people being crowded into fast-growing industrial cities as a separate class of individual, having different and less pressing human needs. This meant that the well-off were able to condone the deterioration of the inner urban area into slums. Ultimately the better off began to see the slum dwellers not just as different but as an *inferior* type of being. This is exactly Richard Wilkinson's argument about the importance of equality for good social cohesion. The more different people are in terms of status and income, the less easy it is for the rich to identify with the predicament of the poor. They then come to see them as different and inferior beings. When reading lots of books on Glasgow I found it dispiriting that the idea that the poor were worthless and contemptible – scum or worms – crops up repeatedly in literature or commentaries on the city. Also, there's evidence that the rich feared that the poor would turn on them in anger.

Authoritarianism

Authoritarianism is the charge commonly levelled at those who ran Glasgow industries. Historical experts argue they were ferocious bosses who, like the Scottish landed aristocracy, were used to being obeyed. They did not confer with their workers who were simply 'tell't' what to do. No wonder workers had an understandable fear of dismissal. Such an approach simply cemented rampant inequality and feelings of powerlessness for those at the bottom of the pile.

The social effects of inequality in the city

A central question for me in *The Tears that Made the Clyde* was whether this inequality, powerlessness and abject poverty led to divisions among the poor themselves and to the type of bicycling reaction described by Wilkinson whereby people kick out at those below them in the hierarchy in order to feel better about themselves. In the book I set out various ways in which this psychological reaction can be seen within the city's culture.

The poor's pecking order

Reading Glasgow's social history, and drawing on my own personal experience, it was evident that there was indeed a pronounced hierarchy in the city's working-class. People were ranked, and ranked others, on the basis of the number of rooms they had, the sanitation (inside or outside toilet), the type of tenement and the area in which they lived. Cleanliness and 'respectability' were major social markers. What I found disconcerting when reading many stories written by Glaswegians is how they simultaneously talk about Glasgow as an egalitarian city and then write disparagingly about the poor and excluded. This is evident in an essay written by the Glaswegian journalist and comedian Cliff Hanley who refers to Glasgow as 'this savagely egalitarian city' and then fills several pages outlining how the 'snob-scruff system' operates in Glasgow and that he grew up 'infused with snobbery'. Hanley came from a working-class family.

Disunited we stand

What about the workplace in Glasgow? Did it also have pronounced stratification? After World War I Glasgow was seen internationally as a militant city – Red Clydeside was legendary. But in reality Glasgow had not been a stronghold of political radicalism. From the mid 1850s England developed strong national unions, which exhibited a great deal of militancy, whereas Scotland tended to form federations of small, independent unions supported by Trades Councils. When Beatrice Webb visited Scotland in 1892 she was distinctly unimpressed by Glasgow trade unionists, noting, in her diary, their divisiveness: 'The Scottish nature does not lend itself to combination; the strong men seek to rise and push for themselves and not serve others.' Indeed one of the reasons why Glasgow workers did not form strong unions is that there was considerable division in the workplace. Demarcation disputes, between various occupational specialisms, were common. Skilled men jealously guarded their position by fighting to continue wage differentials between themselves and semi or unskilled workers.

Sectarianism

One labour historian, in a review of working class politics in Glasgow up to World War I, argues, 'The fragmentation of the city's working class, and in particular the persistence of ethnic and sectarian loyalties, meant that working-class unity was difficult to achieve and still more to maintain.' Undoubtedly a strong divisive feature within the Glasgow working class was religion. For example, it is claimed that the Amalgamated Society of Engineers did not have one Catholic member until 1931. Some higher status jobs such as train drivers or other railway jobs were more likely to go to Ulster Protestant Scots rather than the Catholic Irish. The same was true of the skilled jobs in the shipyards. The historian Tom Devine asserts 'boys from unskilled Catholic families would be permanently excluded from the best jobs'. This is why the question 'what school did you go to?' was infused in Glasgow with so much meaning and potential discrimination.

Sectarianism also operated at the family level. In fact, I know personally how a 'mixed marriage' of a Catholic and a Protestant could irretrievably divide families.

Us and them

There was yet another division in Glasgow. The aggressive management style of the bosses and their huge wealth meant that a pronounced 'us and them' attitude and strong sense of solidarity against the rich was evident in Glasgow's working-class. There was, and still is, a great deal of reverse snobbery: folk who are successful, or who do not behave the same as everyone else, are criticised or ostracised. They become the butt of jokes because they talk 'posh' and so must be snobs. The historian Richard Finlay argues that Scotland as a whole 'was plagued by a small-town mentality in which "I kent his faither" was used to rubbish social mobility.' He attributes the problem in part to 'jealousy' of those who come from the same background but still manage to get on. So it's not difficult to see how traditionally in the city there was a hostility to 'getting on'.

Violence

Given Glasgow's extreme inequality, it's hardly surprising that the city has a long history of gang-related violence and knife crime. But what's interesting is that Glasgow's particular claim to fame lay in mundane types of everyday aggression and violence – punch ups, alcohol-fuelled social disorder, and domestic violence. Reading through copious historical material for the book, I was taken aback by the amount of everyday aggressive, violent behaviour. Violence seems to have permeated so much of Glasgow life. Ralph Glasser, raised in the Gorbals in the 1920s and 30s, recounts in his autobiography: 'We grew up with violence. It simmered and bubbled and boiled over in street and close, outside the pubs, at the dance halls . . . ' According to one social historian, it was common, for example, for 'ordinary workers' to 'unhesitatingly go out the back-court, take their jackets off and have a "square go" with whoever had offended them'.

Piers Dudgeon in his book *Our Glasgow* (2009), based on interviews with people who grew up in the city, portrays Glasgow's violence as fuelled by two things – drink and feelings of inferiority. The working men, recalled in the book, knew they were the bottom of the pile and were fed up with a life of toil for very little reward. They aimed to get the respect they craved, and enhance their self-image, by being tough. This is exactly the argument set out by Richard Wilkinson in his work on why inequality leads to violence.

So there's little doubt that historically, at least, Glasgow was a fractured, socially divided society which exhibited in a number of ways the bicycling reaction which Wilkinson argues happens in unequal societies.

Women and children last

When reading histories and stories (both literature and autobiography) about Glasgow, it quickly became evident that this was a city which was divided by gender and where women were treated abysmally. I didn't set out to look for this but it was one of the most striking features of the history of Glasgow. For the sake of brevity, I outline here two interrelated reasons why women's position was worse in Glasgow than in equivalent industrial cities.

First, Glasgow's industrial jobs were overwhelmingly in heavy industries and these usually excluded women. In the south of England, by contrast, there were lots of jobs for women in light industries, many of them producing consumer goods. In Dundee, it was women who predominated in the jute industry. Of course, Glasgow women often had 'wee jobs', as domestic cleaners for example, but they were economically dependent on their husbands and the men liked it that way. Male workers in Glasgow fought hard to keep women out of workplaces for fear that it would undermine their role as breadwinner.

But here's the problem: many Glasgow men did not regard their wages as family money. It was 'his money'. That's why many women in the city queued up outside industrial premises or pubs to retrieve any of the pay packet for themselves and the family. This was a common sight in Glasgow. By contrast, in many coal-mining communities men ceremoniously handed over their complete pay packets to their wives who then gave their husbands pocket money. The macho Glasgow man would have seen this ritual as humiliating.

Second, the squalid, overcrowded housing conditions in Glasgow militated against family life. It was better for men to spend time in the pub with their mates than at home in one room with a large family. Male absence led to quarrelling between men and women, making it more likely that men wouldn't want to be at home. I'm going to return to the topic of Scotland and alcohol in later chapters, but it's important to point out here that Glasgow had a love affair with drink, particularly heavy liquor. In the early days of industrialisation both men and women frequented the pub to numb the pain of their terrible existence but one consequence of the temperance movement in the early nineteenth century was that it removed women from pubs. It hardly made a dent on male drinking. As Piers Dudgeon points out in his book on Glasgow, the city's drunken, macho culture exacted a heavy toll on family life, writing: 'Pumped-up and indignant, a man would turn his resentment on his family . . .'

Glasgow is commonly portrayed as matriarchal with the family headed by a strong woman who makes the decisions. I disagree with this idea. Historically what we see in Glasgow is the detached man, absent from the family and spending 'his money' on himself and his own interests – football, betting and drink. I call him 'the Lone Ranger'. A woman headed up the family not because she had the power but because her man wasn't physically or emotionally present. He wasn't interested. In contrast to the absent, uncaring father, Glasgow working-class mothers often sacrificed themselves for their children.

I am not suggesting that this picture was unique to Glasgow. What I've described here could be found in slum communities not just in the UK but internationally. My argument is that this gender hostility was a more pronounced part of Glasgow's culture as it flowed from particularly robust structural factors – male heavy industry and terrible, overcrowded living conditions for the mass of the working population. So what I describe in the book enveloped a greater percentage of the population than elsewhere. In Glasgow there was simply too much aggression, quarrels and anger and not enough love and gentleness. It was a culture driven by the behaviour and values of hard-drinking macho males which didn't value a home-centred life, or provide space for, softness, nurturing and femininity. There's little doubt that many Glasgow women suffered terribly at the hands of selfish, uncaring and often violent men.

These are the circumstances which can lead women to feel ill and depressed. But men suffered too. Research shows that a good marriage can have a very positive effect on men's physical and mental health. One study showed that when men with cardiovascular disease were asked 'Does your wife show you her love?', those who responded positively had half as many symptoms as those who said no. Women who had breast cancer and said they lacked affection in their lives were twice as likely to be dead in five years than those who were similarly afflicted but reported affection. Again it has been found that healthy women who say that their husbands despise them are much more likely to suffer ill health than those in loving marriages.

I cohabited for over twenty years so I don't have a moralistic view of marriage but, looking at the data, it's clear that being married has a very positive effect particularly on men's physical and mental health. In fact, it's more important than employment and income. So if we want to undesrtand why 'Shettleston Man', as he has been called, has an average life expectancy of 64, the lowest figure for Western Europe and worse than some third world countries – we need to look at marriage and relationships. Sadly the tale that emerges from *The Tears that Made the Clyde* is that the city has a long history of bitterness and alienation between the sexes and that this must contribute to the city's poor health. And I'm not alone in thinking that.

In 2014 a BBC World Service correspondent, Lucy Ash, made an *Assignment* programme entitled 'The Mystery of Glasgow's Health Problems'. She interviewed me and spoke to a variety of residents in some of the poorest areas of the city. In one pub in Bridgeton she asked a local man why he thought many of the men in his area were dying earlier than other places. 'Nine out of ten men don't love their wives so much. Men will die if they don't love anybody,' was his swift reply. He's right.

Publishing the book

As I neared the end of writing the book I began thinking about possible publishers. Fortunately, I decided to turn first to Argyll Publishing and emailed them one night with an outline of the book. Much to my surprise I received an immediate response from the owner, Derek Rodger, who wrote that what I described sounded like the book he was 'most keen to publish'.

Derek is not a typical publisher. He is the son of a Fife miner. After university he went into teaching and social work and in 1986 he started a magazine called *Scottish Child*. This encouraged his desire to enter publishing and he later moved to Glendaruel and started Argyll Publishing. Unlike many publishers who are primarily driven by commerce Derek was most keen to publish books which reflected his own commitment to understanding social issues and illustrating the need for change. My proposed book was completely in tune with his personal mission.

When I approached Derek I knew that I wanted to call the book and he was happy with this. The line 'it was tears that made the Clyde' came from Archie Fisher's song 'The Fairfield Crane'. He gracefully gave me permission to use it as the book's title. Derek and I were also agreed on the need for an arresting cover which did not play into the city's macho, hardman image. We wanted something which spoke of human vulnerability and need for tenderness. Fortunately, I was friendly with Gill Scott, a social policy lecturer. Her husband was the wonderful artist Michael Scott who had died all too young a few years before. Michael was a prolific figurative painter whose work was infused by mysticism and mythology. Gill generously gave me access to Mick's archive to see if there was a picture that we could use as a cover illustration. We chose a beautiful, and strangely evocative picture which worked well with the title and the book's contents. I'm eternally grateful to Gill and her two sons for allowing us to use 'Night Magic' for the book's cover. The book was finally published in 2010.

Reaction to *The Tears that Made the Clyde*

Professor Tom Devine contributed a supportive foreword to the book. He writes that I 'conclusively demonstrate' that conventional analysis will not help us understand why Glasgow is suffering more than other deindustrialised cities and accepts my contention that we must 'dig deeper and wider'. He then goes on to write that my approach is:

> . . . nothing less than a new model of interpretation. A central contention in the book is that the real answers to the key questions lie far back in time. The social problems under consideration have a long lineage and so historical analysis of the Glaswegian past, she suggests, is an essential approach to them.

> Using many of the results of the recent revolution in Scottish history writing, Dr. Craig provides a total picture of Glaswegian life over the centuries which includes discussion of economy, male culture, drinking habits, urban modes of life, middle class ideologies and much else. It is an exhilarating brew.

Tom Devine also commends me for simply diagnosing the cause of Glasgow's problems but also ending the book with some recommendations.

In his afterword Professor Phil Hanlon calls it 'an important book and a vital contribution to the debate about the causes of Glasgow's many health and social problems.' He particularly welcomes that I have broken out of the straitjacket of reductionism. However, he also predicts that my analysis may not be popular for two reasons. First because city leaders are intent on selling Glasgow as a success story and this book is underscoring the city's problems. Secondly, academics are wedded to their reductionist analysis, whatever that may be, and will resent my multifaceted approach.

The book attracted a number of favourable reviews and one which was excoriating and to which I'll return. Phil's prediction was accurate in the short term at least, that my book would not be welcomed universally by many leaders in the city. When I wrote *The Scots' Crisis of Confidence* I was asked to speak about the book at hundreds of events. Not so with this one. The book sold well but invitations to speak were limited. When I did talk about it, for example at a big session at the annual Glasgow book festival Aye Write!, it was clear that many readers appreciated the book. Many told me that it helped them understand and come to terms with difficult relationships with their fathers. But those running Glasgow organisations preferred not to discuss its contents. So, ten years after publication, it was great to be asked to speak at a couple of events run by psychologists and therapists who told me how much they valued *The Tears that Made the Clyde*.

That review

I have been in two minds about whether to write something about the review of *The Tears that Made the Clyde* in the Winter 2011 edition of *Scottish Affairs*, a quasi-academic journal. I've decided to express my view as it was so scurrilous that it even led to a news story in *The Times*. The headline, taken from the review itself, was 'pernicious mince'. Now it's reasonable to ask why a journal would include a seven-page review on a book that the reviewer thought, not to mince my words here, was crap. And it's quite clear that I was being tell't. Put in my place. Put back in my box. Like thousands of Scottish women before me I was being silenced. Or so they hoped.

The review's author was Sean Damer who has written a number of books about Glasgow and who sees himself as *the* expert on the history of Glasgow's working-class. Much of the review is a Marxist critique which I didn't care about, but it then descends into vitriol and attacks me personally for 'bad faith' as I'm allegedly trying to sell self-esteem to the poor people of Glasgow! So, it's quite clear Damer hadn't read the whole book before jumping on his high horse. From there he pats me on the head at one point for my analysis of women and this is something I've experienced before. In the past I was lauded and patronised by men for my feminist views but as soon as I entered their territory and expressed a different view from them, they either didn't want to listen or became unpleasant.

At the time the main problem I had with the review wasn't so much about the author as his reputation preceded him. Google Sean Damer and Symi, a Greek island he wrote about after living there for research purposes, and you'll see just how much he angered the residents. So much so they were threatening legal action. What really bothered me was that the editor of *Scottish Affairs*, a well-known Scottish academic and previous friend of mine, thought it an acceptable review for his journal. I wrote to him to complain and ask for an apology but all I got in return was an outline of the usual complaints procedure: I could write an article of the same length but Sean Damer would get the final word. In other words, there was no acceptance on his part that I had been wronged in anyway. However, he did publish a letter from Harry Reid, former editor of *The Herald* complaining about the review. (Reid had written a book on the Church of Scotland and was very enthusiastic about *The Scots' Crisis of Confidence*.)

I've subsequently been told by a couple of male academics that lots of their colleagues loved the review. After all, how dare I get all that publicity and support and express views that were different from the real experts? Some of these academics can talk a good game about the valuable tradition of Scottish generalism and the democratic intellect but they're keen to slap down those who do not play to the standard academic rules. Particularly women.

My board were very supportive of me after the review was published and helped to write a statement for our website. But the main support I received was from other women. Some got in touch to say how sexist they found the review and that the journal wouldn't have treated a man like that. I'm very grateful for the support I received from one woman in particular who is sadly, now deceased.

Tessa Ransford, a famous, visionary Scottish poet and the founder of the Scottish Poetry Library emailed to ask if we could meet for lunch. We had never met before but I was happy to meet up with such an interesting woman. What I didn't know, until we sat down at the table, was that Tessa was on a mercy mission. She wanted to tell me how much she liked my book, give me a copy of the malicious review, commiserate and tell me how she found out about it. This was all new to me as I didn't know about the review until that lunch.

Tessa's story was interesting, but chilling. She participated in a regular seminar in the politics department at Edinburgh University (where I had once worked). It was convened by the man who was at that time the book review editor for *Scottish Affairs*. During the discussion Tessa reached into her bag, brought out a copy of *The Tears* and said how much she loved it. As she did so the convenor started shouting 'get that out of here' as if the book was going to contaminate those present. But what Tessa found most challenging was that he hadn't even read it and wouldn't listen to anything positive she had to say about the book. Another woman being silenced.

At the time I thought the review, and Tessa's story, evidence of sexism. After all, academic research shows that readers judge written work more harshly if they know it has been written by a woman than they do if there's no name attached or it carries a male name. This is called 'implicit bias' and women can also be guilty of negative judgements about other women. Implicit bias against women can take many forms and is why women will often say that to be perceived as competent they have to be twice as good as men.

With the passage of time, I can see that Damer's review and its publication wasn't simply sexist. It was misogynist. And I say this because it used a common misogynist trope that there's something dirty and unclean about women. The article is full of allusions to contamination and my book, indeed my whole person, is portrayed as a dangerous vector to be avoided at all costs.

I recount this incident not to portray myself as a victim but as a survivor. Despite the odious review, and the attempt to silence me and put me in my place, I carried on. I wrote another three books, I organised events and published more books in our *Postcards* series. I wrote an influential article on independence and I'm now writing this book on the history of the Centre. I'm proud to say I didn't wheesht.

I know that many people who read *The Tears* get a lot out of it. It gives them a context for understanding their family's history. It gives them a better understanding of some of the problems they are having to deal with in Glasgow. I'm proud of the book and the fact that many who work in the city think it's essential reading.

CHAPTER 12

Enough is enough: challenging materialist values

A memorable workshop in Greenock;
Professor Tim Kasser's research on materialism;
background to *Postcards from Scotland;*
Professor Phil Hanlon and the first book in the series – *AfterNow;*
Centre events on materialism;
TEDx talk on materialism;
The Great Takeover;
the well-being challenge of consumer culture;
The True Cost film on fast fashion;
signs of hope;
why the Centre didn't take forward a campaign on materialism.

'YOU NEVER HAVE enough, you're never good enough and you never get there.' That's how many people responded in workshops when I asked why they thought there was a significant rise in depression in contemporary times. And one group's belief that consumerism was eroding their lives was so poignant I can never forget our discussion.

In 2013, Ian English, a lecturer at James Watt College in Greenock, asked to see me for a discussion. After he aired his concerns, we agreed that I would run a half-day workshop on materialism with some of his health and social care students – six men and four women. The men were aged late 20s to early 40s and in a previous era most would have worked in the shipyards lining the Clyde. Two of the women were in their 40s and the other two were late teens.

After a very short introduction at that workshop, I simply explained that researchers have found that the more people pursue materialist values in life, the worse their well-being. I gave them the common definition of materialism used by researchers: the pursuit of money and what it can buy, and a focus on appearance, image, status and popularity. I then asked them to form two groups, discuss why materialist values could undermine well-being and record their main discussion points on flip chart paper.

The students themselves decided to divide into groups of men and women. The men covered four or five sheets of paper in a very short space of time. Intuitively they knew how detrimental these values were to the quality of their lives. They didn't need to hear about research summarised by Professor Tim Kasser in his book *The High Price of Materialism* (2003), for the simple reason that they lived it. As they summarised their discussions one of the men even said 'welcome to our lives and it's crap'. They knew all about the inherent dissatisfaction of consumer culture, the envy it breeds and how it takes you away from the things that really contribute to life satisfaction such as relationships or doing things you find interesting or enjoyable. They thought that a life based on materialist values – their own lives – was shallow and depressing. It's no exaggeration to say that they despaired for themselves and particularly despaired for their children. If I had introduced Professor Bruce Alexander's term 'poverty of the spirit' I'm sure they would have agreed that this summed up their despair.

The men had a sense that life hadn't always been so materialistic – they could remember times when community was strong, when pride could be gained from skilled labour and institutions like the church, the labour movement and robust youth organisations inculcated healthier and more human values.

The women had a more divided response. The older women

largely echoed the male students, but the younger women struggled to grasp the issue. They thought the problem was that people couldn't afford the brands they coveted and suggested ways round this. As they did so the rest of the group sighed and shook their heads.

All the older students agreed that the issues we were focusing on were vitally important for them personally, yet they never discussed the topic with anyone. These weren't the concerns you raised with family members and you certainly didn't talk about them while at work or when socialising. Without my prompting, all the parents resolved to try and rear their children differently. A number of the men said they were going to buy a kitchen table for family meals. Most resolved to turn off the television more and take their children out more frequently for country walks or to participate in different activities.

I have no idea if anyone put their resolutions into practice, but I have never doubted the impact our discussion on materialism had on those students in Greenock. And I know it had a profound effect on me.

I first understood the toxic nature of consumerism in the 1980s when I ran assertiveness workshops with women and became acutely aware of how dissatisfied they were with their lives. They often attributed some of this to advertising and the media. Even before the advent of 24-hour television and social media, the content of women's magazines encouraged unhelpful social comparisons that had a negative impact on how their readers felt about themselves and their lives. As a result of these discussions, I've never bought another woman's magazine.

So it's easy to see why I would be attracted initially to Seligman's work and positive psychology more generally. These thinkers attempted to put money in its place and warned of the dangers of a 'hedonic treadmill' whereby we get used to new things in our lives and they stop having a positive effect. They also pointed out that meaning in life is eroded if we are too focused on individual wants and desires. And it was these ideas that materialist values were detrimental to well-being that came to the fore in the Centre's new book series.

Postcards from Scotland

I am a great believer in the power of books. What I've learned from books over the years has contributed enormously to how I see the world. And it was the publication of my first book *The Scots' Crisis of Confidence* which literally transformed my working life and led to the establishment of the Centre. So, it's hardly surprising that I was eager for the Centre to have its own book series. I approached Derek Rodger from Argyll Publishing and he was keen to partner us in this venture. We launched *Postcards from Scotland* and the first three books in March 2012.

We wanted the series to address some mounting problems we all faced. The Centre's publicity for the series reads:

> In the face of huge challenges such as climate change, resource depletion, financial melt-down, globalisation, falling living standards, rising inequality and mental health problems, it's becoming increasingly clear that Western societies will have to make huge changes. In short, we cannot go on in the same vein: we need to envision and enact a radically different future.
>
> This period in Western culture and Scottish political culture requires outlets for new ideas across a whole range of topics – environmental, social, organisational, political, cultural, psychological, economic and spiritual – as well as new frameworks and ways of conceptualising. *Postcards from Scotland* aims to help develop this new thinking in a readable and accessible format and publicise, to a much greater audience, some of the projects in Scotland which are already aiming to help bring about a new way of living.

We also believed that Scotland is well-placed in some respects to make a significant contribution to this new thinking: Scots played a major part in the eighteenth century Enlightenment and many of the factors which facilitated Scotland's leading role are still in place. Namely, we are a small, networked society with strong commitment to social improvement and where it's easy to have conversations across subjects and sectors.

One of the founding ideas of the series was that they would be slim books of between 25,000 and 30,000 words – hence the title. But we haven't been able to maintain this objective and some of the more recent books are weightier volumes.

The first book in the series was called *AfterNow* but before outlining its contents let me say something about its main author, Professor Phil Hanlon.

Phil Hanlon and his ideas

I was first introduced to Phil in 2003 and met him from time to time for various discussions. He became a board member of the Centre in 2006 and then took over as board Chair in 2014, a role he still holds at the time of writing. Phil is not your typical university professor. He is a captivating orator who rarely speaks from prepared notes and his forte is engaging his audience with spontaneous reflections and questions. When he was a full-time academic Phil cared about evidence but he was also clearly committed to large scale social and cultural change. Like many I consider Phil to be a visionary.

Phil's visionary strengths were much in evidence in the AfterNow website project he launched with his colleague Dr Sandra Carlisle at Glasgow University in March 2010. It contained six introductory videos, 30 short papers and a dozen 10-minute podcasts. The website was part funded by the Scottish Government's National Programme for Improving Mental Health and Well-being run by Geoff Huggins who was also supporting the Centre financially at this time. Some of the thinking behind AfterNow is summarised in Box 10 overleaf.

AfterNow: What's next for a healthy Scotland?

Given the radical perspective underlying the AfterNow project, and the focus on social change, it was appropriate that Phil Hanlon and his colleague Sandra Carlisle should write the first *Postcard from Scotland*. Their book focused on Scotland and demonstrated how severely affected the population is by addictions, obesity, loss of well-being and inequality. It suggested that Scotland had experienced one of the most intense periods of industrialisation in the world and that this had been followed by one of the most severe manifestations of deindustrialisation. The resultant economic and cultural forces gave Scotland a set of health challenges greater than any other comparable part of Europe.

At the core of the *AfterNow* book is a critique of Western culture. Hanlon and Carlisle write: '. . . the values of modernity – materialism, individualism, consumerism, scientism and economism – have a considerable hold on our society and our leaders.' And they add, 'Like the frog sitting in water slowly being heated to boiling point, we seem oblivious to the malign effect of this environment.'

As it is these values which have led to the 'dis-eases' of modernity if we want to address public health problems such as rising rates of depression and anxiety, addictions, obesity, health inequalities and the loss of well-being, then we have to think differently, adopt new values and move towards a radically different culture. After all, these values are not just damaging human lives but are having a potentially catastrophic environmental impact.

The authors argue that something more substantial than government policy is required to address these challenges and suggest that the great ecological and economic challenges of our age represent an opportunity to reframe our current assumptions and ethos. In other words, while these challenges are a threat, nonetheless they may also represent our best opportunity. Indeed, the crux of the book is the authors' probing question that if change is inevitable, if we are forced to change by larger forces, can we use this to create opportunities for improved health and well-being? After all, humanity itself now faces a series of linked external threats, derived from exponential growth in a number of key areas. Exponential growth cannot continue indefinitely in a finite system so these forces will lead to certain decline and possible collapse unless we change trajectory rapidly. The book concludes by asking 'who is showing the way?' and reports on innovative thinking about the future that is emerging in Scotland. They also express their hope that positive change is possible and cite various times in history when humans have risen to the challenge of large-scale change.

Box 10: The Thinking Behind *AfterNow*, outlined by Phil Hanlon

The Afternow project was based on the idea that the UK has seen several phases of public health improvement since the Industrial Revolution, each of which emerged from major shifts in thinking about the nature of society and health itself. We suggested that each phase of health improvement can be conceptualised, in metaphorical terms, as a 'wave'. The first wave is associated with Great Public Works and other developments arising from responses to the social disruptions which followed the industrial revolution. The second wave saw the emergence of medicine as science. The third wave involved the redesign of our social institutions during the twentieth century and gave birth to the Welfare State. The fourth wave has been dominated by efforts to combat disease risk factors and decrease the level of chronic diseases like heart disease, strokes and cancers. Although a trough of public health activity continues from each wave, none exerts the same impact as when it first emerged. We then turned to current and emerging public health challenges, in light of the above analysis. We focused on obesity, addictions, inequalities, and the loss of well-being and argued that these are not amenable to earlier or current strategies. However, the intractability of these public health challenges needed to be framed in the light of wider trends – in particular, exponential growth in a number of key human systems which, together with climate change, points to the imminence of inevitable and involuntary change. Our conclusion was that a 'fifth wave' of development was necessary, but will need to differ radically from its forerunners in order to have any chance of tackling such problems. Much of the work of the project was an exploration of small-scale examples of how a fifth wave might emerge.

I took the view in 2012 that the inevitability of change could be a catalyst to bring people together to collectively change the way we live. That is what was achieved in earlier waves of public health improvement. If the Victorians could re-engineer their society and a multiplicity of people create progressive institutions to confront the problems they faced, why could we not do the same?

I developed some of Phil and Sandra's critique of consumerism in the second book in the series but before outlining its argument I want to recount a number of events we held which were important, and motivational, for the Centre's work on materialism.

Centre events related to consumerism and materialism

As part of the Vanguard Programme in 2005 we recorded a webinar with Professor Barry Schwartz, an American psychologist whose 2004 book *The Paradox of Choice: Why more is less*, deservedly attracted a great deal of attention. The lecture proved so popular that we invited him to Glasgow and in May 2009 we held a half-day masterclass with him called **The Choices Worth Having**. Over 140 people, from various sectors, attended on the day. I know it had a large impact on many participants as years later some could still remember some of the stories he recounted.

Schwartz's basic premise, drawing on extensive empirical research, is that choice is paradoxical in that some choice is important to freedom, feelings of personal control and self-expression. But increasing choice for people does not necessarily mean that they experience more control or freedom: in fact, the opposite is often the case. The more choice we have the more we feel overwhelmed and the less able we are to feel fulfilled and satisfied.

Like many social scientists Schwartz is acutely aware that many people in the West now have a great deal of disposable income and previously unheard of opportunities, yet there is a huge rise in depression. What's more, the happiness levels for the majority have hardly shifted. He thinks that one of the reasons for this is that what brings people real happiness is spending time with close friends and family, yet so much of our psychic energy is wasted on consumer decisions which are intrinsically unsatisfying.

Schwartz advises that if we want to lead more satisfied and meaningful lives, we should stop trying to maximise our choices. In other words, stop trying to get the best job, the best hotel, the best meal, or the best phone as the pursuit of 'perfect' or 'the best' becomes unfulfilling and self-defeating. Instead, we should simply settle for 'good enough' and as much as possible opt out from consumerist culture.

Schwartz also argued at the event that while modern life overburdens people with choice in some areas, it deprives them of choice in other much more meaningful areas such as work. I'll explore this important idea in the chapter on organisations.

In October 2011 we ran a stimulating webinar with Professor Tim Kasser, whose book *The High Price of Materialism* is mentioned earlier in the chapter. Kasser's work was particularly important for materialism as he had undertaken considerable research into how the pursuit of materialist values and goals undermines both children's and adults' well-being. Again these ideas were so well-received by our audience that we resolved to do more on materialism. This resolve was boosted when we learned that Tim was going to be in Scotland two months later to speak at a 'Common Cause' event. As Tim had spoken at one of our events so recently we decided to have a slightly different focus and relate his ideas to Glasgow. So as Christmas shopping was in full swing, we held an event in the heart of the city called **Glasgow: well-being, materialism and the values of consumer capitalism** with Tim as the main speaker. I had explored how materialist values contribute to Glasgow's problems the previous year in *The Tears that Made the Clyde* but Tim's fresh perspective on the subject was particularly welcome.

This was a late afternoon event during a bout of very bad weather yet we had 110 registrations and 125 actual attendees. Some people came from the north of Scotland specifically for the event. One of the common complaints people voiced was how Glasgow Council had marketed the city since 2005. 'Glasgow – Scotland with style' was the favoured slogan. Most of those present thought it a travesty that a city once renowned for making things of real quality should now be promoted on the basis of shallow consumerist values which sowed division and competition.

Phil Hanlon and I were critical of the slogan both in our books and when we spoke at events and I hope that our opposition contributed to the Council's decision to drop the slogan in 2013 and replace it with the much friendlier 'People Make Glasgow'.

In February 2012 we then ran an event in Glasgow called **Well-being and Body Confidence** with Jo Swinson MP, who at that time was chair of the all-party parliamentary group on well-being at Westminster. Jo set out her support for national well-being indicators as this helped politicians to move us away from an obsession with economic growth and to concentrate their minds on things that mattered much more to human well-being. She then spoke about why she helped set up the Body Confidence Campaign, and why manipulating media images is a political issue worthy of politicians' attention.

The following month the Centre held an event jointly with Glasgow's Aye Write! book festival. It was called **Watching, Wanting and Well-being** and the main speaker was Agnes Nairn, a marketing professor and author of a recent book on children and consumerism. Many parents were part of the 120 strong audience. The event was very popular and sold out several days before.

We asked Professor Nairn to speak about recent UNICEF research on materialism and inequality which she had undertaken. The research compared young people in the UK with those in Spain and Sweden and showed that UK parents were particularly materialistic in comparison with their Swedish and Spanish counterparts. Given that materialist values undermine well-being, this may help explain why UK youngsters had, at that time, according to a UNICEF survey, the worst well-being in 20 rich OECD countries.

TEDx

A few weeks later in April 2012 I was invited to give the opening talk at the first TEDx event in Glasgow. As their overarching theme was Enlightenment 2.0 I thought it appropriate to call my talk 'Enlightenment in the Age of Materialism' and to begin by talking about the work of eighteenth century Scottish philosopher and economist, Adam Smith.

Commonly people see a discrepancy in Smith's work between the ethics and emphasis on sympathy in *The Theory of Moral*

Sentiments (1812) and the free market ideology of *The Wealth of Nations* (1811). In reality there is less division than is often thought and there is at least one major thread running through both books – Smith's concern for the poor. Even in *The Wealth of Nations* he shows he cares passionately for the plight of the poor – arguing that they had most to gain from wealth creation. His concern was not simply that people should have their basic needs met but that they were able to live 'without shame'. One of the examples he gave is of a day labourer owning a 'linen shirt' so that he could appear in public without feeling 'ashamed'.

For all that Smith was in favour of wealth creation he was actually very judgemental in *The Wealth of Nations* about how people spend money – disparaging the rich who squandered their fortune on 'frivolous objects: ornaments of dress, trinkets, jewels, gew-gaws.' And he saw this use of money as indicating 'not only a trifling but a base and selfish disposition'.

In my talk I also pointed out that the eighteenth century Enlightenment project was to shine the light of reason into dark places and root out what these scholars saw as the problems of their day – religious fanaticism, superstition and irrationality. I then asserted that in the twenty first century we need to embark on a similar project of enlightenment and that our darkest, murkiest place is the way in which base materialist values have come to saturate our culture. These values are leading to gross inequality; extreme individualism and narcissism; a raft of social problems; overuse of resources and environmental degradation; and a loss of well-being.

However, this does not mean that it has to be like this. Most of us have a strong sense that there is something profoundly wrong with our current value system, but we currently lack encouragement to express our concern, clear leadership on a broad-based anti-materialist agenda, and empowering information to help us realise what is going on.

I was the first speaker of the day and slightly nervous, which was unusual for me, and I don't consider it one of my best talks. Nonetheless by 2022 it had attracted over 37,000 hits which I am happy enough with, though that's a modest number of views in comparison with the millions of views for many of the main TED speakers. There's little doubt that the talk introduced our ideas to a wider audience. A couple of weeks later, as a result of my TEDx talk, there was a two and a half page spread in the *Sunday Herald* newspaper called 'How We Sold Our Souls' about the Centre's approach to materialism.

The Great Takeover: How materialism, the media and markets now dominate our lives

As the Centre was so concerned about how materialist values could undermine well-being it was appropriate that we devoted the second book in our new series to this theme but, as the subtitle suggests, the book's focus is much wider than subjective well-being.

In the first chapter of the book, 'Counting the Costs' I summarise TIm Kasser's research and the content of his Centre talks in 2011. I also set out, and use, his definition of materialist values and goals pointing out that what these values have in common is a preoccupation with how you are seen through the eyes of other people. In other words, these values are 'extrinsic' rather than 'intrinsic' and this is in part why they are so unsatisfying and can stunt our personal development.

In that first chapter I also make clear that as human beings are social creatures who inhabit a material world some degree of materialism is not only natural but necessary. Materialism only becomes a problem when it is grossly overdone and distracts people from what really matters in life for well-being – relationships, meaning, purpose, community, nature, challenge, learning for its own sake, exercise and other factors.

In subsequent chapters I look at why we feel compelled to buy and the mass psychology underlying consumer capitalism. I particularly enjoyed reading some of the classic texts on consumerism and was very interested, if depressed, by books such as *The Rebel Sell* (2004) in which the authors argue that the hippy, counterculture values of the 1970s invigorated, rather than challenged, American capitalism.

In some of these early chapters I also focus on how the media have contributed to the societal switch from the collective values of my parents' generation to the individual focus of 'Generation Me', described by Jean Twenge and outlined in Chapter 3. A move which has been toxic for young people's mental health, particularly in Anglo-American societies heavily influenced by American media.

Advertising is obviously a main conduit of materialist values, as is TV and print media which routinely communicate the values of celebrity culture. But outwith these obvious communication channels we can detect the rise and virtual hegemony of materialist values in all walks of life.

This is obvious in business. The collapse of the gold standard in 1971 and the subsequent increase in footloose capital meant that many businesses became driven solely by profit. Investors – frequently foreign – increasingly wanted short-term results and they were largely indifferent to what the organisation was about. Money, and shareholder value, not the product, the employees or the wider community, now became all that mattered in many businesses.

The rise of businesses completely dominated by the profit motive was boosted in the early 1980s with the rise of 'market triumphalism': politicians now believed that it was the market, rather than political decisions, which held the key to a better society. But, as the gifted philosopher Michael Sandel argues, market philosophy is not bounded by notions of right and wrong so embracing it with gusto leads to significant political problems as it drains 'public discourse of moral and civic energy' and ultimately undermines democracy.

Business methods and ideology also dominate the internal workings of government. Even the right-wing columnist, Charles Moore, objects writing: 'Government now affects a business style. At meetings which are not, and should not be, commercial, modern Civil Service language insists on what is "the business case" for a particular course of action.'

The personalisation and choice agenda, which were at the heart of Labour Government policies under Tony Blair, also borrowed from American marketing. But, as we know from Professor Barry Schwartz, choice can be a double-edged sword burdening people with decision-making for which they are not equipped. What people want is access to quality services and everyone should be entitled to this, not just the privileged few who know how to get the best out of the system.

What all these examples have in common is that what primarily matters in today's world is money and questions of intrinsic values, fairness, equality or morality have become almost irrelevant.

Sadly, the predominance of materialist values is far wider than the operation of business, or public sector institutions. Sport, particularly football, has been a casualty of rising materialism and commercialisation. Many football clubs are now the playthings of millionaire businessmen; top footballers are celebrities who can negotiate multi-million pound contracts; and money regularly trumps principle, decency or fairness.

Large charities are also enthralled by money-making and copying business. In 2010 a number of large UK charities including WWF, Oxfam and Friends of the Earth published a report based on a lengthy piece of research and consultancy called 'Common Cause'. Tim Kasser was one of the main advisers. The report uses the term 'extrinsic' rather than materialist but it is essentially the same issue I've been outlining here.

The report is important as it is an open acknowledgement from this sector that the problems they address (world poverty and environmental challenges) are driven by self-centred materialist values – money, appearance and status. These big charities admit that there will not be sizeable inroads into these problems unless people undergo a values shift and become less focused on themselves and more concerned with what they call 'bigger-than-self' problems.

What's encouraging about the Common Cause report is the frank admission that currently these big charities are doing little, if anything, to bring about this value shift. The reason is simple: in their communications and campaigns they use techniques devised by business, advertising and the media – one of the main drivers of the problems they are trying to address. In other words, as these big charities engage with the public for their good causes, they have mainly reinforced materialist values rather than actively try to supplant them or encourage other ideas. For example, large charity dinners often display the values of celebrity culture in the encouragement of over-the-top dressing, the rich displaying their wealth in conspicuous bidding at auctions, and the word 'luxury' appearing on most raffle prizes.

What I'm arguing may seem impractical and 'hair shirt' but human beings are moral creatures. As Barry Schwartz argues: 'nothing motivates people to do the right thing other than the desire to do the right thing'. So when charities use instrumental, self-serving or narcissistic reasons in their advertising and fund-raising they are distracting people from these wider philanthropic goals.

And what about the contribution made by the personal development or New Age movement? Undoubtedly some of this focuses on matters relevant to what we've covered here – namely how people can live satisfying lives which 'do not cost the earth'. Some books or practices on eastern religious and spiritual beliefs, or offshoots such as mindfulness, encourage people to find satisfaction within and live in harmony with others and the environment. But much of the personal development world is obsessed with individual success and making money.

Finally, what about the churches? In the UK, but emphatically not the USA, churches contain staunch critics of materialism. The former Archbishop of Canterbury Rowan Williams, for example, has been an outspoken critic of the present economic system and materialism. The General Assembly of the Church of Scotland famously took Mrs Thatcher to task for her speech praising the free market, often referred to as 'the sermon on the Mound'. I know from my talks that people involved in many churches in Scotland are sympathetic to the arguments advanced in my book but, up till now, they have not been very vocal on the topic and have limited influence anyway.

Tim Kasser's academic work is particularly good on the damage materialist values wreak on individuals' well-being but, following on from Common Cause, I took this further and looked at the damage to collective, or societal, well-being. The UK, like the USA, is particularly scarred by inequality and the widespread social problems it engenders. Inequality was boosted enormously in the UK as a result of the economic policies introduced by the 1979 Thatcher Government. Top executives, both in the private and public sectors, received huge salary increases and large bonuses, often irrespective of performance. In 2011 the High Pay report pointed out: 'Over the last thirty years we have lost touch with what fair pay is. Indeed it has been undermined by a process that simplified individual motivation to that of self-interest.' It's true that financial incentives are needed when people are carrying out physical or mundane factory work, but countless psychological studies show that for jobs involving intellectual skills it is job satisfaction, recognition, opportunities for advancement and doing something meaningful which are much more motivating than money.

As we have lost a sense of justice and fairness it's hardly surprising that many workers have lost out financially. Many of those classed as 'living in poverty' are in work and the government has to help out low paid workers by giving them some financial support – support that wouldn't be needed if there was fair pay and which is effectively a subsidy to employers who aren't paying their workers properly. What's more, low pay in an aspirational consumer society like ours, inevitably means a burgeoning of personal debt as this is the only way many people can get access to the products they want.

Writing the book in 2010 I was acutely aware of how the 2008 crash happened in part because financial gain became much more important than integrity, justice, or fairness: the collapse of the financial sector was linked to the extensive use of debt as a way to compensate for low wages; the highly questionable, if not immoral, lending of money to people who were unlikely to be able to repay (e.g. sub-prime mortgages); and a deliberate masking and then passing on of bad debt to other institutions.

I end this section of the book by raising environmental problems and linking these to the materialism of our age and our politicians' fixation with economic growth.

The True Cost

In 2016 we produced a second edition of the book as our first print run had sold out. I was keen to add an afterword as a result of an experience a year earlier. Glasgow's Merchant City Festival showed a full- length documentary on the fashion industry called 'The True Cost' and I was asked to be part of the panel. It's one of the most shocking, troubling films I've ever seen. Westerners pay a high price for their pursuit of materialist values but the real cost is borne by the one in six workers worldwide who are engaged in the clothing industry and feeding the West's lust for unsustainable fashion.

As was evident at this showing the film elicits strong emotions in viewers – anger, disgust and moral outrage – as well as an almost overwhelming sense of sympathy and compassion for the victims of 'fast fashion'. We might think our desire for consumer goods, mainly clothes, is good for third world countries as it provides them with much needed jobs but in reality most of these workers are not paid a living wage. The film also showed that sometimes these poor garment workers are locked into the factory and forced to work through the night to fulfil pressing orders. If they make mistakes, understandable given their exhaustion and the pressure on them, they are physically and/or verbally abused by management.

As well as these types of tragedies, toxins and environmental contamination cause another range of problems. In some areas significant numbers of children are born with birth defects as a result of the toxins used in various manufacturing processes, particularly in the production of leather.

As so few people attended that afternoon showing in Glasgow, I resolved to run a larger scale Centre event where we would **screen *The True Cost* movie** and then hold a discussion. Over 120 people attended this screening which took place on a very cold evening at the end of January 2016 in Websters Theatre. The audience's response to the film was both angry and emotional and we had a very lively discussion facilitated by Phil Hanlon.

One of the things many in the audience agreed on was that we need to satisfy our understandable human desire to look good in a way that does not damage the environment and destroy the health and well-being of people in poor countries. We heard that one of the ways to do this is to heed the messages from the 'Love Your Clothes' campaign which encourages consumers to pay more attention to where their clothes are made and who has made them. Rather than taking them for granted we should love, cherish and mend our clothes and appreciate the labour that has gone into making them.

This was such a satisfying and useful event that the board discussed whether we should run other events or publish a *Postcards* book on the theme. Eventually we decided that we didn't have any specialist knowledge or understanding to make this viable and that other groups were much better placed to focus on the topic.

Hope

In the first edition I end the book with a chapter called 'Hope'. In it I outline lots of research which shows how disillusioned people in Anglo-American countries are with consumerism and the dominance of materialist values and how they hanker after something different.

For example, in 2009 a firm of 'consumer anthropologists' conducted quantitative research in the USA with a small, representative sample of citizens. It shows that 78 per cent of their respondents thought that the American dream, as expressed through the pursuit of material possessions, had 'died' and now needed to be pursued through 'freedom and ideals'. Over 80 per cent were spending less, often through necessity but also choice.

Following the May 2010 election in the UK an American pollster and political strategist, Stanley Greenberg, conducted a post-election poll of a cross-section of voters. It showed that neither of the main parties' agendas convinced voters. Greenberg said of their findings: 'People were looking for a vision, a direction for the country and a new set of values. They were looking for strategies for Britain to be successful and new definitions of the word success and they didn't see any of it.'

The Australian academic Professor Clive Hamilton has conducted research on downshifting and found that in the UK over 30 per cent of respondents had taken action to spend more time with their family or gain more life satisfaction even though it cost them money. Interestingly this was true across the social classes. This trend has been confirmed by other studies in the UK and research in the USA and Australia. As Clive Hamilton points out, 'The emergence of a large class of downshifters in Britain challenges the main political parties to question their most fundamental assumptions about what makes for a better society.' Indeed these downshifters have made these changes despite the pressures within the system: they did so without any encouragement from politicians or the mainstream media.

I end the book by listing eleven steps individuals can take to protect themselves and their families from the negative effects of materialist values. I include in this list a number of suggestions for discussing the topic with other people and taking social action.

Next steps for the Centre

As is clear from this chapter, for the best part of a decade, the Centre did a lot to alert people to the dangers of materialist values both for themselves and their society. By the time we published *The Great Takeover* in 2012 many people who attended Centre events or heard me speak at meetings were expressing a passionate interest in the topic. Indeed many of those who attended the 'Body Confidence' event in February 2012 expressed an interest in joining a movement to try and counter materialist values.

At board meetings we regularly discussed whether we should try to set up a campaign to help channel and build on this mounting interest. But we never did. It's easy for me to claim that lack of staff and an obvious source of funding provide the reason. The truth is we could not do everythng.

But in May 2014 we did hold an evening discussion event in Babbity Bowsters in Glasgow's Merchant City called **Talking about our generation: Baby booming 2.0**. I have not yet reported that the Centre's clientele was mainly drawn from the generation born between 1946 and 1964. Indeed a few of our speakers commented on how the Centre attracted 'an older age group' and they found this unusual. This clientele also reflected the Centre's management. I was born in 1951 and was in my early 50s when I set up the Centre. The board was also drawn from the Baby Boomers' generation and so too were most of our associates and *Postcards* authors. At the discussion event, those present were aware that while our generation had copious advantages and personal freedom when we were young, our legacy was not beneficial. They knew that the me-centred values which developed in our youth has had a very negative effect on our society. They particularly lamented the loss of values such as integrity in public life and the rise of inequality.

As I reviewed the material in this chapter in 2024, I thought about those care students from Greenock. When I spoke to them eleven years ago they were most concerned about the negative, materialistic values they were passing on to their children. But sadly, in today's world, such concerns may be a luxury. The cost-of-living crisis which started in 2021, coupled with a large rise in child poverty, means that what's now foremost in many parents' minds is not values but paying for basic essentials such as food and heating. These money worries must mean that ordinary people are less receptive to the idea that materialist values undermine their family's well-being. Nonetheless the relevance of this message hasn't gone away. It's an obsession with money, fame and success which drives our competitive culture, fuelling inequality and undermining political and organisational integrity. There's little doubt that a society in which the rich get richer while a growing number of people can't meet their basic needs has something seriously wrong with its values.

CHAPTER 13

Organisational performance and well-being at work

Standardisation and targets in modern workplaces;
Centre event with John Seddon on how targets and bureaucracy undermine efficiency, morale and staff well-being;
the Unreasonable Learners' network;
other perspectives the Centre promoted to improve organisations;
publication of *Letting Go: Breathing new life into organisations*;
the self-interest fallacy;
publication of *Conviction* by John Carnochan on the Violence Reduction Unit;
the scale of the challenge and how the VRU achieved its success;
a new era for *Postcards from Scotland*.

AT HIS MASTERCLASS for the Centre in May 2009, Professor Barry Schwartz told a memorable story which could serve as a parable for our time.

An academic took his seven-year-old son to a baseball game. The boy wanted lemonade so the father went to a kiosk. They had sold out and only had 'Mike's hard lemonade'. The father didn't realise this contained alcohol (7 per cent) and took it back to his son. A security guard noted what the boy was drinking and called the police. Before assessing the incident the police called an ambulance and as soon as it arrived the boy was taken off to hospital.

The doctors pronounced the boy fit and well and said he only had a negligible amount of alcohol in his blood. They were happy to discharge him into the care of his father. But the police and the welfare workers would not agree. The boy was placed in foster care for a few days and then a judge pronounced that he was only able to go home if his father was banned from the family home and lived elsewhere until the case was examined further. It was a full month before this decision was overturned and the father was allowed to see his son and return home.

Schwartz recounted how the judge, the police and the ambulance driver all said the same thing: 'We hate to do this, but we have to follow procedure.' Gone are the days when professionals are allowed to use their common sense or experience. They must follow rules and obey protocols even when to do so is nonsensical.

And these types of incidents are happening here in contemporary Scotland. I know of one recent case where a woman slapped her abusive husband back after he hit her. The husband called the police and said he had been attacked. The police then excluded the woman from the house and she had to live elsewhere, without access to her home, for several weeks. The police were apologetic as they knew exactly what had happened but they had no discretion and had to follow protocol and treat the abusive husband as the victim.

Schwartz's interest in this type of case flows from his research into choice. He thinks it ironic that we are now bombarded by consumer choices which undermine us as individuals yet we are deprived of choice in many workplaces where the expectation is simply to follow centrally derived protocols and rules. This is why he called his masterclass 'The choices worth having'.

It is not just rules and standardised practices which now regulate so much of public sector life in the UK and beyond. Targets are another aspect of this centralised control. Central government departments, often under pressure from a small côterie of advisers, senior politicians and civil servants, issue targets and edicts on how services should be delivered. This is often presented as efficient government but it's anything but. Centralised control leads to a huge bureaucracy of planners, checkers, inspectors, and reporters. It also demoralises staff who often end up doing things which they know instinctively are wrong but have little say in how or what should be done. Rigid targets – in Accident & Emergency departments, for example – easily end up undermining, not improving, patient safety or care.

As the well-being agenda rose to the fore in public sector organisations it also became commonplace for staff to be given 'well-being targets'. As far as the Centre is concerned this is a contradiction in terms: target-driven work cultures undermine staff well-being.

As I had worked with teams prior to setting up the Centre, I inevitably had an interest in issues related to organisational performance but I was aided considerably in this by Zoe Van Zwanenberg. Zoe had worked in a large number of public sector organisations and set up and ran the Scottish Leadership Foundation (SLF). She joined the Centre's board in 2005 but came off the board to become the Centre's Project Co-ordinator three years later.

Zoe was very knowledgeable on different approaches to leadership and at that time was particularly taken by the work of John Seddon, an occupational psychologist, writer and organisational consultant. In 2008 he published an influential book called *Systems Thinking in the Public Sector.*

At that point the Centre's financial settlement from the Scottish Government asked us to contribute to an independent perspective on cultural changes required to underpin their 'overarching economic strategy'. We thought that John Seddon's work most relevant to this. What's more, Jim Mather who was at that time Minister for Enterprise, Energy and Tourism was a fan of Seddon's work.

So on 12th May 2009 we held a half day masterclass with Professor John Seddon entitled **Beyond targets – improving efficiency, morale and staff well-being in the public sector**. Zoe chaired the event which we held in Òran Mór, Glasgow. It attracted 150 participants from a wide variety of public sector organisations and businesses including manufacturing.

In his forceful presentation John Seddon argued that many of the assumptions underpinning modern management practices such as the efficacy of targets, specifications, financial incentives, inspection, and shared back-office functions do not result in enhanced services. Indeed he argued that this type of command and control management is wasteful and time-consuming and leads paradoxically to reduced efficiency and service. At the event he stated:

> Targets always make performance worse. Any arbitrary measure in a system will suboptimise the system. . . When you derive the measures from the purpose of the service from a customer's point of view and put them in the hands of the people who do the work and give those people the means to understand and improve the work you get a level of performance you never would have dreamed of setting as a target. . . There is a systemic relationship between purpose, measures and method. . . If you impose arbitrary measures into a system you create a *de facto* purpose – make the target. That is how we've destroyed the public sector.

This approach to management also lowers staff morale and motivation. Seddon argued convincingly that it was because organisations demoralise staff through their use of illogical and inefficient work practices that they then have to spend so much time and money trying to boost staff motivation, positivity and creativity.

The Department for Enterprise, Energy and Tourism gave us some financial support to run the masterclass with John Seddon as did Glasgow Housing Association. Its Chief Executive, Taroub Zahran, spoke at the event to explain how they were using Seddon's ideas to improve services to tenants. Jim Mather MSP and Minister for Enterprise, Energy and Tourism was the final speaker, outlining what he saw as the benefits to Scotland if Scottish organisations embraced Seddon's approach.

Unreasonable Learners' network

As a result of running the Seddon event we got to know a number of people who were involved in a new network committed to advancing the Seddon type of thinking in organisations. Jim Mather encouraged Gordon Hall, who led the Deming Network, to contact various organisations and interested individuals in Scotland to see if they would be interested in attending a meeting to talk about collaborating on 'new thinking'. The Centre offered to host the meeting at our office and over 20 attended the day-long meeting on 28th June 2010. Some were senior managers from a range of small but influential organisations such as the Scottish Council Development and Industry and the Social Enterprise Academy. A range of academics and consultants also attended. Jim Mather facilitated some of the meeting which was initially chaired by Professor John Carlisle from Sheffield University. As is often the case at this type of event, there was a lot of discussion but few tangible outcomes other than a desire for further discussions under the banner of 'Unreasonable Learners'. Two larger meetings of the network followed, both organised by the Centre. And we did this despite our belief that the name of the new network would discourage participation.

Other Phase 2 Centre offerings on organisations

At the Centre we were supportive of the type of systems thinking approach promoted by John Seddon and the Unreasonable Learners' network but we were also aware this wasn't going to appeal to lots of managers or organisations. We still thought that there was a role for some of the ideas we had already been promoting, such as Professor Carol Dweck's 'mindsets' and in 2009, while in Phase 2, we were still collaborating with her researchers in Stanford University on a Brainology project in schools. These actions were completely in tune with the integral approach we favoured, i.e. encouraging respect for a variety of different ideas and philosophies.

During my time as a trainer/consultant I was aware that there was a major barrier to giving and receiving good feedback in

Scottish organisations and that this was critical to improving performance. On 16th September 2010 myself and two Centre associates, Isobel MacNaughtan and Derek Goldman, collaborated to put on an interactive training session which we called **Creating a Feedback and Learning Culture**. The event proved very popular and quickly attracted 50 participants, the maximum number we could accommodate. As was the case with most Centre events they came from across sectors – education, health, business, skills development bodies etc. Isobel, Derek and I pooled our collective insights and experience of working with Dweck's theory of mindset, as well as assertiveness training, coaching and various personal development techniques to provide participants with some of the skills required to give good feedback and create what was then termed a 'learning culture'.

This was the first time that we had worked together as facilitators with this material and we ultimately felt that we could have structured the day better. Nonetheless we had various people telling us that the event had a major impact on them. For example, Joan Johnson, Deputy Chief Executive of Health in Mind, who participated in the event emailed to tell us: 'I have worked in social work and social care for over 30 years and this one day in Glasgow with you stands out with a handful of other days as having been one of the great door opening learning experiences of my life.' Susan McAvoy, a lecturer at Dundee College also wrote to say: 'The whole feedback culture day is continuing to have an impact. There was a lot on the day and it takes time for that to be processed. I am finding it incredibly useful and only realise now how radical it was actually.'

On reflection I am disappointed that the Centre didn't offer more of these training sessions as they could have been enormously helpful for potential participants. However, it was difficult for me, or the Centre more widely, to keep focused on one topic given our enormous agenda. Besides I had plenty of opportunities to talk about these ideas with lots of different groups. For example, in October 2010 I was asked to run a 'masterclass session' primarily on mindsets with the Scottish Institute of Business Leaders. I also gave a talk on mindset to over a hundred 'learning coordinators' with the PCS Union that same year.

Letting Go: Breathing new life into organisations

With the launch of *Postcards from Scotland* in 2012, and our initial involvement with the Unreasonable Learners network, we were very keen to publish a book on organisations and how they could be improved. I approached Gordon Hall, who had set up the network and one of its main thinkers, Tony Miller, to see if they would be interested in contributing a book to the series. Gordon was CEO of the Deming Network, a group dedicated to learning about the ideas of William Edwards Deming, a statistician and business consultant widely credited with Japan's recovery after World War II. Deming was the founder of 'total quality management' which was instrumental in the creation of the just-in-time production system used by Toyota. At that time Tony Miller was an electrical engineer who lectured on engineering as well the science of management at Robert Gordon University in Aberdeen. He also lectured on Deming.

Twenty or thirty years ago a common assumption was that hierarchy at work was becoming less important and employees were becoming better placed to direct their own activities. But just as the promised 'leisured society' never materialised, freedom from command and control at work hasn't either. If anything, in some areas of employment, control has increased. This isn't about power hungry bosses but the style of management they now routinely use – a style based on performance management techniques, particularly targets.

Performance management practices have a large impact at work both on how organisations go about their business and employees' well-being yet there is little discussion of the issues or questioning of how we got here. And this is precisely what the fourth book in the series, *Letting Go,* aimed to do.

Unfortunately, shortly after I commissioned both Gordon Hall and Tony Miller to write the book, Gordon suffered a serious stroke. Tony continued with the assignment himself, content that he could do justice to Gordon's views and that Gordon had given him his whole-hearted support for this course of action.

In the introduction to the book Tony Miller sets out what he sees as the central challenge for managers: how they 'can manage people without destroying their natural motivation for doing a good job.' Miller argues that at present both private and public sector organisations are bureaucratic pyramids and that managers are obsessed by an analytical, numbers-based approach. This management style fails to treat employees as human beings and inevitably leads to alienation and dehumanisation. What's more, it means that a small group of people far removed from day-to-day operations make all, or most, of the decisions. This then leads to poor performance and dissatisfaction for those receiving services or buying products.

In what I regard as the most important chapter in the book, Miller argues that a central plank of management thinking flows from the pervasive belief in economics that people are essentially self-interested. He also shows that this belief can be traced back to a partial, and somewhat distorted, reading of Adam Smith, as this Scottish Enlightenment thinker also argued that sympathy for our fellow creatures is central to human nature.

The idea that humans are essentially selfish and self-motivated was given a boost in the 1980s when Thatcher and Reagan were in power and pursued policies to promote private, rather than, national wealth. One of the main exponents of self-interest was the influential American philosopher and novelist Ayn Rand. One survey in the 1990s found that her novel *Atlas Shrugged* (1992) was the most influential book in the USA, after the Bible. Rand believed passionately not just that people were self-interested but also that they should be.

Another American who promoted the idea that people are selfish was the Nobel-prize winning economist Professor James Buchanan. His 'Public Choice Theory' maintains that voters, politicians and bureaucrats do not, as they claim, act in the public interest as they are primarily focused on furthering their own interests. Ideas like these were influential in the public sector reforms initiated in the UK by the Thatcher Government.

This prevalent economic belief in human self-interest has enormous consequences for organisations. If everyone is self-interested then how can managers trust their staff? And this lack of trust inevitably means that managers must not only continually direct and monitor employees but also motivate them via bonuses and incentives.

It is important to point out that this belief in pervasive self-interest flies in the face of copious psychological research on human beings which shows that we are intrinsically motivated and want to do a good job. Indeed, there is considerable research which shows that unless people are engaged in manual or repetitive tasks, such as on an assembly line, incentives often demotivate by undermining employees' intrinsic motivation.

The Centre launched *Letting Go* in Glasgow's Trades Hall on 2nd December 2013. Around 150 people attended. Jean Urquhart MSP, who owned the Ceilidh Place, a celebrated small hotel and events venue in Ullapool, chaired the event. Jean is listed in the first series of *Postcards* books as part of the advisory committee. This was informal and consisted of me having frequent, individual discussions with Jean and the two other advisors (Fred Shedden and Phil Hanlon) about possible titles. So it seemed appropriate for Jean to have a role at one of our events. Tony Miller spoke, as did Stephen Boyd who was at that time Assistant Secretary at the STUC. He outlined a disturbing report they had just published, 'Performance Management and the New Workplace Tyranny' which fitted well with the arguments presented in *Letting Go*.

Conviction

Two years later, in 2015, we published one of the most successful and popular books in the *Postcards* series – *Conviction: Violence, culture and a shared public service agenda* by John Carnochan. John had been the first head of the Violence Reduction Unit run by Strathclyde Police and later Police Scotland but was now retired and had the time to write a book. I am including this book here, in the chapter on organisations rather than alongside work on social problems, for one simple reason: it illustrates perfectly what can be achieved when employees are able to initiate meaningful actions and are freed up from direct control from the top.

In some respects, *Conviction* is John Carnochan's story. It starts when he is a Detective Superintendent working in the CID in Lanarkshire. Prior to this he had twenty-seven years' experience working in areas of Glasgow with high levels of violence. At that time Glasgow had the highest rate of murder in Europe per head of population and murder committed with a knife was three and a half times higher than the rate for England and Wales. Most of these murders were the result of feuding gangs. The violence was largely 'recreational' – it was what they did. Rather than questioning why this was the case, John, his colleagues and local residents accepted that this was a fact of life.

But this complacency was about to change thanks to the visionary leadership of Sir Willie Rae, the Chief Constable. In 2004 he appointed John head of the new Violence Reduction Unit (VRU). John describes Willie Rae as 'a very thoughtful, inclusive and modest man who actively encouraged innovation and collaboration. He was not a "command and control" style of leader. He believed in "command and convince".'

With the slogan 'violence is preventable – not inevitable' John and his deputy Karyn McCluskey set about finding allies and looking for ideas on how they could stop the violence. The book sets out clearly how they went about that mammoth task.

Their approach was innovative not only because it stressed the importance of prevention but also because they saw partnership as a key part of their strategy. Potential partners were those 'working in education, social work, prisons, courts, health and other organisations or individuals with a genuine interest in reducing violence'.

John and Karyn came into the Centre on various occasions for discussions with myself and Phil Hanlon. They were particularly taken by Phil's emphasis on culture and health and his analysis of 'the Scottish effect'. They both attended the Centre's Vanguard Programme in 2005. I'm glad to confirm that this exposure to positive psychology did not encourage them to minimise Glasgow's, and indeed Scotland's, problem with violence.

I suspect that the VRU would have achieved little if those involved had tried to cover up the extent of the problem they were grappling with. John and Karyn repeatedly told people not only that Scotland's violence figures were much worse than comparable countries, but also that the data underestimated the country's problem given the scale of under-reporting. And this brutal honesty helped to galvanise potential partners into action.

But this is not to say that John and Karyn were relentlessly negative. They weren't. They were always full of optimism and hope that things could get better: that lives could be saved. They inspired people to work together, to change their work practices. This was a difficult task. Indeed John reports that the VRU team regularly quoted from Machiavelli's *The Prince* (1532):

> There is nothing more difficult to carry out, nor more doubtful of success, nor more dangerous to conduct than to initiate a new order of things. For the reformer has enemies in all who profit by the old order and only lukewarm defenders in all those who profit by the new order.

Thanks to the VRU the Scottish murder rate halved in the following decade. During this period violence fell in most Western countries but the Scottish figures were much more dramatic and mainly as a result of the VRU's activities.

The reduction in the Scottish violence figures attracted considerable media attention throughout the UK. Newspapers regularly profile the VRU and the inspirational figures who are integral to the story. John and Karyn McLuskey, who led the Unit once he retired, are much in demand as presenters at conferences – not just in Scotland but internationally – as there is so much interest in their success story.

Conviction takes us into new territory. In many places *Conviction* reads like a voyage of discovery. It describes in detail how the VRU worked and the ideas and theories which influenced them. This detail could have resulted in a dull, unreadable book. Instead John wrote an electrifying story. This explains why numerous readers recount reading the book in one sitting as they simply couldn't put it down.

James Mitchell, Professor of Governance at the University of

Edinburgh, was so impressed by *Conviction* that he organised an event at the university in 2016 so John could talk about it. He also wrote the foreword to the 2021 edition of *Conviction*. James was one of the members of the Christie Commission on the future of public services. Their 2011 report stressed, amongst other things, the importance of partnership working, prevention strategies and decentralisation of power. So it's hardly surprising that James was so inspired by the VRU story.

In his foreword James Mitchell writes perceptively:

> Violence cannot be eradicated like smallpox. Wicked problems need to be re-solved, solved on a daily basis and that requires a very different approach as is powerfully articulated here. There is much that is remarkable about this book and while it would be a mistake to attempt to replicate the approach in its entirety elsewhere, there is plenty to stimulate, provoke and learn from for anyone interested in policy making and delivering public services. There is no magic bullet or lever to be pulled and there can be no final resolution. There is always more to learn, more opportunities to improve. This is a work in progress. The VRU is, as all the best organisations, a learning institution.

Future of the *Postcards from Scotland* series

There was one reader who did not like *Conviction* – Kay Strang, the new owner of Argyll Publishing. Derek Rodger retired and sold his business to her in 2014 and she had published three titles with us. As Commissioning Editor (and copy editor once Derek retired) I worked reasonably well with her. However, she had no serious background in publishing and little feel for Scottish public life. This became obvious when she read *Conviction* and didn't like it as she thought it was simply 'one man's opinions'. She particularly objected to one paragraph John had written as it would offend many of her professional friends and she thought it libellous (it isn't):

> Revolution was not the plan, at least not then. But we became more revolutionary when we started to broaden our thinking

> on territorialism and gangs and the corrosive impact this was having on progress. As we started to look at the territorial youth gangs in Glasgow we noted a remarkable and surprising similarity between their behaviour and the behaviour of the professional 'gangs' we were trying to engage with. The professional or agency gangs were territorial and resolutely protected their turf. Many were aloof and displayed a conceit about the importance and uniqueness of their role that often led to arrogance. They often failed to, or refused to, recognise and acknowledge the shared agenda and the influence and impact their work had on other agencies.

I argued that this was an important part of the VRU thinking and that it must remain. However, when the book came back from the printers, I soon realised that Kay Strang had removed that paragraph from the final text. I was angry as was my board. We wanted to publish books with a radical slant where warranted; we weren't prepared for the final say to lie with someone with such conventional sensitivities. The board decided that we had to sever links with Kay Strang and I was about to write to tell her this when I received an email from her saying that, given my attitude, she no longer wanted to work with us. She offered to sell us the rights to all of the *Postcards* books at a very reasonable price and we seized the opportunity eagerly.

Conviction sold well and very soon after its initial release we reprinted with the offending paragraph reinstated. From the second edition of *Conviction* on we have listed CCWB Press as the publisher on *Postcards from Scotland* books. I found working with printers rather challenging and was delighted when in 2016, Derek Rodger returned to publishing after winning a legal battle with Kay Strang. Derek now acts as our publishing manager.

Being the sole publisher of *Postcards from Scotland* means we now make some money from our books. We have used this to fund other titles and different aspects of our work. More importantly it has given us more control. And, as most employees will tell you these days, being able to make your own decisions is rare and highly valued. Just think of all those trying to meet top down, and often counterproductive, targets. Or Professor Barry Schwartz's tale of those poor public servants who had to take a child into care and separate him from his father for weeks just because his dad mistakenly bought the wrong bottle of lemonade.

Chapter 14

Paving the way for the new road: the environment, nature and community

Three *Postcards from Scotland* books – *The New Road, Scotland's Local Food Revolution*, and *Raising Spirits*;
the importance of nature and the outdoors in the Centre's work;
the Centre's psychology researcher Emily Cutts;
Emily's book, *The Dear Wild Place*;
a David and Goliath struggle;
G20 Youth Project;
Centre events at the Children's Wood.

IN 2011 when I was thinking about the first few *Postcards from Scotland* books, my older son, Ewan, was working for the Ullapool Community Trust. This meant that I was acutely aware of some of the inspiring local community projects across Scotland. Unfortunately, Scottish national newspapers, much weakened by a loss of revenue and sales, rarely profiled such organisations. So, unless you lived in an area with a lot of community activity, you could be completely unaware of these inspiring projects. This is why I thought a book featuring what was happening in some of these innovative communities would be a great addition to the series.

Box 11: *The New Road* – projects and interviewees

Dunbar community bakery : Philip Revell, Janet Barnes

Twecher Community Action : Sandra Sutton

The Fife Diet : Mike Small

Vivarium (community housing for the elderly): Clare du Boulay and Monika Holton

A Thousand Huts (Falkland): Ninian Stuart

Fintry Development Trust : Kelly McIntyre, Gordon Cowtan

GalGael (Govan): Alastair McIntosh, Gehan Macleod

Neilston Development Trust : Pauline Gallagher

Renton (housing and development projects): Archie Thomson

Comrie Development Trust : Cathy Tilbrook, David McCall, Peter Jones, Emma Margrett

Dundee International Women's Centre : Gwendoline Telford

Transition Town Forres : Carin Schwartz

Sleat Community Trust : Angus Robertson

Isle of Eigg Heritage Trust : Maggie Fyffe, Eddie Scott

Knoydart Foundation : Angela Williams

Ullapool Community Trust : Susan Leslie, Chrissy Boyd, Diane Campbell

There was one big problem with this idea – I couldn't think of anyone I could ask to write the book. The Centre could commission a journalist but that would cost money we simply didn't have. And then I realised the solution to this problem lay close to home. I was living with a retired journalist and, despite chairing both Riverside Inverclyde and Social Investment Scotland at that time, he had some time to spare. Alf didn't immediately warm to the idea when I first raised it with him but he agreed to talk to Ewan. Between the three of us we hatched a plan: father and son would spend a week visiting a variety of interesting and inspiring community projects in Scotland. Ewan would choose them and ask the questions during the visits and Alf would take the lead role in writing up their experiences and observations. So this is how the third book in the *Postcards* series – *The New Road: Charting Scotland's inspirational communities* by Alf Young and Ewan Young came about.

The New Road

The book describes how over the course of a very hot week in May 2012 father and son travelled from Dunbar in the south east to the Knoydart peninsula in the north west. They visited fifteen different projects on their travels: travels made much more challenging by their decision to use public transport whenever possible. The chosen projects were both urban and rural and encompassed a range of different activities – housing, regeneration, wind turbines, local food, employment skills, hutting, community ownership and so much more. See Box 11 for a list of projects Alf and Ewan visited and the people they spoke to.

Fortunately, the Development Trusts Association Scotland were very keen on the idea as a number of their members were to feature in the book and they agreed to provide some sponsorship to help with travel and accommodation costs.

The book could have been boring, presenting the information in a series of tedious reports. Instead it's an engaging and reflective travelogue which firmly places their 'journey of discovery' in the aftermath of the banking crisis of 2008. In the introduction they write:

> Against a backdrop of nearly five years of financial crisis and economic stagnation across many of the economies of the developed west, we wanted to seek out communities, and individuals within communities, across Scotland, not content with waiting until politicians, central bankers and others in positions of power and authority eventually deliver on their oft-repeated promise to get us all back to something called normal.

In the course of their journey they meet a number of inspirational community leaders – visionaries, go-getters, entrepreneurs, innovators – who were making a genuine difference in their area despite many obstacles in their path. Obstacles often put there by various layers of local and national government bureaucracy. Ultimately the authors argue that 'We need to think more radically about what assets communities might aspire to control' and suggest that 'more local communities within our great cities could benefit hugely by looking more closely at what development trusts in the rest of Scotland are already achieving.' They conclude by saying: 'It will take both commitment and vision by many, many people, if all the natural communities across Scotland are to reclaim more control over their own destinies and be all they can be. A new road perhaps. But one all can aspire to set foot on.'

We launched *The New Road* alongside Phil Hanlon and Sandra Carlisle's book *AfterNow* and my own book *The Great Takeover* at the CCA in Glasgow in November 2012. *The New Road* was a huge hit with the Development Trusts Association and we quickly sold out of the initial print run of 1000 and had to reprint.

Scotland's Local Food Revolution

One of the most impressive projects Alf and Ewan visited was the Fife Diet which had been set up and was still being managed at that time by Mike Small. The topic merited much more attention than it could get in *The New Road* so it seemed sensible to agree to an entire book on the subject when Mike suggested it to me. *Scotland's Local Food Revolution* thus became the fourth book in the series.

Apart from explaining the thinking behind the Fife Diet and

how it works Mike sets out a radical critique of our current food system. In the introduction he writes:

> This book is about our climate crisis and how it's tied to our bloated consumer culture and our dysfunctional food system. It's about how our society has become dominated by values not of most people's making and how the resultant exploitation is leading us into socio-ecological disaster. It's about how we are living through an 'intentional epidemic' of obesity and how the food industry is at odds with the public interest, a reality recently exposed by the horsemeat scandal.

Mike's trenchant analysis could have led to a bleak book but it's not. His description of the local food movement in Scotland and the attempt to recapture control of the food system is profoundly hopeful. He also ends the book by giving readers guidance on how they can play their part in this movement for change.

We published the book in June 2013 with launch events at the Open University in Edinburgh and the community run Glad Cafe in Glasgow.

Raising Spirits

The following summer we published what appears as a companion volume to *Scotland's Local Food Revolution – Raising Spirits* on allotments. When the topic was proposed I was keen so long as the authors didn't just write about food growing but also covered how allotments could advance well-being. This seems rather obvious now but in 2013 there still wasn't the same awareness of the potential contribution that tending an allotment could make not just to physical health but also mental well-being.

The authors were Jenny Mollison, a plot holder who wrote a regular column on allotments for *The Scotsman*, Judy Wilkinson who had, for decades been a Policy Officer with the Glasgow Allotment Forum and her daughter Rona Wilkinson. Rona says she was brought up on an allotment and was now involved in renewable energy and community development. It was Judy who originally approached me with the proposal and with whom I liaised throughout the editing process.

We launched *Raising Spirits: Allotments, well-being and community* in August 2014 at a big event in Trades House, Glasgow with support from the Incorporation of Gardeners. Over a hundred people attended to peruse the exhibition that Judy and others had assembled and listen to a few speeches about the benefits of allotments. The book proved popular as it gave readers ideas for what they could achieve. For example, Lynn Semple, who had worked for the Centre in its founding period, was now involved with the Overtoun Community Growing Project and after purchasing the book at the launch emailed to say '*Raising Spirits* is a tremendous resource for all of us working in community growing initiatives.'

The book sold well and a year later in 2015 we had to reprint. The authors were very keen to add an afterword which they called 'A Happy Ending – how Scotland's allotments were saved for the future.' When they had written the text for the first edition of *Raising Spirits* they stressed the need to reform some outdated laws pertaining to allotments. In 2012/13 the Scottish Government had consulted on this issue and our authors were confident that new legislation would be part of the Community Empowerment Bill. However, when the Scottish Allotments and Gardens Society (SAGS) saw the Bill when it was first published in 2014, after the first edition of *Raising Spirits* was published, they were aghast. In the afterword Jenny, Judy and Rona explain that the Bill 'did not empower the allotment community. In fact it could be considered to dis-empower them and empower local authorities. . .'

The afterword sets out in detail how SAGS tried to secure amendments at various stages of the Bill's progress and how they were fully involved in the legislative process. They thought that they had secured the amendments they required, only to find that the Scottish Government was planning to side with local authorities and remove these amendments at a later stage.

Faced with the prospect of allotments, as we know them, disappearing 'SAGS issued an ultimatum':

> If the Bill was passed without our amendments the allotment community would deem the Act to be a failure. SAGS warned that, if the amendments were rejected, Scotland's allotment community would feel betrayed and abandoned. In effect allotments would have disappeared as an identifiable entity and would have simply become part of the amorphous mass collectively known as 'Community Growing Projects'. Given the significance of this, history and the responsibility for future generations weighed on everyone's mind. We even plotted a mass demonstration outside Holyrood with pitchforks and barrowloads of dung.

The ultimatum worked and soon meetings with the Scottish Government were arranged. A professional facilitator conducted the meetings and ultimately these led to a number of clauses in the new version of the Bill which protect allotments and plotholders.

When the Community Empowerment Act came into force the Minister responsible, Dr Aileen McLeod, stressed that the Scottish Government recognised 'the unique identity of allotments', including their history, contribution to food growing and wider benefits.

The new Act and the fulsome statement of government support allowed our authors to end their Afterword on a positive note. A note which aptly reflects the book's title and sentiments:

> All of us who had worked so hard to secure this recognition and the protection afforded by the Act could now breathe easily. We had achieved what we set out to do. Our spirits, like the numerous seeds we had sown in our allotments over many years, were well and truly raised.

The importance of nature

I read many psychology books in the first five years of the Centre's life and one passage lodged in my mind. 'When highly stressed people are asked to visualise a soothing scene, nobody imagines a freeway or shopping mall. Rather, images of wilderness, forest, seascape, and starry skies invariably emerge.' These are the words of Theodore Roszak, the man who first coined the term 'ecopsychology' and who was ahead of his time in arguing for the importance of nature to people's health and well-being.

These ideas resonated strongly with me. I have always loved nature and being outdoors walking or gardening and when I lived in a Glasgow tenement I had a hut at Carbeth. I intuitively knew that the natural world is not only an anti-depressant but also soothes anxiety. It didn't take much to convince those involved with the Centre of the well-being effects of nature. We were also all aware that there's no point in critiquing materialist values unless there are alternative values to promote. And being in nature is for most of us an important antidote to meaningless consumption.

As I explained in Chapter 10, in 2009 we embarked on creating a section of our website called 'Flourishing Lives' and used an unfinished jigsaw as a way to convey that there are various things that contribute to well-being. One of the main sections in the children and youth part of 'Flourishing Lives' was called 'outdoors'. The resources here included summaries of extensive empirical research showing the importance of being in nature to mental health and well-being, as well as tips and other practical help for teachers and parents on how to utilise the outdoors for learning, play and well-being.

We did some of the research and writing ourselves but we didn't have the expertise to compile the information about how to get children outdoors for playing and learning. So we commissioned Juliet Robertson of 'Creative Star', one of Scotland's most accomplished and celebrated outdoor educators, to write these sections for us. She did a brilliant job and I was always very proud of the free resources we were providing for teachers and parents on what I considered a very important topic for young people's well-being.

Nature Connection: Nurturing Hope

Given the value the Centre placed on being outdoors in nature it made sense for us to provide training on the topic for those interested in working outdoors on nature and well-being themes. Fortunately, a young woman came into the Centre to see me and this was exactly the type of training she provided. Her name was Maeve Gavin and she had undertaken training at leading nature connection schools in America.

We ran two taster sessions for practitioners/professionals on **Nature Connection** on 2/3 September 2010 at Pollok Park, Glasgow. The first of these was aimed at those working with young people. In the course of the day Maeve introduced the 20 participants (the maximum number) to a variety of techniques which they can use to enhance young people's well-being through connecting with nature. The second session was aimed at those working with adults in a variety of settings. This proved to be less popular and only attracted around ten participants.

Participants evaluated both courses very highly. Many reported boosts to their own well-being as well as gaining tools to use with young people or adult clients:

> The day was just wonderful and I had the best sleep ever when I got home. [We] . . . are going to take our Eco committee children over to do a team building exercise based on the day. The children will then peer teach the activities to the children in their schools.

> I am very fortunate in that I live and work in an area where I am surrounded by nature every day, but I don't always take the time to truly appreciate it. The day helped me to look at how I can do that again, both for myself and for the families I have contact with. I will pass on some of the ideas from the day to my groups of volunteers so that they can perhaps utilize them in their befriending.

Some participants were keen to have other staff members trained, and while we thought the courses a great success, given the other things we were doing, we just didn't have the capacity to organise more. Therefore, we encouraged Maeve to provide this training herself and we committed to advertising her courses on the external events section of our website.

Within a few years there was much general acceptance of the link between nature and well-being and many more providers of training. The mounting environmental crisis also ensured that courses on how to use the outdoors for learning and mental health became more prominent.

However, while the Centre did not do more on the topic of being outdoors in nature we were, indirectly, behind a large campaign and project in Glasgow's west end on precisely this topic, thanks to the activities of an original staff member.

Emily Cutts

In late 2005, shortly after the Centre moved into new offices in Union Street, we interviewed for the post of psychology researcher. Emily Cutts impressed us with her energy, commitment and enthusiasm. Given our temporary funding the post was a short-term contract but we employed Emily till 2010 when she left to go to the USA with her husband, Quintin, who was on sabbatical. She had another child when she returned and worked for the next few years for the Centre in a freelance capacity.

During her early days at the Centre Emily became very interested in positive psychology and was one of the first students to take an MSc in the topic at the University of East London. Like myself, she ultimately decided that she preferred a more holistic, rather than an exclusively psychological, approach to well-being.

While full time at the Centre Emily put together some great PowerPoint presentations that we allowed other organisations to use, collaborated with Glasgow University on some original research into mindset and wrote material for the Centre's burgeoning website. Latterly we had a feature on the website called 'Emily's News' where she would summarise some of the latest research on well-being and other topics of interest to the Centre and its followers.

When Emily and Quintin returned to Glasgow in 2012 they became involved in community activity related to North Kelvin Meadow. 'The Meadow' as it is usually called is a four acre site of open space in Glasgow's west end which borders the much poorer, working-class area of Maryhill. The Meadow had a variety of uses over the years and until 1992 it was mainly school playing fields. In 1996 the Scottish Government had refused the Council permission to develop the site for housing. Plans for a community sports complex were also knocked back and the area slowly reverted to nature, becoming wilder and greener. At this point community involvement with the site was mainly picking up litter and creating raised beds for a community garden.

This all changed in 2012 when a local developer, with support from Glasgow Council, submitted a proposal for a high-end housing development covering the whole site. As the Council owned the land they stood to make £10 million on its sale as well as significant sums annually in council tax once the houses were occupied.

The Dear Wild Place

Emily didn't just join the campaign to oppose this development: she ultimately led and masterminded it. She tells the story of what they did and why in her *Postcards from Scotland* book which we published in 2019. It's called appropriately *The Dear Wild Place* (echoing the famous Archie Hind novel about Glasgow – *The Dear Green Place*) and we added the subtitle *Green spaces, community and campaigning*.

In her introduction Emily describes the Centre and her involvement with it. She even mentions writing 'Emily's News' and then tells readers 'It was only in 2011 and 2012 that I could see a way to use what I was learning to make a practical difference to people's lives.'

> I believed the key was to get people from near and far on the land. I organised a series of events for children and the community, every two weeks, and then monthly. I organised mass den building, recycling events, bow and arrow making and much more. All free. Walking from nursery to nursery I invited parents, carers, teachers to use the land. We also became highly skilled at trowelling dog mess as this was one of the main barriers to people coming to the land. Events got

> more eye-catching: lighting up the Meadow for Halloween; bringing in reindeer at Christmas. These activities had a dual purpose – to entice more folk onto the land as well as raise the profile in the media. . . As we could see the importance of getting young people outside on this piece of land we started to call a portion of the site 'the Children's Wood' but there were also events aimed at getting people involved in the wider Meadow.

The sheer volume of activities Emily initiated on the site is breathtaking. She had learned about 'Forest Schools' while working at the Centre so she sought out local practitioners and soon had a Saturday club running founded on these principles. She approached teachers in local schools to see if they might want to use 'the Children's Wood' with some of their classes: most of the schools in the area had concrete playgrounds. And Emily and others provided some training for teachers on how to use the outdoors for learning and encouraging children's imagination and how to assess risk.

Throughout the book it is easy to see the passion and skill of Emily, the researcher. She provides teachers and parents with the evidence for the importance of outdoor learning. For example, she gives them information on what's called 'loose parts play', and Professor Howard Gardner's notion of 'multiple intelligences', particularly what he calls 'nature smart'. In Emily's work in the Meadow these are not just abstract ideas to communicate to others but an integral part of practical projects which help transform people's lives.

This is also true of Emily's ideas on community and how to address some of the big challenges of our time. In the chapter called 'Community Matters' she writes:

> I wanted to actively build community feeling by involving people in defending our patch of land from the threat of development. I also viewed our land as a place to commune with each other, an outdoor community centre, a modern day church without the religion, and a town square without the shops. In short I saw it as a place where people can gather together informally and formally and connect with one another.

Emily is so sure footed and confident in her ideas because she has read widely on the topic. For example, in *The Dear Wild Place* she gives a short summary of Robert Putnam's famous book *Bowling Alone* (2000) and she summarises the latest Office for National Statistics (ONS) research on the extent of loneliness in the UK. She also gives a short summary of Professor Tim Kasser's research on materialism and how the shift from intrinsic to extrinsic values undermines well-being in both children and adults. She then tells us that she learned from Kasser 'that one of the best ways to undermine materialist values is to promote intrinsic ones and to encourage people to see how satisfying they can be.'

Another galvanising idea for Emily was the importance of meaning and purpose. She had learned about the importance of this from Viktor Frankl's famous book *Man's Search for Meaning* (1946) but she also found the focus on meaning one of the most important, and attractive aspects of Martin Seligman's work. Emily intuitively knew: 'A strong sense of meaning and purpose helps people and their community develop a collective aim and this in turns helps to overcome naysayers, risk aversion or fatalism.'

And there was a lot of fatalism and pessimism around. Given how much money the Council would make from the housing development it was easy for people to believe that the developers would defeat the community. But they didn't. Emily portrays the battle like a David and Goliath struggle. The inspiring news is that once again David won.

Campaigners found out that the development had been turned down for good in December 2016. Emily recalls that some of her fellow campaigners worried that now the land had been secured they would 'lose' their 'shared vision and sense of purpose.' However Emily tells us, 'this wasn't my concern. Now we had won that battle, we could concentrate on a bigger war about wider societal problems such as materialist values and the restrictions on children's freedom to play outside.'

Emily is very clear that during the campaign she drew on, and applied, the knowledge she gained during her time at the Centre. Later she states 'I believe what we have achieved with our wild place is part of the Centre's legacy. In the acknowledgements she writes, 'Carol has been my role model and inspiration since I began working at the Centre for Confidence & Well-being.'

I am flattered by Emily's generous acknowledgement of my influence on her life and thoughts. I am delighted to read about how she applied the ideas we learned about together in her community and I'm proud to think that what she describes in *The Dear Wild Place* is part of the Centre's legacy. But I also want to highlight that Emily achieved so much because *she* is truly an exceptional woman. And this is clear for everyone to see in Emily's personal priorities and what she did next.

G20 Youth Project

The Meadow is near to the Botanic Gardens in Glasgow's leafy, wealthy Kelvinside but is technically in the historically working-class area of Maryhill. Emily reports that this is one of the 'most deprived wards in Europe'. She writes: 'So in our area there are those who have lots of resources, money and amenities and those who have nothing. From early on in our campaign I wanted to highlight the importance of inequality.'

One of the things Emily and other campaigners did was show the documentary film *The Divide* on income inequality which had been inspired by *The Spirit Level*. More importantly Emily knew that one of the ways that children are disadvantaged by poverty is via their lack of access to play areas and green spaces. This is why she was always keen for children from poor backgrounds in the neighbourhood to use the land. She also wanted to see more social mixing of people, both adults and children, from different backgrounds; something which doesn't happen much in our very class stratified society.

This could have been a problem for Emily. Some of the local children and youth come from fairly traumatic backgrounds. Many of them have parents who misuse alcohol and/or drugs and, as a result of these adversities, can be aggressive and anti-social. Many of them have problems with school and can get into trouble with police. But this didn't stop Emily befriending them. She tells us about one particular ten-year-old who teachers couldn't work with and who had been aggressive on numerous occasions. However, he wasn't like that in the Meadow because, as he told Emily, he feels 'relaxed here'.

> [One] day when I was on the land celebrating my daughter's seventh birthday the same boy turned up and we asked him to join us. He happily played hide and seek, tag and other games with us. He was like any other child his age – a complete contrast to the times when he threw a brick through a car window or attacked another schoolmate. This boy needs to play and relax in a natural environment where he feels safe.

Emily recounts how the anti-social behaviour of some of the Maryhill kids 'makes others feel scared of them' and they don't want to get involved. But, as the above passage from *The Dear Wild Place* shows, Emily stepped towards these youngsters, not away from them. She soon understood that their challenging behaviour was linked to their circumstances and that they were in need of help. 'They are bored, have little money, and are very stressed and vulnerable,' writes Emily and they deserved the 'opportunities to participate in various activities.' And soon this is exactly what Emily and others provided:

> We spoke to a new police officer at Maryhill Police station and between us we managed to bring together others in the local area who are also concerned about our young people – McDonalds, Partick Thistle football club, local teachers and community members. . . We have started monthly meetings to discuss how we can best support these vulnerable young people. We are now planning community football matches and over the winter we moved our youth club into McDonalds so we could start working where the young people like to hang out. We are building positive strong relationships between the young people and ourselves. . . The young people we have been working with have demonstrated some positive changes like trying to reduce aggressive behaviour in their peers. They are also showing a willingness to help out within the community.

Emily was soon able to secure a temporary building for a youth club for this group and managed to raise some funding. It is called the G20 Youth Project and from the outset provided opportunities for the young people ranging from hill walking to the arts. Increasingly it was with this group that Emily wanted to work and in the summer of 2022 she left the Children's Wood to work exclusively with them, particularly G20 Works. This provides training and employment opportunities 'to support young people over 16 who may have experienced or be at risk of addiction, unemployment and imprisonment, to improve their life chances and become valued, contributing members of the community.' From their great new base in the Wyndford, in the heart of Maryhill, the project runs a car wash, cafe and barbers shop! The project has a close working relationship with the Violence Reduction Unit but none of this would have happened without Emily, her involvement with the Meadow and her limitless empathy for a group of youngsters society at large prefers to ignore or punish.

Publication and related events

The Centre published *The Dear Wild Place* in March 2019. We managed to secure a slot for Emily to speak about the book at Aye Write!, Glasgow's book festival. We had our launch party in the Meadow at the end of March with a bonfire and food. The Centre was planning to host an event there the following spring but unfortunately the pandemic prevented us from doing this. However, in late June 2022, just before Emily left the Children's Wood, we held a Saturday afternoon event which we called a ***Postcards from Scotland* Social Gathering and Discussion**. We let people know that Emily and Sue Palmer (more of Sue and the *Postcard* book she edited in a later chapter) would speak and Phil Hanlon would chair the discussion. We also referred to the event as a 'post-pandemic get together to discuss some of the big issues of our times.' Just over 30 people attended despite the day being not just chilly but rainy for June. Some had travelled a fair distance to be there – Inverness, South Ayrshire, Edinburgh and Lanarkshire. People's desperate need for a meaningful discussion with others after a few years of lockdowns and isolation was palpable.

After the event formally came to an end, 20 of us went to a local bar for a meal and to continue the conversation. The major issues on people's minds became clear during the formal and informal discussions – children's well-being, the loss of nature and environmental threats, the looming cost of living crisis, political dysfunction and the war in Ukraine which had commenced a few months earlier. I am happy to report that the Centre donated all the money it made from the event to support the people of Ukraine.

I had one simple regret about the day – family commitments meant that my son Ewan wasn't able to come down from Ullapool to attend. Having journeyed round Scotland in 2012 to look at fifteen different projects as part of the research for *The New Road,* he would have appreciated seeing the Meadow and would have been impressed by what that community has achieved.

CHAPTER 15

Inequality and poverty, drugs and alcohol

Perspectives on inequality;
Creating Good Lives event with Professor William Julius Wilson;
Centre's event on 'The Wire';
the Independent Enquiry into Drugs and Alcohol;
subsequent Centre events;
Darren McGarvey's *Poverty Safari*;
the Poverty Truth Commission.

IN MARCH 2011 I heard a memorable talk by the social geographer and inequality expert, Danny Dorling. We were both speaking at the same session of Aye Write! Danny was talking about his book *Injustice; Why social inequality persists* (2011) and I was presenting the main arguments in my book *The Tears that Made the Clyde.*

I had read Danny's book a few months before. But it was his talk which had much more impact on me as he distilled his findings into a few key facts. He explained that progressive taxation and various government policies meant that from 1918 to 1980 the income gap in the UK narrowed substantially. In short, Britain became fairer during this period and there was increased social mobility. However, this then changed from the 1980s on with the expansion of the economy, and the 'greed is good' philosophy unleashed by Thatcherism. The big bonuses paid to top executives soon followed. Dorling calculates that sadly we are now back to levels of income inequality which pertained in the mid nineteenth century when Charles Dickens wrote *Hard Times* (1854)! Social mobility has also decreased considerably as inequality has risen.

I certainly benefited from the social mobility of the post-war era. I remember the 1960s as a period when the old class order was being ridiculed and attacked and there were lots of opportunities for people like me to get on. The Robbins Report led to a massive expansion of university education in the mid-1960s, creating many more places for people from working class backgrounds. In those days the music scene was dominated, not by middle class people who attended public schools, but people from very ordinary families.

What I particularly like about Dorling's book *Injustice* is that he tries to explain the mechanisms which lead to, and perpetuate, injustice and inequality. He identifies them as being – elitism, exclusion, prejudice, greed and despair. I am particularly interested in his ideas on elitism. He argues, rightly in my view, that one of the ways in which inequality is justified is via the belief that there is a group of particularly talented individuals with high IQ and innate abilities who need to be rewarded for their efforts. The assumption here is that many people just don't have much innate ability and so we shouldn't waste our resources educating or training them or paying them well; they simply don't have what it takes. So it's the myth of the talented few which justifies the big bonuses to bankers and top executives.

This mentality is endemic in our society and yet it's simply wrong. Mounting research shows that the brain is not fixed. We are not born with an innate amount of ability or talent – this is cultivated through good teaching and hard work. Of course, people require to be motivated to grow their potential but this is very different from arguing, as the elitists do, that you either have it or you don't. Indeed one of the reasons the Centre particularly valued Professor Carol Dweck's work on the growth mindset is that it challenges rather than reinforces innate elitism.

At the time of Dorling's research there were only three advanced, industrial societies – the US, Portugal and Singapore – which were more unequal than the UK. And what of Scotland? How did we fare on inequality? Scotland performed slightly better but it was marginal: at that time the top ten per cent of earners in Scotland had 29 per cent of the total income whereas in the UK as whole the figure was 31 per cent. Not a great record for a country that prides itself on its egalitarian beliefs.

I wrote a large number of blogs on inequality and the erosion of social mobility and I always tried to mention the topic in my many talks. I saw, and continue to see, the UK's level of inequality as a blight not only on the lives of the poor but on our whole society. As a Centre we never shied away from the evidence or the idea that inequality detracts hugely from well-being.

Creating Good Lives event

The Centre saw its role as a catalyst for change: we wanted to introduce new ideas and speakers on topics of relevance to well-being in Scotland. Understandably, we were keen to do something on class inequality and poverty. On 29th October 2010 we held a one-day event in the Strathclyde Suite of Glasgow's Concert Hall. We called it **Creating Good Lives: class, inequality, work, family, education, environment, well-being, drugs and alcohol**. Around 260 people, mainly professionals from different sectors and geographical areas, attended. Eight organisations leant their support to the event – Drumchapel Life, Oxfam, the Glasgow Centre for Population Health, the Social Justice Foundation, Learning Link Scotland, the Nurture Group Network, Scottish Community Development Centre, Faith in the Community Scotland and Share, the training organisation for housing associations.

Here's how we described the aims of the day's programme:

> The event aims to boost our chances of solving contemporary urban problems by:
>
> - helping to widen participants' normal focus of interest and attention

- placing due emphasis on cultural factors such as historical background and belief systems

- giving more prominence to family, gender and relationship issues

- discouraging people from looking for 'silver bullets' or panacea programmes of action which are then discarded when they don't deliver

- showing how centralised, government responses can unwittingly become part of the problem, not the solution

- encouraging policy makers and practitioners to think through how they can tackle the causes of problems rather than treating symptoms

- encouraging more respectful dialogue and giving more weight to collaboration and partnership working

- forging new, dynamic links across sectors

- encouraging new thinking, learning and independent action.

Looking back I can see that many of these aims, and the topics covered at the event, were linked to much of the analysis I had presented in *The Tears that Made the Clyde*.

In that book I quote the work of Harvard Professor William Julius Wilson, one of the most celebrated academics researching and writing about urban poverty and worklessness. He was author of some of the most influential sociology texts on race, work and the urban poor. In the mid 1990s *Time* magazine described him as the 26th most influential person in America. So it made perfect sense to invite Professor Wilson to be the keynote speaker.

At Creating Good Lives, Professor Wilson explained the rise of worklessness in the USA and how this had resulted from deindustrialisation and the practice of 'off-shoring' – manufacturing items more cheaply in third world countries. These practices have taken hold throughout the modern world and have led to a decline in the demand for traditional working-class labour, a development

Box 12: Breakout sessions, facilitators or speakers at Creating Good Lives

Early Years and Education – Alan Sinclair and Susan Deacon;

Work Employability and Skills – Professor Stephanie Young of Skills Development Scotland;

Regenerating Real Communities – Andy Milne of the Scottish Urban Regeneration Forum facilitated with input from Russell Jones (GCPH), Petra Biberbach (Planning Aid), Liz Gardiner (Fablevision) and Dairmaid Lawlor (Architecture and Design Scotland);

Drugs and Alcohol – John Carnochan, Phil Hanlon, John Matthews and Mike McCarron;

Families, Relationship and Health – Carol Craig and Peter Lynas;

New Thinking, New Action – Andrew Lyon of the International Futures Forum and the celebrated community activist Cathy McCormack.

with negative consequences for families and communities worldwide. In the US there is a prevalent tendency to play down the importance of structural factors, such as employment opportunities, housing and transport and to see worklessness and poverty as a result of individuals' personal failings. These punitive attitudes are not nearly as common in Europe, including the UK, where there is widespread acceptance that the poor are not to blame for their predicament.

Professor Wilson does not want to weaken the argument about the importance of structural factors as he is loath to encourage people to blame the poor for their misfortune. But, nonetheless, as a social scientist, he thinks it important to point out that cultural factors do play some part in the continuation of poverty and worklessness. For example, in the black communities he has studied children often grow up with poor verbal skills and are often taught 'norms of resignation' as a result of their parents' experience of racism and disrespect.

He ended his talk by telling the audience about an inspirational and 'spectacularly' successful programme called 'the Harlem Children's Zone' (HCZ) which was set up by the visionary Geoffrey Canada. The programme introduced into an area of Harlem a range of structural and cultural interventions on education and health including kindergarten places and a 'baby college' for expectant parents and those with children under three. And it has been the success of HCZ which has led Wilson to call for a 'holistic analysis of inner-city poverty' – an analysis which stresses the salience of structural factors while still acknowledging the part culture plays.

At the event I spoke after Professor Wilson and the title of my talk was 'Why the long title?' I explained how as a Centre we did not believe there was a single solution or approach to the problems we faced in Glasgow or other Scottish cities and gave examples of the factors I considered in *The Tears that Made the Clyde*. After my talk we had four speakers on very different themes.

Professor Harry Burns, who at that time was Scotland's Chief Medical Officer, was one of these four speakers and he chose to talk about the importance of 'a sense of coherence', a term coined by the sociologist Aaron Antonovski. Drawing on a range of evidence Harry argued that without a sense of meaning and control the human brain experiences great stress and this chronic stress is undermining the health of so many poor people in Scotland.

Professor Susan Deacon spoke about the assignment she had been given by the Scottish Government to make recommendations on the early years – a very relevant topic given Professor Wilson's conclusion and one we shall return to in Chapter 18.

Peter Lynas from the Relationship Foundation spoke about research on the importance of marriage for mental and physical health as well as the instability of cohabiting relationships.

Professor George Morris talked about 'Environment, Health and Equity'. He was particularly critical of his own discipline of environmental health which he claimed was still focused on 'hazards' rather than on those factors which contribute to 'health promoting places'. He ended with a great quote from the musician and composer John Cage: 'I don't know why people are frightened of new ideas. I'm frightened of the old ones.'

After lunch there were six different break-out sessions set out in Box 12 for individuals to attend with facilitators and/or speakers:

The Centre received detailed notes of the discussions and recommendations for most of these sessions and we put them on our website. At the event we also gave all participants two postcards and asked them to comment on the question 'What I and others need to do differently?' as well as writing some general comments. We also put these responses on our website.

Following these sessions Phil Hanlon facilitated a discussion with all those who attended which we called 'questions, observations and closing remarks'. Phil did this in his usual spontaneous and articulate way giving people his observations on the day before soliciting comments from participants.

The morning plenary session of the event was chaired by Baroness Helena Kennedy. Helena grew up in a working-class family in Glasgow and is now one of England's leading barristers and a famous human rights lawyer. She had contacted me a few months before to say how much she valued *The Tears that Made the Clyde.* She was eager to support the Centre and readily agreed to chair this event. Everyone I spoke to was impressed by her authoritative air and the way she stamped her personality on the conference. 'Don't think you are asking me to come all the way to Scotland and then not expect me to put my tuppence worth in,' she said at one point. Her comments were lucid, articulate and often very radical.

I wrote a blog after the event in which I record a couple of gratifying comments from participants. One was from a man who works for a think tank. 'I think that something special is happening here today – I don't just mean the numbers of folk you've managed to get along,' he told me. And then added, 'There is an atmosphere, an urgency about the need to change, that I haven't detected before. It is as if we've turned a corner.'

A senior civil servant stopped on the way out to tell me how much she had enjoyed the whole day, adding: 'I really admire your knack of getting people to talk about things that we don't normally discuss.' This was exactly what I had hoped would happen as I knew that if we were going to address some of the big challenges facing us we required to have a better analysis and had to be honest about the scale of the problems.

I am particularly proud of the fact that we managed to keep the entry fee to this event to only £60 as one day conferences were usually much more expensive than that. We also had reductions and free places for organisations and individuals who couldn't afford this fee.

After events the Centre usually organised an informal dinner with the main speaker if they were staying in town that evening. With this one we had a more formal dinner in a private room in a local restaurant and Geoff Huggins, Head of Mental Health Division in the Scottish Government chaired the discussion. Most of the main speakers attended, as did Helena Kennedy and Sir Peter Housden who had recently taken up his appointment as Permanent Secretary to the Scottish Government. Professor Wilson spoke with great passion about the importance to the structure of family life of one parent being employed. This was followed by a lively discussion which William Julius Wilson particularly appreciated as not one person present blamed the poor for their bleak situation. This would not have been true of an equivalent gathering in America, he told us.

Evening talk on *The Wire*

When I spoke to Professor Wilson on the phone about the Creating Good Lives event and our desire for him to be the keynote speaker, he told me that he would not accept a fee and that he would pay his own expenses out of his Harvard University travel budget. He also said that he would bring a postgraduate student with him. The student's name was Anmol Chadhha and he was co-teacher on a course on '*The Wire* and social policy' at Harvard. Like millions of others, I was a huge fan of the tv series and so quickly arranged for Anmol to give a talk called **What *The Wire* can tell us about complex urban problems and their solutions**. We held the event in the Teacher Building in central Glasgow, early evening the day before the big event. It was such a popular topic it sold out within days of our publicity.

For those who didn't watch *The Wire* it is a celebrated American television drama series set in Baltimore. It was written by David Simon, an American journalist who worked on the *Baltimore Sun* and mainly reported on police stories. There are five series in total – sixty episodes. Some critics have hailed *The Wire* as the best television series ever made. It's particularly acclaimed for its script, acting, rounded and complex characters and realistic portrayal of urban problems.

Professor Julius Wilson, like many social policy specialists, is enthusiastic about *The Wire*. Indeed Professor Wilson claims that the programme 'has done more to enhance our understanding of the challenges of urban life and the problems of urban inequality than any other media event or scholarly publications, including studies by social scientists.'

David Simon, the programme's creator, was delighted that it was seen as social commentary as this was his intention. He has outlined its themes as being 'the fraud of the drug war, the evisceration of the working-class, our inability to reform our political infrastructure, the inequality of educational opportunity and, lastly, the declining ambitions and viability of high-end journalism.'

David Simon has also confirmed that Professor Wilson's book – *When Work Disappears: the World of the New Urban Poor* (1997) – was the inspiration for Series Two which focuses on the plight of dock workers in Baltimore. What I loved about the series is the way the programmes slowly build up a picture of life in the city – we get to know the kingpins of the drugs world but also the youngsters sitting out on the corners selling. We get to know the dockers, the unions, the lawyers, the police, the teachers, the politicians and the press. . . What's more, these characters are complex. Some of the heroes that we are expected to care about are capable of the most crass, self-serving acts and some of the violent drug dealers can, in their own terms, act with principle and even compassion.

One of the most poignant aspects of the stories is the way they repeatedly show how many of the characters may ostensibly be free yet they are trapped in a nightmarish world. Unexpectedly, one of *The Wire's* strongest themes is one very close to my heart – how the work done by government agencies such as the police and schools is completely distorted by targets. Indeed in the series the target-driven culture in which the police operate is one of the main reasons not just for police cynicism and disaffection but also poor performance.

In the course of his talk Anmol described and commented on some scenes in the series, and their importance, but in the main gave us some sociological background to life in the type of urban communities on which *The Wire* focuses. Studies show that many who grow up in these communities are trapped as a result of poor language skills, lack of education, and access to jobs. Yet in the USA two thirds of white folk believe that the root cause of African American poverty is related to individual factors such as the lack of a work ethic. Even a slight majority of black people believe this.

Anmol finished his talk referring to one of the most moving scenes in the series. Two young black drug dealers are talking about the dire circumstances in which they live. One of them says that not everyone lives like this – there is another world out there. The other replies: 'and how do you get to that world from here?' The skill of the series is to show how difficult that transition is for many poor black youths. (As I write this I'm aware that an escape route is what Emily Cutts is providing in her G20 Works project for the young people in Maryhill.)

The next speaker at this event was John Carnochan who was at that point still head of Scotland's Violence Reduction Unit. I had been keen to give John the chance to speak, not just because he is a big fan of *The Wire*, but also because I thought we needed someone to say that while we could learn something from discussing the series, Glasgow is not Baltimore. This John did with great insight and humour. Glasgow has a major violence problem, he acknowledged, but went on to stress that it's not criminal gangs but territorial gangs that plague our streets. He also said, controversially, that some of the most dangerous gangs were those of social work, education, the police and other professions protecting their own disciplines rather than working for the common good.

Drugs and alcohol

When Emily Cutts started working with the youth of Maryhill she was aware that so many of them came from families where parents suffered from addiction to drink and/or drugs. In the neighbouring area of Ruchill, the local Church of Scotland minister, John Matthews, had very similar concerns about many of the people living in his parish as these problems are so much more acute in poorer neighbourhoods in Scotland, like Ruchill.

John was an unusual Church of Scotland minister. He had once held top positions in business and worked in America with General Electric. As he came from a working-class background in Glasgow, he began to feel unfulfilled by his business role and returned to Scotland in his early 40s to study and ultimately became a minister.

In early 2010 John accepted the invitation to Chair 'the Independent Enquiry into Maximising Recovery from Dependent Drug Use in Scotland'. He invited Phil Hanlon to become one of the Enquiry members and also its principal advisor. John also asked me to join the Enquiry Team. I originally refused as this wasn't a subject I knew much about but I was persuaded: John thought that my writings on Scottish culture and Glasgow's social problems, as well as the resources of the Centre, would ensure that I was a useful team member.

One of the Enquiry's first decisions was to widen the scope of study to include Scotland's problematic relationship with alcohol. In October 2010 the Enquiry published its report entitled 'Melting the iceberg of Scotland's drug and alcohol problem'. The Enquiry chose this title as the dominant theme of its report as Scotland's involvement with drink and drugs can be likened to an iceberg. The people who have problems with these substances are 'the tip of the iceberg'. What we don't see so readily is the culture which lies beneath – the values, beliefs and practices endemic in Scotland which unwittingly encourage people to turn to drink and drugs. Of course, we need to help those whose lives are blighted by drugs and alcohol but the report argues that as Scots we need to start facing up to the scale of the challenge and ask what we can do individually and collectively to 'raise the temperature of the water'.

In short, we need to change Scottish culture to make it less likely that people will feel the need to drink and take drugs.

The report acknowledges that there are different ways to understand addiction and different models. The one that the Enquiry Team found most useful is Bruce Alexander's – a psychologist with decades of experience in addiction and author of an important book on the topic, *The Globalization of Addiction: A Study in the Poverty of the Spirit* which I introduced in Chapter 10. At the time he was Professor Emeritus at the Simon Fraser University in Vancouver. As we learned in that earlier chapter, Bruce Alexander argues that addiction happens when people become 'overwhelmingly involved' with substances or activities which are ultimately destructive to them or their society. Of vital importance is Alexander's assertion that people are much more prone to addiction when their psychological needs are not met as a result of cultural erosion, loneliness or other forms of social fragmentation. 'Dislocation' is the term he often uses.

There is much I could write about the Independent Enquiry, such as the evidence it acquired, its conclusions and its recommendations. However, this book is primarily about the Centre for Confidence and Well-being so much of this is not relevant. Except for one thing. Once the Enquiry published its report it wanted to hold a large public event to communicate its ideas and findings. This could easily have been organised by STRADA (Scottish Training – Drugs and Alcohol) as their head, Joy Barlow, was a member of the Enquiry Team and STRADA provided executive support to the Enquiry. However, the Team decided that since the whole purpose of the report was to try and involve a much wider group of people in Scotland in discussions about drugs and alcohol it was much better if the Centre held the event. We were particularly well placed to do this not just because we had run a number of very successful large-scale events, such as Creating Good Lives only six months earlier, but also because we were one of the few organisations in Scotland to attract people regularly from a wide range of sectors to our conferences.

Tackling Scotland's drink and drug culture event

So on March 14th 2011 the Centre held a half-day event in the Hilton Grosvenor Hotel in Glasgow. The precise title of the event was **Tackling Scotland's drink and drug culture – what next?** It proved to be hugely attractive and 300 people, the maximum permitted in the venue, registered to attend. As we anticipated, participants came from a wide variety of sectors. Joy Barlow from Scottish Training – Drugs and Alcohol introduced the programme and appropriately, the keynote speaker was Professor Bruce Alexander.

Professor Alexander outlined his 'dislocation theory of addiction' whereby a fragmented society, which does not satisfy individual's psychological needs, leads to mass dislocation and mass addictions. One of the most powerful parts of Professor Alexander's speech was his argument that those who take heroin are less damaging to society than CEOs whose addiction to money and power can have drastic social and economic consequences. Because Professor Alexander argues that addiction happens when people's psychological needs are not met, the problem can easily change from one substance or activity to another. For example, a person can move from an addiction to alcohol to gambling or drugs. This is why he was particularly generous in his praise for the Independent Enquiry report since the authors recognise that the issue is *cultural*.

I spoke next and in my talk I outlined some of the theories, ideas and research I used in *The Tears that Made the Clyde* to help explain why historically Glasgow's population had such an addiction to alcohol. I specifically talked about inequality, materialist values, adverse childhood experiences and poor relationships between men and women.

Following this there were short, informative and moving talks on how children in Scotland are affected by alcohol. Pete Seaman, from the Glasgow Centre for Population Health, talked about young people's 'drinking to belong' culture. Alison Wales presented the findings from a Childline survey called 'Untold Stories: children's accounts of living with harmful parental drinking'. Another speaker outlined the links between substance misuse and violence and finally we heard about hope and recovery from Kim McGinley who had personally made this journey. These short talks were given under the heading of 'Postcards from Scotland's Young People'. I had completely forgotten this until I started to write this section in 2023. But the title Postcards from Scotland must have lodged subliminally in my mind to emerge a year later as a good name for our series of short books.

The final main session was facilitated by Professor Phil Hanlon. During this interactive session Phil invited the audience to form small groups to discuss the full range of changes required to help 'melt the iceberg' and 'raise the temperature of the water'. There was a huge amount of energy, focus and commitment during these discussions. Phil also asked participants to record some of the most important points on paper. After the event, the Centre grouped these responses into eight categories covering structural and cultural changes, children, family and early years, schools, what needs to happen at the individual level and what those involved in drugs and alcohol work need to do differently. We then put this feedback on our website. The Enquiry Team also considered these responses in detail.

John Matthews, the Independent Enquiry Chair, gave the closing remarks. He started by talking about the Centre's 'Tipping Point' event and how the keynote speaker, Malcolm Gladwell, told such inspiring stories, that listeners left believing that transformational change in Scotland was possible. Echoing Gladwell, he also argued that the change needed was not so much political as personal and social:

> The Enquiry Report. . . strongly encourages a change away from our usual reliance on political and economic power to bring about a step-change to what we now recognise as 'social power' – that is the influence of each of us in combination – which is much more effective in bringing about transformational change. It was the Enquiry's view that there is much more room for manoeuvre than we often allow and that the change we seek is often more within the 'personal' than the political sphere. It was Rudyard Kipling who perceptively suggested that, 'the strength of the pack is the wolf, and the strength of the wolf is the pack'.

Follow up event: Communities that Can!

The Enquiry Team decided that a follow-up event six months later would keep the momentum going. The Centre organised this and we held the half-day event in the Roxburghe Hotel, Edinburgh on 3rd October 2011. We chose this venue as McDonald Hotels allowed us to use it for free and we only had to pay for catering and audio-visual support.

The event was free for participants but only 90 people registered – more than 200 fewer than for the Glasgow event six months earlier. John Matthews chaired the event again and Joy Barlow gave an introduction. She outlined progress to date with the Independent Enquiry and then particularly focused on one aspect of the report's recommendations – 'the circle of care'. Phil Hanlon also spoke and reiterated the thinking behind the report particularly the need for a 'whole population approach'. Phil also facilitated a 'what's next?' discussion at the end of the afternoon.

The main speaker and facilitator was Dr Tam Lundy from Vancouver, Canada. Tam had extensive experience in large-scale capacity building and community involvement in health promotion. She had played a leadership role in the start-up phase of BC (British Columbia) Healthy Communities and was now using this practical experience, together with her scholarship on human and social development and an 'integral approach', to create a framework she called 'Communities that Can!'

On paper Tam's proposal for how she would facilitate her session at the event looked perfect and exactly what we needed to move forward. For example, in her programme notes she says that 'Communities that Can! provides a comprehensive action framework and capacity building approach to support the change-making work of practitioners, policy makers, multisectoral leaders and engaged citizens working in diverse organisational and community contexts.' And she also pledged to link her framework to the complex change challenge – widespread drug and alcohol misuse – that we were facing in Scotland. But at the event Tam's approach came over as too abstract and theoretical and many participants left feeling more frustrated than inspired.

I have found it challenging to be honest here as I spent two days with Tam when she was in Scotland and really warmed to her as a person. I also thought that she was very knowledgeable about how to work with diverse people in large-scale transformational change projects. Nonetheless at the event her input and facilitation style did not work well for the audience.

Fresh ideas

In 2017 a Scottish figure took the UK by storm and even won the prestigious Orwell prize in 2018. He is Darren McGarvey, aka Loki, and that prize-winning book was *Poverty Safari* (2017). In January 2018 I wrote two articles on it for the website *Sceptical Scot* created and managed by David Gow and Fay Young who had been giving Darren opportunities to promote his ideas before the publication of his book. The first of my articles is called 'The Man o' Independent Mind' and I give a summary of it here as I think its arguments are so important to the issues I've addressed in this chapter.

I begin by lamenting that we now live in a world which is increasingly intolerant of others' views and that chasms have opened up between those with opposing ideas. This makes new thinking almost impossible. But this is what Darren McGarvey, who grew up in a deprived community in Glasgow's Pollok and has never attended university, gives us in his book.

McGarvey identifies with the left and repeatedly links the challenges of people living in places like Pollok to deindustrialisation, poverty and inequality. He also returns frequently to issues of unfairness and exclusion and believes it right for the poor to feel angry. He is excoriating about the 'poverty industry' and what happens under the banner of 'regeneration'.

But while McGarvey accepts a left-wing analysis he is also aware of how little it has to offer:

> On the left, I see constant talk of new economic systems, of overthrowing elites or of increasing public spending. I see endless debate about the overlapping, interdependent structural oppressions of western society and the symbolic violence inherent in capitalism. But I rarely see anyone talking

> about emotional literacy. It's rare to see a debate about overeating. I never see activists being more open about their drink problems and drug habits or the psychological problems fuelling them.

Later he adds it is as if 'somehow we can postpone action on the things that are demoralising, incapacitating and killing us until after the hypothetical revolution.' In short, for the left abstract structural solutions always trump discussion of vital problems related to what McGarvey calls 'mind, body and spirit'. This wasn't always the case. Just look at the Independent Labour Party (ILP), influential in Glasgow in the early part of the twentieth century, and you will see socialist idealists who also talked about spirituality. What's more, many were passionate teetotallers who campaigned for prohibition because they saw the damage alcohol caused in their communities.

McGarvey is particularly interested in agency and personal responsibility. He is acutely aware that as the left abandoned this agenda it has become the preserve of the right. It is to McGarvey's credit that he ventures bravely into this contested territory. It's not surprising that some of the critical comments about *Poverty Safari* have been about how McGarvey is 'individualising' the problem.

McGarvey also makes clear that he was brought up to blame others for anything he disliked about his own life. 'All my life I was told that the system was to blame for the problems in my family and that my family were to blame for the problems in mine', he writes. He then adds, 'This belief that it was always someone else's fault was reinforced by the poverty industry and politicians. . .'

McGarvey is a thoughtful man who understands that blaming others for everything you don't like about your life is a dead-end. It renders you powerless and unable to grow and develop as an individual. After all, development results from taking action and learning from mistakes and this can only happen if we accept some responsibility for what we do. What's more, our happiness and mental health depend on our personal relationships with family and friends, as well as the state of our inner lives. And the choices we make on a daily basis have an enormous impact both on our relationships and how we feel.

McGarvey is not being simplistic, telling members of his community to stop moaning and pull themselves up by their proverbial bootstraps. He is all too aware that childhood trauma can lead people to be angry and aggressive, trying to numb the pain by overeating or abusing substances. He knows first-hand how constant poverty and feelings of inferiority grind people down and encourage them to take decisions which are ultimately self-defeating. But he sees how toxic it is for people to believe that the choices they make in life don't matter. It's this realisation that helped him turn his own life around.

Instead of continuing to blame the middle classes or his mental illness for everything he disliked about himself or his life McGarvey started to see his own complicity. In one *Scotsman* article he succinctly described the connection between his own behaviour and his feelings:

> If I am growing overly fond of red wine or codeine has found its way into my diet or I spend two hours a day watching violent pornography then I shouldn't act confused as to why I feel tired, paranoid, agitated and emotionally distant from my partner – and myself.
>
> If I sleep in late, wake up and drink three cups of industrial coffee, smoke five cigarettes and have a fudge doughnut for breakfast, then I have to be prepared to accept that I may experience what feels like a mild downer later that afternoon.

Since he argues that blaming others was a major feature of his upbringing, how did Darren McGarvey develop such insight? There's little doubt that his referral for anger management to the Notre Dame Centre when he was an adolescent and the work he did with his psychologist Marilyn was a major turning point. This doesn't save him from sliding into alcohol and drug addiction. But it sows the seeds of self-awareness. Eventually this helps him to make better, more responsible choices for himself.

I was a personal development trainer for many years and know that self-awareness and the insights it brings are in short supply in Scotland. So when I read McGarvey's book I was taken aback at his level of self-awareness and his willingness to analyse his own motivations. As can be common in someone who was maltreated as a child, he has a great capacity to read other people's behaviour. Of course, these skills can make someone appear narcissistic and manipulative, and McGarvey acknowledges that danger. However, on the basis of what he writes I take a more generous view.

Some of his critique on the limited focus of the left could be extended to academia. Partly as a result of subject specialisation and fragmentation, academics focus narrowly on specific topics. The way academics operate means they are not going to come up with a broad view of any social problem: they can't help us out of the either/or trap – the idea that the main problems facing impoverished communities either come from structural problems or what McGarvey calls 'mind, body and spirit'. It's all these things, as McGarvey helps us to see.

His critique could also be extended to some professional groups who take an exclusively structuralist view, believing that improvement is only possible if there are economic changes. Some public health analysts in Scotland, for example, see alcohol addiction only as an outcome of income inequality and not as an additional factor blighting people's lives.

I fully support McGarvey's view that the problems facing poor communities are complex and stubborn. Of course, we need to press for better welfare, more jobs, and houses but there are some things people must do for themselves as individuals, and more importantly, as part of families and communities, to improve their own lives. To believe otherwise is to reinforce powerlessness; to believe that what people do in their lives doesn't matter and to rob them of agency.

That perspective inevitably means that I also support the approach of the Poverty Truth Commission. Faith in Community Scotland established the first one of these in Glasgow in 2009 and Darren McGarvey was initially involved. One of the main founders of this movement is Martin Johnstone, then a Church of Scotland minister in Glasgow and someone I met on a frequent basis. Faith in Community Scotland was one of the supporting organisations for the Centre's Creating Good Lives event and Martin and others attended.

The Poverty Truth Commission has grown considerably since its first Glasgow meeting. Now there's a network of Commissions across the UK. Faith in Community Scotland takes an asset-based approach to community development and always believed that poor people themselves must be at the heart of any change:

> It is our conviction that we cannot hope to understand, let alone address, the causes and symptoms of poverty unless we involve the experts. In this context, the experts are those who have a direct experience of poverty; living with the reality day in and day out. To use our motto, taken from the South African post-apartheid process, 'Nothing about us – without us – is for us'. We believe real progress towards overcoming poverty will be made when those who experience poverty are central to the development, delivery and evaluation of solutions.

2024 postscript

So much has happened since we held our Creating Good Lives event in 2010 and Darren McGarvey published *Poverty Safari* in 2017 that it seemed appropriate to add a postscript. In the past ten years poverty has become a much bigger issue and more and more families and children are living in extremely hard times. Official Westminster Government estimates showed that 30 per cent of all UK children were in poverty in 2022/23 – a much higher number than in 2010/11. Around 69 per cent of these poor children were in working families.

The Conservative Government introduced a benefit cap in 2013 and then the two-child limit for benefits in 2017. These reductions in financial support for families, together with low pay, limited and insecure work, and rising living costs have pushed many more children into poverty. The COVID-19 pandemic and then Russia's invasion of Ukraine have led to large increases in energy and food prices and a cost-of-living crisis. Many families are having to choose between heating and eating. Inflation has also been exacerbated in the UK by a housing crisis.

What many of these families need above all else to live good lives is more money and security.

Chapter 16
Equality, diversity and positive ageing

My background in equal opportunities;
managing diversity;
the Centre's work with the Equalities and Human Rights Commission;
Postcards from Scotland and gender;
publication of *She, He, They: Families, gender and coping with transition*;
background to *Working with Equality*; themes and contributors;
positive ageing event and resources; personal reflection on ageing well.

IN 1991 I attended a meeting, and if I hadn't, I doubt there would have been a Centre for Confidence and Well-being and I would have no need to write this book. In other words, it was one of my 'sliding doors' moments as it set in train a number of important developments for my life and career. I am recounting it here as it's relevant for this chapter on equality and diversity.

The meeting in question was organised by Action for Women at BBC Scotland. I had worked there as a researcher/reporter from 1979 to 1985 before becoming the Continuing Education Officer, Scotland for BBC Education in London. This was a post I held part-time as part of a job share. I was a busy, young, working mother and I hadn't been to one of the Action for Women meetings before. The group's focus was women's pay and promotion prospects in BBC Scotland and that was the only topic on the agenda. I asked if they had ever thought about the portrayal of women in BBC

Scotland's output as this could help make the case for having more women involved in production. They hadn't and those present encouraged me to do something on their behalf if I had the motivation and time.

I picked a week at random and set my VHS machine to record all BBC Scotland's news, current affairs and sports output. I then set about counting the number of participants on these programmes and what percentage was female. As expected, it was shockingly low. I wrote a report on my findings and Action for Women presented it to BBC Scotland management. Its newly appointed Controller, John McCormick, was most impressed. He was keen to pursue a new approach and equality issues were high on his agenda.

John McCormick then asked me to become Chair of his new BBC Scotland Equal Opportunities Committee and to write a detailed strategy report. This was a tricky request for me as my post with BBC Education had just been axed in a major restructuring exercise. John suggested that I still take on the role and they would pay me as a consultant. I had recently trained to deliver assertiveness courses and was considering a freelance career. But there's little doubt that John's offer made this a much more attractive prospect. And it was all this freelance experience I accumulated which prompted me to write *The Scots' Crisis of Confidence* ten years later.

I chaired BBC Scotland's Equal Opportunities Committee for five years and learned a lot as I had to become aware of current disability and race issues as well as gender. I also enjoyed working with a number of great people – particularly Pat Davers, Annie Woods and Colin Cameron who was then Head of Television. I write this as a preamble to saying that very quickly I did not like the world of equal opportunities and the steps organisations were taking under this banner at the time. This is a big topic, and not completely relevant here, so suffice to say that one reason I felt uncomfortable with the equal opportunities approach is that it tended to reinforce, rather than counter stereotyping. So, according to this perspective, women need assertiveness or management training and men don't or we should be giving support to working mothers but not working fathers and so on. I also knew from my own experience and talking to women that most of the barriers they perceived were cultural rather than structural – for example, presenteeism and cloning whereby a particular type of man is promoted as he fits the mould. What's more, I could see that staff were increasingly hostile to equalities work in organisations as they saw it as a 'management' agenda, and something that was complicating their job, rather than something they particularly valued.

So, under my leadership, BBC Scotland became an early adopter of a 'managing diversity' rather than a conventional equalities approach. This is founded on the idea that there is a strong business case for having a diverse workforce and that diversity includes a broad range of differences between people including race, gender, age, cultural heritage, physical ability, class, sexual orientation, religion, lifestyle (parents, carers etc), education, work preferences and personality. We no longer provided training aimed at specific groups and started to place more emphasis on fair selection processes, flexible working, appreciation of diversity and team building. There's little doubt that this approach demanded much more of managers and leaders than traditional equal opportunities.

So what did the Centre I was later to set up do to promote equality and diversity, other than what I have already covered in this book?

Work with the Equalities and Human Rights Commission in Scotland

In 2009 the Centre won a competitive bid for funding from the Equalities and Human Rights Commission (EHRC) in Scotland. The bid was won and the work undertaken principally by Zoe Van Zwanenberg, the Centre's project manager.

The EHRC funded this piece of work as it was aware that leadership statistics across the public, private and third sectors showed that certain groups, specifically minority groups within the population, are under-represented. The project was designed to explore issues of equalities and leadership through the processes of action inquiry, appreciative inquiry and desk-based review. Zoe engaged a wide range of individuals from across all sectors of the Scottish economy, but with a particular focus on the public and voluntary sectors. A group of Scottish government employees was involved in the action inquiry process and submitted a report on their findings on equalities and leadership in the organisation.

Leaders recruited to take part in the project were asked to pose incisive questions about the 'whys' that lie behind the disparity in leadership figures and what could make a difference. By listening to the stories of colleagues and business associates analysing their own experiences, and applying objective research techniques to their situation, these leaders contributed insights into past barriers and came up with practical ideas for future change.

During this eighteen-month long project, the Centre produced a DVD featuring some of the people involved in carrying out the action inquiries. Zoe also produced a 40-page report on the project which was available in a newly created section of the Centre's website. From all the stories Zoe collected from the 75 appreciative inquiry interviewees it's possible to distill a number of lessons. These form the core recommendations for policy makers and development practitioners.

For leadership development to be truly inclusive organisations must:

- Offer leadership development opportunities in school, youth groups etc;

- Make recruitment processes open so that they value experience that is different;

- Focus on the importance and impact of opportunities for growth and development offered in people's first jobs;

- Value self-awareness in all members of the organisation and group;

- Pay attention to organisational culture and how difference is truly valued.

The report also stressed the importance of strong peer learning networks and mentoring programmes for good leadership development. It highlighted the crucial need for all staff to feel respected and valued; for communication skills to be given a high priority in organisations; and for learning communities to be actively supported and nurtured.

On 28th September 2010 the Centre held a conference at the Albany Centre in Glasgow to conclude the 18-month joint collaboration with the EHRC in Scotland. This half day event – **Leadership is a people business: towards a fairer Britain** – attracted over 40 participants. Professor Steve Reicher from St Andrew's University talked about leadership issues. I spoke about equality, confidence and well-being. Zoe talked about the outcomes of the research based on her appreciative inquiry interviews. Delegates also viewed the DVD which the Centre had produced as part of the project featuring some of the people involved in carrying out the action inquiries. It was a fitting end to what had been a complex and satisfying project.

Postcards from Scotland and gender

Given my background I was acutely aware of the gender balance of *Postcards from Scotland*. In the early days I approached a number of women to see if they would like to write a book for the series. I was in frequent contact with several of them but ultimately these books never materialised. That also happened with a few men but undoubtedly it was more of an issue with prospective women authors, some of whom were going to write about gender issues in Scotland.

At the time of writing this chapter, we have published 17 different volumes and the gender breakdown is fairly healthy: seven books carry only women's names on the cover; eight have only men as authors; and two have both male and female names. However, early in the series the books had significantly more male authors. After the publication of *Conviction* there were six books written by men, two written by women (and one of them was me) and one jointly written by a man and a woman. It wasn't only me who felt frustrated and embarrassed by this male bias; the Centre's board did too and we resolved not to publish another book until it was by a woman. I wrote an email to our database explaining that we were particularly looking for women to contribute to the series. Happily, this solicited an immediate response and the tenth book in the series is by a woman though it did mean a fifteen-month gap between number nine in the series and number ten.

She, He, They

Shirley Young is the name of the woman who got in touch as a result of my email. We had met a few years before when I spoke at a conference and was then seated beside her at lunch and we had a very engaging conversation. Shirley contacted me as she thought she had an interesting, and topical story to recount. She certainly did. What's more, she was an instinctive and powerful story-teller. This is how Shirley starts her book:

> The night I lost my beautiful, fine-boned, pixie-faced, blue-eyed, lesbian daughter there was no ambulance whisking her to A&E, no sad-eyed police constables with suitably arranged facial expressions at the door to break the bad news of her passing. Nor was there a kindly consultant saying they tried everything, but sadly she was no more. There was just, in the silence of midnight, the simple statement, spoken in an agony of fear and trepidation – 'I need to be a man, mum. I am a man.'

Shirley's story is simple and powerful. Eleven years earlier, before Jane's confession, she was the mother of a son and a daughter. Then Jane made her transition to a different gender and Shirley was now the mother of two sons. In 2016 there had been a fair amount of coverage of trans issues but I had never read much about the impact that gender transition can have on parents and siblings. In the book Shirley explains why she had invested a lot emotionally in having a daughter and why losing her was so painful.

Sadly, trans issues cannot be discussed openly nowadays and trying to do so can lead to accusations of transphobia. I'm a great believer in free speech and so profoundly dislike the idea that we should not be discussing the subject. Fortunately, trans issues were much less controversial in 2016.

I have also had concerns for a number of years now about the number of young girls who want to become boys and wonder if 'social contagion', particularly on social media, is part of the explanation. So, I would have been deterred from publishing the book if the young person in question – Jane who becomes Nathan– – had been under 18. But when Jane announces to her mum that she is a man, she was 20 – old enough to make this decision for herself and to grasp its consequences.

In her book Shirley does not gloss over the difficulties of gender transition or how hard the journey can be for the individual and the family. Nathan was very troubled by his breasts and so his parents paid £5000 for a double mastectomy. However, his positive view of his new chest was short-lived and the operation led him to feel so bad that he had three attempts at suicide. Shirley wonders if expediting the operation by going privately meant that he had less time to process his feelings. She also recounts how she too felt suicidal at times and admits that she started to drink too much.

There was yet more change to come, though it was not as challenging for the family. Nathan eventually decided that he is non-binary and has 'both masculine and feminine parts of his gender'. Shirley says the biggest challenge now is remembering to use the pronouns 'they' and 'them'. This is why we called the book *She, He They: Families, gender and coping with transition.* We launched the book in the Project Cafe, Glasgow on 25th October 2016.

The book is very challenging in parts but it has a strong narrative structure which means that the reader wants to find out what happens next. It's ultimately a hopeful book as the various ordeals Shirley recounts bring them closer together as a family.

Working for Equality: Policy, Politics, People

In the spring of 2016 I received an email from Professor James Mitchell. He explained that a colleague of his in the Academy of Government at Edinburgh University, Professor Richard Freeman, had picked up a copy of *Conviction* in his office and was now wondering if we might be interested in producing a book on one of his projects. I quickly arranged to meet up with Richard to hear his proposal. We published a book on this project called *Working for Equality: Policy, politics, people* in the autumn of 2017. It was the first edited, multi-authored book in the *Postcards* series. The rest of this section explains how the project came about and the content of the book.

At the end of 2015 Richard had convened a group which he called 'the Reference group on In/Equalities'. The group continued to meet every couple of months in 2016 to discuss the topic which included poverty, homelessness and public health as well as the usual equality subjects. As you can see from the list of chapters and authors (Box 13) group members worked in a variety of different sectors and organisations. In the introduction to *Working for Equality,* Richard explains the purpose of the group and how it operated:

> The idea was to talk. We wanted to share experiences, explore challenges and note successes, develop new, critical and constructive perspectives in the fields in which we worked. To do that we had to leave the silos of our professional and organisational fields, finding a new space in which to engage directly with others we might otherwise never have met – but who, we found, shared remarkably similar problems. In this way, we came to discuss concepts of equality and intersectionality, regulation and legislation, performance management, electoral and many other kinds of politics, arts and culture, administrative systems and the life stories of individual human beings.

As talking was the central purpose of the group they thought a lot about how they should go about it. Discussions took place over a couple of days and involved a dinner. At each meeting a group

Box 13 Working for Equality

I Equalities

1. What we talk about when we talk about equality
   Philip Cook , Political Theory Lecturer, Edinburgh University

2. Liberty equality and fraternity in Scotland's schools
   Danny Murphy, Retired Headteacher

3. Intersectionality and why it matters
   Ashlee Christoffersen, Former equality researcher and now PhD student

4. Equality, instrumentality, uncertainty
   Darcy Leigh, Law lecturer, Sussex University

II Policy

5. Fairness Commissions
   Robert McGregor, Community Planning Manager, Fife Council

6. The business of a Living Wage
   Rachel McEwen, Director of Sustainability at SSE

7. Information or ideas?
   Katherine Smith, Reader in the Global Public Health Unit, Edinburgh University

8. The role of rules
   Richard Freeman, Professor of Social Science and Public Policy, Edinburgh University

9. The inefficiencies of mainstreaming
   Helen Chambers, co-founder Inspiring Scotland

10. Policy talk
    Madelaine Simpkin, Independent social researcher

11. Policy and voice
    Elinor Mitchell, Scottish Government

III Politics

12. Political action on inequality
    Gerry McCartney, Head of Scottish Public Health Observatory

13. Jock Tamson's bairns'
    Jatin Haria, Coalition for Racial Equality and Rights

14. Women in politics: why quotas matter
    Meryl Kennedy, Lecturer in Gender and Politics, Edinburgh University

15. Visibility and vigilance
    Ann Henderson, Assistant Secretary, STUC

16. Achieving LGBT equality
    Fergus McMillan, LGBT Youth Scotland

17. Doing research, doing politics
    Fiona McHardy, Poverty Alliance Scotland

IV People

18. Let me tell you about Tommy
    Ewan Aitken, former Leader of Edinburgh Council and CEO of Cyrenians

19. Every child
    Celine Sinclair, CEO of the Yard

20. People and places – from Mapira to Govan
    Jamie Livingstone, Head of Oxfam Scotland

21. Shared spaces
    Diarmaid Lawlor, Head of Urbanism at Architecture and Design Scotland

22. Small steps, slow journeys
    Caroline Gibb, Development worker for the Edinburgh Equality RIghts Network

Reflections
Danny Murphy, Richard Freeman and Fiona McHardy

member presented 'a case study'. Richard describes the process as 'a report from the field' whereby the individual described 'their work in general terms and then some aspect of it they found difficult or significant, and which they wanted to recognise and reflect upon.' I had the good fortune to be invited to one of these sessions and the dinner which followed. It was an enlightening and convivial experience.

At that meeting I talked about the series and the style of the books. Group members then committed to each contributing a 1,000 word essay which would reflect their own views, rather than their organisations'. In his introduction Richard tells us that these written contributions are 'meant as interventions in the continuing conversation about inequalities in Scotland, as invitations to pick up these thoughts and ideas and take them somewhere new.' In their reflections at the end of the book the three editors named on the cover – Richard Freeman, Fiona McHardy and Danny Murphy – describe the contributions as 'postcards from the frontline as well as from the backstage': the frontline being equalities work in contemporary Scotland.

There is a rich seam of material in this book for anyone who wants to know more about some fundamental ideas about equality, such as intersectionality, and some practical measures, like quotas, Fairness Commissions or the Living Wage, to help bring it about. As there are 22 individual chapters in the book, with different voices and contributions, it's impossible for me to do justice to them in this short section. So I have just selected a few that I found particularly interesting or compelling.

The first of these is the chapter by Jatin Haria of the Coalition of Racial Equality and Rights which he calls 'Jock Tamson's bairns'. Jatin's argument is straightforward: Scotland likes to perceive itself as an egalitarian country where everyone is recorded respect and equality but the rhetoric does not match the reality. He quotes statistics showing a worrying level of racial attacks, including murders, in Scotland. Crime isn't the only problem as Black and Minority Ethnic (BME) people are also much more likely to be poor and face more barriers in finding employment. Political representation is also low. At the time of writing 25 of the 32 local authorities in Scotland had no BME councillors. Jatin thinks there is a very limited understanding of racism in Scotland, political complacency from the top of government and a 'lack of pressure on public bodies and wider Scottish society to take meaningful action to achieve change.'

Madelaine Simpkin, a public policy researcher, begins her contribution by asking why so many government policies 'fail to be fully realised'. She argues that in a complex world people have to make sense of what the changes actually mean and the way this is done is through 'talk' which she sees as the 'unrecognised . . . heartbeat sustaining policy making'. Yet talk is routinely dismissed as unimportant. 'I often hear people in Scotland grumbling about "talking shops" taking up all of our time, of meetings and email exchanges dragging on and taking away from the "real work",' she writes. Adding 'Those perspectives miss the point. . . Those actions are significant aspects of the work. Arguably, much of the rest is some form of documentation.' She ends her article by reminding us:

> . . . the Enlightenment did not happen on paper; it came about in coffee shops and other public fora and was powerful precisely because it was a period of exchanging and challenging ideas. We need a 21st century enlightenment, one which is deeply concerned about the insidious and pervasive inequalities that we continue to face. Talking will not be the only means of overcoming them, but it will allow us to go back to basics, shining light into dark corners, and drawing out the ideas that support meaningful, substantive change.

While I think Madelaine is right to talk about the power of ideas for change, she is primarily talking about public servants in her article, mainly in the civil service. And in the present Scottish context there is so much centralised control, and groupthink, that there is not the free exchange of ideas and challenge that Madelaine maintains is an essential part of the change process. That being said, Elinor Mitchell, who works for the Scottish Government, refreshingly states in her article that 'the role I see for myself, is disrupting the current way we do things – the accepted norms of who does what in our society, and whose voice matters most.' She sees a central part of her job as 'listening'.

A number of other contributors stress the importance of relationships and personal growth for change. This is the view of Ewan Aitken, a former Church of Scotland minister and Labour Leader of Edinburgh City Council, who is now the head of the Cyrenians in Scotland – a charity designed to tackle the cause and consequences of homelessness. He calls his article 'Let me tell you about Tommy', an alcoholic who had lost everything and become homeless. Ewan goes on to tell us about Freddie and Grace too. Once he recounts their stories of transformation he tells us:

> Cyrenians see our task as being simply to journey with those we serve, so they can find the spaces to discover in themselves the strength and resilience to be who they can be. The tipping points described here . . . were all moments when those on the journey responded to a change they experienced in their inner lives; when they were ready, on their terms, in their time. It wasn't simply that their material or other external circumstances had changed: their inner well was filled again and the move from exclusion to inclusion had begun.

Indeed one of the things I particularly like about *Working for Equality* is that it contains lots of stories and an emphasis on people and relationships in the journey towards a more equal, inclusive society.

In the last chapter I wrote about the importance of structural and cultural factors in addressing inequality. In *Working for Equality* there is a great deal of emphasis on behavioural and psychological factors. Equality is not simply about material issues, it is also about how we talk and interact with one another. This is made clear in the opening chapter, written by the political theorist Philip Cook:

> In our discussions at the Reference Group we talked less about equalising income, and more about building boats; less about equalising opportunities, and more about people chatting together on playground swings; less about equalising outcomes, and more about sharing a communal meal. When we talked about equality, we talked about relationships. When we talked about relationships, we talked about respect. Equalising income, opportunities and outcomes is important.

> But a world of equal incomes, opportunities and outcomes in which communities are estranged, in which single mums are stigmatised, and in which vulnerable adults are socially isolated remains unequal.

We launched the book on 2nd November 2017 at an inspiring event in Edinburgh University organised by Professor Richard Freeman. Phil Hanlon spoke on behalf of the Centre and we heard various contributions from authors. I was sorry to part company with this amicable and thoughtful group of people.

Ageism

In Chapter 10 I mentioned that I had written a Ph.D. thesis on Simone de Beauvoir's *The Second Sex.* Many still view this as an essential text on women's subordination but few are aware that Beauvoir also turned her attention to another group who, she claims, are also seen as 'the other' and robbed of their humanity – old people. In *La Vieillesse* (1970) Beauvoir argues that the elderly are seen as a 'foreign species' and that there is 'a conspiracy of silence' in acknowledging this fact. She astutely points out that unless we die young we will eventually join this disdained group so it makes no sense for us to treat the old so badly.

By the new millennium attitudes to older people were beginning to change but not on grounds of fairness. Policy makers and politicians were increasingly aware that we are living in a society where almost a quarter of the population is over 60. In fact, 35 per cent of the Scottish population in 2007 was aged 50 or over. What's more, the number of people in the population aged 80 or over was due to increase sharply thanks to the large baby boomers' generation. For economic reasons, as well as concern for the well-being of older people themselves, everyone needed to start seeing ageing in a more positive light.

In 2007 the Scottish Executive, as the Scottish Government was then called, published a report called 'All our Futures: Planning for a Scotland with an Ageing Population'. The Scottish Parliament's think tank – Scotland's Future Forum – had produced a report on positive ageing and called for a national debate on the issues involved. Their report even claimed: ' A new social contract must be drawn up between government, business and individual citizens: a contract which promotes a culture where older people will be recognised for their value and tremendous potential to businesses, the economy and society.'

Positive ageing

Aware that policy makers were increasingly interested in older people, the Centre held a conference on positive ageing as part of our three 'Vanguard stages' events. We called it **Wisdom and Flamboyance: Flourishing in older life** and held it in Òran Mór, Glasgow on 11th October 2007. Over 40 people, mainly from the caring professions, attended.

The programme was primarily designed by Angus Skinner who had joined the Centre as an Associate Consultant at the beginning of 2007. Angus was previously Chief Social Work Inspector to Scottish Ministers and had helped in the founding of the Centre in 2004/5. Angus was very keen on positive psychology and had spent time at the University of Pennsylvania doing a masters in positive psychology with Professor Martin Seligman.

Positive psychology had a lot to offer those concerned about the upwards trend in ageing so Angus was able to attract financial support from the Scottish Executive so that we could bring to Scotland international speakers for our October event.

Angus and I both chaired the conference. The keynote speaker was Professor Corey Keyes from Emory University who is an expert on flourishing and had co-authored a book on the topic. At the event, he set out his theory that mental health is not just the absence of mental illness. Though they are closely related, they do not lie on a continuum with mental health at one end and mental illness at the other. Instead we need to create the conditions which promote flourishing.

Flourishing at any age of life, according to Keyes, is the presence of both hedonic and eudemonic well-being. Hedonic well-being is what we often think of as happiness: pleasant emotions and satisfaction with life. Eudemonic well-being, by contrast, has eleven components including meaning, purpose in life, personal growth, and autonomy. When we don't have these components in our lives, we are in a state Keyes describes as 'languishing'. In the older years this means boosting positive emotion but also looking at how to create meaning and purpose in life.

The other main speaker was Professor Mary Gilhooley, then President of the British Society of Gerontology and also Professor of Health Studies at Brunel University. She is author of several books on dementia. Professor Gilhooley also established Scotland's first centre of social gerontology at the University of Paisley. Understandably Professor Gilhooley pointed out that positive ageing may not be in the grasp of those with health, social or economic problems.

Jacquie Roberts was Chief Executive of the Care Commission which oversees the standard of care provided for children, adults and older people across Scotland. She assured the audience that her organisation aims to improve the quality of care for the elderly. This was partly about factors such as infection control and supervision of medical care but more importantly it was about staff paying attention to three mantras: 'Know me for who I am; respect me for who I am; treat me how you would want me to treat you.' Jacquie also talked about the importance of self-development, self-care and family and community connections.

At the conference we discussed with participants how we can create a state of flourishing in older people. Participants mainly took the view that we must tap into what the older generation have to give to others and society as a whole. We have much to learn from older people and this can help them cultivate a sense of meaning and purpose. Participants suggested this could be achieved through intergenerational communication and story-telling.

The Centre put most of the material related to the conference onto our website. The following year we created a jigsaw piece in the Flourishing Lives section of our website, called 'later years'. This contained information on what positive ageing looks like and how to foster it. For example, we summarised a variety of studies which show how negative stereotypes of older people have a direct influence on their health and well-being. Conversely, we reported a 2002 study by Becca Levy *et al* which showed that over a 23 year study period individuals, both males and females, who have a positive view of their own ageing lived longer.

In Chapter 7 I reported that there is a replicability crisis in psychology so I was interested to see if this type of finding is still reliable. A meta-analysis conducted by Westerhof *et al* and published in 2023 in *Psychology and Ageing* showed that all of the 100 plus studies they analysed found that measures of subjective ageing – how a person perceives, interprets and evaluates their own ageing – has an effect on health outcomes later in life. In other words, having a positive view of the ageing process can support your mental and physical health and even improve longevity. This means that talking positively to older people about ageing and countering ageist stereotypes can have a significant effect on their lives. And in societies where people are living longer this is hugely important for all of us.

Personal reflection

Ageing, positive or otherwise, is also a topic of great personal relevance for me. When the Centre started in 2005 I was 53 and would have been included in the older age group in some studies. At the time of writing, I'm 72 and most definitely in the 'elderly' category.

More importantly, most of what I've learned about what contributes to good ageing comes not just from positive psychology and academic studies but also from observing my parents' lives, particularly my mother's. When I was asked by Age Scotland to address their large annual gathering in Perth in 2014 about well-being in later life I agreed so long as I could illustrate my talk with reference to my parents. They had both died the year before in their 90s. The audience appreciated what I had to say as they thought my parents' stories brought the research on well-being to life and rendered it much more meaningful.

My mother came from a very ordinary working-class background, and left school at 14. She had a very traumatic childhood, poor mental health from her 60s on and didn't have great physical health. Despite this she lived a good, full life in her own home, until she was 92 with little obvious cognitive decline.

Research now shows that loneliness has a very negative effect on people's health and life prospects in a way that's similar to smoking 15 cigarettes a day or being obese. Some researchers conclude that it may not be the feeling of loneliness which is important; it's the social interaction which really matters. This is something my mother had in spades. She had three daughters and four grandchildren who loved her dearly. She had great neighbours and was involved in community activities. In short, my mother was part of a web of ***social and family connections.*** This is fundamentally important for health.

A sense of meaning and purpose is also important for well-being at any stage of life. And again, this is something my mother experienced in her later years: she helped her two daughters who lived locally with childcare and babysitting. She was then enthusiastic about looking after pets when required. So my mother felt needed throughout her 70s and most of her 80s.

And finally, my mother had another two things going for her as she aged. First, she had an ***active mind*** as she did puzzles on a daily basis, particularly crosswords and second, she had a ***positive view of ageing***. I talked to my mother a lot about the Centre's work but she didn't pick this up from me. In her later years she got it from a BBC television documentary series aired in 2010 called *The Young Ones*. This was based on research conducted by the American psychologist Ellen Langer which shows that people's perception of ageing has a major impact on their cognitive and physical abilities. The importance of ***independence*** was another key learning point of the series and one which resonated strongly with my mother who then made a point of doing as much as possible for herself.

My father came from a working-class Glaswegian background and lived a longer life than any of his five siblings despite the fact he didn't have good physical health. He smoked heavily until he had a heart attack in his 60s and suffered a stroke in his mid 80s. He died aged 90, much older than would have been predicted given his background and chronic physical complaints.

So, what kept him going? One of the remarkable things about my father was that he was extremely motivated by ***hobbies and activities***: he was a great example of what Martin Seligman described in *Authentic Happiness* as 'the engaged life', full of 'flow' and a sense of achievement from learning new skills. He could 'knock a tune' out of most musical instruments, and he was always involved in different activities: making jam or home-made wine, finding wild flowers, gardening, building stone dykes and compiling quizzes. . . Pursuing hobbies is another important way to cultivate a sense of well-being and vitality. And, of course, my father also benefited from having family close by.

Both my parents would frequently say that despite their physical age they felt that 'deep down' or 'inside' they were the same person they had always been. I understand completely what they mean: despite everything I have done and learned in the past three decades I am still that young mother who attended an Action for Women event in 1991 – an event which had a remarkable impact on my future life and career.

CHAPTER 17

Developing ourselves and others

What the Centre did to continue warning of
the dangers of artificial self-esteem building;
four webinars including one with Professor Carol Dweck;
the Centre's *Bounce Back!* courses;
Alan McLean's involvement with the Centre and his work on motivation;
McLean's *Postcards from Scotland* book – *Knowing and Growing;*
another *Postcards* book *The Golden Mean;*
what the Centre did to promote authoritative parenting.

'TRANSCEND AND INCLUDE' – that was our mantra towards the end of 2008 when we moved out of our Phase 1 activities. In other words, we weren't completely turning our backs on what we had been doing but we were also going to embrace new, and varied, activities. And this new work would involve non-psychological approaches to well-being. But as this chapter shows we still did an impressive amount on psychology and continued with a number of strands of activity.

Self-esteem

Advancing a critique of artificial self-esteem building had been central to what we had done in the first phase of activity and had prompted me to write *Creating Confidence* in 2007. In 2010 we were still encouraging people to talk about the topic. On March 30th that year we held a highly popular and very lively half-day event in the Hilton Grosvenor Hotel, Glasgow. We called it **Self-esteem: the facts, myths, challenges and alternatives**. The event was oversubscribed with 450 registered participants. Attendees weren't all school teachers and the event also attracted people working in further and higher education, mental health, careers, sports and the arts.

The main speaker was Keith Campbell, an American psychology professor and expert on narcissism. He had just co-authored an influential book with Jean Twenge called *The Narcissism Epidemic: Living in the age of entitlement* (2009). The focus of his talk was the negative impact that a growing sense of entitlement has on mental health and skills. We also wanted to include Professor Jennifer Crocker on the programme as we had been influenced by her seminal paper 'The Costly Pursuit of Self-esteem'. Unfortunately, she wasn't available but Dr Amy Canevello, her co-researcher at the University of Michigan, accepted our invitation and during her presentation talked through their results. One of the most memorable was that the more students concentrated on how they felt about themselves, and were seen by others, the more unhappy and underconfident they felt.

I also spoke about the Centre's views, the research we had undertaken on self-esteem using the Rosenberg self-esteem scale and what we saw as better alternatives to fostering confidence and good mental health. This included more focus on skills and achievements rather than simply how you felt about yourself.

2011: Autumn series of webinars

The following autumn we ran four webinars – internet-based seminars. One of them was with Professor Jennifer Crocker who updated viewers on their research on the negative effects of focusing on your self-esteem. She set out their findings and concluded her talk by saying that when individuals pursue 'compassionate goals' which are about serving others' needs, they boost their own self-esteem as well as encouraging other people to regard them highly.

The famous Harvard psychology professor Carol Dweck was

the speaker on another webinar. As I recounted in Chapter 3, we ran large events with Carol Dweck in 2007 and 2008. I also outline in Chapter 6 the Centre's research project with Dweck and her colleagues into the effect of her *Brainology* programme on primary school pupils. But I have not yet outlined what Dweck's mindset theory actually involves.

According to Carol Dweck's research, published in 2000, people adopt one of two mindsets towards their intelligence or natural abilities. The first is that intelligence is fixed and doesn't change much over time and the second is that intelligence grows and improves with hard work and effort. People who endorse a growth mindset will attempt challenging tasks, persevere at them, respond positively to criticism and feel optimistic about the future. Those who endorse a fixed mindset will give up when the going gets tough, will not attempt certain tasks in case they fail, become depressed after setbacks, get anxious about both success and failure, and seek to prove themselves to others.

In her webinar Dweck described the fixed and the growth mindsets and her original research before going on to talk about recent research projects. One of them has important, real-life consequences. Gunderson *et al* observed parents interacting with their one to three year olds and the way they praised their children and showed that this had an impact on these children's motivation when they were seven or eight. In essence, the parents who praised their children for effort and encouraged them to struggle with a task or praised them for specific ways of doing things ('good throw') were much more likely to have children who showed a growth mindset (described as an 'incremental framework in this paper) in later years. This was not true for the children whose parents routinely praised them for fixed traits such as 'you're a clever boy', or 'good girl'. These results were independent of socio-economic background and the parents' own mindset. The researchers, which included Carol Dweck, conclude:

> The relative amount of process praise (e.g., 'good job', 'good try') that parents produced during naturalistic interactions when their children were 14 to 38 months of age was a significant predictor of children's incremental framework –

> including believing that traits are malleable, preferring challenging tasks, attributing success and failure to effort, and generating strategies for improvement – at ages 7 to 8 years.

The other two webinars, given by Tim Kasser and Richard Eckersley were related to materialist values and cultural influences on well-being and I covered these topics in Chapter 12.

Bounce Back!

The Australian resiliency programme *Bounce Back!* is another good example of Centre work which spanned both phases. I had first met Toni Noble, its co-creator, in Italy at a European Positive Psychology conference in 2004 and was very impressed by her presentation on *Bounce Back!* She was a skilled facilitator and, as a trained teacher, psychologist and lecturer in teacher education, spoke with great authority about the programme. *Bounce Back!* was extremely relevant to so many teachers as most were struggling on a daily basis with children's lack of resilience. The *Bounce Back!* courses offered classroom teachers practical strategies on how to help all children and young people cope with the complexity of their everyday lives and learn to 'bounce back' when they experience sadness, difficulties, frustrations, failures and hard times. The programme also encouraged schools to listen to children and foster supportive communities.

In Phase 1 we held training courses on *Bounce Back!* in 2007 and 2008. In Phase 2 we held another *Bounce Back!* course in Glasgow in June 2010 and 60 people, mainly teachers and educators from various parts of Scotland, attended and evaluated the course highly. As a result of the Centre's previous work on *Bounce Back!* there was increasing interest in Scotland in the programme. Educational psychologists in Perth and Kinross, Sarah Axford and Kirsty Blyth, were also rolling it out to all primary schools in their area.

In January 2011 when Toni Noble was back in Scotland we held a free recall event for anyone who had ever attended a previous *Bounce Back!* event. Thirty people attended. The two educational psychologists from Perth and Kinross talked about their use of the programme. They also presented their results which showed some improvement in pupil's well-being in the schools using *Bounce Back!* and improvements in teacher well-being.

We held one last training session with Toni in the City of Glasgow College in June 2014 and attracted around 50 participants. We chose the venue not just because it was in the city centre but because it was a college: we were aware that while the focus of all Toni's workshops in Scotland was on schools, they still attracted people from the college and youth work sectors. And these college attendees told us how much they got out of the courses.

The big self-esteem conference, the webinars and *Bounce Back!* have not been our only offerings on psychological approaches to well-being, resilience and personal development in Phase 2. In 2017 we published a *Postcard from Scotland* called *Knowing and Growing: Insights for developing ourselves and others* by Alan McLean.

Tapping into local expertise

I first got to hear about Alan when I was involved in training courses with schools. He had created an award-winning programme, 'Bullyproofing Our School', and another staff development programme called 'Promoting Positive Behaviour'. He was a Principal Psychologist in Glasgow City Council until 2011. He also wrote frequent education columns for the *Times Educational Supplement* in Scotland and *The Scotsman*.

Almost a decade earlier he had become interested in motivation. In the Preface to the book he wrote for the *Postcards* series he explains why:

> About fifteen years ago I found myself struggling to motivate my eight- and ten-year-old sons to take up the guitar. At one point I even said: 'That guitar is getting thrown out in the morning and that's £100 I've wasted on you two.' After two degrees, six years of training in psychology and 20 years' experience as a psychologist, the only way I knew how to motivate my sons was to try to make them feel guilty.

> That's when I realised I knew little about motivation. I had been working in education too long! I knew how to control, manipulate, reward and punish young people but I didn't know how to motivate them.

Alan then studied what was known about motivation, reflected on the topic himself and wrote a book called *The Motivated School* (2003), which was published by SAGE, a global academic publisher. SAGE also published his next book *Motivating Every Learner* (2009). In 2005 the Scottish Government commissioned him to produce a training programme on motivation. Alan has worked with schools not only in Scotland, but also in England, Northern Ireland and the Republic of Ireland. His work has been translated into Chinese, Italian and Ukrainian; educators from Japan, New Zealand, Spain and Denmark have visited Scotland to study his work.

Alan was involved with the Centre in its early years – giving a presentation at one of our first network meetings; co-authoring with me the short booklet published by npower and the Scottish Football Association; and writing a section on motivation for the Centre's website. But our paths diverged over the following decade: Alan was busy writing and speaking on motivation and, from 2008, the Centre was much less focused on psychology. But a chance meeting in a supermarket in 2016 changed that. He told me that he was wanting to break out of an exclusive focus on motivation and look more generally at personal growth and development. As he was struggling to put these ideas on paper, I offered to read and comment. *Knowing and Growing: Insights for developing ourselves and others* was the happy result.

Knowing and Growing

At various points in the preceding chapters I have lamented how the academic world is fragmented into narrow subject specialisms and scholars rarely read beyond their own disciplines. I know from reading many psychology and personal development books over the years that they are often too narrow to be satisfactory: the author is an expert on one specific topic and tries to convince us that this one thing – self-esteem, confidence, mindset, grit, emotional intelligence, optimism or whatever – is 'the answer' we need.

Alan does not fall into this trap as he draws on his extensive experience of working with thousands of individuals and groups as well as on a large academic literature not just from across psychology but the social sciences and philosophy. More importantly he does not just look at one small aspect of human behaviour and development. Instead he creates a schema, based on underlying principles which he sets our clearly, and which helps us to navigate relationships better and chart our own, and others', development. One of the things I particularly like about this book is that it covers almost everything I taught in the twelve years I spent working with individuals, teams and organisations on development issues. So, one of the remarkable features of *Knowing and Growing* is that it provides an all-encompassing theory of human interaction and development. The fact this is contained within 160 pages is extraordinary.

Throughout the book various diagrams powerfully convey the importance of balance and context: we can overdo strengths so that they become not only a liability but our own undoing. He also continually urges us to know ourselves better and to welcome rather than deflect critical feedback. The fact that we can locate our behaviour or feelings on Alan's various diagrams means that we are provided with an objective, and largely non-judgemental, framework, to analyse our own and others' behaviour. Thanks to Alan's insights it becomes easy to see how we end up adopting 'stances' such as 'sulking' or 'people pleasing', which are unproductive if they become our everyday way of dealing with other people.

As a result of this thinking and research Alan, an analytical thinker, has become a convert to the power of emotions. Here's how important he thinks they are:

> We would all like to have a group of close friends who support us. People who know us inside out, have our best interests at heart, candidly advise us what we should be doing, tell us what other people think of us and help us make up our mind about matters of life-changing significance. Well we all have this

> support – our emotions! Emotions, like friends, bring unsurpassable benefits but at times they can also get us into trouble. Emotions can be a blessing or a curse but without them we would have no colour or meaning in our lives. Few phenomena are more complex than emotions but given their central role in our lives it's worth the effort to try to understand them.

In the pages of the book Alan helps us to do just that. And he also helps us to understand how our own and others' development is affected by our attitudes, motives, personality, and identity as well as our emotions.

At the core of the book is his 'Ring of Preferences'. This is based on his theory that we are all driven to experience 'feel good' emotions and that these can be derived from both 'making our mark' and 'being part of things'. However, when these preferences get out of balance with one another then we become either arrogant and selfish or compliant and submissive depending on which preference is dominating. I find this a useful concept because it takes us straight into the balance between the individual and the collective which, as I argued at the end of Chapter 10, is fundamental to well-being. And I'm not alone in thinking that. Ayako Ito, Associate Professor at the Ochanomizu University in Tokyo, commends the book for this very reason:

> McLean's Ring of Preferences gives us a deep understanding of ourselves and our relationships. How to balance these preferences is an essential theme to be pursued by all not only in Eastern culture but in Western countries. The preferences are powerful concepts for increasing happiness, peace and productivity.

Ayako Ito is right to point out the depth of the book: despite its brevity and simplicity its insights are profound. Armed with this book and with a willingness to engage with the practical exercises we would undoubtedly grow and develop as individuals, enhance our relationships and have a dramatic effect on our children's, students' and colleagues' development. And, yes, to paraphrase Ayako Ito, this could have important societal consequences.

A delicate balance

Alan's thinking in *Knowing and Growing* chimes so much with the Centre's perspective that it led not only to the publication a few years later of another book in the series but also its title. He writes in one key paragraph:

> . . . Aristotle's notion of the *golden mean* shows that any desirable quality is the mid-point between two extremes – a balance between too much and too little. For example, courage is good, but if taken too far it becomes recklessness or if it is diminished cowardice results.
>
> The golden mean also implies that most virtues are inter-dependent qualities that shouldn't be considered separately. In fact the positive psychologists Barry Schwartz and Kenneth Sharpe argue that concentrating on one strength in isolation can produce deformations of character. To achieve moderation each quality requires to be paired with a counterbalancing quality. For example, kindness moderates the harshness and potentially devastating impact of honesty when giving someone critical feedback.

It is this idea of balance – how strengths can be overdone so that they become liabilities – and the power of context that is in tune with the position the Centre adopted on a range of topics. It particularly resonates with the approach we thought adults should adopt with young people. In the chapter called 'Styles of influence' Alan looks at the type of leadership, teaching or parenting style to bring the best out in those for whom we are responsible. He counsels that in these situations we must build relationships and balance *support* and *challenge*; he refers to those who manage this balance as 'warmly demanding'.

In essence, what Alan argues in *Knowing and Growing* is a more sophisticated version of what I was outlining in my talks and writings on how we should promote young people's resilience. This then led to the idea that the Centre should publish a book outlining how we should be mindful of this vital interplay between support and challenge in our interactions with young people. I asked Morag Kerr if she would like to edit the book and we soon agreed that it should be called *The Golden Mean: Fostering young people's resilience, confidence and well-being.*

Morag was a consistent supporter of the Centre and attended most of the conferences, training courses and networking events we held. In 2014, we asked her to review the Flourishing Lives section of the website to see how it could be improved. After we put on the last workshop facilitated by Toni Noble in 2014, and with Toni's approval, the Centre then provided *Bounce Back!* in-house training courses for schools. Morag was our choice of facilitator for these courses.

Morag had worked in colleges for years before working for Scotland's Further Education Unit. In her role there she helped Alan McLean produce 'the Motivated College'. Given all this experience, Morag was an ideal person to edit a book on young people's resilience, confidence, and well-being.

The Golden Mean

The first article in Morag's book is by Alan McLean and is called 'Building resilience through support and challenge – the Golden Mean in action'. In it he welcomes how schools have moved away from 'cold control' towards 'collaboration' and how much more empathy teachers show towards their pupils. However, he thinks the level of support teachers now give risks 'overprotection':

> Support is vital but when we try to help too much we can unwittingly create dependency. We can also empathise too much and our attempts to understand some young people can become intrusive. While many will welcome professionals' interest in what has happened to them some may resent what they see as adults prying into their personal lives. Some may also *take liberties* in an attempt to provoke the controlling response they are used to.

Alan is clear, however, that support is vitally necessary. Without support it's inevitable that young people will perceive challenge as threatening. Indeed, he argues cogently that professionals need to balance support and challenge and that support must come first. Teachers and others can achieve this balance by attending to what Alan calls the 'WISE principles' – warmth, independence, sharing the reins and encouragement.

I follow up these arguments by looking at parents' behaviour. As I want to explain how my view on Scottish parenting developed, as well as summarise other work the Centre undertook on parenting, I shall come back to my article in *The Golden Mean* at the end of this chapter.

The third chapter in the book is called 'The Silence of the Weans' and is by Sue Palmer who is the editor of the then future *Postcards* book, *Play is the Way*. Sue wrote her article for Morag's book before we started to discuss a volume exclusively on play. In *The Golden Mean* she argues cogently that children's play is fundamental to their well-being and that their silence outdoors should worry us. Specifically addressing the focus of this book, Sue explains how self-directed play can provide the challenge that young children require. She writes:

> Play provides opportunities for every growing child to discover his or her own strengths, to experiment with small manageable risks, to learn through trial and error how to cope with setbacks, to rise to challenges and bounce back from difficulties.

The remaining six chapters describe varied projects, or approaches, currently happening in Scotland which provide opportunities for professionals to both support and challenge the young people they work with.

The first of these chapters is by Chalmers Smith and is about the value of outdoor education – a subject very close to the Centre's heart given how much we had done on this in the past. (See Chapters 6 and 14)

Ian McDermott, headteacher of Whitdale Primary School describes what they have done to create a supportive, yet challenging, learning environment as well as their experience of using *Bounce Back!* with pupils.

Claire Newman writes about Room 13, an inspirational Scottish education project, originally founded in Caol Primary School, which not only fosters real confidence but also creativity and enterprise. Room 13 allows pupils to go to a creative space, a studio, within the school which is completely controlled by the young people themselves. This then provides the opportunity for them to become artists (award-winning in some cases) or entrepreneurs or simply to fulfil a goal such as going on trips and expeditions.[1] No wonder this project has spawned around 80 Room 13s studios worldwide, including Nepal, South Africa and the USA. Sadly, it has not taken off to the same extent in Scotland, possibly because Room 13 is too imaginative for an education system which values top-down control. Yet, as Claire has acknowledged elsewhere on Room 13, 'the potential of this open space' is that it's not 'in conflict with the more controlled, directed curriculum of the school' but is able 'to complement it, to free the imagination rather than constrain it.'[2]

Kathryn Jourdan of Sistema Scotland, which has been inspired by the world-famous Venezuelan music education project, then describes how their four 'Big Noise' orchestras in poor areas in Scotland help to transform the lives of individuals and communities. And they do this by giving the young people lots of support and encouragement while the youngsters learn how to play musical instruments and take part in classical music concerts – something that is 'challenging' and confirmed in the interviews with young people Kathryn carried out.

The next article by Heather Kajac, describes how the Rock Trust support vulnerable young people who are not only care-experienced but homeless or in danger of becoming homeless – another type of serious challenge.

The final chapter is by Charis Robertson of the Hot Chocolate Trust, an innovative grass-roots youth work organisation at the Steeple Church in the heart of Dundee. Daniel, one of the young people who attended the project, is not only given his place as a

---

1. The art is not only visual but also includes poetry and different types of writing.

2. Claire was speaking to Danny Murphy in his tour for his Postcards book, *Schooling Scotland*. See p. 333ff.

co-author but also the article begins with his words: 'Back then we were like a pack of wolves'. Later he writes: 'I used to be the guy who caused trouble and picked fights, now I'm the person who stops others from doing that – I go out of my way to make sure that other young people are safe.'

The article on Hot Chocolate is called 'Community Approaches to Growing Resilience'. In it Charis acknowledges the importance of adverse childhood experiences (ACEs) as well as their prevalence in the group of young people who attend the project. She also clearly spells out that resilience isn't something that individuals possess, rather it grows in a supportive community. Providing lots of support plus an appropriate amount of challenge is how Charis and her colleagues interact with young people:

> When the team did have to 'bring challenge' (normally asking them to leave due to threatening or violent behaviours towards others), this was always framed with regret, with love, with the promise of second chances (and third and fourth ones), and with affirmations about the skills, talents and potential we saw in them. This was especially important, to not feed into the group's negative sense of self-worth.

We know that *The Golden Mean's* first reader was Derek Rodger as he was typesetting the book. As he had previously worked as a teacher and youth worker he was particularly interested in the topic and enthusiastic about what he was reading. So much so that Morag and I asked him to write a foreword. In it he writes about how hope emanates from the projects described in the book and the voices of young people themselves. He then asserts:

> The discussion . . . on finding the balance between a caring support of the young and a challenging approach to stretch them on to high achievements is lost on many parents, teachers, policy makers and yes, politicians. They would do well to read and digest the thoughts and truly inspiring, touching and life-affirming practices and experiences they can encounter in the following pages.

My article in *The Golden Mean* explores what support and challenge means for parenting but before summarising my contribution I want to explain what the Centre had done previously to educate parents on children's resilience and why it was a topic of interest.

Parents and children's resilience

As I outline in Chapters 20 and 21, traditionally Scotland had a harsh and punitive attitude towards children and, like countless others, I suffered in the 1950s and 60s from this culture. I can clearly remember that when my first son was born in 1982 I consciously resolved that he would never experience any unhappiness and pain. In short, I wanted to protect him from the negative experiences of my own childhood.

I was not alone in harbouring a strong desire to protect my son from the way I had been treated as a child. In the 1980s and 90s I ran a large number of personal development courses involving thousands of people, the vast majority of whom were Scots. During our discussions many would say that while they loved their parents and felt indebted to them, they had often been harsh, cold and excessively critical. There was little encouragement or praise. Like me they resolved to bring their children up differently. They weren't just going to hug them and tell them repeatedly that they were loved, they were also going to shower them with compliments and praise. And they were not going to let teachers punish or talk negatively to their children.

So Scots of my generation (and later) vowed to bring up their children differently. This was a quiet revolution which happened behind closed doors and without public discussion. There was no 'Truth and Reconciliation' process to help us get over the punitive years of Scotland's traditional approach to child-rearing. We simply moved on.

I might never have thought more about the topic if it I hadn't spent time running assertiveness courses for teachers. During role-plays they would often choose an interaction with one of their pupil's parents. This was enlightening as these role-plays showed that parents now complained if their child experienced any disappointment or frustration. Indeed, parents now saw anything that challenged their children as something that had to stop. And I understood this mindset perfectly. I had been one of these parents.

At first, I simply thought that this development was making teachers' lives impossible. But, following Seligman's warning on self-esteem which I outlined in Chapter 3, I now understood that this was also bad for children.

In the first decade of the Centre's existence, I was regularly asked to give talks to lots of different parents' groups on children's confidence. When I spoke, I would always take them through how artificial self-esteem building and only wanting your child to experience positive emotions undermines the development of resilience as well as the learning process. The Centre produced a handout on our recommendations on how to foster young people's resilience and we eventually produced this as a sticker. In these talks I also outlined the dangers of materialist values for children's well-being.

I gave a talk on the subject at a parents' conference in Ayr in 2012. I was then invited to give the same presentation to 700 members of staff. Senior education managers at South Ayrshire council were so taken by what I was saying that they arranged to film me giving the presentation. They then sent this to every group of parents in their schools. In 2014 education staff in Angus Council likewise were keen for parents in their schools to hear my presentation. So, they commissioned me to give an evening talk in both Arbroath and Forfar to parents from a cluster of schools in the area.

I remember clearly that in the open discussion after my talk in both Arbroath and Forfar that many of the parents said that having heard me speak they were now going to let their children play outside. I hadn't mentioned play or the outdoors in my talk and that's why it was particularly memorable. At that time, I really didn't appreciate how the lack of outdoor play was undermining young people's resilience.

Parenting styles

I believe that the impetus in Scotland for an excessively protective and positive approach came originally from parents, not schools, so it's worth looking at different ways parents can behave towards their children. The idea that there are four basic parenting styles has been supported by considerable research and is the foundation for most parent education. (See Table 2) Parents don't always adhere to one style and can move from one to another. And this alone can present serious problems for children as it means their lives are unpredictable.

Table 2: Parenting styles

Authoritarian	**Authoritative**
Cold and firm	Warm and firm
Neglectful/uninvolved	**Permissive/indulgent**
Cold and soft	Warm and soft

The worst style for children's emotional health and future academic success is neglectful or uninvolved. Authoritarian parenting is also detrimental to young people and it's this style which usually prevailed in traditional Scottish culture. Research clearly shows that, at least in Western countries, authoritarian parenting undermines children and young people's emotional development. Some studies link authoritarian parenting with future depression, although this depends on the degree of parental coldness.

Extensive research shows that the best type of parenting for children is authoritative. What this means is that the parent is child-centred, loving and focused on the child's welfare but has clear rules and boundaries. Such parents let their children know what's expected but they are also prepared to reason with them – explaining and discussing the rules – and deliberately try to foster independence and responsibility.

Research shows that for children from European or American backgrounds authoritative parenting is best as it encourages the development of healthy characteristics such as self-control and autonomy. It also helps to foster positive mental health.

An insight into the extent of Scotland's permissive parenting?

We can already see how overprotective, permissive parenting is having a negative health impact on Scotland's children. In 2016 an international survey of 38 countries on children's physical activity ranked Scotland joint last even though the country scored second top for national policy on physical activity. What children do at school is obviously important but the report's author, Professor John Reilly, has said that protective parents stopping kids from being physically active outdoors in Scotland is part of the problem. Scotland was also joint first on the amount of time children spent watching screens and this is partly a reflection of parental permissiveness – a failure to set healthy limits and boundaries. Other parts of the UK did not score well either but they were still ahead of Scotland.

Permissive or indulgent parents by contrast are very involved with their children but they don't place many restrictions on them and don't exercise discipline. Such parents believe that children know what's best and so let them make decisions for themselves. But this is clearly not in children's long-term interests. Children's minds are heavily influenced by daily exposure to advertising. When it comes to food, bedtime and screen time children don't know what's in their best interest.

The children of permissive parents benefit from their parents' warmth, love and interest in them, but they suffer in other ways from the lack of rules or boundaries. As a result such children struggle to learn self-control and do not have such good psychosocial skills as peers with authoritative parents.

Some of the parents in Scotland who deliberately decided not to emulate their own parents adopted an authoritative style. But as far as I can see they were a small minority for the simple reason that the predominance of strong authoritarian parenting meant there were very few examples of authoritative parenting to copy. What's more, in wider Scottish society – education and the prevailing work culture in particular – there wasn't an ethos of negotiation or compromise to learn from. This was the land of the 'wee hard men' to use the artist and novelist Alasdair Gray's term.

In Scotland people were (and still are to some extent) just 'tellt'.

Of course, Scotland still has its share of neglectful parents, perhaps more than its fair share given the numbers affected by drugs and alcohol. But it's wrong to see neglectful parenting as a problem only for children living in poor communities. As Alan Sinclair argues so persuasively in his book *Right from the Start* many middle-class parents can be too busy with their own careers or lives to be good parents to their children. A few have also continued to be as harsh and authoritarian as their own parents. But in my experience of talking to thousands of parents and teachers in Scotland those who wanted to be different from their own parents went from an authoritarian style to one that is permissive and indulgent. That's why I called my article in *The Golden Mean* 'From One Extreme to Another'.

This wholesale adoption of permissive parenting doesn't just have implications for children's well-being and social skills: academic skills are also at stake. Children and adolescents with authoritative parents generally perform better academically than those with parents who adopt different styles. Indeed, a systematic literature review of 131 papers on parenting styles and academic achievement by Masud *et al* concluded that 'Authoritative parenting tends to promote better and positive outcomes in child development.'

The main reason why permissive parents undermine their children's academic achievement is because they see challenge and frustration as something their child must avoid. Professor Carol Dweck, of Mindset fame, is fond of saying that we need to redeem the idea of struggle and challenge. We must move away from the idea that easy praise and easy tasks are beneficial to youngsters' development. They aren't. So it's worrying that school staff have repeatedly told me about parents writing to secondary teachers to say that they shouldn't try to teach their child French (or maths, music or sport) because 'they can't do it and it's stressing them'. As Alan McLean argues convincingly in his article, apathy often results from removing challenge from young people's lives.

I am not arguing for a return to strict rules and punishments. Nor do I think that children and young people must endure situations that constantly stress them. Young people must be supported through challenges. Indeed, having a network of support is a key aspect of resilience. But parents must become aware of the difference between supporting young people through challenges and trying to prevent them from ever experiencing 'difficult' feelings or challenges in the first place.

I also accept that this move from authoritarian to permissive parenting hasn't just taken place in Scotland. It has also happened in the USA and some Western European countries. My argument is that, given the punitive way children were routinely treated in Scotland, both at home and at school, the reaction and move towards permissiveness is understandably more noticeable and intense than in other countries.

ACEs, resilience and parenting

In another chapter I look at the importance of adverse childhood experiences (ACEs) for physical and emotional health and I want to end my comments on parenting by clarifying that there is nothing in the ACE research which contradicts the evidence that authoritative parenting is best. Dr Suzanne Zeedyk is aware of these issues. Indeed she has written about parenting styles. She thinks that if parents avoid confronting hurt from their own childhood they can easily become overly anxious about their children experiencing painful feelings. She doesn't think that trying to protect children from all negative emotion is good for their development.

As I have argued in various chapters in this book, children's resilience requires them to learn that life inevitably has emotionally challenging moments. Resilience can't be fostered if those challenges are avoided completely. This being the case it's worth noting that Suzanne Zeedyk argues that one challenge for the ACE movement:

> . . . is for us to distinguish between stress and toxic stress. It won't help our children or families if we confuse the two. The science of ACEs shows us that stress turns toxic when children have to handle hard times alone, because they end up feeling overwhelmed. It is up to us adults to realise that, for healthy

> development, children really do need emotional challenges, but they also need to know that they can seek help when the challenges feel too tough. Help is different from protection.

So yet again this is a variation of Alan McLean's plea for an interaction between support and challenge – a golden mean.

And finally

I expected to finish this chapter by pointing out that back in 2008 the Centre may have resolved to transcend psychological approaches to well-being by broadening our focus but in the following years we still managed to include a reasonable amount of activity on those issues: issues which had been our bread and butter in Phase 1. However, while that remains true, I want to end on an update to Alan McLean's *Postcards* book.

During lockdown a Ukrainian publisher approached Alan to ask if they could produce a Ukrainian edition of *Knowing and Growing*. We both welcomed this idea. The translation is now complete and the book appeared at the end of 2023. As I had written a foreword to our *Postcards* edition, Bohdan Publishing asked both of us to write the foreword to the Ukrainian publication and we were delighted to oblige. In it we write: 'As author, and series editor, we are pleased to discover that this work is of interest to people in another country but we are particularly proud of this Ukrainian edition as the plight of the country and its citizens is so often in our thoughts.'

The publisher also asked for photographs – lots of them. They wanted pictures of Alan as a child, Alan with his own children, and Alan in working mode as well as the usual author portrait not just of him but of myself as well.

Alan tells me that the Ukrainian edition of *The Motivated School* is filled with images and pictures and looks completely different from the English version. What conclusion can we draw from this? That visual information has more importance to Ukrainians than it does for those of us in Britain? Or is it that culture – shared beliefs, values and history – though often hidden and difficult to grasp, is much more important than we think?

Chapter 18

Prioritising early years and play

Alan Sinclair's professional journey;
the influence of Professor James Heckman;
the evidence showing the importance of the first 1,000 days of a child's life;
the extent of Scotland's problems with inadequate parenting;
Family Nurse Partnerships and Baby Boxes;
the 'Promise' and its limited vision;
inadequate Scottish Government delivery;
the background to Sue Palmer's development as a childhood campaigner;
the importance of school starting age and the foundation of Upstart;
the 'Play not Tests for P1 campaign';
contents of *Play is the Way Postcards* book; the book's impact.

ALAN SINCLAIR has been a close associate of the Centre since its early days. Shortly after we set up our new base in Union Street Alan took a desk in our office. He also undertook projects with us, had a regular blog on our website, acted as an associate and eventually wrote one of our *Postcards from Scotland* books – *Right from the Start: Investing in parents and babies* (2018). In the book he explains how he became a leading, if unlikely, proponent in Scotland for investment in the early years.

Alan's journey

After graduating from St Andrews University with a degree in economics and philosophy Alan worked in international development. He then set up Scottish Education and Action for Development or SEAD as it was usually called. In 1983 when Scotland was gripped by deindustrialisation, Alan and others started a company called Heatwise Glasgow. Its aim was to draught-proof and insulate houses while at the same time helping long-term unemployed people back into work. This was decades before politicians started to talk about climate change and so this initiative seems remarkably prescient. Other environmental projects followed, including Glasgow's first glass recycling centre. Over time these job creation schemes were consolidated into the Wise Group with Alan as its Chief Executive. As the organisation was hugely successful in training thousands of people each year and getting them ready to work it became a beacon of social enterprise and Alan was much sought after north and south of the border as an advisor. In 2001 he left to become Senior Director for Skills and Learning at Scottish Enterprise (SE).

Moving to his SE post he became acutely aware of a problem that had been highlighted in a survey of 22,000 public and private sector employers in Scotland: those that had recruited at least one employee in the previous year reported that these. . .

> . . . new recruits were poor at talking and listening, working with one another and the public, and poor at elementary planning or problem solving. Employers of people in lower paid jobs, for example working in care or retail jobs, had the greatest dissatisfaction. Graduates, we were told, had the same soft skills shortage, just to a lesser extent.

This rang true for Alan as a significant proportion of trainees at the Wise Group lacked these skills. But he also realised this is a difficult message for government (and parents) to accept as they are investing more and more money in higher education. What decision makers fail to grasp, he concluded, is that it's soft skills, or what we could call life skills, that are increasingly needed in the economy and which are in short supply in Scottish young people. The SE board were somewhat taken aback at these findings and asked Alan to find out how these soft skills were acquired. He quickly discovered that they were mainly developed in early childhood!

As Alan was in the midst of learning about the importance of early years to the skills employers said they needed, he attended a lecture which had a huge impact on his future career. The lecture was held in Glasgow in May 2004 and was part of 'the Allander series' organised by the Labour politician and future academic, Wendy Alexander. She had designed the series to encourage new thinking on Scotland's economic future and featured heavyweight speakers, including two Nobel laureates, James Heckman and Paul Krugman. It was the lecture by James Heckman, a famous Chicago economics professor, which had such an impact on Alan. And I know this from personal experience as I too was at the lecture and gave Alan a lift home after the event. In *Right from the Start* he recounts that I asked him what he thought of Heckman's thesis. 'Perplexed' was his reply as he needed to think a lot more about what he had heard. I remember the conversation well as Alan was so visibly affected.

Here's Alan's own explanation for why he found Heckman's thesis so challenging:

> In his presentation that night, Heckman laid it on the line that from the big data he analysed, the most significant gains in human capital and human development came very early in life, way before school. Heckman demonstrated that the rate of return from public investment in these vital early years was around 7-10 % for higher risk families: a higher rate of return than from other types of state spend.

And this mattered to Alan not only because he was economically literate and cared about returns on investment but also because it meant that what he had been doing at the Wise Group with unemployed people was much less important to solving social problems than he had thought. He now knew that it was what happened in the first few years of a child's life that truly mattered. This put parents centre stage for developing skills and relegated universities to a supporting role.

The Heckman lecture literally changed Alan's life: instead of focusing on employability, skills and training he ultimately left SE and immersed himself in learning all he could about the importance of the early years. He became a visiting Fellow at the London-based Work Foundation led by the journalist and economist Will Hutton. In 2007 Alan wrote a 'provocation' for them called '0-5 How Small Children Make a Big Difference'. During his period with the Work Foundation he worked out of our Centre's office in Union Street.

All this research into babies and small children fitted nicely into Alan's personal trajectory. He married late and didn't become a father until he was working at SE, aged 47. Fatherhood followed what he calls 'a dark time' when they lost a baby in pregnancy to a neural tube defect. Alan later discovered that the chances of this happening can be reduced radically by folate supplementation prior to pregnancy – something that requires proper preconception intervention.

In 2011 Alan was awarded a Churchill Travelling Scholarship and spent time in the Netherlands and Finland – both countries that score high for child well-being. Later that year the Centre published his report entitled 'Early Years and transformational Change'. We also collaborated with the NSPCC to hold dissemination meetings in both Edinburgh and Glasgow so that Alan could present his findings, particularly to important 'influencers'. At these two seminars attendees heard about Dutch Mother and Baby Well-being Clinics, their Finnish equivalents, Baby Boxes, and other initiatives to ensure children thrive in the first few years of life.

The Centre launched the *Postcards* series in 2012 and we were always keen to publish a book by Alan. He wanted to contribute yet we didn't finally publish *Right from the Start* until 2018. Alan's difficulty was that he kept on learning and generating new ideas and perspectives and this wasn't conducive to him finishing a book. A mutual friend of ours, Alastair Balfour, agreed to help. Alastair had been a journalist and had the skills, as well as the commitment to the topic, to help Alan finalise the manuscript. As Alan explained in his acknowledgements, Alastair 'encouraged, engaged, dug me out of holes and made the whole text more readable', he then adds, 'Babies and books both need helpful people.'

The evidence

In *Right from the Start* Alan explains many processes which affect the health and well-being not only of a growing foetus, but also a new-born and infant as it develops. He tells us that scientific evidence now shows that the womb is not the haven that we once envisaged it to be: not only is the foetus adversely affected by the substances the mother consumes or smokes, but also the mother's feelings and environment influence its development. For example, the stress of poverty or the fear caused by intimate partner violence can adversely affect the growing foetus.

In the womb and after birth, growth of the brain, body and behaviour is sequential with one step being the foundation for the next stage. It's not good for the child's well-being if a stage is skipped. This critical foundation stage stretches from before conception through pregnancy till about two years of age. *Right from the Start* is mainly about these transformative first 1,000 days.

The attachment of the mother to the infant and *vice versa* is critical for the child's development during this vitally important period. 'Attachment theory' was laid out by the British psychiatrist John Bowlby in the 1940s. If the primary carer is available for the infant as well as sensitive and responsive to his/her needs then this healthy attachment allows the child to form a secure foundation, and from this base to explore the world. Children who are securely attached are able to form and maintain healthy relationships as they develop empathy and good social skills. They also do better at school and have better mental health than those with inconsistent or 'avoidant' parents.

Alan also quotes well-designed longitudinal studies which show that good early years' experiences can have a significant effect on life chances – not just employment, drug taking and mental health but also whether someone is likely to end up in prison. One of these studies was conducted in Dunedin, New Zealand, where academics started studying new-borns from a range of socio-economic backgrounds in 1972. Researchers followed the children every two years up to the age of 11 and then at 15, 18, 21, 26, 32 and 38.

The study found that poor brain development when a child

was three was linked to poorer mental health in adolescence and adulthood as well as poorer long-term cardiovascular health and faster biological ageing in midlife. It also showed that the children with poor brain development at three went on to 'represent a disproportionate share of the economic costs associated with crime, social welfare, hospitalisations, prescriptions, and other indicators of poor health and social dysfunction.' In fact, 20 per cent of study participants accounted for 80 per cent of the economic costs the state had to pay for these types of services.

Another of the Dunedin study's findings concerns the importance of self-control in childhood. This is about the ability to delay gratification, control impulses, persist with challenging activities and regulate your emotions. And the results on the importance of this are startling. The researchers conclude from their data that 'Self-control in childhood is more important than socio-economic status or IQ in predicting adults' physical health, wealth, life satisfaction, addiction, crime, and the parenting of the next generation.' It's good brain development and early years experiences that lead children to develop self-control.

Alan is aware that it was partly a lack of self-control that led some of the Wise Group trainees to be difficult to work with. These were the ones who displayed behaviours such as 'speaking before you think, saying what hurts or is inappropriate, acting out, jumping to conclusions, not resisting temptations and pre-emptive tit-for-tat – hurt someone before they hurt you.' And he found it particularly worrying that most of these young men were already fathers – another manifestation of impulsivity.

Scotland

The findings from Dunedin and other studies should worry us about what's going on in Scotland. We have the worst health in Europe, and not that long ago Glasgow was described as the murder capital of Europe. We have significant problems with addictions, obesity, teenage pregnancies, mental health and suicide. Could poor parenting be part of the explanation? Alan certainly thinks so and it worries him: 'In allowing generation after generation to experience damage in the womb and trauma and uncertainty in their first 1,000 days, we are condemning many of them to lives of poor quality with huge cost to society and the state.'

Alan is particularly concerned about the likely prevalence of Foetal Alcohol Spectrum Disorders (FASD) given the amount of binge drinking in Scotland. Official Scottish estimates suggest that between 500 and 1500 babies are born each year with FASD. Alan thinks it's likely to be much higher and that it accounts for the impulsivity he regularly saw in Wise Group trainees. He also knows that many higher income women drink in pregnancy yet scientific research suggests that there's no safe level of alcohol consumption for foetal health.

Other problems are easier to quantify. Scotland has the highest rate of looked-after children in the UK. In fact, our rate is approximately twice England's. Apart from the tragedy for these children themselves, this is a huge burden on the public finances as Alan outlines in *Right from the Start*. In Glasgow the scale of this spend is so large that it takes up 44 per cent of the Children and Families budget in the city and leaves little scope for preventative or therapeutic work for the even larger group of 'drowning' parents and children.

It's easy to believe that the problem of inadequate parenting is largely socio-economic but that's not what important Scottish data tells us. Professor John Frank and colleagues used an international tool called the 'Early Development Instrument' in East Lothian in 2012-13 to assess every P1 pupil's 'social competence, emotional maturity, language and cognitive ability, physical health and well-being, fine motor skills and communication skills.' Each child was then given a score. The results showed that 73 per cent of these five-year-olds were on track but this meant that 27 per cent were assessed as 'vulnerable'. And those assessed as in this way were not exclusively from poor backgrounds. In fact, almost half came from middle- and high-income earners.

Alan points out that similar results were found in an in-depth, longitudinal survey:

> The Growing Up in Scotland survey has found that at age five, below average vocabulary ability is found in 20% of the children

> from the homes that are in the top income bracket. It is worse in the homes with the bottom 20% of income where 54% of the children have below average ability with vocabulary. Problem-solving, one of the key characteristics sought by Scottish employers, is below average for 29% of the children in the top income bracket and 53% of the children at the bottom earnings scale.

Part of the explanation must be that these children, though from backgrounds with a good income, don't get the love and attention they need for healthy development. Alan, who comes from a working-class family himself, acknowledges that poverty is a problem but cautions that we need to keep this in perspective: 'it's what parents do and don't do that matters. It is not about how much money they have. Too little money is a problem and, so it seems, is too much money. There's a danger that we become too hung up on money.'

'As a society we don't appreciate the benefits, or the damage, that parenting can bring upon our youngest citizens, even before they are born. We have barely started to understand the personal burdens and economic costs of unplanned pregnancies and childhood neglect and trauma', writes Alan. He continues, 'In Scotland our personal views and the views embedded in our institutions are child blind.' He argues that this has a cumulative effect on each of us and on the fabric and feel of our communities.

One of the most memorable lines in *Right from the Start* is a quote from a woman who spent the first half of her life in the Netherlands and the second half in Scotland. 'In Holland we love children,' she told Alan, adding, 'in Scotland you tolerate children.'

Changes to public policy

From 2007 to 2012 Alan acted as an unpaid advisor to Noel Dolan who was at that time principal advisor to Nicola Sturgeon, then Health Minister in the Scottish Government. Asked to draw up a 'short list of practical measures with outline costs' that could help tackle Scotland's endemic health and parenting problems, his list included more health visitors, Family Nurse Partnerships from the USA and Baby Boxes, a Finnish initiative.

In 2008 the Scottish Government committed itself to testing the Family Nurse Partnership programme by providing intensive support for women who were most at risk of having babies with poor outcomes. This support was given to first-time young mothers under the age of 19 and some vulnerable 20–24-year-olds. The nurse continues to work with the family until the child is two. This programme is now provided by every health board in Scotland. In 2015 the Scottish Government announced the creation of a Universal Health Visiting Pathway. This guarantees every family 11 home visits – '8 within the first year of life and 3 Child Health Reviews between 13 months and 4-5 years'.

These are real tangible changes the Scottish Government has made that give families with babies and young children support and advice. Nicola Sturgeon's Government also introduced Baby Boxes in 2017 and, when she resigned in 2023, she said that the introduction of the scheme was one of the things her government had done that made her proud. She even claimed that Baby Boxes, which included clothes, nappies and other things required by newborns, meant 'every baby in Scotland literally has the same start'. Some have criticised this claim as it completely ignores the importance of real inequalities in babies' lives. Researchers have also struggled to detect any improvements in child or maternal health since the boxes were introduced. In *Right from the Start*, Alan is mildly critical of the way the Scottish scheme operates: unlike Finland where the box is a way of strengthening the link with support services during pregnancy, Scottish mothers simply receive a box through the post. Alan writes, 'A box of stuff from the postman – however well meaning – is no substitute for supportive relationships.'

However, Alan is impressed by what the Scottish Government has done to address child poverty. In 2021 they introduced a £10-a-week payment for every child under six in families receiving income-related benefits. After a couple of rises, in 2023 it's £25-a-week and every child under 16 is eligible. I agree that the Scottish Government deserves recognition for a measure which has a tangible impact on children's lives in Scotland and is a welcome departure from the punitive and niggardly approach taken in recent years by the Westminster Government.

Promises v. delivery

In 2016 First Minister Nicola Sturgeon had a conversation with 1,000 young people about their experiences of care and says it had a profound effect on her. She knew that the system was failing children and that the outcomes for 'care-experienced' young people were poor but the stories she heard troubled her and she thought the system 'broken'. 'We – government, society – too often let our most vulnerable children down at the time they need us most, ' she wrote in an article. The nub of the problem was, and still is, that despite some committed staff the system repeatedly puts its own interests before the needs of these vulnerable children. In fact, the system often acts as it if is blind to the type of development issues Alan outlines in *Right from the Start*.

Sturgeon set up an Independent Care Review which reported in February 2020 claiming that the current system was 'fractured, bureaucratic and unfeeling'. It demanded system changes to ensure that by 2030 care-experienced children will grow up 'loved, safe and respected'. The Review framed its recommendations as a 'promise' that Scotland is making to its young people and includes, for example, assurances that siblings will be kept together. The First Minister endorsed 'the Promise' which also attracted cross party support. The Scottish Government has allocated £500 million to a Whole Family Support fund and some other measures like bursaries for care experienced young people. However, a leaked document in July 2023 showed that local authorities were not making the progress required of them for the 2030 deadline and that the necessary funding is not available. Some fear that the system is now worse for children, not better.

Alan is critical of the thinking behind 'the Promise' and how the Care Review formulated the challenge of children in care. Their priority was to listen to the voice of children and adults who have been in care and ultimately to improve the care experience. But around 50 per cent of children going into care do so in their first year of life. These babies are preverbal and literally this means that they have no voice. So for Alan the primary challenge ought to be reducing the number of children going into care, rather than improving care itself – though, of course, he isn't arguing against changes such as keeping siblings together.

Glasgow City Council is now on the road to demonstrating how to reduce the number of children going into care. In the past seven years Mike Burns, assistant head of Children's Services, and his team have halved the number of children going into institutional care. They have achieved this through perseverance and managing risk. In 2018 Glasgow's Children Services had 1,350 children in care, at an annual cost of £95 million and within that group were a subset of 239 children costing £42 million a year, at an average cost of £175,000.

By reducing the number of children going into care and saving on care costs, Glasgow Council can redirect money to supporting parents, kinship carers, foster parents and the parents of adopted children. It has deployed more health visitors and added small amounts of money to the family budgets of those struggling to look after children. It has also enlisted teams of voluntary sector workers to engage and support families. The evidence is now clearly coming through that it's possible to strengthen relationships between parents, carers and children, thereby ensuring that fewer relationships break down.

But while there are glimmers of hope on potential improvements to children's lives in Glasgow, across the board the SNP Government attracts considerable criticism that its rhetoric far exceeds its delivery; that it fails to realise its grand ambitions. Sadly, this includes 'the Promise' as well as its vision for Scotland to become 'the best country in the world to grow up'. When Bruce Adamson stepped down in 2023 as Scotland's Children's commissioner, he claimed that Nicola Sturgeon 'absolutely failed' to deliver for young people. In January 2024 Sturgeon acknowledged that the SNP Government was failing to deliver 'the Promise'.

In numerous blogs I have expressed my scepticism on the SNP Government's vision for us to become the best country in the world to grow up. Indeed, I've always seen it as a smokescreen to obscure the ugly truth that historically we've been one of the worst countries in Europe for the treatment of children – a claim I'll justify in Chapters 20 and 21. In his book Alan is more measured, pointing out that for the Scottish Government's vision to be realised there 'would have to be dramatic financial and managerial improvements, and a major investment in creating a better-trained, skilful and motivated' staff. And he is also right to point out that 'in the real world our collective aspiration would need to change, political decision-making would need to re-orientate, health services re-calibrate and above all our personal and communal parenting approach would need to up its game.'

Few could doubt Alan Sinclair's commitment to improve the lives of Scotland's children. But, as I've written this section, I've continually thought what a remarkable person he is. How many men have made it their life's work to argue for investment in parents and the early years? Particularly when Alan's research and proselytising has been undertaken not because it's part of his job but because it comes from his passion. Children would undoubtedly benefit from the changes Alan seeks but in the long-term all of us in Scotland would too. Without substantial improvements in how Scotland raises its children our atrocious health and social statistics will continue to haunt us. And we shall pay dearly for our lame attempts to rescue people from problems created years earlier in their childhood; problems we should have tried to prevent in the first place.

Given the important work Alan has done in the past twenty years I'm particularly proud to know that he chose to do so much of this through the Centre and that for years we helped to amplify his voice.

Sue Palmer

Another exceptional person working for the betterment of Scotland's children is Sue Palmer who has already made an appearance in this book thanks to speaking at Centre events and contributing a chapter to our *Postcards* book, *The Golden Mean*. The Centre's association with Sue ultimately led to our most successful book to date – *Play is the Way* (2020).

Sue grew up in Lancashire and moved to Edinburgh in the late 1960s. She undertook teacher training at Moray House in the early 1970s and then had various posts in Scotland as a teacher and headteacher before going to Manchester to study for a masters degree. Sue then had a high profile and influential role as a literacy

centre for
confidence
and well-being

www.postcardsfromscotland.co.uk

Some of the 300 participants enrolled in the Centre's Vanguard Programme, September 2005, the Radisson Hotel, Glasgow

Line up of guests and speakers, including First Minister Alex Salmond and ex-footballer Alan Hansen at a Scottish Manufacturing dinner in October 2007. Carol Craig (pictured) spoke on the importance of optimism and confidence at the event

Carol Craig with Professor Martin Seligman at the European Positive Psychology conference, Italy, July 2004

Debbie Knight, Hazel Black and Emily Cutts, Centre staff, at the registration desk at the Centre's Vanguard Series, Dundee event, September 2006

Willy Roe, Chair of the Centre's board 2004–2007 and Chair of the Vanguard Programme

Go Dundee Learning Journey, September 2009

(left) Go Dundee event, Apex Hotel, June 2008

Press coverage of Go Dundee event with Dr Tal Ben Shah, January 2008

Get motivated about Dundee

ALMOST 300 people heard a lecture by top US motivator Tal Ben-Shahar (left) in Dundee's Apex Hotel.

Dr Ben-Shahar is a former international squash player who has become the most popular lecturer at Harvard University.

He lectures in positive psychology and leadership psychology. He was brought to the city by the Go Dundee network and the Glasgow-based Centre for Well-Being and Confidence.

Go Dundee members Tom Shepherd of CXR Biosciences, the Care Commission's Jacquie Roberts and Joe Lafferty of Life Tree also spoke.

The organisation brings together people from all areas of community life to accentuate all that is positive about Dundee. Yesterday Mr Lafferty, a team development and leadership specialist, said Go Dundee will look at how to apply the content of the lecture to the city to make it more positive and confident.

Session with three *Postcards* authors at Aye Write! book festival, Glasgow, May 2018. From left to right, Carol Craig on *Hiding in Plain Sight*, John Carnochan on *Conviction* and Alan Sinclair on *Right from the Start*

Edinburgh Book Festival, August 2007 at an event to launch the Centre's publication, *Creating Confidence: A handbook for professionals working with young people* by Carol Craig

The Centre for Confidence and Well-being's office, 45 Union Street, Glasgow from September 2005 for six years

Launch of *Postcards* book *Raising Spirits: Allotments, well-being and community*, Trades Hall, Glasgow, August 2014. Carol Craig and Dr Michael Mattel, the Deacon of the Incorporaton of Gardeners, Glasgow, stand behind the three seated authors. From left to right: Judy Wilkinson, Jenny Mollison and Rona Wilkinson

The people who made the Centre what it was – a mix of full and part-time staff members, associates, freelances and volunteers

Hazel Black Business development manager 2005–2007. Seconded from Scottish Enterprise and loves the Centre so much she's still involved with the board

Morag Kerr Associate 2013–2017, main trainer on *Bounce Back!* Helped to reconfigure Flourishing Lives. Also Postcards author

Pete Fletcher Graphic designer 2004–2017 Worked closely with the Centre for over a decade. His designs were behind all the Centre's visuals till 2017

Lynn Semple Centre administrator/PA 2004–2006 Enjoyed working in such an innovative organisation and helping to organise large-scale events

Zoe Conlin Event manager for the Vanguard Programme 2005. Seconded from Standard Life for what proved to be a challenging, but enjoyable, learning experience

Debbie Knight PA to CEO and office manager 2006–2009 As a new graduate, working at the Centre helped Debbie to develop her own confidence

Emily Cutts Centre's psychology researcher 2006–2013 in full and part-time role. Postcards author. Completed MSc in positive psychology while at the Centre. Then used what she learned in campaigning/charitable work

Dr Elaine Duncan Centre's psychology adviser 2005–2011 and trainer on Centre's action research courses. Psychology lecturer at Caledonian Uni. Inspired by Centre's positive psychology work

Zoe Van Zwanenberg Centre's project manager from 2007–2011 (full & part time). Previously ran the Scottish Leadership Foundation. Enjoyed the range of projects she managed

Will Craigie Volunteer 2007–2011 and then training consultant. Volunteered a day a week after hearing Carol speak. Reports that the Centre 'changed his life'

Helen Carmichael Admin support 2015–2022 Particularly loved the inspiration provided by the Postcards series

Isobel MacNaughtan Associate/consultant 2005–2012 (Napier University project and various training courses) Inspired by the Centre's optimism and 'the hunger to learn' she encountered in events and courses

Keith Hunter Associate 2005–2007 involved in running courses for Centre . Says it was a pleasure to be involved in such a large-scale cultural change project

Derek Goldman Associate 2007–2013 involved in research and training. Highlight for Derek – research into mindset with Stanford Uni and being at the forefront of this work

Stewart McIntosh Freelance writer for the Centre. Wrote newsletters and copy for Flourishing Lives section of website. Loved learning and so really valued his writing role at the Centre. Died in 2021

Alan Sinclair Associate 2006–2011, based in the Centre, undertaking research and then a Postcards author. Grateful to the Centre for support to develop his knowledge and thinking on the early years

In this visionary book, Phil Hanlon and Sandra Carlisle look beyond health in Scotland to the main social, economic, environmental and cultural challenges of our times

The dominance of materalist values in the media and business in all our lives leads to a loss of individual and collective well-being. Sets an agenda for change

Mike Small exposes the reality of food, the movement of food round the globe, and how supermarket shopping generates waste. He finds hope in Scotland's local food movement

Father and son Alf and Ewan Young make a journey round Scotland to see at first hand some great environmental, social, employment and regeneration projects

Tony Miller and Gordon Hall explore why employees feel frustrated at work. Effective leaders,should 'let go' of controlling staff and nurture intrinsic motivation

A fascinating look at how allotments came about; and why they can make such a substantial contribution to health, well-being, community & producing food

Calls for a better partnership of parent, child, school, government and society – one to which all Scotland can contribute and from which all children can benefit

This guide to human achievements and future challenges is designed to help young people consider the future their children and grandchildren will inhabit

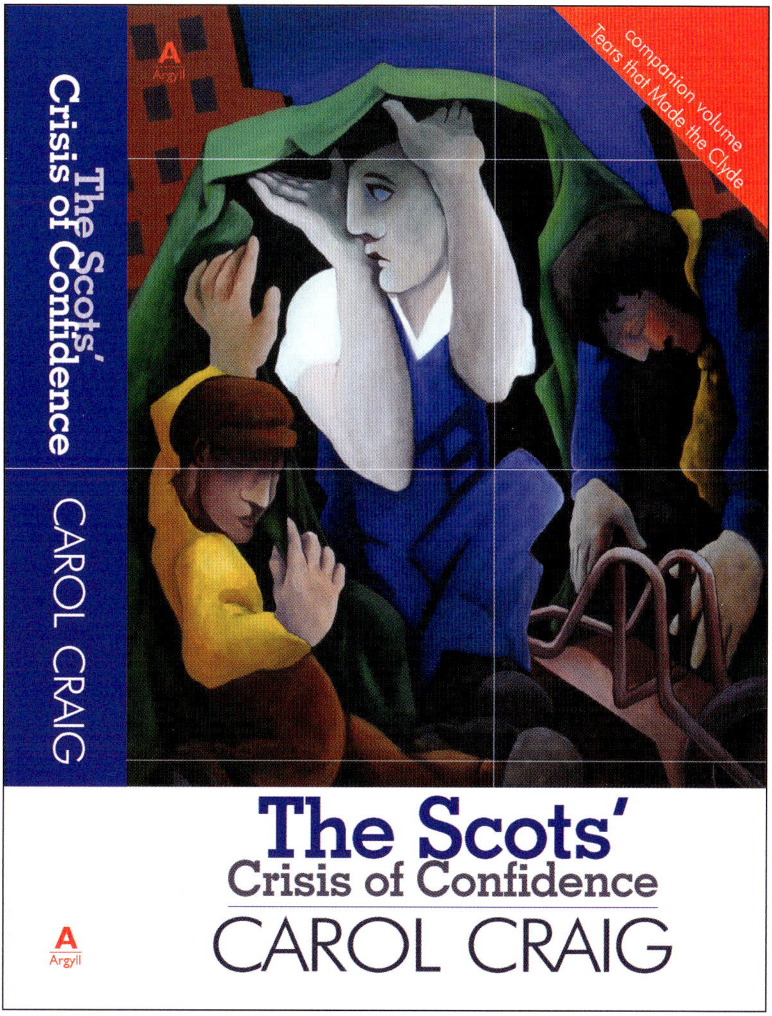

First published to great acclaim in 2003, in the current 2011 edition, since reprinted, Carol Craig examines again Scots' attitudes to and predeliction for negativity. She offers a refreshingly different analysis of the big themes of Scottish culture. The front cover artwork 'Raising the Tarpaulin' is by the late artist Michael Scott and is reproduced here with permission of the artist's estate

How challenging can gender transition be for both parents and siblings? Shirley Young's story shows how parents can move beyond the shock of transition

This extraordinary book provides insights and practical tools to help you navigate everyday human interactions, balance your own and others' needs and create a more fulfilling life

Brings together 22 experienced practitioners to reflect on class, race, gender, poverty, disability and homelessness as well as health and education

A collection of views from activists and young people provides a compelling answer – a healthy balance between support and challenge – 'the golden mean'

Former policeman John Carnochan takes us on a memorable journey of discovery as he comes to grips with violence and Scotland's traditionally high murder rate. He also gives a fascinating insight into the work of Scotland's Violence Reduction Unit and why it has been so spectacularly successful. This compelling book is not about high visibility policing or more officers but the importance of empathy and children's early years

POSTCARDS FROM SCOTLAND
PA22 3AE

www.postcardsfromscotland.co.uk

Scotland languishes in the second division of global child well-being. One child in every four is judged to be 'vulnerable' when they enter primary school. Alan Sinclair reveals the harm inflicted on so many of our youngest, most defenceless citizens through a toxic mix of poor parenting, bad health and a society focused on dealing with consequences rather than causes. He also sets out a routemap for us to start putting children first by helping us all to become better parents

Emily Cutts recounts the frenetic campaign to protect a magical oasis in the heart of a busy city from housing development – a David and Goliath struggle. She shows how a grassroots initiative can address the intensive materialism of modern life, improve children's lives, provide precious outdoor space for play and health, build a vibrant community and break down barriers caused by pronounced income inequality. An inspiration to all

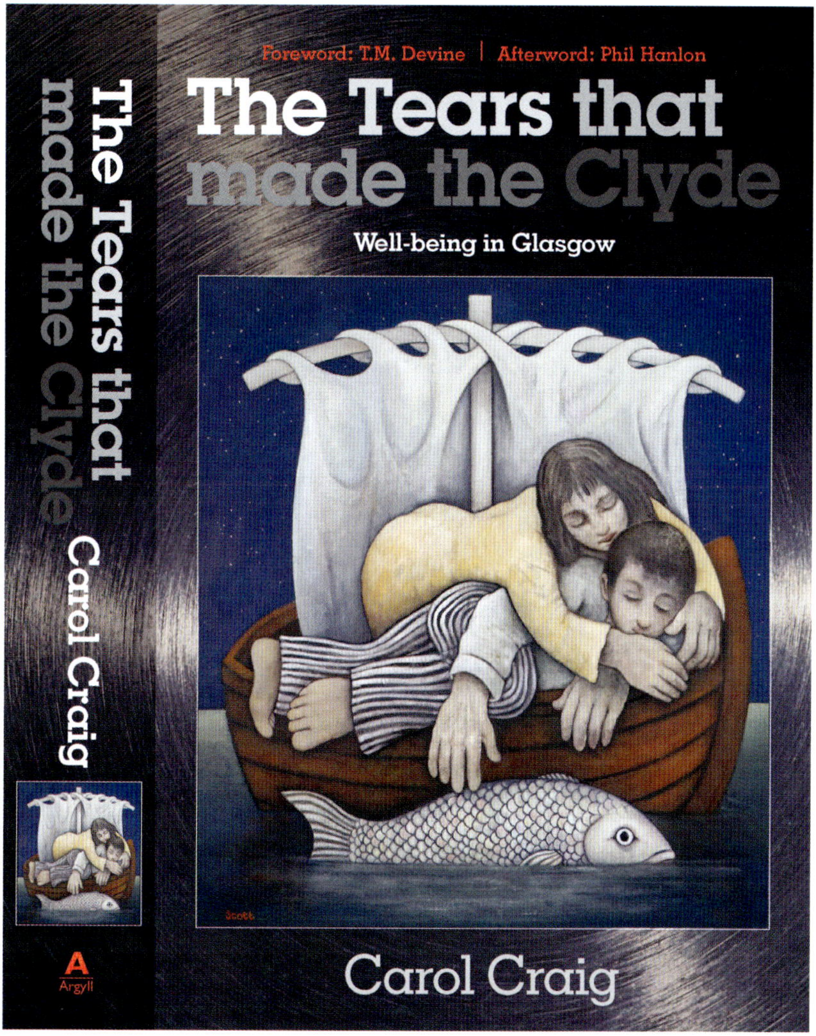

In this hard-hitting and profoundly thoughtful book first published in 2010, Carol Craig subjects Glasgow's post-industrial image as 'Scotland with style' to a long-overdue and honest scrutiny. The city's motto rings out 'Let Glasgow Flourish' yet this book powerfully shows that many citizens have languished as a result of mental ill-health, illness, deprivation, worklessness, gangs, drink and family breakdown.

Many Glaswegians are profoundly damaged by a culture of inequality and a corrosive dynamic within the family. Blending history, politics, literature, sociology and psychology this important book changes forever the way we see the city. It is now regarded as essential reading for anyone brought up in Glasgow as well as those searching for ways to heal this fractured city.

Cover artwork 'Night Magic' is by the late Michael Scott

Always the Cinderella of the education system, the significance of early years has been seriously under-estimated. Play is the Way brings together leading practitioners, policy-makers and academics to explain how a coherent approach to early years – centred on positive relationships and play – will not only result in better educational performance but in greatly improved health and well-being for future Scottish citizens. They challenge the deeply-ingrained cultural acceptance, throughout Scotland and the rest of the UK, that formal instruction in the three Rs (reading, 'riting and 'rithmetic) should begin at the age of four or five – at least a year before other European countries

Scotland. A country that prides itself on its modernity and progressive instincts. Yet this is a nation whose mental and physical health outcomes are poor by European standards. This book asks why? Grippingly readable yet challenging, Carol Craig offers an answer which is glaringly obvious. Generations of Scottish children have suffered in ways that undermine the nation's health. Starting from her own and her neighbours' lives, she explores the growing awareness internationally of the impact of Adverse Childhood Experiences that are hiding in plain sight.

Cover artwork 'Siren Song' is by the late Michael Scott

consultant and an adviser to the Westminster Government's National Literacy Strategy. She also wrote books on literacy as well as hundreds of articles for the educational and national press. She was a regular contributor and advisor to BBC schools programmes.

During this time Sue was in frequent contact with teachers and heard them repeatedly say that children's behaviour had undergone subtle but worrying changes. This then led her into intensive research into child development. From this she concluded that the modern world fails to provide children with what they need to live healthy lives; that cultural and technological changes, such as screens, fast food and car infested streets are undermining children's mental and physical health.

Her book *Toxic Childhood* was published in 2006 to much acclaim. It attracted considerable media attention and sparked an international debate on children's well-being. She followed this with a self-help book for parents, *Detoxing Childhood* (2008) and then *21st Century Boys (*2009) and *21st Century Girls* (2013).

From the publication of *Toxic Childhood* on, Sue ceased being seen primarily as a literacy expert and became increasingly involved in campaigns about early years, play and the commercialisation of childhood. Since 2014 she has been listed in *Who's Who* as a childhood campaigner. She frequently travelled abroad, particularly to Scandinavia, and was often asked why UK children start school so early. This simple question eventually led to her latest passion – play in the early years.

School starting date

When she started to look at why the UK had a school starting age of five, and often four, Sue Palmer discovered that:

> . . . starting ages for formal schooling around the world were chosen by politicians, as opposed to educational experts. And even for most politicians, the thought of putting four- and five-year-olds into a formal school environment seems to have been unpalatable. During the late nineteenth and early twentieth centuries, the governments of 66 per cent of countries

> worldwide chose six as the school starting age, while in 22 per cent (including some of the most educationally successful nations) they preferred seven years old.

That left only 12 per cent of countries worldwide where children start school at five or younger. Interestingly, this 12 per cent consists of the four nations of the United Kingdom, and a selection of its ex-colonies and protectorates, including Australia and New Zealand. In effect, 'every wide-eyed, wondering child around the world who starts compulsory schooling before the age of six is the great-great-grandson or daughter of the British Empire.'

It was in 1870 that Victorian politicians in the UK decided to send such young children to school. Parliament had recently abolished child labour so something had to be done to get children off the streets as factories needed their mothers. A start date of five eased this problem. England effectively reduced this to four in the late 1980s, partly to address concerns about levels of literacy and partly to help get women back into the workplace.

This story about school starting age worried Sue as it makes clear that it's not based on an understanding of child development but on the needs of industry or society. What's more, there's a huge amount of research which shows that it's informal play which the under-sevens need for proper cognitive, emotional and social development – not formal schooling.

The Upstart campaign – Onwards and upwards!

This then led Sue to write a subsequent book – *Upstart: the case for raising the school starting age and providing what the under-sevens really need* (2016). This issue then became the primary focus of Sue's intellectual and campaigning skills. By then she was back living full time in Scotland so when she set up Upstart, a charitable organisation, its campaign mission was to introduce a kindergarten phase in Scottish education. Sue became chair of the Upstart board.

On her return to Scotland Sue was immediately welcomed into the early years world. She was invited to chair the Scottish Play

Commission and serve on the Scottish Government's Early Years Task Force set up by the then Chief Medical Officer, Sir Harry Burns.

I had met Sue personally as she had spoken at a few Centre events but our friendship developed as the result of frequent meetings in the Ceilidh Place in Ullapool for the 'Changin Scotland' twice yearly discussion events organised by its owner, and future SNP MSP, Jean Urquhart and Gerry Hassan. As I write I have a copy of *Toxic Childhood* on my desk and Sue has personally inscribed the title page with the words 'Here's to fellow travelling! Ullapool March 08'. And how right she's been. Since 2008 we have indeed been fellow travellers, contributing in different ways to a shared goal of trying to improve children's lives. In the past seven years our personal crusades have intertwined as Upstart started to feature in my own life as well as in the Centre's story.

In 2017 Sue asked me to become a trustee of Upstart. I was still very involved in Centre business, and my own writing, so I hesitated in case I didn't have the time, but Sue assured me that the meetings weren't too frequent and my role would mainly be advisory. So with my own board's blessing I became an Upstart trustee.

Having a role in Upstart was also in tune with my personal life. In 2015 I became a grandmother. I now have four grandchildren. Parents are often too busy, and too immersed in everyday care, to pay close attention to their child's development but that's not true of most grandparents. We not only have the time and distance to notice but also to relish the unfolding stages and see that a child's play is key to growing up strong and resilient.

But I had another reason to become interested in play. My daughter-in law, Merlin, was brought up in a wood near Ullapool and returned there after art school with my son Ewan. After the birth of their two sons Merlin started to ask local friends with children to come to play in the wood and soon she had the vision of opening a forest nursery. Within a year or so it had become a thriving Community Interest Company called Kinder Croft. All four of my grandchildren have benefited from their experiences there. What's more, my other daughter-in-law, Rhiannon, has now undertaken early years training and is happily working in the forest nursery. Rhiannon also went to art school and has designed the covers for some of the *Postcards from Scotland* books, most notably *Play is the Way*.

'Play not tests for P1'

When I joined the Upstart board the organisation was in the midst of a vigorous campaign against standardised assessments in P1.

In 2015 it was becoming increasingly clear that Scotland's educational attainment gap was widening. Indeed Scotland lagged the rest of the UK both in terms of the numbers of students from poorer backgrounds going to university and also in its higher drop-out rates. Given that Scotland had once prided itself on its good performance on educational equality, this was an affront to the country's values and a stain on the SNP, as it had been in government for eight years. The First Minister announced she was appalled and committed to take action. She also asked Scots to judge her personally on the country's future education record. The Scottish Government then awarded more money to schools in poor areas, which was certainly welcome but it also did something which many educationalists did not support – it introduced more standardised national tests. And the most controversial of these was what quickly became known as the 'P1 tests'.

At that time, partly as a result of 'the early level' of the Curriculum for Excellence, some teachers were providing a play-based curriculum in P1. The introduction of standardised literacy and numeracy tests in P1 greatly increased the likelihood that P1 teachers would feel obliged to 'teach to the test' thus reverting to the formal teaching of four- and five-year-old pupils. The Scottish Government also introduced P1 literacy and numeracy 'bench-marks' which set out the standards these infants were expected to achieve.

As Sue had done extensive research into the impact of school starting date on children's emotional well-being and educational attainment for her *Upstart* book, she knew that these standardised tests had no statistical reliability for this age group. The distinguish-ed educationalist Professor Dylan Williams put his finger on the problem when he said: 'The unreliability of the assessments, combined with the unreliability of five-year-olds, means these assessments are almost completely useless as guides to the achievement and needs of five-year-olds.' More importantly such tests inevitably downgrade play and put academic pressure on children even though this may be detrimental to longer term attainment. Sue writes:

> A growing number of research studies have linked an early start on formal education to social, emotional and mental health problems in later childhood and beyond. An increasing number of Scotland's children and young people now suffer from developmental disorders and mental health conditions. The reasons behind these problems are complex, but we cannot ignore the impact of pressure for early academic attainment.

Yet there is no educational advantage to an early start. Indeed, in 88 per cent of countries worldwide, children don't start school till they are six or seven – and countries that wait till seven (such as Finland, Estonia and Switzerland) always do well in international comparisons of educational achievement. Research has found that children who are taught literacy skills from the age of five do no better in the long run than those who start at seven. The results even out by the time they're 10 or 11, and thereafter the late starters tend to have better comprehension skills and are more likely to enjoy reading.

Fortunately, Upstart, the organisation she had set up, was an ideal vehicle to disseminate this research to a wider audience. Before long there were Upstart leaflets, opt-out postcards for parents of P1 pupils to complete and extensive information on the organisation's website. Sue and Kate Johnston, a former nursery head and energetic Upstart board member, were also very good at spreading the message on social media. Upstart spearheaded a very successful 'chalking campaign' resulting in people all over Scotland chalking 'Play, Not tests for P1', in locations throughout the country and then posting pictures online.

Upstart was not a lone voice and its leaflets and postcards carried logos of supporting organisations including the EIS, Children in Scotland and Connect, formerly the Scottish Parent

Teacher Council, and later the Scottish Childminding Association.

The Scottish Government pressed ahead with the P1 tests even though the International Council of Educational Experts which it had established had doubts about this measure. So too did the majority of teachers, indeed 66 per cent were opposed and only 3 per cent in favour. Many thought the tests 'a waste of time' and stressful for many children, even the most confident.

As a result of the growing antipathy to the tests, in September 2018 the Scottish Conservatives tabled a motion in the Scottish Parliament calling on the Education Secretary, John Swinney, to scrap them. The motion received support from opposition parties and, following a tetchy debate, passed by 63 votes to 61. The Scottish Government would not listen to the arguments, maintaining fiercely that the Conservatives' motion was 'politically motivated': the Tories had always supported standardised testing and the fact they had changed their tune showed they were not to be trusted. However, what's clear from the debate is that Conservative MSPs had changed their views. They still fully supported the tests for older age groups but had been persuaded, partly by the type of arguments that Upstart had been advancing as well as by teachers' comments, that P1 testing was not appropriate. This was also the view of the other opposition parties, including the Greens.

The Education Secretary, and the SNP, were not for turning and would not respect the will of parliament by cancelling the tests. But they did initiate a review. This reported in 2019 and, unsurprisingly, supported the tests despite the views advanced by the majority of teachers and educationalists.

So it was in this febrile environment that the idea of a *Postcards from Scotland* book, setting out the case for a play-based curriculum for the under sevens, emerged. I can't recall if it was my idea, or Sue's, but we were both convinced that a collection of essays on this topic, edited by her, would be an important and timely contribution to the debate on the importance of play in P1 and P2. Fortunately, the Centre's board agreed.

Play is the Way

We published *Play is the Way: Child development, early years and the future of Scottish education* in November 2020. With permission, we borrowed the book's main title from Falkirk Council who use it as the name of their early years strategy. The book is 216 pages long so one of the thicker volumes in the series. There are 15 different contributors in the first edition and 16 in the 2021 edition. Box 14 overleaf lists the chapter titles and authors.

Sue did a very good job in identifying and then commissioning an impressive list of expert contributors. Indeed some of the contributors, such as Professor Aline-Wendy Dunlop, are the most important thought leaders on early years in Scotland. There isn't space here for me to summarise the content of each chapter so I'm only going to refer to a few of the different contributions to help readers get a feel for the breadth and depth of the arguments presented in *Play is the Way*.

In her introduction Sue explains the background to Upstart – its successes and challenges:

> In 2015, we had high hopes that [we could achieve] a kindergarten stage fairly easily . . . However, we soon recognised there was a potential barrier – the deeply ingrained cultural acceptance in Scotland that instruction in the three Rs should begin at the age of four or five.

And this cultural barrier is then explored in more depth in the first chapter by developmental neuroscientist Dr Suzanne Zeedyk. Suzanne was born and grew up in Texas and moved to live and work in Dundee in 1993. As a result she melds an astute sense of being part of Scottish culture with the clarity of an outside observer. She begins her article by reminding us of the pride Scots take in having once been the most educated country in the world. This means that criticising the fact that we begin formal teaching with children as young as five, or even four, can easily provoke a negative reaction. Some find it disagreeable that these critics, or upstarts to be more precise, want to replace the 3Rs with play. Suzanne argues that those same religious roots which encouraged Scots to value book learning also ensure that we feel squeamish about play: 'That

Box 14 Contents of *Play is the Way*

Calvinist ethos was opposed to frivolity, on the grounds that fun did not offer a suitable path to God. In fact, it was dangerous. Play led you straight into the arms of the Devil himself.'

Suzanne also quotes from the talk John Carnochan gave at the 2018 Upstart AGM: 'There's something about us, about our Calvinist genes. Why is it we don't like to be enjoying ourselves? Kids laughing and playing football. . . We don't like the idea, because they're a bit noisy. We don't enjoy the laughter.'

Ultimately Suzanne is hopeful not only because progress is being made but also because the developments Upstart seeks would not just bring about a change in children's school experience but help 'to shift Scotland's sense of self'.

Dr Pam Jarvis, a chartered psychologist and teacher, debunks 'the myth of early acceleration' in her chapter. She argues that the top-down pedagogical approach forces all infants on a formal learning path before they are developmentally ready and, given what we now know about brain development, this makes no sense. Before the age of six, most children do not have 'the cognitive architecture' to use the knowledge being imparted to them as 'there is little for the incoming constructs to hang upon'. She explains:

> It's like throwing a piece of clothing into a wardrobe with no suitable hangers – such 'transmissions' fall to the bottom and lie tangled together in the darkness. To continue the wardrobe analogy, when a new garment arrives that could be coordinated with existing items, it's difficult or impossible to find them in the tangle that lies at the bottom.

Jarvis cites both neuroscientists and the developmental psychologist, Piaget, to explain how children's minds develop:

> As children build their knowledge base, they become able to process larger amounts of information more quickly by flexibly 'chunking' ideas. For example, as childhood unfolds, cats will be linked both to a 'domestic pets' schema which will also include dogs and rabbits and then later to a 'feline animals' schema which will take in lions and tigers. As the child gains

> further in maturity and experience she will form yet more abstract connections, for example to the musical 'Cats'.
>
> To continue the 'brain as wardrobe' analogy, the hangers slowly appear and the garments are coordinated into mix and match outfits in the wardrobe: incoming information now enters a network of connections. As this process unfolds, the child becomes increasingly able to follow adult agendas because they have many more routes in existing cognition through which they are able to 'connect'.

Jarvis then swaps her wardrobe metaphor for a new one: an overworked, partially built, car. This is how she envisages the way educators are treating young children when they overburden them with formal learning before they're ready. This idea is crucial to the case for play for the under sevens:

> The stress will be even greater if – due to age-related expectations and standardised assessments – they come to feel that they are a source of disappointment. And such experiences do not only have an effect upon the emotions, but also upon the cognitive process as stress hormones fill the body and brain. Hence attempts to accelerate children risk creating the opposite effect to the one that is intended – it can actually *damage* their readiness to learn.

Jarvis ends by pointing out the variation in age in a P1 classroom. A four-year-old, for example, has had '25 per cent less time in the world' than a five-year-old. She argues, this is yet another reason for dealing with a child 'where s/he is' rather than through standardised 'instructional' procedures.

It's also another reason why parents should think seriously about delaying their four-year-old child's school start date. This crucially important issue is the focus of one of the chapters in *Play is the Way* – 'Parent Power: how a grass-roots campaign secured a promise to change the law'. Patricia Anderson and Diane Delaney, both parents and Upstart supporters, recount their experience of establishing a Facebook group called 'Deferral Support Scotland' in 2018 to provide parents with a clear understanding of their legal rights. This then became the 'Give Them Time' campaign which has been spectacularly successful in lobbying government.

In Scotland there is no legal requirement to start children at school until they are five. But there was considerable variation in how local authorities responded to a request from parents to defer their four-year-old. What Give Them Time has managed to do is secure an automatic entitlement for all children, who would be four when starting school, to a further year of funded nursery or childcare.

Returning to *Play is the Way*, there's also a chapter by Alan Sinclair which he calls 'The three Ps before the three Rs'. From what we know of Alan's thinking it isn't surprising that his three Ps are 'preconception, pregnancy and parents'. There's also a chapter by Professor John Frank and Dr Rosemary Geddes titled 'A public health perspective on child development'. As well as being a professor of public health at the University of Edinburgh, John is a member of the Upstart board. I referred to him in the section on Alan Sinclair above as he was the lead researcher on the East Lothian study of P1s' development in 2012-13 which showed that 27 per cent of children in this cohort were assessed as 'vulnerable' and many of them came from middle-class backgrounds.

In their chapter the authors explain the benefits of using the internationally renowned tool, the Early Development Instrument (EDI) which assesses 'social competence, emotional maturity, language and cognitive ability, physical health and well-being, fine motor skills and communication skills'. They then set out how it has been used to very good effect in other countries, particularly Australia, to assess and then support the developmental needs of birth cohorts. Frank and Geddes also outline how their articles on this Scottish research passed rigorous peer-review and were published in prestigious journals yet this had no influence on Scottish policy-makers who remained uninterested in the potential benefits of the EDI.

Originally the researchers thought that the problem might be due to their concern about how to use the EDI findings to allocate resources based on varied developmental needs in local authority areas. But they soon realised that this wasn't the problem. The

Scottish Government and others weren't interested as they were already committed to the introduction of P1 tests on educational attainment. Frank and Geddes think this is the wrong priority: not only are these tests too narrow and don't look at the child's whole development but also they preclude the knowledge that P1 teachers have of their pupils. And none of this makes sense to these public health experts. They write: '. . . the scientific literature argues strongly that. . . indicators, based on what the child can do "in everyday life", are much more powerful predictors of both later school and career success, than three Rs test results at age 5-6.'

But the Scottish Government remained impervious to such arguments. Indeed they demonstrated their commitment to the P1 tests when in 2021, in the midst of the Covid-19 pandemic and following multiple school closures, the Education Secretary told teachers to undertake the P1 assessments.

Publication and sales

Covid-19 had a significant influence on *Play is the Way*. We published the book in the autumn of 2020 during a lockdown and so were unable to hold a proper book launch as gatherings were forbidden. We had to make do with a launch event online.

The book received glowing reviews from a wide range of influencers and readers. It also received considerable press coverage and was named as a 'Book of the Year' in *Scottish Review*. Very quickly the book generated a large number of internet sales. Upstart was not well placed to cater for these so it was the Centre that dealt with the demand. Helen Smith, who worked a few hours a week as my assistant, did an excellent job in fulfilling the thousands of book orders placed on the *Postcards from Scotland* website. Alf Young, who was an enthusiastic supporter of Upstart, dealt with bulk sales and spent many hours packing boxes and delivering them to courier companies. I had fractured my left hip and shoulder in September that year so I did what I could to help.

Sue Palmer and Kate Johnston promoted the book constantly on social media and no doubt many of the sales resulted from this activity. Between February and October 2023 Upstart also held nine 'book club' events on *Play is the Way* with the various authors summarising and presenting their articles. Hundreds of people participated in these sessions on the online platform Zoom. This too proved a great way to maintain interest in the book and generate sales. Upstart also organised a crowd-funded campaign of its supporters and made enough money to send a copy of the book, ostensibly as a 'Christmas present', to every MSP and Director of Education in Scotland.

As a small charity the Centre doesn't pay royalties to its authors but, after giving authors a generous number of free copies, we let them purchase their books at cost price to sell at talks or events thus making some money from direct sales. This has worked well for some of our authors but lockdown meant it wouldn't for *Play is the Way*. Events were forbidden and Upstart didn't have the capacity to sell online. As so many of the book sales were generated by Upstart's activities, we had to devise a way to ensure that the organisation benefited financially from its popularity. So, with our accountant's approval, the Centre's board decided to split the profits from the book and pay this directly to Upstart as a series of donations.

In January 2024 *Play is the Way* has sold just over 4000 copies. In Scotland a sale of 500 is considered impressive so this is exceptional. It is significantly more than our second most popular book – *Hiding in Plain Sight* – which has sold 2,300 copies. We hadn't anticipated these sales figures and so had to keep reprinting.

Impact

There's little doubt that *Play is the Way* had considerable impact on the early years sector and on some parents of young children. Scotland, and the UK more generally, does not understand what neuroscience and development psychology tells us about what children need for healthy development. If we understood properly we would follow the lead of other countries in Scandinavia and elsewhere and defer formal schooling to at least six and preferably seven. So, for many readers *Play is the Way* was their first encounter with this evidence. It also helped to bolster the confidence of those working in early years who were aware of these arguments but knew they were being ignored by policy makers and the wider Scottish public.

It's important to point out that there is what Sue Palmer calls 'double think' at the heart of the SNP Government's approach to early years. In February 2020 Education Scotland and the Scottish Government published 'Realising the Ambition: Being Me', a document setting out detailed 'practice guidance' for early years professionals, and teachers, working with children up to age six. Sue is hugely enthusiastic about this guidance as she considers it 'wonderfully developmentally appropriate'. However, the continuation of the P1 tests and benchmarks on literacy and numeracy mean that, despite 'Realising the Ambition', teachers are being given very mixed messages about the importance of play. This will only change when the Scottish Government breaks out of the corner into which it has painted itself and scraps the P1 tests.

Sue Palmer stepped down as Chair of Upstart and became its President in 2023. I took this opportunity to resign from the board feeling that I had made my contribution to the organisation and the campaign. Besides I had a large book to write. But it now looks as if the Centre's involvement with Upstart and play is not quite at an end. In March 2025 we shall publish another *Postcards* book on play edited by Tam Baillie, a former Children's Commissioner and Upstart board member, and Professor John McKendrick, an expert on poverty and play. The book is called *Born to Play*, an echo of *Born to Fail?* published in 1973. Our new book looks at the issue of play and inequality but also focuses on the biological imperative all young animals have to play. This is nature's way of ensuring that the young develop healthy brains and bodies. The book also covers how play helps children process stress and trauma. This is one reason why children commonly play in the rubble of war.

In the UK, which scores very badly for child well-being, we rarely hear the sound of children playing and laughing outdoors, unless we're passing a school playground. And this should worry us for children's well-being depends on their active, independent, outdoor play. And, as we know from this chapter and Alan Sinclair's work, Scotland needs to make child well-being a genuine priority.

Chapter 19
Schooling Scotland

Danny Murphy's offer;
the background to *Schooling Scotland*;
defining and tackling inequity;
a plea to raise the school entrance age to five;
Danny's 'inspiring schools'; building on the positives;
the importance of community; publication and reaction;
Nicola Sturgeon's 'defining mission';
Scotland's declining educational standards; Seligman's warning;
the Curriculum for Excellence;
the problem with the term 'confident individuals';
Derek Brown; *Shaping our Global Future*; publication and reflections.

'WOULD YOU like a book on education for your series?' That was the question Danny Murphy asked me when we were at a Scottish Education Leadership, Management and Administration Society (SELMAS) event at Stirling University in November 2012. We were both speakers at the conference and as the Centre had just launched the *Postcards* series I mentioned this in my talk. Of course, I was interested in learning more about Danny's proposal. In the first five years of the Centre many of our activities were aimed at education staff: talks to schools and workshops on confidence; *Creating Confidence: A handbook for professionals working with young people*; conferences aimed at teachers and educationalists with keynote speakers such as Professor Martin Seligman and Professor Carol Dweck; and our large number of *Bounce Back!* training courses on resilience.

I met up with Danny a few weeks later and had a memorable discussion. He was an ideal contributor for a book on Scottish education. For over thirty years he had worked as a teacher, head of department, local authority adviser, and headteacher of three different Scottish secondary schools. Now retired from school education he was Senior Teaching Fellow at the University of Edinburgh. He was also the author of *Professional School Leadership: Dealing with Dilemmas* (2007). What's more, he was an experienced creative writer. I wasn't surprised when he won the Costa short story prize in 2016 and then the Exeter story prize in 2018. Danny knows how to write. Readers with good memories will be aware that we met Danny in an earlier chapter as he is one of the editors of *Working for Equality*.

None of this means that Danny found it easy to write *Schooling Scotland*. He didn't. Scottish education is a large topic and focusing on something that could be written about clearly in 25-30,000 words was a challenge. He had been inspired by what Ewan and Alf Young had done for their book *The New Road* and so he wanted to visit various educational establishments to see what they were doing well and this added another layer of complexity.

In the year following our initial meeting we were in regular email contact debating ideas and discussing the focus and structure of the book. We agreed that the book should look primarily at educational inequality, something that was growing in Scottish schools. Indeed Scotland then had the widest educational attainment gap in the OECD, the largest NEET (Not in Employment, Education or Training) group and some of the worst health inequalities. Taken together these data suggested there was something wrong with the way that Scotland equipped people at the lower end of the social spectrum with the skills not just for work but to lead healthy lives. Danny believed that the main problem was secondary, not primary education, though he thought changes were needed to early years provision.

We also agreed that he would not tackle the subject in an abstract way and his starting point would be the everyday experiences of pupils, teachers and perhaps parents. This approach would inevitably mean a focus on social interaction, behaviour, relationships and personal psychology – not the usual fare for Scottish analysts. Danny would also set out what he saw as the most important things to change as well as his priorities.

All the hard work was worth it. I've been proud to be involved in the publication of all the *Postcards from Scotland* books. But I've been particularly proud of *Schooling Scotland: Education, equity and community* by Daniel Murphy.

Schooling Scotland

At the time of writing, we have published 17 books in the series and the cumulative page count runs into tens of thousands. But for me there are a couple of pages that stand out and they are from *Schooling Scotland.* Danny asks us to imagine that we are standing with him as headteacher at a comprehensive school house assembly looking at 'the sea of faces'. In the book the subsequent passage runs to almost two and a half pages and I intended to simply give readers a flavour of it here. However, as I read it again, I thought that every word mattered: each word is needed to help us see the complexity of Scotland's comprehensive schools and the issues facing many pupils.

> There's a girl who is worried about exam results – will she get the five A passes she needs to apply to study medicine at university? Next to her is a boy whose preoccupation is working out how to speak to a girl he fancies. Many here haven't thought about school since the 4.00 bell yesterday. One helped his uncle in his plumbing business at the weekend and wishes he was still there. Some spent the weekend at Boys Brigade camp, some attended Mass, one played the organ at Methodist Church, four attended Islamic centre classes, some visited an ageing relative, some went with their dad and his dad to watch football in Glasgow. Some are on special diets, two with nut allergies, some vegetarians, some diabetic, some superfit, some superfat. Two proudly sport new tattoos, some fiddle with nose piercings, some have piercings that can't be seen. Twenty or thirty years ago, three children with Asperger's Syndrome would, along with another forty or more others with various

learning difficulties or physical disabilities, have been in a separate school, but they are well kent here, among their peers, and we and they understand our humanity better as a result. Some drink alcohol regularly, a few drink recklessly; some smoke fags and some smoke weed: two or three do so regularly with their mothers' dealer boyfriends – and one of these regularly disrupts classes, a victim of drug-induced psychosis. A few are on a slippery slope with cocaine. Some breakfasted on crisps on their way to school; some had porridge, toast and orange juice. Some left home angry but arrived smiling with their pals. Some forgot their homework, one hasn't done it because they ended up sleeping at their dad's house and their school bag is at their mum's. Two girls spent the whole evening with their mother, herself a teacher in another school, revising a piece of work they want to get 'just right'. Some watch every episode of East Enders and some none. Some went to Turkey for their Easter holiday, several have been to Australia and some have never been as far as Glasgow. Three newly arrived Latvians stick together; they speak little English. Some spend a lot of time in their bedrooms, online, unsupervised, perhaps at risk but more often just learning. Some would be happy to play football all day every day and others would do anything to avoid getting changed into sports gear. After years of domestic violence, two sisters are trying to hold their lives together, working through a programme with CEDAR (Children Experiencing Domestic Abuse Recovery) which includes rebuilding their relationship with their abused mother. Another two sisters have come to school together planning how they will surprise their mother for her 40th birthday. Some are on to their third Ipad, some have no broadband at home. All live in houses with running hot and cold water but two are in a house where there was no money to feed the meter this morning – in fact there is often only cold water – while four live in homeless hostel accommodation. One girl had a letter about the humanitarian consequences of the Syrian conflict published in the Observer at the weekend, a group of boys are making money from their own commercial gaming website, but some sitting in the same hall can barely read at all. Some will forever believe they are 'no good at

> maths'. Five have parents who are solicitors, four have parents who are refuse collectors, one has a parent who is an MSP, thirty five have parents who work in shops, many have parents whose jobs lack security, a few have relatives in the forces, and some don't know their parents at all. One girl is sitting worrying whether she should ask the teacher she confides in about the 'morning after pill'. There are two in care whose father is in Carstairs for life on account of murdering their mother a few years back. There are many more whose fathers cook at the weekends. Almost no-one ate 'five a day' yesterday and half a dozen have had no fruit or veg in the past week. Two children in wheelchairs will be the first to scoot out of assembly and make their way to the lifts. One, with athetoid cerebral palsy, uses a hand switch to operate his chair and a different switch for the communication device he uses to speak and which goes everywhere with him. He often brings a smile to our faces with his pre-programmed jokes. . .

This passage shows clearly that the author is in modern parlance an 'empath'. He's particularly good at tuning into others' feelings and motivations. It also shows that he respects, values, indeed cherishes, individual differences.

Defining and tackling inequity

But Danny Murphy is also a sophisticated thinker, adept at philosophising where appropriate. And he does this admirably in relation to the main topic of the book – educational inequality. He contrasts the life chances of two fictitious boys born on the same date in 1997 – Jim and Ian. Jim was born into a middle-class family, is doing well academically and has benefited in many different ways from his parents' ability to pay for 'school-based learning activities beyond the classroom' such as music lessons. Ian, by contrast, has achieved minimal academic qualifications and, for a variety of reasons outside his family's control, looks destined for 'insecure work'. Ian is also much more likely to suffer from ill health, substance misuse and mental health problems than his wealthier peer. Danny writes that he could tell a very similar story about Catherine and Elaine.

Danny is very keen to point out that there are very many good teachers in Scotland who are motivated to make a difference to the Ians or Elaines in their class. But despite this good work it's still true that the wealthier you are, the more you benefit from school education:

> The very things that improve the chances of the very poorest – individual support, continuing professional development for teachers, a warm and supportive ethos, high expectations – also improve the learning of all other pupils. In a competitive system, when those at the bottom of the ladder improve, those above them may work harder to maintain their advantage. Even if every pupil in Scotland attained five Highers in their school examinations, do we imagine that the children of doctors, lawyers and bankers would then take up equal numbers of low-paid insecure service sector jobs? Is it not likely that the threshold for entry to desirable university courses in medicine and law would increase to five Advanced Highers, that richer parents would pay for more tutoring, more internship experience?

The problem – 'the elephant in the room' that we refuse to acknowledge – is our unequal society. It's not schools in themselves that cause the problem of educational inequality, it's the inequality in the wider society which is the problem. Indeed, research by the OECD on Scottish education, published in 2007, concluded that it's not the quality of schools which has most impact on pupils' attainment. It's 'who you are'. In other words, it's socio-economic background which is of most importance.

Danny philosophises on the meaning of equality in education. He argues that the weakest form is 'equality of opportunity' as this takes no account of the individual's ability to make use of the opportunities he or she has ostensibly been given. But 'equality of outcome' is impractical in a democratic society which values freedom and individual choice. He breaks out of the problem of balancing equality and freedom by focusing on *equity* which is about our sense of 'fairness' and not about 'precise statistics'.

This leads him to argue that 'it takes *all* Scotland to raise a child' – that all of us in civic Scotland share in that responsibility. If

Scotland wants Scotland's children to have a better start in life, there is nothing we can do that would have a greater effect than to *ensure that poor families have sufficient money*, that they are above... [the] 'threshold', where choices are easier, where it is possible to live more autonomous, less reactive, lives. Increasing the income of poor families may well be a much more effective educational intervention than any of the work done by teachers or in schools. How this should be done, Danny believes, is a job for politicians – that it *should* be done should be a demand from all of us in a civilised society, committed to equity in our democratic life.

Danny Murphy's views on early years

Given pupils' unequal start in life, Danny is particularly keen to ensure that children from poor backgrounds have access to excellent early years provision. But for him, just as for Alan Sinclair, this means involving parents as much as possible in rearing their children well: it's not about trying to replace parents with professionals. Indeed, Danny argues that parents need to be 'inside the tent' when possible.

He knows this is being done well in some places in Scotland. I said earlier that Danny Murphy was inspired by the journey Alf and Ewan Young undertook for their book *The New Road* and so he embarked on a similar journey. (See Box 15 for a list of places

Box 15: Postcards from some of Scotland's Inspiring Schools

A journal of a tour round Scottish schools, 2013, written to accompany the book *Schooling Scotland: Education, equity and community*. Daniel Murphy

- 'Wee Pans' (Prestonpans Infant School): community and school working together
- Bucksburn Academy, Aberdeen: what will we do when the oil runs out?
- Room 13 – artistic flourishing in Caol [see page 300]
- St Bernadette's Primary School, Larbert: great teaching and great design
- Perth and Kinross – schools as community hubs
- Auchenharvie Academy – a fine comprehensive school
- Scottish Borders – the teaching profession of the 21st Century

he visited on his tour.) And it's in one of these schools that he encountered inspiring early years' practice:

> At 'Wee Pans', in my school tour, I saw mothers and fathers going into school from the earliest stages, effective programmes of study support to young mothers and no walls between school and community. Some of what is happening there costs money, but some of it is about opening up the right doors, making the right connections, putting people, parents, professional services, third sector organisations, in touch with each other, with the school as a community hub. While there is a lot of this kind of practice in early years, showing a new way for school and community to work together, the aims, standards, management and governance of early years provision – whether private or public – vary greatly.

It's interesting that in the first section on inequalities in education Danny starts by outlining one issue which was hardly acknowledged in 2014 let alone discussed: age when starting school. He points out that those commencing school at four and a half are disadvantaged not just in P1 but right the way throughout school 'up to and including national examinations at age 15/16'.

As a secondary school headteacher Danny was very aware that those youngsters from poorer backgrounds are further penalised as they leave school:

> In a final unfair throw of the dice, those born after September in a given intake year, and who wish to leave school to seek employment at the end of S4, have to stay on an extra half year till Christmas of S5. In many schools, it is inefficient to provide a special August to December curriculum for the 'Christmas leavers', so, after eleven years when they never quite catch up with their older peers, they experience a poorer curriculum in their final, additional, half year.

Throughout the book Danny comes up with nine specific recommendations for action. The first of these is that the Scottish Government should not permit any child under the age of five to start school. He also recommends abolishing the two-stage leaving date. Danny is so convinced of the damage that is done to children who start school when they are four that he believes 'this change alone. . . could enhance the educational experience of the largest number of pupils.'

I have little doubt that if Danny were writing today he would take an even harder line on the inequity of Scotland's school starting age. The Scottish Government still has not formally excluded four-year-olds from P1 but has given an automatic entitlement for all children, who would be four when starting school, to a further year of funded nursery or childcare. Undoubtedly this will assuage concerned parents of four-year-olds and allow them to defer. One of my grandsons has undoubtedly benefited already from this provision. But as more middle-class parents become aware that it's not in their child's best interest to go to school at four, and defer his/her entry, this will worsen educational inequality. Indeed some P1 teachers are already reporting a difficult mix in their classrooms of very young disadvantaged four-year-old pupils alongside some older middle-class pupils who are almost six on their first day at school. This means that poor four-year-olds will suffer even more than currently as they will be so much younger than some of the older, sturdier, more cognitively developed middle-class children in their class. And remember this inequality isn't simply a problem in P1 as it can persist well into teenage years.

Building on the positives

Danny Murphy has many ideas for how schooling can be improved in Scotland but at every turn he's keen to acknowledge and celebrate its many strengths. He believes that Scottish schools are much more inclusive and supportive than when he entered the profession and that there's an impressive number of dedicated, enthusiastic and informed teachers. In the work he was then doing at Moray House with senior school leaders, and on his 2013 tour of Scottish schools, he found 'inspiration and optimism aplenty'.

Nonetheless Danny believes there's plenty scope for improvement and at the heart of his suggestions is his belief that schools can't on their own deliver the changes that are required. He thinks the emphasis should be on 'the quality of experience', not simply the measurement of academic achievement:

> The current schooling system, particularly secondary, builds in, for some, alienation, inequity and division. Despite the many personal relationships of care and affection within a school, at its end point the system ranks children formally on only one measure of what it means to be a fully flourishing human being, and anticipation of this ranking feeds its way back through the system, in parental memory and in the anticipation of current pupils. Current hierarchical management structures and complicated professional routines exaggerate distances between home and school. For some in our society this is schooling by regulation (*done to*) rather than schooling by participation (*done with and for*).

For Danny, the aphorism 'It takes all Scotland to raise a child' sums up the philosophy underpinning *Schooling Scotland*. He thinks we need a better understanding, and balance between 'the forces of liberty and equality, autonomy and control, "bottom-up and top-down" ' and makes a few suggestions for how this might be done.

One of these concerns the role of standardised testing. Danny is passionate about the importance of literacy and numeracy and thinks it vitally important that all children are equipped with these skills when they leave primary school and that they maintain these skills in the first three years of secondary. To ensure each pupil's steady progress Danny recommends that schools use standardised assessments of literacy and numeracy but that these annual assessments are used confidentially as they are in a medical setting. This means that the result of a test would only be known by the teacher, parent and pupil. These results would not be aggregated and used as a way to judge schools and create a 'schools market' based on league tables. These annual interviews with parents on the results would lead to a plan for remediation and improvement. Danny thinks that well-being measures could also be included allowing for discussions on obesity, for example.

The importance of community

Of fundamental importance to Danny's desire to improve the 'quality of school experience' is his various suggestions for giving communities a role in what happens in schools. The first of these is for the creation of 'community learning hubs'. Schools would still retain their identity and most learning would take place there but there would be different types of learning within different community locations:

> . . . people of all ages will work together to enquire, to develop their knowledge and understanding, to learn from each other and work with each other to answer the difficult questions they face in their lives and their civic choices. The support some young people need will come not just from professional services but from closer relationships within the community, suitably structured and quality assured. In community learning hubs, school pupils can break out of the age-segregated insularities of school society and work across the generations.

This may seem pie-in-the-sky but Danny saw schools operating like this on his tour. Nonetheless he agrees that these types of educational experiences are not mainstream and that for progress there would need to be a long-term national vision.

Another recommendation is that 'parents and the school community should have a stronger role in governance, reducing the role of top-down inspection, but with elected authorities with sufficient capacity providing strategic oversight and resourcing'.

The third of Danny's recommendations for wholesale community involvement is the introduction of a 'high stakes' Scottish Graduation Certificate for both primary and secondary schools. This is simpler for the primary sector and simply involves recognising each child's unique talents and achievements along with their attainment in learning. The introduction of the certificate would be more complicated for secondary schools. He argues that at present 'the current examination system drives so much practice in secondary school because it is the *only* national high-stakes process through which schoolwork is valued.'

Let's be clear what the absence of a general graduation certificate indicates about the current system: a child who is not capable academically or who misses examinations could leave secondary school with no record of what he or she might have achieved whilst there. It also means that a youngster can reach the date at which they are formally permitted to leave school (16) and then just slope off with no recognition of what they achieved while there or even that they attended the school for over four years. This is why Danny also argues for the introduction of graduation ceremonies as a formal rite of passage.

> What would a Scottish child have to do to graduate? We already have a robust model in programmes such as the Duke of Edinburgh Award, where candidates have to attain a standard in a number of broad categories, with flexible options within each category. It would not be either/or, separating academic and vocational routes, but both recognising the value of different types of learning experience and achievement. The certificate should be sufficiently challenging that it requires effort and commitment, sufficiently flexible that it can reflect the diversity of individual talent and sufficiently structured to reflect the breadth of outcomes and experiences at which Curriculum for Excellence aims. The certificate should be created *with* the pupil, not something done *to* them.

Danny includes a table outlining the various elements of a 'possible' Scottish Secondary Graduation certificate. This would recognise *academic progress, community service, skills* (including practical and performance such as music or drama), *working life* (including paid or unpaid work experience), *challenging experiences* (such as an expedition), *personal assessment* (including health and well-being). The certificate would also recognise different pathways pupils take into the adult world.

Until I spoke to Danny I had not realised how unjust it is for youngsters to leave school without proper recognition of these types of skills and experiences. And, of course, it's the non-academic pupils, usually from poorer backgrounds, who miss out most. It's also easy to see from Danny's table how important it is for pupils to have access to a range of what he calls 'free, stimulating outwith-classroom learning experiences'. Indeed it's because private schools can provide their pupils with so many of these that make them so good at equipping them with confidence.

Danny provides readers with a useful guide to the current pros and cons of Scottish secondary schools and comes up with nine broad recommendations which he refers to as 'issues'. I cannot do justice to all of them here so I simply want to conclude this summary of *Schooling Scotland* with how he himself sums up the main argument in the book. He writes: 'Each and every one of the issues I have raised can contribute to the evolution of a stronger, fairer system of schooling, within a broader concept of education as a collaborative activity in which all Scotland plays its part in supporting the education of all Scotland's children.'

Publication and reaction

We published the book in November 2014 and held two launch events – one at Moray House in Edinburgh and the other in the Project Cafe, Glasgow. There's little doubt that readers liked the book, particularly Danny's voice. For example, Eileen Prior, then head of the Scottish Parent Teacher Council, said of *Schooling Scotland* 'the author's passion for education, for schooling but most of all for children shone through on every page'. Ken Cunningham, then General Secretary of School Leaders Scotland, thought it 'well researched' and 'persuasive' and a 'must read for every adult in Scotland.' James Mitchell, Professor of Governance at the University of Edinburgh emailed me to say that he thought it a 'refreshing read' and that he had recommended it in a recent talk to local authority chief executives. The book received a very positive response in the *Scottish Educational Review* and many headteachers recommended it in newsletters to their colleagues.

Fred Shedden, who was then Chair of the Centre's board and informal chief proof reader for our book series, was so motivated by the main ideas Danny presented in *Schooling Scotland* that he gave us a donation to send some free copies to key influencers. We then dispatched 35 copies to Directors of Education and people we thought had some influence over educational policy. SELMAS held a 'brains trust' session in September 2015 in a school in

Edinburgh called *Postcards from Scotland*: Equity in Education and Danny was the main speaker.

In 2015 the organisers of the West Dunbartonshire Book Festival – 'Booked' – gave *Postcards from Scotland* a slot in their programme. Alf Young, Danny Murphy, John Carnochan and I all spoke about our *Postcards* books and it was a heart-warming event attended by over 90 people. Many of them were middle aged or elderly and were so eager to engage with us on the issues we raised on materialism, community and how to support today's youth. We came away even more convinced that there was an appetite for the type of material we were producing.

Danny reports that the book was well-received by those who read it and that it prompted lots of discussion. But sadly *Schooling Scotland* had no discernible influence on Scottish Government education policy. Less than a year after the launch of Danny's book Nicola Sturgeon's Government was heading off in a different direction.

Education: Nicola Sturgeon's 'defining mission'

In August 2015, a year after becoming First Minister, Nicola Sturgeon made a speech in Wester Hailes, Edinburgh committing her government to raise educational standards and effectively eliminate the attainment gap between rich and poor. She proclaimed that education was her Government's 'defining mission'. Indeed she went further: 'Let me be clear, I want to be judged on this.' Undoubtedly there was a big problem for the Government to address and it wasn't simply the yawning attainment gap. A year earlier national data showed that literacy rates for pupils in primary and early secondary in Scotland were falling.

The Scottish Government subsequently established a 'pupil attainment fund' to help narrow the poverty attainment gap but one of its main tools to drive up academic attainment and narrow the gap was the introduction of 'standardised assessments' in primary school, including the P1 tests which I looked at in the previous chapter.

This was nothing like the standardised assessments proposed in *Schooling Scotland* which test the child, not the school and which are diagnostic rather than judgemental. These new assessments echoed the reforms previously advanced by the then Conservative Secretary of State for Scotland, Michael Forsyth. At a press conference after her announcement Nicola Sturgeon indirectly acknowledged this when she told the press that while her government would not produce league tables 'I'm not going to stop you guys . . . trying to put it into league tables.'

After the Sturgeon announcement I was in contact with education faculty staff from universities, headteachers and teachers. Their prevailing view was that Nicola Sturgeon's decision to reintroduce standardised national tests in primary schools was, as some put it, 'a return to square one'. 'The politicians have bottled it,' one educational expert told me, adding 'they've given up on the basic thinking behind the Curriculum for Excellence.' After all, a major impetus for this reform of Scottish education was the desire to escape from tests and a narrow focus on academic skills and to replace standardisation with learning more appropriate to specific circumstances. Interestingly none of the education people I spoke to could understand why the Scottish Government was reintroducing tests as the move is not underpinned by sound educational theory. They could not think of a single educational theorist who would recommend such a course of action.

This response from people I respect in education, and my previous involvement with *Schooling Scotland*, led me to write a much-read, and circulated blog called 'Standardised testing – cawin the feet from the CfE?' In it I argue that social class, the devastating effects of poverty and the expectations and values inherent in our education system and wider society play a major part in the Scottish figures. This meant that standardised national testing will not only fail to address the main problem but also that type of top-down governance, with its capacity to alienate, threaten and divide, is destined to backfire.

I also use John Kay's fascinating concept of 'obliquity' to elaborate on why I think the First Minister's approach was destined to fail. Kay, a Scottish economist, set out his ideas in an influential

2010 article and later in a book of the same name. Giving a variety of examples from business, public and personal life Kay argues that goals are more likely to be achieved obliquely: 'If you want to go in one direction, the best route may involve going in the other,' he writes. 'Paradoxical as it sounds goals are more likely to be achieved when pursued indirectly. So the most profitable companies are not the most profit-oriented, and the happiest people are not those who make happiness their main aim.' Obliquity is particularly relevant in complex systems which 'change as we engage with them.' Kay writes:

> Obliquity is relevant whenever complex systems evolve in an uncertain environment, and whenever the effect of our actions depends on the ways in which others respond to them. There is a role for carrots and sticks, but to rely on carrots and sticks alone is effective only when we employ donkeys and when goals are simple.

This insight is pertinent to the reintroduction of standardised testing in Scotland. While it might notionally improve results, any small gain would come at the expense of wider educational goals and pupil and teacher motivation. In health, some professionals have described this type of top-down initiative as 'hitting the target but missing the point'. Schools in areas of deprivation and those with a significant percentage of pupils from poor backgrounds will be particularly damaged by these comparisons.

Over the years Nicola Sturgeon's government attracted criticism on how it spent so much time and effort on pointless conversations with stakeholders and tinkering with the machinery of government rather than prioritising the actions which will bring about real results. But in this instance, I didn't think that the politicians could achieve tangible results unless reform became a defining mission of the Scottish people, not the Scottish Government. At the very minimum this would require a large-scale national consultation on what's underlying Scotland's educational inequality figures and what needs to be done to remedy them. The priority here would be to involve and listen to those parents and youngsters living in areas where the figures are so poor. I also recommended soliciting feedback and suggestions from individual teachers and their organisations and other professionals working with young people.

The overall purpose of this consultation would be to cultivate a real sense of involvement across Scotland in this vitally important agenda.

In the blog I also urged Nicola Sturgeon to look at the recommendations Danny Murphy makes in his book *Schooling Scotland* – recommendations he specifically advances to help close the inequality gap.

Scotland's declining educational standards

It gives me no satisfaction to report that almost ten years on we can see that Nicola Sturgeon's education reforms have been an abject failure. She asked us to judge her on this defining mission and all we can do is judge, at least this part of her governmental mission, harshly.

In 2017 the Scottish Government set out its targets for closing the attainment gap. At the end of 2023 data showed that it's falling well short of its targets. The Government blames the pandemic but analysts are not persuaded by this argument. Indeed, the *Herald's* education correspondent, James McEnaney, suggests there is an element of 'delusion' in the idea that it was ever going to meet these targets as they are falling so short. He also dismisses the whole exercise as 'more about an ongoing political circus than any serious attempt to transform Scottish education for the better.'

But potentially more worrying data emerged in the autumn of 2023. Scotland's educational decline in science, literacy and maths became evident around 2012 but with the publication of the 2022 Programme for International Student Assessment (PISA) results it became clear that the slow erosion of Scotland's educational performance was now accelerating. And the problem wasn't simply that poor pupils were performing badly. In the words of education professor, Lindsay Paterson: 'Scottish performance is now lower than in England at all points in the distribution of attainment, but it is particularly poor for the highest-attaining pupils – Scotland is not serving its most able students well.'

There was noticeable angst in Scotland as it became clear we were falling down the international league table for education.

For centuries academic attainment was one of Scotland's greatest achievements, so this reduction in school performance was akin to losing our superpower.

These results prompted me to do something I had considered for some time: publish an article on the warning Seligman gave me almost twenty years ago about the dangers of artificial self-esteem building and how it would undermine young people's well-being and academic standards. That's what had happened in the USA and some of these practices were happening here too.

In early January 2024 I sent a draft article to the editor of *The Times* newspaper in Scotland asking if he would be interested in publishing it. He was and used it as the long weekend essay in the paper on January 13th. The two-page spread was entitled 'The fear of challenging children has broken education in Scotland'.

In Chapter 3 I set out how Seligman's warning led me to undertake considerable desk research into the effects of self-esteem boosting measures in American schools and how the Centre's understanding of these dangers informed our various activities including the publication of *Creating Confidence.* The standfirst used by *The Times* may help jog readers' memories of my arguments: 'The blinkered drive to make pupils more confident and for no one to feel bad about themselves in the face of healthy competition has morphed into the damaging promotion of US-style self-esteem.'

I was very grateful to *The Times* editor for giving me so much space in the newspaper to outline my views but the inevitable editing process meant that there were some additions and omissions which affected the way my argument came across. Ultimately, I felt that it didn't fully represent my views. For example, I think there's already too much competition inherent in education in the UK and I'm not arguing for more. I'm also not suggesting that what I focus on in the article is the sole reason for a decline in Scottish attainment. Of course, there may well be other factors such as the downgrading of knowledge in the Curriculum for Excellence. What troubled me most, however, was that some of my examples were removed. In the essay I write that over the years teachers had told me that 'parents were increasingly visiting schools to complain about their child's mental state.' In my original article I then used the following examples:

> 'My son failed his spelling test and it's bad for his self-esteem'; 'my daughter didn't get the lead part in the pantomime and she's devastated'; 'my angelic daughter has fallen out with her friends so what's the school going to do about it?' One lovely primary headteacher even told me: 'So many parents seem to think I'm trying to make their children's lives difficult that when I look in the mirror I expect to see Cruella de Vil.' Many secondary teachers recounted notes from parents which say please don't try to teach my child maths or French (or anything challenging) as he can't do it and is feeling stressed. For many parents challenge has become a dirty word. And I understand this completely as I too had been a parent who wanted to protect my sons from any negative feelings.

Apart from the sentence about Cruella de Vil that whole paragraph was removed. But these examples were vitally important in helping readers understand what I meant. Currently many children have poor mental health and excessive anxiety and, of course, parents will want to inform teachers when this is the case. I wasn't referring to these types of serious problems but to everyday set-backs and challenges which should be normalised so that children develop resilience and are prepared for real life. Without these examples, I'm the one that looks like Cruella de Vil.

Nonetheless the article received very positive comments on the newspaper's website and a number of people I know, mainly grandparents, got in touch to say how much they agreed. But there are generational differences in how we raise children and I wonder if many young parents would have agreed wholeheartedly if they had read the article. Given this, I was particularly heartened by the email I received from one nursery headteacher telling me that I raised important issues for her and that she sees so much meaningless, routine praise from her young staff that they might as well shower children with praise for breathing! I was also greatly indebted to a primary headteacher who read the article pre-publication and not only corroborated the argument but also stiffened my resolve to publish.

Curriculum for Excellence (CfE)

And what of CfE which has dominated Scottish education since it was implemented in 2010? In the early days of the Centre, when we received a Scottish Government grant, I didn't think it politic to say what I really thought given this was a flagship government policy, though I would express my reservations on some aspects. But freed from this limitation more should be said.

From my encounters with staff who were putting together some of the materials for CfE in the early days I didn't think that they had deeply considered the implications of what they proposed This feeling that it was built on rather shaky foundations has only grown in recent years.

I was influenced in part by Keir Bloomer who had been a member of the original Curriculum Review Group which looked at the views coming out the National Debate on Education in Scotland in 2002 and came up with the initial outline for CfE. Keir had been a Director of Education and then Chief Executive for Clackmannanshire Council. He was then an educational consultant and is currently chair of Reform Scotland. At the 'Towards a Confident Scotland' conference in 2003 Keir was the main speaker in the workshop session on education. He also spoke at the Centre's 'Creating Confident Individuals masterclass on the Curriculum for Excellence' which we held with Professor Carol Dweck in 2008.

Keir Bloomer may have been involved in the original thinking of CfE but he became more and more critical. In one of his talks he recounted that he hadn't been keen on the name and that it had really been the choice of the civil servants involved in the group. He then added, 'The word I was worried about was Excellence. The word I should have been worried about was Curriculum. We never thought that what we were proposing was a new curriculum. We were only setting out the principles which we thought should underpin the curriculum.'

The Scottish Executive then built on these deliberations and made the purpose of Scottish education to 'focus classroom practice upon the child and around the four capacities of education which provide opportunities for children and young people to develop as: successful learners, confident individuals, responsible citizens, and effective contributors.'

In an interesting paper in the *Oxford Review of Education* (June, 2010) called 'The development of Scotland's Curriculum for Excellence: Amnesia and Déjà Vu', educationalists Dr Mark Priestley and Professor Walter Humes examine the thinking underpinning CfE . They conclude that it's essentially 'an ahistorical and atheoretical document' and lacks 'conceptual clarity'. Curriculum design and planning is not something I am equipped to evaluate but the authors' judgement on 'the four capacities' really struck a chord with my own thinking:

> These capacities have quickly become a kind of mantra in Scottish education, regularly cited at conferences and CPD [Continuous Professional Development] events, and have been subject to little in the way of critical interrogation. For example, how crucial are the particular combinations of adjectives and nouns? Would it make much difference if the capacities were given as effective learners, responsible individuals, successful citizens and confident contributors? A Curriculum for Excellence does not offer much in the way of extended justification for either its terminology or its recommendations.

I always believed there was *no* coherent rationale for the term 'confident individuals'; that the word individuals was only there as a noun was required to work alongside learners, citizens and contributors and form the core of a diagram. I would have had no objection if those nouns hadn't been there at all and the purpose of education had been expressed as learning, contribution, citizenship and confidence. I would also have been content if the nouns had been shifted around to give 'confident learners' or even 'contributors' or 'citizens'. But everything I knew about confidence led me to believe that the 'confident individuals' formulation in CfE was not simply unhelpful but could also lead to well-meaning but ill-judged classroom practice which could easily backfire, eroding confidence. Why?

The problem with the label 'confident individuals'

As I explained in Chapter 6 confidence is not a term used much by psychologists as it's multifaceted and not easy to measure. After working with the concept for a few years the Centre defined confidence primarily as self-efficacy. We saw confidence as contextual, meaning that a person could be confident in some situations but not others and that confidence was usually dependent on skills and experience and the feeling that goals were achievable.

When I ran countless workshops with teachers on confidence in the period between CfE being launched and implemented (2004-10) I asked teachers to define a 'confident individual'. The most common response was 'someone who is confident all the time'. Given the words that's a perfectly reasonable definition but it makes no sense as it defies everyday experience. Who is that person who is always confident? Many people would describe me as a confident individual as I would speak confidently in public, often without notes and to a large audience, and I was also confident in social interactions. But I'm emphatically not confident about a large number of other activities: running a marathon, hosting a big dinner party, singing, dancing, drawing, finishing *The Times* crossword, doing maths calculations. . . The list of things I don't feel confident about is endless.

So the first problem with the label 'confident individual' is that it's usually defined as speaking in groups and/or social confidence. At one of my workshops on confidence one well-meaning teacher said in passing: 'I'll know I'm doing my best to create confident individuals when each one of the children in my class can get up in front of their classmates, give a talk and enjoy it'. As the other teachers in the group nodded in agreement, my heart sank. Not only was this teacher unlikely to achieve her goal, but also she was likely to undermine some of her pupils' feelings of self-worth in the process for what she's talking about largely reflects the child's personality. So confidence building in schools can easily become another way of labelling children negatively and letting them know that they're not ok. And historically negative labelling has been one of the major downsides of Scottish education.

To elaborate on the likelihood of demonising quiet pupils I want to introduce my son, Jamie. When he was young he was always a quiet, reflective boy. In class he never presented a problem for the teacher and with his peer group he was popular but happy to fit in with others. He had no need to be in the limelight. As an assertiveness trainer it would have been very easy for me to look at my quiet son and believe he was lacking something – confidence. I could have concluded that what he needed was to be more confident and outgoing with others – particularly in class or at social events. I could then have tried to make him more talkative, outwardly confident or assertive. In other words, I could have communicated to my son that he wasn't all right the way he was and that he should become a different person.

Fortunately, I didn't do this. Thanks to my understanding of Jungian psychological type, with its explanation of introversion and extraversion, I could see that Jamie's quietness in class was about being an introvert, not about being underconfident.[1] Rather than communicating to him that he was lacking, I valued and supported the person he was. One of Jamie's real strengths, and his type of confidence, became very apparent when he left school. He wanted to travel and arranged a four-month trip which involved flying to Chile and joining a group of people to travel around Latin America in a truck. His father and I were anxious. I doubt that I could have done this when I was 30, let alone 17. But Jamie looked at both of us and said with great conviction, 'I'm totally confident that I can do this'. All those years of mulling things over in his head and being quiet meant he had developed enormous inner resources. He was confident that he was able to travel to the other side of the world, and even if he hardly spoke to another person, and things were tough, he would cope. And he did.

I often told the story about Jamie when I spoke to parents and teachers and many parents were eager to tell me a similar story about their child. One mother, who was also a teacher, told me that her eight-year-old daughter was very quiet and reflective. She was a conscientious, meticulous young girl who worked hard and

---

1. I'm using extravert, rather than the everyday spelling extrovert, as this is what Jung uses in his book *Psychological Types* (1921).

excelled at written work. The girl earned lots of praise for this at school but – in the era of CfE – teachers were no longer seeing her strengths as enough and wanted her to set goals to interact and talk much more in class. 'Rather than understanding my daughter's strengths and respecting who she is,' this mother told me, 'the teacher is focusing on what she is not and telling her she's not ok.' The mother then added, 'If she were seventeen and about to enter higher education or work, then it would be fair enough to encourage her to make an effort to develop oral communication skills but I just don't think it's appropriate to do this to a girl of eight.'

I also have no difficulty with pupils being expected to talk and be assessed on this in senior exams. Oral communication is vitally important. But we should not equate the desire to communicate in groups with confidence. Confidence is not a type of activity; it is a person's belief, in a specific context, that she or he can reach their self-determined goal.

But there is yet another problem with the attempt to create confident individuals in Scottish classrooms. Some teachers give pupils, as young as eight, worksheets so they can write down how they are, or could become, confident individuals. Teachers can also require pupils to set goals for boosting their confidence. They also just keep talking about confidence to pupils and how important it is – after all it's one of the four capacities and so one of the main purposes of education. But these direct ways to boost confidence have the capacity to backfire and produce paradoxical effects.

In Chapter 5, I summarised some of the research carried out by social psychologist Dan Wegner and his team on 'ironic processes of mental control'. This research shows that if we try to not think about being anxious, for example, the mind will automatically set up a monitoring process for this goal so that it knows if success has been achieved. So the very thing we are trying not to think about (anxiety) keeps coming into our thoughts. We are particularly prone to ironic effects in stressful situations or if our brains are being taxed, as they often are in educational contexts.

Ironic effects are particularly common around relaxation – the more we try to relax the more aware we become of being tense. Wegner *et al* write: '. . . too often our efforts to cool down, withdraw, or calm ourselves seem to backfire – producing greater agitation than we had suffered before we even tried to relax.' Wegner suggests that it may be better for professionals to take much more indirect approaches and 'disguise the overall aim of relaxation procedures in some way.'

This insight is of great relevance to policy makers and practitioners in education. If they want to achieve certain outcomes they must be aware of the need for subtlety. If teachers keep raising the importance of confidence with children and young people the youngsters will become more aware of any lack of confidence they have and this may increase anxiety about their confidence. I've been told by many teachers and sports coaches that this is exactly what's happening as there's now a much larger group of pupils who won't even try something, like public speaking, drama or a new sport, because they aren't confident. In other words, the emphasis on confidence is creating a barrier to participation and learning skills. Rather than think you can only do something if you feel confident it's much better to adopt the mantra 'feel the fear and do it anyway'.

John Kay's concept of 'obliquity' echoes ancient wisdom in pointing out that goals are often best achieved through 'oblique, rather than direct methods'. For example, many philosophers and religious thinkers have argued that deliberately trying to be happy is counterproductive. Thus we should never make happiness our goal as we can only attain it indirectly. This piece of wisdom is now supported by extensive psychological research. Kay thinks we're in danger of forgetting the importance of indirect, subtle methods because we now live in a world so dominated by management by objectives and centralised planning. And, of course, in schools by constant assessment.

So, we need to tread warily with the confidence agenda. Of course, we can make it one of the purposes of education and create a climate in schools which fosters it. Essentially, it's about teachers valuing each individual pupil and giving lots of encouragement and helpful feedback as well as extensive opportunities for them to grow and develop skills in a broad range of subjects and activities. But none of that means lecturing on the importance of confidence or asking pupils to fill in worksheets or set confidence targets. Scotland was the birthplace for a fantastic project, now international, called Room 13 which shows how this can be done as I explained on page 300.

Shaping our Global Future: A guide for young people

In 2015 we branched out and undertook some work on another of the four capacities – citizenship. Derek Brown is one of the most insightful and thoughtful people I know so in the summer of 2014 when he suggested that he could contribute a book to *Postcards from Scotland* I was keen to hear more. I first met Derek when I was undertaking lots of training courses with staff at Jordanhill School. He was an English teacher and we had a mutual interest in Scottish literature. This was the late 1990s and it was clear to me even then that Derek was destined for senior management roles. So, it came as no surprise when in 2023, after many career moves in education and local authorities, he became Chief Executive of Highland Council.

When we first discussed his book proposal in 2014 he was a headteacher in a school in Aberdeen. In this capacity he had been researching and creating educational materials on some of the big global issues of our time to use at school assemblies. There's a lot of information around on global problems such as human rights abuses, world poverty and hunger thanks to the many development organisations and the work of international agencies such as the UN. But the sheer volume of this material can be daunting to a headteacher or teacher who needs something more specific for the classroom or an assembly. So Derek's proposal was for him to write a book on global issues aimed at young people, mainly teenagers. He envisaged writing the book primarily for youngsters to read if they were interested in global issues but that it could also be used as a resource by teachers or others working with young people.

As the Commissioning Editor for the *Postcards from Scotland* series I was aware that a conventional publisher would have automatically turned down Derek's suggestion on the basis that it was at odds with our target readership – adults. However, the more I thought about it the more I considered this was an untenable response. All our books had been directed at adults so why wouldn't we want at least one book in the series to be aimed at young people, particularly when it was completely in tune with our desire to publish ideas about the future and how we needed to adapt?

So my response to Derek was positive. But what was the best way to cover global issues for teenagers? Derek was aware that a book exclusively devoted to some of the big global problems such as climate change, lack of resources or human rights would be exceedingly negative for adults to handle, let alone young people. So he came up with the idea of structuring the book round seven global 'challenges' and seven global 'wonders'. For the latter he chose topics such as the Rights of the Child, the Olympic Games and the International Space Station – projects which have involved a large amount of international cooperation.

By choosing this structure Derek had set himself a daunting task. He had to cover 14 chunky topics but so concisely that his contribution would still fit in with a book series of slim volumes. To make the book more readable he decided to present it as a letter to his 16-year-old daughter. In the preface he writes: 'This is a wee book about your human future. It's a father's gift. An act of hope.'

Remarkably Derek managed to pull it off. His book is a bit longer than others in the series but not by much. More importantly he manages to distil each topic into essential information and some basic questions, particularly on the ethical issues likely to engage young minds. He also wanted to write the book in such a way that it could be a jumping off point for teenagers to do their own research. This meant that he used source material that was easily available online, such as TED talks, newspaper articles and websites.

The Scottish education system now places a great emphasis on interdisciplinary learning so the book could be a useful resource as it weaves together information on a wide range of topics and curriculum areas – science and technology, politics and current

Box 16: *Shaping our Global Future: 7 Wonders and 7 Challenges*

The wonders

The international Space Station

Olympic Games

Genetic Engineering

Telecommunications

CERN (the European Organisation for Nuclear Reserch)

Electronic Gaming

The United Nations Declaration of the Rights of the Child

The challenges

Global War

Terrorism

Disease (pandemic)

Future Resources

Climate Change

Gap between Rich and Poor

affairs, religious and moral education, geography. . .

In the book, Derek alternates a global wonder with a global challenge to give the text a more optimistic feel. But for ease of assimilation, I present them in Box 16 as a list of wonders and challenges. Derek is aware that some of the global challenges provide 'sources of hope and optimism' and that some of the wonders 'contain some terrifying or problematic aspects'.

Dr Alan Britton, at that time Director of the Education for Global Citizenship at the University of Glasgow, was hugely enthusiastic about the book and wrote the afterword. In it he describes the younger Derek Brown, whom he had met a decade before, as being someone who worried that while schools may equip pupils academically, these youngsters still lacked 'resilience, autonomy and a clear values framework . . . to interrogate the world they would inhabit.' He also talks about Derek's 'restless curiosity'. Britton also laments the paucity of 'long term thinking' in the teaching profession and commends the book as an antidote to a culture where 'our attention spans are eroded by ephemeral stimuli and short term gratification'.

Britton also sums up Derek's goal and conclusions:

> He wants to equip young people with an understanding that recognises both the challenges and opportunities that lie ahead of them individually and as members of a global society, and to help them make the right choices for themselves and others. Along the way Derek deals unflinchingly with both the light and the dark in humanity, and paints a picture that at times might appear rather pessimistic. However it is notable that he concludes on a note of cautious optimism, grounded in an enlightened sceptical humanism.

I learned so much while editing the book that I ultimately believed that adults, not just young people, would benefit from reading it.

Publication and reflections

The Centre published *Shaping our Global Future* in June 2015 and launched the book in the Teachers' Building in Glasgow. Derek had always advised that young people would prefer to read the book online as this would facilitate the use of live links for research. So we published only a few hundred copies and immediately created a downloadable file for purchase.

Before Derek had finished the manuscript he left his head-teacher's post in Aberdeen and became Head of Education for Fife Council and within a few years he was employed in a series of promoted posts in North Lanarkshire. He was a busy man: too busy to do much to promote *Shaping our Global Future.* Besides, the need for a resource like this was understandably receding in his rear-view mirror. Selling to schools wasn't something I knew anything about though I made some effort. I even went to a Saturday morning network meeting of Modern Studies teachers to sell some copies. But I also gave up on the idea of selling the book as I was aware that, given its subject matter, it was destined to date very quickly. Only an author who was prepared to keep amending for new editions could have avoided this problem. Derek was not that author and we were not that publisher. In the end the Centre just had to accept that this was our most elusive book and that any future collectors of the *Postcards from Scotland* series may struggle to get their hands on book number eight by Derek Brown.

When writing this section I reflected on what had changed since Derek wrote the book and began to wonder if he could have managed to sound a note of 'cautious optimism' at the end if he had finished writing it ten years later: in 2024 not 2014. Climate change is now wreaking devastation round the world. Russia's invasion of Ukraine and the crisis now engulfing the Middle East, means that the prospect of global war is casting a shadow over all our lives. Every day in the media we witness scenes of carnage and atrocity reminding us of Robert Burns' famous lines – 'Man's inhumanity to man/ Makes countless thousands mourn!'

No wonder that in 2023 the 'Oxford children's word of the year' was 'climate change' (33 per cent) closely followed by 'war' (31 per cent). In 2015 the year we published Derek's book it was 'hashtag'. Tragically it's now very difficult for anyone to sound a realistic note of optimism for children and young people, even in the UK where we are not in the front line of global catastrophes.

Sadly we're no longer in that hopeful world where Danny Murphy, and then Derek Brown, felt inspired to write a book for *Postcards from Scotland*; a world where it was easier to believe that things could get better.

Chapter 20
Childhood adversities: Scotland's dismal record

The health challenges of Milngavie's council estate;
Scott, 'Garvie Crescent' and the fate of his peers;
GCPH's explanation for ill health in the West of Scotland;
Scott's story of a drunken father and a prevailing drink culture;
my miserable childhood;
the research behind adverse childhood experiences (ACEs);
why ACEs are so toxic;
Scotland's binge drinking and drug taking culture;
verbal abuse and emotional neglect;
ACEs in Scotland's stories; the rise of an ACE perspective.

'MY FATHER was a maniac. He frightened away the best of our health', writes Andrew O'Hagan in his Scottish novel *Our Fathers* (1999). Sadly, in Scotland it hasn't just been fathers that have been frightening away children's health. Until recently many parents, teachers and institutions may have unwittingly contributed to children's long-term physical and mental ill health.

The catalyst for turning my attention on Scotland's poor health came from meeting up again with two men whom I'd known when growing up. I met the first in 2015 as he was driving a taxi I'd ordered. 'You're Carol Craig from Milngavie. You lived round the corner from us,' he said as soon as I sat down. As I looked closely at the man sitting behind the wheel, I could see the wee boy who lived over the back.

During the thirty-minute journey my driver could only talk about the fortunes of those who grew up with us in Milngavie's council estate where he still lived. It was a litany of premature death, heart problems, cancer, disability and alcoholism. It was easy to see that the ill health of our generation really troubled him and that he was desperate to know *why* we had fared so badly.

Some readers may be surprised by what they are reading as Milngavie, seven miles north of Glasgow, has a reputation for being middle-class: a reputation burnished by many comedians. And the casual visitor can remain unaware of the large council estate which lies at a distance from the town centre.

In the following year I had numerous discussions with another man from Milngavie whom I also knew when we were young. Scott (not his real name) also wanted to talk about the deaths and poor health of our generation.

These conversations happened at a point when I was coming to terms with my own ill health. In 2011, after a string of what I assumed were minor illnesses, my doctor decided to do a blood test. This revealed that I had been infected by the potentially fatal liver disease, hepatitis C.[1] This helped to explain various ailments I had suffered from over the years. Fortunately, within two years I was part of a drug trial for new anti-viral drugs and cleared the virus. Nonetheless I can see that having had hepatitis for 35 years and undergoing lengthy treatment to eradicate it had undermined my health.

But by 2015 other things were having a negative impact on my health. I had been diagnosed with migraine when I was seven and it was now having a profound effect on my life. I also had erratic and often dangerously high blood pressure. I had good

1. I had received a blood transfusion in 1976 and was therefore one of the victims of 'contaminated blood' which is routinely portrayed as the biggest scandal in NHS history.

reason to believe that both debilitating conditions were related to my unhappy childhood.[2] My parents had died two years earlier. I was very close to my mother and her death gave me permission to confront the various ways I had suffered as a child. This would have been too painful for her to bear and I just couldn't have faced it while she was alive. The time now seemed right to acknowledge and explore how I had felt when I was growing up.

When Scott started to talk to me about had happened to his peers, he did not know that I had written *The Tears that Made the Clyde* and had any particular interest in the health and well-being of people in the West of Scotland. Nor did he know how I felt about my own childhood. He just wanted to talk because we had known each other as teenagers. During our conversations I could see that Scott had three great gifts: an exceptional memory, a facility to analyse and a real interest in people.

'Garvie Crescent', Milngavie

Scott grew up in a crescent of just under 90 attractive but quite densely built houses (many of them terraces) first occupied a few years after the end of World War II. The houses in this crescent were, and still are, high quality and spacious. All the houses have gardens and the whole Clober housing estate has many positive features and easy access to attractive countryside. There is no derelict land. Nor is geographical isolation a problem. Schooling, at least from the point of view of education and aspirations, was also good. Dunbartonshire had comprehensive education prior to the 1965 Act so, apart from the religious divide, everyone went to the same school and many left with qualifications or went straight into apprenticeships.

Scott estimates that a fifth of the families in his crescent came from Clydebank as a result of the 1941 Blitz. Others came from Maryhill but most were from Milngavie which (like many places in Scotland) had once been a centre of industry with grossly inadequate houses (small cottages and tenements) for local

---

2. See the book by the cardiologist Samuel J. Mann, *Hidden Within Us: A radical new understanding of the mind-body connection.*

workers. As Garvie Crescent was one of the first streets to be built in the Clober estate it was families in greatest need who were allocated houses there and living in slum conditions prior to moving to their new house may be one of the reasons why health has been so poor in this particular crescent.

Nonetheless, Scott maintains, and this chimes with my own experience, that real hardship and poverty wasn't an issue for most families when our generation was growing up. The vast majority of families from the 1950s on had at least one adult working and worklessness was uncommon. Many of the children's fathers were in skilled or semi-skilled jobs.

The fate of so many of Scott's peers

None of what I've described so far suggests that many of the children who grew up there would suffer from poor physical and mental health and that some would die very prematurely. But they did and we both wanted to work out why.

So we sat down together, Scott reeled off the names of those who had grown up in his street and were now dead and I took notes. He also knew the cause of death (at least in layman's terms), age (within a year or so) and for the male victims their occupation. We drew up a table. At a later date we added another two variables – where their families hailed from and what their fathers had done during the war. We also gave his street the fictitious name of Garvie Crescent. This was not an attempt to create rigorous statistics. Rather we were painting as accurate a picture as we could of what had happened to Scott's peers.

Scott was able to name around 200 children growing up in the street in the late 1940s right through to the early 1960s. To his knowledge 42 of them had died by their late 60s. Many of them died much younger than that – from their 20s on. For example, one young man died at the age of 23 from alcohol abuse. In fact, eight of the 42 have died of excessive alcohol consumption. Of the 42 fatalities, three were murdered, five died in accidents, and three by suicide. The remainder died of natural causes – mainly heart problems, strokes, and cancer. Scott recounts that in this group there were another six heavy drinkers and two drug users.

A huge amount of research has shown that Scotland, and particularly the West of Scotland, has substantial problems with health. Indeed we have the worst life expectancy figures in Europe. Scotland's 'excess mortality' is driven particularly by deaths in the working age population from chronic disease but also, more importantly, from alcohol, drugs and violence, including suicide. This is what Scott was observing in his peers.

Health bodies define premature mortality as death before the age of 75. Scotland has the highest premature mortality rate in the UK and the worst in Western Europe. As most of the children who grew up in the crescent in the early days were, at the time of Scott's calculations, still in their 60s and could die before the age of 75 the final tally of those dying prematurely is likely to be much higher.

I am, of course, not seeking to make a statistical argument from one small community. Rather I am demonstrating that the area in which I was brought up starkly illustrates what epidemiology is telling us about health in Scotland.

Scott talks about the ill health of his peers in terms of premature death as this is easy to see and quantify. But, of course, Scotland's health problems are much more extensive than that. Indeed, currently a staggering 46 per cent of Scots over the age of 16 suffer from one long term condition such as cancer, heart disease, diabetes, asthma, chronic obstructive pulmonary disorder, mental health problems and so forth. So, the burden of disease, not just premature death, will also be high in our old schoolmates.

It's worth reminding readers of the Glasgow Centre for Population Health's research which I cited in Chapter 11 when looking at ill health in Glasgow. This research shows that after controlling for poverty and inequality (factors well-known to undermine health) Scotland has proportionately 5,000 more deaths each year than England. In one GCPH study researchers compared Glasgow, Liverpool and Manchester, remarkably similar cities in terms of poverty and inequality. This shows that Glasgow has 30 per cent higher premature mortality than the English cities.

In the summer of 2016, while Scott and I were in the midst of our discussions, the Glasgow Centre for Population Health published a report in which David Walsh *et al* give for the first time their explanation for Glasgow's and more generally Scotland's 'excess mortality'. Their main thesis is that for a variety of historical reasons Glaswegians, and Scots as a whole, were rendered particularly 'vulnerable' to the negative effects of deindustrialisation and other social, political and economic forces particularly unleashed by Thatcherism and neoliberal policies.[3] They argue that Scotland's homegrown New Towns policy had been particularly detrimental to Glasgow and that the city had been the victim of 'political attack' by Westminster politicians.

Leaving aside the part of their argument where they discuss 'the lagged effect of overcrowding', both Scott and I simply could not see the relevance of their structural, political and economic explanations to what had happened to his neighbours as these explanations mostly applied to the city of Glasgow.

Scott's explanations

Scott has thought a lot about why so many of his peers have died prematurely or have serious health challenges and the first explanation he advances is the legacy of World War II. Many of the families housed in the estate, but particularly in his crescent, contained men who had returned home from active service. Indeed 27 of the 33 deceased men's fathers were in the services during the war. Scott maintains that many of the fathers were suffering from what is now called Post Traumatic Stress Disorder (PTSD). This meant that many of these men's behaviour was unpredictable – they could be sullen, withdrawn or aggressive. According to Scott many of these men were violent and domestic abuse was rife particularly when they had been drinking.

When Scott talks about his childhood he describes a world where children either witnessed or personally experienced routine abuse and violence. This was Scott's own personal experience.

---

3. In the report the authors acknowledge that research is needed into early years and childhood experiences as these may be contributory factors. See the end of this Chapter for their research findings.

His father had been in the war and had been traumatised by what he saw. He drank a lot at weekends and regularly beat up Scott's mother. He also hit his sons and could even put the whole family out of the house when in a drunken rage. The only time Scott becomes emotional talking about his experiences is when he says that his father could be a good dad when he hadn't been drinking.

Peter Mullan, the Scottish actor, grew up in the 1950s in Glasgow's Mosspark, another 'posh' council housing estate and he would concur with Scott's observations as he too had a drunken, violent father:

> To be fair to him, I believe that his whole generation were completely screwed. They were war casualties; they came back from the Second World War to no counselling, they were all running around barking mad. I'm convinced they had no clue how to relate to their wives, their kids or themselves. I know virtually no one of my age who can remember a hug, or a smile from their father, or a 'Let's go play football'.

Growing up in a culture 'steeped in alcohol' is another of Scott's explanations for his contemporaries' ill health. He maintains that they were raised to see heavy drinking as the norm. This was not only the main way that their fathers managed stress but also drinking in a pub was how many chose to spend their free time, thereby undermining family life. He also maintains that many of them were heavy drinkers if not alcoholics. Perhaps in the spirit of 'if you can't beat them, join them' some women in the street also drank heavily.

New council estates in Glasgow were not allowed to have pubs until 1964 but not so older working-class areas like Maryhill or Govan or small towns like Milngavie. Its town centre, less than a mile from Garvie Crescent, had four pubs, a hotel that was open on a Sunday and two off-licences. There were also three licensed clubs. No wonder Milngavie was hoatching with drunk men every weekend. My mother worked in the hotel pub which was packed every Sunday, so I knew about this drink culture first hand.

Scott cites remote difficult fathers, alcohol and domestic violence as an explanation for ill health because they resonate with his own 'lived experience' and basic intuition of what's gone wrong in the lives of so many of his peers. Does this mirror my own experience?

My miserable childhood

My father was different from those Scott describes. He was a railwayman so he wasn't called up in the war and didn't see active service. His father had been a drinker and this had put him off alcohol. He didn't hit my mother but he could hit his daughters hard for misbehaviour which often simply meant getting on his nerves. Even without this physical abuse he was a scary dad. You never knew when he could explode in anger at something you had done. He was often verbally abusive and cursed and swore a lot. He had lots of clashes, some of them violent, with my older sister when she was a teenager and I found watching this particularly stressful and painful.

I don't want to be too hard on him as a father. He was a good worker and provider. He could have been a drunk who thumped my mum and spent his wages in the pub and he didn't. I also sense that he didn't know how to be a good father because he didn't know what this looked or felt like. But he improved with age. He was a much better father to my sister who is ten years younger than me; he was also a good grandfather.

I was in an isolation hospital for six weeks with scarlet fever when I was five and the experience was unbearable. In fact, hospitals and medical procedures featured heavily in my young life. When I was about seven my paternal grandfather sexually assaulted me. He threatened to murder me if I told anyone, so I kept quiet. Given these painful experiences it's hardly surprising that when I was seven I developed stomach pains and headaches and generally felt unwell. I was hospitalised on two occasions for investigations – more stressful experiences.

I have little doubt that school played a big part in my psychosomatic illnesses. I detested primary school. When I was in my late thirties I discovered why I had found it so difficult: I am dyslexic. I knew that I had found learning hard when I was a child and would have called myself a late developer. However, as a result of my two sons both being diagnosed with dyslexia in primary school I took them to see an educational psychologist. He tested me too and the results showed that I am indeed dyslexic.

Research now suggests there are specific strengths associated with dyslexia. Nevertheless being dyslexic in 1950s Scotland, primary school was a frightening experience. In those days a child could be belted for academic mistakes and I lived in terror of that.

Life improved for me in my teenage years. Learning became easier. The shocks and abuses which dogged my early years receded. Looking back I can see that I was a particularly troubled soul in my childhood as my father was scary and my dyslexia intensified the fear of corporal punishment in primary school. A series of unfortunate incidents and hospitalisations added to my stress. But I was certainly not alone and some suffered much more.

In a family who lived nearby the mother used to tell her daughter when she did something naughty 'wait till your father gets home'. The girl would then languish, often for a whole day, in her bedroom waiting for his return. He would then assault her with a belt and even from the street we could hear her screams. No wonder her behaviour was odd and that we used to say she wasn't 'right in the head'. Another school friend's parents both got steaming drunk every weekend and spent whole days in bed leaving her and her siblings to fend for themselves.

Of course, there were children with a good home life: children with fathers and mothers who were loving, gentle and teetotal. I can think of a few friends who came from that kind of family. But I now wonder if they were the minority. Even these lucky children would have suffered from the brutality of school, a topic I'll return to in the next chapter.

I've always seen my upbringing as 'ordinary'. Given the pain I know I suffered in childhood I began to wonder if lots of Scots of my generation suffered too – many of them much worse than I did. Reflecting on my own and Scott's experiences I started to discuss these issues with friends and acquaintances and I've been bowled over by some of the stories people told me. When I put these stories alongside my growing understanding of how stress in childhood damages health, and my knowledge of how modern Scottish novels and films are awash with childhood adversities, I had an epiphany: childhood suffering is the key to Scotland's excessively poor health. In fact it is so evident – staring us in the face almost everywhere we look – could we say that it is 'hiding in plain sight'?

This epiphany then led me to write my fifth book, and the twelfth book in the *Postcards* series – *Hiding in Plain Sight: Exploring Scotland's ill health* (2017).[4] It starts with information about Milngavie and Garvie Crescent.

Adverse childhood experiences (ACEs)

The girl near us who languished in her room till her father got home and belted her moved away. But our mothers kept in touch for decades. In her early twenties the girl developed serious gynaecological problems. Then mental health problems. Both were so severe that she couldn't have children or hold down a job.

Until the 1980s it would have been difficult to say that this scared girl's childhood experiences and future ill health were little more than happenstance. But in the past thirty years an impressive amount of research has shown conclusively that 'adverse childhood experiences' (ACEs) have a significant bearing on long-term physical and mental health.

One of the two doctors at the centre of the ACE research is Vincent J. Felitti. He stumbled upon the link between childhood experiences and health almost by accident. In the mid 1980s he was working with patients on an obesity programme. So many of them referred to traumas in childhood, particularly sexual abuse, that he wondered if there was a link. Felitti joined forces with another doctor, Robert Anda, who was interested in heart disease and depression. They then teamed up with one of the USA's biggest

4. When I chose this title in 2017 this expression was hardly used in everyday speech.

private health insurance companies and went on to survey 17,000 patients to see if there was indeed a link between childhood experiences and later health.

The ACE survey questions focus on two different types of adversity. Some are physical or emotional stressors that we can face as children or teenagers – physical, verbal and sexual abuse. The questionnaire also asks whether you were physically or emotionally neglected. The next set of questions asks about what was happening in the family. Did your parents divorce or separate; was your mother hit or threatened; was someone 'a problem drinker' or alcoholic or use street drugs; was someone suicidal or suffer from depression or another mental health problem; or was a family member sent to prison? Respondents get a point for every category of the ten adversities they experienced.[5]

Respondents in the first ACE study were mainly white, middle-class Americans. Three quarters of them were college educated and in stable jobs. Yet the number of ACEs they recorded was much higher than researchers predicted. Only one third scored zero. The connection between the number of ACEs and physical and mental health was so powerful that it shocked the researchers. Anda says he 'wept' at seeing how much people had suffered from what had happened to them in childhood. Felitti recalls: 'Our findings exceeded anything we had conceived. The correlation between having a difficult childhood and facing illness as an adult offered a whole new lens through which we could view human health and disease.' Of course, ill health has a variety of causes – germs, accidents and genetic weakness, for example – but the ACE research demonstrates that childhood adversities play an important part.

Between 1998 and 2018 a total of 789 articles on ACEs appeared in 351 different academic journals. These show that there is a relationship between ACEs and various physical and mental health outcomes. Having ACEs increases the risk of heart disease, chronic lung disease, liver disease, depression, suicide, injuries, HIV and other risks which are the leading causes of death.

---

5. See Appendix 2 for the original questionnaire.

There are now numerous studies which show that there is a graded relationship between ACEs and health. For example, those who score one are more likely to suffer from depression than those who score zero. Indeed 50 per cent of people who score four or more suffer from chronic depression. When it comes to suicide the results are more startling. Studies show that only 1 per cent of those with an ACE score of zero have attempted suicide but someone with an ACE score of four or more is 1220 times more likely to attempt suicide than someone who scores zero.

It is not just mental health which shows this graded relationship. Physical health does too. A Welsh ACE study conducted by Bellis *et al* shows that compared with people who scored zero those with four or more ACEs were three times more likely to develop heart disease and respiratory conditions and four times more likely to develop Type 2 diabetes. The American research shows that a child who scores seven or more ACEs grows up with a 360 per cent higher chance of developing heart disease. People with an ACE score of six or higher are at risk of their lifespan being shortened by 20 years.

It's really important to understand that it's not just those with very high ACE scores who are at risk. People are more likely to suffer physical ill health even if they score a relatively low number of ACEs. For example, a study published in the *Journal of Psychosomatic Medicine* in 2009 found that one ACE correlated to a 31 per cent increased risk for women to be hospitalised for diseases linked to autoimmunity. The figure for men was 34 per cent. Those who scored two or more adverse events had a staggering 70-80 per cent increased risk of hospitalisation so there was still a strongly graded relationship.

Why adverse events in childhood are so toxic

So why are ACEs damaging to mental and physical health? Recent research in neuroscience on the impact traumatic stress in childhood can have on neurodevelopment helps us to understand why. The US science journalist Donna Jackson Nakazawa devoted her book *Childhood Disrupted* (2015) to outlining research into

ACEs and giving relevant case studies. She explains the problem with ACEs in ways that the layperson can more easily understand:

> In young and growing children, the HPA (hypothalamic-pituitary-adrenal) stress axis is developing – and healthy maturation is heavily influenced by the safety or lack of safety we encounter in the day-to-day environment. When a young brain is repeatedly thrust into a state of hyperarousal or anxiety because of what is happening at a child's home, community, or school, the stress axis gets tipped into reaction over and over again, and the body becomes routinely flooded with inflammatory stress neurochemicals. This can lead to deep physiological changes that lead to long-lasting inflammation and disease.

Nakazawa later elaborates that part of the problem is that chronic stress in a developing child's brain leads to 'epigenetic' changes that can essentially set the child up for a lifetime of chronic stress and inflammation. In short, the child who experiences regular adversity is permanently alert to danger.

It's not just the brain that is potentially affected by ACEs. Various research studies demonstrate that these childhood experiences can affect a person's body at a cellular level and that there's a link between ACE scores and a variety of biomarkers of inflammation such as C-reactive protein. Inflammation is now considered a leading cause of ill health.

The brain changes outlined above also set up individuals with high ACE scores for another set of health problems. If you feel you can never switch off or relax, if you always feel on edge, then it is tempting to self-medicate – turn to substances which can make you feel better. This is why ACEs correlate so closely with smoking, alcohol consumption, and illicit drug taking. The Welsh study particularly looked at the link between ACEs and 'health harming behaviours' and showed really strong correlations between adversities in childhood and later alcohol and drug use. It's also worth mentioning that learning and behaviour are also compromised by childhood adversities, thereby having the potential to affect children's whole lives.

Everything I have presented so far suggests that it's the fear provoked in the young brain which makes ACEs so damaging. So are some ACEs more damaging than others because they generate more fear? Is child sexual abuse, for example, worse than physical neglect or watching your father beating your mother? But when ACE researchers simply looked at whether there were long term consequences from an individual's ACE score they mainly concluded that the type of adversity wasn't the issue. What seemed to have most impact was whether the stresses children endured were 'unpredictable'.

The ACE questionnaire is an imperfect instrument. It doesn't include all the factors that can lead to serious childhood adversity. Nor does it ask about poverty or discrimination, yet these are undoubtedly serious adversities. By relying on childhood memory, the ACE questionnaire also potentially plays down the importance of infant experiences such as attachment and the kind of factors Alan Sinclair highlights in his *Postcards* book *Right from the Start*; factors vital not just for babies' health but also for longer term health and well-being. The questionnaire also depends on respondents understanding what emotional neglect or emotional abuse looks like. But these weaknesses mean that the questionnaire is likely to minimise, not maximise, people's ACE score.

It's also worth saying that the questionnaire cannot predict how an individual will fare given the ACEs they have accumulated while young. Some people may be more genetically predisposed to mental and physical changes following adversities. There are also resilience factors, which help protect individuals from the damaging effects of ACEs. The most important of these is whether there's one adult in the child's life that is reliably supportive.

GIven all these limitations it's vitally important to bear in mind that the ACE questionnaire is simply a research tool to ascertain the prevalence of potentially damaging experiences in specific populations and to see how these translate into various health outcomes. It should never be used to diagnose an individual's problems or be used to decide their access to services or treatment.

So let's now move on and apply this research on ACEs to Scotland. First let me be clear that childhood adversities happen in all countries and cultures and they remain a hidden source of mental and physical ill health everywhere. But the prevalence of ACEs varies from country to country – culture has a significant impact. And it's perfectly plausible, though painful to accept, that the Scots have experienced more ACEs than people in other Western countries and that this helps us to explain our poor health. This is the topic I explore in *Hiding in Plain Sight* in chapters dedicated to looking at: alcohol and drugs; domestic conflict; punishment and violence; and emotional abuse and neglect. I outline some of that material here. The specific issue of punishment and physical abuse is the focus of the following chapter.

Alcohol

Scotland is 'a nation of drunks'. So claimed First Minister Alex Salmond in 2014 much to the surprise of his political foes. A year later his successor as First Minister, Nicola Sturgeon, claimed that Scotland's relationship with alcohol is 'unhealthy' and that drink was too much of 'an ever present' in people's lives. By this she meant that 'we identify having a good time with drinking alcohol, having a shit time with drinking alcohol, being happy with drinking alcohol, being sad with drinking alcohol.'

The 2016 Scottish Health Survey reports that one in four Scots drink at 'hazardous or harmful' levels. So it's hardly surprising that 84 per cent of Scots think that alcohol causes either a 'great deal' of or 'quite a lot' of harm in Scotland. Since we know this I'm not going to labour the point about the level of drinking or demonstrate how much more we drink than our neighbours.

From the point of view of childhood adversities what matters most is how people drink – the culture around alcohol. A man living in Spain, Italy or France can drink a few glasses of wine with lunch and more with dinner on a daily basis and never get drunk. When imbibed in this way alcohol may damage health and lead to death but is less likely to contribute to arguments or violence. If no voices are raised, and family members simply accept that this type of drinking is part of life, then it's not a contributing factor to childhood adversities.

But this has never been the Scottish pattern of drinking. Historically many commentators observed that many Scots drank to get drunk. In other words, drink was not about savouring, enjoyment, socialising or pleasure; it was much more about oblivion. Drinkers wanted alcohol to be anaesthetic – to help them forget and numb pain as well as providing a longed-for release from the stress of everyday life. And this appears still to be the case. Recent figures show that Scotland's particular problem with alcohol is *binge drinking* and *drinking to get drunk.*

This type of alcohol consumption doesn't just undermine the drinker's health, it's a major slayer of intimate partner relationships and is responsible for ACEs. One of the ACE questions specifically asks if, when you were growing up, you lived with a 'problem drinker or alcoholic'. But the difficulty is much greater than having to deal with a drunk parent. Alcohol (and drugs) is a major driver of other childhood adversities. ACE research shows that if one household member abuses alcohol then the child is much more likely to be physically, emotionally and sexually abused.

Scotland's proclivity for excess alcohol consumption was effectively kept in check for over a hundred years by licensing restrictions. From the 1960s on Scotland, like the rest of the UK, began to liberalise its drinking laws. This meant that alcohol in Scotland became much more widely available and much cheaper. Some call this 'the grocerisation' of alcohol as people could now buy it in supermarkets and small shops and then take it home to consume.

Proponents of the liberalisation of alcohol in Scotland thought that it would lead us to adopt continental attitudes to drinking. But it hasn't. Indeed, given Scots' love affair with drink, it has been akin to handing a convicted arsonist a box of matches and a gallon of paraffin. In 1991, about thirty years after the start of liberalisation, Scotland saw a very worrying trend emerging – 'the fourfold increase in male deaths and a doubling of female deaths from alcohol-related harm.' Indeed one of the main problems with the new drink culture is that many women are now heavy drinkers, something that was rare pre-liberalisation.

As living with a problematic drinker can lead children to have a fistful of ACEs, Scotland's new drink culture has been particularly disastrous for children and young people as it seriously undermines their long term physical and mental health. Yet there has been no public acknowledgement of this fact.

Drugs

Scotland's problem with drugs echoes its problem with drink. Commentators used to say that Scotland would escape a serious drugs problem as it was so enthralled by alcohol: sadly they were wrong. Scotland is high in the international league table for illicit drug use – top for cocaine and in the top ten for use of opioids such as heroin. And just as with alcohol, the holy grail for drug users is oblivion.

In recent years Scotland has had more drug deaths per annum than any other European country. Our figure is, pro rata, twice that of England and Wales. These figures have mainly focused minds on structural ways to reduce deaths such as drug consumption rooms, legalisation of possession and various harm reduction methods. We simply haven't heard enough about recovery which those of us involved with the Independent Inquiry into Drugs and Alcohol thought vitally important. In Scotland most of the money is spent on harm reduction, such as methadone programmes and clean needles and now safe consumption rooms. Recovery and treatment programmes have received little funding. It's as if Scots don't think that addicts can recover even though there are people in our midst who have recovered and want to tell their stories.

An emphasis on culture was also at the heart of the Independent Inquiry's report but is hardly mentioned these days. In as much as commentators like Irvine Welsh, author of *Trainspotting* (1993), question why we have so many addicts they always cite unemployment and deprivation (particularly the legacy of Thatcherism) as the cause. Of course, they have contributed but they aren't the whole story: other countries have also deindustrialised without it leading to such high levels of binge drinking, drug taking and drug deaths.

ACEs are undoubtedly part of the explanation of why Scotland has such a problem with drink and drugs. Children who grow up in households with problematic users often walk a similar path when they are older as they too want to self-medicate to soothe the pain. This is why we can see such problems ricocheting down the generations. And, of course, the ACEs problem in Scotland is much wider than drugs and alcohol.

Verbal abuse and emotional neglect

The first question on the ACE questionnaire asks: 'How often did a parent or adult in your home ever swear at you, insult you, or put you down?' This question used to be called 'emotional abuse' but it's now verbal abuse and respondents score a point even if they answer 'once or twice'. I believe there are few Scots of my generation, at least from the central belt, who would score zero for this question as verbal abuse was endemic in homes, communities and schools.

In Scotland verbal abuse is an inherent part of everyday life. If a comedian from elsewhere wants to impersonate a Scotsman all he needs to do is put on his best Scottish accent and then, peppering his speech with expletives, say something like 'See you, you're a wee . . .' and then add his choice of Scottish insults. The preponderance of negative, critical words is not just an aspect of Glasgow's patter. 'The Scots language is rich in words that can be used as insults,' writes the lexicographer, Betty Kirkpatrick, adding later, 'Scots is not lacking in ways of indicating our disapproval or contempt for others.' What's more, there are few terms of endearment. Scots don't tend to see this as a problem and we are often proud of our rich vocabulary of insults. Just think of all those mugs in gift shops brandishing words like 'numpty' and 'eejit'.

Parents being verbally abusive to their children is considered an ACE. In fact, ACE researchers have found that verbal abuse (which involves swearing and humiliation) is the biggest predictor of adult depression and has been correlated with a slightly higher level of adult health outcome than other ACEs. The ACE questionnaire does not allow a nuanced reply to questions so it's worth noting that a more refined instrument, the Childhood Trauma Questionnaire (CTQ), which researchers use with individuals aged twelve or older, also shows that what might appear as fairly low doses of parental or family unkindness, emotional abuse or emotional neglect can have a negative effect on children's later mental and physical health.

And what about emotional neglect? Another ACE question asks if as a child you felt loved, special or important. It's fairly common now for people to tell their children that they love them and to display affection but that wasn't true when I was growing up. And previous generations suffered even more from this lack of affection.

Again if I return to the discussions I had in workshops with thousands of Scots, mainly of my generation, many reported that parents rarely, or never, said they loved or admired them. Many reported that their parents rarely hugged or kissed them. This may be why the Scots can't resist saying of animals or children who are physically affectionate, 'They're nothing but a big sook.'

Emotional neglect exacts a heavy price but this can be difficult to see. Indeed we have to remember that negative childhood experiences need not look too damaging on the surface. The original ACE question on emotional neglect asks 'Did you often or very often feel that . . . no one in your family loved you or thought you were important or special? or Your family didn't look out for each other, feel close to each other, or support each other?' The problem many Scots face in answering this particular ACE question is that they aren't aware that they lacked a loving, emotional environment as this was so common it was the norm.

In 1989 a German academic, Peter Zenzinger, published an essay on contemporary Scottish fiction. He attributed the negativity inherent in most Scottish books he studied to a variety of factors but he singled out Scotland's 'Calvinist heritage' with its 'negative attitude towards sexuality' claiming it 'has crippled the Scots emotionally'. And interestingly he goes on to state: '**The inability to love is. . . the primary curse of Scottish life**.' (My emphasis)

The problems of childhood emotional neglect need not result in what we define as mental illness. It can simply affect our sense of self. We need to have been seen, heard and validated as children by our parents or caregivers for us to feel good about ourselves as adults.

Parents who are emotionally neglectful are often good people who just don't know how to support their children emotionally. These are the mothers who can physically care for their children but can't help them to develop emotionally. Or the fathers who don't want to repeat their own father's abuse and deliberately don't drink and provide materially for their children but, nonetheless, just don't know how to engage positively with their family. This is why it's so easy for emotional neglect to reverberate through time.

Stories about the damage done by ACEs in Scotland

Milngavie has only one novelist it can call its own – Agnes Owens, born in the town in 1926. Her novel, *A Working Mother*(1994), set in a 1950s council estate, is about a woman married to a hard-drinking man haunted by World War II. Ultimately, she descends into alcoholism and ends up in a mental institution.

This was not the author's fate and she lived till she was 88. Nonetheless Owens clearly wrote about familiar characters and situations. They are uncannily like Scott's version of growing up in Milngavie's Garvie Crescent. And this makes sense: authors usually write about what they know, particularly in first novels. Given this, it's hardly surprising that modern Scottish novels, plays and films contain countless examples of childhood adversities. Indeed, in *Hiding in Plain Sight* I had no shortage of examples from Scottish literature to support my argument about alcohol, drugs, conflicted marriages, domineering or absent fathers, domestic violence, psychopathic teachers, gangs, verbal abuse, emotional neglect – all of it is there in spade-loads in the stories Scots have told about their lives.

Given the predominance of these types of experiences in modern novels and films, and our liking for them as readers and viewers, it's evident that *childhood adversities are an important aspect of our history and culture. Yet we have failed to acknowledge this fact, never mind confront it.* Recognising how common these experiences were for many Scots is, for me, a necessary precondition for real cultural change.

The prevalence of childhood adversities and their negative

legacy is ignored for two main reasons. First such experiences in Scotland are so common and normal that we don't see them as remarkable. They are just life. And secondly commentators and academics tend to look at Scottish books and films through the prism of history and politics. When literary characters have problems in their personal relationships – becoming addicted or having a mental breakdown, for example – critics tend not to recognise these problems as the result of family dynamics or dysfunction. Indeed such critics tend to ignore what's happening with individual characters and discuss novels in terms of Scotland's difficulties with identity and voice or some specific aspect of the country's political history.

When I was writing *Hiding in Plain Sight* I explained the subject matter to a friend and revealed that I was including my own experience. 'Would you not be better to write a novel?' he asked. 'Surely you would get a better audience.' A reasonable yet ridiculous suggestion. For over a century Scottish writers and film-makers, much more talented than me, have told hundreds of stories about childhood trauma, neglect, authoritarian fathers and household dysfunction yet these stories have hardly made a dent on Scottish consciousness. In fact, you could say that the writers have had as much chance of being heard as a horse whisperer in a force ten gale.

I find it astonishing that as a people we fail to grasp just how abusive family life is in much of our literature. Just think about that much lauded Scottish classic, *The House with the Green Shutters* (1901) or Scotland's favourite novel *Sunset Song* (1932) by Lewis Grassic Gibbon. Its admirers often portray it as a beautiful, lyrical account of the eclipse of Scotland's agricultural way of life. But there's so much physical and mental cruelty in heroine Chris Guthrie's home that once readers are 'ACE aware' and have an understanding of just how damaging an abusive family culture can be to children, they are compelled to see *Sunset Song* in a very different light.

The rise of an ACE perspective

Many professionals in Scotland heard about ACEs for the first time at a Violence Reduction Unit (VRU) conference at Scotland's Police College in 2007. Dr Felitti was one of the keynote speakers at the three-day event. I wasn't there but Alan Sinclair was and I remember vividly him handing me a copy of the original ACE study shortly thereafter. When I read it I knew that this research had enormous significance both for understanding my own life and for an analysis of Scotland's poor health statistics. I then devoted four pages to explaining ACEs in *The Tears that Made the Clyde* in 2010.

The original ACE research was published in 1998. Anda and Felitti report that it angered many doctors who didn't want to engage with its findings. But that changed over the next ten years and there was considerable activity throughout the USA by the time the VRU held their event in 2007. The fact that the VRU adopted a public health approach to violence is evidenced in their call for more health visitors, not police officers.

In 2014 Professor Mark Bellis and colleagues published an ACE prevalence study for England and Professor Bellis published a similar study for Wales in 2015 and again in 2017. In that year the Welsh Government funded the establishment of an ACE Support Hub for Wales and set itself the mission of becoming a leader in the field. Since then an enormous amount of research, policy development and awareness-raising on ACEs has taken place throughout Wales.

Scotland was not far behind in seeing the significance of the research. In 2016 the Scottish Public Health Network brought out a paper called 'Polishing the Diamonds: Addressing adverse childhood experiences.'[6] In it the authors, Sarah Couper and Phil Mackie, outline the original ACE research and the prevalence studies for England and Wales. It also set out ways Scotland could benefit from an ACE perspective and how it could be used in health settings. And the following year NHS Health Scotland organised a

6. The report explains that the title 'Polishing the Diamonds' refers to the idea of a Health Visitor that while children, like diamonds, have inherent value, they need to be polished with 'care and attention'.

large event in Edinburgh on ACEs. The chair was Professor Michael Marmot who has gained considerable fame for his work on inequality and health. Professor Mark Bellis also spoke.

In 2016 Public Health Scotland set up a Scottish ACE Hub and the Scottish Government committed itself to tackling ACEs in three of its programmes – 2017/18, 2018/19 and 2019/20. The Glasgow Centre for Population Health now lead an ACE research group. The 2019 Scottish Health Study, a population-level study, included questions on ACEs thus giving Scotland its first prevalence data.

ACE-Aware Nation

Scotland's distinctive engagement with ACEs has come from considerable grassroots interest and involvement. This primarily started as a result of an American documentary made by campaigner James Redford, son of the famous Hollywood actor Robert Redford. It is called *Resilience: The biology of stress and the science of hope* and was released in the UK in 2017. The Scottish premiere was a sell-out and the vigour with which Scotland embraced the film took the producers by surprise. In September of that year a group of local women, supported by Children 1st, screened the film in Glasgow's Citizens Theatre and Scotland's First Minister Nicola Sturgeon chaired the subsequent discussion, pledging her government to become 'trauma aware'.

In the two months following its premier, in April 2017, more than twenty-five showings of *Resilience* were held all over Scotland – not just in the main population centres but also in the Highlands and Islands, the Borders and small towns in between. These showings mainly took place in community and church halls. Nearly all sold out within days of their announcement.

The spark for all this activity came from two determined and inspiring women – Dr Suzanne Zeedyk, whom we met in the previous chapter, and Tina Hendry a former police officer who worked with organisations to help them understand how early trauma affects a child's biology and behaviour. Tragically Tina died in 2020, aged only 52. Pauline Scott, Managing Director of the TIGERS group, then became Suzanne's main partner. They founded and led a Scotland-wide movement of people interested in tackling childhood trauma called 'ACE-Aware Scotland'. In September 2018 over 2000 people gathered at the SEC in Glasgow for a large-scale event on ACEs. I attended and can attest that it was an inspirational, and well-run event that captured and developed the growing public interest in this agenda. The Centre had a book stall at the conference and sold hundreds of copies of relevant *Postcards* books. This movement is largely responsible for why *Hiding in Plain Sight* has sold over 3000 copies.

By the time this big conference took place there was both growing interest in this agenda as well as increasing criticism. The Centre believed that there was a need for both support and critique of ACEs and in February 2019 we held a half-day event in the Lighthouse, Glasgow called **The Insights, Benefits and Risks of an ACE Perspective**. The maximum number of participants allowed by the venue (100) quickly signed up and the event was ultimately judged to be a helpful contribution to the discussion we need to have on ACEs. I chaired the event, and we heard contributions from Dr Suzanne Zeedyk of Ace-Aware Scotland and Professor Jane Callaghan who is critical of the ACE movement for 'individualising' the problem of childhood adversity. Phil Hanlon facilitated the discussion.

There's little doubt that ACE-Aware Scotland has had an enormous impact not just in Scotland but internationally. In an article called 'The history of Scotland's ACEs movement: Grounded in a focus on relationships', Suzanne Zeedyk outlines the various activities that have taken place under the ACE banner, both in the public sector and at grassroots. I doubt she is exaggerating when she says that what has happened in Scotland has been an inspiration for other countries – Northern Ireland, Netherlands, Australia, New Zealand, Turkey, Portugal, and Canada. She also argues that, unlike America where the approach is epidemiological and the questionnaire used as a screening tool, Scotland has highlighted the importance of relationships, particularly attachment.

I agree with Suzanne that the thrust of ACEs work should be relational, and not epidemiological. Nonetheless I think that the ACE questionnaire provides a very useful research tool, particularly for a country like Scotland with such poor health outcomes, high levels of violence, and an inadequate understanding of why this is the case. Prevalence matters and this data can give us valuable insights into national culture and why so many Scots have suffered.

The prevalence of ACEs in Scotland

In 2019 the Scottish Health Survey (SHeS) included questions on adverse childhood experiences. These questions were then put to almost 5,000 adults (18 and over) involved in the research. The authors advise that as there were some differences in the nature of this survey and the wording and scoring of two ACE questions, 'Caution should therefore be used in making direct comparisons between the ACE data reported in SHeS and the ACE data reported in the English 2014 and Welsh 2015 ACE studies.' Following these cautionary words they attempt no comparison.

I consulted two public health experts on whether a comparison of these prevalence studies is valid. The first is Professor John Frank who has co-authored an article on ACEs and teaches students epidemiology, including how to compare studies. The other is Professor Mark Bellis, the main researcher on the English and Welsh prevalence studies and a host of other ACE studies. Both experts thought that comparing the Scottish Health Survey results with the prevalence studies carried out south of the border was valid. Both also expressed surprise at the large differences between Scottish respondents and those in England and Wales. These results have received little attention in Scotland.

In Table 3 I highlight the most pertinent results for now and tackle the issue of physical abuse in the next chapter. The most striking result in Table 3 is the Scottish response for verbal abuse (47 per cent) – more than twice the English and Welsh figures. I don't find this surprising given what I've written in earlier pages about our extensive, abusive vocabulary. National stereotypes usually have some foundation in fact and, like it or not, foreigners often stereotype the Scots as verbally abusive as well as violent. What's more the verbally abusive father, and sometimes mother, emerges strongly in Scottish literature and films.

Table 3: Comparison of ACE prevalence studies for England, Wales and Scotland

ACE	England 2015 n=3885 %	Wales 2017 n= 2497 %	Scotland 2019 n= 4903 %
1. Verbal abuse	17	20	47
2. Physical abuse	14	16	28
3. Household domestic violence	12	17	24
4. Household mental illness	12	18	19
5. Household alcohol abuse	9	13	16
6. Household drug abuse	4	6	5
8. Sexual abuse	6	7	7
9. Incarceration of a household member	4	4	3
10. Parental separation	23	25	23

Here's another small piece of corroborating evidence. At the 2017 'Polishing Our Gems' ACE conference in Edinburgh mentioned above, Dr Michael Smith asked those present to complete the ACE questionnaire online and 172 obliged. The result for verbal abuse is startling – 60 per cent of those present registered this as an ACE. Of course, this conference audience was not representative of the wider population in Scotland and not all of them will have grown up here. It's also well known that when people at ACE events complete questionnaires the prevalence of ACEs is always higher than population findings. Nonetheless 60 per cent registering verbal abuse at a Scottish conference of middle-class professionals is exceptionally high.

So too was their response on witnessing domestic violence – 40 per cent of the audience in Edinburgh said yes to this question. It was also high in the Scottish prevalence study – 24 per cent, double the figure for England (12 per cent) and substantially higher than the Welsh figure (17 per cent). And, again, this makes perfect sense given how common violence and abuse are in Scottish culture.

In the Scottish Health Study (SHeS) the ACE score for parents abusing drugs or alcohol is not as high as I would have expected given our health data. If we combine the two figures, 21 per cent of Scots say their parents abused alcohol or drugs and that is only slightly higher than Wales (19 per cent) but significantly higher than the English figure (13 per cent). But it's worth pointing out that this still indicates that more than a fifth of Scots report growing up in a household with a problem drinker or drug user.

In the Scottish study 71 per cent of respondents registered at least one ACE and that is substantially higher than England's 48 per cent and Wales's 50 per cent. This means that there are fewer people in Scotland unaffected by adverse childhood experiences than in England and Wales. And this matters. Professor Mark Bellis *et al* have conducted an analysis of five English and Welsh studies, including 22,361 respondents, to see if one ACE can have a negative effect on health. They specifically look at the impact that a single ACE has on some health-related outcomes: smoking, binge drinking, obesity, cannabis use, sexually transmitted infection, teenage pregnancy, low mental well-being, violence perpetration, incarceration and violence victimisation. Their study leads them to write: 'We find that exposure to a single ACE type... is significantly associated with multiple poorer health and behavioural outcomes and that such associations vary according to ACE type.'

Some of their specific findings are important for Scotland given our poor health outcomes. For example, having a problem drinker in the household 'was more strongly related to binge drinking than any other ACE'. As I outlined above, binge drinking is a widespread problem in Scotland. Living with a problem drinker is also strongly related to being involved with violence. But it's their comments on verbal abuse, something that 47 per cent of Scots recorded in the Scottish Health Study (SHeS), which should make us sit up and take notice. They write:

> A number of studies link verbal and emotional abuse in childhood to poor outcomes, in particular relating to mental health, and also outline social and physiological pathways through which these effects may occur. Despite this, verbal abuse has received relatively little attention in comparison to other ACEs. . . Results here support substantive impacts on life course health and behaviour associated with verbal abuse even in the absence of other ACEs. Thus, verbal abuse was associated with low mental well-being levels comparable with those reporting sexual abuse in childhood or growing up with someone with mental illness. Verbal abuse was also associated with higher levels of binge drinking, cannabis use, violence and incarceration; all of which can be linked with poorer mental health. Without evidence specifically on the impact of verbal abuse, parents, health and education services may underestimate the toxic impacts.

All the health outcomes listed above are high in Scotland. Indeed Scotland's atrocious health statistics and data on other factors such as violence, make it an ideal country for research into the impact this has on long term health-related outcomes given that so many people reported verbal abuse in the Scottish prevalence study.

Bellis *et al*'s single ACE study was a deliberate attempt to get away from the predominant notion that it's only acquiring four or more ACEs which has considerable impact on health. And it's certainly true that most papers focus on four plus ACEs, including the Welsh, English and Scottish prevalence studies. So how do Scots fare on this measure?

The figure given in SHeS for four or more ACES is 15 per cent and that's almost double England's 8 per cent but only 1 per cent higher than Wales' figure of 14 per cent. And this is where we run into problems with comparisons. England and Scotland didn't ask questions on physical neglect or emotional neglect but Wales did in its 2017 survey. But just as I was proven correct in predicting in a couple of my books that Scots would score high for verbal abuse in ACE surveys, I'm also predicting that, historically at least, emotional neglect would be high.

To avoid going into more justification for this assertion let me quote the case of Ireland. A prevalence study in the Republic found that the Irish score for verbal abuse was 36 per cent, that's more than twice England's figure, substantially above Wales and much lower than Scotland's 47 per cent. Ireland included the question on emotional neglect and 30 per cent of respondents registered this as an ACE. I'm not saying that Scotland's figure would be as high but, given similarities between Ireland and Scotland on verbal abuse and physical abuse, I'm sure the emotional neglect figure would be high and would therefore increase the percentage of Scots scoring four or more ACEs.

The Irish study also showed that emotional neglect has important consequences for individuals and that 'those who experience emotional neglect were nearly two times more likely to abuse substances' and we know that substance abuse is an issue in Scotland. The authors also report that 'emotional neglect had a stronger association with mental health than all other ACEs.' Unfortunately, the Bellis single ACE study did not look at emotional neglect presumably because it has been omitted in a number of the studies they considered.

Explanatory factors

ACE studies usually analyse results by some measure of socio-economic status and there's little doubt that across the board those from poorer backgrounds score more ACEs. That makes sense: poverty is stressful for families and this can make household dysfunction of various kinds more likely. It's also easy to see how in poor communities childhood adversities can easily pass from one generation to the next.

In the SHeS, the ACE data is analysed by the deprivation status of respondents. Those in the most deprived area were almost twice as likely to experience four or more ACEs than those living in the least deprived area. (See Table 4)

However, there is something significant going on here that cannot obviously be attributed to deprivation: a substantial number of those who live in the two most affluent areas suffered from four or more ACEs. The average for those living in the top two areas is 13 per cent whereas it is 18.5 per cent for those in the bottom two areas.

Table 4: Those experiencing four or more ACEs by deprivation status

5th least deprived	11%
4th least deprived	15%
3rd least deprived	13%
2nd least deprived	17%
1st most deprived	20%

This resonates with one of the findings from the GCPH's three cities survey referenced earlier. This shows that Glasgow has 30 per cent higher premature mortality than Liverpool and Manchester and that these deaths are not confined to poor Glaswegians: even middle-class Glaswegians do not fare as well as their counterparts in Liverpool and Manchester. In short, the poor health of Glaswegians, and those more generally in the West of Scotland, cannot simply be attributed to socio-economic factors. As Scott and myself know only too well, culture matters – values, beliefs, relationships and behaviours which have all been shaped by our collective history. This means that we could never see the relevance of the GCPH's explanatory model for poor health in our part of Scotland: a model which *exclusively* emphasises the importance of economic and political factors.

I know that my taxi driver wouldn't have considered it plausible either. Like Scott, his father was badly affected by his war service and was a violent alcoholic who regularly hit his wife. But abuse was rife in Scottish family life and that's why so many children suffered adversity and why so many of us are blind to this feature of Scottish culture.

In 2013 GCPH published a report by Martin Taulbut and David Walsh called 'Poverty, parenting and poor health: comparing early years' experiences in Scotland, England and three city regions'. This looked at four cohort studies ranging from 1946-2000 as well as other 'routine data' and large-scale surveys. Essentially this report examined variations in children's experiences in Merseyside, Greater Manchester and Glasgow and the Clyde Valley to see if these could help to explain the variation in life expectancy across these regions which GCPH authors found in an earlier analysis, already summarised in this chapter.

Taulbut and Walsh report that there was little difference across the three regions in the type of early years' experiences that can have a negative impact on children's lives. They also write: 'There was also little evidence to suggest poorer gender relations or a lack of shared parental responsibilities in the Scottish areas.' From the data they analysed the authors also report that 'it remains unclear whether childhood and early years in Scotland and Glasgow and the Clyde Valley are characterised by less warm relationships and more use of shouting to discipline children.' They call for further research including a UK-wide ACE study.

However, the publication of the 2019 Scottish Health Survey and the fact that we can now use English and Welsh prevalence studies to compare Scots' experiences in childhood with respondents south of the border, suggests that children *have* been treated differently across the UK when it comes to verbal and physical abuse and witnessing domestic violence. And it is to the physical abuse of Scottish children that we now turn.

CHAPTER 21

Illuminating the darkness: Scotland's physical abuse of children

Kenneth Roy's chronicles of twentieth century Scotland;
the belt culture; corporal punishment elsewhere;
the consequences of being belted;
institutionalised fear; why Scotland had to ban corporal punishment;
the role of religion; hitting children at home;
the prevalence of corporal punishment; the evidence of harm;
Scotland's smacking ban;
the abuse of children in Scottish institutions;
Kenneth Roy's experience of abuse at school.

WHEN I WROTE *The Scots' Crisis of Confidence* I made great play of our fear of failure and making mistakes but I didn't attribute any responsibility for this to Scottish education and the extensive use of the belt, or the tawse to give it its official name. Of course, I knew the belt was used in Scottish schools, as I had been belted myself, but I thought this practice standard fare across the world. In that book I also disagreed with those who argued that Scotland had a particularly authoritarian streak. I was wrong on both counts.

The person who opened my eyes to how much the belt was used in Scottish schools and the country's predilection for cruelty to young children was Kenneth Roy. He was a former BBC newsreader and presenter and I knew him well as we had worked together at BBC Scotland in the 1980s. Our paths crossed again as he went on to found a very successful online journal called *Scottish Review*. But it's his two history books on modern Scotland, *The Invisible Spirit* (2013) and *The Broken Journey* (2016) which had a pronounced influence on me.

Kenneth's chronicles of Scotland tell the country's story from 1945-1999. In both books he devotes a chapter to each year and this structure makes his portrayal of Scotland's past fresh and original. What's more, most of his material comes from contemporary newspaper reports giving the books a wide-ranging and lively perspective. This approach allows him to record not just what happened in Scotland but how events were seen and presented by the press, so Kenneth's account also reflects public opinion.

Scotland's belt culture

However, it's the routine way ordinary Scottish schoolchildren were belted to which Kenneth repeatedly refers. Some of these references are to court cases where, despite evident harm, the teacher or headteacher was often exonerated. He reports evidence which shows that corporal punishment was much more common in state schools in Scotland than in England and Wales. Indeed, extrapolating from Edinburgh data on the incidence of corporal punishment in the city's schools during one term, he claims that in the mid 1970s there would be an 'annual total of 30,000 beatings in Edinburgh alone'.

Kenneth reports that in the 1970s Secretaries of State for Scotland advocated 'a consensual approach to abolition' but felt no pressure to ban it. 'They had no cause to fear public disapproval,' he writes, 'for the Scots as a whole were almost as keen on the idea of corporal punishment as the teachers.'

It was reading Kenneth's two-part history of Scotland which encouraged me to look into the topic and I presented my views in *Hiding in Plain Sight: Exploring Scotland's ill health*. The following year (2018) I wrote an article for *Scottish Review* on Scotland's use of corporal punishment. As editor, he chose to title it: 'Scotland the cruel'.

Once I started thinking about corporal punishment in Scottish schools I asked almost everyone I met about their experience. And I hardly encountered one Scot of my generation who wasn't belted at some point in their school days – most of them multiple times. As well as the belt many recounted other incidents of teacher violence such as having wooden blackboard dusters thrown at them, being struck over the knuckles with a ruler, repeatedly jabbed in the back or ribs with a finger or pencil or slapped forcefully on the legs. One friend told me that his technical teacher struck him on the head from behind with a block of wood and he fell to the floor unconscious. My maths teacher threw blackboard compasses at a girl in the class and grazed her hand. We never saw him again but he was employed in other schools.

Many remember teachers at secondary school wearing their belts over their shoulders like scarves or under their gowns so they could whip them out at the slightest provocation. Some talk about having to bandage their hand after being belted. Scott, whom we met in the previous chapter, has a permanently disfigured finger from being belted at the age of seven. Lots of people claim that some teachers in their school, both primary and secondary, were sadists or psychopaths. Some, both men and women, believe that some teachers belted them as they were 'kinky'.

Official guidance in Scotland said that the belt should only be given for disciplinary offences and not for poor academic performance but people were certainly belted for that. In some teachers' classes spelling mistakes, errors in sums, not knowing French vocabulary, forgetting poems. . . all warranted a good belting. One man I know was belted every Monday morning at his Catholic school for not remembering the catechism. I was belted, aged seven, for losing the place in reading. In an interview for a BBC Scotland programme, first aired in 2017, called 'Growing up in Scotland' Professor Tom Devine states, 'Corporal punishment was actually used not just for reasons of discipline but also for academic reasons. There's plenty of evidence that if you failed to gain a certain mark then the belt would be produced.' As Liz

Lochhead, a former teacher, points out in this programme the whole culture was terrible for dyslexic pupils, as I know only too well.

As most of the people I spoke to performed well at school and went on to university I've been surprised by how many of them recounted numerous incidents. At secondary school these beltings were often for lateness or because the teacher had decided to belt the whole class and in primary school for talking or misbehaving in line. Or it could be for some bizarre and totally unpredictable reason.

I have also been surprised by how many girls my age were belted at primary school. One woman, now a GP, told me that when she was seven she put one foot on the road when out on a school trip; the teacher belted her when they returned to school. Another female doctor recounts being belted when she was five for pleating the hair of the girl in front of her in class. My close friend, latterly a professor, says she was belted every week in primary school because she was giggling or talking (i.e. behaving like a child) or the teacher wanted to put her in her place. Another said she was continually belted or hit with a ruler for 'dumb insolence'.

There were much worse incidents than the ones I've heard from friends. Someone posted the following question on a Glasgow discussion board online: 'Did you get the belt at school, how many, what for and did it work?' The last time I looked there were 571 comments. Many of the incidents people relate are awful. For example, a woman recounts that she was so frightened of her Primary 1 teacher she didn't ask to go to the toilet and wet the floor. The teacher then belted the scared infant. A man recounts that in his first day at secondary school one of the teachers belted him as they shared the same surname and the teacher wanted to prove to the class there would be no favouritism. Another woman tells us that she got the belt seven times one morning in Primary 2 for not being able to remember a prayer. Some recounted getting twelve strokes of the belt, others say they had to put their hands above a desk so their knuckles hit it thus doubling the pain.

Evidence for the use of corporal punishment is not just

anecdotal. Kenneth Roy quotes studies which corroborate the extensive use of corporal punishment in Scottish schools. For example, a study of 40,000 school leavers conducted in 1980 found that only 1 in 20 Scottish boys went through secondary school without being belted. A 1977 study found that more than a third of 12–15-year-old boys received the belt at least once in ten school days. A fifth received it three or more times during this period: a figure which undermines the argument that the belt had a deterrent effect.

Any way you look at the issue, institutionalised violence was endemic in Scottish schools and, as far as I can see, it happened across Scotland. One of the most chilling accounts I've read of teacher violence to pupils is in Calum Ferguson's book *Children of the Black House* (2003) about life in Lewis in the nineteenth and early twentieth centuries. His mother Mairead reports that when she was at school, 'Shouting abuse at pupils and slapping their faces was commonplace.' But that was the least of it:

> One male teacher, born and brought up in Garrabost. . . was terribly harsh in his treatment of children. For example, it was customary for him to heat the spokes of the tawse in the fire so as to make its bite the fiercer. As he slammed the crossed hands of those who had earned his displeasure, he added insult to injury by describing his victims as 'unspeakable wretches', 'stupid idiots' or 'odious villains'.

When I raised the subject of the belt with a friend who went to school in Lewis in the 1960s and 70s she confirmed that corporal punishment was commonplace in both primary and secondary school but, like me, she thought this was only a reflection of how children everywhere were treated. It wasn't.

Corporal punishment elsewhere

Once I started to look at corporal punishment here, I realised how my assumption that children were belted everywhere was wrong. Poland was the first country to ban corporal punishment in schools and it did this in 1783! Corporal punishment of any kind ceased in French schools in 1887, Russia abolished it in 1917 and China in

1949. If we look at the progressive European countries we would like to emulate, we'll find that they abolished corporal punishment in schools decades ago – Finland (1914); Netherlands (1920); Italy (1928); Sweden (1928); Norway (1936); Luxembourg (1945); and Denmark (1947).

The English-speaking world was not as eager to outlaw corporal punishment in schools – New Zealand banned it in 1989, Canadian provinces followed suit in the 1990s and there is one state in Australia and 16 American states (mainly in the south) which still permit it.

There's little doubt that posh independent schools in the UK were the world leaders in physically punishing pupils, particularly with the cane. A disturbing book by Alex Renton called *Stiff Upper Lip: Secrets, Crimes and the Schooling of a Ruling Class* (2017) exposes the severe physical punishment meted out to pupils in UK public schools, particularly boarding schools, right up to the turn of this century. Canings and similar types of punishment weren't just the preserve of school masters and headteachers. In many private fee-paying establishments, including prep schools, prefects were also given the power to beat their younger peers. Indeed Renton argues that the British establishment had to be forced to ban corporal punishment in schools because it had been so much part of their schooling that they thought it 'normal'.

Some state schools in England also used the cane and corporal punishment was widespread throughout the country until the Westminster Parliament banned it in 1986, one year before Scotland. Some local authority areas banned caning decades before but permitted use of the slipper or a slap with the hand. Newcastle schools used a Scottish style belt. What is clear is that while corporal punishment was widely used in English state schools it wasn't nearly as prevalent as it was in Scotland. Some local authorities didn't allow girls to be disciplined in this way, primary school children were much less likely to be hit and some secondary schools didn't use corporal punishment at all. Indeed, Colin Farrell in an article for 'the Corpun' website maintains that the Scottish prevalence levels for corporal punishment, cited earlier, suggest 'a considerably higher level of usage of CP overall in Scotland than in England and Wales.' This chimes with the experiences of many people I've spoken to. For example, Sue Palmer, editor of *Play is the Way*, was educated in England, then trained as a teacher at Moray House in Edinburgh. Sue subsequently worked extensively in education both north and south of the border. She maintains that at least from the 1960s corporal punishment was less frequently employed (and less harsh) in English than in Scottish state schools. When she was a student at Moray House in the 1970s she was taken aback by the small classroom where trainee teachers were shown how to use the belt.

The consequences

It's commonplace for people to recount adverse events such as physical punishment at school and then dismiss what happened as it 'didn't do me any harm'. Indeed, victims sometimes argue that such events toughened them up and boosted their resilience. Nonetheless we know that many Scots feel angry at what happened to them and don't agree with this conclusion.

The 2018 article I wrote for *Scottish Review* about Scotland's belt culture was read by the journalist Ian Jack who then responded by devoting one of his columns for *The Guardian* to the topic. Ian Jack, a Scot himself, did not take issue with the prevalence of corporal punishment in Scottish schools though he (wrongly) asserted that girls didn't get belted. The main point of his column was to argue that being given the belt had felt 'unfair' but that it had 'done me no harm'.

Within an hour of people reading *The Guardian* over breakfast the paper's website was inundated with comments. In fact, on the Saturday that Ian Jack's column appeared, readers' responses were coming in at a rate of around 200 an hour. By Sunday evening there were 1,849 and *Guardian* website staff disabled the comments facility.

The vast majority of those who commented disagreed with Ian Jack. Indeed *The Guardian* chose the following comment by an Australian to put at the end of the article: 'The number of traumatic experiences being poured out on these pages in the last few hours shows just how harmful it was/is. Hopefully some are finding comfort in sharing stories but don't forget there's help out there if you're upset by any of this – and you're not alone.' Some commentators pointed out wryly that if anyone says that they weren't harmed by corporal punishment it's incontrovertible evidence that they were.

The majority of comments were posted by Scots on their experience of the belt even though the newspaper is not widely read north of the border. What's more, the readership tends to be educated, if not intellectual. Yet here were people who had presumably done fairly well at school recounting their negative experiences of corporal punishment. Can you imagine what the response would have been if it had come from adults who had hated school, who were not motivated by academic work and who were more likely to make errors for which they could have been belted?

I knew Ian Jack, sadly now deceased. I always saw him as a decent, gentle man with laudable values. He had considerable empathy. Yet in this column he directed that empathy only towards the teachers and not the pupils. At one point he writes:

> I sympathised with a good friend, a teacher in a rough Glasgow school, who said: 'Basically it's a matter of convenience. . . when you're faced with a class of 40 15-year-old boys who don't want to be there anyway, pelting you with paper balls, the quickest, surest way to get some kind of attention is to belt somebody. Then you can get on with the history of U-boat warfare or why the UN is a good thing.

What puzzles me about this is that Ian acknowledges in his column that other European countries abolished corporal punishment in schools long before Scotland was forced to abandon the practice by the European Court of Human Rights. So how were they managing to keep order in class without resorting to the belt? Did Ian simply have no understanding that there are other ways of fostering respect for the teaching staff or for learning itself?

Another of *The Guardian's* chosen comments shows how this could be done:

> The best teacher at my school by a country mile was also the strictest and best respected. She never even shouted let alone hit anyone. Her method was simple. Respect, for ourselves, our education and for others. She would ask us to stand up when she entered the room, and we did, only for her not any other teacher. She would always begin the lesson on the right note – professional, prepared and really caring about our progress, stretching us. Her great care for our education and the technical brilliance she gave to her lessons (English Literature) made everyone in that class improve. And our grades improved across other subjects as well. There is absolutely no place for hitting in society and that includes children.

Institutionalised fear

Whatever way you look at Scottish education's 'addiction' to the belt (to quote Ian) it was an indictment of the whole system. It institutionalised violence towards children, as young as five. The fact that young children and adolescents were not only punished for gross disobedience but also minor misdemeanours and errors in schoolwork is, to my mind, unforgivable. I sympathise with the respondent to Ian's article who wrote: 'Nicola Sturgeon should stand up in parliament and apologise to all those Scots who were physically abused by the teaching profession for "crimes" such as failing their spelling test or forgetting their PE kit.'

From the comments it's also clear I'm not alone in now thinking that the Scottish education system led to a fear of making mistakes and affected young people's relationships with adults. This then impeded confidence. Indeed one reader, recounting the extent of corporal punishment in her Dungannon primary school, stated: 'Like Scotland, Northern Irish kids grew up shy, unconfident and angry.'

I was belted a couple of times in primary school for minor academic failures but I believe that the real damage was done by Mrs Buchanan, my P2 teacher who never laid a finger on me. She was in her late 50s or early 60s and the product of a different, and more brutal, era in Scottish education. Mrs Buchanan didn't belt six-year-olds: she assaulted them. Her method of corporal punishment was to take infants over her knee, pull up their short trousers or knickers and slap them very hard on the buttocks and legs. She didn't just do this to rumbustious, cheeky boys creating havoc in her class (not that this would have been excusable): everyone was vulnerable and every day I lived in fear that I could be next. With good reason – Mrs Buchanan even smacked my nervous, mild-mannered friend Patricia in front of the whole class for not having a clean handkerchief. It was terrible to witness our dragon teacher meting out this punishment to classmates for trivial, unpredictable offences. I'm sure I wasn't the only six-year-old child sitting, holding my breath (the freeze response) and experiencing 'toxic stress' for the simple reason that there was no escape.

If a young person's only exposure to teacher violence was a few beltings at secondary school this may not have affected them too badly. But, when I was young, minimal exposure was uncommon. Many pupils, from the infant class on, were repeatedly belted. What's more, in Scotland the education system was designed to instil fear. This is why Scottish teachers were encouraged to use the belt on a pupil in front of the whole class. And it's fear that is so toxic to young minds. The idea that the frequent use of corporal punishment in schools didn't do pupils any harm is preposterous. Neuroimaging now shows that unpredictable, fearful events can leave a mark on the brains of developing children.

It's also important to point out that when I was at school, when teachers weren't belting children they were often lashing them with their tongues. Verbal abuse, strong criticism and humiliation of pupils in front of the whole class was an integral part of many teachers' pedagogy.

Of course, there were always a few Scottish teachers who didn't resort to this type of discipline or abuse. For example, two men whom we met in earlier chapters – Alf Young and Alan McLean – were school teachers at the beginning of their careers and they refused to use the belt in their classrooms. No doubt many of their colleagues considered them 'odd' for not controlling their classes in this way. There were also some inspiring figures like the educationalist and headteacher R.F. MacKenzie who argued passionately against the use of corporal punishment. However, he was sacked in 1974 for banning the belting of girls in his school.

Banning corporal punishment in Scotland

Scotland didn't change its mind about belting children at school and there was never a widespread public campaign against it. It was the principled objection of two mothers – Grace Campbell and Jane Cosans – which ultimately brought about its demise. Jane's 15-year-old son Jeffrey had refused to be belted for taking a short-cut when going home from school on the basis that his parents were opposed to corporal punishment. He was then suspended and never allowed back.

Grace, the other mother, argued that she should be allowed to decide whether her seven-year-old child should be subjected to corporal punishment. Strathclyde Council wouldn't agree. She appealed to councillors and MPs but they wouldn't help. The predominant view was that you couldn't teach children if you didn't threaten them with the use of corporal punishment.

Both women appealed to the European Court of Human Rights. Scottish education authorities and the British state fought hard for the status quo but ultimately the mothers won, though it took five years from their application to the judgement in 1982.

This case was primarily about parents' right to decide on how their child should be disciplined and whether a child should be suspended from school for refusing physical punishment. So the judgement did not automatically mean that belting was outlawed. Scottish authorities tried to find a way to keep the belt given this new parental right but this proved impossible and corporal punishment in Scottish state schools finally ended in 1987 and in independent schools in 2000.

In 2017, to mark the 40-year anniversary of the beginning of his mother's campaign to end corporal punishment in Scotland's state schools, one of Grace's two sons, Andrew Campbell, wrote a moving and informative article in the *Times Educational Supplement* entitled 'If you didn't get the belt, you can thank my mum'. He explains why both his parents felt strongly on the issue:

> My parents' memories of their school days – like those of a lot of people – were far from those of a loving, caring education system that put the child first. Rather, they remembered the brutalising effect of being hit and humiliated repeatedly, arbitrarily, sometimes day after day, often for getting something wrong and – on one traumatic occasion – just for recovering from serious illness.

By the time Andrew's brother was in P3 he had witnessed several pupils in his class being belted and this 'affected' him and made him fearful that he would be next. And this is why Grace began her appeal to the local authority and finally took the issue to the European Court.

Andrew tells us that there were some supportive people, including teachers, but 'generally people were openly hostile to the idea that someone might challenge corporal punishment and might get it removed from schools altogether.' The family came under enormous pressure. Some neighbours stopped talking to them. Graffiti was painted on their front door; they even got a brick through their window; and the children were verbally abused by other pupils. Their telephone was tapped.

Understandably Grace felt under enormous pressure not just with the court case but with the negative reaction the family was attracting. Aged 40, the year of her victory at the European Court, she had a stroke. She died a few years later, aged 47, and should perhaps be seen as a casualty of Scotland's authoritarian culture.

It's worth reading Kenneth Roy's account of the case at the European Court of Human Rights in his book *The Broken Journey* and the reaction in Scotland to the possibility that schools would be prevented from using corporal punishment. For example, Glasgow's *Evening Times* wrote on Jeffrey Cosan's case that the headmaster and education authority had '. . . set a good example. It's probably symptomatic of today's attitudes that the situation ever arose: it almost certainly wouldn't have in the days when stepping out of line brought swift retribution and no one dreamed of challenging it.' We also learn that in 1976 the Labour MP Dennis Canavan, a former teacher, introduced a Ten Minute Rule Bill in the Commons to outlaw corporal punishment throughout the UK.

It received little support from Scottish MPs. Scottish Labour was solidly pro corporal punishment. According to Kenneth the only support came from MPs in London and the South-East of England.

Religion

In an interview for the BBC Scotland series to which I referred earlier, Professor Lindsay Paterson, who does not even mention corporal punishment in an article entitled 'Scottish education in the twentieth century', was forced to accept that it had been used in schools. But he then tacitly justifies its use: 'The threat of physical violence was present in schools but then it was present in families, it was present in communities and present through the church,' and then added 'schools simply saw themselves as reproducing that – that ethics were to be instilled partly by the threat of violence.'

But it wasn't the threat of violence that was the only problem: it was also its frequent use. And the idea that this was always linked to the instillation of 'ethics ' is absurd. What's ethical about hitting infants with a leather strap for mistakes or trivial actions or thinking that the only way to get children to learn is by threatening them with a belt? I have more sympathy with Kenneth Roy's views that some teachers were sadistic and some got a perverse sexual pleasure from hitting pupils.

Nonetheless Paterson is right to link the use of corporal punishment in schools to the church. It's easy to overlook Scotland's former religiosity as it's now one of the most secular countries in the world. But until the late 1950s Scotland was a very religious society with high levels of church membership and attendance. And until the mid-twentieth century religion played a bigger part in Scottish life than it did south of the border. Also 'discipline' was fundamental to the religious practices brought into force in Scotland after the Reformation. Traditionally Scottish Presbyterianism was more influenced by the Old, not the New, Testament and this matters as it's this part of the Bible which exhorts parents to punish their children. After all Proverbs tells us: 'He who spares the rod hates his son, but he who loves him is careful to discipline him.'

In his book on public schools Alex Renton argues that it was Christian values and the supposed adherence to the Bible that initially lay behind British boarding schools' extensive use of corporal punishment. In my private discussions I was also surprised by the number of people from religious backgrounds who reported that their 'nice', 'gentle' churchgoing parents not only smacked them but struck them with a belt for disobedience.

America's southern Bible Belt states share some of Scotland's heritage as they too have a deeply religious past influenced by the Old Testament. Many of these states were even founded by Ulster Scots or the 'Scots Irish' as the Americans say. Sixteen of these states still use corporal punishment in schools and people in these states argue ferociously for parents' right to hit their children.

The home front

Indeed one of the reasons why parents rarely challenged schools' extensive use of corporal punishment is that so many of them were also using it at home. The social historian Richard Finlay makes some interesting observations about Scottish childhood in the 1930s:

> There was an unusually wide range of words associated with physical punishment. 'Leathering', 'battering', 'tanning', 'skelping', 'bleaching', 'whipping', 'hammering', 'roasting', 'hiding' and 'thrashing' were familiar expressions for most children, as was the term 'doing' – as in 'You'll get a doing'.

These words were also current in the 1950s and 60s when I was growing up. Finlay also points out that physical punishment was so much the norm that neighbours, shopkeepers and the police would also give kids a 'clout on the ear or a kick in the arse'. Youngsters would not want their parents to know that they had been hit by teachers or other adults because they were likely to get another belting.

The comedian Billy Connolly, who was severely abused as a child both at school and home, joked about the 'strange things' parents said to children. 'Can I go out on my bike. What? Bike? I'll give you bike. . . Can I go to the pictures? What, pictures is it? I'll pictures you my lad. . . I'll make you smile on the other side of your face. . . I'll take my hand off your face.'

When I was young it was common to see parents hitting their children in public, mostly in the street or in shops. And I'm not talking about a gentle smacking but an aggressive and sustained physical attack often accompanied by verbal abuse.

Of course, this type of punishment was (and still is) doled out to children in other countries of the world but there are reasons, other than religious beliefs, that may have made this type of punishment more likely in this country. First, Scotland had atrocious overcrowding and poor housing conditions right up to the middle of the twentieth century, so there was lots of family stress which can easily lead to violence and frustration. Second, Scotland had high levels of street violence – people took offence easily and were quick to use their hands. And, because there was so much violence towards children, it was easy to think it was normal.

I certainly did. That's why I didn't include anything about it in *The Scots' Crisis of Confidence*. In *The Tears that Made the Clyde* a few years later I write a fair amount about the belt in schools but little about parents smacking or physically abusing their children apart from the doings they could get from their drunken fathers. And I must confess I smacked my two sons on a couple of occasions out of sheer frustration. I felt guilty almost immediately. I apologised and I hope I managed to heal the rupture in our relationship but nonetheless I should not have acted in this way.

Scottish parents and corporal punishment

My use of corporal punishment was in the mid 1980s or early 90s and it was so much part of Scottish culture it was unremarkable. Sensibilities have changed considerably since then and now fewer parents hit their children. This can be seen in Table 5 which I have extracted from a 2015 report called 'Equally Protected' which includes data on parents' use of smacking from 2005 – 2013.

Table 5: Prevalence of Parental Smacking of children in Scotland 2005-2013

Study	Respondents/question asked	Prevalence
Growing up in Scotland Study2005/06	Parental endorsement of smacking: 'It may not be a good thing to smack but sometimes it is the only thing that will work' – agree/strongly agree	For parents of children 34.5 months – 42% For parents of children 10.5 months – 30%
Millennium Cohort Study 2006 & 2008	'How often do you smack (child) when he/she is naughty?'	Any smacking reported: Age 5: 58% Age 7: 48%
Growing up in Scotland Study 2012/13	'My parents smack me when I have done something wrong' – child respondent born 2004/05	Age 7: 56 %

There are a few things in these figures which are noteworthy. First, almost a third of parents admit to smacking babies of just over ten months old. I find that shocking. Second, leaving aside parents' willingness to smack infants, smacking tends to decrease as children become older. Also, parental reporting of smacking is lower than children's reports. This is well known by researchers, presumably because some parents won't admit to smacking as they know that, in our progressively child-centred world, it's now frowned upon.

So what did the 2019 Scottish Health Study (SHeS) – Scotland's ACE prevalence study – tell us about how many parents hit their children in Scotland and how does that compare with the English and Welsh prevalence studies?

The original question in the ACE study is on physical abuse rather than physical punishment and it reads as follows: 'Did a parent or other adult in the household often or very often. . . Push, grab, slap, or throw something at you? or Ever hit you so hard that you had marks or were injured?' This was then changed by the researchers to 'how often did a parent or adult in your home ever hit, beat, kick, or physically hurt you in any way? Do not include spanking.' Once or more than once indicated an ACE. In the Engish and Welsh prevalence studies the sentence 'Do not include spanking' has been changed to 'This does not include gentle smacking for punishment.'

In the questionnaire used in the SHeS, this short sentence was dropped completely. The authors explain that they did this to 'reflect the introduction of legislation related to smacking in Scotland (the Children (Equal Protection from Assault) (Scotland) Act). This came into law in November 2019, the same year as the Health study enquired about ACEs.

It's a pity that there is this variation between the questionnaires used in Scotland, England and Wales. However, I'm unsure if this would have made a substantial difference. The wording used in the English and Welsh question implies that the parent tapped the child's hand or lightly tapped their legs or bottom. I doubt that in such circumstances the child would remember the event as it was so low key. But we know that this is not generally how parents discipline children. Professor George Holden has spent years studying discipline in the home and he maintains that parents usually hit their children when they are 'stressed, frustrated or angry with their child.' In such cases, 'gentle smacking for punishment' is unlikely to describe an incident which is charged with emotion. In the 'Equally Protected?' report quoted above the authors also argue that it's difficult to distinguish the effects of physical punishment such as smacking and physical abuse and that attempts to do so reflect cultural attitudes towards hitting children. And as I argue earlier in this chapter on the use of corporal punishment in schools, Scottish parents generally supported the idea that it was good to hit children for punishment and the way this was done, could rarely be described as 'gentle'.

If there were only a few points of difference between responses in Scotland in the ACE study and those south of the border this may be dismissed as the effect of leaving out smacking. But the difference is large: 28 per cent scored an ACE for physical abuse in Scotland whereas the English figure was 14 per cent and the 2017 Welsh figure 16 per cent.

Even if you think that a comparison is invalid given the difference in how this question was posed north and south of the border it's worth reflecting for a moment that **over a quarter of Scots (28 per cent) report they had been physically abused before the age of 18: that their parents had hit, beaten, kicked or physically hurt them in some way**. Obviously, few would defend parents physically assaulting their children in such a manner but what about smacking?

The evidence of harm

Some readers may think that smacking isn't a problem and may even be good for children but this isn't what research tells us. A meta-analysis of 50 years' worth of studies, encompassing more than 160,000 children, by Elizabeth Gershoff and Andrew Grogan-Kaylor found that spanking was associated with long lasting effects into adulthood including more mental health problems, aggression, lower self- esteem and poor relationships with parents. Of course,

Box 17: Key outcomes of physical punishment

- Physical punishment is not effective in achieving parenting goals.
- There is strong and consistent evidence for a link between physical punishment and childhood aggression, antisocial behaviour and delinquency.
- There is good evidence for a reciprocal relationship between physical punishment and problem behaviour. Physical punishment exacerbates existing problem behaviour, leading to a vicious circle of cascading conflict.
- Childhood physical punishment is linked to adult aggression and antisocial behaviour, including aggression and sexual violence within intimate partner relationships.
- Physical punishment is related to depressive symptoms and anxiety among children. There is also some less consistent evidence for links with depressive symptoms and reduced self-esteem in later life.
- Other negative outcomes that were shown to be related to physical punishment are parent-child conflict, adult mental illness and adult substance abuse.

not everyone suffers long-term effects from physical chastisement, but many do.

This is corroborated by the 'Equally Protected?' report published in November 2015. It's subtitled 'A review of the evidence on the physical punishment of children' and had been commissioned by NSPCC Scotland, Children 1st and the Children and Young People's Commissioner Scotland who was at that time Tam Baillie.

As well as reviewing the evidence on the prevalence of physical punishment in Scotland, which I have already summarised, the authors (Anja Heilman, Yvonne Kelly and G Watt) analyse a range of studies on the effects of smacking on children. As Box 17 shows, their extensive research corroborates the finding that physical punishment leads to worse outcomes for children and for adults who were physically punished when they were young.

Scotland's smacking ban

In 2019 the Scottish Parliament passed the Children (Equal Protection from Assault) (Scotland) Bill which removed parents' right to hit their children on the grounds of 'reasonable chastisement'. This started out as a private members' bill presented by the Green MP, John Finnie, but was then adopted by the SNP Government.

By 2019 over 50 countries in the world had made it illegal for parents to hit their children. The Scottish Parliament wanted to follow suit but was initially met with considerable opposition. The Catholic Church in Scotland mounted a stout attack on a ban even though many Catholic countries had legislated against physical punishment. The Church of Scotland gave support to the Scottish Bill but many small Protestant churches, including the Free Church of Scotland lodged objections. An umbrella group – Be Reasonable – representing many of the organisations who were opposed to the ban argued in favour of what they called 'loving parental discipline' and against what they considered unreasonable interference by the state in family life. Many of the groups opposed to the legislation were encouraged to do so because they believed their views were in tune with public opinion. A ComRes poll published in 2017 showed that three-quarters of respondents opposed a ban.

Jillian van Turnhout was an Irish senator and is now a children's rights advocate. She was responsible for the implementation of a smacking ban in Ireland and in 2017 spoke at Holyrood on Scotland's proposed legislation. Interestingly she told *Holyrood* magazine that there was not the same level of opposition to a ban in Ireland than there was at that time in Scotland. 'In Ireland, we didn't have a concentrated campaign in opposition, though we had some individuals who spoke out against it,' she reported. The Catholic Church in Ireland decided not to campaign and remained silent. So why did so many Scots still support the idea of hitting children?

Van Turnhout also said that in Ireland even those individuals who hadn't been in favour of a ban supported it within a few years. I am sure that there are still some Scots who are opposed to the legislation but I think most now support the ban and find it difficult to justify hitting children. It's worth noting that Jersey and Wales have both voted for similar legislation but in 2023 smacking is still legal in Northern Ireland and England.

It would be good if I could finish this chapter on this upbeat note about Scotland. But to do so would be a disservice not just to the memory of Kenneth Roy but also to the countless children who were abused in Scotland – not in homes or schools but while in the care of the state or living in a wide variety of residential settings.

Child abuse in institutions

In May 2019 I wrote another article for *Scottish Review*, this time called 'Scotland has treated its children badly'. I was motivated to write this for three main reasons. First, Kenneth Roy died after a short illness in November 2017 aged only 73. I thought it a great pity that we had lost his distinctive voice in support of Scottish children's right to be treated humanely. I also thought it appropriate to celebrate his contribution in an article in *Scottish Review*.[1] Finally

1. The last edition of Scottish Review was published on 1st November 2023.

I wanted to draw attention to our loss, particularly when there were two current issues which warranted attention – the Scottish and English child abuse inquiries and the campaign against the proposed smacking legislation which I've outlined above.

In 2019 I had understood for a while that there were Independent Inquiries into child abuse running in both Scotland and England. What I hadn't fully appreciated was the difference. The English Inquiry was appointed in 2014 by Theresa May when she was Home Secretary and had been prompted by the Jimmy Saville sexual abuse scandal. Its remit was to look at how English and Welsh institutions carried out their 'duty of care' to protect children from sexual abuse in any setting. The Scottish Inquiry was appointed in 2015 to look at all forms of maltreatment of children but only in residential settings such as care homes, List-D schools, school hostels, foster care, religious institutions, and residential, including fee-paying, schools.

The broader remit of the Scottish Inquiry is not surprising: until recent times Scotland had an abusive, authoritarian culture which was so ingrained that native Scots thought it unremarkable. Given that Scottish education normalised the punitive treatment of children, and that so many Scottish parents not only accepted this but also hit their own children, it was hardly surprising that many youngsters in Scotland's institutional care were treated abysmally.

Kenneth Roy highlights some of this abuse in his two historical accounts of Scotland from 1945-1999. For example, guidance for teachers on use of the belt specified that it could only be used on hands. Not so in approved schools mainly for 'delinquents' where teachers could apply the stout Lochgelly tawse to the buttocks. Scottish Education Department documents from the 1970s, published under the 30-year rule, show that corporal punishment was used ten times more often in Scotland's approved schools than their English equivalents.

That is one shameful fact amongst many that Kenneth features. For example, in 1958 dozens of teenage girls 'incarcerated' in the Lochburn House and Laundry in Glasgow's Maryhill managed to escape. The home's original name was the 'Magdalene Institution for the Repression of Vice and Reformation of Penitent Females'.

The Magdalene laundries in Ireland, whose brutality we know about thanks to film maker Peter Mullan, were under the control of the Catholic religious orders. Lochburn was non-denominational but had close contact with the Church of Scotland and was partly funded by public subscription. None of the 1958 escapees had been convicted of wrong-doing yet they were hunted down and treated as if they posed a public danger. It soon emerged that the girls were regularly beaten and drenched with cold water and their letters censored.

The Scottish Home Department investigated. The laundry closed at the end of the year. But there was no official public inquiry and the department never published its findings. No one was ever held accountable for the maltreatment. What I find particularly chilling is that, after studying contemporary newspaper reports, Roy states 'in the Glasgow of 1958 there was no public sympathy for the victims of Lochburn.'

In 1962 another maltreatment case emerged. The South Inch detention Centre in Perth, which dealt with young offenders from 17 to 21 had such a draconian regime that there were seven serious incidents of attempted suicide by inmates. According to Roy these lads 'would rather have cut their wrists and bled to death than submit to the brutality.' A private inquiry was held but, as with Lochburn, the report was never published. No action was taken against the prison officers involved.

In the 1990s some of those who had been in care in Scotland began to meet up, support one another and speak publicly about what they had endured. It was only at this point that the scale of the suffering and abuse of so many children became evident and pressure mounted for an inquiry. As Kenneth Roy mainly confined his historical accounts of post-war Scotland to what was reported in the newspapers of the day it's understandable that he wasn't able to mention this hidden institutional child abuse in *The Invisible Spirit* and *The Broken Journey*. It certainly wouldn't have surprised him. His strong sense of just how punitive Scotland could be to the vulnerable meant that he couldn't resist making some barbed comments about his native land. '. . . if Hell was the ultimate sanction in authoritarian Scotland, there was never a shortage of shorter-term earthly alternatives,' he writes. Reporting on a 1976

Glasgow Citizens play on the Marquis of Sade, which some Scottish critics thought didn't feature much sadism, Roy quips: 'In Scotland, however, there was no need for sadism on the stage when there was so much of it in real life.'

In October 2018 Scotland's Child Abuse Inquiry published its first set of findings relating to two residential homes run by the Daughters of Charity of St Vincent de Paul. It found that the children did suffer abuse. Lady Smith, Chair of the Scottish Child Abuse Inquiry, said: 'For many children who were in Smyllum and Bellevue, the homes were places of fear, coercive control, threat, excessive discipline and emotional, physical and sexual abuse, where they found no love, no compassion, no dignity and no comfort.'

Lady Smith also reported that some of the children were beaten every day with a variety of implements, including the Lochgelly tawse, regularly used in schools. This first report is an indictment of Catholic religious orders, and much of the abuse was carried out by nuns, but there have been allegations of abuse in homes run by the Church of Scotland and medical institutions. When I wrote my article the Inquiry was investigating allegations of child abuse in over 80 individual establishments. At the end of 2023 they had announced 112 investigations and completed 11 case studies. In November 2023 they released details of shocking abuse which took place at Loretto's – one of Scotland's leading boarding schools. This was soon followed by evidence of sexual, physical and psychological abuse of pupils at Edinburgh Academy between 1968 and 1992. One of the victims included the broadcaster Nicky Campbell. In December 2023 police arrested and charged five men in connection with these crimes.

Personal reflections

By the time the Scottish Child Abuse Inquiry published its first findings Kenneth Roy was seriously ill and no longer writing weekly columns. Sadly, we shall never hear his distinctive voice on the topic. But it's telling that when he knew his death was imminent he chose 'the girls on the bridge' to represent his journalism. This was the tragic story of two teenage girls in care in the Good

Shepherd Centre in Bishopton who jumped to their deaths from the Erskine Bridge in 2009. Kenneth personally undertook an in-depth inquiry and paints a bleak picture of professional incompetence and indifference. He disagrees with the Fatal Accident Inquiry report as he concludes that their deaths were 'preventable'.

Kenneth died in November 2018 and while in hospital in the last stages of his illness he wrote *In Case of Any News* (2019). As Sally Magnusson says in her foreword, the book reads like 'a love letter to the doctors and nurses of the NHS' who cared for him in his final weeks. I was so glad to learn that he died feeling surrounded by 'overwhelming love'. As well as charting his final days he wanted to use his writing 'to achieve some internal resolution of the past'. He specifically sought an answer to a very personal question that had troubled him throughout life. 'How was a clever boy of 12 consistently second in his class throughout his primary education, so disastrously unable to cope with secondary school? How did he end up leaving at the age of 15 with no qualifications?'

In the book Kenneth tells us that his 'waster' of a father was a drinker who spent his money in the pub and short-changed his wife, creating intense stress for the family. His father also put pressure on his son to 'Be Somebody'. But it's not his homelife that he thinks responsible for his academic failure. This he pins squarely on his school. As Kenneth was a very intelligent child, he was placed in the A stream of his local high school and could have expected 'a glittering five years, followed by a place at Glasgow University to study English.'

Instead he couldn't cope with the school's 'institutional brutality', and truanted every day, behind his parents back, for months on end. He never recovered from all this lost education.

Kenneth particularly feared one teacher (Mrs Smith) who would belt all the boys in the class, on the tips of their fingers, for academic mistakes. 'This was not mathematics', he writes. 'This was the theatre of cruelty.' He confesses that nothing ever happened in his life that made him as 'miserable' as he was at that high school. He also tells us that the maths teacher 'continued to haunt me. She would appear as a monstrous figure in nightmares. . . Even as I prepare to die she is the one human being I cannot find it in my heart to forgive.'

Despite facing up to the terrible impact high school had on his life he knows that these memories do not help him explain why he did so badly academically:

> . . . how come I couldn't hack it when everybody else could? What was so special – so uniquely sensitive – about me that I couldn't put up with Smith for a few hours a week, take the sting of her tawse, and the bite of her tongue, and then forget about her? How did this malevolent woman get under my skin that she altered the course of my life, making me an altogether darker personality? I go on searching, but I receive no answer. Except that the problem was not Smith. It was essentially me.

Maybe it was simply because he was a sensitive child with an overdeveloped sense of unfairness (thanks to the antics of his drunken father) that meant he couldn't cope with the terror deliberately inflicted by his teacher. Perhaps this, coupled with the injunction to 'Be Somebody', led to unbearable stress. Was it so much easier for the young teenager to opt out than struggle to succeed?

Towards the end of the book Kenneth asks what had made him 'so driven a personality'? When I read this I understood why I had felt not just empathy for Kenneth but resonance. As this book testifies, I am a *driven* woman. I too desperately wanted to understand the person I have become – not out of narcissism but because I often didn't like myself and wanted to understand my inner imperatives. In this respect I agreed wholeheartedly with the famous Socrates quote: 'The unexamined life is not worth living.' For me this quest involved years of leading workshops on assertiveness and on personality type and writing *The Scots' Crisis of Confidence*. As I've always considered my background as fairly ordinary I also thought that lots of people shared my childhood experiences. And this fuelled my desire to use my insights to help others and not just myself.

Much has changed in Scottish education and households since

those dark, punitive times. Schools are radically different from the ones that my generation attended. But as a people we have never collectively faced up to the cruel way Scotland raised its children. This failure to acknowledge the wrongs of the past is one reason why I argue in Chapter 17 that in raising or educating children many Scots have gone from one extreme to another: removing some healthy challenge in youngsters' lives, being overly protective and unwittingly undermining their resilience.

I certainly don't want Scots to wallow in victimhood but it's cathartic to acknowledge what has happened to you in the past, to confront or at least honour buried feelings and only then to move on with greater insight and empathy for both yourself and others.

Chapter 22

The *zeitgeist* – trauma and abuse

My own journey from confidence to trauma and abuse;
how this was shaped by the *zeitgeist*;
the idea of concept creep;
the rise of interest in trauma in the US and internationally;
defining trauma and Post Traumatic Stress Disorder (PTSD);
widening definitions of abuse;
reasons for this cultural shift;
the rise of victimhood and 'safetyism'
and why trigger warnings don't make sense;
how all this leads to division and extremist politics;
what concept creep and victimhood mean for this book.

AS I WROTE the last two chapters six words echoed in my head: *from confidence to trauma and abuse*. In this book that's the trajectory of my thinking: from my concern about a lack of confidence in Scottish life when the Centre started in 2004 to a more recent concern about the adversities and abuse Scottish children have suffered.

It would be easy to pass off the evolution of our ideas as my own personal journey. When I wrote *The Scots' Crisis of Confidence* I was a personal development trainer and there was a considerable emphasis throughout society on believing in ourselves and becoming all we can be. There's little doubt that such interests and passions travelled to these shores from the USA and its highly influential self-esteem movement. But this type of personal development was also an offshoot of the women's movement and I had been involved in that. In the early 1990s I trained as a Redwood assertiveness trainer. This approach had been inspired by American psychologist Anne Dickson's book *A woman in your own right: Assertiveness and you* (1983).

As I explain in Chapter 20, I had a miserable childhood. I tried to keep the lid on my emotions about this but, a decade ago following the deaths of both of my parents, that lid blew off. I then became much more intimate with the literature on the physical and mental health impacts of childhood adversities. So, from pondering abuse in my own life, it was a hop, skip and a jump to writing about the preponderance of adverse childhood experiences (ACEs) in Scottish culture, the atrocious use of physical punishment in Scottish schools, and the type of cruelty to children later revealed by the Scottish Childhood Abuse Inquiry.

But my personal journey is not a sufficient explanation for the arc from confidence to abuse and trauma. My work on confidence at the beginning of the 1990s and the early years of the new millennium reflected the *zeitgeist*. But by definition the mood and spirit of the times continually change and a few decades on they're now in sync with my own current interests. However, this is hardly surprising as new ideas create new labels and these then affect how individuals see themselves and interpret their lives. When individuals embody the label devised by professionals this then encourages more research or extensions of the term. A Canadian philosopher, Ian Hacking, was the first to describe this phenomenon and called it 'looping effects'.

Another relevant term is 'concept creep' first outlined by Professor Nick Haslam in 2016. In his landmark paper, 'Concept Creep: Psychology's expanding concepts of harm and pathology' he outlines his argument:

> Many of psychology's concepts have undergone semantic shifts in recent years. These conceptual changes follow a consistent trend. Concepts that refer to the negative aspects of human

> experience and behavior have expanded their meanings so that they now encompass a much broader range of phenomena than before. This expansion takes 'horizontal' and 'vertical' forms: concepts extend outward to capture qualitatively new phenomena and downward to capture quantitatively less extreme phenomena.

Haslam then focuses on six psychological concepts: abuse, bullying, trauma, mental disorder, addiction and prejudice. Two are particularly relevant here – abuse and trauma. The word trauma is now having a huge impact on society, particularly in America, and it's now part of the *zeitgeist*. So, in this chapter I look at how the word has evolved and the impact this is having on our culture, even in Scotland.

Trauma

'The national trauma complex', a riff on the much-loved, left-wing phrase 'the military-industrial complex', is how some commentators describe the overwhelming interest in trauma in America. Some call it the 'word of the decade' though its popularity can be traced back to at least 2001 and the 9/11 terror attacks.

In most articles on the popularity of the word, Bessel van der Kolk's book *The Body Keeps the Score: Brain, mind and body in the healing of trauma* (2014) is usually presented as the epitome of how trauma has established itself in popular consciousness. It's a dense, academic book written by a psychiatrist on his research and treatment of patients suffering from Post Traumatic Stress Disorder (PTSD) yet it made a splash on publication and from 2018 on began to climb the *New York Times* bestsellers list. It remained on the list for almost five years (c 245 weeks) and for 27 of these weeks was No.1.

Some trauma experts think the book's popularity is simply because trauma is so common. Others attribute it to the pandemic but van der Kolk himself disagrees. He takes this view not only because the book's rise predates Covid-19 but also because he thinks the pandemic was challenging but not traumatic. Yes, there was an increase in anxiety and depression as a result of the pandemic but these are not necessarily indicative of trauma. Indeed van der Kolk set out an alternative explanation for the spectacular success of his book in America in an interview in August 2023. He thinks that people's interest in trauma was piqued by Trump's election as President in 2016. Trump 'is so clearly an abusive man and he must remind a lot of people about the lying and manipulation and bullying of their own parents,' he told the interviewer. Perhaps of even more importance is how Trump was received by some politicians and press commentators and by many Republican voters:

> What traumatized people suffer from is that people don't believe them or people minimize it or say, 'it didn't really happen'. People go through terrible things and the world around them says, 'just get over it, keep moving, it doesn't matter'. Trump's supporters. . . are known for either downplaying or condoning his behavior, which could remind trauma survivors of their own stories of being ignored.

So let's be clear, van der Kolk is not saying Trump's election was traumatising, simply that it stimulated memories many people had of being badly treated by parents and their ardent desire for them to answer for their bad behaviour.

The interest in trauma is at its most intense in the US – 'the country's favourite diagnosis', according to some. But there's interest in trauma worldwide as is evidenced by *The Body Keeps the Score*'s translation into 43 different languages. It's very easy to detect concept creep: the word is no longer used to refer to experiences which psychiatrists originally considered to be traumatic but to anything that people find distressing or even mildly challenging. Hence people, even in the UK, will say 'I had a traumatic morning as I was stuck in traffic and late for work'. Young people are very keen on the word, maintaining that hearing or reading ideas on racism or slavery, for example, is traumatic. Indeed, cancel culture is fuelled by the sense that ideas can 'trigger' traumatic experiences. No wonder many critics now argue that trauma has been 'weaponised'.

Van der Kolk does not think that he can be held responsible

for how people now use the term trauma but is concerned. One of his collaborators, Janina Fisher, argues that if we keep using the word so much 'we will dilute the term trauma so that it no longer has meaning.' Inevitably this will downgrade the experiences of those who have been most affected by trauma.

Defining trauma

Given the predominance of ideas about trauma, it's worth looking briefly at its original definition and how this has evolved.

The ancient Greeks used the word trauma to describe a physical wound and doctors still use it in this way. The main psychiatric use of the word traumatic occurred in the USA in the 1970s when so many soldiers who had served in Vietnam were returning with obvious psychiatric problems. One of their main symptoms was recurrent intrusive memories of their combat experiences such as nightmares and flashbacks. When an individual experiences severe trauma their symptoms can last and they can barely function in everyday life unless they receive help. Soldiers from previous wars experienced such symptoms and were diagnosed with 'shell shock' and sometimes denounced as malingerers or cowards. However new tests, such as brain imaging which can measure damage to the brain and body resulting from extreme stress, allowed a new definition to emerge.

Post traumatic stress disorder (PTSD) was the new diagnosis and it was listed in 1980 in the *Diagnostic and Statistical Manual (DSM)-111*. There was now an official recognition of the harm caused not just by combat experiences but also other extreme life-threatening, out of the ordinary events such as a severe car crash or rape. But within a few years new versions of *DSM-111* stated that learning about the severe threat to the lives of close relatives could also give rise to PTSD as could 'indirect exposure' such as witnessing life threatening events happening to others. *DSM-IV* then included 'developmentally inappropriate sexual experiences' thus removing the acceptance that a trauma must involve a threat of serious injury or death. So psychiatrists themselves widened their use of the word trauma and trauma researchers started to include childbirth, infidelity, marital breakdown and sexual harassment as potentially traumatic experiences. Haslam summarises how much the concept changed from the original conception of PTSD:

> A traumatic event need not be a discrete event, need not involve serious threats to life or limb, need not be outside normal experience, need not be likely to create marked distress in almost everyone, and need not even produce marked distress in the traumatized person, who must merely experience it as 'harmful'. Under this definition the concept of trauma is rendered much broader and more subjective than it was even three decades ago.

Meanwhile the public was finding the term 'trauma' useful. Indeed, by the 1990s the term trauma was being used widely in the USA partly as a response to the civil rights movement and the fight against racial injustice. The women's movement also took the word trauma to heart as it helped describe the harm wreaked on women by domestic and sexual violence as well as the lasting damage of child sexual abuse. According to Lexi Pandell, this growing popularity meant that 'terms such as "cultural trauma", "collective trauma", "historical trauma", and "intergenerational trauma" were on the rise, particularly in connection to genocide, enslavement and war.'

In 2005 van der Kolk devised the term 'developmental trauma disorders' and argued this applied to children and adolescents. He asserts that repeated and prolonged abuse and trauma in childhood profoundly alters 'the mind and the brain'. This then sets in train subsequent problems with stress and leads to a host of physical and mental health problems, criminal acts, addictions and other social issues.

Michael Scheeringa, author of *The Trouble with Trauma* (2022), is a trenchant critic of the current conceptualisations of trauma, particularly van der Kolk's pronouncements on children and the term 'complex PTSD' which is extensively used by researchers and practitioners. He has considerable experience of the topic as he was a practising psychiatrist and researcher into children and adolescents with PTSD.[1] He asserts that van der Kolk and other trauma researchers simply don't have the evidence that traumatic events permanently 'change neurobiology'; that their claims don't meet the rigorous demands of proper scientific research. He acknowledges that the brain scans of people who have suffered traumatic events show abnormalities but argues that these may not have been caused by the event. Individuals could have been born with these abnormalities and this on its own could explain the disorder or at least some of the symptoms. Only longitudinal studies showing individuals' brains, pre and post the traumatic incident, could show definitively the lasting neurobiological effects of trauma. Scheeringa claims such studies either don't exist or don't unequivocally support the claim. It's certainly true that van der Kolk argues that 'borderline personality disorder', for example, results from trauma when researchers have shown that in some cases the condition is genetic in origin. Indeed, the British psychologist and writer Lucy Foulkes asserts in her insightful and compassionate book *Losing our Minds* (2021) 'all psychiatric disorders are genetic to some extent'. That's why individuals respond in very different ways to traumatic events.

Abuse

It isn't difficult to see how attitudes to children have changed markedly over time. In the UK in the nineteenth century children worked in factories and on farms and six-year-olds were even used to sweep chimneys, a practice outlawed in 1875. Until recently it was also routine for adults to hit children. Even nowadays adults often shout or talk to children in ways that would be denounced if they were speaking to their peers.

In the past adults were able to treat children badly as they were

1. The term, 'complex PTSD' was devised by Judith Herman who argued that clinicians needed a new term to apply to victims who suffered from prolonged and repeated trauma such as chronic sexual abuse. She claimed that those suffering from this disorder had a much wider range of symptoms. This term has still not been listed in any version of the DSM in the US as the authors argue it overlaps with other disorders. But it has been accepted by World Health Organisation member states, including the UK.

generally seen as an inferior class of being with few rights. Various professional groups and children's rights activists have helped bring about legislative and cultural change and Scotland has even incorporated the United Nations Convention on the Rights of the Child (UNCRC). Some of this has come about as a result of a growing understanding of the damage adults can unwittingly inflict on children.

In his concept creep paper Haslam points out that classic psychologists recognised two forms of abuse, 'physical and sexual'. The first involved deliberate bodily harm while the second involved 'inappropriate sexual contact'. Research showed that both types of abuse led to relationship difficulties, poor adult health and various psychopathologies. In the 1990s the term was widened to include 'emotional abuse' which includes 'verbal aggression and other behaviour that is domineering, intimidating, threatening, degrading, possessive, inconsistent or emotionally unresponsive.' At first this was mainly used to describe negative domestic relationships but was then extended to encompass adults' behaviour toward children. Then neglect was classified as a form of abuse and was no longer a separate category of maltreatment. Haslam argues that these new ways of using the word abuse allow an element of subjectivity. Unlike a physical wound which can be seen, an emotional wound is experienced by the individual and may even be unnoticed by an observer. The term also now covers acts not carried out (looking after) and not simply to what has been done to the child.

A culture shift

Haslam states that more extensive use of terms like abuse and trauma do not appear to result from psychological ideas in general gaining more prominence in society. Instead he thinks concept creep is due to a 'broader cultural shift'. So just as my interest in trauma is part of the *zeitgeist,* so is my frequent use of the word abuse. But what has caused this shift? Haslam is partially persuaded by Professor Steven Pinker's argument in *The Better Angels of our Nature* (2011) that movements for the rights of women and minorities can be seen as a 'civilising offensive targeting forms of aggression and inequity that had previously been accepted'. These campaigns have been 'propelled' by what Pinker calls 'an increasing sensitivity to new forms of harm'.

Should we be concerned about these developments? Haslam weighs up whether the concept creep of the six terms he studies are beneficial to society at large:

> Those drawn to a pessimistic assessment of these changes might argue that the expanding meaning of concepts such as abuse, bullying, and mental disorder is creating a culture of weakness, fragility, and excuse-making, in which everyone is a victim and no one is responsible for their predicament. Those drawn to a more optimistic assessment might applaud the growing sensitivity to suffering and maltreatment. A balanced evaluation of concept creep would be more ambivalent, falling somewhere between conservative reaction and liberal celebration.

Surely, it's good that, as a society, we're more aware of the harm being done to individuals and groups and want to take action to eliminate this whenever possible? However, it's easy to see how an emphasis on trauma, abuse and mental disorders could have a major effect on people's sense of self, thus leading individuals, or whole groups, to typecast themselves as 'victims', devoid of agency.

This is no idle speculation as it's already happening and it's outlined in Bradley Campbell and Jason Manning's book *The Rise of Victimhood Culture* (2018). The two sociologists examine the dominant morality upheld by students in American universities and show that it's 'victimhood, a kind of moral status based on suffering and neediness'. They also claim that 'if victimhood is a virtue, privilege is a vice'. It's not possible to read this book and think that this culture only affects American institutions as the authors cite examples from the UK, including Edinburgh University. What I'm about to describe is now commonplace in corporations, public sector organisations and charities for, as students have moved into jobs, they have taken their ideas with them.

One of the main features of victimhood culture is 'low tolerance for slight'. Hence the current emphasis on tackling 'micro-aggressions' and punishing the often-unwitting perpetrators. Contemporary young people also have a low tolerance for anything which may lead to discomfort, such as hearing views contrary to their own. They often now demand that authorities 'implement trigger warnings that protect people from coming into contact with words, images, or ideas that might cause them distress'. In short, they are intent on protecting themselves from harm – harm that previous generations would simply have ignored. Indeed older people often used the adage 'sticks and stones may break my bones but words can never hurt me' to minimise the importance of interpersonal conflict.

Another book on this theme is *The Coddling of the American Mind: How good intentions and bad ideas are setting up a generation for failure* (2018) by Greg Lukianoff, a free speech campaigner, and Jonathan Haidt, one of America's most distinguished psychologists. This book tackles in a much more sophisticated and in-depth way the types of concerns I've expressed in various chapters about the erosion of young people's resilience. My concern was initially triggered by the reading I did back in 2005 on how attempts to artificially boost young people's self-esteem in the US was leading to an unhealthy obsession with protecting them from any bad feelings; how this was happening here too and particularly underscored what the Social and Emotional Aspects of Learning (SEAL) programme in England was attempting to achieve.

Lukianoff and Haidt's primary focus is how young people are now raised in a culture of 'safetyism'. When it comes to physical safety this has generally been a good thing and has saved lives. (Just think about how children used to travel in cars before seat belt legislation.) But the authors argue that concern for children's safety has led to the curtailment of free play and has prevented them from opportunities to 'dose themselves with risk' and has important consequences for their development. 'Children like other mammals, need free play in order to finish the intricate wiring process of neural development,' they argue. This means that those who are deprived of free play will be 'less competent' both physically and socially as adults. 'They are less likely to be tolerant of risk, and more prone to anxiety disorders'.[2] This then makes them both a product of safetyism and its future advocates.

The authors argue that safety is another word that has been subject to concept creep as it has now been expanded to mean '*emotional* safety' – making sure that people's feelings aren't hurt and they don't feel discomfort. This is why, throughout American campuses, words are seen as 'sources of danger' and that there are constant demands for trigger warnings and 'safe spaces'. But these, and the thinking underpinning safetyism, are 'based on a fundamental misunderstanding of human nature and the dynamics of trauma and recovery'.

Lukianoff and Haidt point out that human beings are not fragile like china teacups and echo the thinking of the famous Lebanese statistician and polymath, Nassim Nicholas Taleb, who argues that humans are 'antifragile'. Whereas the word resilience suggests that human beings can withstand shocks, antifragile means that we '*require* stressors and challenges in order to learn, adapt and grow'. This is true of our immune system, our muscles and bones and the way our brains work. Hence the authors' use of Nietzsche's famous line, 'what doesn't kill you makes you stronger'. So overprotective parents may think they're helping their children but they're actually undermining their healthy development and setting them up for anxiety and victimhood. The same applies to what university administrators are doing to students when they accede to their demands for emotional safety. Indeed, in the process they are changing the role of higher education: we never used to see universities' role as making students feel comfortable. We thought they were about making students think.

There's a further tragic irony in the use of trigger warnings. The authors write: 'Avoiding triggers is a *symptom* of PTSD, not a treatment for it.' In support they quote a distinguished clinical psychologist who points out that 'Trigger warnings are counter-therapeutic because they encourage avoidance of reminders of trauma'. Students who are suffering from PTSD need to overcome

2. This is such a concern for Haidt that in March 2024 he published a new book called *The Anxious Generation* in which he emphasises once again the importance of free play to healthy development.

their trauma through therapies which involve 'gradual, systematic exposure to traumatic memories until their capacity to trigger distress diminishes.' Students who have not suffered from serious trauma will benefit from emotional discomfort and should not seek to avoid it.

But perhaps the most worrying aspect of the analysis presented in both *The Coddling of the American Mind* and *Victimhood Culture* is the threat these cultural trends pose to democracy. Micro-aggression complaints stoke tension and animosity and can make ethnic tension, and other divisions, worse. A culture of victimhood and safetyism fuels intolerance, threatens free speech and leads to censorship and cancellation. For the champions of this culture, discussion is not to be tolerated. In the UK this has been apparent in the row over trans rights. In the USA critical race theory, which has replaced the thinking behind the civil rights movement, is stoking a culture of victimhood and, in the name of safety for black people, racial segregation.

This type of culture divides the world simplistically into goodies and baddies. Victims are morally superior to the perpetrators – mainly straight white people, particularly white men, who epitomise privilege. But this is not how most working-class white men view their lives – so there's rising anger at such views, particularly when life is hard for most working-class people as is witnessed by the proliferation of food banks, a cost of living and housing crisis, a gig economy and steeply rising economic inequality. In America there are also barriers to basic health care.

Campbell and Manning argue that this vilification of white men is a particular issue for those who do not have a college education and they fear it may drive such men 'to greater support for those who champion the superiority of these groups'. This can result in misogyny, something that's rising in British schools. and boosts 'the alt right' with its ideas of white supremacy. This is why these sociologists predict that 'white identity politics' is likely to grow as 'victimhood culture expands' and will lead to extremist politics. It's interesting that one of Donald Trump's main electoral appeals is that he speaks his mind and doesn't care about political correctness.

Increasingly writers concerned about how tribalism is undermining democracy argue that part of the problem is identity politics: ideas that one group identity is qualitatively different from others. It's easy to see how this is eroding universalism – the notion of a common humanity – once the cornerstone of progressive ideas. Identity politics, where we are all marooned in our own groups and focused on our self-interest, prevents us as human beings from even trying to pull together, despite conflicts and difference, to improve society and our shared planet.

What concept creep and victimhood mean for this book

I did my research for *Hiding in Plain Sight* between 2015 and 2016 and was not aware of 'concept creep' and the way the word trauma was being used much more loosely even by psychiatrists. So I used the term generously in those pages though not as often as childhood adversities or abuse. But in the last few chapters I have refrained from using trauma wherever possible as I accept that it's now so overused that it's becoming meaningless and downgrading the experience and symptoms of those who have suffered from PTSD.[3]

When I now think about what happened to me as a child I believe that only one experience would, even in my own view, qualify as being truly traumatic and that's the violent sexual assault by my grandfather and his threat to murder me if I told anyone. I genuinely feared for my life. I'm sure that some of the health problems from which I subsequently suffered resulted from that attack and its impact. But I'm also aware that even before this event I was an anxious child.

Van der Kolk includes in his examples of traumatic experiences an adult hitting a child so hard that it left a mark. So, with his blessing, we could certainly use the word trauma when describing

3. I still stand by my teenaged neighbour Scott's use of the term traumatised and PTSD to describe the suffering of some of the fathers who lived in Milngavie's council estate after returning from active service in the Second World War. My mother worked in a bar and she would often recount how some of these men seemed to relive terrifying war memories when they got drunk.

many Scottish children's experience of punishment at school as belts commonly left red welts on the skin. On some occasions, or for some particularly sensitive pupils, being belted could have been traumatic but I don't believe this was generally the case: getting the belt was such a routine experience in Scottish schools that it was institutionalised, and children had no reason to feel that their lives were in danger. This could have been different in schools or institutions for young offenders where the regime was much more brutal. From what I've read about the way senior pupils behaved in private schools, and how younger pupils often feared for their lives in bizarre and brutal rituals, the word traumatic seems warranted in those cases.

However, while I'm mindful of the way the word trauma has suffered so much dilution and I'm now careful about using it, I defend my liberal use of the word abuse when discussing the ways that many Scottish children were traditionally brought up. And I'm making this defence for two main reasons. First, there's now extensive international research which shows the physical and mental damage that can be done to children who are raised by parents who are not just physically but also emotionally and verbally abusive. We now know that abuse of various kinds can lead to poor physical and mental ill health. Second, and more importantly, Scotland has serious health problems in comparison with other Western European countries and the reasons for this have never been pinned down. I simply want us to consider whether Scottish culture plays a part in the country's health problems, particularly our penchant for verbal abuse.

I realise that tackling the issue of various types of childhood abuse and adversity means walking a tightrope: that it would be all too easy for what I'm writing to encourage even more over-protective parenting and to fuel the obsession with safety, harm and victimhood that's already undermining young people's resilience and challenging their mental health.

I have now laid out what the Centre did in Phases 1 and 2 thus giving an overview of our activities from 2004-2024. In this chapter I've also provided a commentary on how the development in our thinking has mirrored changes in the zeitgeist over the past 20 years.

However, one important topic remains outstanding. The Centre was born as a result of the publication of my book *The Scots' Crisis of Confidence.* In other words, it evolved from my thinking on Scottish culture and its influence on Scots, individually and collectively. As the Centre has now undertaken a great deal of work in the past two decades has my thinking on Scotland changed? The answer is a resounding yes. Some of this new thinking has been clear in previous chapters but, for clarity, I want to say more. I also want to write about the 2014 Scottish independence referendum as it's the most important event to take place in Scotland during the period under review.

So, with all of this in mind, I've included a final part to this book called *Reflections on Scotland.* In it I outline my new thinking about Scotland in three fairly lengthy chapters. The first two build on what I've concluded on early years (Chapter 18), childhood adversities (Chapter 20) and physical punishment of children (Chapter 21). The first of the reflection chapters specifically looks at whether Scotland has suffered from a national trauma which would help to explain why Scottish children have been treated badly. I don't find this a convincing argument but, given the emphasis on trauma in Western culture, the notion of a Scottish national trauma is likely to grow in the coming years. The second chapter looks at the legacy of Scotland's Protestant Reformation. In it I argue that the country's religious past – specifically the Calvinist notion of human worthlessness and the ambitious attempt to build the New Jerusalem – have contributed enormously to what I term a 'Scottish mentality'. I then move on to the independence referendum, applying where relevant some of the material covered in the preceding two chapters, and specifically focus on the Scottish yearning for collective redemption.

Following these reflections I include a chapter called 'the final analysis'. Given the scope of the book I don't try to weave together the separate strands of activity outlined in Phases 1 & 2. Instead, I set out how the Centre's belief system evolved and assess its impact and potential legacy.

Part 3

Reflections on Scotland

CHAPTER 23

A national trauma?

Some positive features of contemporary Scotland;
turbulent times in the seventeenth century;
the Darien disaster;
the 1707 Union;
Scottish victimhood and exceptionalism;
colonisation and slavery;
the obsession with politics;
clearances and market capitalism;
the effect on the victims;
urbanisation, industrialisation and dislocation;
twentieth century restructuring.

IN 2017 WHEN readers of that travel classic, *The Rough Guide*, voted Scotland 'the most beautiful country in the world', the organisers simply asked, 'Who can deny that these wild beaches, deep lochs and craggy castles are some of the most wonderful and beautiful sights in the world?' Few indeed. As a proud, native Scot I also celebrate the charm and beauty of our cities and the sheer variety of our breathtaking landscape – the Hebrides, Sutherland, the Trossachs, the Borders. . .

When *Rough Guide* readers were asked to vote on the world's 'most welcoming country', Scotland topped the list for that too. Of course, it can be difficult to generalise, but the Scots are a hospitable people. We don't go in for stiff formalities, we often go out of our way for strangers and are noted for our humour.

This sociability runs deep within our culture – 'We're all Jock Tamson's bairns.' Enlightenment figures like Adam Smith and Adam Ferguson rejected the conception of people as isolated individuals and argued that we are fundamentally social beings. Indeed, Scotland's contribution to the Enlightenment was the foundation of *social* science. What's more, the Scots are a patriotic people with a strong sense of national identity and commitment to their country.

So, there are various aspects of Scottish life to admire and feel proud of. Unfortunately, as I have argued in the last two chapters, nurturing children is not one of them. I believe this is a problem Scots have encountered for centuries and that, by failing to provide the right emotional support for children, the country's overall health and well-being has been adversely affected.

When I have discussed this thesis with people, individually or at events, many immediately wanted to discuss 'why?' They were prepared to accept the idea, but they wanted to discuss and advance their own theories. The Union with England, the Highland Clearances and the Reformation/Calvinism are the three explanations people were most likely to advance as they saw these events as a source of national trauma.

In Chapter 11 on Glasgow and Chapter 20 on adverse childhood experiences I give various historical explanations, such as rapid industrialisation, poor housing and a developing alcohol culture, to show that Scottish living conditions created adverse environments for children. But, given people's strong desire to come up with explanations I hadn't explored, I thought it necessary to include a chapter in *Hiding in Plain Sight* which looked at whether it was plausible that such past events *caused* a Scotland-wide trauma which then created adverse environments for children. I set out, and update, these arguments in this and the following chapter. In this one I examine the Union with England, clearances and dislocation. In the following chapter I look at the Reformation and Calvinism.

Turbulent times before the Union

Before looking at the important topic of the Union of 1707 it's worth setting out some information about Scotland's challenges in the seventeenth century.

For centuries it was commonplace for Scottish historians to portray the country pre-union as backward and inward-looking and the Union with England as having a civilising effect. This is incorrect and it's right that this aspect of Scottish history has been revised. Thanks to the Reformation in 1560 and John Knox's insistence on Scots being able to read the Bible for themselves, and on having a 'school in every parish', Scotland was the most educated country in Europe. Scotland was not insular but an outward looking European country. It's also common for those arguing that Scotland was a dark, backward place to maintain that the nation's system of food production was medieval and improvement much needed. But evidence now shows that for most of the seventeenth century Scotland was able to feed its population.

That all changed in the period known as 'the seven ill years' of the 1690s. A combination of grain shortage, economic turbulence and weather changes led to widespread famine. Between 1694 and 1698 there were four years of cold weather which led to crop failures. This happened in France and elsewhere in Northern Europe but England did not suffer greatly. Scottish agriculture was devastated. It's estimated that about 15 per cent of Scotland's population (150,000 people) perished between 1695 and 1699. In the words of one contemporary commentator: 'Everyone may see Death in the face of the Poor that abound everywhere.'

Mass movement was also a consequence of the famines. Tenant farmers, no longer able to pay their rents, were evicted. Fletcher of Saltoun, one of the most vocal critics of union, argued that there was a large rise in 'vagabonds' and people 'begging from door to door'. During this period many emigrated to England, Ulster and America. It wasn't just the poor who suffered during this period of Scottish history. So did the better off. It's estimated that between 1660 and 1710 as many as one in four Scottish estates had to be sold because of bankruptcy.

Between 1689 and 1697 England's war with France had a negative effect on Scottish commerce. The Royal Navy rigorously implemented the Navigation Acts which prevented 'illicit' Scottish trade with England's American colonies. Since Scots believed that they needed plantations to source raw materials and colonies to access customers, the country's response was to set up its own trading colony. The chosen location was Darien, in the Isthmus of Panama. This was a national project and large sums of money were raised in Scotland to fund it. In 1695 the ships sailed off with great fanfare and optimism.

The whole Darien project was a humanitarian and financial disaster. It's estimated that around 2,000 Scots died and that the country lost a quarter of its liquid capital. Poor planning and reconnaissance were undoubtedly factors: the area to be colonised was a malarial swamp and many died of tropical diseases. It was also in the middle of territory claimed by Spain which was hostile to the Presbyterian Scots.

Ultimately, many Scots blamed England for exacerbating their problems as, fearing they might alienate Spain, the English refused to send help or provisions. Many Scots were particularly angry that their king – a king shared with England – betrayed his country by refusing to send them aid.

John McKendrick in his book *Darien: A journey in search of empire* (2007) argues: 'Darien had a profound psychological effect on Scotland. It robbed the country of confidence. It was a loss that would have been felt by everyone. Every Scot at the time would likely have known someone lost or known someone who lost money investing in the colony.'

The Union of 1707

In his comprehensive, ground-breaking book, *The Scots and the Union* (2014) Professor Christopher Whatley argues that there are lots of myths about the Union; one of the most enduring is the notion that Scots parliamentarians were 'bought and sold for English gold'. He presents historical evidence to show that few were bribed to accept the loss of the Scottish Parliament and that, in the 1690s, a time marked by 'extraordinary levels of anxiety and pessimism', most had strong reasons to willingly support an incorporating union. These were mainly due to the 'parlous condition' of the Scottish economy caused in part by the disastrous Darien scheme. He estimates that in 'late 1699 and early 1700, it looked as if at least half of the nation's financial resources had simply disappeared.' So famine, mounting debt, the potential collapse of municipal government and the Scots' limited opportunities for legal trade weighed heavily with Scottish parliamentarians and predisposed them to vote for Union. Religion also played a major part with many influential Scots supporting Union to ensure the Protestant succession, resist Jacobinism and stop an invasion by Catholic France or Spain.

But Whatley is also clear that those who wanted an incorporating union were in the minority. A sizeable number of Scots were undecided and many, perhaps even the majority, were strongly opposed. In fact, there was considerable unrest and even rioting in both Edinburgh and Glasgow and as talks took place 'the country [was] ablaze with disorder'. Whatley asserts that some saw union as 'a betrayal of Scotland's national interest' and that there was considerable antipathy towards the English.

Presbyterian ministers used the pulpit to agitate against union but many ministers changed their minds. As the Church at that time was the most powerful institution in the country, the Act of Union would not have happened without its approval. The Kirk was won round in part because Scottish negotiators extracted guarantees of its continued independence. Those negotiating the Union terms managed to ensure not just the continued independence of the Scottish Kirk but also the independence of the country's legal and education systems and local government. England paid money to the Scottish Parliament, including a sum to compensate investors who had lost money in Darien.

Nonetheless when union came about many Scots mourned the loss of national sovereignty and there was little celebration when the Act of Union received Royal Assent. The much-vaunted economic advantages did not materialise for decades and in 1713 parliamentarians, some of whom had been staunch supporters of union and were now sitting as Scottish MPs in Westminster, moved for a repeal of the act.

I had always thought that after 1707 life for most Scots continued very much as before but there were changes in everyday life which ordinary people disliked. Scotland now had new imperial weights and measures and much-resented customs and excise duties to pay in a country where tax collection pre-union had been chaotic. Smuggling and a black economy skyrocketed as did popular protests provoked by an increase in the malt tax. Whatley writes, 'The fact is that Scotland had become virtually ungovernable.'

There was also considerable friction between Scotland and England in the eighteenth century and not just over taxation. A mere five years after union, England legislated to give landowners the power to choose Church ministers, something that Scotland itself had abolished in 1690. Worse still, England's action appeared to be against the spirit of the 1707 Act of Union which guaranteed the Kirk's independence.

There's little doubt that the main casualties of the Protestant Union of Scotland and England were Highlanders. Following the 1715 and 1745 Jacobite uprisings, Highland culture itself was brutally undermined both by the English and Scottish Lowlanders. The vicious attack on the Gaelic language and Highland culture which ultimately ensued was very damaging for many Highlanders. Even those who fought for the King in the 1745 uprising were persecuted.

So if we put these events together – famines, Darien, loss of sovereignty and a brutal attack on Gaeldom – we can see that, as there was a considerable loss of life, money, national pride, confidence and optimism, this period could be categorised as a desperate time for the country. But can we construe the events in question as constituting a national trauma?

Victimhood and Scottish exceptionalism

In Scotland there's a strong sense of national victimhood: a prevailing sense that bad things have happened to the Scottish people that we have been powerless to stop. This means that we can blame these adverse events on other people – namely, the English. Indeed, it's commonplace for Scots to present their country as a victim of English imperialism. There's also a prevailing sense of Scottish exceptionalism; that our historical experiences have been different from what people in other countries have endured. This is what I was readily picking up when people were quick to claim that national trauma is the reason why Scotland has treated its children badly.

It's easy to read Whatley's book on the considerable resistance to the 1707 Union and the erosion of national sovereignty and feel aggrieved on Scotland's behalf. But what Scots endured, in comparison with what other European peoples have experienced, was less in scale. Our closest neighbours – Wales and Ireland – were invaded and colonised by the English.

Scottish historian, Dr John Young, has made a particular study of Scotland's involvement in Ulster and rejects the idea that Scots were a 'victim' of Empire. Indeed, when Scotland's King James VI became England's King James 1 in 1603, he expedited the colonisation of Ireland and encouraged Scots to migrate to Ulster to 'civilise' the Gaelic people whom he regarded as 'Barbarians'. By 1640 there were around 30,000 Protestant Scots in Ulster. Another 40,000 Scots emigrated there during the famines of the 1690s. This large-scale immigration of Scots meant that Belfast was a largely Scottish town. These Ulster Scots challenged a distinctive Irish culture and laid the foundations for Ireland's enduring political problems. These still persist today in Northern Ireland in the tension between Protestants and Catholics.

Professor Norman Davis' exceptional book *Vanished Kingdoms: The History of Half-forgotten Europe* (2012) helps us to remember all those states, such as Aragon, Burgundy and Prussia that once thrived but were ultimately taken over or swallowed up by aggressive neighbours or eliminated from the map in post-war treaties. Whatley points out there are several Baltic states which, like Scotland, 'boast ancient lineages' but unlike our country, they 'have also been incorporated through conquest, and endured oppression and repression in its most brutal, culturally constricting manifestation.'

Also, within living memory many European countries were exposed to events that appear much more traumatic than Scotland's largely peaceful route to union – the brutality of the Spanish Civil War, particularly what happened at Guernica, or the wars in Yugoslavia in the 1990s when ethnic conflicts led to the death of 140,000 people including terrible acts of genocide in Kosovo.

Or what about the military occupation of many Western European countries in World War II when France, Belgium, the Netherlands, Luxembourg, Denmark, Norway, Greece, Northern Italy and the Channel Islands were all occupied by Nazis? Many people in these occupied countries suffered not just psychological trauma resulting from a cruel, occupying army and intensive civilian bombardment, but also from the severe curtailment of food, if not starvation. Yet patterns of life expectancy and health statistics in all these countries suggest that they have not suffered from the long-term effects of historical trauma. So why would Scotland, particularly when the supposed traumatic events involve a minority of the population and are much further back in time?

Slavery and colonisation

If we look at what happened to peoples in countries outwith Europe the picture becomes more grim as we are now faced with the horrors of slavery and brutal colonisation. Scotland's leading, and nationalist, intellectual Tom Nairn was always contemptuous of the idea that Scotland was, or ever had been, an English colony.

Nonetheless, for decades, many Scottish nationalists liked to portray Scotland as a country that had been 'colonised' by the English. Many particularly warmed to the book *Internal colonialism* (1975) by Michael Hechter in which he expounds the idea of England as the domineering 'national core' and the periphery, the Celtic fringe, inferior and marginalised.

In 1989 Craig Beveridge and Ronald Turnbull published a highly influential book called *The Eclipse of Scottish Culture.* Drawing on Frantz Fanon's *The Wretched of the Earth* (1961), they argue it is 'inferiorism', the type of mindset third world peoples develop as a result of colonisation, which leads some commentators to disparage Scottish culture and represent it as deformed or pathological.

However, in recent years the idea that the Scots were active colonisers is receiving considerable academic attention. In his book, *The Scots in Australia 1788-1988* (2017), Dr Benjamin Wilkie tells us that his research 'uncovered harrowing accounts of children in Western Victoria being beaten to death and burned alive by Scottish farm labourers, their overseers poisoning entire families.' Wilkie, who describes himself as a 'historian of the Scottish diaspora', also refutes the idea that somehow Scots settlers were nicer to native people: 'Scots were not significantly more generous or benevolent than the norm for British or European settlers in their relations with indigenous peoples or in their attitudes towards the appropriation of their land.' He also adds, 'In Africa, Australasia and North America they were as complicit as other nationalities in their racial discrimination.'

This growing knowledge that Scots were some of the most active and enthusiastic participants in what has been described as 'the greatest single period of land theft, cultural pillage, and casual genocide in world history' weakens the Scots' claim to victimhood. Research into slavery has dented it further.

In 2023 Stephen Mullen and Ewan Gibbs published an academic article called 'Scotland, Atlantic slavery and the Scottish National Party: From colonised to coloniser in the political imagination'. As the title suggests their article charts the shift that has taken place in nationalist circles on attitudes to both slavery and colonisation. They explain that historians of Scotland have been slow to realise the importance of slavery to the country's economic and social development. But that changed with the publication of *Recovering Scotland's Slavery Past* (2015), edited by Professor Tom Devine. Mullen and Gibbs write:

> Whilst historians of Scotland were late to recognise the centrality of Atlantic slavery to the development of Scotland, this new

> orthodoxy represents the final refutation of Scotland as 'periphery'. Rather than an 'internal colony', Scotland's invitation to the core meant imperialism played a proportionately greater effect on national development compared with England, whose empire Scots infiltrated. In 40 years, the empirical evidence of Scots as colonisers has rendered the narrative of colonised Scotland obsolete in historiographical terms.

Mullen and Gibbs show that the Scottish National Party has moved considerably towards accepting, and apologising for, Scotland's role in slavery. However, they argue that 'nationalists also adopted a historical balancing act, often qualifying acknowledgment of the role of Scots as perpetrator by insisting on simultaneously presented narratives of victimhood.' And that victimhood is linked to the Highland Clearances.

Political obsessions

Before moving on to the second set of events Scots cite as a national trauma – the Highland Clearances – I want to make an observation. The Union with England may have been a rather mild affair in comparison with what happened to other countries with a larger neighbour, but there's little doubt that it left Scotland in a political situation which is unlike other nations. Professor Richard Finlay in his book *Scottish Nationalism* (2022) argues that the Union created a 'constitutional twilight zone': Scotland wasn't completely assimilated after 1707 but neither did it remain a completely independent state.

This anomalous position has led to two things. First, there have been recurrent Scottish fears of Anglicisation. Indeed, Scotland has a large library of books where the author asserts that, unless Scots wake up and take action to avert impending catastrophe, Scotland will die as a nation and Scottish identity will be lost. Second, our unconventional constitutional status has led to an obsession with politics, particularly constitutional politics. Over the centuries commentators on Scotland have come to see Scottish experience mainly through a political lens and to believe that positive change can only happen from politics. Such a belief ignores or downplays other factors which contribute to the quality of people's lives – though they do have political dimensions – such as personal relationships or childrearing. This is something to which I shall return at the end of the next chapter.

Clearances and the arrival of market capitalism in the eighteenth and nineteenth centuries

Until the mid-eighteenth century the vast majority of Scots throughout the country had some place on the land as tenants, subtenants or cottars. But within a hundred years that had changed. Scotland went through a period of intense agricultural 'improvement' which led to mass dispossession of land. Cottars who had made up a quarter to a third of rural parishes in the Lowlands ceased to exist.

Professor Tom Devine has published a comprehensive study of the topic – *The Scottish Clearances: A history of the dispossessed 1600-1900* (2018). Devine believes that in the Lowlands, 'The loss of landholding must have caused stress, pain and anxiety as a centuries old way of life came to an end in the eighteenth century.' But this story of clearances in the Scottish Lowlands is hardly known. Highland dispossession, a story we all know, tended to be later, more geographically varied and 'more convulsive'. Some Highlanders were brutally cleared.

The reasons for the Highland Clearances are complex but in Scotland, and internationally, most people only know a very simplified story. The first academic studies of Highland Clearance didn't appear until the middle of the twentieth century. This allowed popular accounts of these events, by writers such as John Prebble, to enter popular consciousness. Prebble begins his bestseller, *The Highland Clearances* (1963), by telling readers: 'This . . . is the story of how Highlanders were deserted and then betrayed. It concerns itself with how sheep were preferred to them, and how bayonet, truncheon and fire were used to drive them from the land.'

Prebble subsequently tells a classic story of good and evil, villains and victims where the baddies are mainly former chieftains of the clans who, in becoming commercial landowners, betrayed their people for profit. They're aided in their brutal enterprise by nasty estate managers and factors. This popular notion of the Highland Clearances has also been conveyed by various Scottish novelists and, of course, by the playwright John McGrath in his smash 1970s hit *The Cheviot, the Stag and the Black, Black Oil*.

From the 1970s on, the rise of nationalist thinking in Scotland and anti-Union sentiment means that Prebble's version has been bastardised: many now think it was the English that were clearing Highlanders, thus giving the story a sense of national victimhood. But as Neal Ascherson in *Stone Voices* (2003) explains, '. . . with few exceptions, the clearing landlords were not incomers from south of the border. They were traditional clan chiefs, Highland gentlemen or Lowland capitalists and speculators. . . Scots cleared other Scots'.

Devine argues that the dominant narrative in Scotland about the Highland Clearances focuses exclusively on 'human wickedness' but that this does not fit with the true historical causes. He lists these as:

> . . . the limitations of natural endowment in the Highlands; a marked increase in population on poor land with no long-term alternative for subsistence or employment for a people who had always lived close to the edge of subsistence in the old clan-based society; the destruction of infant Highland manufacturing by Lowland competition; bankruptcy of the traditional landed class; the overwhelming power of market capitalism; and the absence of any viable long-term alternative to pastoral husbandry.

Professor Eric Richards was one of the world's foremost scholars on migration and in his book *The Highland Clearances* (2016) he too provides evidence to show that much of what happened in the Highlands was partly the result of large increases in population (threefold in some areas between 1770 and 1850) and that the Clearances were an attempt to deal with some of the significant demographic and economic problems facing the Highlands. He shows that emigration from the Highlands pre-dated the Clearances and much emigration (post-1870) was not 'directly associated' with Clearances. Indeed, he writes, 'People would have left the Highlands in any case.'

As to the notorious forced Clearances he maintains that there were cruel, uncaring landlords but some had to act or face economic ruin. Indeed, some landlords who didn't evict tenants became bankrupt and it was ultimately the receivers who removed their crofters. To substantiate his claim that landlords were not all as bad as they are portrayed, he points out that while the Highlands were particularly susceptible to famine, the actions of many Highland landowners meant that the potato famines of the mid-nineteenth centuries killed very few Highlanders. This is in stark contrast to the political conditions in Ireland where millions either lost their lives or emigrated.

Earlier we learned that Devine does not believe that the Highland Clearances were caused by landowners' wickedness, but this does not mean that he thinks them all innocent of wrongdoing. He argues that many Highland lairds proved to be incapable of 'living within their means' and wanted to ape the lavish spending they witnessed in the south of England. And this splurging on fancy houses and expensive consumer goods was, in some cases, akin to 'financial suicide'. Moreover, some Highland landlords made shortsighted decisions on restructuring their land and others made poor economic decisions which undermined their estates and led ultimately to enforced clearance.

There's little doubt that some countries managed rural depopulation better than we did in both Lowland and Highland Scotland. Indeed, what happened in Scotland in the eighteenth and nineteenth centuries was in contrast to Denmark, for example, where the Danish Government ensured that whole-scale rural transformation was planned and more humane. The speed with which landowners could force tenants off the land in Scotland was possible because of the powers the old Scottish Parliament gave to landowners – the most extensive landowner powers in Europe.

Impact on the victims of Clearances

The complexity of the causes for the Highland Clearances does not mean that the impact on Highlanders was slight. Indeed, Richards believes that 'emigration was a trauma for the departing people' even when they left voluntarily, adding 'in times of famine and clearance it became a nightmare.' He regularly uses the words trauma, traumatic and shock to describe Highlanders' experiences during this period of abrupt change. Devine argues that 'social transformation in Gaeldom was more traumatic and cataclysmic than anywhere else in Scotland' and regularly uses the word trauma when describing what happened in the Highlands.

Dr Joni Buchanan's celebratory, but often poignant, book *Women of the Hebrides* (2024) recounts some of the terrible things that happened to families as townships were 'swept' to make way for the 'big holdings': roofs taken off houses, looms destroyed, cattle taken and occupants evicted even if the woman was in the midst of childbirth. One witness recalled, 'I have seen the women putting their children into the carts . . . while their husbands lay bound in the pen and were weeping beside them without power to give them a helping hand, though the women themselves were crying aloud and their children wailing like to break their hearts.'

One of the things I've found shocking when reading about the Highland Clearances is the attitude of Lowlanders who commonly believed that as Anglo-Saxons they were not just racially different to the Celts but racially superior. 'Latent racism' came to the fore in the period of famine in the 1840s as this had led to considerable charity support from Lowland churches and other organisations. But, as Devine points out, the *Glasgow Herald* and the *Scotsman* were now full of worry about how 'industrious' Lowlanders were supporting 'indolent' Highlanders. There was much written about 'Celtic laziness'. A 'destitution test' and accompanying bureaucracy was introduced to ensure that Highlanders could only receive food in exchange for hard labour.

Devine tells us that part of the problem was that Highlanders' work patterns were shaped by 'seasonal rhythms of a pastoral economy' and the climatic challenges of the area. But this clashed with:

> . . . the Victorian belief in the moral and material value of regular and disciplined toil. Also offensive to this mentality was the traditionalist expectation of the Celt that his social superiors had the responsibility to offer social support in times of need. It was a conflict of two world views but in which only those who were committed to the virtues of self-help, independence and initiative had the monopoly of power and authority. For, unlike the pattern of Lowland rural society, where rulers and ruled shared broadly similar sets of social and cultural expectations, the Highland experience seems more akin to one of colonial dominion imposed on the region by outside forces.

When you put these experiences of dispossession and clearance alongside the official government attack on clan culture after the 1745 rebellion it's easy to conclude that Highlanders suffered from colonisation. This is what Dr Iain McKinnon argues in his 2017 article 'Colonialism and the Highland Clearances' and what many nationalists believe. But Devine rejects this interpretation, writing: 'The Gaels were not being dominated by a foreign power.' It was the English government, Lowland Scots, and indigenous landlords who, in their enthusiasm for market capitalism, destroyed the traditional way of life for so many Highlanders, though forces such as population growth and famine also played a part.

In 1851 the *Scotsman* newspaper supported the idea that enforced expulsion was the solution to the problems posed by the Celts, asserting: 'Collective emigration is, therefore, the removal of a diseased and damaged part of our population. It is a relief to the rest of the population to be rid of this part.'

But sympathy for the Highlanders started to grow in the nineteenth century with the rise of romanticism. This favourable view accelerated in the 1880s throughout the UK as crofting rebellions generated widespread publicity for their cause and various organisations campaigned for their protection. The Westminster Government appointed a Royal Commission and this was followed by the Crofters Act of 1886 which outlawed old-style clearances. It also guaranteed that some Highlanders managed to hold onto a piece of land, something that Lowlanders had not achieved. Antipathy to Highlanders also melted away as romanticism took hold and Scots were eager to portray themselves not only as descendants of the clans but of a culture which Lowlanders had once belittled, if not despised. Yet there's little doubt that the culture which had once been reviled by southerners was extremely rich in poetry, song and story and that the language deserved protection.

Did the Highland Clearances constitute a national trauma?

It is apparent that for many people compelled to leave their homes in the Highlands the experience was traumatic in the psychiatric, not just popular, use of the term. They may have feared the death of themselves or their loved ones and what they endured was so intense that they may have had recurrent flashbacks. In addition, some of them may have had such profound feelings of loss and betrayal that they could not function in day-to-day life, would have displayed serious psychiatric symptoms or resorted to alcohol to numb the pain. And it must have been awful for those who weren't 'traumatised' in the strict psychiatric sense but who were profoundly shaken and shocked by what they personally experienced or witnessed.

Some of those threatened with dispossession fought back, particularly the women, but until the 1880s it was to no avail and there was understandably a prevailing sense of hopelessness as the terrible events unfolded. Devine argues that the strict Calvinist doctrines which influenced the Highlands provided spiritual succour in these dark times. They also dampened resistance as they gave 'spiritual certainty during transition from clanship to Clearance as the evangelicals concentrated the minds and emotions of the people on a highly personal struggle for grace and election (to the Kingdom of Heaven).'

Mental health professionals stress that people experience potentially traumatic events differently. Some appear to be immune to serious symptoms whilst others suffer dreadfully. The most important protective factor is social support. If other people share the burden of what you've experienced, and help ease your pain, then you're less likely to suffer lasting effects. And there's little doubt that Highlanders had more social support than those of us living in advanced capitalist society can possibly imagine. In fact, during the Clearances whole Highland communities chose to emigrate *en masse*.

In the traditional story of the Highland Clearances, there is a sense of Scottish exceptionalism; but Richards opposes this view, writing, 'The exceptionalism of the Highlands has been over-rated at the expense of the significance of the Clearances as a well-documented exemplar of the perils facing a poor society located on the edge of industrialisation.' In short, Scotland was not alone in enduring painful evictions as this happened in marginal communities all over Europe. This was the dehumanising logic of market capitalism.

Undoubtedly, the Highland Clearances were a tragedy for those caught up in them and for some this would have been 'traumatic' in any way we define the concept. But I think it's reasonable to only use the term 'national trauma' when the traumatic events would have affected a majority, or at least a sizeable minority, of the country's population. And that's simply not the case here. What's more, many of the Highlanders who were forced to leave emigrated to the colonies and were removed from future Scottish health and social statistics.

In short, it is unlikely that the Highland Clearances are the explanation for why Scotland has brought up its children badly. Nonetheless, this period of Scottish history may lead us to another, more plausible, explanation.

Dislocation, dislocation, dislocation

Bruce Alexander, the Canadian psychologist whose work on addiction I've already quoted, uses the term 'dislocation' to refer to periods of social change when people's psychological need to simultaneously experience 'individual autonomy and social belonging' are not met. Traditional cultures manage to maintain this difficult balance but neither socialist societies, which suppress individual autonomy nor capitalism which eradicates a sense of belonging have provided adequately for these psychological needs.

In its extreme form, or in periods of intense restructuring, capitalism has led to 'mass dislocation'.

According to this theory, dislocation is not only 'socially destructive' but also painful for individuals. The dislocated individual feels empty and overwhelmed by 'the poverty of spirit' or the sense of his or her lost soul. To help fill this void, dislocated individuals don't simply turn, but become addicted, to other things in life to provide a diversion and/or numb the pain. This perspective on addiction helps us to see why historically massive social change, such as colonisation had such a profound effect on people, often leading not just to social breakdown but large-scale addiction to drink, drugs and gambling.

Alexander argues that in Western countries alcohol became a problem with the rise of capitalism and the breakdown of traditional social obligations. England was the first country to industrialise and develop a free market economy so it's hardly surprising that it was also the first to register alcohol addiction as 'a national problem'. According to the distinguished historian Eric Hobsbawm, in the 1800s uncontrolled industrialisation and urbanisation spread a 'pestilence of hard liquor' across Europe, resulting very often in 'mass alcoholism'.

Scotland urbanised much more quickly than England or other European countries. Many Scots, like plants in the fields they once tended, were violently uprooted. They went forcibly, or willingly, to the cities. When we add to this profound psychosocial disintegration, the terrible working and living conditions and the continual feelings of insecurity that characterised their new lives then we can see why urbanisation created ideal conditions for addiction to alcohol – a substance well-known to numb pain and obliterate consciousness. These changes did not just affect the labouring poor: even those who materially benefited from these huge economic changes could suffer from dislocation.

As I recount in *The Tears that Made the Clyde*, Glaswegians in the nineteenth and much of the twentieth centuries experienced some of the worst, overcrowded housing conditions in Europe. Men's jobs in the heavy industries were tough. The heavy drinking which ensued, and men's alienation from a hellish overcrowded, home life led to a fracturing of many urban families. Relations between men and their wives and children were often strained to breaking point. And violence became commonplace in this male-dominated unequal culture.

Glaswegians weren't alone in experiencing the problems of urbanisation but for a variety of reasons I set out in the book, a high proportion of people in this city lived in hellish circumstances and more were caught up in the negative culture which ensued. A blizzard of adverse childhood experiences was the legacy for many growing up with parents suffering such stresses. Indeed, *ACEs are the transmission mechanism whereby trauma is passed from one generation to the next*. What's more, these ACEs can then make people even more vulnerable to future stressors and more likely to be traumatised by events such as military action.

Given the importance of the Highlands to this section of the book, it's worth saying that many Highlanders who migrated to Glasgow were protected, not from the poor housing or disease, but from some of the dislocating effects of the big city. Gaels formed distinct communities in Glasgow, particularly in Partick and Govan. They met socially, not just on a Sunday evening under the bridge at Central Station, known as 'The Heilanman's Umbrella', but in clubs and venues. Ceilidhs were common. These events allowed Highlanders to continue speaking Gaelic as well as maintain an interest in their cultural heritage. It also afforded individual Gaels some protection from incipient Lowland racism which liked to portray people from this community as slow and backward.

Restructuring

Two other periods of extreme dislocation, if not trauma, occurred for many Scots in the twentieth century. The first involved substantial slum clearance, particularly in Glasgow. Experts estimate that by 1975 the Council had demolished 95,000 houses and large areas had been cleared of shops and industries. Effectively this meant that hundreds of thousands of Glaswegians had to move and whole communities and areas, such as the Gorbals, disappeared. Many tenants went willingly and were delighted with their new homes. Many appreciated having an inside toilet or a bathroom, a garden or being surrounded, for the first time, by some green space.

But it's clear from people's memoirs that many felt disoriented. One minute they were living next to neighbours they had known for years, near their extended family and part of a community and the next they were living in a neighbourhood where few people knew one another. Remember in these days most working-class people didn't have telephones so even keeping in touch with family members was difficult. Also transport links were poor. One early resident of the Castlemilk estate recalls that people were at first happy to go but that the move was often beset with problems: 'When people came to Castlemilk, there was a tremendous change to their lives. Some people couldn't take the shock. Others couldn't afford it. We were like early settlers. We needed an extra wage for bus fares to get to visit our families, who were all away in another part of town.'

One of the biggest problems with the Council's response to the housing crisis was their decision to demolish, not refurbish, most of the old tenements. The planners and politicians obviously did not grasp that in moving tenants about in such a wholesale fashion they were breaking vital social ties and family bonds – the very support that people needed to live meaningful and decent lives. The politicians also decided to replace many inner-city dwellings with multi-storey flats. It's now widely recognised by social scientists that housing poor families in tower blocks is a big mistake: they simply don't have the access to facilities, and green spaces, that makes an apartment lifestyle reasonable. Unfortunately, Glasgow built so many high flats that by 1979 the city had a higher percentage of citizens in this type of dwelling than any other equivalent city in Europe.

Boredom stemming from the lack of community and cultural opportunities was also an important negative factor in people's lives. In the early 1960s when the Easterhouse housing scheme was built its population was 58,000. This meant it was bigger than many Scottish towns yet it had absolutely no facilities and inadequate public transport. For example, when I was writing *The*

Tears that Made the Clyde, the town of Ayr had a population of 46,000 and had a cinema, racecourse, sporting facilities, hotels, theatre, library, pubs, shopping centre, hospitals and countless other facilities. This is what we would expect in a place catering for that level of population. Yet Easterhouse started off with nothing. The sheer size of some of these housing schemes encouraged a sense of alienation and estrangement.

Sadly there was more alienation and stress coming down the track as a result of economic restructuring. In the 1970s and 80s heavy industries shrank and many jobs were lost. Whole communities were sometimes affected as jobs in mining, steel and shipbuilding disappeared. This happened from the 1970s on but once the Thatcher Government came to office in 1979 change accelerated. Nothing on this scale of restructuring had happened since the industrial revolution. The West of Scotland was particularly affected by 'deindustrialisation'. By the 1990s there were only a few shipyards left on the Clyde. By 1993, the unthinkable happened – the iconic Ravenscraig steel plant closed. Many of the manufacturing plants fell silent – Singer at Clydebank, Caterpillar in Uddingston and Talbot at Linwood, to name but a few.

Some workers resisted. Some with incredible eloquence. In 1971 Jimmy Reid, one of the leaders of the work-in at Upper Clyde Shipbuilders, became Rector of Glasgow University. The *New York Times* considered his inaugural speech, on alienation, one of the best since the Gettysburg address and published it in full. The most famous passage is when Reid likens modern society to a rat race:

> To the students I address this appeal. Reject these attitudes. Reject the values and false morality that underlie these attitudes. A rat race is for rats. We're not rats. We're human beings. Reject the insidious pressures in society that would blunt your critical faculties to all that is happening around you, that would caution silence in the face of injustice lest it jeopardise your chances of promotion or self-advancement. This is how it starts and before you know where you are, you're a fully paid-up member of the rat-pack.

More opposition was to follow in the form of miners' strikes and a growing clash between industrial areas and the Thatcher Government. As Scotland hadn't voted for Mrs Thatcher there was a growing nationalist character to Scots opposition to Westminster's policies which people now thought an affront to Scottish values. Ministers at Scotland's General Assembly in 1988 let Mrs Thatcher know how opposed they were to her ideas, particularly that there was 'no such thing as society'.

Modern historians generally agree that Scotland came through this grim period remarkably well. The new Scottish economy was much more diversified and by 1987 the country's occupational structure had moved away from a reliance on old, unsustainable heavy industries and was now more similar to England's. It's also accepted that Scotland generally fared better from this period of economic restructuring than Wales or the Northeast of England. However, few would disagree that this period of economic change exacted a huge price: communities suffered as did the individual human beings caught up in the turmoil.

But once again we must guard against Scottish exceptionalism: deindustrialisation happened all over Europe and America where the practice of 'off-shoring' – manufacturing items more cheaply in third world countries – has led to large-scale changes in employment. These practices have taken hold throughout the modern world and have led to a decline in the demand for traditional working-class labour: a development with negative consequences for families and communities worldwide.

So, is national trauma the explanation for why Scotland has brought up its children badly? I don't think we can say that Scotland has had more national trauma than that experienced by many other countries. But I do think it's easy to look at Scottish history and see how economic and social developments, particularly in the nineteenth and twentieth centuries, could affect changes in adults' behaviour and outlook, such as increased alcohol consumption, depression or violence, thereby creating the likelihood of adverse childhood experiences within families. But since other countries also urbanised, industrialised and cleared people from the land

and then deindustrialised in the later decades of the twentieth century, why have Scots fared so badly?

Is it income inequality? If we are comparing UK health statistics with those of our continental neighbours, of course this is a factor as Britain is a country deeply divided by inequality as we've seen in earlier chapters. However, as research by the Glasgow Centre for Population Health shows that inequality cannot explain why Glaswegians have much worse health than their counterparts in Liverpool and Manchester. There must be additional, cultural and psychological factors. So, let's turn now to what these factors may be.

CHAPTER 24

A Scottish mentality

The hidden influence of religion;
impact of the Reformation on Scotland;
Calvinist doctrines – fault finding, predestination, depravity, patriarchy;
Calvinism and Scottish confidence;
blaming the poor;
positive and negative psychology; Calvinism, nurture and ACEs;
Dutch Calvinism;
Scotland's blind spot;
good intentions; secularisation.

WHEN I WROTE *The Scots Crisis of Confidence* I did not argue that the Scots' problem with confidence is mainly the result of England, a negatively defined identity (i.e. not being English) or constitutional politics. Of course, these were factors but I didn't consider them to be the main driver of Scots' lack of confidence. I was much more convinced that the problem lay in Scotland's religious past – it was the Reformation, Calvinist theology and Scottish Presbyterianism to which I continually returned. As religion played such an important part in the book I had regular meetings with a Calvin scholar, Jim Greig, to make sure I didn't make a *faux pas* while tackling such controversial subjects.[1]

With the passage of time even I can see that it seems odd that, in the new millennium when the Church of Scotland had lost its

---

1. Jim Greig translated Calvin's *Economic and Social Thought* (2005) from the original French.

power and Scotland was one of the most atheistic societies in the world, I would put so much emphasis on religion. I certainly didn't start the process of writing with this intention. I'm not religious myself though I attended a United Free Church of Scotland Sunday school when I was young and can still detect some residual influences. But when I contemplated confidence issues in Scotland and read Scotland's religious history, I could not help but see a link. So, most of the chapters in the book draw on this aspect of our past and link it to Scottish society and culture.

In the past twenty years I have not changed my mind. In fact, I now believe that religion has had a much more profound effect on Scotland than the confidence issues I address in my 2003 book. What these effects may have been is the focus of this chapter. In a nutshell I link religion with Scotland's predilection for punishment, blame and shame, the impact of these beliefs on raising children, and the inevitable erosion of individual well-being.

Before getting into this topic, I want to say something about an important, bestselling book which appeared in 2019 – *Dominion: The Making of the Western Mind* by Tom Holland, a historian who has written books and made programmes for television and radio on a variety of topics. In *Dominion* Holland argues that 'increasingly empty though the pews may be,' Western society is 'firmly moored to its Christian past'. This isn't simply because 'Time itself has been Christianised' but because we can see the beliefs of medieval Christianity everywhere, particularly the idea that 'God . . . [is] closer to the weak than to the mighty, to the poor than to the rich.' Indeed, 'the assumptions' we all grow up with. . .

> . . . about how a society should properly be organised, and the principles that it should uphold – were not bred of classical antiquity, still less 'human nature', but very distinctively of that civilisation's Christian past. So profound has been the impact of Christianity on the development of Western civilisation that it has come to be hidden from view.

Unlike the Romans who pursued conquest and were not concerned if this led to the slaughter or enslavement of millions, Christians cared about 'suffering humanity'. Of course, this hasn't meant that Christians always treated others humanely as we know from the enslavement of Africans by Westerners. But those caught up in this horrendous traffic in human beings had to find justification in racism. The abolitionists, led initially by Quakers, didn't agree, and drew heavily on the Bible in their campaign. Holland argues that it's Christian values which underlie the West's concern about human rights and why we are so instinctively repulsed by fascism.

Of course, Christianity is not a unified belief system. It contains various churches which share some core beliefs but nonetheless have distinctly different histories, values, traditions and customs. I'm not simply referring to Christianity's major division into Catholics and Protestants but also the variety of Protestant faiths – Puritans, Lutherans, Calvinists, Presbyterians, Baptists, Methodists, Quakers. . .

Presbyterianism, a form of Calvinism, was for centuries Scotland's dominant faith and, as I'm about to argue, it has left a distinctive mark on the country and its people, irrespective of their own faith group, professed atheism or the emptiness of Scottish pews. In short, we may be unaware of its influence, but religion continues to have a profound effect on Scots – Protestants and Catholics, believers and non-believers alike.

The Reformation

In Scotland, the Reformation was not a one-off event but a series of changes which occurred from 1560 to 1690. The undisputed leader of Scotland's Reformation was John Knox. Formerly a Catholic priest, Knox later converted to Protestantism and became one of the leading rebels against the Catholic Church in Scotland. His rebelliousness meant that life in his home country was dangerous. He was forced to work as a slave on a French galley and then found refuge in England. During this period of exile from Scotland he studied under John Calvin in Geneva. Knox returned to Scotland in 1559 and led Scotland's overthrow of the Catholic Church and the establishment of a new religion – Presbyterianism.

Tom Holland reports that Knox's preaching on his return to Scotland 'inspired an eruption of godly vandalism' across Scotland.

'One congregation, after listening to Knox inveigh against idolatry, had promptly set to dismantling the local cathedral. Other bands of enthusiasts had incinerated abbeys, chopped down the orchards of friaries, and pulled up flowers in monastery gardens.' In comparison with other countries, the Reformation in Scotland was achieved with very little bloodshed. In Europe, millions were slaughtered.

John Knox and his followers fashioned out of Calvinist dogma a religion for the Scottish people which stressed the importance of *understanding*. The key to this new religion was education: the ordinary parishioners in Scotland were to be taught not only how to read the Bible but also how to understand its meaning so that they could enter into debate on the scriptures. The scheme to transform the Scots into a people capable of such understanding was set out in the *First Book of Discipline* written by a commission appointed by the General Assembly in 1560 and led by John Knox. The Book states that all children in Scotland, no matter how poor, should receive an education. It also set out a scheme for the development of the Scottish universities. Provisions were made for children to be publicly examined on the catechism and every year the ministers and elders were to examine each parishioner publicly on the chief points of the Bible.

This emphasis on understanding and debate had important implications for the Scottish Presbyterian church. The core of the Scottish service is the sermon – the singing, prayers and communion are mere appendages. The bareness of the Presbyterian service and the lack of ritual, candles and kneeling obviously appealed to the reformers' taste for logic and understanding but inevitably they created a religion which caters for the mind at the expense of the emotions. The interiors and exteriors of Scottish churches still display the desire for such simplicity. This is no small matter as the Covenanters fought and died for the right to simplicity in their service and against the imposition of English High Church ways.

Scottish Presbyterianism is also a deeply democratic religion. It may have taken hundreds of years, and the spilling of blood during Covenanting days, but the Scots managed to separate their

Kirk from the monarch and state and build it on thoroughly democratic foundations. The power of the Pope was abolished. Bishops were eliminated. Church governance was put in the hands of ordinary parishioners who elected the ministers and elders. *The Book of Discipline* encouraged ministers not to pay too much attention to the rich or to important members of the parish and encouraged respect for the poor.

Even hundreds of years after the Reformation it's easy to look at Scottish institutions and aspects of Scottish culture and still see the hand of John Knox. What's much harder to detect, but in my view is even more important, is how Calvinist doctrines shaped Scots' interior world and how these ideas have affected Scottish society and culture. To get to the heart of this I want to draw on the insights of one of the most important books on Scotland and religion – *Scottish Identity: A Christian Vision* by William Storrar (1990), a Scottish theologian who is now the Director of the Center of Theological Inquiry in Princeton and who has written the foreword to this book.

Storrar argues that John Knox was the architect of an important Scottish vision: Scotland was to become 'a Godly nation where the Kirk and people were one'. The reformed Scotland would be a 'Godly commonwealth' based on 'the word of God', particularly that revealed by the Old Testament which effectively became the country's 'political handbook'. In 1638, with the signing of the National Covenant, Scotland proclaimed to the world that it saw itself as 'having a special covenanted relationship with the Almighty'. This strong sense of a unified, national, religious purpose lasted until the Great Disruption in the Church of Scotland in 1843.

This means that for almost three hundred years Scotland as a nation was animated by a grand, utopian vision. Indeed, some argue that no other nation in the world has set itself the task of creating the kingdom of heaven on earth. And, in this respect, it marks Scotland as different from other countries. I believe this new religious order, which had the best of intentions, has nonetheless profoundly undermined individual and collective well-being in Scotland.

Calvinist doctrines

Calvinism is a substantial belief system, so I've distilled its most important beliefs for understanding Scotland into six discrete topics:

1. Discipline, fault finding and instilling fear

Human beings are imperfect, flawed creatures and they are neither suited to a utopian life nor able to act consistently in accordance 'with the moral and spiritual purpose of godliness'. For the Scottish vision to be realised the Kirk had to ensure strong external control on the individual's behaviour. And this is indeed what happened. Thanks to the eventual adoption of the *First Book of Discipline*, the church not only punished conduct it judged immoral, but also set up a system of mutual prying and spying; ministers, elders and congregation were to correct one another. The esteemed intellectual, Edwin Muir summed up the effect in his book *John Knox: Portrait of a Calvinist* (1930) when he stated:

> A Church such as this, held together by universal and reciprocal fault-finding, could not but have something ambiguous in its piety, and could not but encourage the self-opinionative and the censorious at the expense of the sensitive and the charitable. It did more, however; it substituted for the particular tyranny of the priest a universal and inescapable public tyranny.

This public censure was additional to considerable punishments handed out by the Kirk. Of course, other countries also had various types of puritans and their discipline to contend with, but it's the dominance and unity of Scottish Presbyterianism up to the Great Disruption in the mid-nineteenth century which makes Scotland different from other countries.

As Wallace Notestein observes in *The Scot in History* (1946), the Scottish Church reformers: '. . . organised the censorship of behaviour so that even trivial faults were a matter for criticism. They put a premium on spying. They arranged for continuous moral judgements. . . They raised the scrutiny of one's fellows to a public virtue.' This meant that how much people ate and drank, the kind of clothes they wore, the words they used, how they treated the poor, their sexual behaviour, and what they did on a Sunday – all came under legitimate public scrutiny. In *The Social Life of Scotland in the Eighteenth Century* (1899) a cleric writes of officers, beadles and deacons:

> There was not a place where one was free from their inquisitorial intrusion. They might enter any house and even pry into the rooms. In towns where the patrol of elders or deacons, beadle and officers, paced with solemnity the deserted causeway eagerly eyeing every door and window, craning their necks up every close and lane, the people slunk into the obscurity of shadows and kept hushed silence.

In the Catholic Church, discipline is mainly achieved through private confessional, supported on occasion with public rebukes or excommunication. In Knox's reformed religion this was reversed. *The Book of Discipline* allows for transgressions, which were not widely known to be dealt with in private Kirk sessions, but more commonly, alleged sinners were called before the minister, elders and congregation and publicly rebuked, shamed and punished. The historian T.C. Smout recounts that for sexual misdemeanours the sinner was 'forced to stand dressed in sackcloth, bare-headed and bare-footed, first at the kirk door and then on the public stool of repentance in front of the congregation on every Sunday for six months or occasionally for several years, and sometimes by whipping and fining as well.'

The Kirk had other ways of enforcing conformity. For example, the session appointed the parish schoolteacher and inspected their school and teaching methods. The Church also influenced the universities. Smout argues its power was enormous: 'The emphasis in every home and school on repeating and understanding the catechism impressed on every child the importance of holding the right belief.'

The Church authorities also used prying to ensure the people of Scotland observed the Sabbath. People could even be censured for 'idly gazing out of windows'. A minute from the Edinburgh Kirk session of 1727 describes how each session was instructed 'to take its turn in watching the streets on Sabbath . . . and to visit each suspected house . . . and to pass through the streets and reprove such as transgress and inform on such as do not refrain.' Again, people could be referred to the Civil Magistrates for punishment.

From the Reformation till the early eighteenth century Scotland was a theocracy – the discipline of the church was backed and enforced by the civil authorities as is the case today in many Muslim countries such as Iraq and Afghanistan. Theocracies give the church unassailable power over people's lives. In seventeenth century Scotland a person couldn't even move from one parish to another without a testificate from the local minister certifying his or her good behaviour. One of the benefits of the Union was that this ceased. In 1712 Westminster's Toleration Act 'forbade magistrates to enforce kirk censures or summonses'. This weakened the grip of the Kirk but nonetheless it continued to dominate Scottish life as we can see in the earlier description of the policing of the Sabbath in 1727.

At the turn of the new millennium, Donald Macleod, a Scottish Free church theologian, published an article called 'Scottish Calvinism: a dark repressive force?' Macleod looks specifically at complaints that 'Scottish Calvinism exercised a harsh discipline, probing inquisitorially into private lives and subjecting Scotland to four hundred years of repressive moral tyranny.' It's interesting that he concedes a great deal of ground to the critics, arguing that there was an unfortunate overlap of ecclesiastical and civil courts, Kirk discipline was 'harsh' and outcomes, including use of 'the birch, the stocks and the jouggs', were 'horrific'. But he urges us to see this in context – all over Europe severe punishment was being meted out to offenders. Nonetheless after reflecting on the Kirk's witch burning and executions, he writes: 'No defence is to be offered for such behaviour on the part of a state which professed to regulate its civic life by the teaching of Christ.'

2. Predestination

One fundamental tenet of Calvinism which is difficult for the modern mind to grasp is predestination. Catholicism believes that individuals can win God's grace through good works and the sacraments. For Lutherans, the religion of many Scandinavians, grace can be won through faith alone. But for Calvinists, God alone grants salvation and in his eyes there are two types of people – the 'elect' who God has chosen to go to heaven and the 'damned' who will go to Hell. Even Calvin himself thought the fact that we are all preordained to either heaven or eternal damnation, 'dreadful'.

It may seem paradoxical but 'election' has nothing to do with how the individual behaves. In this sense it is 'unconditional'. However, Calvinists ultimately came to believe that we can tell whether a person is part of the elect by their success in life. As God elects who is saved or damned, irrespective of what they have done, pure Calvinists believe that babies are born into the world with God's judgement already upon them. In short, some are damned.[2]

3. Depravity and Worthlessness

TULIP is the acronym popularly used to explain the five essential Calvinist beliefs. The first of these is 'Total depravity'. So, humans are not just a wee bit depraved but depraved in every fibre of their being. Indeed, because humans are 'fallen', we are unable to resist the temptations of the flesh and eschew evil. As one wit observed, total depravity is like the Christian belief of original sin 'on steroids'. The current teachings of some TULIP Calvinists, like the American pastor Voddie Bauchan, has led to the description of babies as 'vipers in diapers'.

In Calvinism there's also the central tenet of God's magnificence and humankind's abject state. This means that in comparison with the majesty of God even our noblest achievements are worthless. What's more, in Calvinism there's a prevailing sense of human beings as fixed, unchangeable entities who we can judge. This is indeed the Scotland that Bill Duncan, a Scottish teacher and novelist, presents in his satirical appraisal, *The Wee*

2. Some American Calvinists have moved away from predestination as it makes evangelism pointless.

Book of Calvin (2004). Indeed, the most striking feature of Duncan's humorous distillation of the Scottish Calvinist mentality is the way that individuals – often children – are judged and labelled. Needless to say, the labels are mainly damning and suggest worthlessness. One telling example from Duncan's wee book reads: 'Ye can tell the criminal from the face in the crib'. Another is 'Yer sins go down beside yer name in the book o' no rubbin oot.'

Feelings of worthlessness are not equivalent to suffering from low self-esteem. The latter is about how we rate ourselves in comparison to others. If we lived on a desert island, self-esteem would be irrelevant but feelings of worthlessness would not. These are about how we judge ourselves morally, from the perspective of a critical, damning, all-seeing God.

The main purpose of our emotions is to appraise our experience of life and the most highly charged appraisal is of ourselves – our self-worth. Living in a culture that tells us to judge ourselves as *worthless* and of no importance has a profound impact on our well-being.

4. Patriarchy

Calvinism postulates the spiritual equality of the sexes as it makes both men and women responsible for their own salvation. But Lesley A. Orr Macdonald, in her book *A Unique and Glorious Mission* (2000) on women and Scottish Presbyterianism, argues that this 'potentially liberating' aspect of Calvinism for women was not realised for centuries. Indeed, Macdonald argues that the Scottish Reformation ushered in a religion which was deeply masculine in both belief and practice.

Catholicism allows for female religious communities, making it possible for some women to live almost independently of men. The cult of the Virgin Mary and the plethora of female saints also means that Catholicism offers women role-models and emphasises the importance of female compassion. The Reformation swept all this aside. The reformed Kirk didn't simply place the patriarchal Old Testament at the core of its teachings, its most influential figure, John Knox, was utterly opposed to the idea of female authority.

Indeed in 1558, much to the annoyance of John Calvin himself, Knox published *The First Blast of the Trumpet against the Monstrous Regiment of Women* lambasting female rulers as unnatural.

The reformers' God was an authoritarian male figure and absolute masculine authority was considered appropriate not only for Church governance but also for family life. The Kirk believed it was right and proper for women and children to be under the rule and supervision of a patriarch. Indeed, it believed that it was unnatural and 'disorderly' for women to have any authority. As only men could become ministers or elders, the Church discipline was the discipline of men, with women and girls often on the receiving end. So harsh was this discipline that the poet John Keats once remarked, 'I would rather be a wild deer than a girl under the dominion of the Kirk'. As Macdonald shows, much of the Kirk's discipline attempted to keep women submissive and in a subordinate position:

> For a range of offences, from gossiping and slander, to adultery, harlotry and witchcraft, women in the 16th and 17th centuries were subjected to punishments which were intended to silence, to humiliate, to shame, to demonise and above all to control them for behaviour which was not in keeping with the submission required by the defenders of the faith. Those who committed sexual misdemeanours, or who chose to live on their own and not in a male-headed household, were liable to particular pursuit and censure. This atmosphere of repression, abuse and contempt reached its nadir in the periodic witch hunts of the period. In 1727, the last of thousands of Scottish women were tortured and burned.

Between 1560 and 1690 Scotland had numerous waves of persecution for witchcraft. Most of those accused were poor women, often herbalists, over the age of 40 and throughout this period older women must have lived in fear of accusation. Even though Scotland's population was only a quarter of England's it executed at least twice as many witches and was also more likely to torture them. On International Women's Day 2022, Nicola Sturgeon, as First Minister, apologised at Holyrood to 'all those who were accused, convicted, vilified or executed under the Witchcraft Act of 1563'.

However, even when the obsession with witchcraft burnt itself out, Scotland's patriarchal authority remained. In 1847, Thomas Chalmers, the man who led the Great Disruption, said in response to the subject of women's rights: 'I have always looked upon this as a very paltry and distasteful question; I think that it is revolting to the collective mind of the Free Church.'[3]

5. Pleasure, sex and displays of affection

The new reformed religion was all about logic, reasoning and understanding. It was a cerebral religion which not only downplayed the importance of spiritual experience, aesthetic sense and beauty, but eventually demonised enjoyment of any kind. So, the Kingdom of Heaven the Scots pursued was no paradise where people lazed about in beautiful palaces, thinking spiritual thoughts, being artistic, having fun, copulating or eating fruit; it was a world where everyone worked hard, led serious, frugal lives in accordance with the Bible and worshipped the Lord.

For all that John Knox is seen as a killjoy who turned the Scots into a guilt-ridden people, he was not opposed to all forms of enjoyment. Nor was he particularly a promoter of Sabbatarianism. Such Puritanical edicts were a later development in Presbyterianism which gripped the nation with a vengeance – doing anything on a Sunday, other than worshipping the Lord, was forbidden. So was celebrating Christmas or other traditional holidays. 'Gorgeous and vaine apparel' was criticised and people were exhorted to dress in sober colours. 'Hodden grey' was the Kirk's choice. Any form of enjoyment, such as card playing, gluttony, drinking, festive burials or weddings was also attacked. In 1649 the General Assembly of the Church of Scotland passed an act decreeing an end to 'promiscuous dancing'.

Sex, the most natural of all human activities, was seen as vile

---

3. Despite this past, the Church of Scotland voted to ordain women ministers in 1968, much earlier than many Protestant churches.

by the Kirk and any type of sexual activity outside the strict confines of the marriage bed deemed a serious breach of discipline. The elders even quizzed married couples on their sexual relationship. Edwin Muir's study of John Knox led him to claim that to the end of his life his favourite terms were 'fornication, abomination, adultery, idolatry'. Much of the Kirk's obsession with sin concerned sexuality and those who transgressed were punished severely. Many of them were young women accused of fornication. What's more, Calvinism was extremely cerebral and uncomfortable with the body and bodily functions.

These beliefs also deterred Scots, parents included, from physical displays of affection or even warmth in everyday communication. As I reported in Chapter 20 on childhood adversities, the Scots language has a cornucopia of insulting words to label people negatively, but few terms of endearment. Mary Rose Liverani (née Lavery) in her book on growing up in Glasgow in the 1940s writes: 'In our house, the only four letter word never voiced aloud was love.' Thinking of my own father, my response to this is another four letter word – snap.

Indeed, people brought up in Scotland right up to the 1960s report that families were not physically affectionate. In fiction many Scots describe a childhood devoid of hugs, kisses, and cuddles. For example, in Gordon Williams' novel *From Scenes Like These* (1968), set in the West of Scotland, the young protagonist is aware that his experience is different from what he sees in the cinema: 'Funny how in the pictures you often saw kids give their mothers a kiss or a hug. He could no more have done that than shagged a horse.' Glaswegians are still very dismissive of animals or children who are affectionate: 'He's nothing but a big sook,' they'll say. Variations on this theme are calling someone who likes physical contact, a 'plaster' and anyone who shows their emotions may be dismissed as a 'big wean'.

Of the six Calvinist beliefs, outlined here, this is the one which has noticeably waned with time. It's now commonplace for Scots to say 'love you' when leaving someone or ending a phone call. Kissing and hugging, not just children but other relatives and friends, is also a noticeable part of Scottish life.

6. Guilt and Pessimism

Many historians point out that Calvinist teachings did not stop people from fornicating, drinking or partaking in other sensory pleasures, but they made Scots feel guilty about doing so. As Neal Ascherson writes: 'Guilt – formless, unassuageable, darkening all pleasure with dread of what was to follow – entered the Scottish psyche.'

There is also a strong current of pessimism in Scotland which was satirised to good effect by the poet, Alexander Scott:

> **Scotch Optimism**
>
> Through a gless, Darkly.
>
> **Scotch Pessimism**
>
> Nae Gless.

Alastair Reid was a poet and writer who, like many fellow Scots, travelled the world. Born in Whithorn in 1926, he lived in many different countries including the United States, France, Greece, Spain and Central and South America. Reid was a gifted writer – a skill he used for many years as a columnist for the *New Yorker* – and this talent, coupled with his astute observations as both an insider and an outsider, meant he has written some of the most perceptive articles on twentieth century Scotland. In his book *Whereabouts: Notes on Being a Foreigner* (1987) he explains why he chose to leave his native Scotland:

> The spirit of Calvin, far from dead, stalked the countryside, ever present in a pinched wariness, a wringing of the hands. We were taught to expect the worst – miserable sinners, we could not expect more. A rueful doom ruffles the Scottish spirit. It takes various spoken forms. . . a man in Edinburgh said to me, 'See you tomorrow, if we're spared,' bringing me to a horrified standstill . . . The wariness is deep-rooted. I prize the encounter I once had with a local woman on the edge of St Andrews on a heady spring day. I exclaimed my pleasure in the day, at which she darkened and muttered, 'We'll pay for it, we'll pay for it.'

Another prevailing belief is that enjoyment or even happiness is not only unimportant but potentially dangerous as such 'inessentials' divert your attention from life's true purpose. As a result of the Kirk's traditional teaching most Scots in earlier centuries saw 'real' life as being about hard work which should be undertaken, not so much for your own personal benefit, but for the benefit of God and others. This work ethic may have dimmed over time and with the advent of a more hedonistic society but it's still there. Indeed, the Scots are known to have very positive attitudes to work and that's why Scotland for many years has been a favoured site for inward investment.

Many Scots, even today, (myself included) uphold the essentially Calvinist idea that a person's life should be 'a pilgrimage towards an objective'. Just simply living your life unthinkingly is not good enough. To be meaningful, life has to be imbued with a sense of purpose. Andrew Carnegie, the Scottish self-made millionaire, would regularly remind young people, 'we've not been put in this world just to enjoy ourselves'.

Calvinism and Scottish confidence

It's not too difficult for readers to see from this description of Scotland's religious past, why I thought it provided an explanation for the Scots' lack of confidence. In a nutshell our religious history explains why Scots would become excessively worried about making mistakes and drawing attention to themselves as this could easily result in humiliation and punishment. But there's something else at work here which we can see if we compare Scotland and America.

America is still a largely Protestant country with many churches with roots in Calvinism. In 2004 two American psychology professors, Jennifer Crocker and Laura Park, argued that the prevailing Protestant ethic means that Americans link a person's worth with their achievements. When this view is allied with the American emphasis on self-reliance the idea emerges that some individuals are 'worthier' than others. Crocker and Park point out that such a belief system is alien to eastern cultures, such as Japan, where ideas of interdependence and belonging are strong. It's also alien to many indigenous cultures where individuals are an integral part of kinship and social groups. In other words, in some societies people do not have to prove their worth to gain respect or feel they belong to the group. Even the Lutheran version of Protestantism, dominant in Nordic countries, does not take a judgemental view of people's worth, believing anyone who has faith will be saved by God.

Many early colonists in America were deeply religious and came from Protestant denominations influenced by Calvinist theology. The English Puritans were Calvinists as were the Dutch and the Scots. But beliefs can evolve, particularly in a dynamic country like America. Centuries later there is a big difference between this aspect of Scottish and American culture. People in the US are given a simple message – go forth and use the opportunities available to prove your worth through material success. The Scots by contrast are given confused messages in the form of two competing injunctions – prove you are not worthless but don't think you are anybody special and don't look better than anyone else.

These competing messages restrain individual achievement and shape how we see equality. Scottish egalitarian values are based on the notion that if everyone is equal then no one is better than anyone else. At their most negative these values mean that we are all equally worthless. It's hardly surprising that Scots who achieve success can be treated with contempt. The poet Alexander Scott summed this up pithily in his two-line poem:

Scotch Equality

Kaa the feet
Frae thon big bastard.

In the USA, on the other hand, Calvinist beliefs have been overtaken by the more aspirational idea that everyone can achieve. Indeed Americans passionately believe that anyone can become President. Of course, it's a myth – people in the US do not have equal chances in life – but it's a myth most of the population buy into, including poor black Americans. So America's version of Protestantism encourages Americans to pursue success and money.

The Scots' version of egalitarianism, on the other hand, impedes individualism and promotes collective values. This means it has some benefit within the culture, but it exacts a hefty price. Not only does our egalitarianism level down and lead to mediocrity it's also deeply confusing for individuals. Being pushed to prove that you're not worthless while being held back for fear of censure leads to inertia, frustration and feelings of powerlessness. It undermines the opportunity for people to feel both worthwhile and confident.

As a result of exposure to the mass media, the Americanisation of our culture and some positive beliefs emanating from education and the personal development movement, more Scots are comfortable with the idea of personal success. But the confusion around success certainly hasn't disappeared and was a major barrier when I was growing up in the 1950s and 60s. No wonder Scotland's favourite son, Billy Connolly, once said 'I hate my country for the way it holds people back, tells them they're not good enough.' In fact, he could have gone much further.

Blaming the poor

Like many Scots I seriously disliked Thatcherism and, though I wouldn't have admitted it openly, deep down I thought that the Scots were morally superior to the English. In this respect I had been influenced by William McIlvanney's portrayal of Scotland in *Surviving the Shipwreck* (1991) particularly his notion of 'the deep humanity of the Scottish people' and Scots' compassion towards the unfortunate'. So, when I started to read Scottish history, I was shocked at the picture of Scotland that emerged. And, once again, it had been shaped by our Calvinist past.

In the nineteenth century it was common for slum dwellers to be seen, throughout Britain, as 'human vermin'. But, thanks to Scotland's Calvinist belief system this was particularly strong north of the border. Scots believed that poverty and squalor were due to bad character, and not environmental circumstances. This flowed from Calvinist beliefs on predestination and the notion of the elect and the damned. Those leading good Christian lives, with the outward signs of success, were likely to be members of the elect while those living wretched lives demonstrated their abject worthlessness. This is one reason why the Scottish Poor Law of the industrial age had a strong moralistic and judgemental character to it even though mass unemployment in an industrial era was an inevitable consequence of global trade cycles.

The Scottish academic, Allan MacLaren, argued in his book, *Social Class in Scotland: Past and Present* (1976) that, while some individual doctors made contributions to medicine and the understanding of disease, Scotland's strong religious beliefs meant that the country as a whole lagged behind England, by more than a generation, in the movement for public health. MacLaren asserted that strong Calvinist beliefs led to the widespread view in mid-nineteenth century Scotland that cholera, or other such diseases, were the result of God's divine intervention and should not be questioned, let alone interfered with. This gave way to the notion that cholera was 'God's judgement against filth'. These judgemental notions which rob people of human dignity and personal worth resounded throughout Scotland for centuries. So, as well as having to bear the most appalling housing and working conditions, the poor were also told they were worthless and to blame for their predicament.

MacLaren also argued that the notion that spiritual and economic destitution were inextricably linked and 'the incorporation [of] these ideas into middle-class ideology might be seen as one essential distinguishing feature between the Scottish and English bourgeoisie of the nineteenth century.' Ultimately, the challenge to such views came from secular society, specifically from *English* social reformers like Charles Booth and Seebohm Rowntree as well as a host of Royal Commissions on various issues ranging from working conditions and wages to housing and Poor Law. These official reports illustrated the importance of environmental factors. This new sociological perspective ultimately led to the appeal of the new socialist parties and in the long run it was the state which paid for slums to be demolished and new houses built. In Scotland it led to an emphasis on civic responsibility.

The approach which portrayed the poor as victims of poverty and circumstance rather than personally responsible for their plight ultimately triumphed in Scotland. The Church of Scotland's new mission was to improve the lives of poor people, not condemn them. But remnants of old ideas persist and the worthlessness of the poor is one: there's still a prevailing notion in contemporary Scotland that we're all worthless unless we prove we're worthwhile and the poor find that much more challenging than the better off. One Chinese woman living in Scotland summed up the problem thus: 'What's tragic about Scotland and which makes me so sad is your poor people. They feel worthless and they have no hope. Our poor people are simply poor. They don't feel bad about themselves and they hope that one day they will have better lives.'

Positive and negative psychology

Ironical though it may sound, both leaders of the positive psychology movement – Martin Seligman and Mihaly Csikszentmihalyi – argue that the brain tends to prioritise negative information. Indeed, Seligman argues that the brain is 'hard-wired' for negativity. Drawing on the work of evolutionary psychologists he argues that our ancestors needed to be alert to danger to survive and that it's their genes we have inherited – not their happy-go-lucky relatives as they were more likely to have been eaten or drowned in a flood. In short, negative emotion always has the ability, as Seligman describes it, 'to trump' positive emotion. Csikszentmihalyi has studied the importance of what he calls 'flow', engaged concentration, to human satisfaction, and he argues it's important because it helps suppress negative emotions. He writes:

> . . . with nothing to do, the mind is unable to prevent negative thoughts from elbowing their way to center stage. . . Worries about one's love life, health, investments, family and job are always hovering at the periphery of attention, waiting until there is nothing pressing that demands concentration. As soon as the mind is ready to relax, zap! the potential problems that were waiting in the wings take over.

There's something of a paradox here: the brain finds it very easy to be negative but it's very important for human beings to experience positive emotions as it's in this emotional state that we nurture and develop our health, our relationships, and our intellectual and psychological reserves. Such a paradox leads ultimately to the conclusion that it's crucially important for human beings to *learn* how to side-step the natural negativity of the brain and to experience more positive emotion. Traditionally it has been the prevailing culture, particularly religious ideas and practices, which teach people how to keep the negative brain in check and amplify good feelings. In early societies this was often the point of cleansing practices such as the use of sweat lodges. Buddhists by contrast teach acceptance and meditation techniques. New Testament Christianity preaches forgiveness, love and gratitude – emotions which enhance well-being according to various psychological and medical studies. Indeed, as I demonstrate in Chapter 12 on materialism, consumer capitalism has a negative effect on well-being as it encourages us to focus on what we don't have in our lives.

And what of Scotland? Could Scotland have a slew of challenging health and social statistics partly because Scottish culture has never been good at encouraging us to deal with the natural negativity of the human brain? Indeed, rather than encouraging Scots to learn how to experience positive emotions did religion in Scotland, at least in the centuries following the Reformation, encourage them to amplify negative feelings? Yes and no.

Thanks to Calvinism, for centuries Scotland was ruled by an Old Testament God who thundered 'thou shalt not' and punished the human race for original sin rather than being a country which paid attention to the loving God of the New Testament. As Table 6 shows, as Scots we're much more interested in 'an eye for an eye', and punishment, than forgiveness. Gratitude, appreciation and love are mainly expressed in Scottish life on Burns night. Robert Burns is so important to Scotland because he encourages the otherwise cold, critical Scots to celebrate and appreciate what's meaningful to them. This can be simple things from everyday life – daisies, mice, simple family ways, a smile, a sweetheart – but Burns also encourages deep thinking about the nature of happiness as we know from his famous lines, 'But pleasure is like poppies spread. You seize the flower. It's bloom is shed.'

However, the warm, open, appreciative stance displayed on Burns night is not how Scots perceive themselves or are seen by outsiders. 'Dour' is a word that is commonly used to describe the Scots individually or collectively. Even contemporary Scots tend to see people who are upbeat and positive as gushy and superficial. There's also a palpable fear of mistakes in Scotland and nothing to discourage us from paying close attention to the critical, negative inner voice that's part of the human experience. So, is this why we have such a problem with alcohol and drugs, since such substances can help suppress the negative inner voice which berates and negates?

But there was an important aspect to Scottish Calvinism that did help control negative emotions – work. Protestantism in general, but Calvinism in particular, traditionally valued effort and hard work and this is why Protestantism is closely linked to the rise of capitalism. Protestants argued that 'the devil makes work for idle hands' and Csikszentmihalyi would agree that negativity and worry can easily result from an idle brain if not idle hands. So, the Scots' emphasis on activity, learning skills and finding a sense of mission were important ways to avoid negativity and promote a sense of personal satisfaction, mainly through engagement or flow. It's impossible to read Scotland's economic and industrial history and not conclude that learning and using hard won education and skills was an important way in which the Scots experienced satisfaction in life. This is perhaps why the loss of skilled jobs in heavy industry in recent decades has been devastating for so many Scots.

Calvinism, nurture and childhood adversities

As we saw in the chapter on ACEs, how adults behave has a large effect on their children. This means that what I've written in the past few pages has enormous implications for how children in Scotland have been brought up. But I now want to look more specifically at how Scotland's past has specifically affected child-rearing.

George Albee, the distinguished American psychologist of

international renown, died in his 80s in 2006. Albee was principally interested in the prevention of mental illness not the treatment. His research convinced him that the principal cause of mental illness is not brain disease or disorder but poverty, exploitation and lack of love. He often said that the best, single way to improve mental health was to make sure that all children were wanted. He firmly believed that 'if children sense in their bones that they are wanted, loved and appreciated, they develop a great internal self-confidence that resists all kind of stress.'

Given such findings could anyone read my summary of Calvinist beliefs and say that it would lead children to grow up feeling loved and appreciated for who they are as unique individuals? Historically this was a religion which encouraged fear, promoted guilt and emotional repression, detested bodies and bodily functions, was founded on the belief that people are depraved and worthless, and had an extremely judgemental view of people – actually dividing human beings into two distinct camps and saying that one was damned. Not only did it operate via punishment and blame but individuals experienced such discipline and denouncement as humiliation and shame. As we saw in Chapter 21, Scotland was very keen on corporal punishment for children.

Thanks to the ACE research, neuroscience and the evidence on the importance of secure attachment we know what conditions are necessary for babies and young children to thrive. Fear and humiliation are toxic for young minds. We now know that optimism and positive emotions such as love, gratitude, appreciation, and forgiveness are important for well-being in adult life. But, for almost three and a half centuries, until a deliberate softening of its outlook in the twentieth century, the Scottish Kirk preached a belief system which hindered, rather than encouraged, human flourishing. It was also a strongly patriarchal religion which preached against women having any power, even within the home, and amplified male authority. This is no doubt why the life-denying, authoritarian father figure haunts Scottish literature.

The Dutch example

However, it was not inevitable that Calvinism would undermine Scots' well-being and have such a negative effect on child rearing. Other aspects of Scottish life and history, and the personality of leaders such as John Knox, had an impact on how Reformation ideas developed in Scotland. We can see this by looking at the Netherlands – another country with a strongly Calvinist past. This country now scores highly on international happiness surveys for both adults and children. Indeed, in such surveys the latter often register as having the best well-being in the world and Dutch women rarely suffer from depression. This may be the result of women's position in society: from medieval times Dutch women were noted for their strength and independence and even now are often seen to be in charge at home. The nuclear family is also very strong.

Holland's Calvinism was not as pervasive and unchallenged as it was in Scotland. More importantly, religion in the Netherlands consciously evolved in the late nineteenth and early twentieth centuries under the influence of 'Neo-Calvinists'. One important figure was Abraham Kuyper, a churchman and intellectual who, William Storrar claims, helped Dutch citizens rethink their godly vision in the secular and pluralist terms of contemporary Dutch society and Western thought. Kuyper became Prime Minister of the Netherlands at the beginning of the twentieth century. He helped pave the way for Holland to become a tolerant, liberal society as well as grounding Dutch culture in social democratic values. These values also helped twentieth century Netherlands adopt a preventative health care system, which is so beneficial for mothers and children. Indeed, these health policies are the envy of public health specialists the world over. This secular Calvinism may also have encouraged the Dutch to subjugate materialist values in preference for 'quality of life' – one of the most attractive features of their contemporary culture.

The Scottish Kirk did not lead Scotland through an equivalent, cleansing, reforming Neo-Calvinist era. Storrar argues that, after the fragmentation caused by the Great Disruption in 1843, the Scottish Kirk did not come up with, or encourage Scotland to discuss, a new vision for the nation. Under the influence of that great nineteenth century thinker, Thomas Carlyle, who emphasised duty, many Scots who had abandoned orthodox beliefs were inspired to dedicate their lives to others but there was no new national project. Storrar realises this was a tall order in a modern, pluralist, European context but acknowledges that this was exactly what the Netherlands achieved. Scotland's increasing secularisation, without this type of spiritual renewal has, in my view, made us particularly susceptible to the continued effects of a weakened but still palpable Calvinism. It has also made us vulnerable to the toxic materialist values of the contemporary age which I examine in Chapter 12.

Scotland's blind spot

This focus on the Netherlands has another purpose. It helps us to understand an important conundrum – how Scotland's weakness in the nurturing of children could have remained hidden for so long, particularly when I have argued that it's evident almost everywhere we look. Scotland is blind to its child-raising problem in part because it does not compare itself with other European countries where child well-being is high. As a result of language, family connections and shared media, it's America, Canada, Australia, and New Zealand, as well as the other countries of the UK, that are our main point of comparison and most do not fare as well as many European countries on child well-being, or even adult health. In short, we are only marginally worse, and in one case perhaps better, than the societies and cultures with which we are most familiar. Nonetheless, our alcohol, life expectancy and health figures are still more worrying than most of these countries.

England is our most common point of comparison and the English are noted for their maltreatment of children. Indeed, Auberon Waugh once claimed, '. . . the English are famous throughout the entire civilized world for their hatred of children.' England is the land that first introduced child labour in factories and we know from Charles Dickens' portraits of Victorian England that children lived miserable lives. He had been forced to labour himself as a child and so wrote sensitively about children's exploitation.

Table 6: Our Calvinist/Presbyterian legacy?

Social issue	Comparisons and/or comments
Scotland's minimum age of criminal responsibility (MACR) was 8, the lowest age in Europe until 2011. This was raised to 12 by the Scottish Parliament in 2011 for prosecution in court but children aged 8 could still be arrested and charged. The MACR was then raised to 12 in 2019.	Other parts of the UK had, and still have, a MACR of 10. The recommended minimum international standard for criminal prosecution is 14 (not 12) and many countries have 16 as the minimum age of criminal responsibility. Scotland's punitive approach was softened to some extent with the introduction of the Children's Hearings system in 1971.
Council of Europe data show that Scotland is the country in Western Europe with the *highest prison population*.	In 2022 Scotland's adjusted prison population rate was 135.8 per 100,000 people. In Northern Ireland it was 82.6, and in England & Wales it was 98.4.
Scottish state schools used *corporal punishment (the tawse or belt) excessively* for a range of transgressions, including academic mistakes. It was only abolished in 1987 as a result of a ruling from the European Court of Human Rights.	As I outline in Chapter 21 most European countries outlawed corporal punishment for decades, if not centuries, before Scotland. Data show that Scottish state schools physically punished pupils more frequently than their English equivalents.
Physical chastisement of children *(hitting to punish bad behaviour)* was commonplace in Scottish homes. The Scottish Parliament passed a bill outlawing smacking in 2019.	See Chapter 22 for more details.
Per capita Scotland has the highest number of *drug deaths* in Western Europe.	Data published in 2023 shows the Scottish drug death rate as 248 deaths per million, the rate for the UK as a whole was 88. In Estonia it was 40.

[continued over]

Table 1 [continued]

The Scottish Government accepts that Scotland has a far higher rate of *problem drug use* than England and other European countries.	Scotland's rate of problematic drug. use is 1.62% compared with 0.74% in England. In 2015 the UN's Office on Drugs and Crime (UNODC) published a map of drug use internationally. Its research showed that Scotland topped the world for cocaine use, was third top for ecstasy and tenth in the world for opioids – drugs such as heroin and codeine which are often taken to relieve emotional and physical pain.
In Scotland 1 in 5 Scots (22%) drink alcohol 'at hazardous or harmful levels' and Scotland has the highest *rate of alcohol-related deaths* in the UK.	In 2022 the rate of deaths from alcohol per 100,000 people in Scotland was 22.6, and in the UK it was 16.6. The Scottish Government accepts that alcohol presents 'a public health emergency' for the country. People in deprived communities are five times more likely to die from alcohol-related disease than the wealthiest.
Rates of *violence* in Scotland have dropped significantly over the past twenty years. Nonetheless, Scottish figures remain higher than some comparator countries, and Glasgow remains more violent than many cities in Western and Northern Europe.	See Chapter 13 for information on Scotland's successful public health approach to violence reduction. Shame, feelings of humiliation and guilt are often presented as triggers for violent behaviour. American psychiatrist, James Gilligan, maintains that 'shame is the pathogen that causes violence' and considers punishment in childhood another important cause.
Scots are more generous than people in the UK as a whole – taking part in *charitable activities, donating money, sponsoring and volunteering*.	In 2019 'Scotland Giving' reported that 76% of Scots had taken part in a charitable or public service social activity in the past four weeks, 12 percentage points higher than the UK average of 64%.

But perhaps the most shocking aspect of the English ruling class's treatment of children is not how they treated the poor but how they brought up their own children. This is a topic Alex Renton covers in his book about public schools, *Stiff Upper Lip: Secrets, Crimes and the Schooling of a Ruling Class* (2017). He shows how, by the middle of the nineteenth century, the idea had taken hold that children aged eight or younger must be removed from their mothers' 'softening' influence, so that they could be 'toughened up'. Dormitory life, corporal punishment and not being allowed to cry were all designed to ensure that England's top schools would not produce 'effeminate, enfeebled bookworms'. It was widely believed that this supposedly character-forming regime would then stand the child boarders, and the nation, in good stead as these were the strengths required for ruling the Empire. Parents also believed that entering prep schools at a young age would help their offspring get into good public schools thereby ensuring their future privilege. Renton argues that in the nineteenth century many of these institutions were so barbaric that death, including suicide, was common. We now know that many of those who attended prep or boarding schools have ultimately suffered from depression or are unable to form good relationships. Psychotherapist, Joy Schaverien, has written a book entitled *Boarding School Syndrome: The psychological trauma of the 'privileged' child* (2015) based on many of her clients' experiences.

Renton argues that this desire to send very young children away from the family home for extended periods and the tough way they were treated is unique to the English ruling class. (However, as Renton can personally testify, the Anglicised Scottish upper-class followed suit.) 'Nowhere – in societies traditional or modern – are the children separated from their blood relatives for eight or more months of the year for ten years, from the age of seven or eight,' he writes, adding: 'Even in the warrior culture of ancient Sparta, whose legendary hardening of children was so admired... the separation was for days, not months.'

If we leave the upper class and look at England's working classes, we shall find similarities to what I claim happened widely in Scotland, particularly in those areas, such as the North East, where heavy industry dominated and a macho, heavy-drinking, non-child-friendly culture evolved. But, this may have been ameliorated by better housing as well as a different religious inheritance. A similar pattern of heavy industry and heavy drinking could also be found in South Wales and Northern Ireland. Nonetheless Glasgow's premature mortality figures are still the worst in the UK.

If we cast our eyes to the west, we'll see that the Republic of Ireland is not a child-friendly country either as it was historically dominated by a type of Catholicism (Jansenism) which is also based on the notion of human depravity. It too is extremely puritanical about sex and bodily functions. Punishment, humiliation and the importance of respecting authority have traditionally been fundamental to the way Irish children were brought up. This also has resonance with many Scottish Catholics and some describe themselves as 'Catholic Calvinists'.

Thanks to our consumption of American films and television, America is a country with which we are very familiar. It is a wealthy country yet, by European standards, scores poorly on child and adult health and well-being. This is partly the result of its gross inequality and poor health care. There are large variations between the American states in terms of life expectancy. It is low in the 'Bible Belt' southern states for both black and white people. Thanks in part to the influence of what Americans call 'the Scots-Irish' (Ulster Scots), Calvinist attitudes have ensured the dominance of Old Testament religion in the American South as well as a patriarchal, punitive approach as is seen in their continued use of capital punishment. It was these socially conservative Americans who helped to elect Donald Trump in 2016. The ethos in these southern states is certainly not healthy for child well-being. Indeed, US prevalence studies for ACEs show that people raised in these Bible Belt states chalk up significantly more adversities than the American average. If we compare how children were traditionally raised in Scotland with America, particularly the Bible Belt, we would not think we had any particular problem to address. In fact, we look quite good if we compare ourselves to the American South's violent, gun-toting, punishment-driven culture which is now awash with alcohol and drugs and still hits school children.

Political framing

We've also remained so blind to the shadow cast by Calvinism, particularly on the raising of children and our health and social statistics, because we are so fixated on politics. Any problems with Scotland and Scottishness are *only* seen through the prism of political power. This precludes any other understanding of Scotland, even when discussing Scottish literature. For example, Douglas Gifford *et al* in the huge tome *Scottish Literature* (2002) use the terms 'shadowland', 'wastelands', 'blighted nation', 'blighted cities' and 'dystopian visions' as subtitles when discussing Scottish fiction post-1945. They also argue that following the publication of Alasdair Gray's ground-breaking novel *Lanark* (1981) an 'impressive number' of writers also began to focus on 'psychological breakdown and trauma':

> . . . many of the new writers handle what is in essence the same situation – a damaged protagonist (the damage can be physical, but it is the mental harm which matters most), unwilling or unable to face the events which caused the damage, evades reality through various diversionary strategies, these often taking the form of dream escape. These escapes, however, are never successful. . .

When discussing modern Scottish literature the predominant narrative is usually political even though terms or ideas are imported from psychoanalysis. So, Scots have damaged, 'schizophrenic' identities as they are split between being Scottish and British; their feelings and thoughts are divided between Scots and English and they have particular problems with 'voice'. Scots live in the shadow of a more powerful neighbour and feel inferior, or powerless, as a result. What's more, Scots have all been undermined and threatened by deindustrialisation and a change in values forced upon them by the policies of Thatcherism and Scotland's failed 1979 devolution referendum. So when literary characters have problems in their personal relationships – becoming addicted or having a mental breakdown, for example – critics still discuss the novels in terms of Scotland's difficulties with identity and voice or some specific aspect of the country's political history.

In fact, when I read a literary analysis that only discusses political identity and voice, I can't help feeling that the analyst is not simply barking up the wrong tree but has wilfully set up camp under a lamp post with inadequate light and is refusing to move to where the illumination is better. And, certainly for me, it's Calvinism and Scotland's religious past which sheds light on Table 6 on pages 489/490, not politics.

It's also Scotland's religious past which helps us to understand aspects of how we conduct public life in Scotland. There's a preponderance of black and white thinking, absolute certainty and moral judgement which mean that opponents are not seen simply as misguided but as bad, immoral people who are acting in bad faith.

It's also Calvinism which has shaped what we might call a Scots' mentality. Robert Louis Stevenson wrote about 'a strong Scotch accent of the mind'. The novelist and film-maker Alan Sharp claimed that being Scottish is a 'very specific kind of existential event'.

Other commentators on Calvinism

Of course, I'm not alone in arguing that religion is key to understanding Scotland as many commentators in the past took this position. The influential poet and literary critic Edwin Muir, for example, made the Reformation central to his analysis of Scotland and even wrote a biography of John Knox. Tom Nairn's most famous soundbite is that Scotland could only be 'reborn the day the last minister is strangled with the last copy of the *Sunday Post*'. Some twentieth century critics went much further. The novelist George Blake talked about Scotland being 'infected' by Calvinism and the notion that the Reformation ushered in some kind of disease of the mind was commonplace. Willa Muir, the novelist and critic, maintained that 'the Reformation was a kind of spiritual strychnine of which Scotland took an overdose'. But this was mild in comparison to the views of the Scottish playwright and critic, W. Gordon Smith:

> Four hundred years of bloody bigotry bitten deep into the bone.
> Centuries of self-righteousness and extreme unctuousness.

> Slavering hypocrisy and unrepenting smugness. The rape of logic and the murder of reason. Blindness, deafness, and beggared imagination. . . To think that in this age of penicillin and streptomycin there's no antibiotic to cure such a pox of the mind.

While there has been a great deal of comment on the influence of Calvinism, much of this has been about the impact these ideas have had on the arts in Scotland and about our attitudes to beauty or to sexuality. And with good reason. Even Donald Macleod in his article agrees with some of the critics: '. . . there has been no Calvinist aesthetic. An excessive spiritualism has inhibited us from clearly asserting the goodness of the material universe. Terrified of the sensual we have refused to face the deeper question of the sensuous.'

In *The Scots' Crisis of Confidence*, I draw heavily on Scotland's religious history but distance myself from any over-the-top claims about a pox of the mind. I argue that our Calvinist religious inheritance has been both positive and negative – setting up Scotland to be one of the most educated countries in the world, paving the way for the Scottish Enlightenment and, I thought at the time, giving us a strong sense of equality. I also did not want to demonise ministers personally and I quote favourably from Catherine Carswell, the successful novelist who wrote an acclaimed biography of Robert Burns. In this book Carswell was able simultaneously to tell us about the 'fulmination' and fear preached from the pulpit and then remind us that 'other voices with more of pleasantness and peace in them were calling to the people of Scotland. For not all the ministers were stern evangelicals.' And this is the point that Donald Macleod makes when he criticises the attacks on Scottish Calvinism for their 'relentless insinuation that every one of the class is of the same type.'

Macleod was a minister in the Free Church which is most strong in the Hebrides, where he was born. It's commonplace to stereotype the Gaidhealtachd as particularly undermined, by killjoy, Free Church, Calvinist beliefs. That is not my intention here. Indeed I suspect that the intensity of religious beliefs and practice in Gaelic speaking Scotland has not had the deleterious effect on well-being that they may have had on Lowland Scots. My reason for arguing this is simple: there are other aspects of life in the Gaidhealtachd which help buffer well-being – a strong sense of community, family and belonging; a rich oral and literary culture; and a close relationship to nature and the land. These are all important factors for well-being. What's more, unlike Scots which has a paucity of words to convey affection, Gaelic has over 70 terms of endearment. This may explain why the only tender passage written by a Scottish man on his father that I encountered while undertaking research for *Hiding in Plain Sight*, is Finlay J. Macdonald's account of his boyhood on Harris in the 1930s. He writes: 'My father and I had developed a marvellous relationship which puberty, paradoxically, was strengthening rather than abrasing.'

Of course, extreme Calvinist religion with its strong opposition to pleasure has been a feature of Hebridean and Highland life but it's important to eschew caricature. Hebridean poet Derick Thomson was aware of the negative effects of what he terms the Calvinist 'scarecrow' on the culture of the ceilidh-house, yet he also wrote a short poem which begins – '*Although Calvin came/he did not steal the love out of your heart. . .*' As Alastair McIntosh writes in *Poacher's Pilgrimage* (2016), Thomson's poem 'testifies to an underlying island spirituality; to a love that maybe still runs deeper than the injuries.'

I have met many Church of Scotland ministers who are not only benign, warm human beings but who also provide hope and support to their parishioners. I am an atheist myself but I'm not hostile to religion. In fact, I think human beings have a need for religious or spiritual beliefs and I'm aware that something important is lacking in my own life.

Finally, I want to acknowledge that much of what has happened in Scotland in the name of religion has been done with good intentions. Indeed, much of the motivation has been utopian and idealistic. But, counterintuitively, this may be where the problem begins.

In 2019 the Scottish novelist and thinker, Ewan Morrison, wrote an article for *Psychology Today* called, 'The Road to Hell is Paved with Good Intentions'. I found it both enlightening and deeply challenging. It seems stupid, but I didn't appreciate that this phrase has a double meaning. I thought it only meant that people resolve to behave well and then don't. It never occurred to me that it also meant that people's well-meaning acts could have hellish outcomes. I found this challenging as I am by nature an idealist.

In this article, and another on how 'fanaticism' may 'run in families', Morrison sets out why the topic is of such interest to him. His grandmother was a strong Calvinist who routinely condemned others as sinners, and his parents were hippies. Morrison believes his childhood was filled with neglect and abuse as a result of their ideals. His father was also a 'tartan terrorist' supporting those who fire-bombed foreign-owned cottages in Scotland in the 1980s. Morrison himself became a communist. This background has led him to be extremely sensitive to the downside of ideals. In fact, he argues that the problem with idealism is that it blinds people to the negative effects of their actions as they can't face up to the reality of what they've done. These outcomes are often the complete opposite of what they originally intended. Morrison gives lots of examples of how ideals became perverted in various cults and political movements from the Children of God to Pol Pot. What's more, 'unintended consequences' are inevitable if you try to intervene in a complex system.

Secularisation and beyond

The Presbyterian emphasis on understanding and on each parishioner being able to debate the finer points of theology meant that it sowed the seeds of its own destruction. It would have been well-nigh impossible for there to have been one single Church in Scotland given the disputatious nature of the Scots. The fact that the Scottish Kirk survived intact for almost two hundred years is indeed remarkable. But infighting and disputes became commonplace leading ultimately to the Great Disruption of 1843 when Thomas Chalmers and four hundred others walked out *en masse* from the General Assembly.

A Church which encouraged people to think for themselves was also paving the way for agnosticism and atheism and this is precisely what happened in Scotland. In urban areas, even by the nineteenth century, many Scots took the view that religion was a matter of personal belief and conscience. Nonetheless in 1956 the Church of Scotland had an active membership of 1.3 million. It's now around 280,000 and even though the Catholic Church has well over 100,000 active members who attend weekly Mass, Scotland is the most secular part of the UK and one of the most secular countries in Europe.

Tom Holland points out in *Dominion,* that empty pews do not mean that Christian ideas have receded and no longer influence our thoughts. In this chapter I argue that Scotland's past religious ideology continues to affect individual Scots and Scottish institutions. But a religious, or Calvinist, interpretation of Scotland has fallen out of favour. Many Scottish novelists and commentators once saw problems in protagonists' lives as the result of religious ideas but, since the late 1970s, when novelists write about family dysfunction and psychological problems, critics view these novels exclusively through the lens of politics. So they now see these Scottish stories as displaying the negative effects of 'inferiorism', and the schizophrenic, confused identity Scots allegedly have as a result of the Union and Scotland's unusual constitutional status. This change in interpretation mirrors the new identity many Scots have forged in the years post-Thatcher as well as the rise of nationalism. Such views shift any blame for Scotland's problems onto others – notably the English – and enhance a sense of victimhood and grievance. Analysts who want to understand Scottish health and social problems, particularly those inflicting Glasgow and the West of Scotland, also favour theories which are economic and political.

I'm not arguing that there's no merit in such approaches, but I think that in themselves these arguments don't explain **some of** Scotland's enduring health and social problems. They specifically don't help us to understand Scotland's continuing predilection for punishment. Why do we still lock up more people than any other country in Western Europe? Why, within living memory, did we belt infants at school for academic mistakes? Why is our culture so verbally abusive? What lies behind the desire for oblivion that motivates so many Scots, making us top of the table for drug deaths in Western Europe and a leader in binge drinking?

When the psychologist Alan McLean read this chapter he was shocked by the insights it gave into Scottish history and culture. As a Scot, he fully recognised the picture I paint of Calvinism's legacy. McLean has studied emotions for over a decade and in the model he has created, feelings of worthlessness underpin all of the most negative, internal emotional states such as shame, humiliation, depression, feelings of hopelessness and cynicism. Feeling worthless also fuels negative emotions towards others such as hate, contempt, grievance and resentment and the desire for revenge. He also believes that even a diluted version of Scotland's past religious views could plausibly drive our cultural predilection for punishment, addictions and violence and lead to poor health.

But McLean also had a mild criticism of my emphasis in this chapter. He thinks that by presenting the problem of Calvinism's legacy as primarily about the poor nurturing of children, something I do repeatedly in the last few chapters, I diminish the impact it has had as people commonly don't understand how significant childhood is for adult life. I accept that. Rather than rewrite this part of the book at this late stage I simply want to reiterate William Wordsworth's famous line: 'the child is the father of the man'. And to state clearly that if I'm right to argue that for centuries we have not nurtured children well, then this would have had a profound effect both on individual Scots and Scottish culture.

I now want to take my argument on the importance of Scotland's religious history a stage further and argue that the country's mission to build the New Jerusalem has also had a pronounced effect on Scottish politics. And it is to this that I now turn.

Chapter 25
We'll show the world: the independence referendum and collective redemption

The claim that the referendum was about confidence and optimism;
why I voted No; the currency problem; the wider Yes movement;
morality and risk taking;
Scotland's utopian leanings and the quest for redemption;
seeking compromise.

THIS IS A BOOK about the Centre for Confidence and Well-being's work in Scotland from 2004-2024. It's a period which includes one of the most important events in Scotland's constitutional history – the 2014 Scottish independence referendum when an astonishing 85 per cent of the electorate voted. The No side, which campaigned against independence, secured 55 per cent of the vote. Nonetheless few can doubt that it was the Yes campaign which chalked up an impressive victory by energising and enthusing the electorate, 45 per cent of whom voted for Scotland to become an independent country.

The independence referendum was an event that many Yes-minded Scots thought was all about confidence. For many it was a 'time of hope'. Ironically, that was never my view.

The referendum

The Scottish independence referendum was held on September 18th 2014 after a two-year campaign. Throughout that time, I received regular tweets or retweets from Yes supporters saying something like, 'I know you'll agree this referendum is all about confidence or optimism. It's about believing in ourselves as Scots.' Many posted on Twitter the Turnbull cartoon from the 1979 devolution referendum depicting a lion rampant sucking its thumb. 'I'm feart' the caption read. Lack of confidence and the Scottish cringe did play a part in that previous campaign in the 1970s. Even though there was little at stake, there was palpable fear that the Scots would make a mess of devolution.

But by the time of the 2014 Scottish independence referendum, I thought these views on Scotland had largely been expunged as a result of the Scottish Parliament – particularly the two SNP administrations of 2007 and 2011. These governments appeared professional and competent, the senior ministers articulate and presentable. When we add to this the huge success of Glasgow's Commonwealth Games, weeks before the referendum, it was easy to see that most Scots no longer doubted their nation's ability to run its own affairs.

A powerful argument in favour of independence, and hence a Yes vote, was that Scotland and England, once united through common projects such as Empire, world wars and some shared heavy industries, had drifted too far apart. Both countries had founded the welfare state but, thanks to Thatcherism and privatisation, England had changed: it had watered down its commitment to the NHS and public spending and become much more individualistic and more persuaded by market values than Scotland which retained its belief in the importance of the state. All this increasingly mattered when it looked like England would continually return Tory governments to Westminster – governments that a majority of Scots hadn't voted for.

The No campaign was also extremely negative although it was hard for them to be anything else. It would have made a difference if the referendum question had been 'Do you want Scotland to stay in the Union?' as it would then have been easier for those opposed to independence to craft a more positive campaign. But, there's little doubt, the No side exaggerated negativity by arguing irrelevant things such as Scots not being able to watch *Dr Who* after independence. More importantly, unlike the Yes side which had creative and cultural figures supporting the cause, the No campaign's 'celebrities' were boring establishment figures. As no adult likes to be told what to do, bankers, business leaders and British political figures telling Scots that they shouldn't vote Yes was bound to rouse antipathy, particularly when the establishment's reputation had been trashed by the 2008 crash and the years of austerity.

I have little doubt that if I had moved on from being a personal development trainer to a fairly traditional job somewhere in Scotland I would have voted Yes in 2014, particularly when my values and penchant for idealism found resonance in the Yes campaign. But I spent a few years studying Scotland for my book *The Scots' Crisis of Confidence* and started to see the country in a different light, now believing that confidence issues largely flowed from Scotland's religious and cultural history, not English dominance. When I set up the Centre I spent years contemplating the importance and relevance of optimism and pessimism and the weight we should give to facts and reality. This all meant that I brought a critical perspective to Scotland's Yes campaign as this was deliberately crafted to be optimistic.

Nonetheless I prevaricated for most of the two-year campaign and didn't express an opinion in talks, blogs or articles. Some weeks I thought I would vote Yes and then I would change my mind and decide to vote No. For months I would describe myself as undecided. People working closely with the Centre all had different views. Three people with close connections, including the board Chair, Fred Shedden, were not only Yes supporters but SNP members. Other board members were either undecided or No voters. So there was never any chance that the Centre would adopt a formal position either for or against independence.

A few weeks before the vote I finally decided to vote No. As so many people assumed that I was voting Yes, and because authenticity is important to me, I decided to write an article explaining why I was voting No. I contacted Kenneth Roy, editor of *Scottish Review*, to ask if he would be interested in publishing what I was proposing to write on the referendum. He welcomed the idea and used it as the leading article with the heading 'Why this optimist is voting No'. I submitted it as the author of *The Scots' Crisis of Confidence*, not the person who ran the Centre.

On publication Fred contacted me to say he thought the article 'depressing' but nonetheless interesting, sincere and well argued. He suggested that it should be put on the Centre's website, but that I should make clear that it didn't reflect the Centre's views. This I did, but a couple of days later I removed it as I didn't feel it belonged there. To understand arguments I develop later in this chapter, it's important for me to give a short summary of some of my concerns before the vote.

Overoptimism

In 2007 the SNP held workshops with the Really Effective Development Company (REDCO) based in Nottingham. Amongst other things, participants learned about Martin Seligman's academic research on how it's the most optimistic candidate in American presidential elections who wins. From then on, the SNP put optimism at the heart of its message to voters. But the SNP workshop didn't just inform those present on the importance of optimism in elections (at least in the USA) it also included practical exercises. One of these involved giving everyone a bag of pennies and every time they spoke, they had to put a penny on the table if they said anything negative. This major change of approach meant that everything the SNP subsequently said about independence was positive and even in their projected budgets they only used best-case scenarios. The clear implication was that everything would go well for Scotland and other countries would simply agree to what we wanted. As life simply isn't like that, I was sceptical about this and other aspects of the independence offering.

As I write this, almost exactly ten years after the referendum, I find it difficult to believe that something as fundamental as currency in a newly independent Scotland had not been resolved before the campaign launched. Prior to 2009 many nationalists thought the currency problem would be solved by Scotland joining the

Euro but the 2009 Euro debt crisis put an end to that. Sharing the pound was advanced by the Scottish Government in its white paper as its preferred option but all the Westminster parties ruled it out on grounds of financial instability. First Minister, Alex Salmond, refused to come up with a 'Plan B' for currency and threatened to renounce Scotland's share of UK debt if Westminster wouldn't agree to a currency union. This was a serious showdown with important implications for long-term relations between the two countries and financial stability. The main alternative was for Scotland to set up its own currency but this was unpopular with voters and carried significant risks particularly in the transitional period as substantial reserves would be required and this would mean swingeing cuts to public services.

The Yes campaign dismissed any concerns about currency as an insult to Scotland. Other small countries are independent so why not Scotland? But Norway became independent in 1905, Finland in 1917 so they didn't have developed welfare states to pay for or the volatility of financial markets to concern them. In short, establishing their own currencies was relatively easy. The 2008 crash and the 2009 Euro debt crisis taught us just how vulnerable national economies can be. Indeed the economies of Ireland, Iceland, Spain and Greece almost toppled under the weight of debt and seemed little more than the playthings of international markets.

Liz Truss's catastrophic budget in her brief period as Prime Minister in 2022 provides another important lesson on the frightening power of the markets and how they can ruin people's lives through rising interest rates. Even more importantly this episode showed that a currency union, or Scotland continuing to use the pound, could *never* have protected Scotland from England's neoliberal economic policies. Indeed, it was because England would effectively determine Scotland's financial policies and expenditure if we shared the pound that former SNP Vice President James Sillars broke ranks with his party and called their currency proposal 'stupidity on stilts'.

On the eve of the referendum, 55 of the UK's leading academic economists wrote to the *Financial Times*, independently of the No campaign, to say that independence was 'a gamble with very poor odds'. Given the volatility of oil, the difficulties with currency, and Scotland's ageing population they argued that if Scots voted for independence the 'downside risks for current and future generations are huge.'

Independence posed lots of dangers but those who raised them during the campaign were shirracked. The No side were dismissed as Project Fear, naysayers, fearties. They were talking the country down. A frequent complaint of the Yes side was that opponents were insinuating that 'Scotland is too wee, too poor and too stupid' to become independent. During the Brexit referendum in 2016, Vote Leave arguably thought the official Yes campaign so effective that they borrowed its playbook. Not only did they call the Remain campaign, Project Fear, but also Prime Minister Boris Johnson dismissed Remainers as 'doomsters' and gloomsters' and constantly asserted that all the UK had to do to make a success of Brexit was to believe in British (aka English) exceptionalism. It's worth noting that in April 2024 the *Economist* reported that over 60 per cent of UK voters now think that Brexit was a mistake.

The wider Yes movement

So far, I've only mentioned the official SNP Yes campaign but there were thousands of people involved in the wider Yes movement. This was a movement of individuals, groups and most notably cultural figures, inspired by the idea that Scotland could become independent. A few months before the vote, many working-class communities in Scotland were asked to come up with ideas on what the new Scotland would look like. I'm sure that every one of the group in Greenock I wrote about in Chapter 12 on the toxic nature of materialist values would have voted Yes and I understand why. Indeed, it's because I shared the values of much of the popular Yes campaign that I found the referendum period so difficult. When I heard many Yes supporters speak they were talking my language: extremely critical of the Westminster regime, the values of contemporary life and the politics currently on offer. My values chimed with theirs. I also admired the energy and creativity of their campaign.

In the Spring of 2014 the Scottish novelist Ewan Morrison,

quoted in the last chapter, decided, belatedly, to join the Yes movement. A few days before the referendum he wrote an important internet article called 'Why I joined Yes and why I changed to No'. In it he recounts participating in debates where, if a pragmatic question was asked about governance or economics, the questioners were 'quickly silenced by comments such as "We'll sort that out after the referendum"...' The questioners could even be accused of 'being negative' or 'talking the language of the enemy'. He effectively describes the Yes movement as a broad church where anyone's positive idea for Scotland was welcomed. So Yes was prepared to silently accept goals that were inherently incompatible or contradictory such as Scotland becoming a 'world leading Green economy' and a 'world leading petro-chemical economy'. Morrison says that the Yes movement reminded him of his days in the Trotskyite Socialist Workers Party where 'Revolution' was the goal but this was never defined and people could project their own desires on to it thus maintaining unity. Morrison argues that 'the genius' of the Yes campaign was that:

> they've managed to conflate personal self-determination with state power – to shrink the idea of the state down to the self and the question of the future down to 'belief in the self'. You wouldn't want to repress yourself and you personally want to be independent in your own life so, the Yes logic goes, you should ask the same of your country. Every economist has told us that you cannot transpose the micro-economics of your home onto the globe – that micro and macro are different worlds, with different rules, but Yes has managed to blur the two to say 'your country is you'. Your country is an extension of your own personal desires.

Later he writes: 'The Yes camp have managed to make it seem like criticism of their politics is an attack on the individual's right to imagine a better self. To do this, the Yes campaign has had to be emptied of almost all actual political content. It has had to become a form of faith.'

This was a very influential piece. Within two days, and just before the vote itself, the article had more than 300,000 hits. I'm sure it brought many wavering voters down to earth and they understood why the author ended by arguing that the illusion of unity would shatter if there was a Yes vote and 'Scotland will be fighting out its internal battles on a world stage.'

In May 2023 Neil Mackay published an article in *The Herald* in which a former director of Yes Scotland, Ian Dommett, admits the popular (ie. non SNP) campaign was 'naive' and that Yes campaigners didn't agree on what an 'independent Scotland would look like'. In other words, 'the fundamental intellectual and political problem' was that 'we were selling a product we hadn't defined.'

In the end I think that the 45 per cent Yes vote can be attributed to the informal Yes campaign. It was testimony of the type of social power Malcolm Gladwell highlighted in *The Tipping Point*. It was word of mouth, in this case neighbours', friends' and family members' optimism, that boosted the idea that voting Yes would lead to a better future for Scotland and secured much of the vote for independence. Ironically, as I argue in the next chapter, the Centre played a major, albeit indirect, role in this informal movement for Yes.

Morality, selfishness and risk

The referendum was a great experience for those involved with this informal Yes campaign. But woe betide you if you were a No voter as Yes supporters, in my view, ran a decidedly moralistic campaign. Indeed the attitudes of many Yes supporters can be summed up in the phrase, 'holier than thou' and it was possible to detect distinctly Calvinist undertones in many Yes voters' perceptions of the two sides. Yes were the saved, who would go to heaven as a result of their moral superiority, whereas those who voted No were the damned.

Ironically, the SNP's main argument to voters was that independence would make them better off. It was not about heart but pocket. When it was clear that this wasn't going to get Yes over the line, the party changed strategy and started to talk more about social issues such as child poverty.

Prominent nationalists, who had never shown interest in inequality now started to make this their burning issue. For example, Sean Connery told the press that his number one reason for voting Yes was for 'social justice'.

After I made my views public I was on the receiving end of Yes's moral judgement. One woman I knew through work emailed to berate me for being another 'selfish' old person who was voting No and that she never wanted to see me again. A man I had known for years sent an email hectoring me for my 'selfish' position. A woman who was going to accompany me to the Rural Parliament, as I was giving a talk and she had offered to sell *Postcard* books, told me she was no longer going because of 'the stance' I had taken 'for a better, fairer Scotland'. And for months I was denigrated online as a person who 'loved Westminster and the Tories' and was 'in favour of child poverty'.

However, I also received lots of messages from women thanking me for writing my article pointing out the risks of independence. And this is not surprising. One of the biggest disparities in voting, after age, was gender – 53 per of men but only 43 per cent of women voted Yes. This difference may be explained by research which shows that women are considerably more 'risk averse' than men.

As has been clear throughout this book I am by nature a risk taker: I took a big risk both in setting up the Centre and running the expensive Vanguard Programme when finances were uncertain and shaky. Sustaining the work of the Centre for twenty years has been fraught with risk – no government support after the initial period and no private investors. But I thought the risks of independence – not to myself personally – but for Scotland were unacceptably high given the financial context in which we now live. The world is a dangerous place and I don't accept the nationalist argument that there's something exceptional about Scots that means that we would automatically rise above any challenges. In fact, I thought the opposite: Scotland's poor health, ageing population (a much higher proportion of inactive older people than other countries), and low business birth rate[1] would

---

1. In 2022 the Scottish Government published an evidence paper on Scotland's new 'National Strategy for Economic Transformation'. The report points out that 'Scotland ranks low when compared to other OECD countries and the UK'[OVER]

present a serious problem at least in the early days of independence. I was particularly concerned about young people's prospects as they are already facing a challenging future thanks to climate change. Indeed, this may be one reason why 54 per cent of the youngest voters, aged 16-24, voted No.

Of course, in the long run Scotland might have benefited from independence but that's difficult to tell and even if it's true there would have been a lot of pain in the first few decades. However, there was so much idealism and utopianism in the wider Yes movement that the prospect of pain or difficulties hardly featured.

Utopianism and realpolitik

When I wrote *The Scots Crisis of Confidence* I included a chapter on how the Scots are a people with an inclination to utopian dreams. Of course, rationally we know that utopia, or perfection, is unachievable, but lurking behind this understanding is the belief that it *should* be achievable: that the lion should lie down with the lamb and that there is indeed a happy land which we can reach if we just try hard enough.

These utopian longings were evident in the campaign for devolution and resurfaced in the popular Yes campaign. for independence. I'm not arguing that everyone who voted Yes did so because they were animated by the idea of a perfect, just and fair Scotland. Some did so for pragmatic reasons, coming to different conclusions from myself on the risks and advantages to Scotland of independence. But undoubtedly much of the energy behind the Yes campaign was fuelled by the idea that independence would provide Scotland with the opportunity to do something remarkable: to show the world how great we are. Indeed, many argued that voting Yes was like being given a blank sheet of paper and the chance to create a new country. But this was magical thinking. A Yes vote would have immediately plunged Scotland into the world of realpolitik where politicians and civil servants on

---

on measures such as business innovation, investment and total early-stage entrepreneurship (TEA). Scotland needs to increase its TEA 'by around 70% if it is to match the performance of other small advanced economies like Ireland.

both sides of the border negotiated over debt, financial arrangements and trade, rewrote treaties and made legal arrangements, no doubt bickering as they went along, just as with Brexit. Governments across Europe are struggling to fulfil voters' expectations and these are often much lower than the dreams of many in the Yes camp. As the academic Wolfgang Streek argues, Western nations everywhere are living through a 'crisis of democratic capitalism'. Unless you think Scots are 'the chosen people' it's hard to see how we, uniquely, would escape this fate.

Interestingly, Kate Fox in *Watching the English* (2004) never represents her compatriots as having utopian leanings. Indeed the opposite is true. Fox argues that England's grounded empiricism, pragmatism and 'matter-of-factness' are summed up in what she sees as a major English slogan – 'Oh, come off it!'– which is used routinely to squash pretentious or abstract ideas. Of course, many Scots don't like airy-fairy ideas either, but nonetheless, there's a much greater tolerance in Scotland, than England, for philosophising, abtract thought and indeed utopian dreams.

Scotland's utopian leanings

Of course, thanks to personality differences, idealists, utopians, and dreamers can be found in all cultures – even England. The issue here is whether these longings are encouraged or discouraged by the prevailing culture. Given what happened in Scotland just over four hundred years ago it would be remarkable if such utopian tendencies were not evident in Scottish life, for the most striking feature of our past is that Scotland was a nation of religious revolutionaries. In his acclaimed work, *The History of the Scottish People*, T.C. Smout argues that the Protestant reformers in Scotland tried to create on earth 'a perfect mirror of the Kingdom of God in Heaven'. Campbell Maclean, a Scottish minister and broadcaster, believed that Scotland was indeed exceptional in its attempt to build the New Jerusalem:

> Most nations, however Christian, have retreated from this dangerously utopian hope and have been content with more realistic and attainable ends. Where it has been tried, the

> communities have either been territorially smaller, as in Calvin's Geneva, or have opted out of general life in society, like Catholic monastics or like some of the Puritan primitives in the United States. But this is the single instance of a whole nation over centuries, being absorbed by the vision of communal attainment of such ambitious proportions. Only the great Communist states of the twentieth century have shared a like vision.

In Scotland, our Calvinist legacy has predisposed us to the need for redemption. It's a need which fuses the sense of a fallen, corrupted world, with the desire for salvation. In America 'the American Dream' is the result of a fusion of strong Protestant impulses with migrants' ambitions to find a better life. It's primarily a dream of *individual* salvation via hard work and material success – a dream supposedly made possible by a land of opportunity and equality.

As Scotland is no longer a culture dominated by God, nowadays the Scottish dream takes a secular form and is mainly a dream of *collective* redemption and salvation. The Scottish novelist and screenwriter, Alan Sharp, once wrote, 'Scotland lives in the grip of a dream – a dream that originated from the attempt to build the kingdom of heaven on earth.' But it's in politics, that we are most likely to see the Scottish dream in action. and particularly the type of left-wing politics which have dominated the Scottish political landscape for decades. The leading shop steward in the Upper Clyde Shipbuilders work-in of 1971, Jimmy Reid alluded to the dream in one of his newspaper columns when he wrote: 'My dad wept with joy when Labour won in 1945. He was dreaming of a New Jerusalem. John Smith would have understood, but not Blair and Mandelson. Their souls were never seared by the vision splendid.'

'The vision splendid'

Almost all socialist creeds have idealistic or moral underpinnings but, paraphrasing George Orwell, some are more idealistic and moral than others. Marxist-Leninist thought is based on 'dialectical materialism' and sees itself as 'scientific'. As a result it has little time for socialist movements which are simply based on the idea that a socialist society would be morally better or more humane than capitalism. Within the Labour movement which thrived in Britain in the early decades of the twentieth century, there was a huge range of opinion and again some of the parties and sects were more idealistic and moral in their views than others. What's clear is that socialists from Scotland, almost irrespective of grouping or party, had a strong ethical and idealistic base to their beliefs. Indeed, many writers on socialism in Scotland point out that religion played a greater part in the movement's ideology than Marxism. This was certainly true of Keir Hardie, the man credited with founding the Labour Party. He was from Lanarkshire and the influences on him were religious.

Some of the great Scottish socialist politicians of this time – Keir Hardie, John Maclean and James Maxton – passionately tried to improve the living conditions of ordinary people and their campaigns to raise men, women and children out of squalid poverty and inhumane working conditions cannot be seen as idealistic. But inevitably, as Scottish religious thought and history played such a large part in the creation of Scottish Labour ideology, these political reformers were not desiring to win mere palliative, economic measures; they were in their own way also attempting to create the Kingdom of Heaven on Earth. As one Scottish Labour Party pamphlet of the time argued, the change they were pursuing did not simply amount to capitalism being replaced by communism 'but also the greater transition from the semi- human to the wholly human. . . Socialism is the only gospel on earth that makes for the spiritual emancipation of the human race.'

For men like James Maxton, these socialist ideals became entwined with his aspirations for Scotland and the Scottish people. His was a huge vision not just for better lives for working people but also a Scottish Parliament and a 'Scottish Socialist Commonwealth'. In the St Andrew's Hall in Glasgow in 1924 Maxton declared:

> Give us our Parliament in Scotland. Set it up next year. We will start with no traditions. We will start with ideals. We will start with purpose and courage. We will start with the aim and object that there will be 134 men and women, pledged to 134 Scottish constituencies, to spend their whole energy, their whole brain power, their whole courage, and

> their whole soul, in making Scotland into a country in which we can take people from all nations of the earth and say: This is our land, this is our Scotland, these are our people, these are our men, our works, our women and children: can you beat it?

In short, we'll show the world.

Party politics and fallen dreams

I'm not suggesting that the creation of a socialist utopia ever gripped the whole Scottish nation, let alone the whole of Clydeside, in the 1920s. Even in those elections where old-style Labour did exceptionally well, they never won an outright majority of votes in Scotland. And even when their vote was high, many Scots voted Labour because they liked aspects of the socialists' programme not because they shared the whole vision. But the Scottish socialists' vision of utopia owed so much to Knox and the Covenanters that it became entwined with the Scottish dream of collective redemption and still plays a part in the nation's life.

This does not mean that a majority of Scots consciously buy into the notion of collective redemption or live with a sense of utopia. (Sadly many people in contemporary Scotland live in such bleak circumstances that they have little hope or optimism for their own lives, let alone an aspiration for communal perfection.) But what it does mean is that when people feel involved in politics in Scotland they can easily become animated by the Scottish dream.

The early days of the National Party for Scotland, the forerunner of the SNP, were blighted by the political equivalent of snake oil salesmen, all claiming that their idea, if adopted, would at a stroke revitalise Scotland. In his book *Scottish Nationalism* (1969), the New Zealand academic, Harry Hanham, maintained that even in the late 1960s SNP policy was essentially a weird mixture of notions from 'Douglas Social Credit' (a political scheme much loved by Scottish literary figures such as Hugh MacDiarmid and Leslie Mitchell), 'Christian Socialism, anarchism and political Radicalism'. 'Everything,' Hanham caustically adds, 'except a frank acceptance of the modern state and of modern bureaucratised industrial, political, trade union, and commercial empires.' However, many nationalists' commitment to independence is so strong simply because they believe that breaking away from England will instantly solve many of Scotland's problems. Many advocates of devolution, myself included, thought the new parliament would become a beacon of hope and radicalism.

Twenty-five years after the Scottish Parliament was established we're still waiting to see the new Scotland many of us hoped for. Politics professor James Mitchell points out that in the early days of the Scottish Parliament there were significant levels of public spending, reasonable growth and economic stability. This meant that 'Pouring money into services was easier than designing good policies'. So, there was conspicuous Scottish Government largesse – free personal care for the elderly, free prescriptions, free bus passes, an end to bridge tolls, and free university tuition fees. The promised radical change to financing local government to make it fairer didn't materialise. No wonder Mitchell in 2016 described Holyrood 'as a middle-class parliament for a middle-class electorate, though few, if any, of its members would dare admit it.' He accepted that, 'There have . . . been policies designed to address inequalities and efforts to improve the life chances of the least well off' but he adds, 'there can be little doubt that middle-class Scotland has had little to fear from the mythical "radical Scotland".'

The SNP Government in power at the time of writing this book (2024) has introduced child payments and more progressive taxation but the freebies and sweeteners continue to consume a large amount of the annual budget which arguably could be put to better use. And, as James Mitchell points out in his article, once these perks are introduced, they're very difficult to ditch. Even the more limited aspiration for a new style of politics has failed to materialise. Holyrood is every bit as adversarial and nasty as Westminster. As the devolved parliament has not managed to transform Scotland, many Scots' utopian longings have now attached themselves to independence.

The quest for individual and collective redemption

In 2005 Jock Encombe contacted me to request a discussion as he had just read *The Scots' Crisis of Confidence*. At that time Jock was working as a management consultant with organisations but he had trained as a clinical psychologist and had worked for ten years as an adult psychotherapist in Guys and St Thomas NHS Foundation Trust in London. He drew me a model, based on Cognitive Analytic Therapy, that was relevant to his psychotherapy work. It was uncannily like the picture I paint of Scotland in this book, particularly the penchant for black and white thinking, feelings of worthlessness and the drive to prove yourself and utopian dreams. The conversation with Jock helped me see many Scots' attitudes to politics in a new light.

Just before the 2014 independence referendum Jock published an article called 'The psychopathology of everyday nationalism'. In it he writes: 'Psychotherapy teaches us that when people are attracted to visions of a perfect future and then become aggressive towards people who do not buy into their fantasy, they are in denial about some aspect of themselves.' And, he explains, certain processes can evolve which enable some sort of coping with their experiences like narcissism and magical thinking.

> The process works by seeking to avoid unbearable feelings of worthlessness by either angrily projecting them onto others... or by escaping into grandiose fantasies of wholeness and perfection. While providing temporary relief, however, magical thinking is ultimately doomed to fail. The return to reality is always painful and often destructive. Furthermore, it is a pattern of behaviour which, if the underlying psychological hard work of acquiring self-knowledge is not undertaken, is destined to repeat itself. It is perhaps worth noting that middle-aged men seem particularly vulnerable to these kinds of behaviour.

Over the years, I've come up with a model inspired by that conversation with Jock. I'm not claiming that it's psychotherapeutic and offer it here simply as a potentially useful way to see a common pattern of behaviour in Scotland.

Figure 3 relates to our dreams as Scots, not for individual, but

Figure 3 – Collective redemption

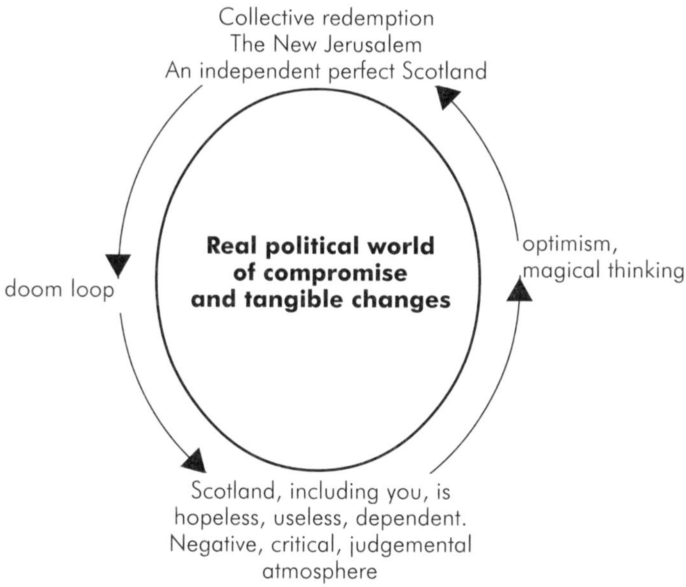

collective redemption. It's about Scots attempting yet again to build the New Jerusalem. The energy here comes from feelings of not being good enough, not just about the self but the country as a whole. A combination of optimism, and magical thinking, propels us to exaggerated views on our own importance and powers.

This is the bumptious, boastful side of Scotland that asks 'wha's like us?' It's the Scotland of the grandiose vision that above all else wants to impress the outside world, just as those planning the ill-fated Darien scheme wanted to do centuries ago and James Maxton dreamed about in the 1920s. This is the Scotland in which Jack McConnell's Government chose the slogan 'Scotland is the best small country in the world'. (The SNP abandoned it when it took power as they didn't think it needed a qualifier. We were simply the best country in the world.) Then the new Scottish Government aimed to become the best country in the world for children to grow up and, at the same time, the best country in the world to do business, with no acknowledgement of how far Scotland was from these goals. In 2008 the Scottish Government announced that its green targets were the 'best in the world' and that Scotland would play 'a leading role in the fight against climate change'. In 2024 it abandoned its 2030 carbon emissions targets, as they were unachievable, and mothballed key parts of its strategy as a result of inadequate planning and consultation. It also accepted that its targets were 'always beyond what was possible'. But nonetheless the Scottish Government is still clinging to the idea of being the best in the world for environmental policies and has retained a more ambitious 2045 target than the UK and most other countries. Those in the know about climate change are sceptical of Scotland's chance of delivering.

The top of Figure 3 is also the home of all those over-the-top aspirations for an independent Scotland to become a perfect, fair, green, economically turbo-charged democracy that would be the envy of the world. When it didn't happen, and it could never have happened even if there had been a Yes vote, people then felt angry and frustrated and lashed out at those who thwarted their fantasy. What's missed out this time is the real world of politics which is about compromise. Things can improve if you devote time and energy to making them better in everyday life.

I admit that so much of my own story is in this model. I was a wee working-class girl who thought she was worthless and, perhaps thanks to her Sunday school days, developed very idealistic views. I can still remember singing the hymn 'There is a happy land' written by Scottish dominie Andrew Young and longing for that perfect place. This idealism fuelled my drive for personal development and I can see that when I started to write books and set up the Centre I was unconsciously motivated by collective redemption. This is why I found Ewan Morrison's article on 'the road to hell', referred to in the previous chapter, so challenging but illuminating. I can see now that a desire to do good can easily backfire and have a negative effect – one that we then feel reluctant to admit since this wasn't what we intended.

Of course **I'm not asserting that everyone in Scotland who voted Yes was in pursuit of collective redemption and completely out of touch with everyday politics**. But many were and I think we can gauge this by their reaction to No voters. Do they see them simply as people entitled to hold a different view and acting in good faith or do they denounce them angrily as bad people who got in the way of their fantasy of a perfectly fair and just, independent Scotland? Ten years on, things have improved slightly but for me a certain narcissism and magical thinking still prevails in our culture. And whatever the political future holds, these impulses and trends need addressing.

Final reflections

When I came out as a No voter, some leading the independence campaign thought it ironic that the head of Scotland's Centre for Confidence and Well-being lacked confidence. How wrong they were. It took a great deal of personal self-confidence for me to publicly disagree with the Yes campaign. Some of this was simply the result of how the question was framed. As the actor Bill Paterson wrote in a humorous article on how difficult it was for those in the arts to do anything other than support Yes, he wrote: 'Yes is a great wee word. It sounds kinder. It's just nicer to say. It's progressive. It's the very definition of positive' whereas 'the negative and Calvinist No. . . seems a particularly dreich option'.

I have never considered myself to be a Unionist. In 1977, when I was a postgraduate at Edinburgh University I joined, former Labour MP, Jim Sillars' new Scottish Labour Party (SLP). It was campaigning for an independent Scotland within the European Union. I remember being somewhat lukewarm about this but not because I wasn't keen on Scottish independence or home rule.[2] I voted No in 2014 as I was concerned about financial stability and the negative impact independence could have on Scotland. As my main concern wasn't about leaving the UK, I could be considered a 'soft No' voter. My views are always open to change. Given this I was intrigued by the conciliatory approach now being adopted by Stephen Noon.

Stephen had worked in the Scottish Government and Parliament, latterly as a senior political advisor for the SNP. He then became

---

2. In those days people on the left were generally anti 'Common Market' as it was dismissed as a 'bosses' club'. The SLP was short-lived, brought down in part by Trotskyite entryism, and I was a member for less than a year.

Chief Strategist for the official, SNP Yes campaign and an enthusiastic believer in the power of optimism. After the vote he left Scotland and trained in Canada to become a Jesuit priest. While he was living in community with Jesuits in Quebec he talked about independence referenda and these mild-mannered men became angry. Stephen told Kenny Farquarson of *The Times* that 'what that did for me – probably for the first time – was make me understand the other side of the experience. Maybe "wound" is a slightly excessive word, but it had left a mark on them.' Stephen decided not to become a priest, returned to Scotland and is now in academia studying for a Ph.D. on a new type of politics.

Having read some articles about Stephen's new ideas I contacted him and suggested we meet up, and we did in April 2024 for what proved to be a deep and amicable discussion. Of course, he's still committed to Scotland and would like to see independence in the long term but thinks that how this happens is vitally important. When working for Yes he thought that 50 per cent of the vote plus one would have been a victory. He now shudders at the thought as he knows that this would have led to a deeply divided Scotland which would have struggled with the challenges facing it. He's acutely aware that the referendum created a binary in Scotland when the reality is that there's a large majority of people, including me, who wanted to build a stronger nation. So, he now thinks that a focus on more powers or a different relationship with Westminster would've been better than an independence referendum for which the country wasn't ready.

During our discussion Stephen accepted that the Yes campaign was one-sided and it shouldn't have tried to be 100 per cent optimistic and acknowledged risks and weaknesses. However, he said the reality of politics is such that the press and other political parties would have magnified any doubt they may have expressed making this impossible. I accept that. In the spirit of give and take, Stephen also agreed that Scottish independence was not all about confidence and optimism.

For Stephen it's 'compromise' and a politics of 'compassion' and 'connection' that will take us to a better Scotland. I wholeheartedly agree.

The Final Analysis

THE FIRST CHAPTER of this book begins with the Scotland's Tipping Point event in Glasgow's Òran Mór on 2nd December 2004 when we launched the Centre and this chapter refers to developments happening in the summer of 2024. I now want to focus on four things during the twenty-year period under review. First, whether the Centre, and myself as a thinker, had a coherent philosophy or approach. Second, what impact our work had on Scotland and beyond. Third, why there has been such a loss of hope. And fourth, whether there might be a lasting legacy from the Centre's work, my books and thinking. To organise this material I have divded this chapter into four sections: beliefs, impact, loss of hope and legacy.

I

The Centre's beliefs and philosophy

Scotland's Tipping Point

Since writing *The Scots' Crisis of Confidence*, my interest in change in Scotland has been cultural, behavioural and psychological, and not framed in constitutional or even political terms. And this is clear in my speech at the Centre's founding event, Scotland's Tipping Point. Not only do I still have a copy of that speech but I wrote a chapter with this title in a book edited by former SNP MSP and Cabinet Secretary for Justice, Kenny MacAskill, called *Agenda for a New Scotland: Visions of Scotland 2020* (2005).

In that article I didn't simply outline what I said at Scotland's Tipping Point but also described the event itself including Malcolm Gladwell's contribution, and how so many left Òran Mór saying how inspirational the day had been. Gladwell set out how social movements come about and how quickly they can reach a tipping point when real change happens. In my speech I addressed the tricky question of what I thought those gathered there wanted to tip. In short, what changes were we pursuing in Scotland?

The first thing I said we needed was more positive attitudes – optimism, praise, appreciation, compassion and gratitude as a counterbalance to the negativity that was so common and, ironically, intense in the first few years of the Scottish Parliament. I specifically said that this is not about being positive all the time as this is 'inhuman' and we don't want to create a nation of Pollyannas. I then move on to confidence, particularly self-acceptance and self-efficacy. Individuality was next on my list and this was about valuing difference and self-expression. I specifically said this isn't about individualism and pursuit of self-interest or the erosion of Scotland's collectivist values. I also mentioned creativity, innovation and recognition of success. And finally, I introduced the importance of well-being which was a little used concept back in 2004.

In the following three or four years the Centre undertook a great deal of work on confidence and positive psychology which I describe in the section of this book devoted to Phase 1 of our activities. From 2009 on (Phase 2) we then broadened our definition of well-being, beyond people's subjective psychological state and looked at how other factors, such as the natural world, inequality and class, alcohol and drugs and a host of other topics, also affected well-being individually and collectively. What I want to do now is summarise how most of this work was underpinned by certain beliefs and philosophical approaches. Some of these have been mentioned in previous chapters but I think it's helpful if I summarise them here and so I've set them out in Box 18.

Box 18: The Centre's beliefs and approach

Many people in Scotland are operating below their capacity: This has always been a fundamental belief for the Centre. We believe that for whatever reason – historical attitudes, upbringing, mindset, education and most importantly rigid, top-down organisational structures which centralise decision-making – many people are capable of achieving more than they are currently. While there may have been some improvements in school pupils' beliefs about their own capacities, the centralised nature of political decision-making in Scotland has removed personal agency from many working people, including professionals.

Well-being is complex: There are many different ways to view well-being but we prefer to stress that well-being has two sides. The first concerns the importance of feelings of belonging to a wider group – family, friends, neighbours, community, work, church, clubs and societies. This is why loneliness is so bad for people's health. But the second side to well-being is the importance of individuality and agency. People want to make decisions for themselves, learn skills and develop themselves as individuals. When people are able to employ their skills and personal experience to advance others' welfare or the greater good, and not just their own lives, this further enhances their well-being. This means that it is particularly beneficial if the two sides of our well-being interact and boost one another.

The golden mean: Almost from the first day of the Centre's existence we understood the importance of balance. So, we wanted to encourage positive feelings such as optimism but never conveyed the idea that pessimism wasn't valid and always said that it was also important for people to be able to express negative feelings. Given the Scots' well-known predilection for negativity and dourness we thought that encouraging more positive feelings would provide a balance but not completely eliminate negativity, particularly Scots' healthy scepticism.

This notion of balance was also central to the work we undertook on young people's confidence and well-being. So, we argued that adults are undermining young people's resilience by focusing too much on avoiding negative feelings and experiences. Thanks to our work with the psychologist Alan McLean, we started to frame this as a judicious balance between support and challenge and finding what Aristotle called 'the golden mean'.

More is not better: Related to this idea of balance is our belief that because a small amount of something can be good, more is not necessarily better. In fact, it may have the opposite effect. So some emphasis on the importance of trauma and abuse can be helpful but constant exposure to the idea that trauma and abuse are particularly harmful can in itself be debilitating if it encourages a strong sense of victimhood.

The way that ideas are constantly reinforced is a major issue in the modern world. As soon as an idea, diagnosis or label has some currency (e.g. depression, self-esteem, adverse childhood experiences, trans identities, attention deficit hyperactivity disorder) then there is a large professional network of support workers and self-help groups to amplify the ideas through the media, particularly social media. As I outlined in Chapter 22 this phenomenon is called 'looping effects'.

We are social animals, and inevitably influenced by others in our peer group, particularly when we are young. Social contagion results when people infect others with their ideas. What's new is that thanks to all the communication channels now open to us, ideas can be amplified and reinforced in a very short period of time. We need to be constantly alert to the potential downside of ideas that we're transmitting.

Ironic effects/unintended consequences/the road to hell: From very early on in our work we understood the importance of 'ironic effects' – that it's not only possible, but also easy, for us to do things which have the opposite effect from what we originally intended. So, relaxation exercises can lead us to feel more stressed and harping on about confidence can encourage others to pay more attention to their lack of confidence and then see this as a barrier to doing something challenging. Unintended consequences are also likely when we intervene in a complex system. In recent years we've seen unintended consequences flowing from people's well-intentioned actions and desire to be helpful and kind. This is why the saying 'the road to hell is paved with good intentions' seems especially apposite in a world where more people are now pursuing their ideals with religious, indeed puritanical, zeal.

Context matters: As a Centre we've always understood that it can be unwise to assert hard and fast rules as context matters enormously. This can refer to historical context, to specific circumstances or to the personalities and experience of those involved. What might work in one context, with a specific group of people, might not translate into other situations. This is why we've never favoured a rigid, programmatic approach to personal development. Nor have we ever thought that you can single out one virtue or character strength and state that this is all that matters. Yet this is precisely what many people and groups have done with kindness. But while kindness is often appropriate, it isn't always and sometimes needs to be tempered by truth and courage and should not undermine justice. As Barry Schwartz has argued so convincingly, it's wisdom that's required to help us balance these competing values or virtues within a specific context.

Goals may be best achieved indirectly: We have always been attracted to the concept advanced by the Scottish economist, John Kay, which he calls 'obliquity'. This echoes ancient thinkers on how goals are often achieved through 'oblique' rather than direct means. So, if a company wants to be profitable it's often more likely to succeed if it puts excellent customer service, developing staff or another laudable goal at its core rather making money. We think that introducing a kindergarten stage in Scottish education is an oblique method to improve both child well-being and, ultimately, academic standards.

To remedy problems there's never one single perspective, discipline or approach: The Centre's thinking here is partly a reaction to the number of professionals, consultants or academics who believe that if their approach were to be adopted then it would instantly provide a 'quick fix' or the much sought after 'silver bullet'. Psychologists, including positive psychologists, were particularly keen to claim that their approach, on its own, could improve child well-being, for example, when there is a range of factors undermining children's mental and physical health. A narrow focus is the inevitable result of academic specialisation.

Given the limitations of reductionism, we were particularly attracted to the quadrants in Ken Wilber's integral theory. This shows that for any issue concerning human beings we must pay attention to factors which are – psychological and spiritual; physiological and behavioural; cultural and relational; and structural and social. We were drawn to Wilber's theory as it encourages respect for different thinkers and approaches as they all have a specific contribution to make to our knowledge and understanding. 'It all matters,' to echo Wilber.

The objective, real world matters: Related to this last point is our firm believe that the real, objective world matters. Of course, subjectivity is important and up to a point we can choose how we see the world. However, we disagreed with the evolution of Martin Seligman's ideas as he ultimately dismissed the importance of external realities such as class, inequality or poverty on an individual's life. Indeed, we were initially attracted to positive psychology because in Seligman's earlier work there's a strong emphasis on facts and objective reality. Nor did we ever accept the type of magical thinking which underlies Rhonda Byrne's best-selling book *The Secret* based on 'the law of attraction' or other forms of largely American positive thinking approaches.

Implications of the Centre's beliefs and approaches

The contents of the box above might seem rather abstract and these beliefs weren't something we talked about often, if at all. These became implicit beliefs which helped us to decide the topics to work on.

Writing them down for the first time I was aware that these beliefs came together in a fairly coherent approach: one that eschews a programmatic, top-down idea of change. Scottish policy thinking, such as it is, usually comes from the centre and then staff are expected to apply it irrespective of the context they're working in, the specific individuals or circumstances involved or the imbalance that might result from the 'intervention' (Not a word we were ever keen on.).

What we need more of in Scotland is really well-trained, supported and thoughtful practitioners who in a particular context, faced with specific individuals, are able to make decisions on the right course of action or the most appropriate response. They may make the wrong decisions sometimes (and of course that happens in the current system) but unlike now they will be encouraged to use their independent judgement and to grow and develop thus becoming more sophisticated and more confident practitioners.

So, as a Centre, we were never keen on the idea of a programmatic approach to change and, apart from starting to design a programme for organisations which we then abandoned, this was not what the Centre was about. We primarily saw ourselves as a catalyst for change. Introducing new ideas, preferably with an evidence base, that were interesting and potentially helpful, and we were always hopeful that bigger and better resourced organisations would pick them up. This is why much of our work consisted of large-scale events with inspiring, first-class speakers and books, including a book series, in which we could provide detailed analysis of the type of changes needed in Scotland and how they may come about, or were in fact happening here or elsewhere.

In the case of self-esteem, or our work on the Westminster Government's SEAL (Social and Emotional Aspects of Learning) programme, we aimed to discourage people from using these approaches and encourage them in what appeared to be a better direction. And without being too pious, we consciously did this even when we knew we could have made lots of money, and grown the organisation, if we had devised a fashionable programme on self-esteem or a Scottish equivalent of SEAL.

But we also believed that more people needed to be involved in decision-making. We fully supported community action and involvement in development issues. Our book *The New Road* by Alf and Ewan Young set out some inspiring examples and argued for more. Those of us working at the Centre thought that centralised, top-down control was undermining organisations, an argument that Tony Miller and Gordon Hall put cogently in *Letting Go*. And we agreed wholeheartedly with the Poverty Truth Commission's slogan, 'Nothing about us – without us – is for us.'

II

The Centre's impact

Government and organisations

It was always very difficult for us to assess the Centre's impact. Even in the early days when we had Scottish Executive funding, we were too wee and too poor, but I hope not too stupid, to commission formal assessment of the impact we were having on either the people involved in Centre activities or the wider society. Of course, we always evaluated responses to our events but that's different from trying to measure impact.

All I can do here is estimate what our impact may have been. For the first seven years we received Scottish government funding and had to submit plans and reports to funding departments. Apart from two specific topics, I doubt that we had much impact on Scottish Governments' thoughts and actions. The first of these is my large SEAL (Social and Emotional Aspects of Learning) report, outlined in Chapter 5, on what I perceived to be an Orwellian development in English education. This seems to have had some impact on Geoff Huggins, Head of Mental Health Division in the then Scottish Executive, who did not then aim to support a similar scheme here. The second concerns the numerous reports written by Alan Sinclair, while a Centre associate, on the importance of the first two years of life and what types of early intervention can make most of a difference. Alan is very much a policy animal and he's still having ongoing conversations on the topic with senior civil servants.

Ironically, I think the biggest impact the Centre had on government was on the Westminster Government's Department for Children, Schools and Families. In 2007 SEAL was an important education project for that department. It wasn't popular with many teachers, particularly in secondary schools, but they were being silenced by the Department's argument that it was based on sound evidence. It wasn't and I revealed this in my in-depth report which was then widely circulated by teachers and other educationalists. I'm not saying that SEAL disappeared and that no aspects of it still remain but there's little doubt that my paper deflated Westminster's Orwellian ambitions for school pupils in England and Wales.

Once we look beyond formal government structures it's very difficult to assess the Centre's impact. Remember, an emphasis on confidence and personal development, and ultimately well-being, would have happened without us as it was part of the *zeitgeist*. We didn't create the interest or focus on these concepts. Rather we were part of this trend. Indeed in Scotland we were funded by Jack McConnell's Labour administration at Holyrood because confidence was a key part of his Government's thinking. For reasons I set out in Chapter 19, I would never have suggested that 'confident individuals' be put at the heart of the Curriculum for Excellence.

Given that we were not in the driving seat with an agenda which was increasingly being adopted by governments, I saw the Centre's role as ensuring, where possible, that decision-makers and practitioners chose approaches which may be successful and were unlikely to have ironic effects, undermining rather than boosting confidence and well-being. Thus, we promoted the idea of self-efficacy and Professor Carol Dweck's growth mindset, rather than self-esteem, and encouragement rather than praise. We provided training on the successful Australian school resiliency project,

Bounce Back! And we talked about indirect methods to boost confidence such as outdoor learning, sport and fitness, music, and in a later stage of the Centre's work, play. Other organisations, such as Winning Scotland, moved into the space once occupied by the Centre and took on the promotion of Dweck's work. We were happy about this as we always saw ourselves as a catalyst for change, and not a delivery organisation. Apart from anything else we didn't have the resources to be this and didn't seek this type of funding as we were happy with our role.

Those who attended our events were often very taken by the speakers and the new ideas to which they were introduced. I'm specifically thinking here of The Vanguard Programme (2005); 'The Brain that Changes Itself' (2009); Professor Barry Schwartz's 'The Choices that matter' (2009); the Centre's big event critiquing self-esteem (2010); our large 'Melting the Iceberg' event on drugs and alcohol (2011); our events on materialism (2011-13); and the 'Creating Good Lives' (2010) conference with Professor Julius Wilson which majored on class and poverty, and which evolved out of my book *The Tears that Made the Clyde*. These all stand out as events with enormous energy behind them and the capacity to change people's perspectives.

As our approach never conveyed the idea that there was a silver bullet and that we needed to understand problems and devise solutions that are multi-disciplinary, the atmosphere we sought to create was respectful and inclusive. This was about Scottish organisations pulling together to deal with some of the big problems in our midst. The Creating Good Lives event was subtitled: class, inequality, work, family, education, environment, well-being, drugs and alcohol and we could have added in poverty, health, violence and child well-being as they were also discussed in workshops. Lots of organisations came together to support the event. There was so much energy in part because there was a sense of shared ownership. It's worth repeating what a senior civil servant said to me at the close of the conference: 'Something special is happening here today – I don't just mean the numbers of folk you've managed to get along. There's an atmosphere, an urgency about the need to change, that I haven't detected before. It's as if we've turned a corner.'

With hindsight I can see that we did our best work, bringing together individuals from lots of different organisations to talk about the problems facing Scotland and how we could individually and collectively challenge them in Phase 2 of our activities when we had broadened our definition of well-being. In April 2011, our Scottish Government funding was reduced to £50,000, from £125,000 per annum and it remained at this level to 2014 and then we received one further payment of £10,000 and that was it.

As a board we meekly accepted our reduced funding as part of austerity. But we didn't give up and even with much less and ultimately no funding we still produced a variety of successful *Postcards* books like John Carnochan's *Conviction* and we also held some events. But there's little doubt that by 2012 the Centre's health was failing. By 2014, to use a more mechanistic metaphor, we'd been holed beneath the waterline. And the damage inflicted on the Centre wasn't simply about funding: Scotland itself was changing. So too were many Scots' priorities and ironically, as we're about to see, the Centre indirectly made a contribution to those changes.

A social movement on the importance of confidence and optimism

We were never funded to influence the public at large, but with hindsight I can see that we did. There's little doubt that the Tipping Point event, when we launched the Centre at the end of 2004, was the beginning of a social movement for change in Scotland: a movement that ultimately touched the lives of tens of thousands of people. We also attracted a great deal of media coverage. Apart from the numerous Centre events I've listed throughout this book, we had an enormous website of resources in an era where there wasn't much material online. I also spoke to people at a variety of events. For the first 5-6 years I was averaging 40 talks a year. So a large number of people listened to me speak about the importance of confidence and optimism.

From even a cursory knowledge of Gladwell's book *The Tipping Point* it's easy to see why the Centre was likely to have a large impact. He outlines the little things that can ultimately cause a large cultural shift in how people come to think about things. He's particularly keen to explain how an idea tips over from being the preserve of some individuals or a few groups into the wider public consciousness. The metaphor he's fond of using is that ideas, products, messages and behaviours spread just like viruses and, in his book, he sets out the reasons why some things 'go viral'.

The first reason Gladwell gives is what he calls '*the law of the few*'. For an epidemic to occur there only needs to be a few very sociable people who have unusual social gifts which they use to communicate ideas and messages. However, these few people need to transmit their messages to three different groups of people who then have an important role to play in creating cultural change.

Connectors are the first group of people Gladwell outlines. They are the ones who bring people together and start a word-of-mouth chain reaction. Gladwell says that when an idea comes into contact with a Connector it has a high chance of spreading. The Centre was a brilliant vehicle for spreading ideas, as we quickly established connections across Scotland – not just geographically but also across sectors. In those days it was commonplace for occupational groups to speak only to themselves. But from 2003 and the Towards a Confident Scotland conference, inspired by *The Scots' Crisis of Confidence*, ideas on confidence attracted people from across all sectors of health and education as well as sport, enterprise, business and central and local government. Once we founded the Centre we only needed a few people from these different sectors for our ideas on the importance of confidence and optimism to then be taken back to the home organisation and from there circulated further afield by word-of-mouth. As I was regularly giving talks to a wide variety of organisations at conferences or workplace events, schools, community groups etc. this heightened the infectious nature of our ideas. I had always seen my role in the Centre as a Connector. As I had been employed by the BBC and then worked across organisations in my role as a trainer, I had a large number of connections and this proved helpful when I wrote my first book and set up the Centre. But I'm not sure that Connector was my main role.

Mavens are the second group Gladwell discusses. These are experts who translate their knowledge into clear messages. They may remain neutral but what they say is important and people listen. Looking back, I can see that as many of our conference speakers were stellar academics and speakers, they played the role of Mavens. But the Centre's hugely important, resident Maven was Professor Phil Hanlon. Phil didn't just attend but spoke at the end of most Centre events. His role was to reflect on what attendees had just heard from speakers, to clarify its relevance and then to draw participants into discussion. Phil facilitated these discussions, so they weren't the usual, annoying, fragmented question and answer sessions. This meant that participants usually left feeling they had not only gained deep insights but also been given the opportunity to contribute and be heard. Phil's role was hugely important in giving Centre events gravitas as he was an inspiring speaker and impressive academic in a subject of relevance to us all – public health. I've always known that I wouldn't have stuck with the Centre through very challenging times if it hadn't been for Phil's intellectual and personal support as a member of the board. But writing this now I can see that he also had a vital, independent role as a Maven at our events and this contributed enormously to the Centre's story and success.

Salesmen (or women) are the third group Gladwell outlines. These are people who can sell an idea by creating messages that understand how subtle things can make a difference. They can tailor their message to have most impact on individuals. This is linked to the second explanation Gladwell gives for ideas going viral and he calls it '*the stickiness factor*'. A fashion or cultural shift must have something memorable at its core so that people pay attention. In short, for a tipping point you need an idea that 'sticks'.

Much as I'm extremely resistant to describe myself in such commercial terms I was undoubtedly the Centre's Salesperson who created the stickiness of its message. *The Scots' Crisis of Confidence* is not all about confidence. It has a lot about confidence in it but it's more an analysis of Scotland or a cultural critique. I hadn't read *The Tipping Point* when I wrote it but intuitively I understood that my book needed the word 'confidence' in the title as it was the word most Scots would relate to. Gladwell would call that 'the stickiness factor'. Optimism, positive psychology and mindset became other sticky words for the Centre.

Given the popularity of many of the events I devised, I was clearly able to tap into what people found interesting at that moment in Scotland's history. I was aided greatly by Pete Fletcher, a graphic designer with marketing experience, who worked closely with the Centre from its foundation. The logo he created for us was brilliant in summing up what we were about – optimism, positive energy, creativity and innovation. But the Centre was not 'slick' – we never gave out freebies or put any emphasis on glitzy presentation at our events. It was authenticity and the quality of the content that was always uppermost and which was appreciated by the people who attended our events.

This leads into the third factor Gladwell thinks necessary for tipping points – 'the power of context'. All this means is that for an idea to really take off you need to create a community, as once people are part of a group they are susceptible to information passed on through other members. In the first few years we achieved this up to a point: we ran some networking events and there were undoubtedly some people who made a point of coming to all Centre events and who consciously felt part of a community. That's why we had a number of volunteers.

But the community dimension of the Centre's work wasn't primarily about creating a self-contained group of Centre followers, it's about these people and thousands of others who were touched by the Centre's work in other ways, taking the ideas out into the wider community. I'm sure they would've tried to influence colleagues, family members, neighbours and other people they met in various walks of life. And the message they would have wanted to broadcast is easy to sum up: confidence and optimism matter and we would have better lives in Scotland if we were more confident and optimistic. Ironically for me, it was in the political domain that these ideas ultimately flourished.

Politics, constitutional change and the Yes campaign

In my article on Scotland's Tipping Point in MacAskill's book, written in 2004, I cover the role of politics in change and wrote that 'the vast majority of Scots keen to see a transformation in Scotland perceived the change they sought as largely political. For many a new, better Scotland would only be brought about by constitutional change.' This is why so much energy in Scotland over the past century has been devoted to the home rule/ devolution/ independence debate. I accept that there's nothing particularly Scottish about the belief that transformational change can only be brought about by politicians. In fact, Gladwell made this point when he said that people play down the importance of social power and overvalue political and economic power. However, I argued that as we didn't have our own parliament until 1999 it was all too easy for Scots to overvalue the importance of politics and only value structural change.

The type of changes I envisaged Scots making as a result of their contact with the Centre and its ideas can be summed up as organisational, community, personal and relational. So I personally didn't see the change that Scotland and the Scots would most benefit from as primarily constitutional. But undoubtedly some of those who attended Scotland's Tipping Point, or who were touched by the Centre's ideas through later events, went on to apply these ideas to the political realm. In fact, some would have already been switched on to constitutional change and that's why they were attracted to these events and the Centre's work, more generally. It didn't matter to them that I played down the importance of constitutional change and wasn't a nationalist. In those years, before the rise of the SNP or talk of a referendum, an individual's view on independence was not a black and white issue. What mattered was whether you were committed to improving life for people in Scotland and, at that time across the independence divide, I was respected for my obvious desire to make Scotland a better place to live.

As I mentioned in the previous chapter, three people who worked closely with the Centre on a daily basis, including the Chair, went on to become members of the SNP and there would have been many more I didn't know about. While writing this book I realised that the Centre's work on the importance of confidence and optimism undoubtedly fed into the informal Yes campaign for the 2014 Scottish independence referendum. It was this grassroots movement which gave much of the Yes campaign its energy and drive and was no doubt responsible for much of the 45 per cent support for independence in the final vote. And that movement was propelled by confidence and optimism.

It's worth pointing out that the two cities which were most influenced by the Centre's work were hotbeds for Yes in the 2014 independence referendum – Glasgow where we were based and held most of our events and Dundee, thanks to Go Dundee which formed as a result of Scotland's Tipping Point. (see Appendix 1)

In 2014 I was too immersed in Centre activity and everyday life to understand what was happening, so this perspective only became visible ten years later while looking in the rear-view mirror for this book. I was never enthusiastic about the referendum and ultimately voted No so it's ironical that the Centre I founded is likely to have boosted the Yes campaign. It certainly looks like yet another example of unintended consequences and the fact that people who espouse ideas, and spearhead movements, have no control over how these ideas are ultimately used.

III

The Loss of Hope

Things are only getting worse

Another way to think about the Centre's impact is to ask if personal confidence and well-being is now higher in Scotland than when we started. It wouldn't be appropriate to start looking in detail at data this late in the concluding chapter so all I want to say is that I doubt any of these would show that we're going in the right direction: the business birth rate in Scotland is still low, Scottish adolescents' confidence has gone down, not up, and data on addictions in Scotland and physical and mental health do not show that the country is on a positive trajectory. And that's understandable given that many problems have increased substantially since we set up the Centre in 2004. I'm specifically thinking of the steep rise in poverty and inequality, the decline of public services, the housing crisis, the pandemic and its consequences, inflation, the cost-of-living crisis and population health issues like the rise of obesity.

There are also important cultural trends such as increased polarisation and division, loss of trust in politicians, and a steep increase in loneliness – all factors that can contribute to a loss of individual and community well-being. When we add to all this the Russian invasion of Ukraine in 2022 and the war in Gaza which started in 2023 – horror stories which rightly dominate the mass media – and the current and future impact of climate change, everyone now knows that we're living in a much more insecure, challenging and dangerous world. All of these issues mean that many people are struggling to feel any hope for the future. This isn't just happening in Scotland but in the rest of the UK and throughout the West. In the early days of the Centre we thought we could increase individual and collective confidence and well-being but such beliefs now appear to belong to a different world.

A worrying direction

Since 2011 SNP governments have steered the country in a very different direction to what the Centre stands for as it has revealed itself, despite rhetoric to the contrary, to be a party of centralised control. Holyrood has increasingly dominated local authorities, centralised the police service and weakened the autonomy of arm's length bodies like Scottish Enterprise. Communities throughout Scotland feel increasingly alienated by, and distant from, Edinburgh.

In August 2015 First Minister Nicola Sturgeon gave a speech indicating that eliminating the attainment gap in education was her 'defining mission' on which she wanted to be 'judged'. I was shocked at the speech as it clearly conveyed her belief that she was going to single-handedly eradicate something that was deeply cultural and structural and simply not in her gift to deliver. It was hubris and completely ill-thought through. Unsurprisingly ten years later her inadequate, top-down reforms, including standardised tests for four- and five-year-olds had achieved little discernible improvement. Making real progress would require the ideas and involvement of tens of thousands of committed people as well as serious resources.

This topic, and many others, illustrate that there was a remarkable superficiality at the heart of Sturgeon's government. The emphasis was on looking and sounding good and not on actual delivery. For me, the defining image of her government is the launch of the *Glen Sannox* in 2017. This was one of the ill-fated, unfinished and much-needed ferries. Yet it was launched with windows painted on and fake funnels. This was undertaken, at considerable public expense, so that the Scottish Government would be boosted by the spectacle of Nicola Sturgeon launching the vessel, with a piper and cheering crowds waving Saltire flags on the quay. The Scottish Government released a PR video of the event.

The term window-dressing has now taken on a completely new, and somewhat sinister, meaning. As Christopher Hedges argues in his prescient book *The Empire of Illusion* (2009) on America's drift from democracy to authoritarianism, spectacle is at the core of the totalitarian project. I'm not asserting that Scotland now has a totalitarian regime. But there are good reasons why commentators are looking at successive SNP administrations and calling their approach 'progressive authoritarianism'. As someone who has always cared about people being able to speak freely, I'm deeply concerned about this development.

I was prompted to write *The Scots' Crisis of Confidence* after years spent working on personal and team development with thousands of people. I routinely witnessed how Scots didn't have the confidence to speak in groups or express an opinion. People from other countries, including England, would often approach me at the end to say 'I don't get it. Why can't people say what they think?' I had observed the same phenomenon when I was a politics tutor at Edinburgh University as there was such a difference between the Scottish and English students, though sometimes this was explained by whether the students had attended state or private schools.

In my experience, Scots remaining silent is about Scots' reticence, not inarticulacy. It's about not having the confidence to draw attention to yourself and express an opinion, particularly if it's controversial. And I understood it completely as I had been one of these students. I sat through various tutorials when an undergraduate at Strathclyde University and didn't say a word despite the fact I had lots of opinions.

Scots' unwillingness to draw attention to themselves in this way worried me. Not only did it suggest confidence problems but also, in a world that was becoming more competitive, and social problems becoming more complex, we needed organisations to perform better and be more intelligent and responsive. That required input from lots of different perspectives. This is why as a Centre we believed so passionately in encouraging more bottom-up approaches.

Progressive authoritarianism

So what has prompted the claims that the Scottish Government has authoritarian tendencies? First there was the Scottish Government's plans for every young person under 18 in Scotland to have a 'named person' as a state guardian to monitor their well-being and share information, even without their parents' consent. In 2016 the UK Supreme Court, accepted the scheme was based on good intentions, but unanimously decided that it interfered 'with the rights of parents to private and family life under article 8 of the European Convention on Human Rights'. In 2012 the Scottish Government introduced flawed and draconian legislation to control sectarianism by effectively criminalising football supporters for expressing their identity by singing songs. The Act was so unpopular and unworkable the Government later repealed its own legislation. The Scottish Parliament then passed the Hate Crime and Public Order (Scotland) Act 2021 which came into force in April 2024. There's existing legislation to criminalise 'harassment' or 'threatening behaviour' and these are properly defined in law. But this new act criminalises 'stirring up hatred' against minority groups (age, race, sexual orientation, religion and transgender identity) but what this means is subjective. A hate crime has been committed if the victim says so and that means writers, performers and comics are vulnerable if anyone takes offence at their views. This is an enactment of the victimhood culture I described in Chapter 22.

The Scottish Police Federation warned the legislation would

'paralyse freedom of expression for individuals and organisations by threatening prosecution for the mere expression of opinion'. To implement the Act, the police have now set up 41 'reporting centres' for hate crimes which sounds like something from Orwell's *Nineteen Eighty-Four*. In 2021, even before this legislation, Kirkcaldy police were ridiculed for tweeting that they wanted information from the public about the appearance of 'controversial' stickers that simply read, 'Women won't wheesht'. Some women were arrested or harassed by police for projecting their feminism, and opposition to gender reform being promoted by the Scottish Government. Sometimes this has been as innocuous as displaying the colours of the Suffragettes.

The controversial stickers illustrated that there was growing opposition from feminists to the way that the Scottish Government was embedding gender identity in public policy. This meant, for example, that the Scottish Prison Service was now willing to place prisoners on the basis of their self-identified gender. In 2021 First Minister Nicola Sturgeon announced that her government intended to legislate on the subject and would introduce self-ID. The Scottish Government then drafted a Bill setting out its proposals to allow anyone from the age of 16, who had been living in their proposed gender for a minimum of three months, to be given a Gender Recognition Certificate.

I have little doubt that these gender reforms, and hate crime legislation, were all about showing that Scotland was the most inclusive country. It was yet another iteration of that old Scottish mantra 'we'll show the world'. But, ironically what it shows of Scotland is not what she intended. Onlookers are scratching their heads in disbelief. How can the political elites in a country that was once known for its Enlightenment rationalism be captured by ill-thought through, unscientific, illiberal ideas?

At the end of May 2024, as I was writing the last few pages, a book appeared explaining the Scottish campaign behind the controversial stickers disliked by the police. It's called *The Women Who Wouldn't Wheesht: Voices from the front-line of Scotland's battle for women's rights* (*Wheesht* for short) and is a collection of essays edited by Susan Dalgety and Lucy Blackburn Hunter. It's a compelling story, told in the voices of over thirty women, some anonymous, from across the political spectrum, about how they risked abuse, reputational damage and often the loss of their livelihood to oppose what they saw as an assault on women's human rights. And, ironically, that assault was spearheaded by the Scottish Government, led by First Minister Nicola Sturgeon who called herself 'a feminist to her fingertips'. One of her fellow SNP politicians, Joanna Cherry has an essay in *Wheesht* lamenting her party's approach and later called Sturgeon a 'Stalinist'. Some in the book argue that many nationalists looked away and didn't criticise what was happening as opposition might undermine the independence cause. A phenomenon known ironically as 'wheesht for indy'.

Wheesht doesn't show the world how democratic we are as a country or how illustrious our institutions are. Instead it shows how politicians from all parties were captured by a small interest group and rather than challenging the mantra of 'no debate' they acted on it by trying to quash the views of a group of courageous women – women who not only had important things to say about proposed policy but who were also in touch with majority opinion. Of course, other countries and other institutions across the UK have also been influenced by gender ideology but the Scottish Government was leading the world in its complete capitulation to it. Politicians in Scotland refused to listen to the activists' concerns and Nicola Sturgeon herself publicly dismissed their views as 'not valid'. She even criticised opponents of the legislation by saying, 'There are people who have opposed this bill that cloak themselves in women's rights to make it acceptable, but just as they're transphobic you'll also find that they're deeply misogynist, often homophobic, possibly some of them racist as well.' Mandy Rhodes, editor of *Holyrood* magazine, and a previous friend of Sturgeon's, argues that on this topic Sturgeon 'didn't ever engage with arguments or bother herself with facts.'

However, a spectacle was about to undermine the Scottish Government position and show how wrong-headed its approach had been. The spectacle in question was Isla Bryson, a double rapist, wearing a wig, pink jacket and tight leggings with male genitals clearly visible, being taken to a female prison. Here was evidence of what many women had been saying for years – the safety of women was being trumped by the feelings of men, some of them violent offenders. Bryson's mother and wife confirmed that the prisoner had never expressed any interest in being a woman till charged with sexual offences. During the trial there were references to 'her penis'.

There was a public outcry about the Bryson case. The First Minister intervened and Bryson was moved to a male prison two days later. Nonetheless Nicola Sturgeon looked foolish when she was uncharacteristically tongue-tied and unable to answer whether Bryson was a man or a woman. She was mocked. Laughed at. She then resigned two weeks later. Of course, there were other reasons for this, such as the police investigation into the SNP's finances and difficulties over progressing independence. But there's little doubt that she could not have continued as First Minister given the Bryson fiasco and the grassroots campaign against her gender legislation, now documented in *Wheesht*.

In *The Scots' Crisis of Confidence* I gently mocked Scotland's famous intellectual Tom Nairn for what I saw as his hyperbolic views. At one point he argued that there was 'no Stalinist like a Scottish Stalinist' and that if the SNP ever won power there would be 'a junta of corporal punishers'. At the time I didn't agree that Scotland was particularly authoritarian, but I now wonder if he was right and I was wrong.

For hundreds of years Scots' lives were controlled by religious orthodoxy. Scottish Enlightenment scholars helped the nation to break away from the superstitious, punitive beliefs of the church by shining the light of reason into dark places. But clearly there are residual authoritarian tendencies in Scotland which, paradoxically, can easily be activated, by a zealous desire to do good.

When I read *Wheesht* I felt inspired. It confirmed that there are still people, who despite the challenges facing them, will make their voices heard and are intent on using the light of reason to help guide discussion. Of course, transgender people have rights and require support. But we can only try to square these with women's rights if we oppose the injunction of 'no debate'. Women must be permitted to talk openly about the potential conflicts as well as their fears without being shouted down as bigots.

IV

Legacy

There's little doubt that the Centre was always a time-limited organisation. It was bound to run out of steam. After all we were a movement of Baby Boomers and at the Centre's peak many of us were in our 60s and at the age to retire. The Centre benefited from this as some of our *Postcards* authors had the time to write because they had retired from formal posts and moved into more freelance activity. But stepping down from formal employment also meant that some of these authors no longer had the influence they once had at the peak of their careers. Given the speed of change in today's world, I know some felt out of touch very quickly with developments in their field.

Ageing brings other challenges and benefits. As we age, our energy wanes and we often divert our attention from work to family, particularly to looking after grandchildren. I was very aware of this in my own life when I reached the official retirement age of 65 in 2016 and became a grandmother. But I was acutely aware of these life changes in some of our board members and our once devoted followers.

At the time of writing, we plan to close the Centre in the spring of 2026. This gives us time to spread the word about this book and to publish *Born to Play* edited by Tam Bailey and Professor John McKendrick in March 2025.

Much of what the Centre has done over the past twenty years could disappear into the proverbial mists of time. The events and projects are mainly over and, apart from paperwork located in an archive, may only live on for a few years in the memories of those who attended. But books are different. They literally have a shelf-life. They continue, not only to exist, but also to have meaning for generations to come.

In the past five years I was aware that the Centre, which had done so much in Scotland for the first fifteen years of its existence, could evaporate without trace if I didn't write down my version of the story. By providing a lot of detail, including dates, places and names, I hope that this book may be used by future historians to understand this important period in Scotland's history.

But I also hope that my other books may continue to have some relevance and usefulness. I have never written for academics. I've always written for people like myself. In other words, for readers who want to understand themselves, the people they worked with or simply their own country better.

When writing books my methodology is unconventional. I read widely across subject disciplines to find ideas that might be useful to further understand a topic which interests me. I then combine these insights from history, social science research or theory with my own experiences and intuitions to help me, and hopefully readers, understand an issue better. My views are speculative, rather than definitive. I very rarely assert this is how things are, or were in the past. Rather I offer a possible explanation or hopefully useful observation. Speculation may be frowned on by empiricists but if there was no speculation where would they get ideas for what to try and measure?

I'm aware that a little knowledge can be dangerous but so too is trying to look at real world problems through the narrow lens offered by subject specialisation. My ideas can, and do, change in the light of further insights or understanding and I see this as a strength not a weakness. When writing I never assume the reader knows much about the topic, I explain ideas and concepts and want my books to be easy to read.

I find the conventional university method, in social science at least, too narrow to be helpful. I find it unsurprising that one of Scotland's most gifted and celebrated thinkers, Darren McGarvey, a rapper who won the Orwell prize in 2018 for *Poverty Safari*, has not been to university. This has freed up his thinking and encouraged him to draw on a wide variety of personal experiences and reflections to create a trenchant critique of politics and society. In the words of one of the judges, his book 'is not just a lament against austerity but as much a hymn in praise of the power of the individual. It's both a big social critique and a big call to individual liberty and empowerment.' No Scottish academic could have written anything as powerful and complex as this.

The journey

I have always seen this book as the record of a 20-year journey – a travelogue with a distinct beginning, middle and end. The journey begins in earnest on the 2nd of December 2004 and ends almost 20 years later. Like all long journeys progress is varied and eventful. In the first ten years of the Centre's life, we undertook lots of activity mainly on different approaches to confidence and well-being. Lots of people journeyed with us during this decade, energised by hope that change was possible and not too difficult to achieve. These fellow travellers came from all walks of life and for many the ultimate destination was a better, more confident and energised Scotland. Undoubtedly some of our supporters always framed their goal in political terms. Independence was their primary objective. Others had more limited ambitions and simply sought improvement in the confidence and well-being of young people, employees or community members.

From the Centre's foundation I regularly queried where our journey would take us for I could see that, despite our good intentions, it may not lead to where we hoped. Ideas, particularly when diluted for transmission to a wider public, can easily backfire and produce ironic effects. Even before the Centre's programme of activity was fully underway in Scotland, parents' and teachers' desire to protect young people from negativity and boost their self-esteem was undermining their resilience and potentially setting them up for mental health problems. It doesn't surprise me that Generation Z (born between 1997 and 2012) are so focused on safe spaces, trigger warnings and victimhood as they grew up in an environment where adults were obsessed by their psychological, not just their physical, safety.

The Centre did its best to warn of the dangers overprotection posed to young people's resilience. Undoubtedly some individuals benefited from what we did and changed not just their minds but their behaviour towards youngsters. But the idea that children's feelings must be protected at all costs was, and still is, so much part of the *zeitgeist* that it was nigh impossible for us to make noticeable progress.

Of course, there are other possible reasons why young people's mental health has declined: the rise of materialist values, the predominance of social media, the pandemic, the rising consumption of ultra-processed foods, a widespread decline in sleep and exercise and the catastrophising which now accompanies discussion of climate change and environmental issues. I've little doubt that if the Centre was active now we would be fully behind the views of Professor Jonathan Haidt, author of *The Anxious Generation* (2024) – endorsing calls to ban smart phones in Scottish schools and warning parents of the potential dangers of social media exposure, particularly to girls. Haidt also argues that the decline in children's independent, risky play is an important reason why their resilience has declined. Readers will be aware that promoting play has been a major aspect of the Centre's work in recent years, so we agree wholeheartedly with Haidt on this as well.

Concern about young people's confidence, resilience and well-being has always played a large part in the Centre's programme of work. But so too did a range of other issues. In fact, as the chapters dedicated to what we did in Phase 2 testify, we did so much that it's impractical for me to summarise. Instead, I've compiled Table 7[1] listing Centre activities according to Ken Wilber's quadrants. (See p. 170 for an explanation of the quadrants.) In other words, I've taken the Centre's major activities on its 20-year journey and assigned them to a box marked – *individual interior, individual exterior, collective interior* and *collective exterior*. As much of the Centre's work can be arranged in this way it provides a reasonable summary and reminder of our main activities.

---

1. Note for Table 7 opposite: As many of our books or events cover the topic from a variety of angles, they could have appeared in more than one quadrant but for simplicity they are allocated only to the quadrant that sums up the essence of the book or activity. There are a few Centre activities, such as the Scotland's Tipping Point and Creating Good Lives events, that included material or approaches appropriate to all four quadrants and these have simply been omitted as they can't be classified in this way.

Table 7:
Main Centre activities and books according to Wilber's quadrants

Individual interior: Inner mental states **Centre topics** Positive psychology including optimism & subjective well-being Confidence, resilience & mindset **Relevant Centre activities** Vanguard events SEAL critique Self-esteem event *Creating Confidence* *Knowing and Growing* *The Golden Mean*	**Individual exterior:** Factors which influence physiology, health & behaviour **Centre topics** Importance of gestation & early years Play Alcohol & drug addiction Impact of environment & nature on health & behaviour **Relevant Centre activities** Foundations of flourishing events Alcohol & drugs events The Brain that Changes Itself event *Raising Spirits* *She, He, They* *Right from the Start* *The Dear Wild Place* *Play is the Way* ACE event & ACE research presented in *Hiding in Plain Sight*
Collective interior: Common values & shared culture **Centre topics** Identifying historical and societal forces which have shaped culture & outlook **Relevant Centre activities** Events on materialist values *The Tears that Made the Clyde* *AfterNow* *The Great Takeover* Baby Boomers event *Hiding in Plain Sight* *A Time of Hope*	**Collective Exterior:** Systems, structures & socio-political factors **Centre topics** Inequality, organisational structures, constitutional & political factors **Relevant Centre activities** Systems thinking in public sector event *The New Road* *Scotland's Local Food Revolution* *Letting Go* *Shaping our Global Future* *Conviction* EHRC project *Schooling Scotland* *Working for Equality*

I'm aware that for many readers, particularly those who have not read all the preceding chapters, this may seem overly complex. But, in reality, all our quadrants perspective meant for the Centre was that we valued different approaches to improving confidence and well-being. It also meant that we were able to create an atmosphere that was inclusive and respectful and allowed every interested person to be part of the journey. After all, everyone has a contribution to make to our understanding of the world around us and how we might bring about change. By generating energy and hope in this way we created a virtuous circle.

Martin Luther King famously said, 'Hope is being able to see that there's light despite all of the darkness.' At the end of 2024, so much of the world is suffering from war and turmoil that it's challenging to see any light. Even in the UK many are suffering from insecurity and inadequate public services and struggling to pay for life's essentials. However, we can see flashes of light if we focus on some of the people previously mentioned in this book and what they're doing to address some of the Scottish problems highlighted in previous chapters.

Alan Sinclair knows what babies need to thrive (see Chapter 18) and he's been talking to the Scottish Government for years, so it's encouraging to note some progress. First Minister John Swinney's Programme for Government 2024-25 not only has a major focus on eliminating child poverty but also commits to assessing the development of two- and three-year-olds. It also pledges to introduce whole family support into local communities. This isn't enough to address Scotland's inadequate approach to child-rearing, but it's a helpful start.

Upstart, under the new leadership of Willie French and Dawn Ewan, is poised to use the publication of the forthcoming *Postcards* book, *Born to Play*, as an opportunity to reinforce the idea that the 'schoolification' of infants is harmful and that play is essential for children's healthy development.

Suzanne Zeedyk and Pauline Scott, the two women behind ACE-Aware Scotland, continue to have ambitious plans for this growing movement and are steering it in a positive direction. They're holding an event in autumn 2024 called 'the power of community' and have plans for a major conference in spring 2025 with international speakers called 'the biology of belonging'.

I'm also delighted that Stephen Noon, director of the Yes campaign for the 2014 independence referendum, whom we met at the end of the previous chapter, is making progress in his attempt to heal the post-referendum divide. In September 2024, the University of Glasgow's Centre for Public Policy published a report written by its Associate Director – former Labour MSP and leader of Scottish Labour – Kezia Dugdale and Stephen Noon called 'Scotland and the Constitution: Agreeing a way forward'. What matters is not its detailed suggestions but the fact that compromise and finding common ground are now being discussed publicly. As Chris Deerin points out in an article about the report in the *New Statesman*, 'There is weariness on all sides at the. . . divisions that have dogged Scottish political and civic life' since the referendum. What's more, cross party collaboration is once again being discussed in the Scottish Parliament. We need more cooperation and respect across public life, so this is welcome.

In the last few chapters, I've argued that utopian dreaming is common in Scotland, thanks to our religious past, and that this is harmful, not only as it saps energy and deflects us from finding solutions to immediate problems, but also because utopian projects ultimately become dystopian. So, it's extremely helpful that we have in our midst a leading thinker on the dangers of utopian thought. Indeed, some now hail Ewan Morrison as one of the UK's most talented novelists. Many of his novels draw creatively on his experience as a child of hippy, utopian parents and his own flirtation with extreme socialist ideas. Ewan gave a compelling TEDx talk on 'why we would be happier without utopia' which creatively interrogates his father's desire for Scotland to become a utopia and his disappointment that it hadn't come to pass. The topic is so important for Ewan that he calls his blog 'Untopia'. If Scotland is to address many of the big challenges it faces it has to pay attention to current reality and reject the appeal of utopia.

Looking back on the Centre's journey I'm proud that those of us involved did so much to encourage many Scots to believe that change was not only desirable but also possible. But I'm also proud that while we encouraged ambitious, optimistic goals we always tempered hope with reality and never stopped asking difficult questions.

The Centre is now reaching the end of its eventful 20-year journey and its story has been told in the pages of this book. Memories have been preserved. Let's hope that in the future other books and chapters will be written to describe what others, outside the realm of politics, have done to inspire Scots to embrace much-needed change.

Afterword
Professor Phil Hanlon

THIS BOOK IS PRIMARILY about the Centre for Confidence and Well-being but, as importantly, it is about Scotland. My expertise is in public health so it is through the lens of health that I look back on the 20-year history outlined by Carol.

When the Centre was launched, we knew that Scotland had the worst health in the United Kingdom, worse even than comparable areas like the industrial North East of England. A group of us looked at why this might be the case. Unsurprisingly, we confirmed that one of the key reasons for Scotland's poor health status was deprivation. However, the deprivation profile of Scottish postcodes compared with England was by then explaining less of the gap in mortality between Scotland and England than was shown previously. An analysis of the 1981 census showed that the vast majority of the excess mortality experienced in Scotland compared to England and Wales could be explained by Scotland's higher levels of deprivation. However, mortality data in the early 1990s showed that, by then, deprivation only accounted for approximately 40 per cent of the excess deaths at all ages. The excess deaths in Scotland which were not accounted for by deprivation became known as the 'Scottish Effect'. Importantly, this effect could be seen across all social groups and geographies in Scotland (although it varied in size considerably) and the phenomenon was seen again when data from the 2001 census became available.

These results inevitably led to a discussion about the reasons for this Scottish Effect. When teaching students about the determinants of health I liked to use the phrase 'it all matters'. This argued that the determinants of health in Scotland were many: economic, material, cultural, psychological, behavioural and much more. These multiple factors interacted and the health of the people of Scotland emerged in a complex manner from these interactions. Others argued that the most important drivers of health were structural and material and so that is where the emphasis should always remain. This is a strong argument but it begs the question why in the previous two decades the wealth gap between England and Scotland had narrowed while the health gap had widened. This important fact called for a widening of the agenda without diminishing the importance of economic drivers of health.

It was about this time that I met Carol and began to become involved in the work of the Centre. The ideas that informed the work of the Centre these past 20 years (Box 18, page 523–526) were there from the start. Carol always used an eclectic mix of perspectives – psychological and spiritual; physiological and behavioural; cultural and relational; and structural and social. In short, she and I had much the same approach even though we came from very different starting points. I enjoyed the way that Carol found new voices with fresh perspectives and brought them to Scotland so that we all benefited. Also, her three great strengths – writing, speaking and networking – were always employed to challenge and encourage reflection. As a consequence, our collaboration seemed entirely natural.

This book demonstrates the impact made by the Centre these past twenty years. However, Scotland's comparative disadvantage in health remains as intractable as ever. Also, targets set by the Scottish Government to 'close the attainment gap' and 'eradicate child poverty' seem no closer to a solution. The legacy of extreme industrialisation followed by profound deindustrialisation just makes it harder to solve some of these problems. In addition, Carol points to our cultural history: it is, surely, equally important.

However, I am convinced that the problems we face in Scotland represent challenges that are not amenable to current strategies despite our best efforts. The challenges we face converge and intertwine. 'Tectonic stresses' in global society include population stresses arising from differences in the population growth rates between rich and poor countries; large scale immigration as a consequence; energy stresses; environmental stresses; climate stresses; and economic stresses. Scotland cannot escape these difficulties and together with the historical and cultural factors outlined in this book, make the search for solutions challenging.

A legacy of the biomechanical approach to health is the idea that a cure can be found for every disease, given time and resources. The difficulty is that, in our rapidly changing and complex world, we now see diminishing returns from formerly successful approaches. Another issue is the tendency to emphasise systems and processes at the expense of the individual and the human spirit. In the world we have created, we appear to behave as if organisations do the work, regardless of human capacities, consciousness, energy, passion and effort. The existing change model might be summarised as: get the organisations and programmes right and change will happen. Much public happiness may be diminished for a lack of care, attention and understanding, as increasingly ineffective bureaucratic arrangements enter a round of tighter and tighter regulation/re-organisation in futile attempts to effectively manage an increasingly complex world. A sense of unease and dissatisfaction is pervasive.

Consequently, the evidence presented in this book leads me to believe that the approach taken by Carol and the Centre these past 20 years is going to be even more important in the next 20. Carol does not overplay the impact of the Centre or pretend that there are easy answers to many of the problems discussed. What she does demonstrate is that a multifaceted approach is needed. So, to whom is Carol going to pass this baton which she has carried so ably? Universities? Political parties? Other established institutions? Probably no, no, and not likely.

Perhaps this book will inspire someone who sits outside the established consensus to rise to the challenge.

Phil Hanlon
September 2024

Phil Hanlon was formerly Professor of Public Health at Glasgow University and served on the board and then was latterly Chair of the Centre for Confidence and Well-being.

References[1]

As this is such a large book we have streamlined the process of references and only included explanatory footnotes within chapters. We have listed the main texts referred to in numerous chapters below and then included a list of references per chapter.

Main books and articles referred to in numerous chapters

Bruce Alexander, *The Globalisation of Addiction: A Study in the Poverty of the Spirit* (Oxford University Press, 2008).

Carol Craig, *The Scots' Crisis of Confidence* (Argyll Publishing, 2003).

Carol Craig, *Creating Confidence: A handbook for professionals working with young people* (Centre for Confidence and Well-being, 2007).

Carol Craig, *The Tears that Made the Clyde* (Argyll Publishing, 2010).

Carol Craig, *Hiding in Plain Sight: Exploring Scotland's ill health* (CCWB Press, 2017).

Carol S. Dweck, *Mindset: The New Psychology of Success* (Random House, 2006).

Malcolm Gladwell, *The Tipping Point: How little things can make a big difference* (Back Bay Books, 2001).

Helen McGrath & Toni Noble, *Bounce Back!: A Classroom Resilience Program* (Pearson, 2003).

Sue Palmer (Editor), *Play is the Way: Child development, early years and the future of Scottish education* (CCWB Press, 2021).

---

1. **Centre for Confidence and Well-being Archive**
The Centre has arranged to deposit its archive in the Mitchell Library, Glasgow. This incudes minutes, reports, official documents, press cuttings, published books and electronic files.

Martin E.P. Seligman, *Learned Optimism: How to Change Your Mind and Your Life* (Pocket Books, 1998).

Martin E.P. Seligman, Karen Reivich, Lisa Jaycox, & Jane Gillham, *The Optimistic Child* (HarperPerennial, 1996).

Martin E.P. Seligman & Mihaly Csikszentmihalyi, 'Positive psychology: An introduction', *American Psychologist* (Vol 55, issue 1, 2000).

Martin E.P. Seligman, *Authentic Happiness* (Nicholas Brealey Publishing, 2003).

Martin E.P. Seligman, *Flourish* (Nicholas Brealey Publishing, 2011).

Individual chapter references

Books and articles are **listed in the order referred to** in the chapter. The list of references excludes books and articles frequently mentioned in the book. These are listed above. Some chapters have no references. Some references are not specifically mentioned in the chapter but are listed as they have been used for research purposes.

Chapter One: The difficult birth of the Centre

Scottish Executive's Strategy Unit, *Confidence in Scotland* (Scottish Executive, 2005).

Ed Diener & Martin Seligman, 'Beyond Money: Toward an Economy of Well-Being', *Psychological Science in the Public Interest* (Vol 5, (1), July 2004).

Chapter Two: In the Vanguard: the early years and the development of positive psychology

Mihaly Csikszentmihalyi, *Flow* (First News, 1990).

B.L. Fredrickson, 'The role of positive emotions in positive psychology', *American Psychology* (Vol 56 (3), March 2001).

Richard Layard, *Happiness* (Penguin, 2005).

Richard Eckersley, *Well & Good: How We Feel & Why it Matters* (Text Publishing, 2004).

Arthur Herman, *How the Scots Invented the Modern World: The True Story of how Western Europe's Poorest Nation Created Our World & Everything in it* (Three Rivers Press, 2001).

Chapter Three: 'The costly pursuit of self-esteem': what every Scottish teacher needs to know

Roy Baumeister *et al*, 'The Self-Esteem Myth', *Scientific American* (January 2005).

N. Emler, *Self Esteem: The Costs and Causes of Low Self Worth* (York Publishing Services, 2001).

Helen McCarthy, *The Self-Esteem Society* (Demos, 2004).

Andy Westwood, *Me, Myself and Work: Self-esteem and the UK Labour Market* (The Work Foundation, 2004).

Charles J. Sykes, *Dumbing Down Our Kids: Why American Children Feel Good About Themselves but Can't Read, Write, or Add* (St. Martin's Publishing Group, 1995).

Maureen Stout, *The Feel-Good Curriculum: The Dumbing Down of America's Kids in the Name of Self-Esteem* (Da Capo Press, 2000).

Jean M. Twenge, *Generation Me: Why Today's Young Americans Are More Confident, Assertive, Entitled – and More Miserable Than Ever Before* (Atria Books, 2006).

Jennifer Crocker & Laura Park, 'The Costly Pursuit of Self-Esteem', *Psychological Bulletin* (Vol 130 (3), 2004).

Chapter Four: Positive organisations, optimism, pessimism and the power of small change

David S. Robb (Editor), *The Collected Poems of Alexander Scott* (Mercat Press, 1994).

T. M. Devine, *To the Ends of the Earth: Scotland's Global Diaspora, 1750 - 2010* (Penguin, 2012).

Stephen R. Covey, *Principle-Centred Leadership* (Rosetta Books, 2009).

Richard Steel, 'Culture and Complexity: New Insights into Organisational Change', *Organisations and People* (Vol 1 (1), 2000).

Chapter Five: The Centre mounts a challenge to an Orwellian development in English education

Primary National Strategy, 'Excellence and enjoyment: social and emotional aspects of learning. Guidance', SureStart, (Department for Education and Skills Publications, 2005).

Social and Emotional Aspects of Learning for Secondary Schools (SEAL), Guidance booklet (Department for Education and Skills, 2007).

Carol Craig, 'The Potential Dangers of a Systematic, Explicit Approach to Teaching Social and Emotional Skills' (Centre for Confidence and Well-being, 2007).

Katherine Weare, *Developing the Emotionally Literate School* (Paul Chapman Publishing, 2004).

Daniel Goleman, *Emotional Intelligence* (Bantam Books, 1995).

J.D. Mayer & C.D. Cobb, 'Educational policy on emotional intelligence: does it make sense?', *Educational Psychology Review,* (Vol 12, 2000).

J.D. Mayer, P. Salovey, P. & D.R. Caruso, 'Models of emotional intelligence', in R.J. Sternberg (Editor), *Handbook of Intelligence* (Cambridge University Press, 2000).

S. Hallam *et al,* 'Evaluation of the primary behaviour and attendance pilot', (Department for Education and Skills Research Report, 2006).

Dan Wegner, 'Ironic processes of mental control', *Psychological Review* (101(1), 1994).

D. Wegner *et al,* 'Ironic Effects of Trying to Relax under Stress', *Behavior Research and Therapy* (Vol 35 (1), 1997).

Dylan Evans, *Emotion: The Science of Sentiment* (Oxford Univ. Press, 2002).

A. Rose *et al*, 'Prospective Associations of Co-Rumination with Friendship and Emotional Adjustment: Considering the Socio-emotional Trade-Offs of Co-Rumination', *Developmental Psychology*, (Vol 43, 2007).

Christina Hoff Sommers & Sally Satel M.D., *One Nation Under Therapy: How Helping Culture Is Eroding Self-Reliance* (St. Martin's Publishing Group, 2006).

Frank Furedi, *Therapy Culture: Cultivating Vulnerability in an Uncertain Age* (Routledge, 2004).

Kathryn Ecclestone & Dennis Hayes, *The Dangerous Rise of Therapeutic Education* (Taylor & Francis, 2009).

Nigel Wigelsworth *et al,* 'A national evaluation of the impact of the secondary Social and Emotional Aspects of Learning (SEAL) programme', *Educational Psychology*, (Vol 32, 2012).

Chapter Seven: The shine goes off positive psychology

Department for Education, 'UK resilience programme evaluation: Final Report' (April 2011).

Stephen M. Brunwasser *et al*, 'A Meta-analytic Review of the Penn Resiliency Program's Effects on Depressive Symptoms', *Journal of Consulting and Clinical Psychology* (Vol 77 (6) 2009).

D. Stephen Lindsay, 'Replication in Psychological Science', *Psychological Science* (Vol 26 (12), 2015).

Monya Baker, 'Over half of psychology studies fail reproducibility', *Nature* (27 August 2015).

Barbara L. Fredrickson, *Positivity: Top-Notch Research Reveals the 3-to-1 Ratio that Will Change Your Life* (Harmony/Rodale, 2009).

Andrew Anthony, 'The British amateur who debunked the mathematics of happiness', *Observer* (19 January, 2014).

N.J.L. Brown *et al*, 'The complex dynamics of wishful thinking', *American Psychologist* (Vol *68* (9), 2013).

Julie K. Norem, *The Positive Power of Negative Thinking* (Basic Books, 2002).

Christopher Peterson & Martin E.P. Seligman, *Character Strengths and Virtues: A Handbook and Classification, Volume 1* (American Psychological Association, 2004).

Barry Schwartz and Kenneth Sharp, 'Practical Wisdom: Aristotle meets positive psychology', *Journal of Happiness Studies* (Vol 7(3), 2006).

Todd Kashdan & Robert Biswas-Diener, *The Upside of Your Dark Side: Why Being Your Whole Self – Not Just Your 'Good' Self – Drives Success and Fulfilment* (Penguin, 2015).

Todd Kashdan & Robert Biswas-Diener, *The Power of Negative Emotion* (One World Publications, 2015).

Brock Bastian, *The Other Side of Happiness* (Allen Lane, 2018).

Rhonda Byrne, *The Secret* (Simon and Schuster, 2006).

Chapter Eight: An untold story: the rift with Martin Seligman

Jane Mayer, *The Dark Side: The Inside Story of how the War on Terror Turned Into a War on American Ideals* (Anchor Books, 2009).

Martin E.P. Seligman, *The Hope of Circuit: A Psychologist's Journey from Helplessness to Optimism* (Public Affairs, 2018).

Jeff Kaye blogged under the name of Valtin. The correspondence quoted took place between December 2006 and July 2007 and was widely available on the internet. Kaye continues to blog under the name of Invictus.

André Comte-Sponville, *A Short Treatise on the Great Virtues: The Uses of Philosophy in Everyday Life* (Heinemann, 2002).

Chapter Nine: Surviving austerity

Ken Wilber, *A Theory of Everything* (Shambhala, 2000).

Chapter Ten: Defining and promoting flourishing lives

Simone de Beauvoir, *The Second Sex* (Knopf, 1953).

Jesse Singal, *The Quick Fix: Why Fad Psychology Can't Cure Our Social Ills* (Farrar, Straus and Giroux, 2021).

Tim Gill, *No Fear: Growing Up in a Risk Averse Society* (Calouste Gulbenkian Foundation, 2007).

Robert Epstein, *The Case Against Adolescence: Rediscovering the Adult in Every Teen* (Quill Driver Books, 2007).

Alex Richardson, *They are what You Feed Them: How Food Can Improve Your Child's Behaviour, Mood and Learning* (Harper Collins UK, 2006).

Norman Doidge, *The Brain that Changes Itself* (Penguin, 2008).

Chapter Eleven: The Tears that Made the Clyde

Richard G. Wilkinson, *The Impact of Inequality: How to Make Sick Societies Better* (New Press, 2005).

Richard G. Wilkinson & Kate Pickett, *The Spirit Level: Why More Equal Societies Almost Always Do Better* (Allen Lane, 2009).

Theodor Adorno *et al, The Authoritarian Personality* (Verso Books, 2019).

D. Walsh *et al, Exploring Potential Reasons for Glasgow's 'Excess' Mortality: Results of a three-year survey of Glasgow, Liverpool and Manchester* (Glasgow Centre for Population Health, 2013.)

D. Walsh *et al, History, Politics and Vulnerability: Explaining excess mortality in Scotland and Glasgow (*Glasgow Centre for Population Health, 2016).

T. C. Smout, *A Century of the Scottish People 1830-1950* (Collins, 1986).

T.M. Devine, *The Scottish Nation* (Allen Lane, 1999).

T.M. Devine, *The Transformation of Rural Scotland* (John Donald, 1994)

Piers Dudgeon, *Our Glasgow: Memories of Life in Disappearing Britain* (Headline, 2009).

Sean Damer, 'The Peculiarites of the Clydesiders', (*Scottish Affairs*, Feb 2011).

Marc Horn, 'Pernicious Mince: One critic on a book about Glasgow', *The Times* (14 May 2011).

Pragya Agarwal, 'Here is How Unconscious Bias Holds Women Back', *Forbes* (17 December, 2018).

Chapter Twelve: Enough is enough: challenging materialist values

Tim Kasser, *The High Price of Materialism* (MIT Press, 2003).

Phil Hanlon & Sandra Carlisle, *Afternow: What's next for a healthy Scotland?* (Argyll Publishing, 2012).

Barry Schwartz, *The Paradox of Choice* (Harper Perennial, 2004).

Adam Smith, *The Theory of Moral Sentiments* (FQ Classics, 2007).

Adam Smith, *The Wealth of Nations* (Capstone, 2010).

Carol Craig, *The Great Takeover: How materialism, the media and markets now dominate our lives* (Argyll Publishing, 2012).

Joseph Heath & Andrew Potter, *The Rebel Sell: Why the Culture Can't be Jammed* (HarperCollins, 2004).

Michael J. Sandel, *What Money Can't Buy: The moral limits of markets* (Penguin, 2013).

Clive Hamilton, *Requiem for a Species* (Allen & Unwin, 2010).

Chapter Thirteen: Organisational performance and well-being at work

John Seddon, *Systems Thinking in the Public Sector* (Triarchy Press, 2008).

Gordon Hall & Tony Miller, *Letting Go: Breathing new life into organisations* (Argyll Publishing, 2013).

Ayn Rand, *Atlas Shrugged* (Dutton,1992).

John Carnochan, *Conviction: Violence, culture and a shared public service agenda* (Argyll Publishing, 2015).

Chapter Fourteen: Paving the way for the new road: the environment, nature and community

Alf Young & Ewan Young, *The New Road: Charting Scotland's inspirational communities* (Argyll Publishing, 2012).

Mike Small, *Scotland's Local Food Revolution* (Argyll Publishing, 2013).

Theodore Roszak, 'The Nature of Sanity', *Psychology Today* (1 January 1996).

Jenny Mollison, Judy Wilkinson & Rona Wilkinson, *Raising Spirits: Allotments, well-being and community* (Argyll Publishing, 2014).

Emily Cutts, *The Dear Wild Place: Green spaces, community and campaigning* (CCWB Press, 2019).

Robert Putnam, *Bowling Alone: The Collapse and Revival of American Community* (Simon & Schuster, 2001).

Viktor E. Frankl, *Man's Search for Meaning (Rider, 2004).*

Chapter Fifteen: Inequality and poverty, drugs and alcohol

Daniel Dorling, *Injustice: Why social inequality persists* (Policy Press, 2011).

William Julius Wilson, *When Work Disappears: The World of the New Urban Poor* (Knopf Doubleday Publishing Group, 2011).

Darren McGarvey, *Poverty Safari* (Pan Macmillan, 2018).

Carol Craig, 'Man O' Independent Mind: Darren McGarvey's *Poverty Safari*', *Sceptical Scot* (25 January, 2018).

Carol Craig, 'Poverty Safari: Growing up with ACEs and toxic stress', *Sceptical Scot* (5 February, 2018).

Chapter Sixteen: Equality, diversity and positive ageing

Shirley Young, *She, He, They: Families, gender and coping with transition* (CCWB Press, 2016).

Richard Freeman, Fiona McHardy, Danny Murphy (Editors) *Working for equality: Policy, politics, people* (CCWB Press, 2017).

Simon de Beauvoir, *La Vieillesse* (Gallimard, 1970).

Becca R. Levy *et al*, 'Longevity increased by positive perceptions of ageing', *Journal of Personality and Social Psychology* (Vol 83 (2), 2002).

G. Westerhof *et al*, 'Longitudinal effects of subjective ageing on health and longevity: An updated meta-analysis', *Psychology and Ageing* (Vol 38 (3), 2023).

Caroline Park *et al*, 'The Effect of Loneliness on Distinct Health Outcomes: A Comprehensive Review and Meta-analysis, *Psychiatry Research* (Vol 294, 2020).

Chapter Seventeen: Developing ourselves and others

Jean M. Twenge & Keith Campbell, *The Narcissism Epidemic: Living in the age of entitlement* (Atria Books, 2010).

Alan McLean, *Knowing and Growing: Insights for developing ourselves and others* (CCWB Press, 2017).

Alan McLean, *The Motivated School* (SAGE, 2003).

Alan McLean, *Motivating Every Learner* (SAGE, 2009).

Morag Kerr (Editor), *The Golden Mean: Fostering young people's resilience, confidence and well-being* (CCWB Press, 2018).

Diana Baumrind, 'Effects of authoritative parental control on child behavior', *Child Development* (Vol. *37*, 1966).

Diana Baumrind, 'Current patterns of parental authority', *Developmental Psychology* (Vol *4*, 1971).

Diana Baumrind, 'Rearing competent children' in W. Damon (Editor), *Child Development Today and Tomorrow* (Jossey-Bass, 1989).

John Reilly *et al*, 'Results from Scotland's 2016 Report Card on Physical Activity for Children and Youth', *Journal of Physical Activity and Health* (Vol 13 (11 Suppl 2), 2016).

E.A. Gunderson *et al*, 'Parent Praise Predicts Children's Motivational Frameworks Five Years Later', *Child Development* (Vol. 85 (5), 2013). Note: Authors include Carol Dweck.

E.E. Maccoby & J. A. Martin, 'Socialization in the context of the family: Parent-child interaction'. In E.M. Hetherington, (Editor), *Handbook of Child Psychology: (Vol. 4.) Socialization, Personality, and Social Development*, 4th Edition. (Routledge 1983).

H. Masud *et al*, 'Parenting styles and academic achievement of young adolescents: A systematic literature review', *Quality and Quantity* (Vol 49 (6), 2014).

Chapter Eighteen: Prioritising early years and play

Alan Sinclair, *Right from the Start: Investing in parents and babies* (CCWB Press, 2018).

Dunedin study. For findings go to: https://dunedinstudy.otago.ac.nz

Rosemary Geddes *et al*, 'Translating research into practice: A cross-sectional study using the Early Development Instrument to assess early years interventions in local level public health practice', *The Lancet* (Vol 384 (Supplement 2), 2014). Note: The article is based on John Frank's work outlined in the chapter.

Sue Palmer, *Detoxing Childhood* (Orion, 2007).

Sue Palmer, *21st Century Boys* (Orion, 2009).

Sue Palmer, *21st Century Girls* (Orion, 2013).

Sue Palmer, *Upstart: The case for raising the school starting age and providing the under-sevens what they really need* (Floris Books, 2016).

Chapter Nineteen: Schooling Scotland

Daniel Murphy, *Professional School Leadership: Dealing with Dilemmas* (Liverpool University Press, 2007).

Daniel Murphy, *Schooling Scotland: Education, equity and community* (CCWB Press, 2014).

Scot MacNab, 'Nicola Sturgeon: Judge me on education record', *The Scotsman* (19 August 2015).

John Kay, *Obliquity: Why our goals are best achieved indirectly* (Profile Books, 2011).

James McEnaney, 'Data shows SNP has failed to close education attainment gap', *The Herald* (12 December 2023).

Lindsay Paterson, 'Scotland's Pisa results: Severe declines in maths, science and reading show "Curriculum for Excellence" isn't working', *The Scotsman* (5 December 2023).

Carol Craig, 'Fear of Challenging children has broken Scottish education', *The Times (*12 January 2024).

Mark Priestley & Walter Humes, 'The development of Scotland's Curriculum for Excellence: Amnesia and Deja Vu', *Oxford Review of Education:* (Vol. 36 (3), 2010).

D. Wegner *et al*, 'Ironic Effects of Trying to Relax under Stress', *Behavior Research and Therapy* (Vol 35 (1) 1997).

Derek Brown, *Shaping our Global Future: A guide for young people* (CCWB Press, 2015).

Chapter Twenty: Childhood adversities: Scotland's dismal record

Andrew O'Hagan, *Our Fathers* (Harcourt Brace & Company,1999).

D. Walsh *et al*, *Exploring Potential Reasons for Glasgow's 'Excess' Mortality: Results of a three-year survey of Glasgow, Liverpool and Manchester* (Glasgow Centre for Population Health, 2013).

D. Walsh *et al*, *History, Politics and Vulnerability: Explaining excess mortality in Scotland and Glasgow* (Glasgow Centre for Population Health, 2016).

Demetrios Matheou, 'Local Hero', *Observer* (7 January 2001). Article on Peter Mullan and includes quote.

V. J. Felitti *et al*, 'Relationship of Childhood Abuse and Household Dysfunction to Many of the Leading Causes of Death in Adults', *American Journal of Preventive Medicine* (Vol 14 (4),1998).

M.H. Teicher *et al,* 'The Neurobiological Consequences of Early Stress and Childhood Maltreatment', *Neuroscience & Biobehavioral Reviews* (Vol 27 (1– 2), 2003).

R. Anda *et al*, 'The Enduring Effects of Abuse and Related Adverse Experiences in Childhood', *European Archives of Psychiatry and Clinical Neuroscience* (Vol 256 (3), 2006).

R.F. Anda, 'The Health and Social Impact of Growing up with Adverse Childhood Experiences: The Human and Economic Costs of the Status Quo' (Centers for Disease Control and Prevention, 2007).

C.A. Courtois & J. D. Ford (Editors), *Treating Complex Traumatic Stress Disorders* (Guildford Press, 2009).

S.R. Dube *et al,* 'Cumulative Childhood Stress and Autoimmune Diseases in Adults', *Psychosomatic Medicine* (Vol 71(2), 2009).

E. Gretchen *et al, Adverse Childhood Experiences are Associated with Migraine and Vascular Biomarkers.* (American Headache Society, 2012).

Robin Karr-Morse, *Scared Sick: The role of childhood trauma in adult disease* (Basic Books, 2012).

Donna Jackson Nakazawa, *Childhood Disrupted: How Your Biography Becomes Your Biology and How You Can Heal* (Atria, 2015).

Robert Anda *et al,* 'Adverse Childhood Experiences, Alcoholic Parents, and Later Risk of Alcoholism and Depression', *Psychiatric Services* (Vol 53 (8), 2002).

Alcohol Focus Scotland, *Unrecognised and Under- reported: The Impact of Alcohol on People Other than the Drinker in Scotland*. (Alcohol Focus Scotland, 2012).

Bessel van der Kolk, *The Body Keeps the Score: Brain, mind, and body in the healing of trauma (*Penguin, 2015).

Irvine Welsh, *Trainspotting* (Secker & Warburg, 1993).

Betty Kirkpatrick, *Favourite Scots Words* (Independent Publishing Platform, 2014).

M. Munro, *The Patter: A guide to current Glasgow usage*. (Glasgow District Libraries, 1985).

P. Zenzinger, 'Contemporary Scottish Fiction' in P. Zenzinger (Editor) *Scotland: Literature, Culture, Politics* (Carl Winter Universitatsverlag, 1989).

Agnes Owens, *A Working Mother* (Bloomsbury Publishing PLC,1994).

George Douglas Brown, *The House with the Green Shutters* (John MacQueen, 1901).

Lewis Grassic Gibbon, *Sunset Song* (Canongate, 2004).

Sarah Couper & Phil Mackie, 'Polishing the Diamonds: Addressing Adverse Childhood Experiences in Scotland' (Scottish Public Health Network, 2016).

Michael Smith *et al*, 'Is there a link between childhood adversity, attachment style and Scotland's excess mortality? Evidence, challenges and potential research, *BMC Public Health* (Vol 16 (655), 2016).

Scottish Health Survey 2019, Volume 1, Chapter 8 (Scottish Government, 2020). Scottish prevalence study for adverse childhood experiences.

A.M. Bellis *et al*, 'National household survey of adverse childhood experiences and their relationship with resilience to health harming behaviours', *BMC Medicine* (Vol 12 (72), 2014). Note: This gives ACE prevalence rates for England.

A.M. Bellis, *et al*, *Adverse Childhood Experiences and their Impact on Health-harming Behaviours in the Welsh Adult Population* (Public Health Wales, 2016). Note: This gives ACE prevalence rates for the first study in Wales.

Karen Elizabeth Hughes *et al*, *Sources of resilience and their moderating relationships with harms from adverse childhood experiences* Report 1: Mental Illness (Public Health Wales, 2018). Note: This gives ACE prevalence rates for the second study in Wales.

Ellis M, Hughes K, Leckenby N, *et al.* 2014b. 'Adverse childhood experiences and associations with health-harming behaviours in young adults: surveys in the European region'. *Bulletin of the World Health Organisation* 92(9): 621-696.

Renner, L & Slack, K. 2006. 'Intimate partner violence and child maltreatment: Understanding intra- and intergenerational connections' *Child Abuse and Neglect* 30(6):

A.M. Bellis, *et al*, 'Adverse Childhood Experiences and their Impact on Health-harming Behaviours in young adults: Surveys in the European region', *Bulletin of the World Health Organisation* (Vol 92 (9), 2014).

Louise Marryat & John Frank, 'Factors associated with adverse childhood experiences in Scottish children: a prospective cohort study', *BMJ Paediatrics Open* (Vol 3 (1), 2019).

Mark A. Bellis *et al*, 'Comparing relationships between single types of adverse childhood experiences and health-related outcomes: a combined primary data study of eight cross-sectional surveys in England and Wales', *BMJ Open* (Vol 13 (4), 2023).

Christa McCutchen *et al,* 'The occurrence and co-occurrence of ACEs and their relationship to mental health in the United States and Ireland', *Child Abuse & Neglect* (Vol 129, 2022).

S.R. Dube *et al*, 'Childhood verbal abuse as a child maltreatment subtype: A systematic review of the current evidence', *Child Abuse & Neglect* (Vol 144, 2023).

Peter Fonagy, 'Think before shouting at your child: To them words can be as harmful as physical blows', *The Guardian* (2nd October, 2023). (One of the authors of the study listed above.)

Martin Taulbut & David Walsh, 'Poverty, parenting and poor health: comparing early years' experiences in Scotland, England and three city regions' (Glasgow Centre for Population Health, 2013).

Chapter Twenty-One: Illuminating the darkness: Scotland's physical abuse of children

Kenneth Roy, The *Invisible Spirit: A Life of Post-War Scotland, 1945-75* (ICS Books, 2013).

Kenneth Roy, *The Broken Journey: A Life of Scotland, 1976-99* (Birlinn, 2016).

Carol Craig, 'Scotland's belt culture', *Scottish Review* (20 March, 2018).

Ian Jack, 'I was belted at school. It felt unfair but was it harmful?', *The Guardian (*24 March, 2018).

Carol Craig, 'Scotland's "addiction" to the belt', *Sceptical Scot (*2 April, 2018).

Calum Ferguson, *Children of the Black House* (Birlinn, 2006).

Corpun website, www.corpun.com. Lists countries' different approaches to corporal punishment.

Richard Finlay, *Modern Scotland* (Profile Books, 2004).

Andrew Campbell, 'If you didn't get the belt, you can thank my mum', *TES magazine* (24 March, 2017).

Alex Renton, *Stiff Upper Lip: Secrets, Crimes and the Schooling of a Ruling Class* (Weidenfeld & Nicolson, 2017).

A Heilmann *et al. Equally Protected? A Review of the Evidence on the Physical Punishment of Children* (NSPCC, 2015).

Scottish Health Survey 2019, Volume 1, Chapter 8 (Scottish Government, 2020). Scottish prevalence study for adverse childhood experiences.

Elizabeth T. Gershoff & Andrew Grogan-Kaylor, 'Spanking and Child Outcomes: Old Controversies and New Meta-Analyses', *Journal of Family Psychology* (30 (4), 2016).

Gemma Fraser, 'Smacking ban: "We don't hit children from a rational place" ', *Holyrood* (23 April, 2019).

George W. Holden, 'Why do parents physically punish their children?', Psychology Benefits Society website, (1 February, 2017).

Carol Craig 'Scotland has treated its children badly', *Scottish Review,* (May 2019).

Scottish Child Abuse Inquiry evidence and reports can be found at: https://www.childabuseinquiry.scot

Kenneth Roy, *In Case of Any News: A Diary of Living and Dying* (ICS Books, 2019).

Chapter Twenty-Two: The zeitgeist – trauma and abuse

Anne Dickson, *A Woman in Your Own Right: Assertiveness and You* (Quartet Books, 1983).

Ian Hacking, 'Making Up People', *London Review of Books* (Vol.28 (16) 17 August 2006).

Nick Haslam, 'Concept Creep: Psychology's Expanding Concepts of Harm and Pathology', *Psychological Inquiry*, (Vol 27, 2016).

Bessel van der Kolk, *The Body Keeps the Score: Brain, mind and body in the healing of trauma* (Penguin, 2015).

Aditi Shrikant, 'Why we're still reading "The Body Keeps the Score" almost a decade later according to author Bessel van der Kolk' (CNBC, 14 August 2023).

Lexi Pandell, 'How trauma became the word of the decade', *Vox* (Jan 25, 2022).

Richard J. McNally, 'Can we salvage the concept of psychological trauma?', *The Psychologist,* (22 May, 2010).

Judith Lewis Herman, 'Complex PTSD: A syndrome in survivors of prolonged trauma', *Journal of Traumatic Stress* (Vol 5 (3), 1992).

Michael Scheeringa, *The Trouble with Trauma: The Search to Discover How Beliefs Become Facts* (Central Recovery Press, 2022).

Lucy Foulkes, *Losing Our Minds: What Mental Illness Really Is – and What It Isn't* (Bodley Head, 2021).

Steven Pinker, *The Better Angels of Our Nature: A History of Violence and Humanity* (Penguin, 2012).

Bradley Campbell & Jason Manning, *The Rise of Victimhood Culture: Microaggressions, Safe Spaces and the New Culture War* (Palgrave Macmillan, 2018).

Nassim Nicholas Taleb, *Antifragile: Things that Gain from Disorder* (Penguin, 2013).

Greg Lukianoff & Johnathon Haidt, *The Coddling of the American Mind: How Good Intentions and Bad Ideas Are Setting Up a Generation for Failure* (Allen Lane, 2018).

Johnathon Haidt, *The Anxious Generation* (Penguin, 2024).

Chapter Twenty-Three: A national trauma?

John McKendrick, *Darien: A Journey in Search of Empire* (Birlinn Ltd, 2018).

Christopher A. Whatley, *The Scots and the Union* (Edinburgh University Press, 2006).

John Young, 'Scotland and Ulster connections in the seventeenth century: Sir Robert Adair of Kinhilt and the Scottish Parliament under the Covenanters', *Journal of Scotch-Irish Studies* (Vol 3 (4), 2013).

Neil Mackay, 'How Scots were foot soldiers in England's colonisation of Ireland', *The Herald* (11 June 2023).

Norman Davies, *Vanished Kingdoms: The History of Half-Forgotten Europe* (Penguin, 2012).

Michael Hechter, *Internal Colonialism: The Celtic Fringe in British National Development, 1536-1966* (University of California Press, 1977).

Craig Beveridge & Ronald Turnbull, *The Eclipse of Scottish Culture: Inferiorism and the Intellectuals* (Polygon, 1989).

Benjamin Wilkie, *The Scots in Australia 1788-1938* (Boydell Press, 2017).

Stephen Mullen & Ewan Gibbs, 'Scotland, Atlantic slavery and the Scottish National Party: From Colonised to Coloniser in the political imagination', *Nations and Nationalism* (Vol 29 (3), 2023).

T.M. Devine, *Recovering Scotland's Slavery Past* (Edinburgh Univ. Press, 2015).

Richard Finlay, *Scottish Nationalism: History, Ideology, and the Question of Independence* (Bloomsbury Academic, 2022).

T.M. Devine, *The Scottish Clearances: A History of the Dispossessed 1600-1900* (Allen Lane, 2018).

John Prebble, *The Highland Clearances* (Martin Secker & Warburg Ltd, 1963).

Neal Ascherson, *Stone Voices* (Granta Books, 2003).

Eric Richards, *The Highland Clearances* (Birlinn General, 2016).

Joni Buchanan, *Women of the Hebrides* (Acair, 2024).

Iain McKinnon, 'Colonialism and the Highland Clearances', *Northern Scotland* (Vol 8 (1), 2017).

Chapter Twenty-Four: A Scottish mentality

Tom Holland, *Dominion:The Making of the Western Mind* (Abacus, 2020).

The First Book of Discipline can be accessed at www.truecovenanter.com.

William Storrar, *Scottish Identity: A Christian Vision* (Handsel Press, 1990).

Edwin Muir, *John Knox: Portrait of a Calvinist* (Jonathan Cape,1930).

Wallace Notestein, *The Scot in History* (Praeger Publishers,1946).

Henry Gray Graham, *The Social Life of Scotland in the Eighteenth Century* (A. & C. Black, 1899).

T.C. Smout, *A History of the Scottish People 1560-1830* (Collins, 1970).

Donald Macleod, 'Scottish Calvinism: a dark repressive force?', *Scottish Bulletin of Evangelical Theology* (Vol 19 (2), 2001).

Bill Duncan, *The Wee Book of Calvin* (Penguin, 2004).

Lesley A. Orr Macdonald, *A Unique and Glorious Mission* (John Donald Publishers, 2000).

Mary Rose Liverani, *Winter Sparrows* (Michael Joseph,1976).

Gordon Williams, *From Scenes Like These* (Secker & Warburg, 1968).

David S. Robb (Editor), *The Collected Poems of Alexander Scott* (Mercat Press, 1994).

Alastair Reid, *Whereabouts: Notes on Being a Foreigner* (North Point Press, 1987).

Jennifer Crocker & Laura Park, 'The Costly Pursuit of Self-Esteem', *Psychological Bulletin* (Vol 130(3), May 2004).

William McIlvanney, *Surviving the Shipwreck* (Mainstream Publishing, 1991).

Allan MacLaren, *Social Class in Scotland: Past and Present* (John Donald Publishers, 1976).

Mihaly Csikszentmihalyi, *Flow* (First News, 1990).

George Albee interview – 'Focus on the Growing Efficacy of Prevention Programs' in *Lifelines: Journal of Centre for Study of Health Disparities* (Vol 1, Fall 1999).

Rina Mae Acosta & Michele Hutchison, *The Happiest Kids in the World: Bringing up children the Dutch way* (Doubleday, 2017).

Joy Schaverien, *Boarding School Syndrome: The psychological trauma of the 'privileged' child* (Routledge, 2015).

Vanessa Sacks & David Murphey, 'The prevalence of adverse childhood experiences, nationally, by state and by race or ethnicity', *Child Trends* (February 12, 2018).

Douglas Gifford *et al* (Editors), *Scottish Literature* (Edinburgh Univ. Press, 2002).

Alasdair Gray, *Lanark* (Canongate,1981).

Tom Nairn, 'The Three Dreams of Scottish Nationalism' in Karl Miller (Editor), *Memoirs of a Modern Scotland* (Faber & Faber, 1970).

W. Gordon Smith, *This is My Country: A Personal Blend of the Purest Scotch* (Souvenir Press: 1976).

Catherine Carswell, *The Life of Robert Burns* (Chatto & Windus, 1951).

Finlay J Macdonald, *Crotal & White: Scenes from a Hebridean Boyhood* (Macdonald & Co 1983).

Alastair McIntosh, *Poacher's Pilgrimage: A Journey into Land and Soul* (Birlinn, 2016).

Ewan Morrison, 'The Road to Hell is Paved with Good Intentions', *Psychology Today (15 April,* 2019).

Ewan Morrison 'Does Fanaticism Run in Families?', *Psychology Today* (11 September, 2020).

D. Walsh *et al*, *History, Politics and Vulnerability: Explaining excess mortality in Scotland and Glasgow* (Glasgow Centre for Population Health, 2016).

Alan McLean, *Knowing and Growing: Insights for developing ourselves and others* (CCWB Press, 2017).

Chapter Twenty-Five: We'll show the world

Iain Macwhirter, *Road to Referendum* (Cargo, 2013).

Carol Craig, 'Why this optimist is voting No', *Scottish Review* (8 September, 2014).

John McDermott, 'An optimist argues for a No vote', *Financial Times* (9 September, 2014).

Daniel Finklestein, 'The penny has dropped on political pessimism, *The Times* (13 September, 2014).

Carol Craig, 'The SNP have become Scotland's Pollyannas', *The Guardian* (10 September, 2014).

Chris Giles, 'Economists warn Scots of 'gamble with very poor odds', *Financial Times* (17 September, 2014).

James Stafford, 'The Revenge of Sovereignty: The SNP, the Financial Crisis and UK Constitutional Reform *Sheffield Political Economy Research Institute* (Paper No. 20, 2014).

Ewan Morrison, 'Yes: Why I Joined Yes and Why I Changed to No', Wakeup Scotland website (15 September, 2014).

Ewan Morrison, 'Why I quit Yes and their disciples of separation', *Daily Mail* (17 September, 2014).

Neil Mackay, 'Ex-Yes Scotland director: SNP trashed us – that's why we lost', *The Herald* (14 May, 2023).

Carol Craig, 'On Selfishness and the Scottish Independence Referendum', Wakeup Scotland website (12 October, 2014).

Scottish Government, 'Scotland National Strategy for Economic Transformation: Evidence paper' (1 March, 2022).

Kate Fox, *Watching the English* (Hodder, 2005).

Campbell McLean, 'Who is Their God' in Alastair M. Dunnett (Editor) *Alistair MacLean Introduces Scotland* (London, 1972).

Jimmy Reid, *Power without Principles* (B&W Publishing: 1999).

Labour Party pamphlet quoted in T.C. Smout, *A Century of the Scottish People 1830-1950 (*Collins, 1986).

James Maxton quoted in Gordon Brown, *Maxton* (Mainstream Publishing, 1986).

Lindsay Paterson 'Scottish Democracy and Scottish Utopias: The First Year of the Scottish Parliament', *Scottish Affairs* (Autumn, 2000).

H.J. Hanham *Scottish Nationalism* (Faber & Faber, 1969).

James Mitchell, 'Scotland's Parties Need to Face Political Reality', Centre on Constitutional Change (18 April, 2016).

Jock Encombe, 'The Psychopathology of Everyday Nationalism', Wakeup Scotland website (13 September 2014).

Bill Paterson, 'Why a celebrity may sit on a fence', *Scottish Review* (September, 2014).

H.M. Drucker, *Breakaway: The Scottish Labour Party* (Polygon, 1978).

Kenny Farquharson, 'Brains behind 2014 Yes campaign is back with hard truths', *The Times* (27 August, 2022).

The Final Analysis

Kenny MacAskill (Editor), *Agenda for a New Scotland: Visions of Scotland 2020* (Luath, 2005).

John Kay, *Obliquity: Why Our Goals are Best Achieved Indirectly* (Profile Books, 2011).

Christopher Hedges, *The Empire of Illusion*: *The End of Literacy and the Triumph of Spectacle* (Nation Books, 2009).

Susan Dalgety & Lucy Blackburn Hunter (Editors), *The Women Who Wouldn't Wheesht: Voices from the front line of the battle for women's rights* (Constable, 2024).

Tom Nairn, 'The Three Dreams of Scottish Nationalism' in Karl Miller (Editor), *Memoirs of a Modern Scotland* (Faber & Faber, 1970).

Tam Baillie and John McKendrick (Editors), *Born to Play (*CCWB Press, 2025) Forthcoming.

Chris Deerin, 'Can the SNP and Labour learn to work together?' *New Statesman* (27 September, 2024).

Appendix 1

Confidence building at a city scale: the background, activities and legacy of Go Dundee

'Go Dundee' was a group of people who started to meet in the city as a result of the Centre's 'Scotland's Tipping Point' conference in Glasgow in December 2004. Here **Stewart Murdoch**, one of the group members and a senior official in Dundee Council's culture department, looks back.

How do you trace the origins of a movement? How do you measure the impact of a social innovation? What are the sources of evidence we can draw on? And how do you guard against false memory, perhaps rose tinted?

This is a reflection on the origins and influences of a movement which both characterised and influenced the direction of the city of Dundee over a period of 20 years or more.

Dundee City Council created a Communities Department in 1999 which brought together the range of public services which were community facing – libraries; community centres; youth work; equalities and community support services like Community Wardens etc. This workforce was charged with working alongside communities to improve quality of life, deliver a decentralisation strategy and develop local community plans for the city. The City Council subsequently approved the establishment of local area teams and area budgets to enable communities to prioritise and implement action at a neighbourhood level. This was in itself a political decision which took a lot of self-confidence.

There was a strong belief in the importance of honouring local decision-making and a lot of effort was put into the establishment of local community forums which were less prescriptive than Community Councils, but which were intended to fulfil a similar function.

During this period the City Council organised a two-day residential staff conference (a real thing of the past). The theme of the conference was 'self-confidence'. Staff selected this topic as they saw lack of self-confidence as a recurring theme confronting those working in communities, particular with young people.

The City Council designed the event to facilitate self-directed learning through group work as well as provide input from prominent speakers who could give different perspectives on self-confidence:

Philosophical and theological – Professor Robert Davidson, Glasgow University;

Psychological – Ian Galloway, Edinburgh University;

Sociological – Professor Ted Millburn, Strathclyde University;

Economic and business — Chris Dawes MD of Michelin, Dundee and Chair of Scottish Enterprise, Tayside.;

Educational – Fraser Patrick, Assistant Director of Education, Dundee City Council.

The after-dinner speaker was Brian Keenan, who had previously trained as a community worker and who had published a book called *An Evil Cradling* (1992) following his release after 18 months of incarceration as a hostage in the Middle East.

This event, as well as the core purposes of the Communities Department, meant that there was a significant number of influencers working at both the grass roots and strategic levels in the city who were already trying to understand what created self-confidence, how it could be damaged, its relationship to resilience and their role in nurturing it.

It was in this context that members of the Dundee Partnership became aware of the emergence of the work of Dr Carol Craig and discussions to set up the Centre for Confidence and Well-being. A number of people who went on to form Go Dundee attended the Scotland's Tipping Point conference she ran on December 2nd 2004.

John Palfreyman, wrote an article in 2005 for the Centre's newsletter, 'Confidence Matters', outlining the challenges faced by Scotland's 'City of Discovery', what Go Dundee was and how it was responding to these challenges:

> Dundee is a funny old place. It has never been on the main route to the Highlands, is not really a very attractive stopping off point for travellers on the way to Aberdeen, was not greatly liked by Samuel Johnson and mostly missed out on the oil industry.
>
> And yet, can you find another city in the UK which has such a fantastic geographical situation? Can you find a comparable cluster of Life Sciences expertise outside London and Cambridge? Or can you find another city which is reinventing itself as rapidly as Dundee has done (and is doing) over the last decade?
>
> But there is a long way to go and much of the development of Dundee has been achieved by incomers to the city who can see the quality of life that Dundee can offer. There is still a selling job both within the city and to the external world and much of this has to do with 'confidence' – confidence of the people of Dundee in themselves and confidence about Dundee.

John goes on to explain that there was a strong representation from Dundee at Scotland's Tipping Point conference and what happened next:

> We had representatives from the local enterprise company, the arts, health, education and industry sectors and a couple of consultants. Some of us knew each other; most of us were new to each other. The Dundee group wanted to do something, though we had little idea other than to have our own 'Tipping Point' conference back in our own city.

> We did have a meeting back in Dundee for those who had been at the Glasgow conference and others, and this group set up an entity called 'Go Dundee' which organised the Dundee 'Tipping Point' conference on February 15th 2005.'

We had speakers from local businesses and organisations, as well as newcomers to the city. More than half of the conference involved people talking to each other. We had three sessions, comprising:

- people's stories of Dundee
- what people would like to see happen in Dundee, and
- how people could contribute to the delivery of some of these ideas.

And that was it, people went home to think about the Go Dundee idea. . .

Learning journeys

The group then alighted on an innovative and practical focus for Go Dundee – a series of 'learning journeys' which would allow people to continue these conversations as well as engage a broader cross-section of citizens. One of our expressed aims was to promote understanding of the different perspectives of those who lived or worked in the city. Dundee Council's Communities Department sponsored and organised these journeys. Without the flexibility to resource and co-ordinate this type of initiative one has to wonder if they would ever have happened.

The work which had already been done in recent years to establish community representative structures ensured that invitations could be sent to such representatives across the city. The Dundee Partnership gave access to public sector representatives and Go Dundee was itself a networking initiative. Filling a double-decker bus was never going to be a problem.

The idea was to take people on a shared journey, promoting dialogue between stops and taking those on the journey behind the facade of organisations to get a better shared understanding of how they operated, what they did, and the challenges they faced. The first couple of journeys were 'conducted' by actors in costume from the communities department of the Dundee REP theatre. Xplore Dundee generously provided a brand new bus and driver for the day at no cost and the organisations which opened up their doors to host visits provided hospitality.

The feedback from those who took part was very positive and the 'journeys' continued for several years with the local bus company continuing to make available buses as part of their community social responsibility.

This initiative reflected the ambition to bring about change that existed in the city. There was a widespread recognition that to drive change in a way which was sustainable it had to be inclusive. There are lots of metaphors which could be employed, but it was clear that those who chose to 'get on the bus' were those from academia, business, health, local government and elected members. In other words, they were people who wanted to understand the perspectives of people working in different institutions which make up a city. The passengers on the journey were asked to sit between stops with people they were meeting for the first time, to share their perspectives on the visit and to have the type of conversation that can be sparked when travelling with strangers. This provided further insights and has led to some lasting relationships.

One recurring theme from these journeys was the importance of the quality of life for those living in poor circumstances, for incoming students and academics and for those looking for a city in which to develop business. This came down to the quality of the local environment and the importance of cultural opportunities which were accessible, relevant, and challenging. Dundee achieved a great deal through its political leadership as they bought into these goals and were helping to develop both range and quality in the cultural sector. At this period the community focus and plethora of organisations involved became a defining characteristic of the city's renaissance.

Many believe that the success of Dundee's later campaigns to be recognised as the UK City of Culture, and subsequently the European Capital of Culture, drew on these aspirations. These were good bids and while for different reasons neither won, in both cases many of the projects listed in the bids were implemented in subsequent years.

Most importantly, initiatives such as 'We Dundee' engaged a huge number of people who helped create a momentum. There was an unwritten consensus that citizens wanted to see cultural opportunities as a right, regardless of income level.

Events

Between 2005 and 2008 we held various large-scale events such as **Dundee's Tipping Point** in February 2005. We followed this up in March 2006 with an event called **Go Dundee. . . the art of the possible** which attracted over 100 participants. The keynote speaker was Sir Brian Langlands, the Principal of Dundee University, and we used interactive techniques from World Cafe to ensure everyone had a chance to contribute and share stories of positive change in the city.

In January 2008 we held a large event with the Centre called **Leadership and the positive city**. The keynote speaker was the famous Harvard positive psychology lecturer, and leadership expert, Dr Tal Ben Shahar. Other speakers included Joe Lafferty, a leadership coach and Go Dundee member, Dr Tom Shepherd from the life sciences sector in the city and Jacquie Roberts who at that time was CEO of the Care Commission which had its office in Dundee. The journalist Iain Macwhirter chaired the event. At one point he thrilled the 300 strong audience with his view that Dundee could plausibly present itself as 'the crucible of the new Scotland'.

This was such a successful event that people wanted more opportunities to get together. So in June 2008 we held a large networking event called **Go Dundee – let's work together** and asked Carol Craig to present her views on how Dundee could become a more confident and optimistic city. There was also time to socialise and listen or dance to the music of local Dundee band 'the Hazy Janes'.

We held all these events in the Apex Hotel – a new boutique hotel on the waterfront. Go Dundee had no funds and its ability to hold large public events in attractive surroundings was due to good fortune. Marcus Kenyon was CEO of Apex Hotels from 2002 to 2011 and he went to Scotland's Tipping Point to hear Malcolm Gladwell. Thereafter he was a supportive Go Dundee member and helped enormously by giving us use of the hotel whenever possible. We only had to pay for hospitality.

The Dundee Contemporary Arts Centre was also supportive and we held a dinner discussion there in March 2009 on the theme of **Challenging the Conventional Wisdom**. In 2014, almost eight years after we first got together, Go Dundee still had a core group of members who met from time to time.

Reflection

What can we take away from our experiences? Dundee at that period in history was the right place, at the right time, on the right scale. Despite the pressures on public finance that have always existed, the City Council created the capacity to innovate and there was the strong political and officer leadership necessary to encourage a culture strongly focused on working in an inclusive way. Go Dundee reflected these drives and contributed to this spirit. It provided the main way for people from different sectors and backgrounds, who wanted to initiate change, to meet and develop the confidence to make Dundee the great place we always knew it could be.

Original team 2005

Amanda Boyle, Dundee-based businesswoman
James Brining, Director Dundee Rep Theatre
Steven Carter, Scottish Enterprise Dundee
Shona Cormack, Manager Scottish Enterprise Dundee
Clive Gillman, Director Dundee Contemporary Arts
Steve Grimmond, Director Dundee City Council
Marcus Kenyon, Manager Apex
Joe Lafferty, Organisational Consultant and Executive Coach, Lifetree
Stewart Murdoch, Director of Communities, Dundee City Council
John Palfreyman, University of Abertay
Lucy Rennie, NHS Tayside
Karen Tinney, Manager Dundee City Council

Later Members

Laurie O'Donnell, adviser, consultant and visiting professor
Jacquie Roberts, CEO Care Commission

Appendix 2

Original ACE Questionnaire

Prior to your 18th birthday:

1. Did a parent or other adult in the household often or very often. . . Swear at you, insult you, put you down, or humiliate you? or Act in a way that made you afraid that you might be physically hurt?

No__ If Yes, enter 1 __

2. Did a parent or other adult in the household often or very often. . . Push, grab, slap, or throw something at you? or Ever hit you so hard that you had marks or were injured?

No__ If Yes, enter 1 __

3. Did an adult or person at least 5 years older than you ever. . . Touch or fondle you or have you touch their body in a sexual way? or Attempt or actually have oral, anal, or vaginal intercourse with you?

No__ If Yes, enter 1 __

4. Did you often or very often feel that. . . No one in your family loved you or thought you were important or special? or Your family didn't look out for each other, feel close to each other, or support each other?

No__ If Yes, enter 1 __

5. Did you often or very often feel that. . . You didn't have enough to eat, had to wear dirty clothes, and had no one to protect you? or Your parents were too drunk or high to take care of you or take you to the doctor if you needed it?
No__ If Yes, enter 1 __

6. Were your parents ever separated or divorced?
No__ If Yes, enter 1 __

7. Was your mother or stepmother:
Often or very often pushed, grabbed, slapped, or had something thrown at her? or Sometimes, often, or very often kicked, bitten, hit with a fist, or hit with something hard? or Ever repeatedly hit over at least a few minutes or threatened with a gun or knife?
No__ If Yes, enter 1 __

8. Did you live with anyone who was a problem drinker or alcoholic, or who used street drugs?
No__ If Yes, enter 1 __

9. Was a household member depressed or mentally ill, or did a household member attempt suicide?
No__ If Yes, enter 1 __

10. Did a household member go to prison?
No__ If Yes, enter 1 __

Now add up your 'Yes' answers: TOTAL ___
This is your ACE Score'

Acknowledgements

I STARTED TO WRITE this book in January 2021 when the UK was in lockdown for the Covid-19 pandemic, and I was recovering from two debilitating accidents. As a result, I needed emotional and intellectual support from a wide variety of people to keep me motivated for the large task I had set myself.

Fortunately, I had lots of people to provide this. First and foremost was the Centre's board who discussed the book at length, read various drafts and encouraged me when necessary. Particularly I want to acknowledge Phil Hanlon for his insightful comments on my drafts, Fred Shedden for his proof-reading, and Taroub Zahran for her encouragement. Hazel Black helped enormously by contacting previous staff members and pulling together that section of the book. And Hugh Anderson, architect turned artist, excelled himself by producing such an inspiring, and apposite, image for the book's cover.

I could not have finished the book without the constant input, interest and companionship of Derek Rodger of Argyll Publishing. Without Derek, at the other end of the phone, writing the book would, at times, have been a very lonely process. I'm particularly grateful to Derek for his editorial guidance, drawn from his extensive experience as a Scottish publisher.

I feel very privileged that three friends, Andrew Bolger, Wendy Alexander and Sue Palmer, devoted considerable time to reading the book and giving me comments on everything from grammar and punctuation to my interpretation of events. I'm also grateful to Annmarie Ward for discussing recovery issues with me, and Professor Mark Bellis and Dr Suzanne Zeedyk for discussions on adverse childhood experiences in Scotland. Professor John Frank was also helpful on public health issues and Stephen Noon likewise on the independence referendum.

I also feel honoured at the interest that Professor William Storrar has shown in my books and the Centre's work. I'm particularly grateful that he was so keen to write such a generous, and illuminating, foreword.

Many people, who feature in the book, also read and commented on some of the material – Gregor Henderson, Alan Sinclair, Alan McLean, Danny Murphy, Emily Cutts, Elaine Duncan, Morag Kerr, Derek Goldman and Isobel MacNaughtan. I would like to thank them for their support. I'm very grateful to Stewart Murdoch, Joe Lafferty and John Palfreyman for helping to put together the section on Go Dundee and to Joe for the excellent photographs.

As the book was going to press I learned that Gregor Henderson had died of cancer on the 9th August 2024 at the young age of 63. He held various senior roles in public mental health and former colleagues described him as a visionary leader and spoke of his 'wisdom, warmth, kindness and energy'. The Centre would not have happened without Gregor's instinctive understanding of the various factors that contribute to good mental health, including confidence and well-being. As I make clear in the opening chapter, it was Gregor who suggested that I set up an organisation to pursue my interests in these topics and he then committed himself to securing Scottish Executive support. I know that Gregor was proud to count the Centre for Confidence and Well-being as part of his considerable legacy.

My two sisters, Marianne and Janice, were also very supportive. Marianne came to lots of the Centre events, particularly in the early days, so it was always useful to get her feedback. But she also diligently read the whole book and helped with corrections. Janice supported me in practical ways by helping promote the book to our database and organise the book launch. My immediate family – my partner Alf and our sons, Ewan and Jamie – were constantly encouraging and accepting of the fact that my time was so taken up with writing. My four grandchildren – Feichin, Cailean, Kafka and Lena – are too young to understand what their grandmother has been up to over the past four years, but I hope that in time they may find the story in this book heartening and encouraging. They have taught their grandmother the importance of play to healthy development and this is a topic to which I devote lots of pages in this book. I sincerely wish that their generation will grow up resilient and also know what it's like to live in a time of hope.

So, to all the people named above, and to everyone who features in the Centre directory, profuse thanks for your support, interest and encouragement. But, of course, I alone am responsible for any errors of fact or judgement.

Finally, there's one person, not named above and hardly mentioned in the book, who was vital for the story I've recounted here – Jack McConnell, who was Scotland's First Minister from 2001 to 2007. To him I owe a particular debt of gratitude. Without his interest and his administration's financial support there would never have been a Centre for Confidence and Well-being and everything outlined here would not have happened. I would've been deprived of all the rich experiences recounted here and, I hope I'm not alone in thinking, Scotland would've missed out on something special.

Current/Recent Board Members

Phil Hanlon

Taroub Zahran

Hugh Anderson

Fred Shedden

Hazel Black

Carol Craig

Current/Recent Centre for Confidence and Well-being Board Members

Professor Phil Hanlon (Chair) November 2005 – present

Carol Craig November 2005 – present

Fred Shedden July 2005 to June 2024

Hugh Anderson December 2011 – present

Taroub Zahran June 2012 – present

Hazel Black (Company Secretary) October 2006 – present

Former Board Members

Kate Dunlop June 2009 – July 2015

Angiolina Foster July 2005 – December 2007

Morinne MacDonald October 2004 – August 2006

Ian McKay April 2007 – November 2010

Charlie Miller December 2007 – December 2011

William Roe (Chair) October 2004 – March 2008

Martin Stepek August 2008 – September 2015

Zoe Van Zwanenberg July 2005 – August 2008

Index

C

D

K

L

Mc

M

N

O

P

R

S

T

U

V

W

Y

Z